WITHDRAWN

D1207029

WITHDRAWN

Crisis and Conflict

Volumes in the history of
international news reporting

by

Robert W. Desmond

The Information Process:
World News Reporting to the Twentieth Century

Windows on the World:
World News Reporting 1900–1920

Crisis and Conflict:
World News Reporting 1920–1940

070
D465c

Crisis and Conflict

World News Reporting Between Two Wars 1920–1940

Robert W. Desmond

University of Iowa Press Iowa City

University of Iowa Press, Iowa City 52242
© *1982 by The University of Iowa. All rights reserved*
Printed in the United States of America

Library of Congress Cataloging in Publication Data

Desmond, Robert William, 1900–
   Crisis and conflict.

   Continues: Windows on the world.   c1980.
   Bibliography: p.
   Includes Index.
   1. Foreign news—History—20th century. 2. News
agencies—History—20th century. 3. Journalism—History
—20th century. I. Title.
PN4784.F6D47 1982   070.44'33   82-8584
ISBN 0-87745-111-7   AACR2

To all "Ink-stained wretches of the Fourth Estate," and to their associates of film and broadcast.

CAT Jun 18 '83

5-17-83 MLS 28.54

82-6564

Contents

Foreword

The importance of current information, accurately and promptly reported to all persons, can scarcely be exaggerated as basic to a proper functioning of the social order. If this has been said before, the passing years make it ever more true.

With that as a thesis, this writer ventured to examine man's effort to understand his environment in a book entitled *The Information Process* (1978), and subtitled "World News Reporting to the Twentieth Century." To recount that effort through a time span of centuries, beginning in the darkness of prehistory, required a volume of some size.

By the year 1900 the world had so changed that any attempt to carry forward a description of the information process demanded attention to so many elements that a period of approximately twenty years was as much as could properly be examined in another volume of about the same size as the first. So it was that the first volume's sequel, *Windows on the World,* was forced to limit its examination of "World News Reporting" to the 1900–20 interval, although with some references to broad developments of the decade following.

This third volume in the sequence, *Crisis and Conflict,* also moves through a second twenty-year period relating to "World News Reporting, 1920–1940." The 1910–20 decade had been dominated by the Great War of 1914–18 and the Russian Revolution. The decade of the 1920s was one of guarded hope for a better world shaped by a generation made wiser by the hardships and tragedy so recently endured, and by a public better informed by an improved press. Yet problems arose and the decade of the 1930s was indeed one of crisis and conflict, bringing a sad reversal of the earlier hope and culminating in another great war.

That second World War may be said to have started in Manchuria in 1931, to have gained momentum in Ethiopia in 1935–36 and in Spain in 1936–39, to have engulfed Europe in 1939–40, and to have reached its apogee in 1941–45. This volume is not concerned with the coverage of those acts of war themselves, even prior to 1940. But the events leading to such belligerency, and certain of the actions, will be examined in matters of chronology and the position of the information media in reporting the progression toward total war.

On a personal note, the writer was active during this 1920–40 period as a working reporter and editor, mostly in the United States, and including periods in New York and Washington, but also in Paris and London, Rome and Berlin, Havana and Geneva. Not a few of those persons whose names appear in the pages following were friends, acquaintances, and colleagues; others were figures in the news itself and sometimes "sources." Those years allowed for observation and research pertinent to the subject-matter of this volume.

As in *The Information Process* and *Windows on the World,* the objective here is to bring together, often for the first time, diverse elements in the reporting of public affairs, internationally, and of history-in-the-making for the period covered. The broad purpose, again, is to clarify the process itself and to underline its significance as relating to public comprehension of events and situations shaping the life of the times and of generations to come.

Robert W. Desmond
La Jolla, California

PART I
The 1920s: Flow of the News

Geneva: Symbol of Hope   1

The outlook for the world's people in 1920 made it appropriate to look first to Geneva. That sober Swiss city, beautifully situated on the shore of its own blue lake, with snow-capped Mont Blanc, highest of the Alpine peaks, on the horizon, then became the home of the League of Nations. A creation of the Paris Peace Conference in 1919, it was a symbol of hope for a permanent peace, deeply desired by the war-weary of many lands.

One of the basic premises in the formation of the League was that it should be prepared to make information fully available concerning its own activities. Also, it was to assist in the exchange of substantive information among the peoples of the world as an aid to a mutually constructive relationship. Accordingly, an Information Section was organized as a part of the League Secretariat. Its first director was Pierre Comert, an experienced French journalist and prewar Berlin correspondent for *Le Temps* of Paris. He was assisted by Arthur Sweetser, then thirty-two, a member of the staff of the *Springfield Republican* of Massachusetts before the war, an Associated Press correspondent in Belgium and France in 1914 and in Washington in 1916–18, covering the Department of State, and later serving as a captain in the U.S. Army Signal Corps. In 1919, he was attached to the American delegation at the Paris Peace Conference as assistant to Ray Stannard Baker in the press department during the period that the League was created.

In 1933 Comert returned to Paris to assist the French Ministry of Foreign Affairs improve its own information practices. Even though the United States had not become a member of the League, and Sweetser was an American, he remained as Comert's successor in the direction of the League's Information Section. Others in that division of the Secretariat, providing active assistance to correspondents in Geneva, included Harry R. Cummings and May Shaw, both of British nationality, Adrian Pelt, Dutch, and others from more than fifteen countries.

Almost 200 correspondents were present in Geneva for the first meeting of the League Assembly in 1920. In the years following until 1939, when the organization ceased to function in a Europe and a world at war, the annual Assembly was reported by from 225 to 500 correspondents representing the world press, and radio as well after 1932. The gatherings were larger, understandably, when critical issues were considered by the Assembly or by the League Council. This was demonstrated when the Japanese invasion of Manchuria in 1931 and the Italian invasion of Ethiopia in 1935 were considered, both in conflict with the League's basic purpose to preserve world peace.

A League-sponsored Disarmament Conference was well attended and carefully reported in 1932. Correspondents also gathered for meetings associated with the League-related International Labor Office (ILO) in Geneva, and for League-sponsored meetings there or elsewhere in Europe relating to world health, food and nutrition, minority groups, mandates, transit, communications, social and humanitarian work, and other subjects.

The presence of the League in Geneva was to draw other international organizations and meetings there, with media coverage following. The University of Geneva became a center for programs in the city where the International Red Cross had been formed in the 1860s.

About twenty correspondents were permanently in residence. Others arrived, mostly from Paris, when the Assembly met or other special meetings occurred. Nearly all became members of an International Association of Journalists Accredited to the League of Nations (Association Internationale des Journalistes Accrédités Auprès de la Société des Nations), as formed in 1921. The first president was H. Wilson Harris of the London *Daily News,* with André Glarner of the British Exchange Telegraph Company (Extel) as secretary.[1]

One of the first acts of the correspondents was to make representations to the League Council to ask formal recognition of the "rights and privileges" of journalists at Geneva, and that "all reasonable facilities" be accorded them for the performance of their duties. Such assurances were given though hardly needed, Harris wrote later, because all journalists "were extremely well looked after by the Information Section of the Secretariat."

The League occupied the former large Hôtel National, facing on the lake at Geneva and remodeled to meet the new requirements. This in-

---

1   Others to head the organization in later years included Henri Ruffin, Agence Havas; Frank Filliol, Agence Télégraphique Suisse; André Glarner, Extel; Ramon de Franch, *La Prensa,* Buenos Aires; Georg Bernhard, *Vossische Zeitung,* Berlin; Wythe Williams, *New York Times;* Wenceslas Oryng, Polska Agencja Telegraficzna (PAT); and Clarence K. Streit, *New York Times.*

cluded work rooms and communications facilities for the press. Virtually all meetings were open to correspondents. They received advance schedules, relevant documents and, later, summaries, texts of addresses, and other publications.

Correspondents had an unusual opportunity to mingle and converse with delegates and with secretariat members in the rooms and corridors of League headquarters, to drink and dine with them in the hotels and restaurants of Geneva, and to meet at many social affairs. Through these opportunities, unmatched at any previous time or place, they were able to acquaint themselves with the business of the League and to establish personal friendships among world leaders and personalities who came to Geneva. It contributed to perceptive news writing bearing upon the entire range of international affairs.

As radio correspondents began to appear in Geneva in the 1930s they were admitted to the International Association of Journalists and received equal treatment in every way. In 1932 the League put its own powerful broadcasting station into operation at Geneva. Known as "Radio Nations," its transmitter was used by the League to report to the world on its activities. Press and radio correspondents also were able to use the facilities to transmit dispatches and to make their broadcasts. A telephone switchboard provided direct connections throughout the world.

The League sponsored some gatherings outside of Geneva, and the Information Section assisted correspondents on those occasions in the same manner as in Geneva. Such meetings occurred at Rapallo, San Remo, the Spa, Genoa, Rome, Brussels, Stresa, Locarno, twice at Lausanne and Paris, four times at London, and at other places as well. One of these sessions, a World Economic Conference in London in the spring of 1933, offering what proved to be vain hopes for a solution to the international crisis of the time, probably had the largest attendance, with 565 correspondents present.

The first ten years of the League's existence represented a period of hope that it might serve as intended to assure permanent peace in the world. It had sixty-three member states at its maximum. The crises that arose after 1931, however, brought both an erosion of that hope and a decline in membership, with Japan, Italy, and Germany among those announcing withdrawal between 1932 and 1937, and the Soviet Union, only admitted in 1934, actually expelled in 1939 following its invasion of Finland.

Nine other member states announced withdrawal, beginning with Costa Rica in 1925 for financial reasons, Spain and Brazil in 1926, followed by Paraguay, Guatemala, Honduras, Nicaragua, El Salvador, Chile, and Venezuela, all between 1935 and 1938. Austria and Czechoslovakia, both original members, were automatically out of the League after 1938 when those countries were made unwilling parts of Nazi Germany. Peru and Hungary withdrew in 1939.

The League, despite its disappointing end, nevertheless represented an important influence in international news gathering. It set an example, through its Information Section, as to how any and all nations might assist the media in reporting public affairs. Both officials and news correspondents from all parts of the world had an opportunity to observe the methods and advantages of expert handling of such matters. While they did not all apply the methods in their own countries, some improvements were made internationally. Unfortunately, some also learned ways to apply the methods in a negative manner to a propaganda purpose.

Until those first years immediately following the war, journalists of the various countries had had only limited opportunity to know one another. It was rare, even among foreign correspondents, for one individual to become more than superficially acquainted with the method of a journalist's work in any country other than his own.

The Paris Peace Conference, with 500 correspondents present, while not the first international gathering of newsmen, was the largest, was continued for the longest time, and was the most diverse in its membership. It did provide an occasion for the press group to become acquainted and to gain some perspective on matters of news availability and coverage in an atmosphere of relative freedom. Other conferences soon to follow, as in Washington and London, added to the Paris experience. Those in Geneva, however, were notably effective.

Dr. Charles Hodges, in *The Background of International Relations* (1931), observed that through the League personal contact between diplomats and heads of state became more direct and constant than ever before, that the meetings and negotiations were dramatized and humanized with issues of peace as well as war brought into the headlines, and that "the international journalist" became a reality in world affairs.

Prior to World War I, in the view of Hodges, "news gatherers were overwhelmingly circumscribed by their national outlook," with little contact between groups, and little opportunity to check on various sources of information except to a limited degree in London, Paris, and New York. The beginning of better press relations, with professional cooperation between working journalists and the closer relations with officials that came at the time of the Paris Peace Conference, he notes, was greatly advanced in the next decade through "the series of post-war conferences and the work of the League of Nations."

The number of delegations at the Peace Conference, along with the "complex character of the negotiations, the secrecy, and the propaganda made news gathering a nightmare at Paris," Hodges says. He quotes Sweetser as noting that "there was little exchange of news or views" between "national and usually nationalistic correspondents compartmented into groups." This situation was modified, however, as the conference continued. The attempt, certainly by Baker and Sweetser of the U.S. delegation, to bring diverse groups together is cited as the beginning of an "integration" of the press in world affairs. "It was a new experience for newspaper men," Sweetser wrote later. "For the first time in history an official document was transmitted without fear of duplication, for simultaneous release to the press of all nations." Relevant also was a news conference conducted by Assistant Secretary of the Navy Franklin D. Roosevelt and its influence upon French newsmen and officials.[2]

The League extended this open provision of information to newsmen of all countries and, as Hodges says, "made Geneva a source of international facts more objective and less liable to nationalistic distortion than any spot on the map of world politics."

To the time Hodges wrote in 1930, the prospects seemed excellent for continued improvement in news exchange contributing to the information and welfare of all peoples, and to prospects for world peace. From 1930 to 1939, however, the situation deteriorated, with the League itself only routinely operative after 1939.

The League, while it existed, had approached basic problems of information, sponsoring a number of meetings specifically concerned with press matters and intended to improve the standards of world news reporting and exchange. It summoned a Committee of Press Experts to meet in Geneva in 1925 to consider means to advance the dissemination of information of substance. Directors of news agencies were brought together in 1926, and a special Committee of Journalists in 1927, along with a Committee on Communications and Press Representatives in 1928. So not only correspondents, but news executives, editors and publishers of various countries were becoming acquainted.

There had been local, regional, and national meetings of editors and publishers in earlier times, and such meetings continued. The League gatherings were designed, however, to explore matters of news pro-

---

2 This was an occasion when Roosevelt conducted a Washington-style news conference in Paris in 1918. Its informality and frankness was a new experience for French and other European newsmen attending. France's Premier Clemenceau protested later, concerned lest French journalists might demand similar opportunities in their relationship to the Paris government. See Robert W. Desmond, *Windows on the World* (Iowa City: University of Iowa Press, 1980), p. 411.

cedures internationally. This was with a view to advancing the dissemination of full and accurate information on matters of importance to all peoples, and in the interest of good world relations.

In 1931, the League Assembly, with the background provided by the earlier meetings under its sponsorship, and with the same constructive purpose, approved a plan to invite press organizations of the world to join with government representatives in a Conference of Directors of Government Press Bureaux and Press Representatives. Called by the Danish government as host, it met in Copenhagen in January 1932.

Questionnaires distributed world-wide by the League in advance of that meeting solicited the views of practicing journalists as to means by which international news reporting and communication might be improved. A considerable response was received by the Secretariat. The returns came between March and July 1932, too late to have value for the Copenhagen meeting, but nevertheless of potential value in providing some of the first broadly based expressions on the issues and on the practices in international news gathering and presentation. Responses came from the American Society of Newspaper Editors (ASNE), the British National Union of Journalists in London, the Maison de Presse in Paris, and editorial groups of other countries.

Analysis and criticism of the press had not been lacking before 1920, but there is no question that more attention was given from that time to the faults and virtues of the media of information, with a view to improvement. Improvement did come in some countries. The League was not alone in sponsoring such self-examination. Press performance on the world stage was examined between 1920 and 1935 in a series of meetings of British and British Empire or Commonwealth publishers, editors, journalists, and government personalities. Indeed, the first such meeting had taken place in London in 1909, sponsored by the British Empire Press Union. The second, an Imperial Press Conference, met at Ottawa in 1921 and was highly important. It brought together editors freshly aware of the experiences of the war and particularly interested in improved press communication at lower rates. If possible, they wished to see that rate set at no more than a penny a word for dispatches moving between any two points in the empire, as an encouragement to unity and understanding. A third empire conference met in Australia in 1925, a fourth in London in 1930, and a fifth in South Africa in 1935. All tended to reinforce the positive and constructive needs expressed at Ottawa, and they explored a variety of other subjects relating to the performance of the press, with a concern for the best possible information service, as well as for the strength of the Commonwealth.

Three so-called Press Congresses of the World during those years gave further attention to the international exchange of information. They originated in discussions among editors assembled in San Francisco in 1915 on the occasion of the Panama-Pacific Exposition, celebrating the opening of the Panama Canal, then seen as holding prospects for a new Pacific era. The first Press Congress of the World, as proposed at San Francisco, met in Honolulu in 1921. A second met in Geneva and Lausanne in 1926, and a third in Mexico City in 1931. No substantive action emerged, but the meetings advanced the acquaintanceship of men and women from various countries with a professional and informed interest in world news reporting and communications. Further, a proposal for a Pan-American Congress of Journalists also emerged from the fifth Pan-American Conference meeting in Santiago, Chile, in 1923. Out of this came a beginning of an Inter-American Press Association (IAPA) in 1928, although its full organization was delayed until 1943.

The results of these various efforts were constructive. In countries where the media were able to operate without government interference, and where standards of literacy and social relations were appropriate, media practices improved. Under such circumstances and on balance, the public was increasingly well served in matters of information through the years from 1920 to about 1933. Beyond that time, unfortunately, such advances as occurred were spotty.

Germany and Central Europe   2

In Germany, the proclamation of a Socialist republic in Berlin on November 9, 1918, contributed toward the country's acceptance of an armistice in the war and to the kaiser's abdication. A provisional government was formed under the leadership of Philip Scheidemann and Friedrich Ebert, both members of the Reichstag.

The authority of the announced government was immediately contested by an extreme left Socialist group known as the Spartacus Union, or the Sparticists, soon espousing the Communist cause, and headed by Karl Liebknecht and Rosa Luxemburg. A Sparticist revolt in Berlin in January 1919 seeking to gain control was crushed by the provisional government using surviving army forces, and both Liebknecht and Luxemburg were killed while under arrest. In February, Kurt Eisner, a Bavarian politician and former Socialist journalist, conspiring to re-establish the monarchy, was shot and killed in Munich. Neither the Monarchist nor the Communist groups, at extremes of the political spectrum, were as yet out of contention in a struggle for control in Germany. The direction matters might take was uncertain.

Under the provisional government, a National Assembly met February 6, 1919, at Weimar in Thuringia. Ebert was chosen as the first president of the German Republic, with Scheidemann as premier. A new cabinet, meeting in June 1919, accepted the terms of the Versailles Treaty submitted to the German delegation there in May. Reluctantly accepted by the Weimar Assembly, the treaty was signed in the Hall of Mirrors June 28 and ratified by the German government on July 7. A constitution was drafted and adopted on July 31, and became effective on August 11.

Meanwhile, the German fleet, due to be surrendered to the Allies under the terms of the Versailles Treaty, had been scuttled by its crew at Scapa Flow in the Orkney Islands, Scotland, on June 21, just a week before the treaty itself was signed. An Allied blockade of German ports was lifted on July 12, but not before many in Germany were near starvation. Allied troops were in occupation in western Germany, along the Rhine River.

The year 1920 had hardly begun when the Weimar government was faced by a double threat in March—a so-called Kapp Putsch, in which a monarchial group seized government buildings in Berlin, and a new Sparticist, or Communist uprising in the Ruhr coal mining and industrial area centering around Essen.

The Kapp Putsch took its name from Wolfgang Kapp, New York-born in 1868 but raised in Germany. He was a member of the Reichstag in 1918, and a strong Monarchist and organizer of the conspiracy to occupy the government buildings. Others involved in the attempted *coup d'état* were General Erich von Ludendorff, a wartime leader, his former chief of staff, Colonel Max Bauer, and General Walther von Lüttwitz.

Ebert and the German government left Berlin for Dresden as former soldiers recruited into an irregular military organization by the Kapp group prepared to overthrow the republic. That effort failed within a few days because of lack of support from other army veterans or parties of the right, and because of outright resistance by labor unions and working-class groups, who called an effective general strike. Lüttwitz and Kapp fled the country. Lüttwitz was never heard of again. Kapp, upon returning in 1922, was arrested for treason, but died before he came to trial. Ludendorff and Bauer, less in the forefront, remained in Germany, and Ludendorff later joined with Adolf Hitler in 1923–24 in the formation of a National Socialist (Nazi) party.

The Spartacist uprising in the Ruhr was no more successful, but it had other significant results. Beginning on March 19, 1920, just after the Kapp Putsch had collapsed, it continued until April 3. The end came as German troops entered the Ruhr and suppressed the revolt with great violence. The very fact that German troops were used was regarded as contrary to the terms of the Versailles Treaty, and France reacted by sending its own forces into some parts of the Ruhr and also occupied the city of Frankfurt.

Still, the Weimar Republic was not secure. Right-wing Nationalists were strongly represented in the Reichstag and often fostered illegal semimilitary groups looking toward the re-establishment of a strong Germany. Their activities led to two political murders. Matthias Erzberger, a Centre party leader for many years, a member of the provisional government in 1918, a signer of the armistice document, and then vice-chancellor, was murdered in August 1921. The second victim was Walther Rathenau, foreign minister in the Weimar government and an industrialist, who was killed in Berlin in June 1922. It was to be 1925, following the death of President Ebert in February and the election of Field Marshal Paul von Hindenburg to that office in April, before the republic was accepted fully by the German people themselves.[1]

Much else had occurred in Germany during those same years. At a conference at the Spa in July 1920, the Weimar government signed documents agreeing to disarmament, as required under the terms of the Versailles Treaty. At the same time, it reached an agreement relating to the payment of reparations calling for payments both in cash and in goods. It was agreed that the reparations would be apportioned between France (52 per cent), Great Britain (22 per cent), Italy (10 per cent), Belgium (8 per cent), and the remaining 8 per cent to be divided among the other Allied and associated powers. The United States, having refused to ratify the Versailles Treaty, was to receive no reparations.

From this time, much of the German problem was financial, relating to the payment of reparations. The Versailles Treaty had specified that Germany, held responsible for starting the war, should pay for all civilian damage caused, with the precise amount to be determined later. Much of its merchant and fishing fleet was to be turned over to the Allies and 200,000 tons of new shipping was to be built annually for five years for the Allied countries. Railroad rolling stock was to be transferred, as well as German cables. Great quantities of coal were to be delivered for ten years to France, Belgium, and Italy. German property in the Allied countries was to be sold to interests in those countries, and the cost of maintaining the Allied armies of occupation in Germany was to be borne.

A Reparations Commission had been created by the Allies at the time of the Spa Conference in 1920. It met in Paris and London in 1921 and assessed the civilian damages at $33 billion, to be paid by Germany over a period of thirty years. The Weimar government under protest was obliged to accept this demand in May 1921, and under threat of a further extension of the occupation unless $1 billion was paid immediately. The Germans were able to borrow that amount in London, and agreed to a schedule for future payments. Even so, failure to pay an asserted default on a $5 billion payment already had brought an extension of the Allied military occupation in March 1921; troops then moved into three Rhine cities, Düsseldorf, Duisburg, and Ruhrort.

It was virtually impossible for Germany, just after 1920, to meet the reparations demands, particularly for cash payments. There was little

---

1   The writer, in Berlin in 1924, observed a tendency among the German people at that time to view President Ebert with something less than full respect.

industry or commerce. The German mark, with a prewar value of 23.8 cents (U.S. currency), had fallen during 1921 to half that figure. The Weimar Republic lacked strength and the political disorders of the time delayed economic reorganization and recovery. The need to set aside funds for reparations payments further blocked an internal recovery that might otherwise have produced revenue.

By the spring of 1922 it had become obvious even to the Allies that the German currency situation was deteriorating, with the mark possibly to lose all value. In the circumstances, the Reparations Commission granted a moratorium on May 31, 1922, excusing Germany from further payments during that year. France protested the action.

France was adamant about payments in goods. Premier Raymond Poincaré proposed that sixty per cent of the capital control in German dyestuff factories and state-owned mines be appropriated. In December 1922, France also declared Germany in default on deliveries of timber and coal. In support of the latter protest, French and Belgian troops occupied the Ruhr coal and industrial district of Germany on January 11, 1923. Great Britain protested this occupation as unauthorized by the Versailles Treaty, and Italy supported that view.

The German government reacted to the occupation by suspending all delivery of goods to the Allies. This led a Franco-Belgian Commission in the Ruhr to arrest mine owners and to take over direction both of the mines and of the railroads in the area. The German government, in turn, supported a policy of passive resistance on the part of miners and of the people in the Ruhr. To assist the many thus out of work, and lacking any income, the Weimar government made cash payments to them, and also to owners of the mines and the idle factories. This so inflated the currency that by September of 1923 the German mark was worthless, and the entire German economy was in disarray.[2] Rental incomes had no meaning and private savings were wiped out. Foreign speculators were able to buy up property, buildings, and industries for a fraction of their true value. The effect, of course, was felt throughout Europe and the world, and the value of the French franc itself was seriously reduced.

Events related to this collapse opened a new chapter in the affairs of Germany, Europe, and the world. First, under the Weimar Republic, a new cabinet was formed in August 1923, the sixth since 1919, although still under Ebert's presidency. Gustav Stresemann, leader of the People's Party, was chancellor, with a mandate to solve the financial problem and with support from the Socialist, Centre, and Democratic parties.

---

2 The price for a copy of a newspaper, for example, rose to 200 billion marks, the equivalent of $4,760,000,000 at the prewar value of the mark.

Under the Stresemann government, passive resistance ended in the Ruhr in September 1923. Dr. Hans Luther became minister of finance in that government, and Hjalmar Horace Greeley Schacht, a banker and economist, was appointed special currency commissioner.[3] It was their particular task to restore the value of the mark. A new so-called "rentenmark" was created. It was secured in principle by all land and industry within the German Reich, upon which the government held a theoretical blanket mortgage. The new currency was issued in the amount of 3.2 billion gold marks ($7,616,000,000), to be exchanged for a trillion of the old marks. Schacht was made president of a new state Reichsbank, and Luther applied drastic means to balance the national budget. By 1924 the economy had assumed an orderly position. Efforts were being made to establish good relations with other countries, including those of the Allies, to stimulate an exchange of goods, and to promote tourism within the Reich.

The complete breakdown in Germany in 1923, with danger of civil war or anarchy and a possible turn to communism, forced even France to make some concessions on coal deliveries from the Ruhr, and to join in two committees organized to restudy the problem of reparations payments. Stanley Baldwin, British prime minister, also had persuaded the United States government to join in a cooperative effort to save Europe and perhaps the world from financial disaster.

Accordingly, one of the committees formed in November 1923 was headed by Charles G. Dawes, a Chicago attorney and banker. He had been commissioned a general on the AEF headquarters staff in France, with responsibility for supplies, and then was the first director of the U.S. Bureau of the Budget in 1921–22. His committee prepared a report proposing a means to deal with the reparations problem, with modifications in the terms of the treaty. This "Dawes Plan" was ready in April 1924. It was accepted by the German government and was adopted at a conference in London in August.

The plan included the specification that French and Belgian troops were to be withdrawn from the Ruhr, as they were by November 1924. The German Reichsbank was reorganized, still headed by Schacht, but under Allied supervision, and the rentenmark became the reichsmark. It was specified that Germany was to pay 1 billion gold marks ($238 million) annually in reparations, rising at the end of five years to 2.5 billion. At the same time, a foreign loan equivalent to 800 million gold marks (about $190 million) was to be made available to Germany to bolster her economy, financed by the sale of German government

---

3   Schacht was born in Germany in 1877. His father had lived in New York in the early 1870s and conceived an admiration for Horace Greeley, editor of the *New York Tribune*.

bonds. Of this, $110 million was provided through bond sales in the United States, and a further substantial amount in Great Britain. Under this arrangement, the German economy was to recover.

When affairs within Germany still remained seriously out of joint in November 1923, before the Dawes Plan was ready, one of a number of extremist political groups in Bavaria attempted a *coup*. Known as the German National Socialist Workers Party (Nationalsozialistische Deutsche Arbeiterpartie) (N.S.D.A.P.) or the Nazi party, it was headed by General Erich von Ludendorff, who had been involved in the 1920 Kapp Putsch in Berlin. Respected by many as a wartime military leader, he had suffered a mental breakdown at the end of the war and had dreams of new power. A leader in the Nazi party group was a former non-commissioned officer, Austrian-born Adolf Hitler, then thirty-four years old.

The group's attempted coup in a so-called "Beer Hall Putsch" in Munich on November 8–11 failed and Hitler, prominently identified with the effort, was arrested. Sentenced to five years in prison, he was released in less than a year. During his imprisonment, he had written *Mein Kampf* (My Struggle) in which he described his life, ideas, and a political program. By the time of his release, Germany was proceeding under the Dawes Plan, with order restored and the National Socialist party group was all but forgotten.

Germany's President Ebert died in 1925. Former Field Marshal von Hindenburg, in retirement since 1919, was elected in his stead. The French left Düsseldorf and the other Rhine cities they had occupied in 1921, and a Locarno Conference in October 1925 added further to a new European sense of security. In 1926 Germany was admitted to the League of Nations, and plans were begun for a world disarmament conference. From 1925 German industry was growing and prospering. The country became active at sea, with a merchant marine and new passenger liners soon plying the Atlantic. Tourist business stimulated the economy.

Germany was having no problem meeting its reparations payments in those years after 1925. The schedule called for the payments to more than double in 1930, however. It seemed timely to re-examine that schedule and also to set up arrangements that would permit the Allies to end their supervision of the Reichsbank, as provided under the Dawes Plan, and to let the Germans assume full responsibility for transferring marks into foreign currencies by way of handling the payments. A new committee to implement this change met in Paris from March to June 1929. It was under the chairmanship of Owen D. Young, who had been a member of the Dawes committee. He was a Boston lawyer, general counsel of the General Electric Company, and chairman of the board of directors of the Radio Corporation of America, and his committee produced the "Young Plan."

The Young Plan called for the establishment of a new financial institution, a Bank for International Settlements, to be set up at Basel, Switzerland. Its directorate would include representatives of ten central banks in European countries and in Great Britain. German reparations payments would be made through that bank. A revised schedule of payments was specified. Germany was to pay 666 million Reichsmarks ($157 million) each year, unconditionally, out of an annual total due of 1,707 million Reichsmarks ($406.2 million), of which the difference might be postponed for two years. These annuities were to be paid until 1988, with the unconditional annuities secured by a mortgage on the German state railway system, financed through a new bond issue. Since Germany had been paying a billion Reichsmarks ($238 million) annually under the Dawes Plan, with no apparent strain, and since its economy had improved greatly, it was believed that payments under the Young Plan would be no problem when handled through the Bank for International Settlements. Germany agreed to the plan at a Hague Conference in August 1929. The last of the Allied troops in occupation of Germany were withdrawn in June 1930. The Bank for International Settlements was formed. With Germany proceeding prosperously, the outlook for a general recovery and peaceful development in Europe and the world seemed at last to be favorable.

Further hope rested in the fact that Aristide Briand, French foreign minister, and Frank B. Kellogg, U.S. secretary of state, had joined in an effort that produced a Pact of Paris, signed by fifteen nations in 1928. It renounced war as "an instrument of national policy" for the solution of international controversies.[4]

Stresemann, the German foreign minister, in 1927 had urged the League of Nations to sponsor a conference seeking a world-wide agreement on disarmament, and such a conference was planned for 1932. Already there had been a Washington Naval Conference of 1921–22, an International Economic Conference at Geneva in 1927, and a London Naval Conference was to meet in 1930. These all offered promise of a better world.

The importance of the events in Germany during the decade of the 1920s, and of the related conferences mentioned, received full attention in the world press. Radio, as a new medium of information, also was providing reports in increasing measure by the end of the decade.

---

4 Kellogg was awarded the Nobel Peace Prize in 1929. Dawes, who had served as vice-president of the United States in the Coolidge cabinet in 1925–29, and then was U.S. ambassador to Great Britain in 1929–32, also had been awarded the Nobel Peace Prize in 1925. Briand and Stresemann shared the prize in 1926.

Foreign reporters in Berlin had reasonably good sources of information among officials and among the people at various levels of society. They were free to move about the country as they wished. A vigorous newspaper and periodical press provided information to the highly literate population and was of great value to correspondents seeking an understanding of the country and the widest range of opinion.

Every move of the Weimar government was reported. It had been possible from the outset to report even those stories of disorder and violence. These, of course, included also the runaway inflation of 1923, the Munich Beer Hall Putsch, and moving tides of population, including an influx of Jews escaping from Poland and Russia, refugees from the civil war and communist regimes in those areas. There were stories relating to the Allied occupation in Germany and the extensions of that occupation. Correspondents based in London, Geneva, Paris, Vienna, and even Washington sometimes joined with those in Berlin to report matters bearing upon the German situation. This also required attention to events in adjacent countries, notably Austria, Hungary, and Czechoslovakia.

Austria

The Austro-Hungarian Empire was dismembered following the war. What had been a monarchy of fifty million population occupying an area of 241,000 square miles became three separate republics, Austria, Hungary, and Czechoslovakia. In the settlements made at the Paris Peace Conference, moreover, nearly half of the original territory and about twenty million persons living in those areas were assigned to Rumania and to the new kingdom of the Serbs, Croats, and Slovenes, later to be called Yugoslavia.

Austria itself, previously the heart of the dual empire, was reduced to a country of just over 32,000 square miles in area, with a population of less than seven million. Of these, about two million lived in Vienna, still a capital city, but a capital without sufficient hinterland to feed the population properly. The structure of the new country was seriously out of balance. The residents of Vienna, seeking a solution to their problems, turned to socialism. This put them at odds with the people of the countryside, who were conservative and greatly influenced by the clergy. There was an almost immediate concern lest Communist influences should prevail.

Under a coalition government originally headed by Karl Renner, a Socialist, with Viktor Adler and then Otto Bauer as foreign minister, a proposal was made for a union with Germany, but this was denied by the Allies under the terms of the treaties. In elections of 1920, Renner was succeeded as chancellor by Michael Mayr, and in 1922 Mayr was succeeded by Ignaz Seipel. There was so sharp an inflation at that time that the League of Nations arranged for an international loan to bolster the economy.

Matters improved somewhat after 1922, aided by exports of textiles, pharmaceuticals, clothing, and other products, and by a growing tourism. Heavy property taxes were imposed to provide low-rent housing for workers, and to support public health and education programs. The Socialist government maintained a defense force (Schutzbund), but a rival force (Heimwehr) was formed by reactionary elements in the provinces. These forces sometimes were in conflict.

Such a clash occurred in January 1927 at Schattendorf, near the Hungarian border, with two civilians shot by the Heimwehr, an elderly man and a child. When their murderers were acquitted by a Vienna jury in July, a mass demonstration by workers resulted in the burning of the Ministry of Justice. In an assertion of authority, Seipel ordered the police to fire on other demonstrators, of whom eighty-five were killed, as well as four police officers. The Social Democrats responded with a general strike lasting four days. While civil peace then was restored, and a Socialist democracy proceeded in a superficially orderly fashion, neither the political nor economic situation in Austria was secure after those episodes of July 1927.

The events and circumstances centering in Vienna were reported by resident correspondents and by the local press. As in earlier times, Vienna also remained a center for the coverage of events throughout the Balkans.

Hungary

Hungary, separated from Austria in November 1918 as the dual empire came to an end, was proclaimed an independent republic at that time, with Budapest continuing as its capital. Count Michael (Mihály) Károlyi, of an ancient family and in the government since 1905, was the first premier. He then was appointed as president in January 1919, but resigned in March. A Socialist-Communist administration followed immediately, but the Socialists were forced out and a Communist dictatorship was formed under Béla Kun, who had been a Lenin associate in Russia. He directed an attack on Czechoslovakia with a view to regaining former Hungarian territory assigned to that new republic, but was forced by the Allies to withdraw. In July, he attacked Rumania for the same reason, but Rumania responded by sending its own forces against Hungary and Béla Kun fled to Vienna on August 1. Rumanian troops reached Budapest on August 4 and remained until November looting the city, and only withdrew from Hungary altogether in February 1920.

With Béla Kun's departure from Hungary, a provisional government was formed by members of the old regime, Archduke Joseph, Admiral Nicholas Horthy, Count Stephen (István) Bethlen, and Count Julius Károlyi, brother of the first Károlyi, who acted briefly as president. Horthy, commander of the military forces, became head of state upon withdrawal of the Rumanian forces. In June 1920, four months later, the Treaty of Trianon assigned almost two-thirds of Hungary's former territory, with almost one-third of its population, variously to Czechoslovakia, Rumania, and Yugoslavia.

Admiral Horthy in March 1920 had proclaimed Hungary a monarchy rather than a republic and styled himself as regent, with the intention of recalling King Charles, who had succeeded Francis Joseph of Austria-Hungary upon his death in 1916. He had ruled as Charles I of Austria and Charles IV of Hungary until the time of the armistice of October 1918, when he took refuge in Switzerland. He was prepared to return, however, to restore the Hapsburg monarchy in Hungary, and he did return to Budapest in March 1921, ready to replace Horthy.

Neither Austria nor other neighboring states favored such a restoration of the monarchy in Hungary, and their objections led the Hungarian National Assembly to vote against it. Charles went back to Switzerland, but returned to Hungary in October 1921 with a small military force supporting what was intended as a *coup* by which he would gain the throne. Czechoslovakia and Yugoslavia began to mobilize, but a Hungarian force itself intervened to capture the former king. On this occasion, he was exiled to the Portuguese island of Madeira, where he died a few months later, although only thirty-five.

Following the first unsuccessful action by which Charles might have taken over power from Horthy in March 1921, a new cabinet was formed by Count Bethlen, formerly in the provisional government of 1919, and a great landowner. He headed the government of the republic for the next ten years, proceeding under a conservative policy that kept order in the country and generally good relations with other countries. Internal opposition groups were dealt with harshly, however, and Jews were persecuted.

The sequence of events in Hungary was reported for the world press chiefly through the Wolff and Havas agencies, but also by visiting correspondents moving primarily out of Vienna.

Czechoslovakia was proclaimed as a new republic in 1918, carved out of the Austrio-Hungarian Empire. It included Bohemia in the west, with Prague as the capital, Moravia-Silesia in the middle section, and mountainous Slovakia and Ruthenia in the east. Occupying a major area of Central Europe, Czechoslovakia was larger (54,000 square miles) and more populous (14.5 million) than either Austria or Hungary.

Basically a Slavic country, with a history of its own dating from the Middle Ages and the Holy Roman Empire, the republic was largely the creation of Thomas G. Masaryk, long a professor at the University of Prague. He enlisted the support of Czechs and Slovaks in the United States during the course of the war, with his efforts centering in Pittsburgh and Washington, where the interest and sympathy of President Wilson also was gained. Masaryk was assisted in his efforts by a former student, Dr. Eduard Beneš.

With the Austrian surrender on October 28, 1918, Masaryk proclaimed in Prague the Republic of Czechoslovakia. He became president two days later, with Beneš as foreign minister. The new nation was recognized by the Allies in the drafting of the peace treaties at Paris. Czechoslovakia became a charter member of the League of Nations, and also joined in the Little Entente, with France, Rumania, and Yugoslavia.

Rich in agriculture and in coal and iron resources, Czechoslovakia was the center for much of the industry that had existed in the Austro-Hungarian Empire, with a large and skilled working force. The new republic proceeded through the next decade, well governed and economically prosperous. A land-reform program also provided opportunities for individual farmers, with the introduction of improved techniques and the establishment of marketing cooperatives. Coal and lumber production grew, as did iron and steel and related manufacturing. Textiles, boots and shoes, beer, glass, chemicals, and other industries contributed further to an active export trade.

The major problem related to the position of minorities within the country. These included persons still counting themselves as Austrians, Hungarians, or Germans. There also was a surviving protest by Hungary and Poland over the assignment to Czechoslovakia of border areas they considered theirs.

The individual or the country in trouble receives attention in the news. Regrettable though it seems, lack of trouble tends to mean lack of attention. A remarkable success or a constructive event also receives attention, and happily there are enough such occasions to provide a certain balance in any day's budget of news. But if nothing unusual happens, good or bad, there is not much occasion for publishing a report that "nothing special happened today." Thus, Czechslovakia, one of the few successful and peaceful countries of the world during the third decade of the century, was seldom in the news. Routine matters and the few departures from it were reported through the news agency services and by stringers in Prague, but it was rare for a special correspondent to visit the country or remain for long during the 1920s.

The Soviet Union and Eastern Europe 3

The Russian Revolution of 1917, in its first phase in March, brought the abdication of Czar Nicholas II. It led to the Bolshevik Revolution of November.[1] This led in turn to the establishment in March of 1918 of a Communist party government based in Moscow, the ancient capital, rather than in St. Petersburg, which had been the capital since 1703. St. Petersburg was renamed Petrograd in 1914, and became Leningrad in 1924, following the death of Nikolai Lenin.

The end of the czarist government, restrictive and backward, was viewed by many as holding promise for something better. The Bolshevik Revolution, bringing an end to Russia's participation in the war as one of the Allied nations, was a different matter, however. As seen by the Allies, at least, it threatened to release German military forces previously occupied on the eastern front for service in France, with prospects of tilting the balance toward victory for the Central Powers. This threat, indeed, was real. Further, the introduction of a Communist government in Russia was viewed with alarm by many, especially as it was accompanied by an avowed intent to extend an untested and disturbing Communist ideology to other countries wherever possible.

The leaders of the new government in Russia were those "old Bolsheviks" who had been advocates for years past of an extreme form of socialism finding its inspiration in the writings of Prussian-born Karl Heinrich Marx (1818–83), son of a Jewish lawyer baptized in the Christian faith with his family in 1824, when Karl was six years old. Karl Marx, educated at the universities of Bonn and Berlin, became a polemical journalist and as such was expelled both from Germany and France. In 1849 he and Friedrich Engels (1820–95), from the same part of Prussia, and with whom he had become associated in Paris, settled

---

1 Under the old Russian (Gregorian) calendar, these two revolutions occurred in February and October 1917, and references sometimes are made to the "October revolution." The western (Julian) calendar was adopted for use in Russia on February 1, 1918. The 1917 dates thus became March and November for Russian use, as well as in the west, with November 7 long observed in Moscow as the date of the revolution.

in London. There Marx became correspondent for the *New York Tribune,* writing a weekly letter during the 1850s, and Engels is believed to have written it for him at times.

The commanding figure among the old Bolsheviks in 1917–18, and much beyond that, was Nikolai Lenin, an alias adopted by Vladimir Ilyich Ulyanov. Such aliases also were adopted by others as a means of self-protection in their careers as social revolutionaries. Among them were Leon Trotsky (Lev Davidovich Bronstein), who became first commissar (or minister) for foreign affairs in the new government, and then commissar for war, organizing the Red Army with impressive results. Georgy V. Chicherin followed Trotsky as commissar for foreign affairs until 1930. He was succeeded in turn by Maxim M. Litvinov from 1930–39, and then by V. M. Molotov. Others holding key positions were L. B. Kamenev (Rosenfeld) and Grigori E. Zinoviev (Radomyslsky), both close associates of Lenin; Joseph V. Stalin (Dzhugashvili), who became secretary-general of the Communist party in 1922 and Lenin's successor as head of the government in 1924; A. V. Lunacharsky, N. I. Bukharin, A. I. Rykov, Karl Radek, and others holding key positions. In their years as political advocates many engaged in writing and speaking. Among these leaders, Lenin, Trotsky, Stalin, Kamenev, Zinoviev, Lunacharsky, and Bukharin all were experienced journalists, although strictly of a polemical variety.

The new Communist regime was insecure in March 1918. It moved to Moscow to be safer from its opposition than in Petrograd. The Treaty of Brest-Litovsk, ending Russia's war with Germany, was signed and ratified in that month. By its terms, Russia lost control of Poland, the Baltic states, Finland, and even the Ukraine. The treaty also required that raw materials be provided to Germany as an indemnity.

The Allies, still at war with Germany, learned that trainloads of war materials were moving from Russia to Germany, including oil, copper, and foodstuffs. To halt this flow, and a possible additional manpower diversion to German support as a labor force, British, French, U.S., and Japanese troops were moved into Russia in 1918, sometimes making common cause with White Russian elements combating the Communist regime. That regime responded by declaring war on Russia's former allies. After the German surrender in November, most of the Allied troops left Russia in 1919, but an Allied blockade was maintained until January 1920, and an effective peace was only restored in March 1921.

Within what had become Soviet Russia, White Russian forces contesting Communist control presented direct threats, even to Petrograd and Moscow, as late as October 1919. Further, an internal right-wing

Social Revolutionary group stood in opposition, and in Moscow a young woman member, Fanny (Anna) Kaplan, on August 30, 1918, shot and wounded Lenin. Another member, on the following day, killed M. S. Uritsky, a Communist leader, in Petrograd.[2]

The Soviet government gained the upper hand in its conflict with the White Russians late in 1919 not only by a reign of terror, but by a growing Red Army under Trotsky's direction, and by some organized local opposition effective in the Communist cause. In Poland and the Baltic states, the battle continued with a Polish army under Marshal Joseph Pilsudski resupplied and reinforced by Allied effort to sustain Peace Conference settlements. From mid-August 1920, as a result, a Red Army advance in northern Europe was turned to a defeat; an armistice was signed with the former Allies in October and peace terms in March 1921. Areas once part of Czarist Russia, including Poland, the Baltic states, Finland, and some of the Ukraine and Byelorussia, lost to Germany in the Brest-Litovsk settlement, were lost again in the 1921 settlement.

At the time of the Russo-German Brest-Litovsk Treaty signature in March 1918, the war was still in progress, and the Communist regime had sought to persuade the Allies to provide support against the Germans. Trotsky made such an approach through R. H. Bruce-Lockhart, an unofficial British representative then in Russia, and also through Raymond Robins of the American Red Cross. This proposal was rejected by the Allies as unrealistic in the circumstances. They also viewed the Brest-Litovsk Treaty as a betrayal. Some Allied leaders, further, suspected possible complicity between the new Communist government and Germany. They were uncertain, too, whether the Communist government would survive the opposition still active inside Russia, and sent their own forces into Russia as described.

With the war at an end in November and the Peace Conference beginning in Paris in January 1919, both the Social Revolutionary group in Russia and the Communist regime sought support from the victorious Allies. For the Soviet government, Chicherin, then the foreign commissar, made an appeal to the U.S. State Department. In Paris, representatives of the "Big Four" discussed a possible plan under which the White Russians, Communists, and other elements in Russia would meet in a neutral area to seek a settlement by which an administration might be established in Russia agreeable to all parties.

---

2 The Communist party had formed an "extraordinary commission" called the Cheka in December 1917 to deal with counter-revolutionary actions and sabotage. On the night following the attack on Lenin, 500 persons selected from among members of the "old regime" in Moscow were shot in reprisal. The same was done in Petrograd after Uritsky's death. With the Cheka acting as a kind of secret police, a reign of terror was thus instituted by the Communist party to help maintain its power.

In support of some such compromise agreement, William C. Bullitt, a member of the U.S. delegation at the Paris conference, went to Russia in March 1919 as a special emissary for President Wilson and Prime Minister Lloyd George, and with the support of Italy's Premier Orlando, although not of France's Premier Clemenceau. Bullitt carried a proposal fashioned by Colonel Edward M. House, Wilson's chief adviser, looking toward a settlement in Russia, with non-Communist elements participating. If some agreement were reached, with any new regime also recognizing the financial obligations of the former czarist government to the Allies, which the Communist regime so far had refused to do, the Allies would withdraw their forces in Russia and end the blockade against the country. Through meetings with Lenin and others, Bullitt also was to obtain information about the existing Soviet regime and its proposed policies for the guidance of negotiators in Paris.

Bullitt returned to France, having accomplished his mission with apparent distinction, and with some conditional agreements by the Communist leaders for consideration. By that time, however, the White Russian forces were making advances, and there was some belief that the Soviet regime might be overthrown. In the circumstances, neither Wilson nor Lloyd George was disposed to discuss compromises with the Communists, and neither man would see Bullitt, and never learned what he had to report. Bullitt himself remained silent, having been on a confidential mission.

One of the members of Bullitt's party visiting Moscow was Lincoln Steffens, known favorably there for his investigations and writing on urban and state government administration in the United States. A classical liberal, he had been sympathetic to the revolution when it occurred. In Russia, he arranged for John Reed to assist him as guide, interpreter, and secretary. Reed was one of the few western journalists remaining in Moscow. He had reported the revolution sympathetically as it occurred, and by 1919 was acting as a spokesman for the Communist government. Through Reed, and also through his participation in meetings with Lenin and others, Steffens was persuaded of the merits of the new regime. Unlike Bullitt, upon returning to Paris, Steffens spoke and wrote of the Russian visit, and had praise for the government. "I have seen the future," he wrote, "and it works."[3]

The civil war proceeding in Russian territory during 1918-20 held

---

3 See William L. Shirer, *20th Century Journey* (1976), pp. 441–47. Shirer also notes that Bullitt in 1923 married Louise Bryant Reed, widow of John Reed, who died in Moscow in 1920. They were divorced in 1930. Bullitt became the first U.S. ambassador to Soviet Russia (1933-36). See also Robert A. Rosenstone, *Romantic Revolutionary* (1975), and Barbara Gelb, *So Short a Time* (1973).

the possibility of a reversal of the Bolshevik Revolution and an end to the new Communist government. By the summer of 1920, however, the Red Army had gained strength, had driven Polish forces out of the Ukraine, and was nearing Warsaw itself. French military units in Poland under General Maxime Weygand to enforce the territorial provisions set by the Treaty of Versailles supported the Polish troops in driving the Red Army back. A treaty was signed at Riga in October. Its definitive terms in March 1921 set a Polish-Russian frontier and ended the war in the east.

Meanwhile, the Soviet Union designated a federated republic in 1918 became a true federation in December 1922, forming the Union of Soviet Socialist Republics (USSR), with a new constitution in 1923. The four federated republics of that time were to become eleven by 1936, and are now fifteen. The constitution gave formal recognition to the Communist party as holding ultimate authority. Membership in the party was not to be attained for the asking, and was always to be restricted to a small fraction of the total population. A tiny fraction of that group, moreover, forming a Central Committee, held the reins of power. The Central Committee members were elected, or re-elected by a party Congress, meeting about every four years. The Central Committee selected candidates for election, as a formality, to a Supreme Soviet, consisting of two chambers, and meeting twice each year in short sessions, if summoned.

The Central Committee members also select from among their number those to serve in a Council of Ministers, consisting of a Politburo (Presidium since 1952), and a party Secretariat. There is duplication among members so serving, but the Presidium with sixteen members exercises authority in practice, even though responsible in theory to the Supreme Soviet.

A member of the Presidium holding title as president of the USSR is formal head of state. The chairman of the Presidium is selected by its members and also is chairman of the party Secretariat. This same member also is chairman of the Council of Ministers, with an alternative title as premier. Occupying these three overlapping positions, but particularly by reason of his chairmanship of the Presidium, he holds major power and speaks with greatest authority. These posts were occupied by Lenin until his death in 1924, and then by Stalin.

The new Soviet government during the 1918–21 period was required to cope with dissatisfaction among the people arising from disorganization caused both by the war and the revolution. Industry and transportation had broken down. Banks and currency had lost meaning. Food, goods, and services were difficult to obtain. This made for great problems among city dwellers. Yet in the rural areas party efforts to control the system of agriculture disrupted established procedures. With forced deliveries of grain and other products, plus a great drought in early 1921, there were food shortages even among the peasants, of whom some ten million seemed likely to die of malnutrition or starvation.

Few of the people were members of the Communist party and therefore lacked dedication to a cause. The vast disorders, hunger, and discontent presented a threat to the regime. This was dramatized in a mutiny among sailors at the Kronstadt naval base near Petrograd in March 1921, only put down with great bloodshed. The loyalty of the army also was in question. With factories closed, workers were ranging the countryside in search of food, but with little to be found.

Europe itself then was in difficulties, with social and economic disruption widespread as a heritage of the war. Even so, shipments of food, medicines, and supplies might have been made to the Soviet Union, as they were being made available in southern Europe and elsewhere. The Soviet Union, however, had broken off normal relations with other peoples and nations; trade was at a virtual standstill. Further, the Communist party in March 1919 had formed a Third International (Comintern), headed by Grigori Zinoviev, with the announced purpose of propagating the Communist doctrine world-wide. This had frightened and antagonized governments, organizations, industrialists, and individuals in many lands. The Communist party also again had disavowed responsibility for the debts of the czarist government, including costs of the war in which many of those other lands had come to its aid. For all these reasons there was no rush to assist the Soviet government. That government also hesitated to seek assistance lest such an appeal to the much maligned capitalist world should reflect upon the Communist pretensions to administrative wisdom and popular support.

The crisis in the Soviet Union was such, however, that Lenin, as a realist, proposed that the Communist party program be modified, at least temporarily, to enable both peasants and workers to improve their own conditions. With no reasonable alternative presented by other members of the party, this change was authorized in a decree of August 9, 1921, and was referred to as a New Economic Policy (NEP). It remained in effect, in some measure, until 1927, and helped to restore and advance the situation in the country.

Before that program was introduced, however, the gravity of the food shortage was dealt with in another compromise. Quite unofficially, Maxim Gorky, world-famed for his contributions to literature, and a friend of Lenin's, was permitted to write a personal letter in July 1921 to Herbert Hoover. Then secretary of commerce in the new

Harding administration in Washington, Hoover also was chairman of the American Relief Administration (ARA), which had organized help for the people of Belgium and northern France in 1915-16. The ARA also had since extended help to people in need in other parts of Europe, in Armenia, and the Middle East. Gorky proposed to Hoover that the ARA provide help for the starving in Russia.

Hoover and the ARA responded. A mission headed by Colonel W. N. Haskell, director of the ARA, was in Riga by August 1921 for discussions with Maxim Litvinov, then assistant commissar for foreign affairs in the Soviet government.

Soviet leaders still were reluctant to have foreigners enter the country, even to bring aid to the millions affected by the famine. "Food is a weapon," Litvinov told ARA representatives. Another Soviet official, even more specific, said that while food was made available to Communist party members, it was a matter of indifference whether others starved, that persons suffering from hunger and malnutrition had little energy or strength to rebel and, meanwhile, the party could further entrench itself. Indeed, while the famine was at its worst, the Soviet government shipped some grain abroad for sale as a means to obtain foreign currency credits.

Desperate as the food situation was, the ARA group was only permitted to enter the Soviet Union in November 1921. Its work continued until late 1923, centering chiefly in the Ukraine. Bringing in foodstuffs, the ARA fed an average of ten million persons a day for that period at a total cost of about $63 million. Although it was estimated that a half million persons may have died before help was made available, perhaps twelve million were saved. In addition, the ARA presence brought an end to deaths from typhus and cholera, both long common in epidemic form in Russia.

The ARA received no cooperation or funds from the Soviet government in these efforts, but rather interference, and no public acknowledgment of its assistance and supplementary aid from the Red Cross and from British sources. After the ARA's withdrawal, some Russians who had worked with the mission were arrested and sent to remote labor camps.

Part of the agreement under which the ARA entered the Soviet Union was that newsmen of various countries also should be admitted so that they might report upon and verify the distribution of food and other supplies. Even though newsmen were admitted in November, none was attached to the ARA in the field. The Soviet government insisted that they remain in Moscow, and that anything they reported should be subject to an advance censorship.

The press of the world in 1920 operated with greater general freedom and a greater sense of responsibility than ever before. The prospects never had been better for a growth of understanding or the creation of a unity of interest among the people, holding promise of a better way of life, including a secure peace.

The Soviet Union was one area, however, where that prospect and promise did not exist. It had halted publication of all newspapers and periodicals existing under the czarist government and began to create its own press structure, wholly party controlled and dedicated to a political ideology, rather than to public understanding.

Official status was given to the former Bolshevik underground paper *Pravda* (Truth) as an organ of the Central Committee and the Moscow Committee of the Communist party. It was sometimes referred to as the "party newspaper." In 1917 *Izvestia* (News) was established and became the organ of the Politburo (Presidium) and the Central Executive Committee of the USSR, and was referred to as the "government newspaper."[4] A Bolshevik paper, *Zvezda* (Star), established in St. Petersburg in 1910, was revived as the organ of the Red Army under the title *Krasnaya Zvezda* (Red Star). Other newspapers and periodicals were introduced, representative of the navy, *Sovetskii Flot,* of labor, *Trud,* of various ministries and agencies of government and of Communist party groups.

The most important of these in their official sponsorship were published in Moscow, but comparable papers spoke for both party and government in other cities, with local editions of *Pravda* in some. By 1922 there were 803 newspapers appearing in the Soviet Union, with many more to come, as well as periodicals. The former Rosta news agency was revived in 1918 as an official service to distribute news and other material to the press, but was replaced by Tass in 1925.

The Communist regime sponsored a campaign of instruction and propaganda in support of the party program and administration. This required a system of education, beginning in youth, but including persons of all ages. It required, also, the development of a network of publications. In the first years, these included "wall newspapers," elaborate bulletin boards using photos and graphics, as well as simple text for display in factories and public places to reach the people, including the illiterate, and covering matter selected and treated to serve the party purposes.

To make that purpose fully effective, the level of literacy had to be raised, with due concern for a variety of languages and dialects in use throughout the vast area of greater Russia. By one estimate, these were fifty-seven in number, with twenty-seven ultimately used in

---

4 Muscovites themselves later sometimes dared to jest that "there is no news in the truth, and no truth in the news." See also James W. Markham, *Voices of the Red Giants* (1967), ch. 3 and following.

print. Literacy of those who could read and write in at least one language, estimated at about 33 per cent in 1918, was reported to have increased to 81 per cent by 1940 in a country by then of about 170 million population. Yet by 1959 the claim was 98 per cent literacy in a population of 218 million. If even approximately accurate, this literacy increase was a triumph of the first order. The primary motivation, however, was not so much to help inform the public or raise understanding, but rather to shape the minds and actions of the people in the interest of party policy.

There was no lack of interest beyond the borders of Russia in what was happening in Moscow and throughout the country in the years immediately after the revolution. But the new Moscow government of March 1918 expelled foreign newsmen and refused officially to admit others until the ARA mission entered in November 1921. Eleven British and U.S. reporters did manage to reach Moscow in the 1918–21 interval, but only two or three were able to work professionally while there. One was expelled, three were imprisoned, one died, and the other six left voluntarily or by request.[5]

For want of any other means to obtain news from the Soviet Union in the first four years of its existence, fragments of information were garnered by reading *Pravda, Izvestia,* and other Soviet publications as they reached such cities as Berlin and Warsaw, Riga, Bucharest, Budapest, and Vienna. There was no radio news broadcasting from Russia. Travelers to and from Russia were queried. These included refugees, as well as persons on special missions. The results, not surprisingly, were unsatisfactory. For want of solid facts, rumors received more attention than they deserved, and many accounts published were superficial, biased, and inaccurate.

The *New York Times,* at that period, was presenting more reports on Soviet affairs than any other publication in the United States. The items necessarily were obtained from a variety of sources, many recog-

---

5   These included Francis McCullagh, *Manchester Guardian* and *New York Herald;* Guy Beringer, Reuters; and Marguerite Harrison, *Baltimore Sun, New York Evening Post,* and Associated Press, all jailed. John Clayton, *Chicago Tribune,* was expelled. John Reed died in Moscow in 1920.

The other six were Frank J. Taylor, United Press; Edwin Ware Hullinger, *Chicago Daily News* and United Press; Isaac Don Levine, *Chicago Daily News;* Michael Farbman, *Chicago Daily News* and *Manchester Guardian;* Samuel Spewack, *New York World;* and Floyd Gibbons, *Chicago Tribune.* Gibbons and Levine were in Moscow on two occasions. Levine, with special qualifications, was the only member of the group to produce notable reports in this period. See his *Eyewitness to History* (1973), ch. 4.

Spewack returned to Moscow for the *World* in 1922. He and his wife Bella wrote a comedy satire for the stage a few years later. Titled "Clear All Wires," and produced in London and New York, it concerned the improbable adventures of a correspondent in Moscow, one "Buckley Joyce Thomas" of a fictitious *"Chicago Press,"* who bore a certain resemblance to Gibbons.

nized as unreliable, and so specified in the accounts. Nevertheless, considering the prestige of the paper and its slogan, "All the News That's Fit to Print," Walter Lippmann and Charles Merz, then associate editors of the *New Republic,* undertook a detailed study of the reports relating to Russia that had appeared in the *Times* between March 1917 and March 1920.

The Lippmann-Merz analysis was presented as a supplement to the *New Republic* of August 4, 1920, under the title, "A Test of the News." It demonstrated the inaccuracy of many of the *Times* accounts, measured against later known facts.

Stung by the report, but making no excuses, the *New York Times* a year later sent Walter Duranty, then second man in its Paris bureau, to Riga. There in August 1921 negotiations began for the admission to the Soviet Union of that group of correspondents technically identified with the ARA. Duranty was to be one of them at last admitted in November. He remained in Moscow as the *Times* correspondent from 1921 until 1934, and returned on several occasions between that time and 1939.

The Soviet Union may have drawn conclusions of its own from the Lippmann-Merz report of 1920, and decided that the interests of the USSR and the Communist party might be better served by permitting foreign correspondents to enter the country. The pretext for their admission came in 1921 with the prospective entrance of the American Relief Administration mission.

While the negotiations were proceeding at Riga, Floyd Gibbons of the *Chicago Tribune* Paris bureau also flew to the Latvian city. There he persuaded Litvinov to arrange for him to fly to Moscow, where he had been briefly in 1919, and go on to see something of the famine area. Gibbons thus became the first correspondent actually to enter Soviet Russia with proper accreditation. He was out before the first accredited group entered in November, and only wrote of his observations after leaving the country.

The correspondents finally admitted in November 1921 included Duranty, for the *New York Times;* McCullagh returning for the *Manchester Guardian* and *New York Herald;* Hullinger for the *Chicago Daily News;* James P. Howe, Associated Press; Raymond Swing, *New York Tribune;* George Seldes, *Chicago Tribune;* Fred A. Mackenzie, London *Daily Mail;* Henry Alsberg, London *Daily Herald;* M. Fusi of the Osaka *Mainichi;* and M. de Marsillac of *Le Journal,* Paris.

Entering briefly later in 1921 and in 1922 were Charles Stephenson Smith of the Associated Press; Spewack, returning for the *New York World;* Isaac Don Levine, returning, but for Hearst's Universal Service; William Henry Chamberlin, who was to remain more than ten years for the *Christian Science Monitor;* Louis Fischer for the *New York Evening Post* and its associated weekly of opinion, the *Nation;* E. Percy Noël, *Philadelphia Public Ledger;* and Paul Scheffer, *Berliner Tageblatt.*

Another who entered in 1921, although not attached to the ARA or the correspondent group, was Anna Louise Strong, an American woman engaged in news and editorial work for Socialist and liberal publications, and who regarded Communist Russia as a "new Utopia." She had managed to get to Poland to aid the American Friends' Service Committee, a Quaker group engaged in postwar relief work there, and proceeded to Russia. She spent most of the following thirty years in the Soviet Union, although sometimes in China where she gave her loyalty to Mao Tse-tung. She acted as a correspondent for *Hearst's International Magazine* for about three years, until that monthly publication suspended in 1925. She gave lessons in English to Trotsky, did considerable freelance writing of articles and books, and lectured on Russia and China in the United States and elsewhere.

Miss Strong was to be instrumental in the conduct of an English-language tabloid newspaper established in 1930, the *Moscow Daily News,* which was published five days a week. Produced with Communist party support, it was designed for British and U.S. engineers and others by then working on construction projects in the USSR as part of the Soviet's first Five Year Plan, and for distribution in English-speaking countries. Also in 1930, Miss Strong married a minor Soviet official, Joel Shubin, who had been at one period press attaché in the Soviet Embassy in Tokyo. Although not herself a member of the Communist party, she aspired to be, and was ever the advocate and propagandist for communism and the Soviet Union. As such, she was permitted to travel widely within the country, largely to obtain impressions and background material for her lecture tours abroad. While she moved on the periphery of the foreign press group, she was hardly a member of that group, and perhaps did not wish to be.

The correspondents admitted to the Soviet Union in 1921 and later were required to proceed directly to Moscow, and to remain there unless granted special permission to travel to other places. They were limited in numbers, ostensibly because of limited housing accommodations. The correspondent was told where he could live, and for most of the first decade, this meant either the Métropole or the Savoy Hotel. Upon arriving, he was to report to the Press Department (Atdel Pyachati), attached to the Central Executive Committee of the Communist party. It was located on the fifth floor of a former apartment building, lacking elevators, and occupied by the Commissariat of

Foreign Affairs (the Narkomindel, or "The Nark"). There he received
a card giving him formal accreditation as a correspondent, with the
right to file dispatches at the government Post & Telegraph Office for
transmission at press rates. The dispatch had to bear a censor's stamp
of approval, however, and the censors were in the Press Department.
The card of accreditation also established the correspondent's identity
for other purposes, both personal and professional. It was, in effect,
his permit to exist so long as he remained within the Soviet Union.

In addition to valid passports, visas were required in the 1920s for
admission to most countries. The Soviet Union often refused to grant
such a visa, or might do so only after unpredictable delay. The visa
had to be renewed at six-month intervals, and might then be denied
even to one already in the country, with no explanation necessarily
given. Further, a correspondent leaving the Soviet Union, supposedly
temporarily, might be denied a re-entry visa.

Czarist Russia had been one of the few countries to expel newsmen,
but this had not occurred often. Indeed, any government taking such
action prior to World War I was likely to court an adverse public
response based on the assumption that it probably was seeking to prevent the reporting of unwelcome truths, which usually was the case.
The Soviet Union expelled correspondents, however, if it so wished,
or denied them entrance or re-entry visas without explanation or apology, and without apparent concern as to whether any explanation was
believed.

News reporting never had been easy in Russia. The great size and
complexity of the country, with the physical problems of travel, contributed to the difficulty. Secretiveness and suspicion on the part of
officials was common. Among members of the Bolshevik or Communist party, raised in a revolutionary tradition and subjected to the
restraints of czarist autocracy, these characteristics were accentuated.
Further, the All-Union Communist party, having established its
power, saw no need to share general information with the people of
the Soviet Union, much less with other peoples. Decisions were made
by the party, and such information as party leaders wanted to have
made known would be presented in an approved form, whether
through the schools and universities, through public meetings, or
through the controlled media.

The foreign correspondent in the Soviet Union was almost as restricted as the Soviet citizen in the information available to him. He
had limited access to officials. General sources were usually "off
limits." There was risk in making photographs. Even assuming a facility in the language, Soviet citizens were discouraged from having

personal relations with foreigners, and especially with journalists and diplomatic representatives.[6] If the correspondent required the assistance of a secretary, translator, courier or chauffeur, a native of the country had to be obtained through official channels. Such an assistant's own life then depended, perhaps literally, upon his or her first loyalty to the Communist regime. This raised inevitable questions as to whether the secretary was reporting back on the correspondent's sources of information, or aspects of his life; whether a translator was providing accurate or representative summaries of matter appearing in the Soviet press; and whether a correspondent who might have displeased the regime was perhaps being misinformed or watched with a view to establishing a basis for his expulsion.

The main source of information most readily available to correspondents day after day was the Soviet newspaper and periodical press, including the official Tass news agency service used by the newspapers and later by the radio. No opposition or independent press was permitted, and foreign publications were not generally available. The most important newspapers, *Pravda* and *Izvestia,* both appeared in mid-morning in Moscow. But there were many others, including some from other cities.

Reading the Soviet publications called for an art unlike that in any other country because of the treatment of what passed for "news" in the Communist style of journalism. Much that would be news in the press of other countries did not appear at all in the Soviet press. If some of the same subjects were reported upon, it might be only after the passage of days, or only in the briefest form. Reports might also be written more in the nature of editorial comment than as straight news, and the facts might be incomplete or distorted to fit a party policy line. The very omission of a report, or part of a report, might be newsworthy in itself, assuming that the correspondent knew of the omission. A small item inconspicuously placed might have a significance far exceeding that suggested by its treatment or position in the paper.

The papers rarely exceeded eight pages. With minor exceptions, there was nothing comparable to advertising in the newspapers or periodicals, because there was no private business to place such advertisements. Much of the space went to special articles, texts of documents or speeches, or to material intended to rally public support to party programs and purposes. There soon were so many publications to be examined, however, that a correspondent hardly had time to do all the

---

6 Some correspondents managed, nevertheless, to marry Russian citizens. Later the Soviet Union temporarily denied exit visas to the wives and their children.

reading himself, even assuming a competence in the language, and so became dependent upon the assistance of a translator.[7]

Beyond what might appear in the newspapers, the correspondent's, dependence and center of activity was the Press Department itself in the Foreign Ministry. There were no press conferences of the sort known in Washington, for example, and questioning of members of the department was rarely productive. But some information was provided. Texts of documents or speeches also sometimes were released. Usually, however, at that period, they were poorly reproduced in mimeograph form, sometimes running as long as eighty pages and in Russian, requiring hasty translation and evaluation. The department also was the point where copy had to be submitted for censorship before it could be accepted for transmission at the telegraph office.

The Press Department was important to the correspondent in another respect. If he wished to meet with any official or with a particular Soviet citizen, to attend a meeting, to visit any office or institution or travel beyond Moscow, specific arrangements had to be made through the department. Such a request was more likely to be rejected than approved, or many applications might have to be made before it was approved, if ever, and delays were usual.

Any travel beyond Moscow that might be approved would require that the correspondent adhere strictly to a fixed itinerary, and that he be accompanied by a courier. Where he went, what he was permitted to see, and whom he met therefore was controlled. Yet the Press Department alone assured him transport, housing, and food. There were sharp limits on making photographs, and whatever he wrote on the basis of such a journey was, of course, subject to censorship.

It was common for the Press Department to make announcements or releases in the early morning hours. Correspondents then were faced with the need, perhaps, to make translations of texts, to determine the significance of information obtained, and to write their reports. This all had to be done under pressure of time, recognizing that whatever was prepared had to be submitted to a censor able to review the dispatch in the language in which it was written, and that all censors were off duty from 2 A.M. to 10 A.M.

The frequency of such night sessions at the Press Department was sufficient to make the Moscow assignment both demanding and arduous. Assuming that the dispatch was prepared in time to pass the

---

7 After World War II, a Joint Press Reading Service was established by the U.S., British, and Canadian embassies in Moscow, with the reading and summarizing done by nationals of those countries as an aid both to correspondents and diplomats. This was an advantage, but the time required for the preparation of the daily report subtracted from its contribution to prompt news reporting.

censorship before 2 A.M., it still had to go to the telegraph office a mile away, carried perhaps in the bitter cold of a long winter night.

If the dispatch was not ready for the censor before 2 A.M. it might mean that the correspondent would lose a day before his report could be transmitted. The probability was that by then it would have lost its primary news value. Another correspondent could have managed to get out an earlier report. If a correspondent represented a morning newspaper, a mid-day transmission of a report the next morning still would be published in afternoon papers or broadcast by radio before another edition of his paper could appear. A Tass agency report, broadcast by Radio Moscow, not uncommon after 1925, and heard in Stockholm, for example, could have provided an early Soviet version of the report.

The existence of the censorship in Moscow made for this sort of delay or distortion in the transmission of correspondents' reports. Yet Litvinov, as Soviet foreign commissar and one of the more approachable officials of that government in the 1920s, sometimes would tell a correspondent, as Press Department officials also did, that there was no censorship in Moscow. In 1923 he also told a group of correspondents that there was no censorship of opinion, but on that occasion conceded that a general censorship was intended merely to eliminate unverified reports or biased or untruthful reporting of "alleged facts." No effective provision was made, however, for correspondents either to verify "alleged facts," or disprove them.

While the Soviet government made little direct effort to foist a propaganda or policy line on correspondents, obstacles were interposed to prevent them getting information the leadership did not wish to have publicized, and the censorship blocked dispatch of such information even if obtained. In the early period, it was generally accepted that anything appearing in a Soviet publication, and particularly in *Pravda* and *Izvestia,* might be cited or quoted in a correspondent's copy and would pass the censorship almost automatically, but this assurance did not continue.

The Communist party and government, almost from the outset, had put emphasis upon a system of so-called domestic self-criticism (samokritka), whereby worker-peasant correspondents (rab'selkor) were assigned to report on faults in the operation of industry, collective farming, distribution of goods, and other aspects of life. A selection of these reports was published in certain papers, although only after they had been investigated, and then accompanied by statements from the appropriate agencies as to what had been done to correct the faults noted. This system was a basis for assertions that the Soviet Union had a "free press."

Correspondents sometimes proceeded on the assumption that anything appearing in the Soviet press might be used, including items reported under the "samokritka" system. This assumption also was ended by objections from the Press Department to what was considered a misuse or a damaging combination of such references. Another theory tested by correspondents was that if they submitted a story otherwise unconfirmed to the censorship, and it was passed, it thereby was verified. This also proved wrong. Even though inaccurate or untrue, such a story might be passed if it did no harm to the Soviet Union. This only hurt the correspondent, when the truth became known. Indeed, such a report sometimes was passed by the censor with the deliberate intent to bring discredit upon a correspondent regarded as "unfriendly" or "hostile," with the hope that he might be recalled as an "incompetent." Further, a correspondent might be purposely misled into sending an inaccurate report as a basis for requesting his recall for sending "false" reports, for writing with "malice," justifying a denial of visa renewal, or for expulsion.

Press Department officials commonly demanded that correspondents report objectively on Soviet affairs. This most were prepared to do, but the word was interpreted to suit the censorship officials.[8] The only alternative left to the correspondent seeking to report as accurately as possible, while still avoiding expulsion, was to use what William Henry Chamberlin, correspondent for the *Christian Science Monitor,* described as "softening euphemisms and compromise phrases." Walter Duranty, *New York Times* correspondent, like Chamberlin, survived in Moscow for more than ten years by following the same procedure. This earned him a jocular reference as "Walter Obscuranty." Some such cautiously written reports were discursive, bland, and dull, and Chamberlin conceded later that the people of the world received only partial information in the day-to-day reports from the Soviet Union during the years he was there, from 1922 to 1934. The same applied to Duranty from 1921 to 1934. This was not a view commonly advanced by correspondents in that period, however. Although they worked under great handicaps in Moscow, most accepted the censorship as inescapable and some even had good things to say about the manner of its conduct and about the censors themselves.

---

8 The conflict in interpretation of the word "objectivity" was given expression some years later by D. Kuzmichev, writing for Soviet journalists in *Problemy Gazetovedeniya* (Problems of Journalism) (1944). He wrote that "All dissertations on 'objective and complete information' are liberal hypocrisy. The aim of information does not consist in commercializing the news, but in educating the great masses of workers, in organizing them under the exclusive direction of the party for clearly defined tasks. Liberty and objectivity of the press—these are fictions. Information is the means of class struggle, not a mirror to reflect events objectively." Cited by John C. Ranney and Gwendolyn M. Carter in *The Major Foreign Powers* (1949), p. 540.

In the first years from 1921 to 1924, the year of Lenin's death, and indeed until 1933, the censorship as handled through the Press Department was direct and "open" in the sense that a correspondent met personally with the censor, learned directly of any objection to a reference in a dispatch, had the opportunity to discuss the point at issue and either persuade the censor to pass it or, alternatively, rephrase it to meet the objection. This meant that the dispatch might be saved from complete rejection, that coherence could be preserved, as against what might result if certain matter was removed arbitrarily, and it assured that the message would bear the censor's stamp and so would be transmitted without further question or undue delay.

If there had to be a censorship at all, this open variety was preferred by correspondents because they could be certain about the content and fate of their dispatches. It also taught them something of what the censors would or would not pass, and so enabled them to write in a manner most likely to be acceptable, as with Chamberlin's "euphemisms and compromise phrases."

The system required that the correspondent prepare each dispatch in triplicate, one copy for his own file and two to be presented to the censor. Those two copies, as finally passed with or without changes and bearing the censor's stamp, would be taken for transmission to the Post and Telegraph Building, carried either by the correspondent himself or by a messenger.

Transmission itself tended to be slow. Correspondents for the U.S. press had to file dispatches no later than 6 A.M. Moscow time if they were to arrive for use in the morning papers in New York and other eastern cities, where time was seven hours behind Moscow. The 6 A.M. deadline in Moscow was 11 P.M. of the previous date in New York, 10 P.M. in Chicago, and 8 P.M. in San Francisco. For morning publication in European cities with a time difference of only one or two hours, Moscow transmission had to be in the early evening. With censors off duty after 2 A.M., however, dispatches normally would be filed at least by that time, which would be 7 P.M. in New York and early afternoon in London or Paris.

Effective telephone communication became possible about 1930 between Moscow and western European capitals. Calls had to be made from the Post and Telegraph Building. Copy to be so transmitted not only had to bear the censor's stamp of approval before a telephone connection would be made, but the call itself was monitored by a censor holding the second copy of the dispatch. Any departure from the approved text would result in the connection being broken. When international radio broadcasting began about 1932, the same system was used, with the radio correspondent preparing a script to be passed by the censor and a copy held by a monitor.

Considering the general dislike of censorship by newsmen, it was surprising that some Moscow correspondents in those early years spoke of the Press Department censors with approval. How far this was sincere and how far intended to soften up the censors is difficult to say. Some of the same correspondents who spoke in those terms were not beyond seeking to evade the censorship at times or to seek its removal. Some became entirely disenchanted with the Moscow assignment and referred to the censorship in other terms following their departure. Some were expelled, in fact, because of conflicts over the censorship.

Hullinger of the United Press typified this experience. Having been one of those in Moscow in 1919 and returning in 1921, he remarked soon after that a correspondent willing to make a careful study even of surface appearances could produce a vast amount of information about Soviet affairs, provided he had some knowledge of conditions in the country and was prepared to dig through a "thick surface stratum of Oriental custom and habits of life," and so perhaps come upon a rewarding "under-vein of news." In that same year he had written that "Samuel B. Cahan, the censor, is the most popular Bolshevik among the American newspaper colony." He referred to Cahan's "genial smile and unruffleable disposition," and of his method of censorship as "more like handing your copy in to your city editor, except that Cahan's pencil is more kindly."[9]

The censor's office in the Press Department, Hullinger added, "is also the correspondent's postoffice for incoming and outgoing mail and telegraph messages. It also is a popular gathering place for foreign newspapermen—a place you like to go at night to hear what the other fellow is doing and thinking, and to gossip about the latest news."

Despite all that, Hullinger was forced to leave Moscow two years later when the Soviet government refused to renew his visa. He had sent a telegram to a professional associate asking him to try to have the Soviet censorship removed through action by the League of Nations. For this, he was accused of consorting with enemies of the Soviet Union, conferring with reactionaries and counter-revolutionaries, and interfering with Soviet internal affairs.

The first of numerous appeals by correspondents for the removal of the censorship had been made in May 1923. It was directed to Litvinov, then assistant foreign commissar, who was regarded as likely to be sympathetic to the request in part because of long previous residence in Great Britain, and because of his British-born wife. Litvinov only replied, however, that the Soviet Union was still in a state of semiwar,

---

9 Cahan's name was tranliterated from the Cyrillic alphabet also as "Kagan" and "Kaghan."

surrounded by enemies, and that the censorship therefore could not be abandoned.

A second appeal was advanced later in that same year by Robert R. McCormick, publisher of the *Chicago Tribune.* He directed George Seldes, the paper's correspondent in Moscow, to deliver a written protest against the censorship to Foreign Commissar Chicherin. Seldes did convey what he later described as McCormick's "ultimatum." It told Chicherin:

> You must abandon the censorship and guarantee freedom of expression. Otherwise our correspondent will be withdrawn and so will the correspondents of other American newspapers, so that Russia will find herself without means of communication with the outer world.

Chicherin was angered. He called Seldes in, protested that "the newspaper speaks to me as if it were a government of equal power." He made it clear that he did not intend to accept any ultimatum from McCormick.[10] Nor was Seldes withdrawn by the *Tribune,* but he was expelled shortly afterward because he had used the American Relief Mission diplomatic pouch as a means to send uncensored copy out of the country. The Soviet Union had no more right to open that pouch, as it had done, than Seldes had to use it for private news transmission. But copy also was found in the pouch from Samuel Spewack, Francis McCullagh, and E. Percy Noël. Spewack and McCullagh also were expelled, and Noël left, apparently of his own volition.

No American correspondents were withdrawn, as McCormick had predicted. Even if they had been, Russia would not have been "without means of communication with the outer world" since there were correspondents in Moscow representing the press of other countries.

With Seldes out of Moscow, McCormick did follow through on his "ultimatum" to the extent that the *Tribune* henceforth relied upon Donald Day, correspondent in Riga, to report the news of the Soviet Union, but with poor results. The paper sent John Clayton again and Larry Rue into the country in 1923 and 1929, but both were expelled. The *Tribune* also announced the closing of what was in fact a nonexistent Moscow bureau, contending with dubious accuracy that correspondents there were obliged to depend for news upon official handouts, and were tolerated only to the extent that they acted as agents for the Soviet government. Henry Wales, chief of the *Tribune* Paris

---

10   By contrast, Melville E. Stone, general manager of the Associated Press, had been more diplomatic in an appeal to Czar Nicholas II in 1903–04, resulting in at least a temporary abandonment of the existing czarist censorship. See Desmond, *Windows on the World,* pp. 117–21.

bureau, visited Russia in 1931, but the paper had no regular representation there after the departure of Seldes in 1923.

Reports occasionally were carried out of Russia in the pockets of
obliging travelers, but at some risk to them. In some instances, code
messages were attempted in dispatches sent by telegraph. The uncer-
tainties there involved, however, were illustrated when Isaac Don
Levine of the INS arranged that in the event of Lenin's death he would
send a service message to the London bureau reading "Send me £50."
When Lenin did die in 1924, Levine sent the message. An editor in
London, uninformed or having forgotten, put the message aside for
later action and eventually queried Levine about his need for the specified amount. Meanwhile, news reports on Lenin's death were held up
by the Moscow censorship for several hours, but INS missed an opportunity for a world beat if the code arrangement had worked
properly.

Because outgoing mail was only spot-checked in Moscow, correspondents sometimes sent uncensored stories in two or three duplicate
copies in separate envelopes, hand-addressed as in personal letters, to
private homes or street numbers in one or more of the western capitals
or suburbs. In most cases, all arrived, but most of the news so transmitted was routine.

While approved texts had to be filed before outgoing telephone connections were completed, it became common in the 1930s for a bureau
in another capital, usually Berlin or Warsaw, to place a call to the
Moscow correspondent of a newspaper or agency at agreed times, perhaps more than once a day. Even though such incoming calls also were
monitored by the censorship, correspondents sometimes managed to
convey information in oblique form by using slang, colloquialisms,
voice emphasis or sports terminology, the significance of which might
escape the monitor.

Such devices, however, were hardly worth the trouble. Even if successful, the effort could boomerang and result in the correspondent
being expelled. This would put his agency or newspaper to the time
and expense of replacing him, costing it also the advantage of such
knowledge as he had gained of the Moscow scene, and with no assurance that his replacement might not encounter the same problems.
These considerations tended to discourage attempts by resident correspondents to evade censorship in Moscow or any other authoritarian
capital.

The most effective procedure for reporting on Soviet affairs without censorship was for the correspondent to leave the country to write
a series of articles, perhaps to be published also as a book. Since this
also could result in the correspondent being denied a re-entry visa, the

procedure usually was reserved for the correspondent already expelled or the correspondent ready to leave Moscow permanently. The efforts then commonly brought harsh words from Moscow.

Many responsible correspondents contended from the outset with considerable justification that censorship was defeating its purpose, whether in Moscow or elsewhere. By closing sources of accurate information and by halting full and prompt transmission of information, they argued, rumors and inaccurate reports gained both currency and credence, whether at home or abroad. Levine, writing in 1931, suggested examples:

> When a village is razed to the ground by a detachment of the Red Army and no mention is made of it in the Moscow newspapers, the event finally reaches Riga or Warsaw in the form of a rumor that a great peasant rebellion has broken out in the Ukraine.
>
> When Stalin goes riding in his Rolls-Royce and a tire blows out with a loud report, the scared eye-witnesses will run away from the scene and describe it as an attempt to shoot the dictator. The newspapers the following morning will contain nothing about the incident. Two months later Warsaw will print a story about an attempt on Stalin's life.
>
> The lies about Russia still occasionally circulated in the outside world spring from the lies inherent in the Soviet information system. They are inherent in any political monopoly which regards the press and all printing as a sharp weapon for the attainment of a definite objective. . . . The lies about Russia are insignificant by contrast with the lies fostered within the country about the rest of the world, for the consumption of the helpless reading public.[11]

Despite the dangers of a mutual misunderstanding or worse arising from such circumstances, if spokesmen for the Communist party or for any other dictatorial regime responded with any civility to objections to censorship after 1924 or 1925 it was common to assert the need for reforms in the country and to work some change on the rather flippant and irresponsible assertion that "you can't make an omelette without breaking some eggs."

In one sense, expulsion might have been viewed as a welcome release by a correspondent if only because of the difficult living conditions in Moscow and the special problems of working there. Housing was scarce, with no choice offered. There was only an assignment of expensive and Spartan hotel space. Food was in limited supply and without much variety. Consumer goods of all types were lacking. These included clothing and such essentials of the correspondent's

---

11   *The American Press* (August 1931), pp. 1, 42–44.

business as paper, pencils, and typewriter ribbons. Medical and dental care could be a problem, in part because of shortages of drugs and supplies. Periodic departure from the Soviet Union sometimes was necessary to obtain such goods and treatment, but with no assurance that a re-entry visa would be granted. Normal family life was almost impossible, especially if the correspondent had children of school age.

Getting about the city required walking, mostly. Automobiles were few in those early years, taxis rare, and trams or buses crowded, inconvenient, and undependable. Correspondents risked arrest if they showed special enterprise in seeking information outside the approved channels. This also placed those with whom they spoke in personal danger. All photos were supposed to come through Sovphoto, the official picture agency, and all were subject to censorship.

Indicative of the tight control over what in other countries would have been routine information was the close attention given by correspondents to some photographs. This applied particularly to those taken on May Day or on the anniversary of the October revolution. Justifiably or not, significance was attached to the presence or the absence of members of the Politburo on the reviewing stand on such occasions, and upon the very order in which they stood, as compared to pictures made in other years.

Except for those occasions, most top officials of the government remained within the walls of the Kremlin. Lenin was available to correspondents only once in an informal group interview following a meeting of the All-Union Soviet Congress in 1923. Correspondents had occasional glimpses of Trotsky, heading the Commissariat of War, and he granted a few interviews. Chicherin and Litvinov, in the Foreign Commissariat, were virtually the only other officials seen by the foreign press representatives, apart from those in the Press Department and such others as they met through arrangements made by that department.

Almost by default, the correspondents associated chiefly with their colleagues of the press from their own and other countries. They also saw diplomatic representatives of their own country and others, and met at least casually with foreign visitors often housed in the same hotels.

The New Economic Policy program introduced in 1921 brought a rapid recovery in the national economy within the Soviet Union. Industrial production approached prewar levels, commercial and banking practices were resumed, levies and taxes on food were removed and independent farming was again permitted, with freedom to trade partially restored. The campaign of terror was eased, and the effort to create a literate public began.

The end of the civil war, coming at that time, brought a strengthening of the federation, the formation of the USSR, and improved relations with other countries. This included participation in international conferences at Genoa and Rapallo, diplomatic recognition by a number of foreign states, an opening of some trade relations, and an invitation to assist the Kuomintang in the unification of China.

Lenin was not well, however, from late 1921. He suffered a serious stroke in May 1922, was forced to reduce his work load, had another stroke in December 1922, resulting in a partial paralysis, and died on January 21, 1924, at age fifty-three. A contest began immediately within the Communist party and government to determine who would assume the top position of power. The two chief candidates were Trotsky and Stalin. It became an open conflict in 1926, with Stalin attaining the necessary support by October.

In gaining and consolidating his power, Stalin forced changes in the Communist hierarchy, with Trotsky, Radek, and Zinoviev among those losing their membership in the Politburo. Then, in December 1927 the Fifteenth All-Union Congress of the party condemned all "deviation from the general party line," as defined by Stalin, with such "deviationists" to be expelled not only from their positions but from the party itself. The most notable victim of this decision was Trotsky. Ruled out of the party, he was exiled from Moscow in 1928 and sent to Alma-Ata in Kazakstan in Asiatic Russia. In January 1929 he was expelled altogether from the Soviet Union and took refuge in Constantinople. Later he went to Norway and then to Mexico in 1937, where he was murdered in 1940, allegedly by a Stalinist agent.

Trotsky's exile and expulsion was, of course, a major event and so treated in the world press. Nothing on the subject appeared in the Soviet press at the time, however. It was only mentioned, ultimately, in an item of less than fifty words minus any headline and buried on an inside page of *Izvestia* early in 1929 when he moved to Constantinople.

In its December 1927 session, the All-Union Congress also made decisions marking the end of the New Economic Policy, which had become faulted by scandals and excesses. It was followed by a new Communist party program of industrialization and a return to the earlier effort to develop collective farming, with the small, independent farmer, or *kulak,* out of favor. This, in turn, led to the introduction in October 1928 of a Five Year Plan intended to advance both industry and agriculture.

The 1924–28 period, disturbed as it was, included the granting of several foreign concessions in 1927. Among these, an Anglo-U.S. group was authorized to undertake the development of gold fields in the Lena River area of Asiatic Russia. In another, Averell Harriman, later to become U.S. ambassador to the Soviet Union (1943-46), headed a group to develop manganese mines in the south. Neither venture continued for long and both were halted during the course of the Five Year Plan.

That plan brought engineers and technicians to Russia from Great Britain and other countries to help design and construct factories and dams to provide hydraulic power. Iron and steel works were projected at Magnitogorsk and Kuznetsk, tractor factories at Stalingrad (formerly Tsaritsyn) and Kharkov, automobile and truck plants at Moscow and Gorki, an agricultural machinery plant at Sverdlovsk, a chemical plant at Berezniki, and a Dnieper River dam and power plants.

During the 1924-26 period, as the internal struggle proceeded to determine Lenin's successor, Soviet officials became even more inaccessible to correspondents in Moscow. Personal information about new members of the government was almost impossible to obtain. Propaganda activities resumed in other countries through the Third International (Comintern), contrary to agreements reached when Great Britain gave diplomatic recognition to the Soviet Union in 1924, led London to break off relations in 1927. They were not resumed again until late 1929.

The Five Year Plan caught the imagination of much of the world, however, and advanced trade and other direct relations internationally. Reports on the developments written by foreign correspondents encountered few censorship problems since they were viewed by the Moscow regime as constructive. Visits to Russia by tourist groups began. Among others organized in the United States were annual pilgrimages sponsored by Scott Nearing, a former professor of sociology at Swarthmore College. He had been defeated as a Socialist party candidate for Congress from a New York City district. His son, calling himself John Scott, then twenty and a former student at the University of Wisconsin, went to work in the steel mills in Siberia from 1932 to 1937. Special news attention went to a visit to the USSR in 1931 by George Bernard Shaw and Lady Astor, both vigorous and outspoken in their inquiries and observations.

In 1926 Stalin granted a first press interview. This was with M. Fusi of the Osaka *Mainichi.* A second interview, in October 1926, was accorded to Professor Jerome Davis of Yale University. He was not a correspondent, but the substance of the interview nevertheless was published in the Hearst newspapers, and quoted elsewhere in the United States and beyond.

A third interview went to Eugene Lyons, United Press correspondent in Moscow, in November 1930. At the Kremlin, he was accompanied by Professor Charles Malamuth of the Slavic Department, University of California, Berkeley, acting as an interpreter. After the interview, Stalin had a search made to find a typewriter with a European alphabet upon which Lyons wrote his story before leaving. Stalin asked to have it read to him in translation, and wrote upon the manuscript, "In general more or less correct. J. Stalin."

A few days later, Walter Duranty of the *New York Times* also interviewed Stalin, and he was to have a second interview in January 1934.

Duranty, a member of the entering group in November 1921 remained in Moscow for thirteen years, except for rare holiday periods out of the country. During his years in the Soviet Union, he learned the language, sought an understanding of the people and the leadership, and was credited with providing as satisfactory a coverage as was possible under existing restrictions. He was awarded a Pulitzer Prize in 1932 for dispassionate, interpretative reporting in the previous year. He made the *Times* one of the most informative sources on events in the Soviet Union, thus reversing the indictment of the Lippmann-Merz "Test of the News" analysis of 1920.

Chamberlin of the *Christian Science Monitor,* in Moscow for twelve years, was another walking a reportorial tightrope. He had arrived in Moscow in 1922 prepared to embrace communism, and remained until 1934. In those years he changed his views. He found the rulers of the USSR

> as sensitive as the most temperamental artist when the effects of their ruthless policies are criticized, or even when they are stated objectively without comment. The foreign correspondent who disregards this sensitiveness, hews to the line of factual reporting, and does not hide behind softening euphemisms and compromise phrases, works under a Sword of Damocles —the threat of expulsion from the country or the refusal of permission to reenter it, which of course amounts to the same thing.[12]

Chamberlin observed that no correspondent could avoid the problems of censorship unless he was prepared to become an outright spokesman for the Communist regime, a propagandist or apologist. This, of course, he could not do. Lack of access to reliable information made his task doubly difficult. To tell the truth was not enough to satisfy the censorship, and often not permitted even where the truth was known. With an awareness of forbidden subjects and words,

---

12 William H. Chamberlin, "Soviet Taboos," *Foreign Affairs* (April 1935), pp. 431–50.

however, and with the use of those "softening euphemisms and compromise phrases," Chamberlin wrote, a correspondent could give readers an understanding of events in the Soviet Union and an understanding enabling many to deduce a great deal more.

Lyons, in Moscow for the United Press from 1927 to 1936, felt able to say in 1931 that routine news passed the censorship promptly and added that "I know of no really essential facts about the Russian situation which the censorship had succeeded in keeping from the world." This was not to say that the "really essential facts" had necessarily been passed by the censorship, on a day-to-day basis. But concerned readers also had access to magazine articles and books by correspondents writing after departure from Moscow. Over a period of time in accumulating such information, a reader gained a background enabling him to understand a day's report.

Lyons had gone to Moscow after working for the Tass agency in New York, possessed of a theoretical interest in communism at that period in 1927. Like Chamberlin, he lost his enthusiasm for the system before he left the Soviet Union in 1936, and like Hullinger, preceding him as UP correspondent, he also had kind words to say about the Press Department. Contact with the censors he described as "usually routine and rarely unpleasant." He spoke of Theodore Rothstein, then the chief censor for correspondents writing in English, as "genial," and his assistant, Joseph Podalsky, as "cordial." Another assistant, however, A. Mironov, he found to be sour, phlegmatic, and sarcastic.

Fred A. Mackenzie of the *Daily Mail* and *Chicago Daily News,* one of the 1921 arrivals in Moscow, not only had good words to say about the censors but found that they also had their own views of the correspondents. For Cahan, of whom Hullinger had approved, he also had "a feeling of the warmest affection and respect." His associate censor, Gregory Weinstein, he described as "a wholly charming and genuine character." His successor, Rothstein, "genial" to Lyons, was also "clever and kind-hearted," in Mackenzie's view.

From these censors, Mackenzie learned that they themselves divided the correspondents into three classes, with some consideration also for the papers or agencies represented.

"First come the representatives of the labor papers, who are genuinely with us. Naturally, we like these best," Mackenzie was told. "Next come the correspondents of the bourgeois foreign press who try to describe us, and we think unfairly; sometimes they make laughable mistakes. If, however, they try to be just, we like to have them. But then come a third class we hate. They are the correspondents who, having no real sympathy with us, come and write, while they are here, what they think will please us. We hate them because we know that once they leave Russia no lie will be too mean for them to invent to discredit us.''

Whether relevant or not, later in 1925, the same year during which he had referred so kindly to the press censors, Mackenzie was denied a re-entry visa to return to Moscow after a holiday abroad.

In 1932 the head of the Press Department was Constantine Oumansky, who also acted as chief censor.[13] In October of that year, the fifteenth anniversary of the revolution, the Press Department played host at a dinner for three U.S. correspondents who had completed ten years in Moscow. These were Duranty, Chamberlin, and Louis Fischer of the *New York Evening Post* and the *Nation.* They were photographed arm-in-arm with Oumansky, the "cordial" Podalsky, and the "phlegmatic" Mironov. By that time, with the Stalin administration well established, Russia was in a new period, marked by purges of party members and a program of internal terror, with correspondents under tighter restraints.

Baltic States,
Finland, and   Latvia, Estonia, and Lithuania, the Baltic Republics as they became in
Poland   1920 by virtue of the peace treaties, Finland, and parts of Poland all had been within the boundaries of czarist Russia. German forces occupied the Baltic states and Poland at the time of the Russian Revolution in 1917. The areas were yielded to Germany under the terms of the Treaty of Brest-Litovsk. Finland, as a czarist province, had been recognized as an independent state by the Russian revolutionary provisional government of March 1917, but the Finns also declared their independence in July. This was officially recognized by the new Soviet government in January 1918, and also by Germany, France, and Sweden. A brief civil war followed, nevertheless, between Finnish Communists, supported by the Russian Bolsheviks, and the Whites within the country who opposed bolshevism and favored a democratic regime. Aided by German troops, the Whites were the victors.

The Austrian and German surrenders in October-November of 1918 resulted in the withdrawal of their troops and the end of their control in all of these areas. A brief war occurred in Finland in June 1919 as the Soviet Union attempted to regain control there. The effort failed

---

13 Oumansky had been foreign editor of the Tass agency. Later he was Soviet ambassador to Mexico, where he was killed in a somewhat mysterious airplane accident in 1945.

and Finland proceeded as an independent democratic republic and a member of the League of Nations. The relationship with the Soviet Union remained delicate, however, and the Finnish government was forced to contend with periodic efforts of internal Communist groups to gain control.

With the Germans out of the Baltic states, the Bolsheviks also tried to regain control there, but lacked the power to do so at the time. With French and British military assistance, justified by the terms of the German surrender in which those occupied areas were yielded to the Allies, the Bolshevik efforts were blocked, and the Baltic states became independent republics under the provisions of the Versailles Treaty. They continued to be harassed, however, both by Communist activities and by territorial and border disputes with Poland, as well as by problems among themselves.

Riga, the capital of Latvia, became a "listening post" for press coverage of events in the Soviet Union, both before and after the admission of correspondents to Moscow itself in 1921. The *Chicago Tribune* and the *Times* of London, refusing to accept the censorship requirements in Moscow, maintained representation in Riga. Donald Day wrote for the *Tribune* and R. O. G. Urch, better qualified by past experience in Russia, for the *Times.*

Poland, which had been partitioned since 1795 between Prussia, Austria-Hungary, and czarist Russia, regained an entity and unity of its own under the terms of the Versailles Treaty. This derived in part from the fact that as World War I began in 1914 the czarist government had promised full independence to Russian Poland in return for its wartime support. One Polish faction based in Warsaw under Roman Dmowski, a member of the Russian Duma, then attempted to provide such support. When German and Austrian troops overran Poland in 1915, Dmowski took refuge in Paris. Germany and Austria, in their turn, then sought Polish support, proclaiming an independent Polish kingdom in 1916 under an interim Council of State. General Joseph Pilsudski, Russian-born, but several times jailed there for revolutionary activity, became a member of that council. He resigned in 1917, however, in protest against a continuing German control. For this, he was jailed by the Germans. Late in that year, the Germans replaced the Council of State with a three-man Regency Council, exercising control in Poland.

With the surrender of Austria and Germany in 1918, Pilsudski was released from German captivity. He joined the anti-Bolshevik White Russian group in the civil war against Soviet Russia in the Ukraine. On November 3, 1918, the Regency Council at Warsaw had proclaimed a Polish Republic. The members of the council presently

granted full political and military power to Pilsudski and then resigned, leaving him in control.

Meanwhile, Dmowski in Paris since 1915 had joined forces with Ignace Jan Paderewski, world-famed Polish concert pianist, to support
the concept of an independent Poland. Paderewski worked to that end
in the United States, rallying the support of the large Polish emigré
community, and also gaining the support of President Wilson. Dmowski and Paderewski, meeting in Lausanne in 1917, formed a Polish
National Committee and established its headquarters in Paris. There it
received recognition as a Polish government-in-exile. It also organized
a Polish Legion, numbering about 100,000, which saw military action
on the western front in France, matching the Czech Legion also organized for that country by Masaryk and Beneš.

Pilsudski in Warsaw reached an agreement in December 1918 with
the Polish National Committee in Paris, and with another provisional
Polish government that had its headquarters in Cracow. This resulted
in the formation of a unified Polish republican government in Warsaw,
with Pilsudski as provisional president and Paderewski as premier.
Pilsudski also continued to direct Polish military forces. The Polish
Legion was transferred from France, where peace had been restored,
and was enlarged so that in 1920 Pilsudski had 600,000 men under his
command. With French military forces added under General
Weygand, the Soviet Red Army was defeated in March 1921. The civil
war ended with the Treaty of Riga defining Polish-Russian frontiers.
Plebicites and treaties with the Baltic states established others.

In 1919 Dmowski and Paderewski had signed the Versailles Treaty
on behalf of Poland, gaining recognition for the independent republic, setting frontiers, and providing for a "Polish corridor" through
East Prussia to the Baltic coast near the port of Danzig, itself made a
"free city" under League of Nations supervision and administration.
Paderewski then resigned as provisional premier to resume his musical
career. Pilsudski, both provisional president and Marshal of Poland,
served in the former office until 1921, yielding then to Gabriel Narutowicz, elected to the presidency by a parliament that was itself elected
by popular vote under the provisions of a new constitution modeled
on that of France.

Poland was disturbed, nonetheless, by internal conflicts and episodes of violence between political and minority groups, with frequent
changes of government through the years. This began at once with
Narutowicz, the first elected president, assassinated after nine days in
office. He was replaced by Stanislas Wojchiechowski, who resigned
before the end of his seven-year term. His successor was forced to
resign in 1926 when Pilsudski himself led a military revolt and became

the effective ruler of the country. Choosing to hold office as premier, he handpicked Ignace Moscicki for the presidency.

Nine years (1926–35) of a virtual dictatorship followed, with sharp repression, the arrest of opposition figures, and the use of decree powers. In those years, Poland began the construction of its own port at Gydnia, a former fishing village on the Baltic seacoast twelve miles northwest of Danzig (now Gdańsk). The new port became fully operative by 1938. With Pilsudski's death in 1935, army commander General Edward Smigly-Rydz became the new strong man in the government still headed nominally by President Moscicki. By then, however, Poland was in a new period.

Turkey, the Mideast, and the Balkans   4

Turkey, with only a small part of Europe remaining within its jurisdiction in 1920, a crumb of the once-vast Ottoman Empire, was nevertheless greatly involved in European affairs. As a member of the wartime Central Powers, Turkey had surrendered in October 1918. Under the terms of the Armistice, an Allied administration was established in Constantinople in December. Sultan Mohammed VI and a cabinet under Premier Damad Ferid followed a policy of cooperation with the Allied Powers.

The Paris Peace Conference began January 18, 1919. The Treaty of Sèvres with Turkey was the last to be completed, on August 20, 1920, and still remained to be ratified by all parties. With some such long interval in prospect from the time the conference began, the Allies authorized the landing of Greek and Italian troops in Turkey in May 1919. It was understood that they would remain to keep order until Turkey actually ratified the prospective treaty. Those landings were made without objection by the Porte, or government of Turkey, but they were protested and resisted by Mustapha Kemal Pasha, a leader of Turkish military forces during the war. His action brought dismissal from his command by the sultan, and an order outlawing him.

Deep in Armenia, in the eastern area of Asiatic Turkey, Kemal responded by calling a Nationalist Congress at Erzurum. In September 1919 that Congress produced a declaration at Sivas, in central Turkey, insisting upon the unity of the country and opposing both the Allied occupation and a proposal arising in treaty discussions at Paris for the formation of an independent Armenia.

The Nationalists gained seats in the Turkish parliament in October 1919 and their influence grew. Sentiments were so aroused by the continued presence of Allied troops in Turkey that the parliament was dissolved by the sultan's action in March 1920. This did not halt the Nationalists, who formed a provisional government of their own at Angora in April, with Mustapha Kemal as president.

The Treaty of Sèvres at last was signed in August 1920, but the sultan and the Porte objected to its terms, as did the Nationalists. Without consent of the sultan, and using arms obtained from the Soviet Union, the Nationalists battled the Greek and Italian occupation forces and moved into Armenia. They reached an agreement with the Soviet Union in October 1920 whereby Turkey gained some territory in exchange for Armenia, which became a Soviet republic. An agreement was reached with France at the same time, gaining its recognition. Italy also reached an agreement with the Nationalists in March 1921, and withdrew all its troops from Turkey.

Greek military forces remained in the Smyrna sector. With some British encouragement, they sought to extend their area of occupation in March 1921, even as the Italians withdrew. This proved to be disastrous, and they failed in an effort to reach Angora. Turkish Nationalist forces under Mustapha Kemal drove them back to Smyrna and captured that city, which was largely destroyed in September 1922. A British supporting force failed to save the Greeks. The Allies made concessions to the Nationalists in October 1922. In November, Mustapha Kemal declared the abolition of the sultanate and Mohammed VI left Constantinople aboard a British warship for Malta. A caliphate was proclaimed under Abdul Mejid, a cousin of the sultan, to conduct the affairs of government.

Meanwhile, the Treaty of Sèvres never was ratified. Instead, a new Treaty of Lausanne was concluded between Turkey and the Allies in July 1923, after eight months of negotiations. Turkey gave up all claims to Middle Eastern territories, but recovered some territory in the European section of the country beyond the Sea of Marmara, and some Aegean islands. The Dodocanese Islands, including Rhodes, seized from Turkey by Italy in the 1911–12 conflict, instead of going to Greece, as had been provided in the Treaty of Sèvres, were retained by Italy, and Cyprus remained British. The Dardanelles strait was to be demilitarized, open to all shipping between the Mediterranean, Constantinople, and the Black Sea. Turkey also was freed of all reparations payments, and agreed to protect all minorities, meaning Christians primarily. An exchange of Christian-Moslem populations was arranged separately between Turkey and Greece.

The Allied occupation administration, primarily British, evacuated Constantinople in August 1923, leaving Turkey again in full possession. Angora became the official capital in October, and a Turkish republic was proclaimed under the Nationalists, with Mustapha Kemal as president and Ismet Pasha as premier. A constitution was adopted in March 1924 and the caliphate of 1922 abolished.

The new state was confronted immediately with a dispute about the status of Mosul, an oil-rich city in Mesopotamia. By agreement, a decision was left to the League of Nations, which assigned the city and area to Iraq, then under British mandate. A second major problem arose early in 1925 in the same area when an insurrection in Kurdistan protesting government policies and seeking autonomy was only suppressed with great bloodshed. Continuing for months, the conflict brought several attempts on the life of Mustapha Kemal and resulted in the introduction of dictatorial rule.

Using those powers, Mustapha Kemal and his administration brought about great changes in Turkey between 1925 and 1930. Polygamy was abolished, civil marriage was made compulsory, but divorce was legalized. The wearing of the fez was abolished and the wearing of the veil by women discouraged. Religious orders were suppressed and the article of the constitution making Islam the state religion was eliminated. Civil, criminal, and commercial law codes based on European systems were introduced.

Most important for the press and for an improved level of understanding by the people, a 1928 decree specified that the Roman alphabet be brought into universal use within the next fifteen years, replacing Arabic and Persian characters and words. All persons under forty were to be required to learn to read such text. The change was applied first to newspapers. Mustapha Kemal himself had established a paper in Angora in 1923, *Hakimiyeti Milliye* (Sovereignty of the People), but its name was changed in 1928 to *Ulus* (Nation). *Cümhuriyet* (Republic) of Constantinople, and *Vatan* (Fatherland) of Angora were other early dailies.[1] A news agency, Anadolu Ajansi (Agence d'Anatolie) (AA) was established with its headquarters in Angora in 1925.

Rulings also were made on the use of place-names and personal names. This brought changes in 1930 of Constantinople to Istanbul, Angora to Ankara, Smyrna to Izmir, and Adrianople to Edirne. For individuals, family names were introduced in 1935. Thus, Mustapha Kemal became Kemal Atatürk, meaning "father of the Turks," and Ismet Pasha, the premier, became Ismet Onönü.

Interest in events in Turkey and in the personality of Atatürk drew correspondents to that country. Other developments and changes included a Turkish alliance with the Soviet Union in 1925, the election and re-election of Atatürk to four-year terms as president in 1927 and 1931, and again in 1935. He served until his death in November 1938.

---

1   The first Turkish paper, official in character, had been *Takvimi Vekayi* (Calendar of Events), established in 1831. The first independent paper, *Tercumani Ahval* (Interpretation of the Situation), appeared in 1859. The effective press, however, began with the republic in 1923.

There were treaties with England (1926), Italy and Persia (1928), Bulgaria and again with the Soviet Union (1929), and with Greece (1930). There were reports of payments to holders of bonds issued by the old Ottoman government, of efforts to develop industry, of suppression of Communist propaganda in the country, and of another Kurdish revolt in 1930.

The Mideast

Much of what had been Turkish territory before the war was reorganized under the provisions of the peace treaties. The Allied Supreme Council in 1920 mandated the areas of Syria and Lebanon to France, and the areas of Palestine and Mesopotamia to Great Britain. These mandates were approved by the League of Nations in 1922. Saudi Arabia and Yemen were proclaimed as an independent Arab state, with Mecca as the center of the Moslem world, and with Ibn Saud as king from 1926.

Persia, also an independent state, Aryan rather than Arab, but also Moslem, and an original member of the League of Nations, was renamed Iran in 1935. A British protectorate over Egypt was ended in 1922, although British military forces remained in the Suez Canal zone. Fuad I became king of an independent Egypt. Upon his death in 1936, his sixteen-year-old son returned from school in England to become King Farouk. Egypt entered the League of Nations in the year following.

The 1920s and 1930s were marked by disorders throughout much of the Middle East.[2] Mesopotamia became the Kingdom of Iraq. Palestine was divided to include that part east of the Jordan River and the Dead Sea, known as Transjordania. Syria and Lebanon were proclaimed as republics in 1926, but were not to become effective as such for another decade. Druse and Kurdish insurrections plagued both countries, and Iraq as well, where a particular question arose as to control of the Mosul area, rich in oil.

Emir Faisal, former king of Syria, was proclaimed king of Iraq in 1921. His death in 1933 brought his son, Ghazi, to the throne. Internal contests for power led to revolts and assassination, and in 1939 King Ghazi was killed in an automobile accident. Some believed the British

---

2 China, Japan, Korea, and adjacent areas had long been referred to as the "Far East." Those areas of southeastern Asia westward to the Arabian peninsula, Turkey, Egypt, the Sudan, Libya, and even the Balkans had been called the "Near East," but from the time of World War I were more often referred to as the "Middle East."

consul in Baghdad had planned the incident, and he was stoned to death. Ghazi's son, then three years old, became King Faisal II.

Persia had attempted to maintain its neutrality during World War I. Russia, campaigning against the Turks, disregarded the northern Persian frontier and moved its forces deep into the country, where they remained after the Russian Revolution. Reza Khan, a Persian officer, through a *coup d'état* in 1921 seized control of the government and concluded a treaty with the new Soviet government whereby the Red Army forces withdrew from Persia. British influence in the country also was ended. A dictatorship established by Reza Khan resulted in the former Shah Ahmad going into exile in Paris in 1923. Because of his absence, he was declared deposed in 1925 by the Majlis, or Assembly, and in 1926 Reza Khan was crowned Reza Shah Pahlavi.

Holding all power, the new shah sought to restore order in Persia, build a strong army, develop roads, rail service, and aviation. In 1931, the government took over the Persian portion of the British-owned Indo-European Telegraph Company line, operating since 1865 between India and Europe. In 1932 it also took over a concession held since 1909 by an Anglo-Persian Oil Company that had made Persia a leader in oil production, with a pipeline built to the port of Abadan on the Persian Gulf. A new concession was granted in 1934 to the Standard Oil Company of California to seek oil in the Bahrein Islands in the gulf.

In the same fashion, the Iraq government had taken over a prewar Anglo-German Turkish Petroleum Company concession. It was renamed the Iraq Petroleum Company in 1925, with British, Dutch, U.S., and French participants. New oil was found near Kirkuk in 1927, and in 1931 the concessions were revised to give the Iraq Petroleum Company full rights to develop oil resources east of the Tigris, and to build pipelines westward to the Mediterranean. In Saudi Arabia, King Ibn Saud granted oil concessions in 1933 and 1939 to U.S. interests to form the Arabian-American Oil Company (Aramco), with oil struck in commercial quantities in 1938.

Significant of future developments as these events were, events in Palestine received major attention in the news through the 1920s and 1930s. Apart from the fact that British troops had occupied Jerusalem in December 1917, two other circumstances shaped the provisions of the mandate held over that country. A secret Anglo-French-Russian agreement of 1916 had specified that a victory in the war should mean an international administration there. Then in November 1917 Arthur Balfour, foreign secretary in the Lloyd George cabinet, announced that the British government favored a national home for Jews in Palestine after the war.

This so-called "Balfour Declaration" became a controversial issue from the time of its pronouncement. Jewish people, living under prejudicial conditions in many countries, began to arrive in Palestine shortly after the war, and many acquired land. Arab residents were alarmed and anti-Jewish riots occurred at intervals after May 1921, and many Jews were killed in a concerted attack in August 1929. Arabs in Palestine, freed of Turkish control, saw their hopes of independence vanishing along with their hopes of acquiring land. Reports by two British commissions and a League of Nations commission in 1930, along with a sharp parliamentary debate in London, only confused the issue and Jewish hopes fell.

Sir Arthur Wauchope was named by the British government in 1931 as high commissioner in Palestine. Jewish immigration and land acquisition continued, although at a lower rate. Protests also continued and in 1933 Arabs introduced a plan of noncooperation and a boycott of British goods, with more protests and riots. This led to a general strike in 1936 and a vain effort to form an Arab High Committee to unite all Arabs in an endeavor to reach an agreement.

A British government proposal in 1937 presented in a Peel Commission Report suggested that the British mandate in Palestine be limited to Jerusalem alone, with the rest of the country formed into Arab and Jewish states. The League Mandates Commission and the League of Nations Assembly accepted that plan in principle. Jewish opinion was considerably divided, however. The plan was approved by the World Zionist Congress, favoring the homeland in Palestine, but still denounced as a violation of the Balfour Declaration. A Pan-Arab Congress meeting in Syria rejected the Peel proposal almost unanimously. That congress proposed an end to the mandate, with Palestine made an independent state and with Jews to have full status along with Arabs, but with immigration to cease and the concept of a national homeland to be ended.

With no agreement on the matter, Palestine was involved through 1938 and 1939 in an undeclared war, with terrorists active on both sides, bombings in Jerusalem, Haifa, and Jaffa, and an Arab seizure of Bethlehem and part of Jerusalem. Both Jews and Arabs were killed, as was the British district commissioner for Galilee. The British administration sought to keep order, deploying some 30,000 troops, maintaining military courts, deporting many Arabs, and executing at least one Jewish terrorist. Wauchope was replaced as high commissioner by Sir Harold MacMichael.

A new commission under Sir John Woodhead returned a report proposing a conference of Arabs and Jews to seek a solution. Such a Palestine Conference met in London during February–March 1939 without result. The British government therefore published its own plan, calling for an independent state of Palestine, with Arabs and Jews to share in the government and Jewish immigration set at 75,000 in the first five years. After that time immigration was to end unless with Arab agreement for it to continue. Land transfers also were to be regulated or prohibited, as the local government decided. Parliament approved the plan, but it met with no favor on the part either of the Arabs or Jews. The outbreak of the European war in September left the Palestine problem unresolved.

The Transjordan area east of Palestine was organized as a kingdom in 1922. The modified British mandate permitted military control to continue, along with some financial control. Beyond that, the state was ruled from 1921 by Emir Abdullah ibn Hussein, son of the Sherif of Mecca. The area did not become known as the Hashemite Kingdom of Jordan until 1949, even though the Emir Abdullah became King Abdullah in 1946.

The Balkans

Greece

The Greek government throughout the war years was beset by political, military, and economic problems. King Alexander, occupying the throne since June 1917, died of blood poisoning at twenty-seven in October 1920 after being bitten by a monkey.

With the war then over and in response to a plebiscite, Alexander's father, Constantine I, who had abdicated in 1917, was restored to the throne and returned from self-exile in Switzerland. Still denied recognition by the French and British governments because of earlier support for Germany, he also was soon unpopular within Greece. Italian forces had been withdrawn from Turkey in 1921, but he chose to continue military action against Turkey until Greek forces were driven ignominiously out of Smyrna in September 1922. At that time, the king was confronted by an insurrection led by General Nikolaos Plastiras heading an anti-royalist element in the army. Again he abdicated, left Athens for Palermo, and died there in January 1923. His eldest son, the pro-German Crown Prince George, whose succession to the throne had been blocked by the Allies in 1917, became king in 1922. Then thirty-three, his wife was the former Princess Elizabeth of Rumania. In that same year his sister, Helen, was married to Crown Prince Carol of Rumania.

Not only was King Constantine forced to abdicate as a result of the Greek military disaster in Turkey, but his premier, Demetrios Gounaris, and five other cabinet ministers and generals were tried or court-martialed and executed in November 1922 by order of General Plastiras. The regime of George II in 1922–23 was marked by internal conflicts and problems. One was a considerable sentiment for the establishment of a republic to replace the monarchy.

The Treaty of Lausanne, when signed in July 1923, provided better terms for Turkey than the preceding Treaty of Sèvres. It deprived Greece of the Dodocanese Islands, even though the people of those islands had voted in favor of union with Greece in a 1919 plebiscite. Instead, they remained Italian. On the other hand, certain Aegean islands, formerly Turkish, became Greek. The Lausanne Treaty provided for a Greek-Turkish exchange of Moslem and Orthodox Catholics supervised by a League of Nations commission. This gave Greece about 1,500,000 persons to assimilate. Many were artisans and farmers potentially able to contribute usefully to the national welfare, but they arrived at a time when Greece was in financial difficulties. Through the League of Nations, $70 million was made available to assist in their support and settlement.

Two other problems arose in 1923. A Conference of Ambassadors in Paris acting as executors of the peace treaties sent out an Inter-Allied Commission to delimit the frontier between Greece and Albania in accordance with a 1921 agreement. Its members were Italian, French, and British. On the morning of August 27, the car bearing the Italian members, having started from Janina in Greece, was fired upon while passing through a forest area. General Enrico Tellini, president of the commission, three Italian members of his staff, and an Albanian interpreter were killed.

The Fascist government of Italy headed by Benito Mussolini directed immediate protests to the Greek government. The Greek island of Corfu was shelled by the Italian navy and troops were sent ashore to occupy the island. The matter was settled in December through the League of Nations under pressure from Great Britain and France. Greece was forced to pay an indemnity, but a world hopeful of peace had observed the first exhibition of international aggression by the new Fascist government of Italy. This Corfu incident received full press attention at the time, but correspondents reported from the capitals of the countries concerned, rather than from Corfu itself.

The second problem in 1923 stemmed from a brief military uprising in Macedonia, the ill-defined district overspreading southern Yugoslavia and extending into northern Greece and western Bulgaria. The uprising was believed to have been advanced by General Ioannis Metaxas, retired Greek chief of staff, and other officers seeking support for George II and for the monarchy at a time when that form of government was itself under attack by General Plastiras, the anti-royalist group in the army, and elements of the civilian population.

The question of whether a monarchial government should be continued in Greece, or whether the country should become a republic was very much an issue during elections in December 1923. Eleutherios Venizelos, almost perpetually in and out of the government since 1898 and favorable to a monarchy, received a strong popular vote indicating that he would become premier again in a new government in January 1924. The December vote, however, had authorized a plebiscite in the spring of 1924 during which the public would vote upon a continuation of the monarchy or the introduction of a republican or federal form of government. General Plastiras was bold enough to approach King George after the December election and ask the king to leave the country so that the question of continuation of the monarchy might be freely debated in the weeks ahead without embarrassment to him and without intimidation or a sense of impropriety so far as the public was concerned. The king responded by leaving the country for London two days after the December election and did not return to Greece for twelve years.

The new government took office on January 11, 1924. Premier Venizelos, even with the assistance of Metaxas, was unable to persuade the anti-royalist army leaders to support the monarchy, and he resigned on February 3 and left the country. When the plebiscite took place on April 13, it produced a vote overwhelmingly in favor of a Greek republic, which was proclaimed on May 1. Admiral Pavlos Koundouriotis became provisional president and George II remained in England.

The ten years following were extremely uneasy with many changes. The first came in June 1925 in a *coup d'état* through which power was seized by General Theodoros Pangalos, an able military leader. Six months later in January 1926, he made himself dictator. Koundouriotis promptly resigned as president, and Pangalos assumed that position. In October 1925 he sent troops into Bulgaria in a reaction to Macedonian or Bulgarian refugee raids across the Greek frontier. A war between the two countries was prevented only by League of Nations intervention, but a fine was assessed against Greece.

A second government change occurred in August 1926 when Pangalos was forced out in a *coup d'état* arranged by General Georgios Kondylis. He had been a member of parliament and had held cabinet posts in governments since 1923, but had been arrested and banished by Pangalos. Returning as head of the government, and backed by a so-called Republican Guard, Kondylis recalled Koundouriotis to the presidency. As premier himself, he reinstituted the constitution, which had been voided by Pangalos, and scheduled a general election for November.

The support for the republic meanwhile had reversed itself and had become so slim, in comparison to a resurgent royalist sentiment, that a coalition government was formed under Alexandros Zaimis, a prewar premier and respected statesman. Kondylis retired voluntarily from the scene and went to France. In July 1928 Venizelos, having returned to Greece, was named by Koundouriotis to replace Zaimis as premier. A general election in August confirmed him in that position where he served more than four years.

During that period, Venizelos restored the senate as part of the legislative machinery and devoted himself particularly to strengthening Greek international relations. This brought treaties with Italy, Albania, Yugoslavia, Bulgaria, Hungary, Austria, and Turkey, and also a meeting in Athens in 1930 of a first Balkan Conference seeking to improve political and economic conditions in the south of Europe. During that time, Koundouriotis retired from the presidency in December 1929, with Zaimis elected as provisional president to succeed him. By 1931 the Greek state and its administration appeared at last to be well established.

Bulgaria

Bulgaria was the first of the Central Powers to surrender during World War I, and it signed an armistice with the Allies at Saloniki on September 30, 1918. Tsar Ferdinand abdicated a few days later. He was succeeded by his son, Boris III. The country was overrun by Bulgarian refugees made homeless by the war, and by others from the Macedonian or Yugoslavian areas. These persons brought violence and disorder to Sofia, the capital, to the countryside, and to adjacent countries. Border raids were common throughout the decade.

Bulgaria's representatives signed the Treaty of Neuilly in 1919 in a formal reestablishment of peace, and the country joined the League of Nations in 1920. The government under Premier Alexander Stamboliski advanced a strong program. Leader of the Peasant party before the war, Stamboliski had opposed Bulgaria's alliance with the Central Powers and had been jailed. As premier, he had his own turn of supporting the conviction and imprisonment of members of the wartime cabinet. He endeavored to divide crown lands among the peasants, introduced a high tax on incomes, closed the university, and curbed freedom of the press. These and other actions naturally created opposition. Members of the Internal Macedonian Revolutionary Organization (IMRO), seeking Macedonian autonomy in an area overlapping Bulgaria and Yugoslavia and part of Greece, and an organization

Stamboliski had attempted to break up, joined in a conspiracy against him throughout 1922 and 1923. This contributed to the overthrow of his government in June 1923, followed by his assassination a few days later.

A new government, headed by Aleksandr Tsankov, reversed some of the Stamboliski measures and freed members of the wartime cabinet whom he had jailed. It was difficult for any government to cope with substantive matters, however, because the country was swayed by internal conflict and high emotion. Much of that derived from the refugee problem. Thousands were victims of peace treaty settlements drawing new frontiers. Others were Macedonians, most of them Bulgarian mountain people seeking a better way of life. There were former soldiers, peasants, and workers without land or employment, and others of the professional and middle classes who suffered by reason of the changes introduced by Stamboliski.

The Tsankov government of 1923–25 was unable to solve this problem, nor were others immediately following. Violence was almost inescapable. In September 1923, a Communist insurrection was put down with great bloodshed; several thousand were killed and others jailed for long periods without trial. In 1924 about 200 persons were assassinated, including Todor Alexandrov, leader of the IMRO. He was killed by a member of a rival faction within the organization.

There was an attempt on April 14, 1925, to kill King Boris, but the next day General Kosta Gheorghiev was a victim. At his funeral ceremonies in Sofia, the Communists struck back in retaliation for their losses in 1923. They exploded a bomb in the cathedral, resulting in 123 persons killed and 323 wounded. Martial law was proclaimed and five persons later were hanged publicly, with many others shot or imprisoned. Communists were outlawed and went underground.

The Macedonian revolutionary organization, having lost Alexandrov as its leader, split into two rival groups, one headed by Nicholoff Protoguerov and the other by Ivan Mihailov. They battled one another without mercy and their members, like some refugees, conducted raids across frontiers to gain treasure and food. This made trouble for the Bulgarian government unable to control them. Protests were received from Yugoslavia, Rumania, and Greece. The latter sent a military force into Bulgaria in October 1925, with a near-war resulting until the crisis was settled through the League of Nations. The IMRO conflict continued and Protoguerov was assassinated in July 1928 by one of the Mihailov faction. This brought the two factions into open warfare. In August 1930 Mihailov was arrested by the government, but the conflict did not end. Mihailov escaped in September 1934 and fled to Turkey.

The violence of 1924-25, culminating in the cathedral bombing and the new repressions following, seemed to bring a greater sobriéty to the country. Even by the end of 1925 there was some belief that a more conciliatory government policy might be appropriate and helpful. Tsankov resigned in January 1926, and Andrey Liapchev, Democratic party leader, became premier.

Through 1926 and until June 1931 the Liapchev administration sponsored acts of a more constructive nature. These began with the release and pardoning of all political prisoners, except Communists. The League of Nations was able to negotiate a loan through the Bank of England to help in the settlement of refugees, and martial law was proclaimed along the frontiers to help curb the border raids. Other loans totalling about $15 million were arranged in Great Britain and the United States to care for Bulgaria's prewar debts. Further aiding the country's financial situation, a conference at The Hague produced an agreement by which Bulgaria's reparations payments were reduced.

A treaty of friendship was signed with Turkey in 1929. In 1930 King Boris married the Princess Giovanna, daughter of King Victor Emmanuel III of Italy. This made for good relations with Italy, and the national outlook was generally improved. The major problems resisting solution related to minority groups within the country, but Communist agitation and frontier incidents continued, in which Macedonian forays from Bulgarian territory created difficulties with Greece and Yugoslavia.

Yugoslavia

Yugoslavia was faced with problems and complexities as difficult to make understandable to the world through press coverage as those existing in Bulgaria. As a political entity, it was a new country. At its heart was Serbia, the target of Austria's attack in 1914 in the first move of World War I.

On October 29, 1918, the day Austria offered to surrender to Italy, a Yugoslav National Council met at Zagreb in Croatia and proclaimed the independence of the Yugoslavs (south Slavs) of Europe. This reverted to the prewar concept of a Pan-Slav union, which included the areas and peoples of the kingdoms of Serbia and Montenegro, the Austrian provinces of Bosnia and Herzegovina, Dalmatia, Croatia and Slavonia, parts of Styria and Carniola, and Voyvodina, a part of Hungary. On December 4, the entire area was proclaimed as the United Kingdom of the Serbs, Croats, and Slovenes, and it was so recognized in the peace treaties of St. Germain, Neuilly, and Trianon, all concluded at Paris in 1919. It became known officially as Yugoslavia in 1929.

Peter I of Serbia became king of the new nation. Then seventy-four and long unwell, he had ruled since 1914 under a regency with his son, Crown Prince Alexander, conducting the affairs of government from Belgrade. Both Peter I and Alexander had demonstrated devotion to their responsibilities, extending to their presence in battle areas during the war years.

In August 1921, King Peter died and the Prince Regent became Alexander I under a constitution only just instituted. In 1922 he married Princess Marie, daughter of King Ferdinand and Queen Marie of Rumania. Thus he became brother-in-law to Crown Prince Carol of Rumania and to King George II of Greece.

Treaties of alliance were concluded with Czechoslovakia and Rumania, bringing the Yugoslav kingdom into the Little Entente shaped by France. Frontier agreements were reached with Italy, Rumania, Austria, and Greece, and treaties of friendship were concluded with Italy, France, Poland, and Greece. A free zone in the Greek port of Saloniki was made available by treaty for Yugoslavian use, with the prewar problem of overland access to the sea at that point also removed by the frontier settlements.

Despite those settlements, there were frontier incidents with Albania. Border raids by Macedonian revolutionaries operating from Bulgarian soil continued to be a problem, and resulted in the formal closure of that frontier from 1929 to 1937. Territorial differences also existed with Hungary, with conflicting claims in the Voyvodina area.

The most serious internal problem was a refusal of the Croats, in the northeastern section of the country adjacent to Hungary, to join in the nation's constituent assembly. They were opposed to the centralized form of government provided for in the constitution, preferring a federal form under which Croatia and other provinces would have greater autonomy.

This controversy resulted in the imprisonment of Croat leader Stephen Radich in December 1924, and the outlawing of his Croat Peasant party. In July 1925, Radich agreed to recognize the constitution. He was freed and was made minister of education in the cabinet, with other Croatians also in cabinet posts. This compromise did not survive, and Radich and the other Croatian members resigned from the cabinet posts in April 1926, but they did remain as members of the assembly.

In June 1928, a Radical party deputy fired upon Radich and other Croat Peasant party members in the assembly chamber. Radich died of his wounds, and Croat deputies withdrew from the assembly and again demanded a federal form of government. When that was not forthcoming, they set up their own parliament at Zagreb in October

1928 and undertook to proceed independently of the Belgrade government.

Seeking to preserve the unity of the kingdom, but unable to heal the breach through compromise or negotiation, King Alexander in January 1929 proclaimed a dictatorship under which he sought to bring the country together. The constitution was suspended, the assembly was dissolved, and a strict censorship was imposed. All political parties were outlawed, a legislative council with only advisory powers was set up, and efforts were made to rid the administration and the military establishment of divisive forces and corruption. This effort involved the arrest in May of Dr. Vladko Machek, successor to Radich as Croat leader, but he was released in June 1930. Meanwhile, in October 1929, the name of the kingdom was changed to the far simpler Yugoslavia. This had the value of eliminating the names of the old divisions which tended to perpetuate a separatist sentiment. The former provinces were reorganized to make nine states with purely geographical names.

Matters proceeded well enough so that in September 1931 the king announced an end to the dictatorship. A new constitution provided for a bicameral legislative body. Political parties were again authorized, except that they were national rather than local or district groups. The party receiving the largest popular vote in open elections was to occupy two-thirds of the seats in the parliament, and its accepted leader would be the premier. The results were disappointing in the November elections, however, and dissatisfaction was general.

The Croat Peasant party ultimately denounced in 1932 what it regarded as a continuing domination by Alexander's own regime. Dr. Machek was jailed again in October, and following his release was once more arrested in April 1933 and sentenced to three years on a charge of treasonable activity. Slovene leaders also were arrested.

The year 1933 brought alarm in much of Europe over the rise of National Socialism in Germany. Alexander had the support of France in seeking to unite the Balkan countries, and a Balkan Pact was concluded in February 1934 between Yugoslavia, Greece, Rumania, and Turkey. Bulgaria refused to join, despite a second visit by Alexander to Sofia in September. A Yugoslav trade agreement with Germany in June led France to send Foreign Minister Barthou to Belgrade later in that month to seek an even firmer French-Yugoslav and Little Entente relationship. Out of this came a return visit to France by Alexander on October 9, 1934.

Met at Marseilles by Barthou, the two rode ceremoniously through the streets of that city. As they did so, they were fired upon by a Macedonian associated with the Croat opponents of Alexander's regime, and both men were killed. The event was witnessed by a crowd of onlookers, including representatives of the press. The assassination brought threat of a war between Yugoslavia and Hungary, where the Croat revolutionary group had its headquarters, but the danger was averted through the intervention of the League of Nations.

Alexander's nine-year-old son succeeded to the Yugoslav throne as Peter II, under a regency headed by Prince Paul, a cousin of Alexander. The Croats offered to cooperate with the new government, Machek was pardoned, but the problems were not ended.

Albania

Albania, the smallest of the postwar countries on the Balkan peninsula, had common frontiers with Yugoslavia on the north and Greece on the south. With a coastline on the Adriatic Sea, it faces the heel of the Italian boot across the relatively narrow Strait of Otranto.

With the support of the European powers, Albania had gained its independence from Turkey in 1912. Prince William of Wied, a German military officer, was offered the crown and accepted, but left the country when the war began in 1914, a victim of intrigue. During the war years, the small country was occupied in various parts and at various times by forces of Italy, Serbia, Montenegro, and Austria.

Just after the war, a national assembly that had been formed in 1912-14 met again and elected a president rather than recalling William. Italy, whose military forces occupied most of the country, and newly established Yugoslavia both sought to establish positions there. Italy withdrew its forces in 1920, at which time Albania also joined the League of Nations. A Conference of Ambassadors in Paris agreed in 1921 to arrange for a settlement of frontiers between Albania and its neighboring countries, but did not act in the matter until 1923. It was at that time that the Italian members of the boundary commission were murdered in Greek territory and that Italy temporarily occupied the Greek island of Corfu.

Albania was proclaimed a republic by its national assembly in 1925, with Ahmed Bey Zogu, a member of the Yugoslav party, president. A constitution was promulgated, a national bank was formed on the basis of a loan from Italy, and the frontiers were redefined in 1926. A treaty in 1927 gave Italy important concessions under which Albania became a virtual protectorate, supported by further loans in later years.

The government was reorganized in 1928, with the republic becoming a kingdom. Ahmed Bey Zogu became King Zog I. His goal was to modernize the country, with Tirana as its capital. Opposition from some who wished to reestablish the republic led to a dictatorial rule and to the arrest of about 200 persons in 1932, seven of whom were sentenced to death. King Zog also contested what he regarded as too great an Italian influence in the country.

Because Albania was out of the mainstream of affairs, news coverage came primarily through stringers in Tirana, and occasional visits by roving correspondents primarily for the press of Italy, Austria, Great Britain, and the United States. Attention tended to center more on the personality of King Zog than on substantive matters.

Rumania

Rumania had entered World War I in support of czarist Russia in August 1916. It invaded Transylvania in Hungary but was forced back by the Austro-Hungarian army and lost half of its own territory by the end of that year. The government moved from Bucharest, the capital, lost in December, to Jassy (Iasi) in the extreme northeast of the country. It was so little able to function that a truce was made with the Central Powers in December 1917, and a peace treaty signed in May 1918 cost the country dearly.

This loss was soon reversed, however. With the Allied successes late in 1918, Bulgaria, Turkey, and Austria-Hungary all signed armistice terms in September and October. Allied troops entered Rumania, and three days before Germany signed armistice terms on November 11, Rumania itself again re-entered the war on the Allied side. This put Rumania in a position to share in the Allied victory. A Rumanian occupation of Hungary followed in 1919. The Paris treaties of the Trianon and Neuilly in 1919 gave Rumania most of the territory it wanted, including Transylvania, Bukovina, and part of Banat, all formerly Hungarian, Bessarabia, formerly a part of Russia, and southern Dobrudja, formerly a part of Bulgaria. The territorial changes brought into being what was referred to as "greater Rumania."

Rumania became a kingdom in 1861, combining the principalities of Moldavia and Wakkachia, formerly under Turkish domination. Karl Eitel, a German-born prince and former Prussian army officer, was offered the throne in 1866 and became King Carol I. Under his administration the country gained full independence from Turkey and status as a constitutional monarchy. Loyal to his native Germany, the king was unable to win the support of the Rumanian legislative body in taking the country into an alliance with the Reich as the war began in 1914. By then seventy-five, he suffered a breakdown and died in October. Carol I was succeeded by his nephew, Ferdinand I. He was German-born and related to Kaiser Wilhelm II, and his wife, Marie, was a granddaughter of Queen Victoria.

In 1914, because of its location between Hungary and Russia, Rumania was under pressure to join the Central Powers, but also to join the Allies in support of Russia. Actually, it maintained its neutrality for the first two years of the war. In that period, Ionel Bratianu, Liberal party leader and premier, had been negotiating with both sides for the most favorable assurances looking toward the territorial expansion later actually attained, plus assurance of military support. In the end, the best assurances came from the Allies, for whom there also was a stronger public feeling. The actual decision in 1916 to cast its lot with the Allies came, however, because British-born Queen Marie, sympathetic to France and Russia and disturbed by the German military successes, was able to persuade Ferdinand to declare war on Austria-Hungary, but not on Germany. For this action, he was disowned by the Hohenzollern family in Germany, and that country declared war on Rumania, with Turkey and Bulgaria following suit, along with Austria-Hungary.

Rumania's decisive defeat, disastrous at the time, was later turned to an effective triumph. The almost incredible creation of a "greater Rumania" was marked by a new coronation ceremony in 1922, making Ferdinand and Marie sovereigns of a united Rumania. A new constitution was adopted in 1923, reforms were made, large estates were divided into landholdings for the peasants and soldiers, and universal suffrage was introduced.

Queen Marie had become a favorite of the Rumanian people through her active participation in charitable enterprises and wartime service as a Red Cross nurse. She was author of several books and had become widely known abroad. In the autumn of 1926, seeking benefits for Rumania, she made a tour of the United States and also made a footnote in the history of journalism.

The queen sailed from Cherbourg October 12, 1926, in the *Leviathan* of the United States Line and returned five weeks later in the *George Washington* of the same line. She was the first reigning queen ever to visit the United States, and received intensive press coverage wherever she went, some of it almost comic in its parochialism.

The coverage began from the time she sailed. Several members of the U.S. press were aboard the ship, by chance as much as by design. She occupied the presidential suite, but moved about the ship and used the public dining saloon. She met each morning with the news correspondents, who filed reports by wireless. Mrs. Woodrow Wilson, another passenger, was virtually ignored.

The press representatives, whom she also entertained at a special luncheon, were Charles Stephenson Smith, returning to New York after a period as Associated Press bureau chief in London; Harold E. Scarborough, *New York Herald Tribune* correspondent there; John Goette, INS; Lorimer Hammond, *Chicago Tribune;* Guy Jones,

NANA: Virginia Sinclair Dakin, *New York Daily News;* Zoë Beckley, Famous Features Syndicate, New York; and May Birkhead, a member of the Paris edition of the *New York Herald* since 1912, but writing of the queen's journey for the *New York Times.*[3]

King Ferdinand died in 1927. Normally he would have been succeeded by his eldest son, Crown Prince Carol, but he had renounced the throne in 1925. Instead, Carol's son, then only five years old, became king. As Michael I, he served under a regency council, of which his mother, the former Greek Princess Helen, was a member. Queen Marie retired from active affairs at this time but lived until 1938.

With a view to establishing a solid mandate for the new regime, the regency council in 1928 authorized Iuliu Maniu, a leader of the National Peasant party, to form a provisional cabinet and arrange for a general election, in which he and his party received a strong mandate. Further reforms were introduced, an existing press censorship was abolished, a consolidation of peasant landholdings took place, and foreign capital investments brought improvements in the country.

Premier Maniu was not satisfied, however, with the manner in which the regency council was functioning under Prince Nicolas, brother of the absent Prince Carol and uncle of the boy-king. He persuaded all political parties to join in inviting Prince Carol to return to the country to assume the throne. There was a distinct understanding that Magda Lepescu, Carol's mistress, would remain in France or England, and that he would seek a reconciliation with his divorced wife, Princess Helen. Carol returned to Bucharest on June 6, 1930, and parliament modified the law of 1925 so that he might assume the throne, which he did on June 9. His son Michael became crown prince. The years following through the decade of the 1930s showed Rumania primarily in decline.

---

3 May Birkhead had requested a leave of absence from the *Herald* to return to the United States on personal business. Eric Hawkins, managing editor of the *Herald,* became uneasy when he learned that she was sailing in the same ship with Queen Marie. This uneasiness turned to "despair," as he tells of it, when the *New York Times* began to publish stories wirelessed from shipboard bearing the Birkhead by-line. They continued to appear in the *Times* as she accompanied the queen to the end of her tour of the United States. This resulted in a request that Birkhead resign from the *Herald* staff after fourteen years. She later returned to Paris and joined the *Chicago Tribune* edition there as a columnist until that paper was sold to the *Herald* in 1934. For her coverage of the sinking of the *Titanic* in 1912 and her early association with the Paris *Herald,* see Desmond, *Windows on the World,* pp. 239, 389, 422.

See Eric Hawkins and Robert N. Sturdevant, *Hawkins of the Paris Herald* (1963), p. 123; Frank O. Braynard, *The Story of the Leviathan,* vol. 3 (New York, 1976), ch. 15.

Queen Marie wrote articles during her U.S. tour, and undertook a short-lived daily column titled "Queen's Counsel."

Great Britain and the Empire   5

London, the first great world news center, retained that position between the two world wars, and the media of the United Kingdom demonstrated the highest professional competence. As a major world capital, a center of international business, finance, and commerce, and a
setting for educational and cultural activities, London provided endless and unrestricted subjects and sources of news and information. In
this, it was more than equal to Washington and New York combined
as news centers in the United States.

Events of news importance originating locally and nationally within
the United Kingdom, and covered by local newspapers and the Press
Association, were reported in other countries so far as interest dictated by Reuters and London representatives for world agencies and
newspapers, and by the growing radio medium. The country was the
center for newsworthy conferences and events. It attracted personalities whose very presence made news. Information poured in from
British Empire or Commonwealth areas and every other part of the
world through the channels of government and private or business
enterprise as well as through British news services and publications,
and largely over British-owned communications facilities. This made
London not only a hub of news, but a relay point in a world exchange.
These circumstances had drawn news representatives to London from
all parts of the globe in the past, and a new influx came after 1920.

Great Britain and the empire never were to be again what they had
been before the war. William L. Langer, professor of history at Harvard, summarizes it in his *Encyclopedia of World History*. He notes
that British war losses, in a population of less 50 million, included
750,000 killed and about 1,500,000 wounded, with thousands more
casualties counted for the empire countries. War costs exceeded £8 billion (nearly $39 billion at the then-existing rate of $4.86 to the pound
sterling). The domestic and foreign debt in 1918 was ten times that of
1914. Of Britain and the empire, Langer goes on to say that Britain
then was

faced with the problem of returning soldiers to industry and introducing social reforms loudly demanded by the laboring classes and was confronted at the same time with increased competition in foreign trade in a world generally disorganized and impoverished. In Ireland, India, Egypt, and Palestine she was confronted with urgent and almost insoluble problems. Even the self-governing Dominions demonstrated an enhanced national feeling and a reluctance to be committed to any share in future European wars.[1]

The postwar period began with a coalition government headed by David Lloyd George as prime minister from 1919 through 1922. Lloyd George at that time held part ownership in the London *Daily Chronicle,* almost certainly the only British first minister ever to have such a direct newspaper relationship.

During those years there was trouble in Ireland, dating from an Easter Rebellion in Dublin in 1916, with the Irish nationalist Sinn Fein organization demanding independence. A Government of Ireland Act passed by Parliament in 1920 provided for a separation of northern and southern Ireland, each to have its own parliament, while also retaining representation in the British Parliament. This was rejected by the south. In 1921 a new agreement provided dominion status for that southern part of Ireland, and the title as the Irish Free State in December 1922. Although approved by the Sinn Fein, controversy continued with the British government.

A strike of coal miners in Great Britain in 1919 was followed by a second in 1921. On behalf of the Allied powers, Great Britain had supported the Greek and Italian military move into Turkey in 1919, and the Italian forces withdrew in 1921. When Greek forces called for support against Turkish units under Mustapha Kemal in 1922, Lloyd George was unable to persuade the Allies to respond and a British force landed in August 1922 failed to save the situation. This brought an end to the Greek regime and the abdication of Constantine I in September 1922, and also ended the government of Lloyd George. He resigned in October in favor of A. Bonar Law. Law in turn resigned in May 1923 because of ill health, and was succeeded by Stanley Baldwin as prime minister.

The prewar position of the United Kingdom as a center for a vigorous world-wide industrial and shipping enterprise, and carrying forward a prosperity by then a century old, had found no revival since the return of peace in 1918. The nostalgia of that period was reflected in an elaborate British Empire Exhibition at Wembley, just northwest of London, in 1924–25. World trade, so far as it revived during the 1920s

---

1 William L. Langer, *An Encyclopedia of World History,* 5th ed. (1972), p. 980.

and later, was shared by other nations to a degree that left not only the United Kingdom but some other prewar industrial nations at a disadvantage.

Meanwhile, a British protectorate over Egypt since 1914 came to an end in 1922, and Egypt was declared independent. Ahmed Fuad, sultan since 1917, became King Fuad I in 1922, but with a constitutional government promulgated in 1923. At the same period, the British mandates in Mesopotamia and Palestine were marked by troubles, and agitation for independence proceeded in India.

Within the United Kingdom, a new general election took place in December 1923 to test a Baldwin government proposal for a high protective tariff as a means to relieve unemployment. It resulted in such a heavy swing to the Labour party candidates as to bring the establishment in January 1924 of Britain's first Labour party government, with J. Ramsay MacDonald as prime minister, Philip Snowden as chancellor of the exchequer, Arthur Henderson as home secretary, and others as new figures in the national leadership. Their first period in office was brief, from January to November, but this was time enough for the administration to extend diplomatic recognition to Soviet Russia, to form trade agreements with that government, and to promise a British loan if former czarist government debts were settled.

These actions and proposals, opposed by Conservative and Liberal party members in parliament, forced a new general election in October 1924. A few days before the voting a letter ostensibly from Grigori Zinoviev, then president of the Communist International (Comintern) in Moscow, addressed to the British Communist party was published in the British press. It urged the party members to work for world revolution and to upset the British government. Although later generally accepted as a forgery, the letter frightened enough voters on the eve of the election to produce a strong Conservative victory, with a second Baldwin ministry following from November 1924 to June 1929.

It was a disturbed period. The new Conservative government began by denouncing the previous Labour government's treaties with the Soviet Union, and the trade agreement was ended in 1927. An Irish boundary agreement was signed in 1925, and Cyprus was made a crown colony. Parliament extended voting rights to women in 1928. The right of the dominions to make treaties of their own with foreign powers had been recognized at an Imperial Conference in 1923. Another such conference in 1926 supported a declaration that Great Britain and the dominions were "autonomous communities within the British Empire, equal in status . . . as members of the British Commonweath of Nations." Thus, the empire became the British Commonwealth through the Statute of Westminster in 1931.

Unemployment remained a major problem. In 1920 an Unemployment Insurance Act had provided for the payment of weekly benefits, popularly referred to as "a dole," to men and women out of work. A more than thirty per cent tariff was placed on imports, as had been proposed in 1923, to protect home industry. Neither measure relieved the unemployment situation, while a tax structure adjusted to provide for payment of the dole placed great burdens on those who were employed and upon the income and estates of the wealthy.

Among workers most seriously affected by the adverse circumstances curtailing British industry and trade were the coal miners, mostly in Wales. Their strikes of 1919 and 1921 had brought the dole into effect, but it was not sufficient, nor was it secure, and a third coal strike began on May 1, 1926. The trade union movement was strong in Great Britain, and the Trade-Union Council supported a general strike in sympathy with the coal miners. From May 3 to 12 about 2,500,000 union members walked out, with rail and bus transport and other essential services interrupted in London and throughout the country. It ended with an understanding that negotiations would be undertaken on wages and hours, and the dole continued. Even so, the coal miners remained on strike until November.

The difficulties within the economy remained persistent to the point where a fourth general election within less than seven years took place in May 1929. It returned a majority for the Labour party again, and a second MacDonald cabinet took office in June and continued until August 1931. Diplomatic relations with the Soviet Union were resumed in October 1929. A desire to return to free trade, while also holding down food prices, led the Labour party government at an Imperial Conference late in 1930 to reject a preferential tariff to aid Canadian wheat exports.

The British government had participated actively in the Washington Naval Conference of 1921-22, with a five-power naval treaty ratified. The Dawes Committee, concerned with a readjustment in German war reparations payments, had met in London in 1924. Modifications of the 1922 naval treaties were discussed at a London Naval Conference in 1930. In preparation, Prime Minister MacDonald had visited the United States as well as Canada, meeting with President Hoover in September 1929.[2]

---

2 The groundwork for the MacDonald-Hoover meeting was laid by Edward Price Bell, director of the *Chicago Daily News* bureau in London from 1900-23. Visiting London again early in 1929 as an "editorial commissioner" for the paper, he persuaded Prime Minister MacDonald to visit Washington to discuss Anglo-American differences on naval matters. The precedent-making conference established a basis for the London

For Great Britain, the 1930s continued to be overshadowed, as the previous decade had been, by economic problems at home and indications of changes in the empire. By 1931, with more than two million still unemployed and a budget deficit in prospect, sharp economies were recommended, including a possible reduction of dole benefits. The economic decline that began with the New York Stock Market collapse of October 1929 had been felt in many other parts of the world by 1931, and not least in Great Britain where the Bank of England felt obliged to abandon the gold standard on September 21, 1931, with the pound sterling declining to $3.49 from its long-time value of $4.86 in relation to the U.S. dollar.

This was an action taken under a new National Coalition government of August-October 1931, including Conservative, Liberal, and Labour party members, with Ramsay MacDonald heading a third cabinet. This cabinet was rejected by the Labour party itself, even though MacDonald and other party members formed the National Labour Group to serve in what was regarded as an emergency period.

The National Coalition Government was approved by the British voters in another general election in October 1931, and remained in office under MacDonald until June 1935. It was the period of an important second India Round Table Conference in 1931 in London, an Ottawa Imperial Economic Conference of July-August 1932, and an World Economic Conference in London during June-July 1933.

King George V died in January 1936 and was succeeded by Edward VIII, who abdicated December 10 to marry the American divorcée, Wallis Warfield Simpson. Edward's brother, the Duke of York, was crowned George VI in May 1937.

The position of the newsmen in London and Great Britain in the 1920s and 1930s differed somewhat from that in the United States. The basic sense of freedom and pride of craft was much the same, which was enormously important in what it meant to the quality of coverage. There was, however, a more formal relationship between the journalist and his news sources. The class system within British society was an element in this relationship, and the foreign correspondent working in London was subject to the same influences felt by British journalists themselves. Another element was the great size of the press corps, both foreign and domestic. Understandably, this made officials and others to whom reporters might turn regularly for information somewhat wary and defensive of their time.

---

meeting in 1930. Bell was nominated for, but did not receive, the Nobel Peace Prize for his part in arranging the MacDonald-Hoover conversations. The conference was one of the first international events reported by shortwave radio. See Desmond, *Windows on the World,* p. 488.

It has been noted that officials in the Soviet Union learned to classify foreign correspondents as friends or enemies of the regime, and to treat them accordingly. The same differentiation arose among officials of the newly formed Fascist government of Italy in the 1920s. To some extent, it probably is fair to assume that this differentiation is made by officials of all governments on every level, and by those others who meet any press or media representatives under almost any circumstance, controversial or not.

Beyond that, it was observed that the journalists in London tended to fall into one of three groups, particularly in their relationship to sources within the government. It was not a friends-or-enemies relationship. But some would be included in what was referred to as an inner circle, others in a middle circle, and many in an outer circle. Informal, unstructured, and loose though it might be, the classification indicated a rough determination of the degree to which the individual journalist had access to news sources, or the manner in which he might be received, if at all, and treated as he sought to obtain information.

Those journalists in the inner circle were a favored few, and identified with the British media. They might be editors and writers who had attended Eton or Harrow, Oxford or Cambridge, wellborn, and members of the "Establishment," originally a British term. If not themselves thus members of the upper class, and perhaps possessed of financial resources and family influence, they would be journalists long in service, and of demonstrated competence and reliability. They probably were representatives of Reuters, the Press Association, the BBC, of such respected publications as the *Times,* the *Sunday Times,* the *Observer,* the *Financial Times,* the *Daily Telegraph,* the *Manchester Guardian,* or the *Economist.* Such journalists and their principals would be likely to accept, share, and follow the concepts put forward by Downing Street, the Foreign Office, other ministries and agencies of government, or the Bank of England. They would not rock the boat in matters of policy, political or economic. If any journalists talked privately with the prime minister, the foreign secretary, or other leaders of party, government, finance, industry, and education, they were of this group. Perhaps as members of the "right" clubs or wearers of the "old school tie," they were trusted, and told nearly all they might ask, some of it off the record and to be held in confidence, but nevertheless providing useful guidance. Foreign correspondents rarely, if ever, gained membership in the inner circle.

Members of the middle circle were more numerous. They included some publishers, editors, and writers for London newspapers and periodicals, for some British provincial papers, either resident in London or visiting, and a very few foreign correspondents representing newspapers or other media judged to be important and responsible. It was rare for a middle circle member to meet with or talk with a cabinet-rank official in office. But by reason of his position and an established reputation for sincerity and reliability, he might meet with a spokesman or public information officer at Downing Street, the Foreign Office, or other important ministries or agencies. The meeting might occur at an informal and friendly luncheon, where the journalist might be told a good deal, some of it possibly off the record for guidance only or not attributable to source if used.

Members of the outer circle included all journalists, British or others, who were not in either of the other groups. Obviously, it was the largest group, with its members the least well informed. Quite aware that they did not share the privileges of those in the other groups, some members referred to themselves as "The Untouchables." This did not please them, but younger members, at least, might hope for promotion to a more favored status. As in all countries, there were some journalists, particularly those for the popular press, who had earned classification as untouchables by failing to demonstrate accuracy or responsibility, or by falsifying reports. Because of this, and to guard their time and privacy, British officials and private citizens alike, including those identified with business and industry, usually managed to keep such outer circle journalists at arm's length. The concept that a man's home or office is his castle was made effective, where possible, by using staff assistants and servants to block the approaches. The telephone, so commonly used in the United States, was rarely effective to the same extent in Great Britain as an instrument in gathering news.

A marked difference between the work of journalists in the United States and the United Kingdom in the 1920s and 1930s, applicable particularly to members of the middle and outer circles in London, related to the kind of information made available. In Washington, officials usually proceeded on the assumption that nearly everything should be made public, unless national security was involved, and national security then was rarely an issue. In London, by contrast, officials proceeded on the theory that only routine information need be made public, and little else unless some essential or desirable purpose was served by making it known. On some occasions, experience suggested, officials even believed that false information best served the government purpose. In any event, it need not necessarily be complete information on a subject, but was to be accepted as the official position.

British journalists, particularly of the outer circle, and some others, confronted with obstacles to obtaining even routine information, whether from government sources or within the private sector, sometimes felt driven to make guesses or assumptions, to invent "facts" or imagine them, occasionally to the point of malice. This practice at times extended to their reporting in other parts of the world. It obviously resulted in inaccuracies, subtracted from the reputation of the press, in general, and contributed to public misunderstanding.

At the same time, all reporters working within the United Kingdom, whether for the British press or others, were obliged to proceed with caution where accounts of criminal offenses, the conduct of the courts, or personal reputations were involved. More than in most countries, the law placed sharp restrictions on what was permitted. The law of libel was strictly interpreted, and citation for contempt of court was a further hazard to be avoided. The Defense of the Realm Act (DORA) and the Official Secrets Acts, passed and amended by Parliament between 1889 and 1939, inhibited the reporter and the British press, although not improperly. Foreign correspondents working in London were subject to most of the restrictions affecting the British journalists, and learned to proceed with equal care.

For the foreign correspondent arriving in London, as in other capitals, a first concern was to gain formal accreditation so that he might approach news sources with the proper *bona fides,* and also establish his right to file news dispatches for transmission at press rates, with the costs to be assumed by his agency, newspaper, or radio network. Accreditation in London followed presentation of his credentials, such as a formal letter of appointment from his principal, to the Foreign Office. The procedure was much the same in other capitals, working through the parallel ministry of government dealing with foreign affairs.[3]

With his accreditation established, the correspondent was authorized to work as an alien in the country. His name was on a list to receive notification of meetings of possible interest and to receive official government releases, or to be able to obtain them, and to be invited to certain gatherings or conferences. He had cards giving him entrée to certain government buildings and meetings, and for use at communications offices, whether in the capital or elsewhere in the country.

In addition, the correspondent in London probably would establish membership in the Foreign Press Association, dating from 1888, or

---

3 Variations existed to this practice, however. In Washington, comparable accreditation for both foreign and domestic reporters was arranged through the Press Gallery of the Congress of the United States, and in Geneva through the Secretariat of the League of Nations. There and in other non-capital news centers such as New York no formal accreditation was involved, but direct arrangements with the communications companies were necessary for the handling of dispatches. Alien residence permits were (and are) almost universally required and an established tax status.

such a group as the Association of American Correspondents in London. He might join the London Press Club, and possibly another club or two, such as the Savage Club or the Reform Club. Thus he would extend his personal acquaintanceship with journalistic colleagues, add to his understanding of attitudes and subject matter, and gain opportunities for a useful exchange of information.

Given time to establish a familiarity with the country and its people, to gain some comprehension of its history and traditions, its governmental structure and current situations and problems, he would at the same time develop his own sources of current information. Possibly the medium he represented would warrant respect in itself, and his own background, attitude, and personality would be such as to make him socially and professionally acceptable. Thus he might hope to attain the middle circle.

Even by 1920, the growing number of correspondents in London had made it almost impossible for officials of government or of banking and business enterprises to find the time to meet with individual newsmen as they might have done in an earlier and simpler era. Out of a need to maintain avenues of communication with the press, the public information officer or the public relations representative in Britain had become a figure both in government and business by the 1930s, much as in the United States.

With the Foreign Office a major source of information, it was not uncommon in the mid-1920s for the correspondent in London to have free range in the corridors of that building and to waylay a familiar member of the press staff in an effort to get some hasty answers to questions. Members of the middle and inner circles had better methods even then. At the same time, the British government was preparing to work more effectively with correspondents of all countries.

Sir Arthur Willert, Washington correspondent for the *Times* from 1911 to 1920, had returned to London in 1921 to become press officer in the Foreign Office. Borrowing something of the Department of State's methods in Washington, he became a spokesman, meeting newsmen in groups to make announcements and respond to questions. In 1934 he was succeeded by Rex Leeper, who had been his assistant. He was followed in turn by William Rigsdale, formerly of the London *Daily News,* and others. At No. 10 Downing Street, the prime minister's office and residence, George Steward became press officer, and other spokesmen were named in other departments or ministries.

This system had results, both good and bad. It became possible to obtain information more promptly and, in some cases, more accurately. For outer circle correspondents, it became easy to depend upon the spokesman to do their work for them, to accept what they were told, perhaps without further inquiry, and so sometimes to be half-informed and even deceived, with the public misled, however unintentionally.

So far as concerned Foreign Office reports, growing world tensions meant correspondents by the mid-1930s ceased to have their former freedom within the building. Instead, they were steered, for a daily, late-morning scheduled group meeting, to a rather shabby first-floor room, poorly ventilated, with equally poor facilities for seeing and hearing what transpired. A random lot of correspondents attending represented agencies and publications of a variety of countries. Questions were asked on unrelated and sometimes trivial matters, often in broken English, and occasionally in other languages. Two or three press officers responded, as spokesmen, but were brief, rarely informative, and clearly bored with the entire procedure.

The alternative for a correspondent sincerely concerned with subjects centering in the Foreign Office was to seek a personal conversation with a press officer in his own room, possibly dank and chilly, even if a small fire burned, or by taking him to lunch if he was willing. Even then, the value of such a meeting, or its very possibility, would depend upon such factors as the length of time the correspondent had been in London, whether he had established himself as a knowledgeable and preferably sympathetic writer on British affairs, and on the standing of his newspaper or agency in terms of quality, importance, and even friendship toward Great Britain. In exceptional cases where this combination seemed right and proper from the British point of view, a correspondent might be advanced to the middle circle. To some others, however, this might suggest that the correspondent had become susceptible to influences that made him less than reliable as an informant. It was for the correspondent to maintain his balance and integrity in that respect, perhaps even in the eyes of his own publisher or of the directors of the medium represented.

The correspondent concerned with policy matters could turn further to a press spokesman at No. 10 Downing Street and others in various ministries. But he could turn also to those members of the diplomatic corps whom he found over a period of time to be reliable and helpful in matters of information and background.

For general information beyond the government itself, important areas of news invited coverage in the United Kingdom. The correspondent might develop sources within the business community, in organizations and associations, political parties and labor unions, in the areas of sports, education and the arts, and among his colleagues of the press and citizens of the country. He could go himself to important meetings and ceremonies to observe and listen, and to the scene of events in London or elsewhere in Britain.

By reading the British press with understanding, and especially those media known to be represented in the inner circle, a correspondent would add to his own information and also find a basis for his own coverage and reporting. Whereas attribution to the source normally is expected to form a part of any news report, that attribution might at times be obscure, and it required some understanding on the correspondent's part to read meaning into such references as "Downing street informants indicate," "the Foreign Office position seems to be," "Whitehall says" or something so vague as "informed quarters."

The royal family, holding interest for many readers throughout the world, is by tradition protected by a formality in its media relations. Members of the royal household staff hold special responsibility for responding to inquiries, arranging for news coverage, and for photographs.

When warranted by the news, foreign correspondents were able to cover cases in the courts. The House of Lords serves as the final court of appeal in the United Kingdom. This it does not as a body, however, but by calling when the need arises, upon three "law lords," peers having held high judicial office, to serve along with the lord chancellor, a cabinet officer.

The prime minister and members of his cabinet are a collective body responsible to Parliament. Whatever they decide on policy matters is to be stated in the House of Commons or in official addresses or releases reflecting official views. If they respond to questions as individuals in the Parliament, they do so normally only to inquiries by members of that House, submitted in written form before that day's session. With the prime minister and others of the cabinet occupying the "government bench" in the well of the House chamber, the opening hour of each session on four days of the week is a question period during which the prime minister and his cabinet respond to such questions. They may take whatever time is needed to consider their replies, to seek information and counsel, and to discuss the subject with advisers or other members of the government. Even having responded, no debate is permitted at the time.

Occasionally it has been possible for a member of the press to arrange through a friendly member of the House to have a question submitted in this way. Since some members of the House are themselves journalists, they could submit questions directly. But the planned delay in responding to questions and their discussion gives the procedure small value for the press as a means of obtaining any quick news reports or clarification.

While there is every other sort of government office building in London, there is none specifically assigned for the use by members of

Parliament, whether lords or commoners. They may have working facilities in their homes or private offices, but if they are to be seen by members of the press without special arrangement, it must be in the lobbies and areas of the Parliament building itself.

British reporters concerning themselves with affairs of government are variously designated as lobby or parliamentary correspondents, gallery correspondents, and diplomatic correspondents. The lobby correspondents are in effect political and legislative reporters. They cover those electoral contests between parties and candidates for seats in Parliament. They cover the business conducted in both houses of Parliament and the general course of the legislation. They see and talk with the members of Parliament in the lobbies and also in the private rooms and restaurants. They form a kind of closed corporation, limited to British journalists only, with special accreditation and rights to move in areas of the building outside the actual legislative chambers, but generally otherwise barred to the public or the press. They meet with members before, between, and after sessions to query them on legislation and on general political subjects. Foreign correspondents are not included among the lobby correspondents and do not enter those areas of the Houses of Parliament except, on occasion, as guests of individual members. In Washington, by contrast, reporters might approach members of the Congress, whether of the House or Senate, either in the halls of the capitol or in their offices in buildings adjacent.

The gallery correspondents, also working in the Parliament building, cover the actual debates in the House of Commons and in the House of Lords. Whereas in Washington those reporters occupy space in galleries directly above the presiding officers in the House and Senate and have work rooms behind the galleries, the facilities in London are more modest. The press galleries are smaller, and there are no work rooms to match those in Washington. The galleries provide accommodations for reporters for Reuters, the Press Association, and the London dailies. Beyond that, only about a dozen other seats must be shared by representatives of the British provincial press, the Commonwealth press, and the foreign press. The fact is that the foreign press is not greatly concerned about direct coverage of parliamentary debates, except when special issues arise, since full coverage is available through Reuters, the British press, and through *Hansard's,* a publication comparable to the *Congressional Record* in Washington. Reporters unable to find space in the Press Gallery, but interested in hearing debates on particular matters may hope to gain admission to the public Visitors' Gallery if space permits, but they are forbidden to make notes there.

The diplomatic correspondents for the British press specialize in the reporting of foreign affairs and broad matters of policy. They are likely to be members of the inner circle, representing Reuters, the Press Association, and the major daily and Sunday quality newspapers of national circulation. They look to sources in the Foreign Office, 10 Downing Street, the Admiralty, and War Office, among informed groups elsewhere, and among members of the world diplomatic and consular corps in London. The term diplomatic correspondent originating in London as bearing upon journalism of a substantive and responsible variety, informed and interpretative, was only adopted in such other capitals as Paris and Washington at about the time of World War II.

Correspondents writing from London or from any other news center are concerned first with the basic reportorial function of telling what has happened or is in prospect, and so to provide the who-what-when-where-why-&-how of an event.

If the event requires some degree of interpretation—enlarging upon the why-&-how and upon what it all means—the reporter's approach is slightly different. If he is reporting upon a situation rather than an event, the approach also is different. In either case, adding the background or factual interpretation, the correspondent produced what sometimes was referred to as a "thumb-sucking piece," a way of saying that it is a story calling for thought and contemplation on his part as he proceeds. It is a kind of story commonly written by diplomatic correspondents, political correspondents, public affairs columnists, and others concerned with substantive matters.

Australia and New Zealand The British Empire changed after World War I. Something has been said above with reference to changes in Ireland, and the Middle East, including Egypt. There were changes also in Australia and New Zealand, Canada, India, and the Union of South Africa.

Both Australia and New Zealand became original members of the League of Nations in 1920. The League mandated German colonies south of the equator to them, with part of New Guinea and islands of the nearby Bismarck Archipelago assigned to the administration of Australia, and West Samoa and the Island of Nauru to New Zealand.

The capital of Australia, previously at Melbourne, was established officially in 1927 at Canberra, a specially designed new city. Between the war years and 1939 governments in Australia were headed by

Premier William M. Hughes, Labour party leader; Stanley Bruce and Earle Page, in a postwar Nationalist and Country party coalition cabinet; James H. Scullin, Labour party; Joseph A. Lyons, of a new United Australian party; and Robert G. Menzies, Liberal party leader.

Both Australia and New Zealand were identified with expeditions to the Antarctic polar regions and also to the extension of aviation to encompass the Pacific. An element in the news reports within the latter category included the reception at Brisbane on June 9, 1928, of Captain Sir Charles Kingsford-Smith, an Australian with four associates who completed the first U.S.–Australian flight, which had started from Oakland, California on May 31. A weekly airmail service between England and Australia, beginning in December 1934, was another element in the news.

New Zealand government leaders included William F. Massey, of the Reform party, followed by Joseph G. Coates; by Sir Joseph Ward and George W. Forbes, both of the United party; and Michael J. Savage, who headed a new Labour party government in 1935.

Some restrictions were placed by both governments upon immigration in the postwar years, with economic as well as racial reasons cited. Both also felt the effects of the world economic depression after 1930. As producers of gold and wool, however, both soon benefitted in those years.

Canada

Canada, with a population of just under nine million in 1920, and a dominion within the British Empire, had as high a general literacy rate as any country in the world. A bilingual nation, nearly one-third of its people, concentrated in eastern provinces, speak French. Territorially the second largest country in the world, with much of the north too cold for settlement, it was and remains primarily agricultural. Rich in other resources, it has a growing industrial development. Its forests provide much of the newsprint used throughout the Western Hemisphere and beyond. Its media organization has been active and of the highest quality.

The country had known a special prosperity during the years of World War I. Its divisions in France had been engaged in some of the bloodiest sectors, and other men were in the royal flying corps and naval service. A sense of strong nationalism emerged from its war experience, and a great feeling for its own autonomy in the world community of nations. This was reflected in the results of the Imperial

Conference of 1926, wherein the dominions were reorganized as equal partners with Great Britain in a commonwealth rather than an empire. It was further exemplified in an independence of action on many matters, including the right to make foreign commitments.

Like many other countries immediately after the war, Canada encountered economic problems bearing upon agriculture, transportation, and trade. Taxes, strikes, and financial difficulties also created political stresses. As in the United States, where similar problems existed, prosperity returned through the period of 1925–29, followed however by an economic depression matching that affecting most countries of the world.

With the government and political system comparable to that in Great Britain, general elections brought changes in 1921, 1925, 1926, 1930, and 1935. Prime ministers in those years were Arthur Meighen and W. L. Mackenzie King, both serving two separate terms, and then Richard B. Bennett, and Mackenzie King again in 1935. Among events during the period, the Imperial Economic Conference at Ottawa in 1932 produced seven bilateral treaties between member states within the British Commonwealth on the exchange of agricultural products and setting tariff rates. It was a conference that brought newsmen to Ottawa from all parts of the commonwealth and from the United States.

That same year brought the signature of a Canadian–U.S. St. Lawrence Deep Waterways Treaty providing for the later construction of canals and electrical generators and facilities to enable ocean-going ships to move by way of the St. Lawrence River into the Great Lakes. King George VI and Queen Elizabeth made a state visit to Canada in May 1939, the first reigning sovereigns to visit the dominion. Accompanied by a large press contingent, they visited the United States, including Washington, en route home.

The Canadian press naturally covered Ottawa, and the U.S. press also was represented there by resident correspondents for the news agencies and some daily newspapers.

A parallel in the Canadian system to that in Great Britain is that a governor-general, appointed by the British sovereign, acts as the sovereign would do in London. For example, he performs such ceremonial acts as summoning and dissolving the Canadian Parliament, names the prime minister, and receives ambassadors. One difference is, however, that the governor-general is appointed on the advice of the Canadian prime minister, with a new appointee about every five years. Lord Byng of Vimy, formerly a career officer and general who had commanded Canadian troops which distinguished themselves in the Vimy Ridge campaign in 1916, was governor general from 1921–26. A successor in 1935 was John Buchan, who had been briefly a war correspondent for the *Times* and was instrumental in the reorganization of the Reuters agency in 1915-16, serving as a member of its board of directors for twenty years. Already the author of many books, knighted, and a member of Parliament since 1927, he was made Lord Tweedsmuir just before taking his Canadian post.

India

There had long been an underlying discontent among people of the sub-continent of India with British rule, but they did support the Allied cause during World War I with both men and money. A desire for freedom and independence had been growing and, from 1917, as in the south of Ireland, a sentiment favoring self-government had become highly vocal, with some advocacy of a Communist regime.

The British government recognized a need for change. Its own first proposals for modifications in administration had been made in 1918 and 1919. These were scorned in India and led to riots. The British response was to suppress the demonstrations and to curb the liberties of the people. This led only to further violence. Mob demonstrations in April 1919 at Amritsar in the Punjab were put down by force, in what later came to be known as a massacre, with 379 persons killed and more than 1,200 wounded.

In London, a Government of India Act was approved by Parliament in December 1919. It provided a plan for the government of British India, which meant most of the country, but excluded certain independent and semi-independent states classified as British protectorates. It was put into effect in 1920, but lacked the approval of many Indians.

Through the years since about 1876 an association of educated Hindus, including lawyers, teachers, and editors, had held a number of "Congresses" to discuss public affairs. Moslems were included also. The association had grown large by the time of World War I and had taken on aspects of a conspiracy, somewhat revolutionary in character.

Because they supported aspirations for home rule after 1916, these gatherings fostered what became known as the Indian National Congress Party, and in 1920 Mohandas Karamchand Gandhi became its leader. Then fifty-one and of a prosperous Hindu family in the western part of the country, he had studied law in London, where he became a member of the bar in 1891, and later practiced law in South Africa from 1893 until 1914, when he returned to India. He became active immediately in the Congress and helped to organize the party.

Gandhi hoped that home rule might be attained through peaceful means, rather than violence or revolution. He conceived the idea of a campaign of non-cooperation with the British administration as a form of pressure intended to win the desired concessions. His idea was put to its first test in 1919, but some participants strayed from non-cooperation into violent demonstrations. The Amritsar massacre was one result, and the effort failed.

Gandhi tried again in Bombay in November 1921, selecting an occasion when the Prince of Wales arrived there on a state visit. Rioting again resulted. For all his good intentions, this seemed to be the story of Gandhi's every effort to use non-cooperation or "civil disobedience" as a means of persuasion. It happened again in 1922, when twenty-two police officers were killed. A few days later Gandhi was arrested and sentenced to six years in prison.

It was not his first arrest, nor his last, and his arrest did not stop rioting and rebellion in India. Actually he was released from prison in 1924 and entered upon a period of fasting, hoping thus to persuade the people of India themselves to end their violent demonstrations. This effort also was unsuccessful.

By then referred to with the honorific title of Mahatma Gandhi, a term for a Brahmin Hindu sage, great-souled and magnanimous and seeking to aid those less advanced, he maintained a year of political silence. This was followed by three or four years of personal visits to villages where he sought to remove class barriers and especially to remove the stigma attaching to the "untouchables." To advance India's independence, he urged the people to spin and weave, so reducing imports of British textiles. Later, in 1930, he campaigned against a salt monopoly maintained by the government.

By 1927 the leaders of the Congress party had decided that home rule was not enough, that India should have its independence. Gandhi was joined in this expression by Jawaharlal Nehru, also educated in England at Harrow and Cambridge, and a practicing lawyer.

The British government was not prepared to grant independence to India, but it was ready to make certain concessions and to grant the country dominion status. A parliamentary commission headed by Sir John Simon, prominent in the British Labour party, visited the country in 1927–30 to explore that arrangement. The proposal was met, however, by a boycott and more violence. Gandhi returned to active party participation and took charge of a new campaign of civil disobedience in particular opposition to the salt monopoly. This was capped by a "salt march" to the sea at Cambay in April 1930, with Gandhi leading and his followers deriving salt from the ocean water. The drama of this march induced many to join it and many others to join in the civil disobedience campaign in a variety of ways. It led to new outbreaks and to arrests. Gandhi and Nehru were imprisoned, causing further violence in protest.

The British government, seeking to break the stalemate, called a Round Table Conference, meeting in London from November 1930 to January 1931. No representative of the Congress party would attend. Others of more moderate view, and representatives of the Indian princely states, did reach some understanding with the British spokesmen, looking toward a measure of self-government.

On that basis, Gandhi, released from prison in January 1931, met with Lord Irwin, then the British viceroy of India. A so-called Delhi Pact resulted in March. It was agreed that the civil disobedience campaign would be discontinued, that the Congress party would join in a second Round Table Conference, and that political prisoners in India not involved in violent action would be released.

The second Round Table Conference met in London in September 1931 with Gandhi present. It ended in December with no progress made, partly because a general election took place and a new coalition government was formed, followed by passage of the Statute of Westminster formalizing the earlier understandings by which the empire would become a commonwealth of nations equal in status.

In January 1932, the Earl of Willingdon replaced Irwin as viceroy of India. The Indian National Congress was declared illegal, and Gandhi and other leaders of the Congress party were again arrested as disorders continued. In London, a parliamentary committee prepared a draft constitution for the country, which would have given the Untouchables a separate political representation, rather than incorporating them into a unified society as Gandhi wished.

Gandhi was released from prison again in 1933. At an All-India Congress at Poona in July, he called for resumption of the civil disobedience campaign on August 1. He was once more arrested and sentenced to a year in prison. In ill health, yet undertaking a hunger strike as he had done on other occasions, he was soon released. He turned his attention almost fully to the production of a weekly newspaper that he had edited for years. He changed its name to *Harijans* (Children of God). It was chiefly concerned with the welfare and recognition of the Untouchables. In 1934 he withdrew from the National Congress, although he remained politically active.

A Government of India Act passed by the Parliament in London in August 1935 did not become effective until 1937, and it still did not solve the India problem.

These events occurring in India from 1918 received extensive attention in the press. Reuters and its subsidiary, the Associated Press of

India, provided coverage both within India and for the rest of the world. Congress party papers were added to others already existing. Gandhi himself was a persuasive pamphleteer and journalist, as well as a speaker. Mrs. Annie Besant, London-born, but long in India as a theosophist and founder of the Central Hindu College at Benares in 1916, had established a paper, *New India,* as a voice of the home rule movement. She was president of the Indian National Congress in 1917, and in 1927 became the sponsor of a Bombay agency, the Free Press of India (FPI). Representing the Congress party and presenting nationalist views, it was more a propaganda service than a news agency. It continued until 1935. Two Congress party papers started in 1930 and using the FPI service were the *Free Press Journal* of Bombay, and the *Indian Express* of Madras. Another nationalist agency, the United Press of India, was started in Calcutta in 1933 and operated with some success through World War II.

Reuters had been represented in India since 1897 by Sir Edward Buck, and he remained until 1933. He was followed by James Strachey Barnes, and by Ion S. Munro in 1938–41. William J. Moloney, Reuters general manager for the Far East from 1932 to 1937, chose to make India his base, with the main Reuter bureau in Calcutta. Everard Cotes, former editor of the *Statesman* of Calcutta, was co-founder with Buck of the Associated Press of India. The agency was purchased and made a subsidiary of Reuters in 1915. Cotes was a member of the London bureau of the *Christian Science Monitor* in the 1930s, and his knowledge of India was put to use there.

British journalists accompanying the Prince of Wales on his visit to India in November 1921 observed the violence growing out of the civil disobedience campaign at that time. They included Sir Harry Perry Robinson and B. K. Long of the *Times.* Sir Stanley Reed of that paper already was in Bombay when the prince arrived. Sir Alfred Watson, editor of the *Statesman* of Calcutta, was a stringer for the *Times* in that city.

Ellis Ashmead-Bartlett of the *Daily Telegraph,* on a roving commission for the paper, was in India at various times between 1920 and his death in 1931. Harry J. Greenwall, representing the *Daily Express,* also made visits to India between 1920 and 1926. Robert Bernays of the *News-Chronicle,* and George Slocombe of the *Daily Herald* were in India in 1930 and later.

Correspondents for the press of the United States or other countries rarely visited India before 1930. Exceptions included Bayard Taylor, undoubtedly the first, who moved through the country in 1854 as a representative of the *New York Tribune.* There were occasional visitors in later years. Following World War I, these included Charles

Merz in 1921 and then with the *New York World,* John Goette of INS in 1924, and James P. Howe of the AP in 1927. Howe returned in 1930 to open an AP bureau in Calcutta, which he directed until 1932. James A. Mills, also of the AP, was in India at the time of the salt march and riots of 1930. He became acquainted with Gandhi, accompanied him to the London Round Table Conference in 1931, was in India again in January 1932 when Gandhi was arrested, and once again in 1933 when he was released from prison.[4]

British Imperial Airways service from London to India was established in 1929, a first venture of long-distance commercial air transportation. Webb Miller, of the United Press, and William L. Shirer, of the *Chicago Tribune,* were perhaps the first correspondents, certainly for the U.S. press, to make the flight to India, as they did in 1930. Miller reported the salt riots, became acquainted with Gandhi, and remained for some time. Shirer remained in India for two years, except for a brief journey to Afghanistan, where he reported the coronation of King Mohammed Nadir Shah at Kabul. During his time in India, he formed a close relationship with Gandhi.

From 1930, the press and people of the United States conceived an interest in events in India, with consistent coverage provided, particularly through the AP and UP.

South Africa and Africa

In South Africa a Nationalist party had been formed in January 1914. Led by General James Hertzog, it represented a rural and Boer element in the population and supported a Boer secessionist sentiment within the country. Although South Africa remained united in its support of Great Britain during the war, full independence for the country was proposed by Hertzog and the Nationalists at the Paris Peace Conference. This was an issue debated within South Africa throughout the 1930s and later, amid domestic and continental changes.

General Louis Botha, Boer leader at the time of the South African War (1899–1902), but the first premier and strong advocate of the Union of South Africa, died there at fifty-seven in August 1919. He was succeeded as leader of the South African party by General Jan Christiaan Smuts, equally experienced in national and empire affairs, and originator in 1917 of the concept for a British Commonwealth of

---

4 Upon leaving the prison in 1933, the first person Gandhi saw was Mills, to whom he said, "When I stand at the gates of heaven, I suppose the first person I'll see will be an AP man."

Nations. He remained in government military and civil service almost to the time of his death at eighty in 1950.

The League of Nations in 1919 assigned German Southwest Africa as a mandate to the Union of South Africa. A popular referendum in Rhodesia in 1922 produced a vote unfavorable to joining the Union, but in 1923 it became a Crown Colony. National elections in 1924 gave power to the Nationalist and Labour party candidates in a coalition government headed by Hertzog. His objective, as summarized by Leonard Monteath Thompson of the University of Capetown, was to free South Africa from imperial control, to "provide greater protection for the whites from the Africans, and for the Afrikaners (Boers) from the British." Legislation was introduced to support these purposes. Smuts agreed with most of Hertzog's objectives, which resulted in a merger of the Smuts South African party and the Hertzog Nationalist party in 1934 to form a United South African Nationalist party (United party), with Hertzog still as prime minister.

British interests in other parts of Africa included Egypt and the Sudan. In spite of the end of the British protectorate in Egypt in 1922, negotiations and agreements with an independent Egypt continued, relating to defense, the security of communications and of foreigners, and the Sudan. A demand was made that Egyptian forces be withdrawn from the Sudan. A new draft treaty in 1927, intended to provide for ten years of British military occupation, was rejected by the Egyptian Parliament in March 1928 as being incompatible with independence. Not until 1936 was a mutually acceptable treaty concluded with the new government of King Farouk.

The German Cameroons and Togoland in West Africa were divided between Great Britain and France under League mandates in 1919, with British Togoland administered through the Gold Coast government. German East Africa also was mandated and became Tanganyika, and British East Africa became Kenya, a crown colony; British Central Africa and Uganda became Nyasaland, and included Swaziland.

France and Northern Europe   6

Paris was the first capital on the European continent to receive consistent coverage by the British press and, in time, by the press of other countries. Its own importance made it the major news center on the continent.

Although the French press made an early beginning, it did not enjoy an assured freedom from government control until 1881. Long before 1920, however, that freedom was well established and Paris itself had more daily and weekly newspapers than any other capital. It also had a larger resident group of foreign staff and stringer correspondents than any except London.

Russia had suffered the greatest manpower losses during the war, with Germany second, but France had been third and, in proportion to its population of about 40 million, had perhaps suffered most, with 1,427,800 dead and 3,044,000 wounded, not counting civilian casualties. Nearly every household had its loss. More than half of a generation of men between the ages of twenty and thirty-two had been killed. With most of the war fought in France, property damage could be estimated in the billions. Farm and forest lands were devastated, more than a half million homes destroyed or damaged, as were factories, workshops, public buildings, railroads and rolling stock, highways, and bridges.

France and its people held Germany responsible for starting the war and for all the suffering it had brought. Neither had they forgotten the Prussian invasion of 1870-71. They were understandably stubborn about demanding that the Treaty of Versailles should provide safeguards against a third invasion and also make provision for reparations in cash, goods, and services. France felt that Germany should not be permitted to rearm, nor was any sort of union between Germany and Austria to be approved. A return of the provinces of Alsace and Lorraine, lost to France in the Franco-Prussian War, was regarded as no more than right, and the mandates granted to France in

Syria and Lebanon and Africa under the League of Nations were incidental to restraint upon future German aggression.

These were circumstances that shaped French policy through the 1920s and beyond. It led to French sponsorship of a Little Entente involving alliances with Czechoslovakia, Rumania, and Yugoslavia. The government, headed by Raymond Poincaré in 1922–24, supported a strong demand for reparations. What was held a failure to make sufficient deliveries of coal resulted in French and Belgian troops extending the existing postwar occupation of German territory in 1923 to include the Ruhr valley, where the coal and iron mines were located. This move had the negative result of producing the vast German currency inflation that made cash reparations impossible. Poincaré resigned in 1924, and the Dawes Plan of that year helped to repair the German economy. France also was forced to modify its reparations demands, as it was again in 1930 when the Young Plan further altered the reparations program and ended the Ruhr occupation.

Meanwhile, a series of treaties had been signed at Locarno in 1925 intended to assure peace in Europe. In these, France joined with Great Britain, Italy, Belgium, Czechoslovakia, Poland, and Germany itself. Germany was admitted to the League of Nations in 1926, providing further safeguards to France and Czechoslovakia. But France signed separate treaties of alliance with Belgium, Czechoslovakia, Poland, Rumania, Yugoslavia, and would add one with the Soviet Union in 1933. France also joined with Spain in 1925 to control tribal insurrections in Morocco.

Not even the Locarno treaties provided complete assurance to France. Artistide Briand, premier in 1926 and then minister of foreign affairs, supported peace efforts through the League of Nations. He joined with U.S. Secretary of State Frank B. Kellogg in sponsoring a Pact of Paris in 1928 by which twenty-three nations agreed to renounce war as an "instrument of national policy," with compulsory arbitration as the alternative.

France nevertheless undertook a reorganization of its army, increased naval construction, and fortified its frontier with Germany in the so-called Maginot Line. The country had not been wholly pleased with those efforts to control or reduce armaments on the basis of agreements supposedly reached through the Washington Naval Conference of 1921–22, the Geneva Protocol of 1924, or the Geneva Naval Parley of 1927. Neither were Italy or Japan satisfied or cooperative, and the United States also was dissatisfied with some of the provisions. The United States was even more disturbed to learn of a secret agreement on naval and military matters between France and Great Britain. This was revealed in September 1928 by Harold J. Horan in

Paris for the Hearst-owned International News Service. He was assisted in obtaining the information by William Randolph Hearst himself, who was expelled from France after publication of the report.

Nonpolitical events of concern in Paris during the 1920s included a contest for the world's heavyweight boxing championship, with France's Georges Carpentier meeting Jack Dempsey, the champion, on July 2, 1921, in Jersey City, in what was described as the first "million dollar gate" in the history of sports. Carpentier was knocked out in the fourth round, but French sports followers were interested in Dempsey's later meetings with Argentina's Luis Firpo in New York in 1923, and in his defeat by Gene Tunney at Philadelphia in 1926, and again in a rematch in Chicago in 1927.

The Olympic Games took place in Paris in 1924, as did a first convention of the American Legion. Soccer was of consistently high interest. A new enthusiasm arose for tennis, with France's Henri Cochet defeating William T. Tilden of the United States, considered the greatest player in 1926. René Lacoste beat him in 1927, and Cochet and Lacoste joined to win the Davis Cup for France in that latter year. Mlle. Suzanne Lenglen also became noted as a tennis professional in 1926, bringing victories to France.

Emotions were greatly wrapped up in an attempt by two leading French aviators to fly from Paris to New York. Charles Eugène Jules Marie Nungesser, a hero of France's wartime air corps, and François Coli took off from Paris on May 8, 1927. They never were heard from again. As it happened, Captain Charles A. Lindbergh, a U.S. Army reserve pilot, took off from Roosevelt Field on Long Island on the morning of May 20, 1927, and arrived at the Paris Le Bourget airport at 10 P.M. May 21, a solo flight of thirty-three and a half hours, in the first uninterrupted flight across the Atlantic Ocean. Despite the French dejection over the Nungesser-Coli loss, Lindbergh was enthusiastically received, and many a newsman in Paris, particularly for the U.S. press, later took pride in recounting his part in the coverage of the story.

In 1927, Admiral Richard E. Byrd, a U.S. Navy pilot, who had made the first flight over the North Pole in 1926, took off from Roosevelt Field on June 29 in a larger plane, carrying three others, plus 800 pounds of payload and the first official transatlantic mail. Reaching Paris at night, and unable to find the Le Bourget airport because of rain and zero visibility, he landed in the Channel surf at Versur-Mer in a flight of just over forty-two hours.

Other stories covered by newsmen from Paris in the same period included the arrival at Cap Gris Nez on the Normandy coast on August 6, 1926, of Gertrude Ederle, the first U.S. woman to swim the English

Channel from Dover. Another story with a more romantic quality covered by Paris newsmen was the marriage in Brussels on November 10, 1926, of Princess Astrid of Sweden to Leopold, eldest son of Belgium's King Albert I. They were to have a daughter, born in 1927, and a son, Prince Baudouin, born in 1930. Tragedy followed in 1934 when Albert I was killed while mountain climbing near Namur, with Leopold thereupon becoming King Leopold III. Worse followed in 1935 when Queen Astrid was killed in a motor accident.

News flowed into Paris from all parts of France, some of it social, often originating on the Riviera. It came also from all parts of Europe and much of Africa, where France had an empire. And news came from the mandated areas of Syria and Lebanon, as well as from distant French Indo-China. It came too from Latin America, through the Havas agency. Paris itself was, of course, an attractive city to which "everybody" came, many of them newsworthy personalities. It was a leading center of the arts, science, education, high fashion, and civilized living. The fashion industry alone produced a volume of information, both for the newspaper press and for specialized periodicals.

The Agence Havas, holding a semi-official relationship to the government through a financial subsidy, provided most of the coverage for the Paris and other French newspapers. Some information papers, with their own reportorial staffs at home and abroad, augmented this coverage and some engaged in that variety of special investigation known as *grand rapportage*. Many Paris dailies were concerned with partisan political matters, and a few with a Catholic sponsorship presented a budget of church-related news, while other daily and weekly papers were concerned with the arts. A very few were rated as "gutter" sheets, sensational in content and not above blackmailing individuals, business firms, and governments.

The papers were generally well written and edited, even allowing for the tendency toward subjectivity and polemicism. This latter style of writing was less used in provincial papers or in the information papers in Paris. For the political papers, nearly all of which appeared in Paris, it was typical, however.

There was no quality paper in Paris or in all of France to match the *Times* of London, for example. Two that were read with special care, however, by those interested in public affairs were *Le Temps* and *Le Journal des Débats,* both dull in appearance and style but serious and well informed. There were two important business papers, *l'Information* and *La Journée Industrielle.*

The so-called big five morning information papers of large circulation were *Le Petit Parisien,* perhaps the best, *l'Echo de Paris,* and three others somewhat suspect because of ownership changes and policies, *Le Matin, Le Journal,* and *Le Quotidien.* Two afternoon information papers, *l'Intransigeant* and *Paris-Soir,* both controlled by Jean Prouvost, were widely read. The first was somewhat sensational, and larger than most, with good advertising volume. *Paris-Soir,* in gaining substance in the early 1930s, became the paper of largest circulation in France, with some two million nationally distributed. It was one of the best information papers. Four others, more specialized in content, *Le Figaro, Le Petit Journal, l'Oeuvre,* and *Excelsior* were at times worthy of attention.

Among many political dailies, three or four were important for what they represented: *Le Populaire,* the Socialist party organ; *l'Humanité,* a Communist party paper; and *l'Avenir* and *La Liberté.* Among periodicals, the *Revue des Deux Mondes* and *l'Illustration* were two likely to be read by correspondents.

The correspondent in Paris, as in any free capital, might go to original sources for the news, seek interviews, establish acquaintanceships and friendships, observe, listen, and cover events directly. He could attend sessions of the French Senate or Chamber of Deputies, the two branches of the National Assembly. He could report cases of special interest in the courts. He might seek private conversations with cabinet members, and even the premier, since the doctrine of cabinet responsibility did not apply in Paris as it did in London. Such meetings were rare, nevertheless.

The French Republic was governed under a constitutional parliamentary system, with an elected president whose duties were mainly ceremonial. The members of the National Assembly were elected by popular vote. The premier represented the political party dominant in the Chamber of Deputies. Directed by the president to act, he named his cabinet members, who became heads of the executive departments, as in the British system. As also in Great Britain, a no-confidence vote on a major issue in the Chamber meant that the existing administration retired from office, with the permanent civil service carrying on until a new premier had formed a new cabinet.

In the years of the Third Republic, from 1871 to 1940, fourteen men served as president of France, but 105 separate governments existed. With a considerable number of parties contesting in national elections, a premier rarely served more than six months in office, and sometimes headed a coalition government even then. Many of the same men appeared and reappeared in the various cabinets, often occupying different ministerial posts, and some served several times as premier. Premiers also became presidents, and former presidents became premiers.

Press representatives in France were not classified as members of an inner, middle, or outer circle, as in London. Reporters for papers supporting the party forming the government, however, might find themselves favored so long as that party's administration continued. More important, six or eight Paris political writers of unquestioned loyalty to the nation did form a favored inner circle group, which continued without reference to government changes. They were experienced and prominent journalists, and included a writer for the Agence Havas, almost certainly writers for *Le Temps,* the *Journal des Débats, Le Petit Parisien,* and several other papers. They met regularly, individually or as a group, with the premier, the minister of foreign affairs, and others of the cabinet. They were well informed and could write with understanding. Some information might be held in confidence, and their sources were not revealed, if there was reason to keep them secret. Out of loyalty to the government and nation, they might put out "trial balloons" to test sentiment at home or abroad, or engage in special ventures in the area of propaganda.

A by-product of this arrangement was a system whereby other reporters for the French press, and correspondents in Paris representing the media of other countries, might be able to receive secondary reports from one of the favored French reporters, possibly paying for what they received.

Pay for information was a practice deriving from the tipster system of seventeenth-century Paris, when civil servants, military men, servants to royalty, and others were sought out by the *nouvellistes* of that period to obtain tid-bits of information for use in oral news reports, as they themselves moved in the public places and collected fees from their listeners.[1]

Officials of the French government were fully aware of the practice under which those favored correspondents, as late as the 1920s and 1930s, passed on information to other journalists. Indeed, they sometimes used the system to serve their own purposes, and with full confidence in the caution the reporters would use, out of loyalty and out of their own self-interest, taking care what they revealed and to whom. The French inner circle journalists thus became intermediaries in providing information and views that the French government wished to have publicized, but without direct attribution. Foreign correspondents, for their part, were sufficiently experienced to realize that they were not necessarily being told everything, that they might even be receiving false or purposefully misleading information. They therefore exercised their own caution, sought verification from other sources, and wrote with appropriate qualifications.

No serious correspondent could approve of this system of tipsterism. Neither could a correspondent depend upon the French press with

---

1   See Robert W. Desmond, *The Information Process* (Iowa City: University of Iowa Press, 1978), p. 25.

complete confidence. The law of libel was far less strict in France than in Great Britain or the United States, and the general reliability of the media was uncertain. The correspondent far preferred to find his own sources of information, so far as possible.

The wartime and immediate postwar experience of British and U.S. correspondents in Paris, with their insistence upon access to original sources, had had some effect. There and in Geneva they had become acquainted with French government leaders and were at times able to talk with them, whether in or out of office. Further, from the time of the war, the Ministry of Foreign Affairs had named information or press officers to receive journalists, to answer questions, and to conduct news conferences. An arrangement was made whereby two daily conferences were held at the Quai d'Orsay, as the ministry was commonly called because of its location on the street of that name along the left bank of the Seine. Such conferences were conducted for French journalists each weekday at twelve noon and at 7 P.M., followed by conferences a half hour later for foreign correspondents. An added conference was held separately each evening for the six or eight favored French reporters, with the foreign minister present, and perhaps the premier himself.

As in London, the group conferences for foreign correspondents tended to be of small value. The press officer himself was not always sufficiently informed. Correspondents commonly were advised to obtain answers to their questions by noting the Havas report due to appear, or by referring them to a particular newspaper, or to something by a particular writer. This discouraged attendance at the conferences. There also was a resentment about the favored treatment of the few French correspondents. Further, information from government departments other than the Foreign Ministry was even more difficult to obtain. The net result was that the French position on events often was not made clear. There was no censorship, but information was often unavailable, poorly presented, possibly misrepresented, and late in being correctly or even officially explained. In this sense, French press relations were notoriously weak, and worked to the disadvantage of the country.

France itself became aware of this and, as tensions rose internationally after 1930, an effort was made to correct the situation. In 1933 the government called upon Pierre Comert, a prewar correspondent in Berlin for *Le Temps* and director of the Information Section of the League of Nations Secretariat since 1920, to try to improve press relations at the Quai d'Orsay. He did provide for easier access to the news at the Foreign Ministry, ended a discrimination felt by some correspondents, and advanced the relationship between journalists and officials, if not necessarily cabinet members themselves. Comert soon was made director of American affairs in the press section of the ministry, with Pierre Bressy assuming the broader responsibilities. Press officers also became available for personal conferences with correspondents, not only at the Foreign Ministry, but in the Ministries of Finance, Air, Marine, Military, and Interior. Documents and reports originating in the executive departments and in the National Assembly became more readily available as part of this general improvement.

There was some tendency to regard a foreign correspondent or his publication as friendly or unfriendly to France. Judgment was made on the basis of how fully the government position on a subject was accepted, with little middle ground allowed. No penalties were visited upon a correspondent judged unfriendly, but neither was he treated with any cordiality or encouraged to seek further information; he might even be subjected to some personal harassment. This had been one basis for those charges of discrimination that Comert had undertaken to correct when he moved into the Foreign Ministry.

The diplomatic and consular sources of information in Paris were useful. Communications were good, except for the telephone service, which was virtually useless as an aid to news gathering. Its value rested primarily in communication between bureaus in various cities and capitals, to transmit, relay and record news, especially in the 1930s. Transportation and travel facilities were generally excellent in Paris and all of France. Housing was satisfactory at this period. Membership in the Anglo-American Press Association, or in comparable groups, provided a useful professional and social benefit for the correspondent.

Members of the Paris bureaus for news agencies and newspapers commonly journeyed to Geneva when the League of Nations Assembly met, or when other conferences occurred there. Members also moved back and forth between Paris and Spain.

Indeed, the larger bureaus maintained in Paris and London provided a reservoir of manpower to permit the prompt reporting of major events throughout Europe in the years between the wars.

*Belgium,
Holland, and
Luxembourg*

Those countries of Europe smaller in size and population were understandably less in the news than the larger countries and the great powers. Fewer events of world interest centered there. This did not mean that they were without importance, of course, and some have been mentioned.

The people of Belgium, Holland, Luxembourg, Switzerland, Denmark, Norway, Sweden, the Baltic states, and Finland were among the most literate in the world, and supported some of the best newspapers, along with national news agencies. A number of the papers had their own correspondents in major capitals. Because the languages were not all widely read or understood, few of the newspapers were seen beyond the frontiers of their own countries. Some were known and respected, however, and quoted in the reports of world news agencies, or those of stringers and resident correspondents. But there were times, of course, when these countries did enter the news because of an event or a situation.

Belgium, having suffered great damage as a first arena of the war, recovered rather quickly after 1919, both in agricultural production and in industry. Possessed of great resources of coal and iron, it was a leader in steel production, and also in chemicals and textiles. Its colonial possessions, notably in the African Congo, in yielding raw materials gave it a further source of revenue. One of the most densely populated countries of the world, it suffered from great unemployment immediately after the war. A need at that time for public assistance, accompanied by social legislation, led to substantial tax increases. With Flemish spoken in parts of the country adjacent to Holland, public pressure brought a new law in 1922 by which it was made an official language of the country, along with French. Financial problems also were sufficiently serious to result in dictatorial powers being given to King Albert for six months in 1926. During that time the Belgian franc was devalued, and the belga was introduced as a new unit of currency, equal to five old francs.

Holland, which had remained neutral during the war, suffered no destruction, but the economy was seriously disrupted by the long wartime interruption of its normal maritime and trade activities. It was in the news in 1918 when the Allies requisitioned Dutch ships and also when it gave refuge to Germany's Kaiser Wilhelm II after his abdication, and when it refused an Allied demand for his surrender in 1920. He lived in Holland, first at Amerongen and then at Doorn, until his death in 1941.

Industry, agriculture, and shipping revived after 1918, and Holland proceeded with a continuing program to reclaim land from the sea. Large unemployment, persistent parliamentary problems, communist-inspired revolts in the Dutch East Indies in 1926–27, and the imposition of a high tax structure to support social reforms and the land-recovery were dealt with through a coalition government under the administration of Queen Wilhelmina. Tariff and trade agreements were concluded at Oslo in 1930 between the Scandinavian countries and between Holland, Belgium, and Luxembourg.

Holland exercised its influence for peace through membership in the League of Nations, as well as through the Permanent Court for International Justice at The Hague.

Denmark, Norway, Sweden, and Finland

Denmark, Norway, and Sweden also had maintained neutrality during World War I, and all entered upon active programs of social legislation in the years following. Although all except Finland were constitutional monarchies, they proceeded on democratic principles, and the governments were strongly socialist. The countries commonly referred to as the Nordic or Scandinavian states worked in close collaboration in the interests of their domestic well-being and in support of world peace through the League of Nations. Greenland remained under Danish sovereignty, but Iceland was granted its independence in 1918. Norway, which undertook to annex part of Greenland in 1931, yielded to a ruling of The Hague Court, which confirmed Danish sovereignty.

Economically, the four states depended upon revenue from agriculture, fisheries, trade, and shipping. Sweden, with resources of coal and iron, was a leader in steel production. With great timber resources, both Sweden and Finland provided much of the paper used by the press in Europe and also exported it to other parts of the world.

Switzerland

Also neutral during the war, Switzerland felt a shortage of food throughout those years, and was beset by internal tensions arising from the relations between its own peoples in districts of German, French, and Italian heritage. Long dependent economically on the production and export of textiles and fine watches, among other things, and upon tourism, it was further at a disadvantage.

These problems ended with the return of peace. With no war damage or war debts as burdens, the country's agriculture, industry, and tourism recovered during the 1920s. The League of Nations, established at Geneva, brought many visitors and Switzerland itself joined the League. Apart from a controversy with France over the location of border customs posts, possibly the chief problem in international relations was with the Soviet Union.

Switzerland broke diplomatic relations with the new Soviet regime in December 1918 because of what it regarded as subversive communist propaganda. In 1923 the relationship suffered further when a Soviet delegate to the Lausanne Conference, V. V. Vorovsky, was assassinated by Maurice Conradi, a Swiss citizen who had been illtreated in Russia. Conradi was acquitted, adding to the tension, which was partially eased in 1927.

Italy, the Iberian Peninsula, and North Africa 7

Italy, a unified nation since 1871, had been well reported by the world press. The importance of Rome as a news center had grown during the years of World War I, because of its position as the capital of one of the Allied nations and as the seat of the Vatican. It was also a vantage point from which to observe the affairs of southern Europe and the Mediterranean basin. As one of the big four at the time of the Paris Peace Conference, Italy was important in the news.

Rome continued to be a base for correspondents after 1920. Some wrote from Milan, a major industrial center, and there were stringers in other cities. The correspondents in Rome were accredited to the Ministry of Foreign Affairs in the Palazzo Chigi. Their numbers were limited, in contrast to London or Paris, but they had no problems of access to information. Relations with officials, politicians, and people in all walks of life were cordial. The daily newspaper and periodical press was advanced and operated freely, presenting a variety of material and opinion. The diplomatic corps was a useful source. Correspondents were free to travel as they wished, and the communications system was as efficient as any in western Europe.

With the end of the war, however, Italy was caught up in discontent. The Paris settlements failed to meet expectations raised in the secret treaty concluded in London in 1915, under which Italy joined the Allies in the war, rather than the Central Powers, as it might logically have done as a member of the Triple Alliance with Germany and Austria-Hungary since 1882.

Italy had gained the Adriatic port of Trieste in the peace settlement. Nationalist sentiments were aroused, however, over aspirations to control the nearby port of Fiume in Bosnia. A position also was desired in the Dalmatian Islands of the Adriatic. Full recognition also had been sought for the nation's position in Libya and in the Dodocanese Islands, as established in its war with Turkey in 1911–12. The prospect was that those islands at least would go to Greece under the terms of the 1920 Treaty of Sèvres.

Gabrielle d'Annunzio, primarily a novelist and poet, conducted both a propaganda and military campaign leading to the capture of Fiume in September 1919. It was returned to the new postwar state of Yugoslavia in 1920, however, under the terms of the Treaty of Rapallo. Italy also was involved in Turkey between 1919 and 1921, with military forces in the country, in accordance with Allied plans, and did retain control of the Dodocanese Islands under the revised Treaty of Lausanne with Turkey in 1923. Italy sent forces temporarily to the Greek island of Corfu that same year.

More critical in the immediate postwar period was a problem of employment in Italy for the thousands of men released from military service. The national economy was disrupted, and such industry as existed, mostly in northern Italy, was affected by strikes. Railroads and agriculture also faced difficulties. Matters were at their worst in 1920 when some factories were seized by their workers who tried to manage them, but without success. High food prices, incidents of violence, budget deficits, and several changes of government under the constitutional monarchy headed by King Victor Emmanuele III, did nothing to give stability to the nation. Industrialists, government officials, and many citizens, aware of what had transpired in Russia since 1917, and observing that Communist ideology was being advanced in Italy by left-wing Socialists, were seriously alarmed.

In these circumstances, a new political group was formed in Milan in March 1919. Known as the Fasci di Combattimento, and opposed to the Socialist party, it was a concept of Benito Mussolini. Then thirty-five and editor of the Milan morning daily *Il Popolo d'Italia,* he publicized the new party through the paper he had established in 1914.

Active as a Socialist writer and editor before the war, he had split with the party in 1914 because of his own advocacy of Italy's entrance to the war on the side of the Allies. He had served with Italy's forces during the war, but had been invalided out and returned to journalism in Milan. Through his newspaper after 1919, he sought to rally those who believed Italy had not been properly recognized in the Paris peace settlements, and those who were disturbed by the disarray in the economy.

Those who responded to Mussolini's appeal included industrialists and property owners fearful of Communist influence in Italy, former military officers and veterans of service who found themselves among the unemployed, some factory workers, and also some publishers, editors, and staff members of other newspapers. Financial support was generously forthcoming. Armed squads (Squadre d'Azione) were formed by the Fasci di Combattimento for both defensive and aggressive action in contests with Socialist groups and others in opposition. Mussolini became the acknowledged leader (Il Duce) and soon became known abroad. This was due in part to his personal attendance as a journalist at international conferences meeting under League of Nations auspices at San Remo (April 1920), Rapallo (November 1920), and Cannes (January 1922).

The Italian Socialist party, meeting at Livorno in January 1921, split, and its more radical wing became Communist. The next month there occurred at Florence the first of many violent clashes between members of that group and the armed squads representing the Fasci di Combattimento. Maneuvering for power, Mussolini in November 1921 organized his followers and met in Rome as a full political party, the Partido Nazionale Fascista (National Fascist Party), which replaced the Fasci di Combattimento.

Through the first months of 1922, the Fascist party gained in numbers, strength, and support. Its armed squads temporarily seized control in Fiume in March, took control in Bologna in May, Milan in August, and Genoa soon after. All this occurred without objection from the national government, which was weak and changed three times between June 1921 and February 1922. Indeed, the government gave its tacit support to the Fascist party actions, with the police and military elements merely standing by.

In October 1922, Mussolini was offered a seat in the cabinet but declined. Instead, at a Fascist Congress in Milan, he demanded that the existing government resign so that he might form a Fascist cabinet. Four days later, on October 28, some 50,000 Fascists were assembled in Rome; the city was then in great disorder because of strikes. There was speculation that they might stage a *coup d'état* to gain control. The king refused to approve the establishment of martial law, but he accepted the resignation of the cabinet, headed since February by Luigi Facta in a coalition government. Three days later Mussolini was summoned by the king and came from Milan to form a cabinet of Fascists and Nationalists. In legend, this became a Fascist "march on Rome." A month later, the king and the parliament granted Mussolini dictatorial power, with a mandate to restore order and bring about reforms in the country.

This was the beginning of twenty years of virtually absolute power for Mussolini and the Fascist party in Italy. As premier, Mussolini had a quadrumvirate of four close associates as advisers. As premier, he also retained for himself the portfolio as minister of foreign affairs and also as minister of the interior. This latter post gave him control of police power, including a secret police organization brought into being, the Organizzione Vigilanza Reati Antifascisti (OVRA). In later years, he was to hold as many as seven ministerial portfolios at once. A Grand Council of Fascism was created in 1923, an outgrowth of the original quadrumvirate, its members all appointed by Mussolini. This was a major force in the government. The king and the army supported Mussolini, but in 1923 the Fascist armed squads also became an official militia for national security, amounting to a private army under his control. In 1926, a so-called Corporazione, or corporative state, was created under Mussolini, with full control of the national economy. In 1929, the king was induced to sign a decree dissolving the parliamentary body. The Grand Council, then with a membership of forty-four, was authorized to act as the supreme legislative and administrative body for the state.

The Fascist armed squads, from the time they were formed in 1919, had used threats, force, and arms to silence or remove opposition. This had recommended the Fascists to those industrial and propertied elements supporting them with funds, and who were afraid of a Communist advance in Italy. After gaining power in October 1922, the established Fascist government also used military power, first in 1923 to put down a rebellion in Tripoli, the Libyan port gained in the action against Turkey in 1912. The murder of the Italian members of the Albanian boundary commission in Greece in 1923 brought the bombardment and occupation of Corfu. Although temporary, it had been accompanied by a warning from Rome that any interference by the League of Nations would result in Italy's withdrawal from that still young organization. In 1924, Italy found reason to return to the port of Fiume, negotiating a treaty with Yugoslavia.

On the face of things, the Fascist government appeared to be fulfilling its mandate to restore order. There was little the Fascists could do to mitigate the results of an eruption of Mount Etna in June 1923 that destroyed nearby villages in Sicily, caused casualties, and left 30,000 homeless. There also remained currency problems, but these were eased in 1925 when the J. P. Morgan Company of New York felt enough confidence in the government to advance a credit of $50 million.

The one serious threat to the Fascist party, its regime and its future, arose in 1924 following the murder of a Socialist deputy, Giacomo Matteoti, who had ventured to oppose Fascist measures in the parliament. Matteoti was kidnapped on June 10, 1924. Three days later his body was found buried some twenty kilometers from Rome. The kidnapping and murder, with its obvious meaning, created a sensation that could have resulted in the fall of the Fascist government. The world climate of opinion in 1924 regarded such actions as unacceptable, especially in a nation counted as one of the freest and most advanced in cultural and intellectual terms.

Mussolini was prompt in disclaiming any part in the Matteoti affair. Four young Fascists were arrested as the kidnappers and murderers, and four other prominent party members were held as accomplices. Criticism of the party, and some defections, brought so strong a Fascist response that it became prudent for critics to drop the issue, as a matter of personal safety. In the end, the Matteoti killers were acquitted or received only light sentences, nor did the accomplices suffer. Mussolini, the party, and the government proceeded almost as though Matteoti had never existed. Yet the affair marked a clear point of departure, leading to full Fascist authoritarianism.

It could not be said that authoritarianism was new in the world; quite the contrary. By 1920, however, it had been supplanted almost entirely by democracies and constitutional monarchies under which the peoples enjoyed individual freedoms, rights, and privileges. The results of the war presumably assured a continuation and an extension of such freedoms. Anything else would have seemed retrogressive.

Except for Venezuela, under a dictatorship since 1899 (and to continue until 1935), the Soviet Union was the only major country in 1920 where civil liberties were denied, along with the right of the people to participate in their own governance. From 1924, however, Italy joined the Soviet Union as the second major country under an authoritarian government, and the first since the war. This was disturbing to many, but there was a disposition to reserve judgment, partly with the thought that Italy might be producing a possible acceptable alternative to communism. The decade to follow, of course, was to see the evaporation of any such prospect. Authoritarianism by then also prevailed in Spain, Poland, Turkey, Bulgaria, Yugoslavia, Germany, Japan, and Brazil.

In the years between 1920 and 1922 in Italy, there was a general press concern with the economic and political problems of the nation. The growth of the Fascist movement was very much a part of the news. Mussolini became of world interest as a personality, and attention went also to others who emerged as members of the party and government.

An Association of Foreign Correspondents in Italy (Associazione della Stampa Estera in Italia) was formed in 1922 with government encouragement. The foreign press corps in Rome then numbered about forty. With the Fascist government just established, there was wide interest in what it might accomplish. Rome became as important as Vienna or Paris as a news center, and the number of resident correspondents increased steadily, reaching 125 in 1935, the peak year in that respect. The Anglo-American representation was large, but by then was outnumbered by the German group, the largest, and by the French group. Robert J. Hodel of the *Neue Zürcher Zeitung* was president of the correspondents' association for several terms.

Another origination of the new Fascist regime was a government Press Office (Ufficio Stampa) established in 1922 in the Ministry of Interior. For a dozen years it was directed successively by Conte Capasso Torre, Gaetano Polverelli, and Lando Ferretti. It became more important every year in its influence upon both domestic and foreign news reports.

The first clear sign of change bearing upon the position of the Italian press and of the foreign correspondents in Italy came in July 1923. At that time, Mussolini issued a decree setting certain press regulations (Il Nuova Regolamento sulla Stampa). It authorized fines and imprisonment for newspaper and magazine editors inciting class hatred, disobedience of the law, vilifying the state or the royal family, the pope or the constitution, officials in charge of national affairs, or friendly foreign powers.

This new regulation, so reasonable on its face, was approved by a parliament already dominated by the Fascist regime. The assumption was that it would be a temporary measure, and would not even be invoked unless it seemed necessary. The decree was not offically promulgated, in fact, until July 1924, about a month after the Matteoti murder, and even then it did not become effective until January 1925.

While holding officially to the pre-Fascist constitution, asserting that "the press shall be free," the new regulations of 1923 nevertheless provided that "the law may suppress abuses of that freedom." By its own interpretation of what constituted abuses, and by adding other regulations, the Fascist regime brought the Italian press under complete control or subjugation by the end of 1926.

Few newspapers in Italy were favorable to the Fascist party or regime at the outset. The regime hesitated at the time to suppress a newspaper outright, but tried to give a legalistic complexion to procedures taken to shape the content. This became possible under the press regulations of 1923, as made fully effective in 1925. Even before that, however, pressures somewhat less than legalistic were brought to bear upon individual writers, editors, and publishers, and these became difficult if not dangerous to resist.

Owners of some papers were induced to sell, with a Fascist leader or loyal party member gaining control, and with editors and staff members changing. One of the first papers to change hands in this fashion, early in 1922, was *Il Giornale d'Italia* of Rome, a morning daily that had gained a high reputation since its establishment in 1900 by Alberto

Bergamini. He was forced to sell to a prominent Fascist party member. That individual, however, was brought into the Court of Justice in 1926 on charges of profiteering. He was succeeded as director of the paper by Dr. Virginio Gayda, who had been editor since 1921 of *Il Messaggero,* also of Rome, a large-circulation popular paper, and something of a scandal sheet.

Gayda had been a supporter of fascism since its first days. As editor of *Il Giornale d'Italia,* he was to become one of the authoritative spokesmen for fascism, particularly in matters of foreign policy.[1] Not even Mussolini's *Popolo d'Italia* of Milan was read more carefully by correspondents and diplomats in Italy seeking clues to government policy.

The Agenzia Telegrafica Stefani, controlled by the Agence Havas of France since 1861, was brought back to full Italian control in July 1924. It was purchased then by Manlio Morgagni of Milan, a man of wealth lacking in journalistic experience but a friend of Mussolini. Promptly ceded to the government, Stefani became an official agency following Fascist party direction.

The press regulation of 1923–25 authorized the prefect, or administrator of any province or district, to confiscate issues of publications which, in his personal judgment, transgressed the provisions of that law in committing "abuses" of freedom. The most prestigious newspapers were not exempt and were repeatedly suppressed or confiscated. The only escape from such harassment was to make changes in the staff, policy, and conduct of the newspaper.

For example, *La Stampa* of Turin, a major daily of high quality, was suspended in September 1925 and only permitted to resume after its staff membership had been changed to make it sympathetic to the Fascist regime. The same change was forced upon *Il Mattino* of Naples, and the practice became general, not by the "suppression" of papers, but by their "suspension" pending change.

In November 1925, *Il Corriere della Sera* of Milan, the most highly regarded and widely circulated newspaper, and one respected throughout Europe, was suspended. The Crespi brothers, owners of the paper, had embraced fascism as a solution to strikes and Communist agitation in their textile mills. They had not interfered with the direction of the paper by its editor, Senator Luigi Albertino, who had conducted it with distinction since 1898. Its independence proved offensive to the Fascist leadership, however, and with its suspension the

---

1 The morning *Giornale d'Italia* and its somewhat sensational noonday edition, *Piccolo,* came to be known in Rome as "Bugiardone" and "Bugiardello," that is, "Big Humbug" and "Little Humbug."

Crespis dismissed Albertino, despite his contract with them. They brought in Aldo Borelli, formerly editor of *La Nazione* of Florence, as the new editor, along with an almost entirely new staff. The paper then was permitted to resume.

Other laws and regulations were to fix Fascist party control'more firmly upon the press. A law of December 31, 1925, established a National Federation of the Press (Federazione Nazionale della Stampa), which became the Fascist Syndicate of Journalists (Sindicato Nationale Fascista die Giornalisti), and still later became a part of the Corporative State organization introduced in 1926. That law determined who was to be permitted to engage in journalism. The right to do so was even more specifically established under regulations of March 4, 1926, and by a royal decree of February 28, 1928, setting up a professional register (Albo) and stating the requirements for inclusion.

Without such approval and registration, no Italian could work professionally as a journalist in the country after 1928. No person who had occupied a position of importance with an anti-Fascist publication at the time of the Matteoti murder in 1924 could be registered. Penalties were specified for criticism of fascism or of Mussolini. Even abroad, any Italian journalist indulging in such criticism might have his citizenship revoked and his property in Italy confiscated. In 1932 it was further decreed that any person working as a journalist in Italy must be a member of the Fascist party.[2]

Italian journalists and publishers in opposition to the Fascist regime, or denied the right to work professionally, either left Italy or retired quietly to some other form of activity. Some were less fortunate. A number were beaten by Fascist hoodlums, fatally in at least one case, were given vast doses of castor oil as a form of torture, or were exiled to the Lipari Islands in the Tyrrhenian Sea, an Italian equivalent of Siberia, though milder in climate.

Those leaving Italy were not necessarily safe from retribution if they continued as journalists. Carlo and Nello Roselli, brothers, publishers of an Italian-language paper in Paris, *Giustizia e Liberta,* were found with their throats cut and their bodies riddled with bullets in 1937, a day after they had published an article about the Matteoti murder on the thirteenth anniversary of that event.

Carlo a'Prato, formerly of *Il Mondo* in Rome, became a stringer in Geneva for the *New York Times,* the *Daily Herald* of London, and a Paris paper. He was forced to leave Geneva in 1937 because the Italian

---

2   In Soviet Russia, it was not required that a journalist necessarily be a member of the Communist party, although only party members were permitted to occupy responsible positions.

government had complained to the Swiss about articles he had written for the *Journal des Nations,* a publication dealing with League of Nations activities. In an unprecedented response, the Swiss government ordered him to leave, contending that his articles disturbed Switzerland's foreign relations. A'Prato moved to Paris, where he published the *Corriere degli Italiani* in association with Guiseppi Donati, formerly of *Il Popolo* of Rome. The paper went to other Italian refugees and was distributed clandestinely in Italy. It had to be discontinued after a few months by order of the French government, which was acting in accordance with terms of a January 1935 treaty of friendship with Italy.

Italy's supplementary press law of December 1925 provided that a newspaper suspended or sequestered for a number of offenses might receive a warning (diffida) from the prefect of its district. If it received two such warnings, it might be suspended permanently. Fifteen newspapers were so suspended in 1926. Under this law, further supported by several so-called "November decrees" of 1926, the last vestiges of internal press criticism of the Fascist regime were effectively ended.

From 1927, accordingly, publications were permitted to exist in Italy only if they could be classified in one of two groups. First were those newspapers or periodicals "which by their origin, their activity on behalf of the Fascist cause, the political loyalty of their directors, editors and administrative staff, give secure guarantee of being worthy to be considered the true and real organs of the regime." Second were those newspapers or periodicals regarded as sympathetic to the regime, even though not organs of it.

In the first group was the original Fascist paper, *Il Popolo d'Italia* of Milan, established by Mussolini in 1914. After he became premier in 1922, it was edited by his brother, Arnaldo Mussolini, until his death in 1931, then by his nephew, Vito Mussolini. Mario Appelius, a later member of the staff, won attention because of his polemical and often abusive articles.

Others in the first group were *Il Messaggero* of Rome, a Fascist paper from 1921, then edited by Dr. Gayda, and *Il Giornale d'Italia,* also of Rome, under party control from 1922 and edited by Gayda from 1926. Still others included *Il Regima Fascista* of Cremona, established in 1922 under the ownership of Roberto Farinacci, who also became general secretary of the Fascist party,[3] and *Il Corriere Padano* of Ferrara, established in 1924 by Italo Balbo, a member of the party leadership and later general of the Italian air force. One other was *Il*

---

3   Farinacci is reputed to have originated the castor oil torture treatment for opponents of fascism.

Telegrafo of Leghorn, owned by Galeazzo Ciano, who held various governmental posts, including that of foreign minister, and who married Mussolini's daughter Edda in 1930. Giovanni Ansaldo, an able writer who had been jailed for several months in 1925-26 because of anti-Fascist references, but who accepted fascism in 1926, became editor of *Il Telegrafo* at that time. He was widely quoted in later years, especially for his vitriolic printed references to the United States and Great Britain.

In the second group of sympathetic publications, those most notable were *Il Corriere della Sera* and *La Stampa,* the two best Italian dailies of pre-Fascist times and the best during the regime. They were quality papers, even with the restrictions under which they were obliged to operate, and were circulated nationally as well as being available throughout Europe.

The *Corriere* retained a respectable editorial integrity even under fascism, which permitted it some liberty as a showpiece. It had the largest circulation of any newspaper in the country, about 500,000 daily. Not even Mussolini's *Il Popolo d'Italia* could overtake it in that respect, even though it made special efforts to do so. The position of the *Corriere* was such that it was able to maintain one of the highest newspaper advertising rates in the world in the 1930s.

La Stampa in Turin became the property of the Fiat automobile and engineering company. With Senator Giovanni Agnelli, director of that company, taking a personal interest in the paper, staffing it well, and encouraging a high standard of performance, *La Stampa* also maintained an admirable news and editorial level and was a second showpiece.

The Fascist party or government felt it to be improper to permit the press in Italy to go its own way, however loyal or sympathetic. Guidance and special instructions, along with words of praise or blame, went regularly to responsible editors. This function was performed, with increasing attention to detail, through the government Press Office.

Daily conferences were introduced at the Press Office. They were held separately for editors of morning and afternoon papers and for the Stefani agency. For editors outside Rome, the instructions given at these conferences went either by telephone, through the Stefani teleprinter service, or through branch offices. Editors were told what news and other material should or should not be published, relating both to text and photographs, to matter received through the Agenzia Stefani, to that prepared by their own reporters and correspondents, or coming from any other sources, including the Press Office itself. Soon editors also were being told when to use certain material, how to write it, and what points to emphasize. Even the position a story was to occupy in the paper and on the page was dictated, and possibly the idea to be stressed in the headline or the picture caption. On occasion, such instructions presumably originated with Mussolini himself, the old journalist.

The readers of newspapers in Italy were not informed that such instructions were being given to the press or, later, to the radio stations as well.[4] Under this system of control supported by laws, regulations, and decrees, no official censorship of the press was necessary in Italy. Rarely was there any departure from approved policy, unless through unintentional error.

The manner in which the press and the entire information process was converted to a political purpose in Italy brought protests and unfavorable comments from other countries. The supposed secrecy by which instructions were given to editors did not remain secret for long. Fascist leaders could not and did not pretend that the press of Italy was free, as it had been previously, or as it was in such countries as the United States or the United Kingdom. But they resorted to a kind of rationalization George Orwell later classified as "newspeak" in his novel *1984*, with assertions made in complete reversal of what formerly had been accepted as proper logic and morality.

While not his first statement on the subject, Mussolini was quoted in Margherita G. Sarfatti's authorized biography, *The Life of Benito Mussolini* (1926), as saying that "Fascism has already stepped, and, if need be, will . . . step once more over the more or less putrid body of the godless Liberty." Of the press, he said, "I consider Italian Fascist journalism like an orchestra," responding to the direction of its conductor and playing the music as written. This was a concept and a figure of speech repeated in the Soviet Union and later in Nazi Germany.

Foreign correspondents in the country were not subject to the pressures felt by Italian journalists in the first years of the Fascist regime. They continued to operate with freedom after 1922, and even received a seventy per cent reduction in fare on the state-owned railroads. Guided tours were made available to them without cost, so that they might view and tell the world about developments of which the Fascist government had reason to be proud.

More correspondents probably were accorded individual interviews with Mussolini in his earlier years in office than with any other head of state. As a journalist, he seemed to enjoy such meetings. He prepared for them, he made them interesting and dramatic, and he used them to

---

4   Comparable controls already were being used in Moscow to shape the content of the press in the Soviet Union.

make propaganda for the regime. The stories resulting were used throughout the world. Correspondents recognized a degree of demagoguery in Mussolini, but many were impressed nonetheless. They deplored incidents of Fascist violence and the suppression of free opinion, but they hoped such excesses might be only temporary. They themselves were able to write in the first years without censorship. There was some disposition to portray Italy's Fascist state as an interesting alternative to democracy, and certainly as a welcome alternative to communism.

Yet all was not well. After the 1924 Matteoti murder, in particular, officials were less accessible. On such occasions as they did appear, individually or in a group, they seldom were prepared or willing to give enough substantial information to support the writing of significant accounts on economic or financial subjects, much less on political topics. They responded to many questions with the phrase "non risulta" (no comment). Government reports and statistics often were confusing and likely to be unreliable, and the Chigi Palace, or Ministry of Foreign Affairs, was of little value as a news source.

Turning to other sources, correspondents tried to read between the lines in reports appearing in the newspapers, as they did in Moscow, and with attention to papers published in cities other than Rome, Milan, and Turin. They sought information from diplomats and other foreigners in the country, including their fellow correspondents. The best of them studied conscientiously and observed what they could. There was so little confidence in official statements, releases, and news reports permitted to appear, so little diversity of viewpoint, and so many rumors, that correspondents became distrustful and skeptical.[5]

Despite the generally inept manner in which the Fascist government dealt with correspondents, it was eager to be portrayed favorably in the world press. This explained Mussolini's early availability for interviews and the guided tours offered to correspondents. A dubious method intended to produce favorable reports was attempted in the first years of the Fascist regime but soon halted and never attempted by any other dictatorial government. This was an offer or bribe to any correspondent reporting in a friendly or favorable vein of an exemption from payment of local taxes, free telegraph or cable transmission

---

5   This in itself led to some curious results. For example, a British correspondent in Florence observed that the Via Tornabuoni had been closed to traffic and pedestrians. He refused to believe a statement that this was to permit street repairs and scraping down peeling stucco walls of buildings. He chose to believe it was a measure taken to control an anticipated popular uprising against the government, and so suggested in a report to his paper. The account both irritated and amused Italian officials, but it was a reflection of a loss of credibility they had earned by failing to deal openly with correspondents on other matters.

of up to 5,000 words of copy a month, and the rebate to the correspondent personally of the transmission charge against his newspaper or agency.

The system was reported by George Seldes, Rome correspondent in 1924-25 for the *Chicago Tribune*. Seldes indicated that Vincenzo De Santo, Italian-born stringer correspondent in Rome for the *Tribune* before his own arrival, had taken advantage of this allowance, but with the *Tribune* aware of it.[6] Seldes estimated that perhaps one hundred writers had received benefits of as much as $100 to $200 a month in this way during the first years of the Fascist regime. This seems unlikely, however, since the number of correspondents in Rome at least was scarcely half a hundred in that period, and no reputable correspondent would have become party to such an arrangement. Some stringers, especially for small papers of little repute, may have benefitted, with or without the knowledge of their papers.

The Fascist government insisted until 1934 that there was no censorship on outgoing dispatches. Correspondents early had reason to believe, however, that dispatches filed for telegraph or cable transmission were being routed by pneumatic tube to be examined prior to transmission by a "board of revision" in the main Post & Telegraph building.

Under this system of *revizione* or control, a routine dispatch would be passed promptly and transmitted. If, however, a message contained words, sentences, references, or statements regarded as unfavorable or inexpedient, the dispatch might be held up long enough before transmission to rob it of news value when it reached its destination or delay its arrival until after deadline and so cause it to be set aside unused. This was a kind of indirect censorship.

A correspondent in Rome, having filed a dispatch at the communications office, had no way of knowing its fate. Unless he received some query from his home office in a service message, or until a copy of his newspaper reached him days or weeks later, and he took the time to check back, he might never know whether his report of a given day had been used, or whether changes had been made in the original message. Even then, he could not know if failure to use a dispatch meant that it had failed to arrive, simply had been forced out of an edition in whole or in part for lack of space, or whether cuts or changes had been made in the home office or perhaps had originated in the *revizione* before transmission.

While the government still denied any censorship, it became clear that the *revizione* was growing bolder and not only delaying transmis-

---

6   George Seldes, *Tell the Truth and Run* (1953), pp. 187-90.

sion of messages, but even making some changes. If the correspondent complained of such actions, the communications office in Rome sometimes would apologize and perhaps credit him with charges for matter not delivered, pleading errors in transmission or technical or administrative difficulties. But the correspondent had to take the initiative, with the time and trouble involved, or delegate somebody to do it for him. In any case, apologies, explanations, and reimbursements did not compensate for failure of the news to reach readers. Difficult as it was for the correspondent to believe the excuses presented by the communications office, it also was difficult to prove them false.

Even filing reports to allow two to five hours for their delivery in Paris, London, New York, or elsewhere provided no assurance against delays and changes. As an alternative, a correspondent in Rome might try to telephone his report to Paris or London for use or for relay, but the clarity of telephone communication was not good until after 1930. The mail provided a reasonably sure way of getting news matter to Paris and other places, even though spot-checked, but it could not be used for news of immediate importance. Correspondents had no hesitation in sending matter out in the pockets of accommodating friends or travelers, but again it could not be news of immediate importance.

Through the first ten years of the Fascist regime, the activities of the government bearing upon media reports related chiefly to domestic affairs. While some correspondents were personally offended by things they observed, and often reported, they could view the party program as still something of a new departure in government to be covered factually, but with a certain restraint. For its part, the Fascist party and government remained sufficiently influenced by the traditions of past decades to take a reasonably tolerant view of the foreign correspondents. Its attitude of the time was interpreted by Herbert L. Matthews of the *New York Times,* even though he wrote somewhat later. He described the Fascist view in these words:

> Leave us alone. We are working out a great experiment with 42,000,000 lives and we want no interference, no advice, no condescension. We will be happiest if you do not write anything at all about us, but if you must write something, we insist that it must be fair and friendly. You have come here of your own free will; you are accorded the privileges of all foreign guests of Italy and many extra ones because of your profession, and you must, if you want to work here, work with us, and not against us. "Everything for the State; nothing outside the State" goes for you as well as for everyone else.[7]

---

7 Herbert L. Matthews, *The New York Times,* Jan. 13, 1933, p. 2E.

This view, without having been so clearly and succinctly expressed in the years immediately following the Fascist assumption of power in 1922, did move the correspondents themselves to keep within certain bounds. They were aware that their conditions of life and work in Rome were infinitely better than those of their fellow correspondents in Moscow, where a dictatorial type of government also existed, and where some correspondents had been expelled for reports unacceptable to the Soviet authorities. Correspondents in Rome reasoned that if the Fascist government should decide to expel any one of them it should not be for any trivial reason, but for a particular story worthy of the risk.

Seldes of the *Chicago Tribune* was expelled from Moscow in 1923, and in 1925 became the first correspondent expelled from Fascist Italy. The second expulsion did not occur until 1935.

From the time of Seldes' expulsion, the pressures under which correspondents worked in Rome increased. The decrees of November 1926, announced as measures applying to the Italian press, carried the implication that a foreign correspondent as well as an Italian journalist might be jailed for reports deemed hostile to the regime. A statement, wholly true or fair by any objective standard, still might be subject to Fascist interpretation as a criminal offense if its effect on public opinion in other countries could conceivably be judged as harmful to Fascist prestige.

No action ever was taken against a foreign correspondent under these decrees, but the possibility induced caution. As with Moscow correspondents, there arose a disposition to use "softening euphemisms and compromise phrases" in accounts. Correspondents, like many persons in Italy, also learned to be careful what they said lest they invite trouble. As Moscow correspondents sometimes referred to the NKVD, or secret police, as the "YMCA," so Rome correspondents referring to Mussolini in conversation in public places, might not speak of Il Duce, but of "the Duke," or "Mr. Smith," or "Mr. Buzz-Buzz." Although they were free to talk with Italian citizens, including "tipsters" offering to sell information in the tradition of early European journalism, such material was almost never of value, and it also became imprudent for Italian citizens to speak at all to foreigners.

In Rome, as in Moscow, the disposition arose at government levels to view a foreign correspondent as either a friend or an enemy of the regime. One of them, cautiously using the pseudonym of "Peter Brooklyn," wrote of the Fascist attitude at that point of change in 1926:

Impartial objectivity in the exercise of the profession of journalism is considered ridiculous in theory and impossible in practice. But realizing the utter futility of confining articles sent abroad to "sympathetic" form and material, the Press Office contents itself with insisting that favorable articles must quantitatively overbalance the unfavorable ones.[8]

Dossiers were kept on the individual correspondents. Early in the Fascist regime, Italian diplomatic and consular officials throughout the world were instructed to watch the local press for references to Italy and Italian affairs, and send to Rome all clippings, whether favorable or unfavorable. In some instances, such reports would be cabled. This, of course, was no unusual assignment for diplomatic officials. Received in Rome, however, the favorable references would be published by the Ministry of Foreign Affairs in a weekly press review, the *Rassenge Settimanale della Stampa Estera*. Distributed widely, it was intended to show how much the world admired the Fascist regime and its activities.

As for the references deemed unfavorable by Fascist standards, four possible results might follow:

First, the offending correspondent could be called aside at the Press Office, or even summoned, perhaps within a day or two after his report had been published. He might be chided and reasoned with, usually in courteous and restrained terms, but sometimes in violent remonstrance, with a warning that further offenses could result in his expulsion. Certain privileges might be withdrawn as a penalty and a reminder. He might be excluded from a group of correspondents being taken on a special journey organized by the government and likely to yield some matter of news interest. A young correspondent, particularly, might hesitate to risk expulsion lest he find himself without another post, and he might also respond to the other pressures, with his reports moderated accordingly.

If a more experienced correspondent ignored a first protest from the Press Office, and a more violent protest also failed, a second measure was applied. This might be to induce the correspondent to leave Italy voluntarily. Unofficial threats of bodily violence to "unfriendly" correspondents sometimes were caused to appear in print, or were hinted at in other ways. These calculated warnings could not be lightly disregarded, because in a few instances correspondents did suffer violence, almost always by design, with intent to frighten them into changing their reporting style or into leaving the country. If the correspondent had a wife and children with him, they also might be subjected to such unpleasantness as to make them wish to leave, thus putting further strain on the correspondent.

Also, the correspondent might be carefully watched. If anything even faintly compromising could be learned about his personal life, it

---

8 *Editor & Publisher*, Dec. 4, 1926, p. 12.

might be used either to blackmail him into taking the "right attitude" in his reports, or be used to discredit him and gain his departure, whether by his own action or that of his home office.

A third alternative or supplementary method intended to move an unfriendly correspondent out of the country was to have the Italian consul, in the foreign city where the correspondent's reports appeared, to protest or arrange protests to his agency or the newspapers using his reports. These protests could take various forms. Local residents of Italian birth or background, or persons sympathetic to the Fascist regime, might be persuaded to protest personally, or write letters protesting the correspondent's stories as "inaccurate," "false," or "malicious." If such persons had relatives or property in Italy, and it was necessary to induce them to protest, even if they had no real knowledge of the issues or reason to protest, they might be pressured into doing so by hints of penalties against those relatives or possible confiscation of their property. For persons engaged in business with Italy, economic pressure might be used. A suggestion might be made to a newspaper itself that advertising for Italian transport services, hotels, and tourist enterprises scarcely belonged in a paper publishing reports that might alarm prospective travelers.

In extreme cases, Italy's ambassador or minister in the capital of the correspondent's country might carry a protest to the foreign ministry of that country, or sometimes even reach the head of state, perhaps on a social occasion, with a plea that good diplomatic and trade relations were threatened by certain "irresponsible" or "sensational" reports. Such protests might then also be relayed, even if only as a matter of information, both to the correspondent's home office and to the diplomatic representative of his country in Rome.

A correspondent whose reports set any such elaborate machinery into motion could not fail to learn of the measures being taken to discredit him. He might become more restrained in his reports, even if he survived the weight of such an attack. These various methods, largely originated by the Fascist government, were used by other governments in some degree. They were by no means always successful—indeed, rarely so. Their very complexity was almost absurd, because the fourth method of dealing with an unwelcome correspondent was so simple.

If all else failed, the correspondent might be expelled from the country. A government possesses a legal right to take such action against any alien. An authoritarian government, in particular, might expel a correspondent or any other person on whatever charge it chose to bring, whether it be inaccuracy, malice, hostility, espionage, improper personal behavior, or an unspecified charge.

Few correspondents had been expelled from the capitals and nations of the world prior to 1920. The Italian Fascist government, adhering to established practices in that respect, was reluctant to expel a foreign correspondent lest the action be interpreted as suggesting an over-sensitivity or that it had something to hide. It did make personal protests to correspondents and subject them to restraints, including a closing of news sources. Some departures may have occurred as a result of the use of the second method described, but none, so far as known, because of the third. Changes appearing on the world scene after 1930 changed that restraint, however. It was symptomatic of a new situation that with only the two expulsions in the fifteen-year period from 1920 to 1935, no fewer than twenty-four correspondents were expelled from Italy in the following three-year period from 1936 to 1939, and still others in 1940–41.

The Vatican

In the unification of Italy and the establishment of the Kingdom of Italy in 1870, the States of the Church, or Papal States, previously occupying a major part of the peninsula between Rome and Venice, were incorporated into the new nation.

Pope Pius IX, then the pontiff, declined to accept the settlement offered, and assumed a role as a "prisoner in the Vatican." This was and is an area of about 100 acres west of the Tiber River, much of it walled, but otherwise surrounded by Rome itself. It includes the great basilica of St. Peter's, the residence of the pope, the Sacred College of Cardinals, the Vatican Museum and library, and related structures. As the world center of the Roman Catholic Church, it was traditionally and remains an area of importance and interest for millions.

Beginning with Pius IX, six popes remained as voluntary "prisoners" in the Vatican between 1870 and 1945. Pius XII, then recognizing a new era following World War II, was the first to leave the confines of Vatican City. Meanwhile, treaties of conciliation and a so-called Lateran Pact or concordat signed in 1929 gave the Vatican a special position independent of the Italian government. The Vatican had its own diplomatic status, postal system, telephone switchboard, railway station at the end of a spur line, and its own radio station built in 1931 under the supervision of Guglielmo Marconi himself and used both for broadcasting and for the exchange of messages, including news reports. The population of the Vatican City State was scarcely a thousand. Those who lived there were free of Fascist government controls, but relations between the Vatican and the Fascist government were strained.

The Vatican always had been a source of news and a subject of news, and this was no less true during the years of the Fascist regime. A strong Catholic press existed in Italy in 1922, but was taken in charge by the Fascist government, along with the lay press. The one exception was *l'Osservatore Romano,* a semi-official afternoon daily newspaper owned by the Holy See and published under the jurisdiction of the pope. Established in July 1841, it was edited during the Fascist period and after by Conte Guiseppe Dalla Torre. Published in Rome until 1930, it was moved to Vatican City in that year and produced from new presses. Although then only four standard pages in size, and naturally giving space to Vatican and clerical subjects, it also received and used news reports from all parts of the world. In addition to its radio station, international telegraph and telephone connections and independent postal facilities were available in Vatican City, all free of censorship.[9] Under Dalla Torre's editorship, and safe from Fascist control, the paper maintained an independence of news judgment and comment that gained it an attentive readership well beyond the confines of Vatican City. This irked the Fascist leadership and led in 1940 to a ban on sale of the paper in Rome and elsewhere in Italy, but it was not possible to prevent copies being circulated privately.

The death of two popes during the Fascist period, Benedict XV in 1922 and Pius XI in 1939, and the selection and coronation of their successors, Pius XI in 1922 and Pius XII in 1939, were matters of major world news. Various papal encyclicals also made news, including one by Pius XI in January 1930 dealing with education. It was 12,000 words in length, was transmitted in its entirety for use by the *New York Times,* and was the longest message transmitted up to that time with reference to Vatican affairs. There were appointments to the College of Cardinals, Vatican statements relating to the course of affairs in the world, and numerous other issues warranting news attention.

Pius XI addressed 120 journalists, including correspondents from seventeen countries, at Vatican City in 1936, and informed them that all were welcome at the Vatican. In a professional sense, however, this was somewhat unrealistic, news being difficult for the average correspondent to pinpoint and obtain there.

In practice, Monsignor Enrico Pucci, domestic prelate to the pope, was then the major source of Vatican news as channeled to the press of the world through the correspondent group in Rome. He operated more as a tipster, however, than as an information officer. His procedure was to provide reports in the form of scarcely legible onion-

---

9 Correspondents in Rome did not use the Vatican City news facilities. To do so would have compromised their positions with the Fascist government and invited retribution, and also would have made difficulties for the Vatican itself.

skin carbon copies of typewritten "handouts," all in Italian. This was somewhat grandiosely designated as a *Servizio Speciale.* For this special service he expected and received a monthly fee from each recipient, and the amount of the fee was determined in part by Pucci's estimate of the prosperity of the correspondent and that of his newspaper or agency.

This "robust, gray-headed priest," as one correspondent described Monsignor Pucci, this "redoubtable yet charming" individual, as another called him, often was cited anonymously in reports as "a Vatican informant," as "a reliable Vatican source," or even as "the Vatican semi-official news service." It was conceded that he had "a tight corner on papal news" through his close relations in the office of the Papal Secretariat of State. By way of protecting his favored position, he was capable of foisting false news by indirection on a correspondent who might attempt to operate independently of his service.

Pucci conducted his news business from his own apartment in Rome and during the 1930s was estimated to have received an income of as much as $1,000 a month. This would have made him one of the highest paid Italian "journalists" of the time, although it was assumed that he returned some of what he received to informants in the Vatican to assure the continuation of his little monopoly.

A few experienced Rome correspondents, before as well as during Pucci's heyday, managed to establish direct Vatican sources of their own. One who did so earlier and with notable success until his retirement in 1931, was Salvatore Cortesi of the Associated Press. Another was Thomas B. Morgan, in Rome before World War I for the AP, and then for the United Press into the 1930s. He was the first newsman to obtain an interview with Pope Pius XI.

Apart from what appeared in *l'Osservatore Romano* and broadcasts over the Vatican radio, most correspondents in Rome during the 1930s seeking information on church matters nevertheless were dependent upon Pucci's services.[10]

---

10 After World War II, Monsignor Pucci was almost literally pushed aside by a new generation of correspondents in Rome. The postwar Italian government also announced that investigations indicated Pucci to have been a member of the OVRA, the Fascist secret police, assigned to report on any anti-Fascist moves made by Catholic Action groups and that he was, in fact, a Fascist government spy in the Vatican. See *Time,* July 22, 1945, and August 1, 1946.

Spain and Portugal, forming the Iberian Peninsula in the southwest of Europe, had been among the first areas of the world to receive organized news attention through the enterprise of the London press, beginning at the time of the Napoleonic wars just after 1800. By 1900 the great world empires created largely by navigators of those two countries, beginning in the late fifteenth century, and followed by military adventurers and missionaries of the Roman Church, had largely vanished. Only in parts of Africa and at island and coastal outposts, including some in Asia and the Pacific, did their flags still fly.

Spain was having trouble in the administration of Spanish Morocco in the first years of the century, and also was at the center of several tense situations when Germany seemed disposed to contest its position there. In 1902 Alfonso XIII assumed the throne in Madrid at the age of sixteen. The internal situation at the time brought the imposition of restraints upon the national press that continued through World War I, during which the country maintained a careful neutrality.

Meanwhile, disorders in Portugal had resulted in the end of its ancient monarchy in 1910. King Manuel II took refuge in England, and a republic was proclaimed. Sympathetic to the Allied cause when the war began in 1914, Portugal seized German ships then in the harbors at Lisbon and Oporto. Both Germany and Austria-Hungary declared war in March 1916, and Portugal sent a small expeditionary force to France early in 1917.

Labor difficulties and social unrest in Spain following the war caused King Alfonso to threaten abdication at that time. The church and the army were the chief props of the monarchy, and the army continued to have difficulty keeping order in Morocco in 1920 because of Riff tribesmen who long had challenged the power of the local sultanate and also resisted control from Madrid. Spanish troops suffered a defeat there in 1921, which accentuated the unrest already existing in Spain itself.

To assure maintenance of order in the country, the king in 1923 called upon Captain-General Miguel Primo de Rivera, military governor of Catalonia, to form a new constitutional government. He established his authority through a bloodless *coup d'état* that gave him dictatorial power. He retained for himself all of the ministerial portfolios, dissolved the Cortes, the legislative body, and ruled under martial law. In 1925 he assumed the title of premier and headed the government until 1930.

The Rivera dictatorship was not severe during its first years. It brought some reforms in government administration and undertook the modernization of the country's internal transportation and communication. This latter included the development of a top-quality telephone system by the International Telephone and Telegraph Company of the United States. The regime encouraged aviation and tourism, sponsored a public works program, and was active in the League of Nations. It conducted a successful campaign against the Riff tribesmen, and so restored order in Morocco.

At the same time, a press censorship was imposed, and civil rights were abrogated. The Agencia Telegrafica Fabra, operating since 1879 as a subsidiary of the Agence Havas, was sold in 1926 to a Spanish banking group and resumed an earlier title as the Agence Espagñol et International. It was subject to government control.

The press itself tended to be more political than informative, and as lacking in objectivity. Newspapers of longest heritage were the *Gaceta de Madrid,* dating from 1661, the *Diario de Barcelona,* semiofficial in character, and *A.B.C.* of Madrid, a prosperous, small tabloid largely pictorial and undistinguished. There were also *El Sol, Debate, Informaciones, La Voz,* and *La Nacion,* all of Madrid, and *La Vanguardia* of Barcelona.

The papers were censored, but not so severely as to prevent them indicating open disapproval of the system. For example, *El Sol,* forced by pre-censorship to remove certain sentences and paragraphs, appeared with the spaces left blank, rather than remaking the pages. Or it inserted a line, "This sentence is deleted by the censor" or "This article is censored" or "This edition has been revised by the censor."

In February 1929, newspapers were ordered to reserve a percentage of space for government material provided by the official Press Bureau. Since the decree did not forbid it, *El Sol* and *La Voz* then added notations saying "We are forced to print this," or "Forced publication, by Royal Decree." In theory, such actions alerted readers to the fact that they were being denied certain information, or were being presented with "approved" information or propaganda.

The events in Spain and Morocco drew correspondents, and some encountered difficulties and hazards comparable to those of an earlier generation. Vincent Sheean of the *Chicago Tribune* was arrested in Madrid in March 1924 and accused, among other things, of writing stories that might imperil the value of Spain's currency in international exchange. Hallet Johnson, chargé d'affaires at the United States embassy, intervened in his behalf. Sheean then obtained an interview with Primo de Rivera and apparently persuaded him to order all surveillance and interference with foreign correspondents to cease. Sheean wrote of his experience, portraying it as possessing aspects of a comic opera.

Other correspondents in Spain at the same general period did not find their experiences in any way comic. A number spent hours or days in jails, and some were threatened with fines and imprisonment for "exaggeration" or other vague offenses. Seeking to avoid censorship, some arranged to have dispatches carried over the frontier to Hendaye, France, or to Gibraltar for transmission. This procedure, however, invited retribution after publication, and gave small satisfaction.

Sheean, after his experience in Madrid during the spring of 1924, went to Morocco for the *Tribune* in December. The Riff War was in progress, with native forces under Abd el-Krim contesting the Spanish and French presence in the area. It was a guerrila-type war, an aspect of those earlier contests with the so-called Barbary pirates, and was to continue until Abd el-Krim's surrender in May 1926.

Paul Scott Mowrer, of the *Chicago Daily News,* and G. Ward Price, of the London *Daily Mail,* far more experienced than Sheean, then only twenty-five and in journalism just three years, already had interviewed Abd el-Krim. Sheean was able, nevertheless, to make contact with the elusive Riff leader, and not only obtained an interview but remained for about ten days as a guest at the secret headquarters, where he met others in the entourage. Out of this, he fashioned a series of highly readable and informative stories that established him as a correspondent with a special flair for a personalized and colorful approach to the news. Even after publication of those accounts, Sheean remained in the Riff country, and in Tangier, for about two months.

Despite certain apparent improvements in Spain, and its success in Morocco in 1926, King Alfonso continued to lose popular support, as did Primo de Rivera, his spokesman. Not only was there a growing disposition on the part of the domestic press to contest the censorship, but, more serious, it appeared that the army was dissatisfied with Rivera. The result was that in 1930 the king dismissed him as premier and appointed in his place another army officer, General Dámaso Berenguer y Fusté, former high commissioner in Morocco.

Madrid editors called upon Berenguer to request that the censorship be removed. He agreed, with the understanding that the acts of Rivera were not to be denounced, and that no attacks were to be made upon the monarchy. In practice, neither of these provisions was observed. The result was a prompt restoration of a stricter censorship. *El Sol* and *La Voz,* the two papers most vigorous in their opposition, were purchased in a forced sale by a syndicate friendly to the king.

Matters still did not improve. There were strikes and revolutionary outbreaks. The king offered a restoration of the old constitution, a restoration of civil liberties, and an open election to permit the formation of a new Cortes. Berenguer resigned in February 1931, succeeded as head of the government by Admiral Juan Bautista Aznar, a monarchist. In April 1931 the promised elections were held throughout the country. The vote revealed so strong a sentiment for a republican form of government that King Alfonso, under pressure, lèft the country rather than risk civil war. He went first to France and then to Italy, where in 1941 he abdicated in favor of his son, Don Juan.

The day of the king's departure for France on April 14, 1931, brought the proclamation of the second Spanish Republic, the first having been in 1870–75. The change was made peaceably, and parliamentary elections were held in June. Niceto Alcalá Zamora y Torres, leader of the revolutionary committee standing for the republic in the earlier April vote, became the first president by formal action of the restored Cortes in December. Manuel Azaña y Dias, a former war minister and provisional president since April, became premier.

Spain's difficulties were by no means over, but were to flare up almost immediately and continue through the 1930s.

Meanwhile, Portugal emerged from the war with certain benefits, but was at the same time in a political turmoil. António Machado Santos, viewed as the founder of the republic in 1910, was among several persons murdered in 1921, victims of an emotional contest in which both military and civilian elements were involved. It had been impossible for any one government to survive for long, with no less than forty cabinets serving between 1910 and 1926.

In 1926 a new provisional government was headed by Commander Joachim Mendes Cabeçadas. He was promptly unseated by General Manoel de Oliveira Gomes da Costa, who lost power in turn to General António Oscar de Fragosa Carmona. Carmona was able to survive a bloody attempt at a new revolution in 1927, and was elected as president in 1928. One of his early cabinet members was Minister of Finance António de Oliveira Salazar, professor of law at Coimbra. In 1933 a so-called "New State" was proclaimed, with a new constitution, to be conducted as a dictatorship by Carmona and, later, by Salazar.

The press in Portugal was without notable strength or distinction, in part because the general literacy rate was below fifty per cent, except in Lisbon, Oporto, and in other large cities. The papers operated with relative freedom until 1933, following which they were under sharp government restrictions. Two of the older morning papers in Lisbon, the *Diario de Noticias* (1864) and *O Seculo* (1880), led in circulation. Other Lisbon papers included the *Jornal do Comercio (1853)*, *Novedades* (1886), *Republica* (1911), and the *Diario Lisboa* (1911). Oporto, among others, had the *Comercio do Porto* (1854), the *Jornal de Noticias* (1888), and *O Primeiro de Janeiro* (1888). The Agence

Havas provided world news for the Portuguese press, and produced most of the reports coming from the country.

References above to Morocco, and elsewhere to Egypt and the Sudan, the Union of South Africa, and other African areas may seem to be negligent in consideration of so great and varied a continent, except within the context of developments there. In the 1920s and 1930s much of it remained colonial territory and figured rarely in the news. Algeria and Tunisia were important French areas on the Mediterranean coast, merging into the vastness of French West Africa, Equatorial Africa, Senegal, the Ivory Coast, and the Cameroons. British interests included Rhodesia, Bechuanaland, Tanganyika, Kenya, Nigeria, and the Gold Coast. Spain had the Rio de Oro as well as Morocco; Portugal had Mozambique and Angola; Belgium had the great central Congo; Italy had Libya, Eritrea, and Somaliland, as well as the recently seized Ethiopia.

Generally speaking, a matter of news interest or importance occurring in any of these areas within colonial holdings was likely to be reported through the press of the country controlling the area.

The United States and the Northern Hemisphere

8

By the end of the Wilson administration in 1921, Washington had become an important news center, both nationally and internationally, and something of a model in its news practices. Many foreign journalists in those years were amazed at the open relationship between press representatives and officials of government. Most foreign correspondents in the United States continued to work in New York, however. It was the business and banking center, the main port and communications center, home of the most prestigious newspapers and headquarters for the news agencies, many syndicates, and important periodicals; it was an active cultural and educational center as well.

Geographical factors placed the common interests of the United States alongside those of Canada, Cuba, the West Indies, Mexico, and Central America. Under British administrative influence were Canada, Bermuda, and the Bahamas, as well as certain other areas touching on the Western Atlantic and the Caribbean. Far across the Pacific, the Philippine Islands were administered by the United States, as were the Hawaiian Islands, Alaska, Guam, and Samoa.

President Wilson was a convalescent as 1920 began, quietly living out his term in the White House. National press representation in Washington had grown considerably. Membership in the Press Gallery of the Congress of the United States, exercising formal accreditation of correspondents, was somewhat in excess of 200, with foreign correspondents included since 1911. A separate and exclusive White House Correspondents Association was only six years old. The National Press Club, started in 1908 by thirty-two capital and Washington newsmen, had become a popular social center, although its membership included at least as many lobbyists and public relations men as working newsmen. Women were admitted only as guests. A separate Women's National Press Club had been established in 1919, reflecting a growth in the number of female journalists in the capital.

Attention was turned in 1920 to the presidential campaign in which, as it happened, two Ohio newspaper publishers contested for that office.[1] James M. Cox, publisher of the *Dayton Daily News* and a former member of Congress and twice governor of the state, was the Democratic nominee. Warren G. Harding, publisher of the *Marion Star*, formerly in the state senate and a member of the United States Senate since 1915, was the Republican party candidate. Franklin D. Roosevelt, former assistant secretary of the navy, was vice-presidential candidate, running with Cox. Calvin Coolidge, then governor of Massachusetts, was the Republican vice-presidential candidate.

Harding was elected in November and inaugurated in March 1921. His cabinet included Secretary of State Charles Evans Hughes, who was defeated for the presidency in 1916 by Wilson. President Harding was prepared to reintroduce the formal presidential news conference, originated by Wilson but suspended during the war. Officers of the White House Correspondents Association, meeting with Harding and with George Christian of his secretarial staff, worked out procedures. Conferences were to be held twice each week, open to all accredited correspondents who might wish to attend. Christian would be available to respond to correspondents' questions at other times.

The conferences began with the highest of hopes for a useful exchange. Meeting in the president's office at the White House, they were informal, with the president providing information and responding to questions. There were only two limitations. The president was not to be quoted directly, unless by special approval. Also, with the clear understanding that it was off the record, some material was given for the background information and guidance of the correspondents, but was not to be reported, or not to be reported with attribution to the source.

Harding was quite prepared to deal frankly and helpfully with the press. As publisher of his own newspaper, he felt among friends. As a member of the Senate, he had been on excellent terms with many of the correspondents and enjoyed their company. He also encouraged a comparable free flow of information in departments and agencies throughout the executive branch of the government. Such a relationship already existed in the legislative branch between correspondents and members of the House and Senate, and their staff assistants. Secretary of State Hughes and Secretary of Commerce Herbert Hoover opened particularly helpful relationships with correspondents.

---

1   Horace Greeley, founding editor and publisher of the *New York Tribune,* a nominee of the splinter party of Liberal Republicans and Democrats in 1872, was the only other journalist previously a candidate for the presidency. Defeated by Ulysses S. Grant, Republican candidate running for a second term, Greeley died less than a month later.

The happy situation at the White House did not survive for long. Abuses occurred because certain persons, other than accredited correspondents, gained admission to the conferences. Some information conveyed in confidence also "leaked," or was revealed to unauthorized persons through tipsters, as had occurred also following Wilson conferences. Such incidents brought prompt caution into the president's responses to questions.

The international conference on Limitation of Armaments met in Washington from November 12, 1921, to February 6, 1922. Involved were the United States, Great Britain, France, Italy, and Japan. Correspondents were present representing the press of those countries. Harding was asked a question at a news conference concerning how the treaty under consideration would affect Japan. His response was somewhat in error. Japan was disturbed, and Secretary of State Hughes had to provide a corrective statement. He also protested privately to the president. Harding took responsibility for the mistake, inadvertent as it was, but he introduced a new provision that correspondents henceforth must submit written questions in advance. This would give the president opportunity to verify facts, when necessary, before facing the correspondents as a group, and also would permit him to pass over questions he might not wish to answer, without making it obvious that he was doing so. The procedure, however, changed the character of the news conferences for more than a decade to follow.

President Harding died in San Francisco in August 1923, following a journey to Alaska. The last year of his term was less satisfactory in the matter of press relations. He objected to some departures from the rule that he was not to be quoted directly without his permission. He became the target of some editorial criticism and the victim of what he considered inaccuracies in press reports. He also was personally disturbed and reluctant to respond to some questions because he became aware that certain of his friends, including members of the cabinet, were taking advantage of their positions and of him. This was demonstrated after his death to be true in the Teapot Dome scandals, a subject of extensive news attention in 1924. Edwin Denby, secretary of the navy, resigned in the face of a Senate investigation. Criminal proceedings were brought against Attorney General Harry M. Daugherty, who escaped prosecution but was forced to resign. Albert B. Fall, secretary of the interior, was found guilty of accepting a $100,000 bribe. He was fined and sentenced to a year in prison (1930–31).

Vice-President Calvin Coolidge completed Harding's term and was re-elected in 1924 to a term of his own. He continued the twice-a-week news conferences at the White House, but with the provision that written questions must be submitted in advance. His conferences lacked intimacy and produced so little news that they were poorly attended. Willis J. Abbot, editor of the *Christian Science Monitor*, referred to them as "symposia of silliness."

Coolidge was insistent upon not being quoted directly, and so objected even to indirect attribution that correspondents were forced to the use of such absurd references as "sources close to the president" or "a White House spokesman" to cover statements by the president himself. He read newspapers carefully for his own information, and also read *Time*, then in its first years as a weekly news magazine. His secretary, C. Bascomb Slemp, an attorney and a former member of Congress from Virginia in 1909–23, was available to correspondents as a source of information. Coolidge entertained some editors and correspondents socially, and granted a few personal interviews. Members of Coolidge's cabinet maintained good relations with the press, notably Hughes and Hoover, who continued throughout his administrations to March 1929.[2]

Herbert Hoover had good relations with the press from the time he entered public life as director of the relief efforts in Belgium and northern France, following the German wartime invasion of 1914, and through his service as secretary of commerce. As Republican party candidate for the presidency in 1928, he defeated Alfred E. Smith, former governor of New York. Between the time of his election in November and his March inauguration, however, signs appeared that his presidential press relations might become less satisfactory. He made a "good will" journey to South America in that interval, with correspondents accompanying him. They were dismayed to find that their dispatches had to be passed upon by a press liaison officer, George Barr Baker, and that some were being censored before transmission.

Actual presidential news conferences began favorably after Hoover entered the White House. The requirement that questions be submitted in writing in advance was continued, but there were none of the problems of attribution that had complicated the Coolidge conferences, and the president responded well to questions.

---

2 Upon leaving office, Coolidge was persuaded to write a brief daily commentary distributed by the McClure Newspaper Syndicate. It went to 200 dailies in 1930–31, with a financial return to him of about $200,000. He also wrote three magazine articles and an autobiography. Writing was difficult for him, and in general the results were undistinguished, in contrast to the post-presidential writing of Theodore Roosevelt, who contributed regularly to the *Kansas City Star* from 1917 until his death in 1919, as well as to the *Outlook* and *Metropolitan* magazines in earlier years, plus writing more than a dozen books.

Deterioration of his press relations soon set in, nevertheless. Some correspondents felt the president was showing favoritism toward older acquaintances among the newsmen, including Mark Sullivan and William Hard, known as writers for *Collier's* and other magazines, Richard V. Oulahan of the *New York Times,* Frank Kent of the *Baltimore Sun,* and Roy Roberts of the *Kansas City Star.* George Akerson, the president's secretary and a secondary White House news source, also drew criticism for eliminating questions from among those submitted for the conferences, and for misinforming or confusing correspondents by his own answers to some questions. Even after Theodore G. Joslin, formerly a Washington correspondent for the *Boston Evening Transcript,* was named as the first specially designated "press secretary" at the White House in January 1931, matters did not improve.

What contributed most to the deterioration of Hoover's press relations, however, was the national economic depression that began, eight months after he took office, with the Wall Street stock market decline of October 1929. Public discontent over failure of the national government to find instant solutions for problems that grew increasingly serious was directed at the president himself.

Like Wilson and Harding, Hoover also became concerned about what he regarded as leaks of information, particularly as touching upon his family and matters of personal privacy, as well as about press references that he viewed not only as critical but as malicious. He became aloof toward correspondents, and even antagonized them. Some news conferences were cancelled, questions on important matters, as submitted in writing, were ignored, and ultimately hardly a half dozen correspondents appeared for such conferences as were held.

News coverage in Washington, otherwise, did not suffer in those years. Congress was well reported, as was the routine of the news. At the executive level, the Department of State remained a good source. Both Frank B. Kellogg, whose term as secretary of state bridged the Coolidge-Hoover period, and Henry L. Stimson, who followed him, conducted regular news conferences, or their assistants did so. Foreign correspondents were among those present, with generally useful results. A Division of Current Information, established at the Department of State during the Taft administration, was useful also. It was directed by Michael J. McDermott, one of the first press relations officers in the government and one of the most competent, and a spokesman for the department until after World War II.

Visits to Washington by British Prime Minister J. Ramsay MacDonald in October 1929, and by French Premier Pierre Laval in October 1931, were the first occasions on which such leaders of state journeyed to the United States. They were accompanied by British and

French news correspondents who were enabled to join their resident colleagues in Washington, and to attend news conferences both at the White House and at the Department of State.

Apart from the presidential campaigns of 1920, 1924, and 1928, the third decade produced a variety of other newsworthy subjects in the United States, of which the Washington Naval Conference of 1921–22 was one of the first. A National Prohibition Act forbidding the manufacture or sale of alcoholic beverages, the eighteenth amendment to the Constitution, had become the law of the land in January 1920. It spawned a growth of criminal activity and an era of gangsterism with endless violence in the illegal provision of liquor to the public. The nineteenth amendment to the Constitution, ratified in August 1920, gave women the right to vote.

As 1920 began, a steel strike was in progress. In 1922 a coal strike brought serious disorders. Railroad and textile strikes followed. The entire national economy was upset through the 1919–21 period by soaring prices, credit expansion and speculation, and reduced inventories, all leading to a sharp postwar deflation, with 5,735,000 unemployed in August 1921, but followed by a strong recovery in 1922–29.

Attention went to a revival of the Ku Klux Klan in many parts of the country, as an extreme manifestation of racial and religious intolerance in the early 1920s, and to the so-called "Scopes trial" in Tennessee in 1925, as another manifestation of intolerance relating to a ban on the "teaching of evolution" in the schools. The 1928 presidential campaign produced a still further show of religious intolerance, with New York's Governor Alfred E. Smith, the Democratic party candidate, a target of attacks because he was a Catholic. Still another was represented in the 1920 arrest and 1927 execution in Massachusetts of Nicola Sacco and Bartolomeo Vanzetti, Brockton workmen charged with a payroll robbery and murder of a factory paymaster and guard. There was serious question of their actual guilt. A bomb explosion in New York's Wall Street in 1920 killed thirty people, injured 100, and caused $2 million in damage.

More constructive news during the decade related to strong industrial development within the country, notably in the automotive field. There was a growth in education and in science and medicine. Germany's Professor Albert Einstein in 1921 lectured at Columbia University in New York, describing his theory of relativity, the basis for the atomic age to come. Events in aviation, making important news stories, marked the decade. These included flights by Rear Admiral Richard E. Byrd over the North Pole in 1926 and the South Pole in 1929; Charles A. Lindbergh's solo flight from New York to Paris in 1927; and a series of other flights over the North and South Atlantic and the Pacific oceans.

The years also brought broadcast radio into the homes of millions, with news as well as entertainment and advertising messages. Motion pictures, including newsreels, became another important medium both of entertainment and information, with voice and sound and color added before the end of the 1930s. Sports became vastly more important, with international contests numerous. World travel increased, and a generation of young Americans discovered Europe, China, and Japan. Popular music, recorded and otherwise, new plays, and books were among influences reshaping the social complexion of the nation. News magazines and other periodicals also contributed to change.

The national economy declined steadily from October 1929, and President Hoover, in the White House until March 1933, endured the agonies of trying to solve the problems of the stubborn depression. Since most questions addressed to him at news conferences related to those problems, and were virtually unanswerable, he dropped the conferences almost entirely. Again the Republican party nominee in 1932, he also faced the hardships of the presidential campaign. He was defeated in the November election by a landslide vote for the Democratic party candidate, Franklin D. Roosevelt, who was inaugurated in March 1933. That date and event marked the beginning of an almost completely new situation in the United States and in the world.

Philippines, Hawaii, and Alaska

A desire for independence had motivated local leaders in the Philippine Islands since before they had been freed from Spanish control in 1898. Cuba, similarly freed at the time of the Spanish-American War, had gained its full independence in 1909. Independence had been promised the Philippines by the United States government when a stable administration had been established in the islands.

The Philippines were granted virtual autonomy in 1916, with a council of state and a legislature working within a civil administration headed by a governor appointed from Washington. In 1934 a major advance toward independence occurred with the establishment of a commonwealth government, under a constitution accepted by the legislature and confirmed by a vote of the people. Manuel Quezon became the first president, elected to a six-year term. It was intended that the commonwealth should be transitional, with full independence to come twelve years later. Meanwhile, the United States retained military and naval bases in the islands, and the right to review decisions by the courts.

In the years between 1900 and 1940 an active press developed in the Philippines, chiefly in Manila. The major newspapers were in English, although others were published in Spanish and in Tagalog, the principal vernacular language. Radio stations were in full operation. The news agencies and radio networks of the United States were represented, and correspondents for U.S. newspapers and periodicals visited the islands.

The Hawaiian Islands and Alaska, as territories of the United States, were active in their own journalistic development and were part of the news agency and radio network organizations. With Pan American clippers flying the Pacific by the mid-1930s, ocean liners moving between major ports, and smaller vessels elsewhere, the Pacific basin was substantially reported for the world media by that decade.

Cuba

News coverage in Cuba, intensive between 1895 and 1905, had been light after that time, even though staff and stringer representation was maintained in Havana, the capital. A sudden change occurred in 1928, first because the sixth International Conference of American States, or Pan-American Conference, met there, and then because of a dictatorial turn of government.

The Pan-American Conference, with important topics on the agenda, took place at a period when the world press was better organized and more enterprising than ever before. It was reported by a larger and more diverse group of journalists than had gathered previously, except for the Paris Peace Conference of 1919 and the Washington Naval Conference of 1921-22. Every country in the Western Hemisphere had correspondents present, and the press of London, Paris, Berlin, Rome, and Moscow also had representation.

Among more than 150 writers, those serving the U.S. press were most numerous. Arriving from Washington were Richard V. Oulahan, *New York Times;* Charles Michelson, *New York World;* Carter Field, *New York Herald Tribune;* Raymond Carroll, *Philadelphia Public Ledger;* Charles G. Ross, *St. Louis Post-Dispatch;* Arthur Sears Henning, *Chicago Tribune;* Drew Pearson, *Christian Science Monitor* and the *United States Daily;* William Philip Simms, Scripps-Howard Newspapers; R. C. Henle, AP; Carl D. Groat, UP; and George Holmes, INS.

Other U.S. writers included Clarence K. Streit, Geneva correspondent for the *New York Times,* along with Russell Owen and Simeon

Strunsky of that paper; Beverly Smith, *New York Herald Tribune;* Henry L. Mencken, Paul Patterson, Stanley M. Reynolds, and John Owen, of the *Baltimore Sun;* Claude O. Poke, *Chicago Daily News;* Nelson J. Riley, AP; Harry W. Frantz, UP; Will Rogers, a syndicated columnist; and Bruce Bliven, writing for the *New Republic* and the *Manchester Guardian.*

Francis Aldham, Washington correspondent for the Canadian Press, was present. For the Cuban press itself, the *Diario de la Marina, El Mundo,* and *El Pais,* all of Havana, had their reporters at the conference. *La Prensa* of Buenos Aires was represented by Ramon da Franch. Dr. Jorge Mitre, director of *La Nación* of Buenos Aires, was present, as were Fernando Ramires de Aguilar of *El Universal,* Mexico City; Lara Pardo of *El Excelsior,* also of Mexico City; and other Latin American editors, publishers, and correspondents. Correspondents writing for the European press included Dr. Max Jordan, then New York representative of the *Berliner Tageblatt;* Dr. H. A. Mattefeldt, *Frankfurter Zeitung;* Mario Appelius, *Il Popolo d'Italia,* Milan; and Stephen Naft, New York representative of Tass.

Cuba itself was in a period of crisis two years later, for the world economic problems of 1930 had brought a prompt decline in the market price for sugar and tobacco, two of the island-nation's major crops and sources of income. Tourism from the U.S. also fell off sharply. Gerardo Machado, elected to the presidency of the republic in 1924 and re-elected in 1928, sought to meet the economic problems and pressures by turning his administration into a dictatorship. It was characterized by corruption and abuses that Machado had no wish to have reported. A variety of controls, accordingly, were imposed upon the press, including a heavy censorship. This so distorted its performance that the three leading Havana dailies mentioned above voluntarily suspended publication on November 13, 1930, in protest against the government policy. Other Cuban papers soon followed their lead.

This action had its effect, and the censorship was lifted on November 28. The papers resumed publication, but on January 9, 1931, Machado suspended twelve leading papers and periodicals and placed uniformed officers at their doors. Correspondents in Cuba were adversely affected by the censorship of the few surviving local publications, and by a censorship imposed upon their own outgoing reports.

Karl A. Bickel, then president of the United Press, went to Havana to discuss this interference with the news. Machado denied that a censorship existed, but shortly afterwards a decree of February 7, 1931, further abrogated what had been the constitutional rights of the people, including those of the press. Notes were addressed to Machado by the U.S. Department of State and also by the directors of the Press

Congress of the World, then planning a regional conference in Mexico City, and dedicated to the principle of press freedom. Whether these notes, along with Bickel's earlier protest, were responsible or not, the twelve suppressed publications were soon permitted to resume.

The troubles were not over, however. Two of the suppressed newspapers chose not to resume, unwilling to submit to the continuing censorship. These were *El Pais* and the *Havana American,* the latter an English-language daily published by John T. Wilford, a U.S. journalist in Cuba for more than twenty years. He left the country voluntarily to circumvent an anticipated order of deportation.

The Machado government policies were objectionable not only to the press, but to others in Cuba. Student riots, street disorders, and shootings occurred, and more than 8,000 persons were jailed between October 1930 and the summer of 1931. Organized revolt brought armed skirmishes near Santiago de Cuba and rebel action in other areas. Machado used the army to block these moves, which were designed to unseat him.

Correspondents moved into Cuba in August 1931 to report the growing rebellion. Every attempt was made to keep them in Havana and away from rebel groups. A censorship on cable and telegraphic dispatches was imposed from August 18 to September 18. By that time, government control was believed to be firm, but newspaper censorship continued.

During the critical August period, James Doyle Phillips, Havana correspondent for the *New York Times* and Harold Norman Denny, who arrived for that paper, and Alva Johnston of the *New York Herald Tribune* contrived to obtain information outside government circles. Denny and Johnston flew to Miami to wire their reports without censorship. They were able to return to Havana, and the Machado government by then was confident enough of its position to permit them to fly to the area of combat to observe what were in fact by then little more than mopping-up operations.

By December 1931 conditions in Cuba seemed sufficiently stabilized for Wilford of the *Havana American* to return and resume publication of his paper. Yet he was again in difficulties by June 1932, and was able to continue only when he agreed to send advance proofs and corrected copies of articles and pages to military censors before the final printing and distribution of any edition. Other papers were subject to the same regulations. Foreign publications were denied distribution or sale in Cuba if they contained material objectionable to the censorship, and newsdealers were made responsible for withholding them.

Some stories unfavorable to the Machado government were permitted to leave Cuba by early 1933, over normal communication channels. These included reports by Lawrence Hass, UP; Thomas Pettey, *New York Herald Tribune;* and Russell Porter, *New York Times.* Even as this occurred, however, Cuban journalists were being arrested.

The rest of the world was paying slight attention to Cuba at this period. Interest was then centering on the Nazi assumption of power in Germany, and on Japan's moves in China. But two experienced U.S. correspondents, William Philip Simms of the Scripps-Howard Newspapers and William G. Shepherd of *Collier's Weekly,* continued to give close coverage to Cuba. They were joined by others in August 1933, when a new uprising finally deposed the Machado regime. The army also turned against him, following excesses in the use of his power. Machado escaped by plane to Nassau and Montreal and went into exile.

This latter period of violence was reported by Phillips of the *New York Times,* Hass of the UP, John P. McKnight of AP, and John D. Montgomery of INS, all bureau chiefs in Havana, and by UP staffer Alex Garcia, Gustavo Reno for the *Chicago Tribune,* and Leo Reisler for the *New York Herald Tribune.* All covered the story under fire, and Reisler was arrested in the course of the action.

Other correspondents flying from the United States to report the events included Pettey, returning for the *New York Herald Tribune;* the greatly experienced Colonel Frederick Palmer, whose war coverage began at the time of the Greco-Turkish conflict in 1897 and had continued through World War I; Robert Casey, arriving for the *Chicago Daily News;* Arthur Evans for the *Chicago Tribune;* William H. Lander, formerly in Madrid and Rio de Janeiro for UP; William H. Hutchinson for INS; and Ted Gill for AP.

News cameramen also were in the center of the action. Exposed to danger were José Garcia and Seymour Rees, AP Photos; David Oliver, *Chicago Daily News* and Universal Newsreel, who was arrested; James B. Buchanan, Euclid Miller, Lou Hutt, and George Westbrook, all of Paramount News newsreel; Sammy Schulmann, International News Photos; Jack Painter and John Keis, Fox Films newsreel; James Pergola, Pathé News newsreel; Louis Hamburg, *New York Times* and Wide World Photos; and R. C. Willets, *Miami Daily News* and Acme Newspictures.

Eye-witness stories, dramatic photos, and motion picture films emerged from the heavy coverage, with photos and films moved by plane to Miami and beyond.

In Cuba, with Machado gone, newspapers regained freedom to publish and comment editorially. Political turmoil continued, however, until effective political power was exercised by Fulgencio Batista, who had risen in the army to the rank of colonel and became its commander-in-chief.

Violence, never far beneath the surface, sometimes erupted. Joseph Gibson, newly arrived for the *Chicago Daily News* and Universal Newsreel, was wounded in a Havana skirmish in September 1933, and AP photographer George Skadding was endangered. Pettey, of the *New York Herald Tribune,* was in danger in another action, and Francis P. Malone and Ralph Willets, both of the *Miami Daily News,* narrowly escaped a firing squad.

Mexico and Central America

Mexico and the Central American states, technically part of North America, received attention in the press of the United States. Mexican elections in August 1920 established General Alvaro Obregón as president, and he was inaugurated on December 1 for a four-year term. General Plutarco Elías Calles, former chief of the cabinet to Obregón, was elected to succeed him in the presidency in 1924-28. Obregón was re-elected, but was assassinated in 1928 before assuming office. The Congress then selected Emilio Portes Gil, minister of the interior, as provisional president. He served until February 1930, when Pascual Ortiz Rubio, elected in November 1929, was inaugurated. In September 1932, halfway through his term, Rubio and his cabinet resigned, with General Abelardo L. Rodriguez chosen by election to complete the term. Lázaro Cárdenas, a member of two previous cabinets and a Calles nominee, was elected and inaugurated in 1934 to serve a six-year term, as provided in a 1933 constitutional amendment. He was succeeded in 1940 by General Manuel Avila Camacho.

All of these administrations from 1920 were devoted largely to efforts intended to correct economic and social problems within the country, stemming largely from the long dictatorial regime of Porfirio Diaz, 1877-80 and 1884-1911. During those years resources of the country had been permitted to pass into foreign control. The nation's finances were in extremely poor condition, and many of the people were living in poverty.

Efforts to correct these matters brought legislation and action affecting established interests within the country, and the changes within Mexico were revolutionary. These events through the years drew more correspondents than ever before, and the Mexican press itself inevitably was affected.

Regulations were established to protect Mexican oil resources from exploitation by foreign companies. Similar regulations were applied to foreign holders of mining concessions. Foreign land owners were required to dispose of most of their properties as part of a program of land distribution to benefit the people of Mexico, especially in the advancement of agriculture. To meet objections by the affected persons and companies, certain compromises were reached short of outright confiscation.[3]

A major element in the revolution related to a reduction in the power long exercised in the country by the Catholic Church. Despite protests at home and abroad, church property was nationalized, education was taken out of church control, and non-Mexican priests, monks, and nuns were ordered deported.

To supplant church domination of education, a system of free public schools administered by the state was introduced. This included a plan for the reduction of illiteracy among adults as well. Plutarco Elías Calles, already teaching school at Guaymas in 1898, established a newsaper, *El Siglo II,* intended to combat ignorance among the Indians and mestizos. It was almost a first step on the way to a remarkable increase in literacy within the nation, which rose from an estimated 15 per cent during the Díaz regime to 37 per cent in 1927, when Calles himself was president, and was 55 per cent by 1938. This, of course, created a growing audience for a growing press.

Measures were introduced to improve working conditions and wages, to provide agricultural land for individuals, to improve health, nutrition, and sanitation, to advance law and order, and to improve transportation and communication. Efforts were made to establish a realistic tax situation, to place the currency and banking system on a sound basis, and to clarify the national and international budgetary, debt, and monetary procedures. All of this added up to a highly ambitious program, which did not proceed without difficulties, but Mexico was in a far better position by 1940 than it had ever been before, and the people were benefitted.

The press of Mexico, although existing in some form since the seventeenth century, had been of small value in advancing the interests or

---

3   More than 90 per cent of Mexico's oil reserves had been controlled by U.S. and British interests. Among foreign property owners, U.S. Senator George Hearst had purchased 200,000 acres in northern Mexico for twenty cents an acre in the 1880s, and this became the Babicora cattle ranch, near Chihuahua. His son, William Randolph Hearst, later acquired another ranch near Campeche, on the Yucatan Peninsula and, along with his mother, Phoebe Apperson Hearst, prior to her death in 1919, also had mining, timber, oil holdings, and chicle property in Mexico. Altogether, the properties were worth millions, and more millions had been put into their development. So long as the Díaz regime continued to 1911, there were no problems for any of the foreign interests, but this began to change in the Carranza period in 1914. By 1930 the Hearst interests had been disposed of at a fraction of their value. The fact that his newspapers had published a series of stories in November–December of 1927 based upon what proved to be forged documents obtained through bribery, and purporting to demonstrate conspiracies by the Mexican government disadvantageous to the United States, did not help Hearst's position in that country.

understanding of the people so long as most of them were illiterate or unable to buy papers. The first newspaper to attain prominence was *El Noticioso,* established in Mexico City in 1894 by Angel Pola. It continued only until 1897. A second paper of greater potential was *El Imparcial,* established as a morning daily in the capital in 1896 by Rafael Reyes Spíndola, already recognized as an able journalist. It became the semi-official organ of the Díaz regime and of his Científico party, and received a government subsidy. This made it possible to sell the paper at two centavos a copy instead of the more usual six centavos, and helped win it a considerable circulation. A paper of some quality stressing news but also providing editorial comment, it is regarded as having marked the beginning of modern journalism in Mexico. Spíndola also established a companion afternoon paper, *El Mundo,* soon retitled *El Heraldo.*

In 1908 Díaz granted an interview to James Creelman, correspondent for the Hearst newspapers. Published in *Pearson's Magazine* of New York, the interview has been cited as a factor in bringing that long dictatorship to an end three years later. Díaz told Creelman that Mexico was ready for democratic government, that he would welcome an opposition party, and would relinquish his power to a legally elected candidate. So it was that Francisco Madero became a candidate in 1910, and was elected. Even then, he was able to assume office in 1911 only by armed military support, with Díaz going into exile in Paris, where he died in 1915.

Madero had promised liberty of the press, if elected. The leading newspapers, all in Mexico City, were Spíndola's *El Imparcial* and *El Heraldo, El Diario, El Pais,* and the *Mexican Herald.* The latter was the third English-language daily to be attempted in Mexico City, and the first to succeed. It had a good circulation, considerable advertising volume, and shared an AP service of 10,000 words a day with *El Imparcial.* Most papers stressed local news, with illustrations, along with editorials, all on page one, with some reports of foreign affairs on inside pages. The *Herald,* however, presented both world news and local news on page one, with business and agricultural news and interviews inside.

A disturbed period of change began for Mexico with the Madero election in 1910. Madero added his own newspaper, *Nueva Era,* and his government started or backed others. The Madero regime was ended in 1913, however, when he was killed following a revolt led by Victoriano Huerta.

Except for *El Independiente,* established in 1911 by members of the wealthy Braniff family seeking to obtain the presidency for one of their own kin, most other papers gave support to Huerta. He seized control in February 1913 and was formally elected in July 1914, but resigned almost immediately with the landing of U.S. military forces at Vera Cruz, and a refusal of the United States to recognize his government.[4]

Already opposed by General Alvaro Obregón, as well as by Venustiano Carranza, with Francisco (Pancho) Villa as his military aide, Huerta was forced out. Carranza became president. A civil war followed, with Carranza opposed by Villa. Carranza was confirmed in office in August 1915, however, and was formally elected in March 1917.

Carranza had echoed Madero in professions of friendship for the press. He did in fact support the drafting of a new and more liberal constitution, to become effective in 1917. Meanwhile, however, the complexion of the press had changed. The Carranza forces, in conflict with the Huerta government, had seized the plant of *El Imparcial* and issued from its presses a paper called *El Mexicano;* the seized *El Pais* plant produced *El Demócrata.* The *Mexican Herald,* transferred to Vera Cruz during the occupation of that city by U.S. forces in April 1914 and through the period of disorder following, was ordered by the Carranza government to cease publication altogether.

Once established in Mexico City, the Carranza regime permitted other former papers to resume. The newer *El Demócrata* continued, and the administration established another paper, *El Pueblo.* In 1916, Félix Palavicini retired as minister of public instruction and founded *El Universal* as a morning paper in the capital. It gained considerable following and influence, largely because of Palavicini's editorials. A critical reference to the government in April 1917 brought a temporary forced suspension. In May 1918 it again caused offense and Palavicini, who received death threats, sold the paper and left the country until after the end of World War I.

Wartime German propaganda efforts were strongly advanced in Mexico during the 1914–18 period, and the Mexican government itself tended to favor the Central Powers. Palavicini's forced departure and the sale of his newspaper, which had been friendly to the Allied cause, were not unrelated to this situation. *El Universal* came under German influence. *El Demócrata* and *El Pueblo,* both with government support, were friendly to the Central Powers. *El Pueblo,* although professing neutrality, was notably hostile to the United States. A new Mexico City morning newspaper, *Excelsior,* started in 1917 by Rafael Alducín, became the strongest pro-Allied paper in the country.

Freedom of expression, including press freedom, assured by the constitution of 1917, still did not make the papers independent of

---

4 See Robert W. Desmond, *Windows on the World,* pp. 257–60.

economic pressures or of restrictions placed upon them by presidential fiat. A government decree of April 12, 1917, established a press law in which a prohibition was placed on "malicious expressions calculated to excite hatred of the authorities, the army, the national guard, or the fundamental institutions of the country." It also forbade publication of news "detrimental to the public good." It was by government interpretation of this law that *El Universal,* for one, had been temporarily closed in April 1917, and under which warnings were issued that forced Palavicini to sell the paper and depart a year later.

Carranza was killed in May 1920 during the internal struggle for power. He was succeeded by General Obregón, who was elected president in September. There then were four dailies of some importance in Mexico City. *Excelsior* was regarded as the best. *El Universal,* having changed its ownership again, was well conducted. The others were *El Demócrata* and *El Pueblo.* Alducín, editor and publisher of *Excelsior,* was killed in a fall from a horse in March 1924, and control of the paper passed to his widow. Having been owned and operated by an employees' cooperative, it became a privately conducted enterprise, although with employees still sharing in the profits, and was continued successfully under the direction of Gilberto Figueroa.

El Universal attained circulation leadership in the 1920s. An afternoon edition, *El Universal Grafico,* was added in 1922. The management of both papers was in the hands of Miguel and Fernanda Lanz Duret, who also were to inherit control of the papers from their father, Miguel Lanz Duret, Sr., upon his death in 1940. The Duret name became prominently identified with the Inter-American Press Association, formed to support the development and maintenance of a free and professional press in Latin America.

Two new papers appeared in Mexico City in the 1920s. *La Prensa* was established in 1928 as a morning daily and an employees' cooperative venture. Directed by Luis Navaro, it soon attained a considerable circulation as a popular-type paper. The second was *El Nacional,* established in 1929 as a government-owned national morning daily to present official information. *El Pueblo* and *El Demócrata,* both originally government-supported, lost ground and were suspended.

The revolutionary events of the 1920s placed pressure on the newspapers. In October 1927 three journalists were charged with aiding a military revolt against the Calles government and were deported. They were José Elguero, chief editorial writer for *Excelsior,* Victoriano Salada Alvarez of the same newspaper, and Félix Palavicini, founder of *El Universal.* He again returned after this second action against him and became an active participant in the Pan-American Press Congress of 1942, from which was to emerge the Inter-American Press Association.

A regional press, "the papers of the states," had existed along with those of Mexico City. These weeklies' and dailies' real growth began after 1917. Most were small in size, emphasizing local news and circulating locally. The largest in the 1920s was *El Informador* of Guadalajara, a morning daily established in 1917. Other dailies included *El Dictaman* of Vera Cruz (1898), *La Opinion,* Torreon (1917), *El Mundo,* Tampico (1918), *La Opinion,* Puebla (1924), *El Correo de Parral,* Parral (1922), *El Noroeste,* Nogales (1926), *El Porvenir* (1919) and *El Sol* (1922), both of Monterrey, the *Diario de Yucatan,* Merida (1912), *El Demócrata,* Mazatlan (1919), *El Continental,* Juarez (1925), *La Gaceta,* Guaymas (1915), and *El Heraldo,* Chihuahua (1927).

Prior to 1935 governments at various levels in Mexico often imposed restrictions on criticism of officials and policies. These restrictions sometimes took the form of threats or even open physical attacks. The ethical standards of the press were not uniformly high, libel laws were lax, and newspapers were in some cases subject to coercion or persuasion by private interests, organizations, or advertisers.

Beginning in 1935, when Lázaro Cardenas was president, there began a period of relative freedom of expression. The national government retained the power under the Press Law of 1917, however, to close a newspaper, but Cardenas took an easier line. Publishers and editors were requested to exercise a voluntary censorship in matters holding possible danger to public order or national security, or occurring in time of crisis. He sometimes called press representatives to the National Palace for conferences at which he requested a policy of restraint on particular subjects.

The government at this period undertook an active program designed to present its policy to the press and people in a favorable light. Officials even talked to children in the schools in the expectation that something of what was said would be conveyed to parents in the home. The official newspaper *El Nacional* was used to disseminate policy views to government employees and officials at all levels, and it was wise for them to receive the paper, whether they read it or not. A government press department was formed, known as the DAPP (Autonomous Department of Press and Publicity), to produce and disseminate government news. In practice, much of it possessed little news value and often was heavy in propaganda content.

Since there was no national news agency in Mexico, the government joined with the Agence Havas in 1935 in forming an Agencia Noticiosa Telegráfica Americana (ANTA) in Mexico City. This Havas subsidiary was semi-official in character and was financed by the Mexican government. It distributed a world service provided by Havas, plus national news prepared by agency staff members. There was some expectation that ANTA might become the first indigenous Latin American news agency operating throughout the hemisphere. When the Havas agency was forced to suspend in June 1940, following the German occupation of Paris and most of France, ANTA turned to Reuters for a world service. This was continued until 1943 and then suspended.

The relative freedom of the 1930s brought new papers into existence in Mexico, both in the capital and in other cities. One of the first, and a departure from the general newspapers, was a morning sports daily, *La Afición*. It was established in Mexico City in 1930 and gained considerable circulation. Among papers stressing current news in Mexico City, *Novedades* began as a morning daily in 1935, established by Ignacio F. Herrerías. It gained quick acceptance as a popular paper and became a circulation leader. Herrarías also established a comic weekly, *Chamaco Chico* (Little Boy Chico), in September 1936. It was the first comic book to use Mexican talent and themes, and became so successful that it was converted in October 1939 into a daily comic magazine.[5] Substantial profits from this publication contributed to the improvement of *Novedades* itself.

Another new morning daily established in 1936 was *El Popular,* the first important labor paper, founded by Lombardo Toledano and conducted by the Confederation of Mexican Workers (Confederacion de Trabajadores de Mexico). In that same year an afternoon edition of *Excelsior* was established, *Ultimas Noticias de Excelsior.* Both papers were directed by Rodrigo de Llano.

Supported by the advanced educational standards and the higher literacy rate in the country, the major newspapers showed enterprise in building circulation and advertising volume. Even from the period of the 1920s, some resembled leading U.S. dailies in content, typography, and general makeup, including also larger Sunday editions with a variety of special features. Emphasis on news increased, as contrasted to editorial expression, in what amounted to an acceptance of a U.S. newspaper pattern distinct from the Paris and general European press pattern. This was accompanied by a growing use of world news reports received from the U.S. news agencies.

The events of the 1920s and 1930s made Mexico City a far more important news center than it had been earlier, and a center also for the coverage of the republics of Central America. Something has been said of representatives of the U.S. press in Mexico City in the 1914–20 period. There also were staff and stringer correspondents for the

---

5   A precedent existed in *Le Charivari,* a daily publication known for its lithographic political and social cartoons and caricatures conducted by Charles Philipon in Paris in 1832-37. It was a direct inspiration for the British magazine *Punch, or the London Charivari,* established in 1841. Philipon also established *Le Journal pour rire,* a daily, in 1848. Honoré Daumier and Paul Gustav Doré were among his contributing artists.

Havas and Reuters agencies. UP and INS representation was added to that of the AP by 1920, or soon after.

As in some other capitals, it was not uncommon for correspondents to maintain close relations with locally published newspapers, often including payment for the right to receive carbon copies or galley proofs of their reporters' stories in advance of publication, as well as rental of working space in such a newspaper office as an added convenience. In the 1930s the Reuters office was in the *La Prensa* building, AP was in the *Excelsior* building, UP in that occupied by *El Universal,* and INS was in the *Novedades* building.

Correspondents assigned to Mexico City in the 1920–40 decades were almost exclusively representatives of the U.S. press organization. The group in Mexico City at various intervals within those years included John Lloyd, John P. McKnight, John Evans, Rafael Ordorica, Fred Krieg, Theodore A. Ediger, and Larry Stuntz for the Associated Press. For the United Press there were Clarence DuBose, Ralph H. Turner, Jacques d'Armand, and John R. Morris. For the International News Service, there were Richard C. Wilson, William Flythe, and Pierre J. Huss.

Newspaper representation included Raymond Daniell, Frank L. Kluckhohn, Arnaldo Cortesi, John W. White, and Harold Norman Denny for the *New York Times,* Jack Starr Hunt for the *New York Herald Tribune* and the *Wall Street Journal,* Betty Kirk and Elizabeth Fagg for the *Christian Science Monitor,* John T. Whitaker and Carroll Binder for the *Chicago Daily News,* and John Cornyn, Frederick Wright, George Seldes, and John Clayton for the *Chicago Tribune.*

Some of these correspondents had been or would be on assignments in South America, Asia, or Europe, and some held broad executive authority. They worked under difficulties in Mexico at times because of emotional reactions to events both in that country and in the United States. For that reason, the general quality of reports occasionally suffered. Two notable series of reports were produced in the mid-1920s, however, by visiting journalists Tom Wallace of the *Louisville Times* and by magazine writer Lincoln Steffens. They wrote of Mexico for the North American Newspaper Alliance, and for their work were made honorary life members of the Foreign Correspondents Club of Mexico City.

With the Mexican press itself freer, the government also asserted that earlier censorship on news transmission had been ended. This was not necessarily so, for correspondents occasionally discovered that a certain page of copy had been unaccountably "lost" or that words had become so smudged that the telegraph operator "could not read them." They found that information available through government channels had little value and that even "original sources" were not always reliable. They therefore questioned nearly every report reaching them.

The Central American countries—Guatemala, Honduras, British Honduras (now Belize), Salvador, Nicaragua, and Costa Rica—were reported by stringers for the most part. The volume of news was small and of a routine nature, but when events justified it resident correspondents in Mexico City moved to the scene. An insurrection and political unrest in Nicaragua between 1925 and 1939, with U.S. military forces landing there in 1926 and remaining for several years, represented a special case and received heavier and more consistent coverage.

Stringer coverage, augmented when justified, also applied to such U.S. territories as Puerto Rico and the Virgin Islands, to Haiti and the Dominican Republic, Jamaica and the other West Indian islands, the Antilles, the Bahamas, and Bermuda.

South America in a Changing Context   9

As World War I ended, the thirteen republics of South America were about to enter upon a new period in their history. All had close ties with Europe because of three centuries of a colonial relationship with Spain or, in the case of Brazil, with Portugal. As in the United States, they had received immigrants from many European countries. British and French capital had helped to build railroads and business enterprises, to extend cables and telegraph lines, to support agricultural development, and to provide ocean transport. Europe provided a major market for products of the continent, and Paris was a favored educational and cultural center for the more prosperous South Americans. The United States also had made contributions toward the development of the continent.

The events of the war and its divisions were keenly felt socially, economically, and politically in the Southern Hemisphere. Most of the countries preserved their neutrality. When the United States entered the war in 1917, Cuba and Panama also declared war on Germany and later on Austria. They were followed in 1918 by Guatemala, Nicaragua, Costa Rica, Haiti, and Honduras. In South America itself, Bolivia was the first to declare war in 1917. It was followed by Brazil, which also sent naval and air units into action, while Peru, Uruguay, and Ecuador broke diplomatic relations with Germany. These actions meant that all of those countries later became members of the League of Nations.

The role of the French Agence Havas in the provision of news to the growing press of South America since 1860, and the returning of a news report from there, had been an element in those European ties. The Reuters agency had a part in that relationship between 1870 and 1890. The press of South America not unnaturally tended to follow a style and pattern characteristic of the European continent, which was basically that of Paris itself, with some adaptations from the press of London. This only began to change after 1918, when the United Press, the Associated Press, and the International News Service, all U.S.

agencies, began to serve the South American newspaper press. This broader exposure was accentuated by the extension of radiotelegraphic service between North and South America in the 1920s and the beginning both of radiotelephonic service and commercial airline service in the 1930s. Buenos Aires became the major news center in South America. Events there and in the other capitals and countries in the 1920–40 period warrant special attention.

Argentina

The people of Argentina were well served by the press of that country in the 1920s and 1930s. Buenos Aires, the capital, was the most literate center on the continent. Its two morning dailies, *La Prensa* and *La Nación,* were among the quality papers of the world and models for the Latin American press in general.

Like most of the South American republics, Argentina operated under a constitution patterned after that of the United States, including assurance of a free press. Like most of the countries, it had proceeded without major troubles for several decades. There had been increasingly persistent complaints in Argentina after about 1900, however, that the national elections were not free or fairly conducted, and that the great land-owning families were dominant, with the middle classes and workers at a disadvantage. Calls for reform led to the organization of a new political party to represent the less-favored. This was the Unión Cívica Radical, or U.C.R. By 1912, also, a new law provided for a secret ballot and even imposed a fine on any person who failed to vote without a satisfactory excuse. The first free election took place under the new law in 1916, with a record ballot cast. The U.C.R. candidate, Hipólito Irogoyen, was elected president and served a constitutional six-year term. In 1922 another U.C.R. candidate, Dr. Marcelo T. de Alvear, was elected and also served his six-year term. In the election of 1928, Irogoyen, again the U.C.R. candidate, was returned for a second term.

The families of wealth and property, who had lost control of the government to the U.C.R. since 1916, formed a new party after 1928, the Partido Demócracia Nacional (P.D.N.). This group staged a *coup d'état* in September 1930 that forced Irogoyen out of office, ending fourteen years of U.C.R. control, and put the conservative P.D.N. representative, José Felix Uriburu, into the Casa Rosada, the Argentine equivalent of the White House. The U.C.R. was subsequently ruled ineligible to enter candidates for the presidency.

Uriburu began as provisional president. On the day he took office, September 6, 1930, a decree abridged civil liberties and a censorship was made effective on telegraph and cable communications. Persons believed in opposition to the new administration were subject to arrest. The press was placed under supervision, and no newspaper was to publish anything of a political nature without prior approval from the prefect of police, who was himself under the authority of the minister of the interior. On that same day, *La Razón* of Buenos Aires, a highly regarded afternoon paper, was suspended.

The censorship was made effective by requiring communications companies in Argentina to bear the responsibility for whatever passed over their facilities. Nothing "alarming or sensational" was to be transmitted, and nothing that might be deemed unfriendly or unfavorable to the new Uriburu government. The companies were made subject to fines or loss of their right to operate. This was a new form of indirect censorship.[1] It left the government technically blameless for any restriction on foreign press coverage of the Argentine situation.

The Western Telegraph Company, a British enterprise, Western Union, All-America Cables, and RCAC, all of the United States, along with French and Italian companies then in South Atlantic communication, felt obliged to protect their own positions. Uncertain as to what the government might find objectionable, they tended to lean over backward to prevent transmission of matter that, by the remotest interpretation, might give offense. In practice, this censorship continued for a week, but was reinstituted in the summer of 1931, with formal notification to the companies through the director of Posts and Telegraph.

The Uriburu government in taking control overlooked the fact that radiotelephonic service had recently become operative between Buenos Aires and New York. The *New York Times* failed to hear from its correspondent John H. White in the Argentine capital and had reason to believe something was wrong because of prior reports of a rebellion against the Irogoyen government. Frederick T. Birchall, acting managing editor, suggested that Harold Denny,[2] formerly in Mexico and Cuba for the paper but then in the New York office, take advantage of the new radiotelephonic service. Denny put through a call to Buenos Aires and was able to reach an editor of *La Nación*. He learned from him details of the rebels' capture of Government House, and Uriburu's assumption of power. This gave the *Times* an exclusive

---

1 This means of using the communications companies as the indirect agents for censorship was borrowed for use by the Nationalist government of China early in 1931.

2 Not to be confused with George Denny of the AP, chiefly in China and Japan.

story, published under the unprecedented credit line, "From a Special Correspondent of The New York Times, by Wireless Telephone," followed by the Buenos Aires dateline.

The AP, UP, and INS, as well as the *New York Times,* used the radiotelephone for several successive days, with Denny even talking with President Uriburu on one call. The calls were made from New York to Buenos Aires, to avoid alerting the government sooner than necessary that it had failed to extend its censorship control to the new facility. It was the first major use of the radiotelephone for news purposes, at a cost of about $10 a minute. Within three or four days, the telephone channel was placed under censorship.

Uriburu continued as provisional president from September 1930 until February 1932. The indirect censorship was maintained through communications companies, and press restraints became more frequent. Two Socialist papers of Buenos Aires, *La Vanguardia* and *Socialiste Independente,* were closed for a time. The popular afternoon paper *La Crítica,* of more than 350,000 circulation and the largest in all of Latin America, was stopped in June 1931. Its plant was seized and the director of the paper and his wife, the advertising director, some members of the news and editorial staff, and a member of the circulation department were imprisoned. As with *La Razón* in 1930, the paper was permitted to resume with its staff a month later. Again suppressed, it resumed once more in August under a new name, *La Jornada.*

Even *La Prensa,* conservative as it was, came under fire for printing what were regarded as critical references to the Uriburu administration without submitting them in advance for examination by the prefect of police. Uriburu threatened to suppress the paper. Dr. Ezequiel Pedro Paz, its director since 1898, gave Uriburu to understand that in such case he would move the paper to Paris, publish there, and let it be known that it had become impossible to print the truth in Argentina. Moreover, he said, he would continue to criticize the Uriburu government when and as he saw fit. That was the last *La Prensa* heard of any threat at that time.

La Prensa was conducted in those years by Don Ezequiel and by Dr. Alberto Gainza ("Tito") Paz, his nephew and a grandson of the founder. Don Ezequiel was childless, and by Argentine law his only sister shared equally in the ownership of the paper founded by their father. She was Doña Zelmira Paz de Anchorena, the mother of Gainza Paz. The Anchorena family held great estates and was among the estimated 2,000 families sometimes said to own Argentina. From the late 1920s, Don Ezequiel had prepared Gainza Paz to direct the paper, and he became codirector in 1934 when Don Ezequiel began to spend about half of each year on a French estate near Biarritz.

The other great quality newspaper of Buenos Aires, *La Nación,* was directed at the time of World War I by Don Jorge Mitre, grandson of that paper's founder. He was followed by his sons, Dr. Luis Mitre and Emilio Mitre, sharing ownership with fifteen members of yet another of the great families of Argentina.

La Nación in 1914 was the first Latin American newspaper to name a resident correspondent in the United States. He was William Willis Davies, an Australian newsman formerly with the *Melbourne Argus,* then in London for the Australian Consolidated Press, and also a representative for *La Nación* before transferring to New York in 1914. There he remained to write for what became the Australian Associated Press, as well as for *La Nación* and other Latin American papers. *La Nación* also received reports from New York from Albert Caprile, Jr.

In the postwar years, both *La Prensa* and *La Nación* had resident correspondents in Paris, London, and some other European centers. Both newspapers were recognized internationally for their high quality, and *La Prensa* was cited in 1930 in the first University of Missouri Honor Awards for Distinguished Service in Journalism. In 1939 the paper received the Maria Moors Cabot Award established for journalism advancing friendship and understanding in the Western Hemisphere by the Trustees of Columbia University in New York as a kind of international parallel to the domestic Pulitzer Prize awards. Cabot awards later went to Dr. Luis Mitre of *La Nación* in 1942, and in 1943 to Angel Bohigas, subdirector of that paper.

Wherever published, most of the Argentine papers were well written and sober in subject matter. Even what might have the appearance of entertainment features tended to be more serious and on a level higher than much that appeared at the time in British, European, and North American papers. This was especially true of Sunday supplements with *La Prensa* and *La Nación.* At the same time, those papers added what were known in North America as comic strips and colored Sunday comic supplements, some produced by Argentine artists and combined with material obtained from North American syndicates, the text translated into Spanish.

Journalists in Argentina generally belonged to a national press association, the Circulo de la Prensa, with headquarters in Buenos Aires. Its membership included nearly every editor, as well as staff members of newspapers and periodicals. Quite independent of the government, it acted to protect the welfare of journalists throughout the country, as well as the press and press freedom in general. It offered free medical, dental, hospital, funeral, and legal services to members and their families.

In his relationship with the press, Uriburu generally tried to stay within the provisions of the constitution, in which Article 32 assured its liberty. That constitution required no parliamentary action, however, for the executive branch of the government to place a control on outgoing news reports, and it afforded no protection to foreign correspondents in Buenos Aires.

Taking office on a provisional basis, Uriburu was obligated to call a new general election, but delayed it until November 1931. General Agustin P. Justo was elected and assumed office in February 1932 for a full six-year term. Most recently commander of the army, Justo had held cabinet posts in the government since the 1920s, and he headed what actually was a conservative coalition administration. He had been a member of the board of directors of *La Crítica*. One of his first acts was to restore civil liberties in the country, and that newspaper was thus enabled to resume publication under its own name, rather than as *La Jornada*.

Economic and political conditions in Argentina became difficult after 1930, as in many other countries. The first hopes of the Justo regime, based upon restoration of civil liberties, faded as the world depression advanced, and before he left office in 1938 the administration had become more dictatorial than that briefer regime under Uriburu.

Brazil

The largest and most populous country of Latin America, Brazil differed from the others in that its European heritage and language was Portuguese, rather than Spanish. A republic since 1889, when Emperor Dom Pedro II adbicated, it had been the only Latin American country directly involved in World War I, with naval forces engaged and pilots flying in France. Among its forty million people in about 1930, beyond those of Portuguese descent, were elements of Italian, German, Japanese, and Russian origin, descendants of African slaves freed in 1888, and native Indians. The national literacy rate stood at about 50 per cent, but was substantially higher in the cities.

The country had been beset by economic difficulties just after the war, leading to disorders and some violence in 1922, and the problems were made worse by the general world economic depression of the 1930s.

Press development began early in Brazil, with the *Diário de Pernambuco* established at Recifé in 1825. Rio de Janeiro became the first center in the new world for the French Agence Havas in 1860, and the first South Atlantic cable was landed at Recifé in 1874. Among the important dailies in Brazil at the time of World War I and after were *O Pais,* the *Jornal do Comercio,* the *Jornal do Brazil,* and the *Correio da Manhã,* all morning newspapers in Rio de Janeiro, with *A Noticia* in the afternoon. In São Paulo, the chief commercial center, *O Estado de São Paulo* was a leading morning paper, with the *Diario Popular, A Gazeta,* and the German-language *Deutsche Nachrichten* appearing in the afternoon.

The 1920s and 1930s brought the establishment of a number of other papers that gained importance. Among them in Rio de Janeiro were *O Globo,* the *Diário Carioca, O Jornal,* and the *Diário de Noticias.* In growing São Paulo there were no fewer than eight new papers, *Folha da Manhã, Folha da Noite, Diário da Noite,* the *Diário de São Paulo,* the *Jornal do São Paulo,* the *Diário da Comercio,* the *Gazeta Mercantil* and the *Diário do Comercio e Industria.*

The press of Brazil, as with other countries in Latin America, had depended upon the Agence Havas for its world service and continued to do so. During the war years, however, it also began to receive service from the United Press and the Associated Press, and later from International News Service. It also had used reports by Brazilian journalists traveling in Europe. One who provided such reports shortly after the war was Francisco Assis Chateaubriand Bandiera de Mello, then about thirty, and known more simply as Assis Chateaubriand, or "Chatô."

Chateaubriand became an important figure in Brazilian and world journalism after 1928, when he began the development of a group of daily newspapers known as the Diários Associados. With its headquarters in Rio de Janeiro, the group by 1938 included fifteen dailies, three magazines, two radio stations, and a news service, the Agencia Meridional, Ltda., formed in 1931 to provide news and feature material exclusively to the associated newspapers and radio stations. The group grew far larger after 1940.[3] Its major newspapers included *O Jornal* and the *Diário da Noite* of Rio de Janeiro, the *Diário da Noite* of São Paulo, and Brazil's oldest paper, the *Diário de Pernambuco* of Recifé. Chateaubriand became a member of Brazil's senate, and also served as ambassador to Great Britain. He and his Diarios Associados received recognition in a Columbia University Maria Moors Cabot award in 1945.

Another highly regarded Brazilian daily was the *Correio da Manhã* of Rio de Janeiro. Established in 1901 by Edmundo Bittencourt, it was owned and directed after 1930 by his son, Dr. Paulo Bittencourt. Silvia de Bittencourt, his wife, was one of the very few women jour-

---

3 The Chateaubriand group was the only one of such size outside the United States until after 1950, when Canadian-born Roy Thomson (Lord Thomson of Fleet) formed an international media group.

nalists in the country and conducted a popular column of comment and information signed "Majoy." The paper and its owners each received Maria Moors Cabot awards in 1941.

The Brazilian press was more fully represented abroad after World War I than that of any other country in Latin America. Such coverage was chiefly in Europe, and primarily in Paris.

Political troubles, and troubles for the press of Brazil, began in May 1930 following a bitterly contested campaign for the presidency. Julio Prestes, who had been governor of São Paulo state, one of twenty-two in the republic, received a heavy majority vote to succeed Washington Luis Pereira de Souza. Running second was Getulio Vargas, governor of Rio Grande do Sul state, the Liberal party candidate. Charges of fraud and other considerations left a considerable dissatisfaction over the outcome of the election, and a revolt began in October. This had the result of establishing Vargas in office as provisional president, supported by an army and navy group.

Vargas began what was to be a fifteen-year period of administration to 1945. Asserting the need to maintain order in the disturbed country, he took dictatorial action, suspending civil rights, naming his own appointees to key positions, and sponsoring a variety of actions intended to restore the economy.

The results were not immediately apparent. The deteriorating world economic conditions brought down the market price of coffee, so important to Brazil. There was rioting and violence in the country in 1931 and 1932, leading to even tighter controls, a revision of the constitution, and dissolution of the legislative Chamber of Deputies.

All of this had an adverse effect upon the national press, depriving it of a traditional freedom and eventually reducing it to a rubber-stamp status. The troubles drew foreign correspondents to the country, but their work was difficult.

The original revolt of October 1930 was not easy to report because incidents occurred in places widely separated, and because a censorship was imposed on outgoing news dispatches. The rebel group was strongest in Vargas's home state, Rio Grande do Sul. Supporting his program, it was interested in having its successes made known to the world. For that reason, correspondents based at Porto Alegre, the provincial capital, were well treated and were able to get news out uncensored through Montevideo and Buenos Aires, the Uruguayan and Argentine capitals, both relatively close at hand. The central area of Brazil was covered from Rio de Janeiro and São Paulo, and the northern area from Recifé and Bahia.

As rebels identified with the Liberal party supporting Vargas seized control of the government, mobs in various cities entered the offices of fifty or sixty newspapers that had opposed the revolution and inflicted great damage on some. The worst and most spectacular harm was done to *A Noite* in Rio de Janeiro. Its magnificent twenty-four story building, the tallest in South America at the time, was invaded on the morning of October 24 by hundreds of men who did millions of dollars damage to offices and equipment. Private offices in the building did not escape. The United Press office, on the fifth floor, was spared when a U.S. flag was hung at the door, even as staff members hastened to remove files, documents, and portable articles to safeguard them. The office of the publisher of *A Noite,* Geraldo Rocha, was sacked, and Ismael Maia, the manager, was roughly treated. The mob tried to burn the building and also to flood it by turning on all water faucets, breaking pipes, and blocking drains.

Six other Rio de Janeiro dailies also suffered mob vandalism. They were *O Pais, A Noticia, Vanguarda, Critica, A Ordem,* and the *Gazeta de Noticias.* Some, trying to salvage newsprint, had the rolls seized, unwound, burned, or wet down with fire hoses. All seven of these papers were obliged to suspend publication pending repairs.

In São Paulo, six dailies were forced to close temporarily because of mob action. They were *Folha da Manhã, A Gazeta, O Combate, Corriero Paulistano, Fanfulla il Piccolo,* an Italian-language paper, and *Deutsche Nachrichten,* the German-language paper. In nearby Santos, *A Tribuna* also was forced to close. There was some doubt at the time as to how many of the newspapers would be able to resume publication, or even be permitted to do so. Newspapers spared by the rioters usually had at least a temporary increase in circulation as the only sources of public information available.

Dictatorial measures used by the Vargas government included strict control over the national press and a strong censorship affecting the work of foreign correspondents. The radio, then becoming important, was likewise under government control. Instructions were issued to the national press and radio and to foreign correspondents late in 1931 establishing eleven prohibitions, violations of which made a journalist subject to arrest and imprisonment for at least twenty-four hours for a first offense, and for an unspecified period for any later offense.

The regulations forbade: (1) blank spaces in newspapers, indicating omission of material censored; (2) references to disturbances of the public order, or threats of such disturbances; (3) news of the movement of military or police forces, except when officially provided; (4) interviews or statements tending "to interfere with government action, to endanger public safety, or to disturb the national economy"; (5) any reference to internal or foreign Communist activities; (6) news and comment bearing upon the financial policy of the government or the economic situation that might harm the national credit position; (7) publication of statements by political exiles that would in any way affect the good relations of Brazil with other nations, or that might disturb internal public order; (8) news and comment on the possibility of certain states seceding from the union; (9) news and comments on internal class difficulties, such as labor strikes or disturbances in factories; (10) news and comment capable of causing unrest among the army and navy ranks, or of producing unsympathetic feeling among such personnel, or between them and the people; (11) news, comments, and editorials capable of provoking scandal—public or private—among government employees, or of shaking confidence in the provisional government.

The government and to some extent the people themselves became sensitive at this period about the manner in which the country was portrayed abroad. There was a concern about anything that might be interpreted as injurious to Brazil. This, of course, affected the work of foreign correspondents.

Censors, operating through the police, tended for a time to be less strict in São Paulo than in Rio de Janeiro. But many were unqualified for their work. Some could scarcely read Portuguese, much less other languages. Correspondents commonly were required to translate their dispatches into Portuguese, or have them translated, which meant delays. Difficulties were compounded when censors disagreed among themselves or were arbitrary in their rulings, going beyond what was injurious in political, economic, or military matters. When they were so uninformed as to make obvious errors, they were possibly supported by equally uninformed superiors.

One victim of such error was George A. Corey, in São Paulo for the *New York Times*. Corey was arrested at his home on December 1, 1931, accused of dispatching news prejudicial to the interests of Brazil, and was sent to Rio de Janeiro and jailed. It developed that the objection was to a story published in the London *Times*. When Corey protested that he had nothing to do with that paper, the chief of police insisted that the *Times* and the *New York Times* were the same, comparable to the Ford Motor Company, as one organization, with offices in various cities. In prison, Corey met Brazilian newspaper publishers and writers held on charges hardly more valid. The United States Embassy intervened in Corey's case, and the Brazilian government, acknowledging no error, agreed to be lenient, provided Corey would leave Brazil immediately.

The Vargas government restrictions were no more acceptable to the established national press than to foreign correspondents. The Brazilian Newspaper Association (Associacao Brasilieria de Imprensa)

(ABI), through its president Herbert Moses, publisher of *O Globo* in Rio de Janeiro, presented a petition to Vargas late in December 1931 requesting that all censorship be abolished. Instead, it actually was tightened later and extended to include mail censorship and regulations to prevent or control the entrance of foreign newspapers and periodicals to Brazil.

Censorship of reports by foreign correspondents remained such that, between 1931 and 1934 in particular, much of the news about events in Brazil reached the rest of the world through Montevideo, Uruguay, a channel through which news of troubled Argentina, to the south, also moved. Some of that news, based upon information available through refugees, exiles, and travelers, inevitably was inaccurate, displeasing the Brazilian government even though itself responsible for the circumstances under which such inaccuracies arose.

In 1934 Vargas was selected by a Constituent Assembly to serve a regular four-year term as president, so ending his provisional status. The year also brought a new constitution under which greater powers were centralized in the national government. This led to further political and press problems in Brazil.

Chile

Chile, linked with Argentina and Brazil in common reference to the "ABC powers" of Latin America, gained early coverage because of its trans-Andes telegraphic connection with Buenos Aires, combined with further telegraph and cable communications on the west coast of the continent. This made it a point through which news flowed to and from some countries of South America and the world. It was the first western center for the expanding Havas service, beginning about 1872, then in association with Reuters.

Chile had a notably free and socially responsible press dating from as early as 1813, and one that became facile both in political and literary expression. Long primarily an opinion press in the continental European tradition, it became more nearly an information press after about 1920. At that period Santiago, the capital, was a key point in the new United Press operation in the western part of South America, with a bureau also at Lima, Peru.

Chile had profited during World War I through the sale of nitrates, but was overtaken almost immediately thereafter by economic difficulties and unemployment. Arturo Alessandri was elected president in 1920, but faced with public discontent he was forced out of office in 1924 in a plot by which a military junta gained control. Returned to office in a second *coup d'état* early in 1925, his program for political and social reform was blocked and he was again forced out and resigned in December. The new president Emiliano Figueroa, equally unsuccessful, remained only briefly in office. He was succeeded by Colonel Carlos Ibañez, a cavalry officer and former minister of war. He served through 1926, was then confirmed in office in a special election in July 1927, and exercised nearly dictatorial power until 1931.

The world economic crisis exacerbated Chile's economic problems after 1930. Riots in July 1931 brought Ibañez's resignation and departure from Chile. Dr. Juan Estaban Montero, elected president in October 1931, was overthrown in a *coup d'état* in June 1932. Another election in October returned Alessandri to the presidency once again. On this occasion, he was able to serve the normal six-year term. Constitutional government was restored, and considerable progress was made in the country, even though unrest continued.

Through the 1920s and 1930s, the Chilean press included some newspapers as progressive as any in South America. *El Mercurio,* since 1827 at Valparaiso, the main seaport, was the oldest existing paper in the country. It had another edition at Santiago from 1900, and a third from 1906 at Antofogasta, a more northerly seaport. Known as the "Mercurio papers," they were all morning dailies, and were well conducted by Agustin and Carlos Edwards. The group also included *Las Ultimas Noticias,* a Santiago noonday paper established there in 1902, *La Segunda,* an afternoon Santiago daily started in 1931, and *La Estrella,* a Valparaiso afternoon paper established in 1921.

Among other dailies, *La Nación,* appearing mornings at Valparaiso since 1885 and with an edition at Santiago since 1917, was published after the war by Carlos Dávila. He was educated in the law and was Chile's ambassador to the United States from 1927–32. He adapted the style and informational emphasis of the U.S. press to his newspapers with great success. Recalled to Chile in 1932, he served at that time as interim president between the time of Montero's overthrow and the election and inauguration of Alessandri. Subsequently, he returned to the United States as an unofficial representative of the government, while also conducting a news service in New York, the Editors Press Service, Inc., with Chilean and other Latin American newspapers as clients.

Three other Santiago papers were *El Diario Ilustrado* (1902), second only to *El Mercurio* in circulation, *La Unión* (1917), a morning daily controlled by the government through a stock company, and *El Imparcial* (1926), an afternoon paper.

The Mercurio papers introduced certain journalistic practices in Chile, and gained success and recognition by so doing. They were departmentalized to some degree even before 1920. Contrary to practice in Argentina and Brazil, this included a society column, also found in some other Chilean papers. It differed from such columns in U.S. newspapers in that a charge was made for items and photos used, and it also included announcements of illness and death.

Early in 1918, Carlos Edwards, publisher of the Mercurio papers, arranged for a representative of the *San Diego Union* (U.S.) to work with the staff of *El Mercurio* in Valparaiso and then in Santiago, and to introduce North American methods into the operation. He supervised changes in the typographical dress of the papers, which began to resemble those of the United States in appearance. A sports page became a regular feature, news of business and finance was increased in volume and departmentalized, and a political column presenting impartial reports of party activities was added. Unusual in Latin America, letters from readers also were given space in a special grouping, regional news coverage was extended, and a concerted program was introduced to increase advertising volume.

Other changes brought the display of telegraphic and world news on page one, in a departure from earlier imitation of the London newspaper practice of using advertising on the first page. Headlines became informative, rather than mere subject-matter labels. Entertaining features were introduced, including translated comic strips obtained through U.S. syndicates. To the Sunday editions were added substantial articles in special sections which were smaller but comparable to those included in *La Prensa* and *La Nación* in Buenos Aires.

Reader response to these innovations by the Mercurio papers was enthusiastic. For example, the changes were extended to the edition in Antofogasta, a city of 60,000 of whom no more than half were literate, and resulted in the paper doubling its circulation within three months, and doubling it again in the nine months following.

Competing papers in the three cities hastened to follow the lead of the Mercurio papers as best they could or lost readers, and some actually ceased to appear. Dávila's *La Nación* in Valparaiso and Santiago was equally progressive and had no problem in keeping pace with the Mercurio papers. The quality of these papers was widely recognized, and *El Mercurio* and Agustin Edwards its publisher received the Maria Moors Cabot award in 1940. *La Nación* and Carlos Dávila received the award in 1941.

The unrest in Chile through the 1920s resulted in certain restrictions on a press formerly as free as any in the Western Hemisphere. Ibañez, president from 1925 through 1931, used his dictatorial powers from 1927 to require newspapers to refrain from comment on public affairs. The press was free again after 1931 in its news function, but felt economic pressures threatening its stability and performance. These included customs duties on imported newsprint and supplies, a sales tax on advertising revenues, and a tax on all salaries. The press appealed to the government to ease this financial drain, expressing fear not only for its freedom but for its very survival. The regulations were not notably changed, however, and the press proceeded under difficulties.

<hr>

Uruguay

Uruguay, the smallest of the South American republics, depended primarily upon agriculture, stock-raising, and meat-packing for income, although it also had mineral and forest resources. With a population approaching two million in 1930, approximately one-third lived in Montevideo, the capital and a seaport. The literacy rate in that city at least was high. Most newspapers were published there in a climate of freedom, although with some restrictions after 1933.

Among the papers, *El Día* (1886), one of the oldest, was regarded as the leader. Owned in the postwar period by Luis Alberto de Hererra, it was edited by José P. Suárez. Other dailies included *El Diario,* an afternoon paper and the largest in circulation, and five morning papers, *La Tribune Popular, La Mañana, El Pais, El Débate* and *La Gaceta Comercial,* a business paper. Two other afternoon papers were *El Imparcial* and *El Plata.* All received world news reports from the Agence Havas and from U.S. agencies, while two, *El Día* and *El Diario,* had resident correspondents in Paris and Berlin.

With political disorders and censorships in neighboring Argentina and Brazil, Montevideo became a listening post for both countries, a haven for some of their journalists, and a point through which their news sometimes was cleared as a means of avoiding censorship. Protests from those governments induced caution on the part of the Uruguayan government.

Uruguay could not escape the influences of the world economic decline after 1930. With Gabriel Terra as president in 1931, the national unrest brought a shift in government policy from that of a liberal democracy to that of a reluctant dictatorship, especially after 1933. One result was that when the seventh Pan-American Conference met in Montevideo in December of 1933, a censorship was imposed on outgoing reports. Even as the conference assembled, the printers' union called a strike in the capital to protest the arrest and exiling of agitators against the Terra regime. The production of newspapers was halted, and outgoing news messages describing the situation were rejected by the communications offices, which were placed under restraints comparable to those introduced in Argentina.

The Pan-American Conference was fully reported, however, after
the first day of its three-week session, perhaps because little of a controversial nature occurred. The conference received the largest coverage of any event in Montevideo,·and reporters for the Uruguayan
press were joined by eighty-four foreign correspondents. Among them
were six representatives of the Havas agency, five for the AP, three
for INS, and ten for the UP. They included Gideon Seymour for the
AP, and Armistead L. Bradford, Charles Farrell, and Arch Rogers
for the UP. Other U.S. correspondents included John W. White,
Harold B. Hinton, and Peter F. Kihss for the *New York Times,* Arthur Ruhl, *New York Herald Tribune,* Hubert G. Herring, *Christian
Science Monitor,* T. B. Ybarra, *Collier's Weekly,* and Jonathan Mitchell, the *New Republic.*

President Terra showed a desire to return to democratic procedures
in Uruguay, but growing tensions led instead to the establishment of a
Press Law in June 1935, subsequently further amended. It set penalties for "the malicious dissemination of false reports which might
result in public alarm, disruption of public order, cause obvious prejudice to the economic interest of the State . . . or prejudice the credit
of the country at home or abroad . . . ." Fines or imprisonment for
up to two years were prescribed as punishment for such offenses. The
law also provided that an editor violating the law three times in any
one year would be removed, and the publication might be suppressed
or otherwise placed under seizure for up to six months. Further, it
granted the right to persons who felt themselves adversely affected by
any published reference to demand space for reply.

Peru

Peru, with common frontiers with Chile, Bolivia, Brazil, Ecuador,
and Colombia, was almost constantly disturbed politically and economically in the years between the wars. The developments were reported for the world press most consistently through the Agence
Havas and the United Press, both with bureaus in Lima.

Peru was engaged in a dispute during the 1920s and 1930s with Chile
over the disposition of the border provinces of Tacna and Arica. It
was a controvery of long standing, stemming from a war between
those countries, and also between Chile and Bolivia, in the early
1880s. Representatives of Chile and Peru met in Washington in 1922
and agreed to arbitration, but not until 1929 was the dispute settled.
Meanwhile a dispute between Peru and Colombia over territorial
frontiers also threatened to cause war, and simmered between 1927

and 1934. Another topic of news concern during these years related to activities of U.S. corporate interests in the country, particularly in copper mining, and to U.S. government loans intended to assist in highway construction and general development, but without notable results.

The eighth Pan-American Conference, meeting at Lima in 1938, brought an influx of correspondents, chiefly from the United States. Among them were news agency staff writers, but others included John W. White of the *New York Times,* coming from Buenos Aires, William Philip Simms of the Scripps-Howard Newspapers, coming from Washington, and Leland Stowe of the *New York Herald Tribune,* arriving from New York. The coverage was shadowed by Peruvian government censorship affecting both incoming and outgoing press matter.

The Peruvian newspaper press, as well as the limited foreign press corps, was concerned with and affected by internal events in the country. More than fifty dailies were appearing in Lima alone, then with a population of about 275,000 in its metropolitan area, and about thirty were published in other cities, but few had circulations exceeding 5,000, including only one outside the capital. The leading Lima daily was *El Comercio,* also considered one of the more important in South America. It was published by Dr. José Antonio Miró Quesada and later directed by his brother, Aurelio Miró Quesada. *La Prensa,* a morning paper in Lima, and *La Cronica,* appearing both in morning and afternoon editions, were favorably regarded. The first was directed by Manuel Velasquez and later by Guillermo Hoyes Osores, the second by Dr. Larco Herrera.

From 1919 to 1930 the Peruvian government was headed by Augusto B. Leguía, actually president since 1908, but operating as a dictator from 1919. The world economic difficulties beginning in 1929 reached crisis proportions almost immediately in Peru and caused disorders that forced Leguía to resign in 1930 and brought his imprisonment. General Luis M. Sánchez Cerro, leader of the revolt against Leguía, took charge as provisional head of the government until March 1931, when he also was forced out. After an interval during which Samenez Ocampo acted provisionally, Sánchez Cerro, a candidate of the Civilist party, was elected president in what was held to be the first free and secret balloting in Peru's history.

Sánchez Cerro's chief competitor in that election was Victor Raúl Haya de la Torre, Oxford-educated founder and leader of a Socialist-oriented party, the Alianza Popular Revolucionaria Americana (APRA). Although failing to elect their candidate for the presidency, and charging corruption in the vote, the Apristas did elect twenty-three delegates to a convention that was to draft a new constitution.

Before that convention met, however, President Sánchez Cerro had Haya de la Torre jailed and the elected delegates deported. This action led to plotting against the government, and on April 30, 1933, President Sánchez Cerro was assassinated.

A constituent congress was summoned to select a new president, and General Oscar Raimundes Benavides, a conservative, was chosen to complete Cerro's term of office. He began by attempting to ease national tensions, with some civil liberties restored and political prisoners freed. Agitation continued, however, and he turned to such stronger measures as deporting the agitators. The results of a new presidential election in October 1936 were annulled when votes favored a candidate backed by APRA, which had been ruled a "foreign organization" because it had originated in Mexico, and so had been officially barred from the ballot. The result was that Benavides was given a mandate to remain in office, holding absolute power until he retired in October 1939.

The dictatorship was felt by the country's press, and *La Prensa* in Lima was closed in November 1930 by its stockholders as a protest against government policy, but publication was resumed later. An attempt was made in January 1935 to dynamite the editorial offices of *El Comercio,* and in May the publisher, Dr. José Antonio Miró Quesada, and his wife were shot and killed. Dr. Quesada's brother, Aurelio Miró Quesada, assumed direction of the paper.

Firm government control was imposed upon the press by the Benavides government in January 1939. This action was taken because of internal problems, including special tensions arising in Peru because of the growing crisis in Europe. It was decreed that newspapers must publish government releases in a prescribed manner. Failure to do so was punishable by fines of up to 10,000 sols ($2,025), payable within twenty-four hours, or the Ministry of the Interior would be empowered to close the offending newspaper.

Colombia

Colombia, with coastline on both the Pacific and the Caribbean, and rich in resources, prospered particularly after 1930, when discoveries of oil introduced a new economic period and when air transport helped overcome geographical barriers. Even though there were political problems and demonstrations, and press criticism was directed at the government and its officials, none of the restrictions felt in most other countries of Latin America were imposed in Colombia.

Prior to World War I, most newspapers in Colombia had been strongly political, with extreme polemics shaping their content. From about 1917, however, modern technology and a greater stress on information brought a more balanced and better quality of journalism. The outstanding daily, and one of the best in the hemisphere, was *El Tiempo* of Bogotá, the capital. A liberal and progressive morning daily, it had been established in 1911, directed almost from the outset by Eduardo Santos, who also became president of Colombia in 1938–42. The paper gained the largest circulation in the country and was widely distributed by air transport. Enrique Santos, brother of the publisher, became one of the nation's leading journalists, writing of public affairs under the name of "Calibán," sometimes even in opposition to the views of Eduardo Santos.

Second in circulation was *El Espectador,* a Bogotá afternoon paper directed by Dr. Luis Cano. Five other dailies in the capital had some importance. *La Razón* enjoyed a sound reputation and a good circulation. *El Siglo,* with an even larger circulation, was edited by Laureano Gómez, leader of the Conservative party. *El Liberal, El Débate,* and *Mundo al Dia* were other substantial dailies.

Outside of Bogotá, *El Colombiano* of Medellín was the largest in circulation. *La Prensa* of Barranquilla and *El Relator* of Cali both had importance. Papers also existed in Cartagena, Manizales, Ibague, Santa Marta, and Pereira.

Ecuador

Ecuador had passed through frequent political changes since its separation from Colombia in 1830. As an independent nation, chiefly agricultural in its economy, it was less in the news than the other Latin American countries so far mentioned. Stringers provided most of the outgoing reports through the Agence Havas and later also through the United Press. Those agencies provided most of the world news reports used by the press of the country.

Daily newspapers were published in about ten cities of Ecuador in the period between the wars, but chiefly in Quito, the capital, and in the Pacific port of Guayaquil, the largest city. *El Telegrafo* of Guayaquil was the oldest existing daily, established in 1884. *El Universo,* also of Guayaquil, a seven-day morning paper dating from 1921, led in circulation. *El Comercio* of Quito was considered the most important daily in the country, however, and also controlled *Ultimas Noticias,* an afternoon paper.

Venezuela was under a strict dictatorship from 1900 until 1935. Such newspapers as existed then and later were chiefly at Caracas, the capital. Because of limited educational opportunities, the literacy rate was low, and the papers were proportionately low in circulation and of little significance. The largest was *El Universal,* a morning daily established at Caracas in 1909, but distributing only about 12,000 copies.

Civil liberties had been suspended in Venezuela during the dictatorships of General Cipriano Castro (1899–1908) and Juan Vincente Gómez (1908–35). Eleazar López Contreras, former minister of war and president from 1935 to 1941, restored some liberties but reversed that action as internal disorders arose. The economy improved, however, as oil and iron ore discoveries were made in that latter period, and the information situation also eased and was to improve further after 1941.

Land-locked Bolivia and Paraguay were seldom in the news, except at time of internal crisis, disorder, or conflict. Much the same could be said of the Guianas, facing the Caribbean. A language variation for the continent was represented in the press of the area. There was an English-language press in British Guiana (Guyana) centered entirely at Georgetown; a Dutch-language press in Dutch Guiana (now Surinam) at Paramaribo; and a small French-language press in French Guiana at Cayenne. A similar variety of English, French, Dutch, and Spanish-language papers also appeared in the offshore island-chain of the Antilles and in the West Indies.

The press of Latin America long had used a heavy volume of news from Europe, because of a strong European heritage and because of the position of the French Agence Havas in the exchange of news. Relatively little news was published which originated in other parts of the world. The entrance of the news agencies of the United States into that exchange during the period of World War I altered the situation. For the first time, a north-south flow of news began in the Western Hemisphere, rather than a movement on a triangular course by way of Europe. It extended the scope of the news and enriched its content, with more news of Latin America moving to the rest of the world press, and with more North American and Asian news reaching Latin America.

This is not to say that any great volume of such news received actually was published, either north or south. A few quality newspapers in the United States, Great Britain, and Europe tried to provide a reasonably consistent report on Latin American affairs. A few in Latin America did the same with reference to the world. Even within that élite press group, a balanced report of substantive value was rare. There was further question as to how much of the material published was read.

Either way, in the selection of news for publication, attention tended to go to reports of the more violent and bizarre events and aspects of human behavior. In reports from the United States, for example, most Latin American papers in the 1920s and 1930s selected for use and emphasis those stories relating to crime, gangsterism, labor disturbances, and personalities of the motion picture world. A dislike of U.S. foreign policy found reflection in Latin American news and editorial columns in matter supporting what some editors regarded as unwarranted U.S. presumption in interpretations of the Monroe Doctrine, hypocrisy, and self-service in what were portrayed as manifestations of "dollar diplomacy" or "Yankee imperialism," and treatments supporting an accepted stereotype of the crude and bumptious "norteamericano" or "gringo." Such portrayals, it must be said, were not confined to the Latin American press, but were to be found in newspapers of some other countries as well.

If there was reason for those in the United States to object to such emphasis in the presentation of affairs, there was equal reason for Latin Americans to object to distortions of their society in the press of the United States, and possibly in some other countries. First of all, very little was published about that great area, and much that was published tended to fit an equally misleading stereotype. This involved, in part, what one Caracas editor observed as including "a guitar, a sombrero, a burro, a song or a dance, a bullfight, a revolution, and a love affair [as] the essential elements."

Even when a revolution or a *coup d'état* occurred, or an assassination or an attempted assassination, all serious events, the reports sometimes were presented in the American press in such a way as to convey the impression that they were part of a "comic opera," rather than substantive news. Again, a change of government, whether violent or orderly, might be reported substantively, but often with no prior reference or with no proper follow-up. Whatever may have been available to a newspaper in advance, through news agencies or other services, may not have been used. Thus a government change, for example, burst suddenly upon an unprepared public. The reader had no frame of reference, the names of persons and places were unfamiliar, the circumstances and background were unexplained. The account therefore contributed more to confusion than to understanding, if read at all, and the subject then also would likely be dropped the following day, or the day after that.

This manner of reporting, operating on a reciprocal basis, and actually between many countries, regrettable as it might be, was not beyond comprehension. It related, and still relates, to elements of news value shaped by distance, time, and assumptions of public interest or disinterest, and by competition for space in the pages of each day's editions of a newspaper. But it still means an essential distortion, a disservice to readers, however unintended, and provides no useful comprehension.

Censorship was at times another factor in obscuring the news of Latin America. The strictest censorship was that in Venezuela from 1900 to 1935. Otherwise, a general freedom existed in 1920, but did not survive much beyond 1930 in some other countries. The effect was more to deny information to the peoples of the southern part of the hemisphere than to prevent correspondents from sending dispatches for use in the world press. Yet they had their problems too, and news agencies selling services in the countries concerned were not inclined to imperil their positions there by contesting local regulations or concepts.

As with any censorship, however, the mere knowledge of its existence made the restrictions somewhat self-defeating. Neither the people of the country nor editors of newspapers in other countries gave full credence to reports placed before them. They also were more inclined to give attention to rumors and unauthenticated reports, from whatever source, and by so doing again contribute more to confusion than to understanding.

In some countries where illiteracy was widespread and educational facilities were lacking, government leaders were disposed to regard it as unwise to inform the general public of matters they were presumably prepared neither to comprehend nor act upon. If informed of some such things, leaders feared, the people might become alarmed or excited and behave in an impulsive fashion that could escalate into disorders sufficient to undo the administration. Editors and publishers, sometimes themselves political figures, could share this view.

Where a departure from this cautious policy occurred, with borderline information published, a government might feel justified in placing an offending newspaper under some form of restraint or control. Even in the freest of circumstances, rationalization might cause a newspaper itself to refrain from criticizing government policies in anything other than mild and perhaps ambiguous terms, if at all.

Prior to 1920, the Latin American press adhered almost entirely to British or European continental patterns, both in appearance and content. After 1920 there was a growing trend toward adoption of typographical practices, at least, that were more typical of daily newspapers in the United States. A European political partisanship often continued, however, with a polemical style and certain literary and cultural pretensions. There also was a tendency to yield to the demands of major advertisers and to political pressures at the cost of full and accurate information.

Even with those faults, inviting distortion in reporting, many daily newspapers in Latin American countries, through their editors and publishers, conducted crusades in support of the public interest, as they saw it. Publishers or editors of such newspapers proceeded with a kind of heroic purpose not common elsewhere in the world, dedicated to the exercise of an influence on public affairs, without regard for financial profit or loss, or even political repercussions. Readers accepted this concept. If an editor or publisher ran into trouble and was fined or jailed as a result, or if his paper was attacked or suppressed, he became something of a martyr, viewed as a high-minded and public-spirited champion of truth and right, facing risk or hardship rather than yielding to a faction in power.

The one irony, in what might seem an admirable if perhaps quixotic position, was that the same editor or publisher who might resist political pressure did not necessarily resist private commercial pressure. Some fell short of distinction on that point. Yet the same might be said of certain newspapers and their makers in other countries. To its credit, the Latin American press included some newspapers of the highest quality and integrity. For those possessing such merit, their performance was never better than in the 1920s.

Japan: A Reaching Out

Japan emerged from the 1914–18 war in a strong position. As one of the Allied nations suffering no casualties, it had prospered through the manufacture of munitions, and its industries were highly developed. Germany's preoccupation with the war in Europe and its defeat enabled Japan to take over its commercial position in Asia. It then also received a postwar mandate through the League of Nations to control the former German-held islands in the Pacific, the Carolines, Marshalls, and Marianas.

The first national census, completed in 1920, showed a Japanese population of about fifty-six million. Great advances had taken place since about 1860, when Japan entered into a full diplomatic and commercial relationship with the world. Among other things, its people had attained the highest literacy rate of any in Asia, and this permitted the growth of an active press.

Japan had acquired the island of Formosa (Taiwan) as a result of victory in the Sino-Japanese War of 1894–95. Victory in the Russo-Japanese War of 1904–05 had given it status as a great power with a naval and military capability. It also had given it control of the southern half of the former all-Russian island of Sakhalin, plus control of rail lines, mines, and coal deposits in Manchuria. In 1910 it had annexed Korea (Chosen), with further access to raw materials and a market among its twenty million people for Japanese products. As Japan's industry developed, those products included iron and steel, silk, wool, cotton, earthenware, and pharmaceuticals. Shipbuilding also was highly developed, as were fisheries and agriculture.

The Japanese government followed a liberal and internationalist policy in the years following World War I, and its representatives were active in the League of Nations. In the Washington Naval Conference of 1921–22, it agreed to reduce its own naval budget by more than $58 million and limit its ships. Relations with China, which had suffered by reason of Japan's 21 Demands of 1915, further demands in 1916, and a move of Japanese troops into Shantung province to take over German assets, were eased by a Sino-Japanese agreement in 1922.

There were problems, however. A move for independence in Korea in 1919, with riots and rebellion opposing Japanese control, was put down with great violence. With many countries of the world in economic difficulties just after the war, Japan's export markets were reduced. This also resulted in unemployment, unrest, and strikes in the cities. Debates relating to that situation and other matters became so heated in the Diet that it was dissolved in February 1919. Although the situation was somewhat repaired by a general election in May, unrest continued and contributed to the murder of Premier Takashi Hara in 1921.

What had been a rather casual interest in Japan among the peoples of the world was suddenly awakened by the drama of the great earthquake and fire occurring there on September 1, 1923, followed by tidal waves and new shocks. Tokyo, Yokohama, and adjacent cities were virtually destroyed—200,000 persons were dead, 43,000 were missing, many were without homes, food, or proper care, and property damage was estimated at $2.5 billion. For perhaps the first time, correspondents in Japan were not instructed to hold down the length of their dispatches. The nations of the world joined to provide help to the people. Efforts to meet their needs and repair damages were the subject of news for months to follow. The great loans required for relief and rebuilding, however, placed such a strain on Japan's national economy that a serious bank crisis occurred as late as 1927.

December of 1923 brought an attempt to assassinate the Crown Prince Hirohito. In 1924 the United States abrogated an existing informal agreement with Japan, and Congress passed a law excluding Asians as eligible to immigrate and gain U.S. citizenship. While applicable to all of Asia, this was especially resented in Japan as discriminatory and placed a strain on relations with the United States.

The Emperor Yoshihito, on the throne since 1912 but unwell since 1921, died on December 25, 1926. So ended the Taisho ("Great Righteousness") era. Prince Hirohito, then twenty, became the new emperor. He had acted as regent since 1921, and had just returned from a tour of Europe, the first prince of such rank ever to leave Japan. This introduced the Showa ("Peace through Justice") era. His formal enthronement in 1928 received world press attention.

Another event of international interest occurred when the German Graf Zeppelin, carrying passengers on an around-the-world flight, made a stop at Tokyo in 1929. The occasion was reported in 20,000 words of copy transmitted out of that capital, a new record. A second well-reported aviation story occurred in October 1931 when Clyde

Pangborn and Hugh Herndon departed from Tokyo on a successful nonstop eastward trans-Pacific flight ending in Wenatchee, Washington. The development of radio occasioned great public interest in Japan in the 1920s, as elsewhere in the world. The beginning of effective broadcasting occurred on March 22, 1925, with a program aired from station JOAK, Tokyo. By the end of the year stations also were operating in Osaka and Nagoya, and the three joined to form the Broadcasting Corporation of Japan (Nippon Hoso Kyokai, or NHK), with a monopoly over broadcasting until 1935, when it was made subject to regulation by the Ministry of Communications.

In the same period, the flow of news was advanced by the introduction of radiotelegraphic communication throughout the world. A general reduction in Pacific press rates in 1929, and a beginning of radiotelephonic communication available in Japan from 1936, further benefitted the Japanese press and people, as well as foreign correspondents in the country.

Japanese military units had joined with British, U.S., and French forces in putting a *cordon* around Russia early in 1918, following its withdrawal from the war, lest the Germans use that nation's resources for military purposes. Following the November armistice, such troops were recalled, except for those of Japan, which remained in Siberia and Manchuria until 1922. Japan also had some conflict with the new Soviet government, relating both to Manchuria and Sakhalin. Tokyo also was concerned by the advance of China's Kuomintang forces between 1926 and 1928, lest the market in China for its own growing industrial output be adversely affected. General Baron Tanaka, in becoming premier in April 1927, sponsored a policy under which Japanese troops entered China's Shantung province in May to block the Kuomintang advance on Peking. The Chinese Nationalist forces nevertheless reached Peking in June 1928, but from another direction.

The Japanese presence in Shantung, and the interference with the Kuomintang, or Nationalist campaign to unify China, brought a boycott against Japanese goods. There was some concern in Tokyo also lest too much pressure drive the Chinese to make common cause with the Soviet Union. British protests about Japan's presence in Shantung resulted in a settlement in 1929. The boycott was removed and the troops were withdrawn.

Uncertainty within Japan about the proper policy to be pursued in the matter of extending its trade, and in the conduct of its relations with China and the Soviet Union, brought no fewer than ten changes of government in the years between 1924 and 1932. Two premiers were assassinated, Yuko Hamaguchi in 1930 and Ki Inukai in 1932. Baron Kijuro Shidehara, foreign minister from 1929, sponsored a policy of conciliation with China, but was criticized by others in Japan who favored stronger measures.

Resident staff correspondents covering the immediate postwar events in Japan were chiefly representatives of news agencies. They included J. Russell Kennedy for Reuters, Joseph E. Sharkey for the Associated Press, Clarence DuBose for United Press, and Duke N. Parry for International News Service. Kennedy was also director of the Kokusai news agency. Others were stringers for newspapers in London and New York, often working as staff members of the *Japan Advertiser* or other English-language papers.

A relatively small group in 1920, most of them met for luncheon each day at the Imperial Hotel, exchanging ideas and information. Out of these meetings there evolved an association in 1923, known as the R.T.P. Club, meaning "receiver-to-pay," a semi-humorous reference to the manner in which dispatches were marked for transmission. As with comparable associations in other capitals, it was to have its value as an organization through which the working interests of its members might be made known to the government. It was formed at a time when the volume of news from Japan and China was about to expand, with a related shifting of correspondents and an increase in their number.

The news of Japan was easier to comprehend and report than that of China or India. It was a smaller country, news sources were usually accessible, travel was possible, and communications were good. The Japanese press itself was active and helpful as an aid to coverage. It operated under laws and restrictions that made for problems within the country, but had little bearing on the work of foreign newsmen. They were under police surveillance, however, and their accreditation was arranged through the government-sponsored International Press Association, foisted upon them in 1909. But they encountered few serious obstacles to obtaining news or transmitting it.

Access to government news was made easier in 1921 when the Ministry of Foreign Affairs (the Gaimusho) established an Information Bureau. Perhaps taking its cue from practices recently introduced at the League of Nations in Geneva, if not in Washington, it provided a center where correspondents might meet with a Foreign Ministry spokesman three or four times a week. Later there was a daily 11 A.M. conference at which announcements were made and questions answered in a somewhat routine fashion.[1] Comparable information bureaus presently were established in other ministries. Correspondents

---

1   One of the spokesmen was Hiroshi Saito, who became Japanese ambassador to the United States and died in Washington in 1939.

also were able to talk with the vice-minister for foreign affairs and other officials in relationships that were pleasant as well as useful. These circumstances were to change for the worse, however. The Japanese press and the correspondents were affected by new legislation in 1925 and 1927 and, especially, by changes in government policy after 1931 that made it difficult for correspondents to see any officials other than the spokesmen.

The first measure, the Peace Preservation Law of 1925, became known colloquially as the "Dangerous Thought Act." It prohibited advocacy of any change in the national constitution, or changes in the private ownership system that might seem to be in the direction of socialism or communism. It established a system of censorship, ostensibly voluntary, prohibiting the publication of protests or of adverse comments with reference to government policy. Immediately suspect under the provisions of this act were Socialists, Communists, or others merely believed to hold subversive views. Labor unions were forbidden.

Under this act, the press was obliged to be extremely cautious in what it published and in editorial comment, lest by interpretation it be judged to be presenting subversive views. Offenders were subject to arrest, fines, and imprisonment. A writer might be jailed for a long term for what in a free country would be no more than innocent speculation, such as advocating a higher wage rate or suggesting a reduction in a twelve-hour work day for nurses.

The home minister could designate by interpretation almost anything as criminal. The police, including the secret police (Koto Keisatsu), also were vested with wide powers. They were authorized, for example, to inquire into the membership of any organization or group of whatever character, to restrict its publications if any, to curtail its use of the telephone or mail service even by such prejudicial means as limiting its equipment or imposing high rates. They were able to demand to see what any person was reading or carrying, and in other ways to seek to control the exchange of ideas and information, printed or otherwise. In addition, they could confiscate any book or publication. Travelers or foreigners were not exempt from such attention, and could, of course, include correspondents.

Offenses of thought were regarded as just as serious as offenses of written, printed, or oral form, or those of action. Persons even suspected of harboring "dangerous thoughts" could be arrested, hence the colloquial name of the law.

This measure was protested at some risk by leading newspapers, but without result. On the contrary, the law was strengthened in 1934 by authorizing a death penalty for advocacy of a change in the constitution. At the same time, the maximum prison term for bringing the system of private property into question was magnanimously reduced to ten years.

The death penalty never was invoked, but some 59,000 persons were arrested under the provisions of these laws even within the brief period of 1933–36, and 2,044 were fined or imprisoned, or both, with another 2,144 given suspended sentences. Many others were held in jail, sometimes for months of questioning and investigation, prior to being released as innocent. There was no *habeas corpus,* and a person arrested was presumed guilty until proved innocent—a reversal of the Anglo-Saxon legal concept.

A second piece of legislation in 1927 was a Publications Bill. It provided for extensive powers of censorship to be exercised through the police, and banned the publication of material falling into seven classifications. These were largely by way of defining restrictions already covered by the act of 1925 and by earlier legislation. Specific prohibitions, nevertheless, were placed on the publication of matter considered by the police to be: (1) derogatory to the dignity of the imperial family; (2) intended to "revolutionize" the national organization; (3) intended to revolutionize the general political system under the constitution, illegally, or to negate the system of private property; (4) calculated to prejudice the interests of the empire with reference to military or diplomatic secrets; (5) calculated to instigate or shield crimes, gain praise or sympathy for criminals, or praise or sympathy for persons accused of or suspected of crimes; (6) calculated, by false or exaggerated paragraphs, to cause social unrest or to have serious effects on the maintenance of order; and (7) immoral, obscene, cruel, or otherwise calculated to prejudice good morals.

Local prefectural authorities had the power and responsibility to act in such matters. In practice, their behavior was inconsistent, unpredictable, and confusing. Decisions of such an authority might be appealed, but the interpretations on appeals could be equally inconsistent. Warnings might be sent to the entire press on some matters, but the warnings could be so vague as to be beyond understanding. Again, a subject might be banned "until further notice," but there never was any "further notice."

Although avoiding forbidden subjects, many of the papers in Japan still were informative, most were well printed, some appeared in a succession of editions, and in certain instances used almost fantastically large reportorial staffs to cover stories considered to be of special interest. Photographs and illustrations were used generously by the 1930s. Papers published in Tokyo and Osaka developed large circulations, in part because of national distribution. This made them prosperous advertising mediums, adding to their size, with a bulk greater than most European dailies. As in China, the absence of any means for mechanical composition applicable to the ideographs used required the employment of many compositors to set the type by hand.

The standard of accuracy, unfortunately, was not high in most Japanese papers, and some advertising accepted for publication was unreliable. The absence of any law of libel also permitted careless and irresponsible references, not to mention displays of bad taste. These factors discouraged public men generally from giving their confidence to the press. It was held in such low esteem, in fact, that few persons even bothered to deny false reports or seek corrections, confident that no reader would give them credence. For the same reason, accurate reports were not necessarily accepted as true by readers. It would be wrong to say that no Japanese newspaper was read with respect and confidence, but they were few.

Seeking to attract large readerships, most papers gave considerable space and display to news involving crimes, scandal, gossip, accidents, disasters, and violence. This was particularly so for some small papers in Tokyo referred to as the "rickshaw" or "geisha" papers, which might also engage in deliberate blackmail.

Even the better papers, however, presented crime news and sensation, but usually grouped such material on one inside page. This was referred to for many years as "the third page," and later, if a different page, sometimes as "the black page." The best newspapers omitted the worst of the personal references, but sought to win and hold readers by presenting human interest stories, sports reports, interviews, magazine-type articles, fiction, special material for women, children, and hobbyists, and even such entertainment features as comic strips and translated pages obtained from U.S. syndicates. The considerable volume of substantial news in the better papers was enlivened and clarified by pictures, maps, diagrams, and charts. Borrowing from the Paris system of *grand rapportage,* writers and teams of writers sometimes were sent to cover important events at home and abroad. Borrowing also from the London *Times* practice, supplements with special advertising were prepared about a subject or a country.

Inexpensive, distributed over most of the country within hours of publication, and made to appeal to every interest, some of the Tokyo and Osaka papers spurred a desire to read, and were among the most widely circulated newspapers in the world. At their best, they contributed usefully to public information.

In 1935, the *Asahi,* with editions in Tokyo and Osaka, claimed 2,450,000 daily, approaching the newspapers of largest circulation in the world at that time, London's Sunday *News of the World,* then claiming a circulation of 3,350,000, and the Sunday edition of the

New York *Daily News* with 2,523,615. The *Mainichi* of Osaka claimed 1,600,000 circulation in 1935. It was a paper that also sponsored sports events and exhibitions, arranged public lectures, financed scientific expeditions, supported traveling hospitals, and donated a music hall to Osaka. *Nichi-Nichi* of Tokyo, with an edition in Kyoto as well, claimed 1,200,000 circulation for both. Since *Mainichi* and *Nichi-Nichi* were allied, the group might have been credited with 2,800,000 daily sales. *Mainichi* also introduced an English-language edition in 1922. Among other Tokyo papers, *Jiji Shimpo* and *Yomiuri Shimbun* each claimed 500,000 circulation, and *Hochi Shimbun,* 400,000.

These seven leading papers, along with *Chugai Shogyo,* a Tokyo business daily of quality, were represented in the core membership of the news agency, Nippon Shimbun Rengo-sha (the Associated Press of Japan). It was formed in 1925 in a reorganization of the Kokumin agency. In 1927 it absorbed the Teikoku agency, the first in the country. Rengo then received the AP service, added to that of Reuters, with its total report going to twenty-six newspapers in Japan, and to radio stations. Its pattern of organization resembled that of the AP in membership arrangement, except that it received government financial support through the Ministry of Foreign Affairs and, after 1929, added an advertising subsidiary.

Rengo was matched by the Nippon Dempo Tsushin-sha (Dentsu) (Japanese Telegraph Agency), founded in 1901 and also conducted as an advertising agency. Both Kokusai and Dentsu had provided the first original foreign coverage for the Japanese press, beginning in the 1920s. Reduced cable rates in 1929 further encouraged such coverage. Rengo might then also have sent correspondents to overseas points, but the problems and tensions of the world economic crisis, then beginning, delayed that until after 1936. At that time, a merger of the Rengo and Dentsu agencies, under consideration in 1931, actually occurred, with the formation of Domei Tsushin-sha (Allied News Agency).

The government by then was dominated by the army. Although Dentsu had been favored earlier by the military as the agency that would survive if a merger occurred, Hoshiro Mitsunaga, its director, remained reluctant to see any such change. The government cautioned him, however, that if he chose to operate Dentsu independently there could be no assurance that telegraphic facilities would remain available for distribution of the service. This was followed soon by what amounted to a government edict whereby Dentsu was forced to merge with Rengo to form Domei.

The government was prepared to finance the establishment of Domei by the provision of 4,000,000 yen (about $18 million) through the Ministry of Foreign Affairs. Yukichi Iwanaga, head of Rengo, rejected the proposal because it would suggest that the agency was no more than an arm of the government, a status he was unwilling to accept. An alternative arrangement was made, however, whereby the same amount was received, but channeled through the Nippon Hoso Kyokai (NHK) (Japan Broadcasting Company). With the NHK itself government-controlled and financed after 1935, the funds so channeled to Domei were classified as a financial credit to the agency in payment for reports to be provided to the NHK over an unspecified period of time for use in the preparation of news broadcasts. As a legitimate return for its service, this left Domei uncompromised in its relation to the government and so met Iwanaga's objection.

Iwanaga used half of this advance payment to recompense Dentsu for its news department, in effect sold to Domei. Dentsu retained its advertising division, Kokoku Kabushiki Kaisa, which continued independently, but with Rengo's advertising division merged with it. Iwanaga was offered 1,800,000 yen (about $8 million) of the NHK credit as compensation for the assignment of the Rengo advertising division to Dentsu, but again he refused because Rengo had been a nonprofit, cooperative organization, which meant that there were no stockholders to be paid off. That money thus remained in Domei's operating fund.

The Domei agency, like Rengo, was concerned exclusively with the news and received both the Reuters and the Associated Press reports. It sent its own staff correspondents abroad, and it engaged stringers. Despite Iwanaga's wish that it remain independent of government, Domei did in fact become a semi-official and then an official agency in 1937. This status was based on official rulings, and involved the provision of subsidies through a new Ministry of Communications.

Iwanaga's direction of the agency ended with his death at fifty-seven in 1939. He was succeeded by Inosuke Furuno, prominently associated through the years with the Kokusai and Rengo agencies, as well as Domei. By 1940 the Domei agency, along with five of the Tokyo and Osaka dailies, had thirty-one correspondents in the United States alone, and other staff or stringer representatives in London, Paris, Moscow, Berlin, Hong Kong, Shanghai, Buenos Aires, Rio de Janeiro, Mexico City, and elsewhere. In retrospect, it seems possible that at that late date some of them may have been engaged in espionage.

The changes occurring in China and Japan alike between 1920 and 1930, and later in that decade, made Tokyo a more important center for coverage by the world press. The changes were political and economic, social, technical, and military. Businessmen, diplomatic personnel, and newsmen arrived from other countries in increasing numbers. More than in any other country, resident correspondents or stringers in Japan were staff members of foreign-language papers appearing there, or continued in association with such papers. In practice, this meant English-language papers. Among several, the *Japan Advertiser* was most notable in quality and in producing contributors in Japan and China for newspapers and news agencies in the United States and Great Britain.

This had been true at least since 1907, when the *Advertiser* already had existed for more than fifteen years in Yokohama. It was purchased in that year by Benjamin W. Fleisher, a Philadelphia businessman recently arrived in Japan. He also found interests in Shanghai, where he helped to establish the *China Press* in 1911, worked with it until 1913, and then returned to Japan. J. Russell Kennedy, then AP correspondent in Tokyo, was owner-of-record of the *Advertiser* from 1909 until Fleisher assumed full direction in 1913. Fleisher then moved the headquarters and publishing office of the paper to Tokyo from Yokohama, where it had been established in 1890.

Hugh Byas, British-born and with London news experience, was editor of the *Advertiser* in 1914–17, again in 1918–22, and also in 1926–30. From 1922 to 1926 Byas was in London and wrote from there for the *Advertiser*. Returning to the editor's post in Tokyo in 1926, he also served as correspondent in Japan for the *Times* and for the *New York Times*. This he continued to do after leaving the *Advertiser* in 1930 and until his retirement and return to London early in 1941.

Editors of the *Advertiser* in these years when Byas was away included Gregory Mason in 1917–18, the first U.S.-born editor since 1909. He had experience as a correspondent for *Outlook* magazine from 1914 in Mexico, Europe, and Russia. R. Lewis Carton was editor in 1922–23, while also serving as correspondent for the *Times*. Frank H. Hedges, another U.S. newsman, formerly of the *Washington Star,* was editor in 1923–26. He also acted as a correspondent for the *Times,* the *Daily Mail,* and the *Christian Science Monitor,* and he remained in Japan for the *Monitor* in 1927–31.

When Byas left the *Advertiser* in 1930, Fleisher himself became editor as well as publisher. His son, Wilfrid Fleisher, became managing editor at the same time, while also acting as Tokyo correspondent for the *New York Herald Tribune* from 1931. He continued in both positions until 1940. Born in Philadelphia in 1897, but involved with the *Advertiser* since his youth, the younger Fleisher had gone to France in 1918–19 as a war correspondent both for the *Advertiser* and for the *New York World* and had remained to cover the Peace Conference. Following study at Columbia University in 1919–21, he was in the Paris bureau of the United Press in 1921-23. Back in Tokyo as business manager of the *Advertiser* in 1923-25, he was also correspondent for the *New York Times*. In the Washington bureau of the *New York Times* in 1925-29, he returned to Tokyo to work from that time for the *Advertiser* and as correspondent for the *New York Herald Tribune*.

Other members of the *Japan Advertiser* staff serving also as correspondents then or later included Glenn Babb in 1915-17. He represented the Associated Press in Japan and in China in 1924-36, when he became cable editor in New York. Roderick O. Matheson, news editor of the *Advertiser*, joined Kokusai and then became Tokyo correspondent for the *Chicago Tribune* in 1921-28. Demaree Bess, having been director of the *Ledger-Post* service in Japan in 1924-26, was news editor of the *Advertiser* in 1927. Later he joined the United Press in China, and held other news positions both in China and in Europe.

While on the *Advertiser* staff, Newton E. Edgers acted as a stringer for the afternoon *New York Sun*, Don E. Brown also wrote for the *Chicago Daily News*, and Hugh Schuck, managing editor, for the *New York Times*. Victor Keen, with the paper in 1923-28, also wrote for the *Chicago Tribune*, but then became *New York Herald Tribune* correspondent in Shanghai. From the *Advertiser* in the 1920s, Henry F. Misselwitz moved to the United Press staff in Japan and China and later to New York; Morris J. Harris began seventeen years of service with the Associated Press in China; John R. Morris began a career with the United Press in China; and Edward S. Hunter moved to the International News Service in China. A number of these men had gone to Japan directly after graduation from the University of Missouri School of Journalism.

James R. Young, a former secretary to E. W. Scripps, and then with the United Press in New York, became business manager of the *Advertiser* in 1931-37. Overlapping this service, he also was International News Service correspondent from 1929 to 1940, and Far Eastern representative of the King Features Service, both Hearst enterprises.

The *Japan Chronicle* of Kobe, another of the English-language papers, was edited by A. Morgan Young. He also wrote as a stringer for the *Manchester Guardian*, the *Baltimore Sun*, and newspapers in Australia.

Established coverage of Japan for the western press had been provided first by Reuters and the *Times*, beginning in the 1870s. J. Russell Kennedy, Reuters representative from 1914 to 1925, as well as director of the Kokusai agency, was succeeded for Reuters by Malcolm Duncan Kennedy (unrelated), while he himself remained in Japan as correspondent for the *Chicago Daily News* from 1927 until his death in the following year. Malcolm Duncan Kennedy served Reuters from 1925 to 1934. He was succeeded by James Melville Cox, a Reuters correspondent in China and other parts of the Far East for thirty years. He was Tokyo correspondent from 1934 until his death in 1940.

The *Times* was chiefly represented in Japan after 1920 by Frank H. Hedges and Hugh Byas. Joseph E. Sharkey, representing the Associated Press since 1913, was succeeded in 1921 by George Denny,[2] who remained for three years. Glenn Babb, although much in China, also represented the AP in Tokyo in 1924-25, 1928-30, and from 1932-36. In the intervening years, Victor G. C. Eubanks was in Tokyo in 1926-28, Joseph Dynan and Max Hill in 1930-32, followed by James A. Mills in 1936-37, and Relman (Pat) Morin in 1937-41.

For the United Press, Miles V. (Peg) Vaughn, foreign editor in New York in 1919-20, became director from 1924-34 of the UP Far Eastern service based in Tokyo. He was followed by Gifford (Ray) Marshall in 1934-39, and then by H. O. Thompson. Other UP correspondents in Japan included Ralph H. Turner and Robert T. Bellaire.

For the International News Service, Luther Huston was in Tokyo in 1927. James R. Young also represented both INS and the King Features Service in the 1929-41 period. Percy Whiteing was a 1940 arrival. Meanwhile, Floyd Gibbons, formerly of the *Chicago Tribune* but a radio personality since the mid-1920s, visited Japan and China in 1931 as a writer also for INS.

For the newspaper press, Demaree Bess had directed the *Ledger-Post* service in Tokyo in 1924-26. Roderick O. Matheson and Victor Keen wrote for the *Chicago Tribune* in the 1921-28 period. St. Clair McKelway, later identified with the *New Yorker* magazine, wrote for the *Tribune* in 1931, and Honolulu-born Kempei Sheba represented the paper in 1937-41. J. Russell Kennedy, who had written for the *Chicago Daily News* in 1927-28, was followed by stringers for that paper, and then by Frank G. Smothers in 1936-37.

Wilbur Forrest of the *New York Herald Tribune,* a veteran European correspondent, visited Japan in 1929. Willard D. Price also was in Tokyo for the *Herald Tribune* before switching to China in 1933. Wilfrid Fleisher, chief representative in 1931-40, was followed by Joseph Newman, who arrived in Tokyo in 1939.

Frank Hedges, representing the *Christian Science Monitor* from the mid-1920s until 1931, was followed in Tokyo for that paper in 1935-39 by William Henry Chamberlin, after long service in Moscow.

The *New York Times* received reports from Fleisher in 1923-25 and from Hugh Byas from 1926 to 1940. Archibald T. Steele, representing

---

2   Not to be confused with Harold Norman Denny of the *New York Times,* chiefly in Latin America and Europe.

the paper in China, also visited Tokyo periodically. When Byas retired early in 1941 and left Japan, he was succeeded there for the New York paper by Otto D. Tolischus, then recently awarded a Pulitzer Prize for his correspondence from Germany.

Byas, a Tokyo correspondent also for the *Times* of London from 1926 to early 1941, was then succeeded for that paper by Vera Redman. The British press also was represented in Tokyo by J. W. T. Mason and Hessell Tiltman, both for the *Daily Express.* Wilhelm Schulze, formerly in New York for the Berlin *Morgenpost* and other Ullstein papers of Germany, arrived in Tokyo in 1932, one of the relatively few non-Anglo-American news representatives in Japan at that time.

The correspondents in Japan and China after 1931 were confronted by situations quite different from those existing in the 1920s, because of military moves in Manchuria and central China by Japan, as well as changes in its government.

China: A Republic Reborn

The formation of the Chinese Republic in 1912 had an uncertain progress through 1923. Dr. Sun Yat-sen, whose efforts had earned him recognition as "the father of the republic," and who had been its first provisional president, was so dissatisfied with its administration by 1913 that he sponsored a new revolution. This failed, and he took refuge in Japan until 1917. Still dissatisfied, he returned to Canton, where he reactivated the National People's Party (Kuomintang), originally formed there in 1898 to advance the concept of the republic. It was 1923 before he felt it was strong enough to challenge the republic as it then existed.

Dr. Sun was in another period of temporary, self-imposed exile in Shanghai that year. There he met an agent of the five-year-old Moscow Communist regime, which had failed in an effort to reach an agreement with the Peking government, but now offered assistance to Dr. Sun. As a result, Moscow sent two representatives to Canton, Michael Borodin (Mikhail M. Grusenberg) and General B. K. Galen, along with other advisers. With Dr. Sun's approval, they proceeded to reshape the Kuomintang and its military forces under a discipline and organization comparable to that of the Communist party of Soviet Russia and of the Red Army. This included the establishment at Canton of a Whampao Military Academy to train leaders to direct forces against the Peking government.

The goal of the Kuomintang under Dr. Sun's leadership was to unite China in full nationhood within a revitalized republic. Sun's aide, with experience in the military campaigns since 1911, was Chiang Kai-shek. He was a graduate of the Paoting Military Academy near Tientsin, and had further training both in Japan and in Russia. Born near Shanghai in 1887, he was thirty-six in 1923.

By the end of 1924 the government of the republic at Peking had become so disorganized that the three leaders, Tuan Ch'i-jui, Chang Tso-lin, and Fêng Yu-hsiang, called for a "Reorganization Conference" to meet in Peking in February 1925. Dr. Sun attended with the hope that he might persuade the triumvirate to join in the Kuomintang program. Already ill with cancer, he died there in March at age sixty. He was survived by his second wife, Ching-ling Soong, whom he had married in 1915, and whose younger sister, Mei-ling Soong, a graduate of Wellesley College, married Chiang Kai-shek in 1927.

A continuing struggle for leadership of the government in Peking left it almost meaningless by 1926. In the interim, the Kuomintang with its Soviet advisers gained a firm organization and a strong military force. Chiang Kai-shek, in succeeding Dr. Sun as head of the party, was joined in the leadership by Mao Tse-tung. Mao came from Hunan province and was an organizer of the Chinese Communist party in Shanghai in 1921. He worked closely with Borodin and Galen.

In the summer of 1926 the Kuomintang forces began a march northward from Canton. Agitators accompanied the armies and persuaded the people at all levels that the Kuomintang held the answer to problems that had beset the country for many years. Without violence, by the end of 1926, the Kuomintang controlled almost half of China, including the major cities of the Yangtze River valley. The party's headquarters were then relocated at Hankow.

The advance proceeded in 1927 and by March had reached Nanking. Serious differences had arisen within the party by then between Chiang's moderate element and Mao's Communist-oriented element under the guidance of Borodin and Galen. Each group had its own concepts and goals for the Kuomintang.

Contrary to the peaceful advance of 1926, the advance to Nanking involved actions by the Communist elements against merchants and others that cost the Kuomintang favor. The advance also was accompanied by violence against foreigners and foreign establishments. Some of these attacks were brought under control by British and U.S. gunboats on the Yangtze. Chiang ordered the Communists expelled from the party, and in Shanghai in April purged Communist elements there. He then brought adjacent areas under control and established a Nationalist or Kuomintang government at Nanking.

The Communist element in the Kuomintang remained based at Hankow, and the rival groups were in sharp conflict from April through August of 1927. Settlement came then in a compromise whereby Chiang, charged with militaristic views and with the intent to make himself dictator of all China, resigned as commander in chief of the Kuomintang forces and retired from public life. Leaders in what had become the Hankow division of the party, charged with radicalism and subservience to Moscow, responded by expelling Communist members and by dismissing the Soviet advisers, who returned to Russia. Those surviving then joined to establish a reorganized Kuomintang party in Nanking.

The Communist element, technically expelled from the Kuomintang, nevertheless retained a unity. They moved south from Hankow to Kiangsi province and formed a Chinese Soviet Republic, with Mao Tse-tung, Chou En-lai, and Chu Teh as leaders of the party organization advised from Moscow. Dr. Sun Yat-sen's widow allied herself with this group and ultimately became vice-chairman of the Central People's Government Council. She maintained a home, however, in the French Concession within Shanghai's International Settlement.

Early in 1928, with the Kuomintang or Nationalist party reorganized in Nanking, Chiang Kai-shek again was placed in command of the armies, as "generalissimo." The Chinese Soviet Republic, under Mao Tse-tung, was forced out of Kiangsi province and its members and adherents made what became known as the "Long March" to the northwest, settling in Shensi province, with headquarters at Yenan. This group never ceased to be of concern to the Nanking government and between 1927 and 1936 it was attacked in five campaigns directed by Chiang Kai-shek.

In addition to its concern with the rival Communist group, the Kuomintang was fully aware that the Republican government was still established at Peking. Marshal Chang Tso-lin, warlord of China's three easternmost provinces forming Manchuria, had been the commanding figure in the coalition directing the republic since 1926. He was assassinated in June 1928 in a bombing of his private train as it was approaching Mukden. The attack was believed to be related to his rejection of advice from Japanese sources. His power in Manchuria was inherited by his son, Chang Hseuh-liang, soon known as the "Young Marshal." He was in sympathy with the Kuomintang, however, rather than with the Peking government. In October 1928 he became a member of the State Council of the Kuomintang, by then the effective Nationalist government in Nanking.

In June 1928 Nationalist forces had occupied Peking, and all of China south of the Great Wall thus was under the effective control of the Kuomintang. The capital of the republic was officially transferred to Nanking, with Chiang Kai-shek as president as well as generalissimo of the armies. Peking was renamed Peiping, variously interpreted as "old capital" and "Northern peace." A constitution of the republic was soon proclaimed, and the Nationalist government at Nanking was recognized by other nations.

The new unity of China was uncertain, for the Nationalist government was to have little opportunity after 1928 to consolidate its power, except in limited areas, or to undertake the intended program of reform, construction, and social change. Instead, it was faced with the problem of maintaining itself in the face of aggression from four quarters.

During four months in 1929 the Nationalist government was engaged in an undeclared war with Soviet Red Army troops along the Chinese Eastern Railway near Harbin in Manchuria arising from different interpretations of the 1924 agreements relating to the operation and maintenance of that rail line. Construction of new rail lines in parts of Manchuria also was opposed by Japan as threatening its own treaty rights in the area, dating from the Sino-Japanese War of 1895, including control of the South Manchuria Railway.

The Nationalist government also was in conflict in several provinces where local warlords had enjoyed power, privilege, and autonomy under the empire and the early republic, and now objected to the kind of centralized government Chiang sought to administer from Nanking. This in itself resulted in almost constant civil war between 1929 and 1932. There also were the Communists in Yenan. Military actions were considered necessary by the Nanking government to curb an extension of Communist power by the Mao regime in and beyond Shensi province.

Even more serious were measures taken by neighboring Japan seeking to protect what it regarded as its economic lifeline and treaty rights in Manchuria and in greater China. This became a major problem from 1931.

News reporting from China, as well as the distribution of news within the country, was complicated by the great distances, limited means of transportation, an incomplete communications system, costs, a variety of languages or dialects, and a high percentage of illiteracy. Events beyond the main centers of commerce were late in becoming known, or might never be reported. Very few western newspapers or news agencies other than Reuters were represented in China prior to 1920, unless by stringer correspondents in certain of the port cities.

This relatively inactive news situation changed in the 1920s, however, spurred particularly by the need to report the Nationalist or Kuomintang military campaign beginning in 1926. The Kuomintang itself recognized a need for an information service in support of its objectives, and established the Chung Yang Sheh (Central News Agency) (CNA) at Canton in 1924. Its main office moved with the Nationalist forces to Hankow in 1926, and to Nanking in 1927. Placed under the direction of the Ministry of the Interior, it held official status, was supervised by the governing board of the Kuomintang's Central Publicity Department within the ministry, and was directed by Yu Wei-yi, soon succeeded by Tung-tze Hsiao.

Another short-lived agency, purportedly representing the Kuomintang, was established at Hankow in 1927 when the military campaign reached that point. Known in translation as the Nationalist News

Agency, it was organized early in that year by William Rupert Prohme, an experienced U.S. newsman, editor of the *People's Tribune* in Hankow, and by his wife, Rayna Prohme, who was working for Borodin. It reflected the views and interests of the Communist-dominated faction of the party. Shortly after it had been started, the Soviet advisory group headed by Borodin was sent back to Moscow, and Rayna Prohme accompanied it. The agency was suspended. Mrs. Prohme died in Moscow in November 1927. Her husband, who had moved to Shanghai, died there.[1]

Few vernacular papers in China had been able to afford to pay for the full world service provided by Reuters, and China did not have a national agency of its own prior to the establishment of the CNA. There had been a few local services, but they were unimportant. One was Ching Mei, originally owned by Americans, but later Chinese-owned. It distributed some freelance articles to vernacular papers, but they were articles on foreign and domestic subjects, rather than news, and they moved by mail. A service called Asia, owned jointly by Chinese and Japanese principals, provided some news of both countries. A third, Dalta, was a service from the Soviet Far Eastern Siberian Republic at Chita, and was one of several semi-official propaganda services.

The Toho agency of Japan, operating in China through the period of World War I and then in Tokyo until it was absorbed by the Kokusai agency in 1925, made reports available to the vernacular press of China at little or no cost, with a view to advancing Japan's political and economic position in China. The Tass service of Soviet Russia became available after 1925 at no cost, for similar reasons. The Transozean service, moved by wireless from Germany, and also available at little or no cost, had some merit between 1920 and 1933, but then became a Nazi government propaganda service.

The Central News Agency established branch offices after 1928 at Shanghai, Peiping, Tientsin, Hankow, and Canton. Correspondents were appointed in other larger cities of China, in Hong Kong, and also in Tokyo, London, Paris, New York, and some other cities of the world. The CNA was a member of the Ring Combination until its demise in 1934, entered into news exchange with Reuters, and held a right to distribute the Reuters report to the vernacular press in China.

The CNA was supplemented by two smaller, semi-official services formed in 1928. Kuo Wen of Canton circulated its reports in Cantonese in the south of China. Kuo Min of Shanghai did the same in Man-

---

1 See Vincent Sheean, *Personal History* (1935), pp. 214ff. Their son, Rupert Prohme, Jr., graduated from Stanford University a decade later, became a U.S. Foreign Service officer.

darin in the north. In translation, both were known as the National People's News Agency. They were sponsored by the Ministry of Foreign Affairs and directed by Lee Choy. The services handled releases from the ministry and matter from foreign and vernacular newspapers.

The editors of vernacular newspapers were aware of the faults and virtues of the various services available to them before 1928, and used them cautiously, if at all. Another practice was to translate and rewrite news from foreign-language publications appearing in Hong Kong, Shanghai, and Tientsin, but often this was done without notable accuracy and with inevitable delay in the news reports.

The vernacular papers had two major production problems. The complexity of the language, with 44,000 characters in a dictionary compiled 300 years earlier, required the use of 5,000 to 7,000 in print. This not only hampered the development of literacy in the country, but it introduced difficulties in the composition of printed text matter, and it ruled out the use of typewriters, mechanical type-setting, and news transmission by telegraph, code, or teleprinter. Copy had to be prepared by hand in brush strokes. Compositors then set the copy by hand, requiring the services of many men, each serving a long apprenticeship to learn the layout of the type cases, and walking as much as three miles a day, by one estimate, to put the copy into type.

To mitigate that problem, a spoken language was adapted to printing after about 1919 in a simplified, somewhat phonetic style, known as *pai-hua*. It was devised by Lu Hsun, Dr. Hu Shih, and Chen Tu-hsiu. Only thirty-nine symbols, rather than more than 200 as before in the simplest usage, could be combined to make about 4,000 characters or "words," to give a sufficient flexibility and variety. Some publications using that style were made to appeal to a popular audience. A so-called "mosquito press," appearing first in Shanghai in about 1930, depended upon this method and found readers. Even that system had limitations. Some complex typewriters and composing machines were devised in the 1930s, but were not in general use.

The second production problem arose because transmission of news or other messages by telegraph, using Chinese, was impossible. The existing telegraph codes were based upon the twenty-six-letter alphabet used by most of the western world. For dispatch by telegraph, a message had to be in English or some other European language, and translated into Chinese at the receiving end. An alternative was to use a numerical code, with each number representing a character, but there were so many numbers that a telegraph operator had difficulty recording them all and then decoding them.

Literacy remained low in China, in a population exceeding 400 million in 1930. Yet if no more than 30 per cent were literate, that represented 120 million, one of the largest potential reading audiences in the world, although still divided between Mandarin and Cantonese, to say nothing of dialects. Since most literate persons lived in the cities where the papers were published, there was a concentration of potential readership.

The more important vernacular papers in the 1920s and 1930s included *Shun Pao* (Shanghai Gazette), a daily since 1873, and *Sin Wan Pao* (News Gazette) of Shanghai, dating from 1893. Both "flew the foreign flag," in that they were registered at the British consulate. During this period, both claimed 150,000 daily circulation. Few other vernacular papers circulated more than a few hundred copies. Even the largest foreign-language paper then distributed no more than 10,000 copies a day to a far smaller potential audience.

A third important daily was *Ta Kung Pao* (Impartial Gazette) of Tientsin, dating from 1902. Regarded in 1930 as the leading vernacular paper, it was read far beyond Tientsin, but it was of such high quality that its circulation was no more than 50,000. A fourth daily of some quality, and also important by reason of its sponsorship, was *Chung Yang Jih Pao* (Central Daily News), established at Nanking in 1929. Directed by the Kuomintang's Central Publicity Department, it was regarded as an official paper, representing party and government views and interests.

Prior to the establishment of the Nationalist government in Nanking there were few reliable news sources in China to which foreign newsmen might turn for official information. In seeking information, they had some advantages under the extraterritorial treaties, and some opportunities not necessarily available to Chinese journalists. These might include interviews with Peking officials, whether of the imperial government, in its time, or of the republic. They could arrange to travel, although it was difficult, hazardous, and virtually impossible in some areas. Yet to verify or disprove certain rumors or reports, or to cover a special situation, correspondents did move to and from Peking on one of the better rail lines, and even ventured into the interior.

At times, the hardships and risk outweighed the value of such journeys. In 1923, for example, Lloyd Lehrbas, then representing INS, and John B. Powell of the *Chicago Tribune* were captured by bandits and held for ransom. Gareth Jones of the *Manchester Guardian* and Herbert Mueller of the German DNB agency had a somewhat similar experience as late as 1935. In 1927, Frank Basil Riley of the *Times* disappeared in Manchuria, presumably killed. In the summer of 1929, during the conflict between Chinese Nationalist and Soviet troops along the Chinese Eastern Railway on the frontier between North Manchuria and Siberia, some sixteen correspondents were held at Harbin and saw nothing.

Correspondents were handicapped in many cases by unfamiliarity with the language. They might have difficulties also in obtaining or verifying information, even under the best of circumstances. Rumors were plentiful, but reports often were contradictory. They might know Chinese business and professional men, scholars, officials, military men, and warlords, but such persons, moved by concepts both of expediency and courtesy, did not always deem it necessary to answer questions with exact or truthful replies. Adding a possible difference of opinion concerning the meaning of events, as between Chinese and foreign residents, there was every possibility that a correspondent, however conscientious, might be accused of inaccuracy, falsification, or even deliberate malice in whatever he wrote.

Correspondents had sources of information among foreign businessmen, missionaries, educators, and diplomatic and consular representatives. They read an assortment of books and publications, using translation services if necessary. There was no press club, but they gathered with fellow correspondents, editors, and others at such favored centers as the bars in the Cathay, Palace, and Park hotels in Shanghai's International Settlement, or in comparable places in Peking, Tientsin, Nanking, or Hong Kong. All of this provided a perspective on the news, but was no substitute for original news sources or direct observation, which was rarely possible, or for hard facts and figures, which were not always available, or reliable when they were. The effectiveness of reporting depended greatly upon the experience and judgment of the correspondent. This was true at any post, of course, but perhaps more so in China than in most others.

Once having gathered information, the correspondent had to consider the communications rates from China as weighed against the limited public interest of the western world in Asian affairs. The rate between China (or Japan) and New York, London, and Paris was so high until 1921 as to discourage extensive telegraphic or cable transmission. The rate remained substantial until radiotelegraphic communication was well established in 1929. Until that time, correspondents were given to understand that the news transmitted was to be kept to a minimum, even though the volume edged up to permit reporting the Kuomintang military advances after 1926.

Only a few newspapers of the world were willing to use reports delivered by mail, even including airmail. For the most part, they proceeded on the theory that only those reports received by cable and telegraph were really *news* acceptable for publication in a daily newspaper. Magazines used mail copy but, even so, articles from Asia were few. Among newspapers, only four were prepared to use longer stories received by mail. These were the *Times* and the *Manchester Guardian* in the United Kingdom, the *Christian Science Monitor* in Boston, and

La Prensa in Buenos Aires. The latter paper gave little attention to Asia, however. The willingness of the other three to use mail copy from China and Japan, and other parts of the world commonly slighted by the general newspaper press, gave them high standing among that important minority of readers eager to have background reports providing a substantial understanding of current affairs in areas lacking full coverage.

From 1928, the new Nationalist government was prepared to aid both foreign reporters and those for the vernacular press itself to a degree never before known in China. The Central Publicity Board of the Kuomintang and the Central Publicity Department provided answers to some questions, at least, and helped arrange meetings and interviews with officials. The Ministry of Foreign Affairs set up a Department of Intelligence and Publicity at Nanking, with a branch office in Shanghai. The Central News Agency provided material such as had not previously been available.

It soon became apparent, however, that the government policy was to reveal only such information as was deemed favorable to its purposes or its image. Experience demonstrated that even official statements might be inaccurate and unreliable, and intended to create a desired impression, with no essential relation to fact. Yet a correspondent attempting to put such statements into a context to give them meaning, however objectively, could find himself in difficulty.

An example arose in the summer of 1929 when the Nanking government charged Hallett E. Abend, *New York Times* correspondent, with willful misrepresentation and "insulting" references to the government and to the people of China. Dr. C. T. Wang, the foreign minister, addressed a letter to Nelson T. Johnson, U.S. minister to China, requesting that Abend be deported from China. Since Abend lived in Shanghai's International Settlement, he could not be expelled outright and, in fact, he never was deported. But the case was pending for nearly two years, during which time the Foreign Ministry denied Abend certain facilities.

The incident was closed only when Abend at last agreed on April 28, 1931, to write a letter expressing his regret that a "misunderstanding" had occurred. The Foreign Ministry then restored to him the facilities for obtaining information that had been withdrawn. At the same time, the ministry released a statement for publication distorting Abend's letter regretting a "misunderstanding" to make it appear that he had expressed regret for "unfair, false news reports."

In a further exercise of its authority, the Nationalist government established a Press Law effective December 13, 1930. This included the creation of a Censorship Board, operated as a part of the Ministry of the Interior. It included members of the Executive Yüan and of the Central Kuomintang, and representatives of the Military Council, headed by Chiang Kai-shek. The board set certain limitations on reporting, on editorial discussion of specified political topics, and sometimes on economic and social matters. It placed a ban on the import of such foreign publications as it found objectionable, authorized the suspension of publications transgressing specified limitations, and set fines and jail terms for such transgressions.

These new regulations did not apply, however, to foreign-owned publications printed in the international settlements of Shanghai, Tientsin, Peiping, and Hankow, all operating under the provisions of the treaties granting extraterritorial rights. The exemption also extended to vernacular papers "flying the foreign flag."

For reasons of tact and prudence, publishers within the international settlements proceeded with caution. They were obliged to work with officials of the government in a variety of ways, and so were the foreign correspondents based in the settlements. This recommended the maintenance of friendly relations. The publications, further, were dependent upon the Chinese postal service for some part of their distribution, which could be halted beyond the limits of the International Settlement, if the government saw fit to take such action.

Despite the caution with which both publishers and correspondents proceeded, the Shanghai International Settlement offered no certain sanctuary for free news reporting after May 15, 1931. The Nationalist government on that date announced that the Ministry of Communications had established censors in the offices of the commercial communications companies within the Settlement, as well as elsewhere in China. Even though the companies doing business there were technically beyond the jurisidiction of the government, other agreements respecting their rights to operate in greater China were due for early renewal. To protect their own positions, the companies felt obliged to cooperate with the Nanking government by yielding to the establishment of a censorship within their offices.[2] From this time, the problems of news coverage in Shanghai and in all of China became progressively more difficult.

Among foreign-owned newspapers in Hong Kong and China in the 1920s and 1930s, those of importance, under British sponsorship, included the *South China Morning Post* of Hong Kong, the *North China Daily News* of Shanghai, and the *Peking & Tientsin Times* of

---

2   The Chinese government was adapting a method first used by the Argentine government in Buenos Aires in the previous September (1930), and further extended in the summer of 1931. The method enabled the government to deny any application of an official censorship of its own.

Tientsin. A number of newspapers and periodicals also were conducted by U.S. sponsors, and a few by French sponsors. The U.S. group included the *China Press* of Shanghai, established in 1911, the *Shanghai Evening Post & Mercury,* dating from 1867 but only taking that name in 1931 following a series of mergers, the *North China Star* of Tientsin, and the *Peking Leader,* both dating from 1920. In addition, vernacular papers were associated with the *Post & Mercury.* The most important of the French-language newspapers, although not the first, was *Le Journal de Shanghai,* established in 1927 under ownership of a corporation formed by the French Chamber of Commerce in the International Settlement. Another was *Le Journal du Pékin,* dating from 1911.

The *China Press* and the *Shanghai Evening Post & Mercury* became great training grounds for correspondents reporting in Asia. The *China Press* was established in 1911 by Thomas F. Millard, a former correspondent for the *New York Herald* who had reported the Boxer Rebellion in 1900 and the Russo-Japanese War. He was in partnership with Dr. Wu Ting-fang, former Chinese ambassador to the United States. They also had financial support from Charles R. Crane, Chicago manufacturer, later to become U.S. minister to China in 1920–21, and from Benjamin W. Fleisher of Philadelphia, owner of the *Japan Advertiser* since 1908 and general manager of the *China Press* in 1911–13, before turning full attention to his paper in Japan.

Most staff members of the *China Press* were from the United States, and many became stringers or staff correspondents in the Far East for U.S. news agencies, newspapers, and magazines. Millard himself served as editor of the paper in its first several years. Following him came Carl Crow, Charles Laval, and Hollington K. (Holly) Tong, a graduate of the University of Missouri School of Journalism and also of the Columbia University Graduate School of Journalism, where he was a member of the first class, graduated in 1913.

Millard also had established the weekly *Millard's Review of the Far East* in Shanghai in 1917. Herbert Webb served briefly as editor. He was succeeded by John B. Powell, a graduate of the Missouri School of Journalism, who arrived in China in 1917. In 1919 Powell bought the paper and changed its name to the *China Weekly Review.* It became highly regarded throughout the world for the light it threw on affairs in the Far East. Powell also became a correspondent for the *Chicago Tribune* and a stringer for the *Manchester Guardian.*

In 1922 Millard sold his interest in the *China Press* to Edward Ezra, a Shanghai merchant, who died soon afterward. Mrs. Ezra and her brothers retained control of the paper until 1930. It was sold then to a Chinese syndicate, of which Hollington Tong was a member. He became editor and managing director of the paper until 1936, as well as chairman of the board of directors. Other members of that board included Chang Chu-ping, manager of *Shun Pao* of Shanghai, Carl Crow, a former editor, and William Henry Donald, former correspondent in China for the *New York Herald* and the *Times* of London.

The *Shanghai Post & Mercury* had had its origin in what was called the *Shanghai News-Letter,* published from 1867 to 1869 by two Americans, John Thorne, agent in China for Wells, Fargo & Company, and Howard Twombly, a missionary. In 1869 it was absorbed by the *Shanghai Evening Courier.* In due course, the *Courier* was absorbed by the *Shanghai Mercury,* established in 1879 and owned by British interests. The *Mercury* continued independently until 1931. Meanwhile, a *Shanghai Gazette* had been established in 1918 by Eugene Chen, ten years later to become minister of foreign affairs in the Nanking government. The *Gazette* ownership changed several times, with both Chinese and foreign principals involved, and the name itself had been changed to the *Shanghai Evening Post.* In April 1928 it became the property of the American Newspaper Company, Federal Incorporated, U.S.A. This was a company directed by Cornelius Vander Starr, a Californian who had entered the insurance business in China and was identified with the American Asiatic Underwriters. In 1931 the American Newspaper Company bought the *Shanghai Mercury,* which had become an organ of Japanese interests, and the two papers were merged in that year as the *Evening Post & Mercury.*

Starr, the controlling owner, did not direct the paper personally. His activities in the insurance field, and later as president of the U.S. Life Insurance Company of New York, required nearly all of his attention, and he was in New York much of the time. Carl Crow, formerly of the *China Press,* and also publisher of the *Evening Post* since 1929, directed the combined *Post & Mercury* for a time after the 1931 merger. By then also the owner of an advertising business of his own, Crow almost immediately yielded the position of editor and manager to Theodore Olin (Ted) Thackrey, also with the *Evening Post* since 1929.

Thackrey, who had arrived in China bringing experience as an editor with the Scripps-Howard Newspapers in the United States, directed the *Post & Mercury* in 1931–35, after which he resumed his journalistic career in the United States. Succeeding him as editor and manager of the *Evening Post & Mercury* was Randall C. Gould, in China since 1923, first with the *Peking Daily News* and then as correspondent for the UP and for the *Philadelphia Public Ledger–New York Evening Post* service. Editing the *Evening Post & Mercury* from

1935 until December 1941, Gould also was stringer correspondent in Shanghai for the *Christian Science Monitor.*

A vernacular edition of the *Evening Post, Ta Mei Wan Pao,* was continued under the *Post & Mercury,* with U.S.-educated Samuel H. Chang (Chang Shih-hseuh) as general manager, and Chu Hsin-kung as editor. A morning edition, *Ta Mai Pao,* was added, and the two vernacular papers claimed a combined circulation of nearly 100,000 in 1938.

The *North China Star* of Tientsin was controlled by Charles J. Fox, an American attorney. The *Peking Leader* was established in 1920 by a Chinese group, but in 1925 it came into the ownership of Grover Clark, an American journalist. After 1928, with the capital moved from Peking to Nanking, Clark sold the paper to Chinese interests once again. It was continued, with Dr. Philip Tyau of the new Chinese Nationalist Foreign Ministry as managing director. Edward Bing-shuey, Canadian-born and educated, but formerly with the Central Publicity Department of the Nanking government, was editor. The *Leader* was subsidized by the Nanking government, but was suspended in January 1931 following a demand upon the government from Tokyo.

One other vernacular daily with which an American was identified was *Chang Pao* of Shanghai, established during the period of World War I. It was sponsored by a Chinese merchant group, and concerned chiefly with business and commerce. The paper was organized by George E. Sokolsky, an early graduate of the Columbia University Graduate School of Journalism. He arrived in China just before World War I by way of Russia, and remained for more than a decade. In addition to his work with *Chang Pao,* Sokolsky served as an editor of the *Far Eastern Review,* established as a monthly in 1904 in Manila by George Bronson Rae. Sokolsky was also a stringer for the London *Daily Express* and other newspapers, and a correspondent for the *Ledger-Post* service, as well as a writer for magazines. In 1932, he returned to the United States to become a syndicated columnist on foreign affairs.

Most foreigners resident in China, especially those engaged in commercial undertakings, were strongly in favor of the extraterritorial privileges assured by the treaties concluded originally by Great Britain with the Chinese imperial government, and continued with some modifications under the republic from 1912 and under the Nationalist government from 1928.

There were those, however, who believed the treaties should be abrogated, or at least further modified, after the Nationalist government seemed well established. Some editors of foreign-language newspapers showed so much sympathy with this viewpoint in the 1930 period that they were obliged to retire from their positions under pressure from opposite-minded members in the foreign community. Among them was Henry G. W. Woodhead, editor since 1916 of the *Peking & Tientsin Times,* editor during the 1920s of the *China Year Book,* and a stringer both for British and U.S. agencies or newspapers. Such opposition also explained the early retirement of Jean Fontenoy as editor of *Le Journal de Shanghai* after previous service in Moscow for the Agence Havas and direction of that agency's China coverage. He was succeeded by G. S. Moresthe, formerly of *Le Petit Parisien.*

Prior to the establishment of the Nanking government in 1928, foreign press representation in China was largely British, and British coverage remained strong. For Reuters, William J. Moloney, based in Shanghai, directed that service in 1919–22. He was followed by William Turner in 1922–31, and Christopher J. Chancellor in 1931–39. James Melville Cox, formerly in Bombay and Colombo, was in Hong Kong from 1909 to 1930 and in Shanghai in 1930–34, when he moved to Tokyo. Geoffrey Imeson, in Shanghai from 1934–37, was chief editor in the Far East, and Spencer Moosa followed as acting chief. Longest in service, Frank Oliver was a staff member from 1927 to 1940.

For the *Times,* David Fraser, in Shanghai since the time of the Russo-Japanese War, was chief correspondent from 1912 until after World War I. He was then followed by Colin Malcolm MacDonald, Peter Fleming, and Frank Basil Riley until his death in Manchuria in 1927. For the *Daily Telegraph,* Woodhead of the *Peking & Tientsin Times* of Tientsin was a stringer for many years prior to his retirement in 1930, and Ellis Ashmead-Bartlett and George Gorman wrote from China for the *Telegraph* as roving correspondents. The *Manchester Guardian* received reports in the 1920s from Herbert B. Elliston, who wrote later also for the *Daily Herald.* John B. Powell also wrote later for the *Herald,* as did G. Lowes Dickinson and, in the 1930s, H. J. Timperley. Sir Percival Phillips and L. Impey were in China as roving correspondents for the *Daily Mail.* Sokolsky wrote as a stringer for the *Daily Express,* and Guenther Stein for the *News-Chronicle.* Some of these individuals also wrote for other papers and services in the United States and the United Kingdom.

The Associated Press had been represented in Shanghai during the war by Charles Stephenson Smith. Walter C. Whiffen was in Peking in 1918–21. James Pomeroy Howe, a freelance in China in 1911, was in Peking as staff correspondent for the AP in 1928 and in Shanghai in 1932. Morris J. Harris, formerly with the *Japan Advertiser,* was in Peking and Shanghai for the AP for the long period from 1924 to 1941, and Glenn Babb, another former *Japan Advertiser* staffer, also was in Peking and Shanghai during most of the years between 1926 and 1936.

The United Press was represented by Carl Crow, in Shanghai as early as 1910 as a stringer for at least a decade before becoming involved in his own advertising business and work with the *China Press* and the *Shanghai Evening Post.* Raymond Gifford (Ray) Marshall was in Peking for the UP in 1921-25, and was followed by Randall Gould until 1927, Demaree Bess until 1932, and by Herbert R. (Bud) Ekins until 1936. Burt L. Kuhn was in China in 1925, and Henry Mizzelwitz, formerly of the *Japan Advertiser,* was in Shanghai in 1927-30.

For the International News Service, John Goette was in Peking in 1924-41, and was dean of correspondents there; Lloyd Lehrbas was in Shanghai in 1923. Edna Lee Booker, beginning work on the *China Press* in 1922, also wrote for the INS from Shanghai from that time until 1943. From 1925, Dixon Hoste was in Shanghai for INS and Universal Service for nearly ten years. Duke N. Parry and Alfred Meyer were early staff members, and Kuhn was with INS before switching to UP in 1925. Thackrey was a stringer in 1929, while also with the *Evening Post,* and Edward Hunter, formerly of the *Japan Advertiser,* was with INS in 1931-33.

For newspapers of the United States, Gould and Bess wrote for the *Christian Science Monitor,* Powell for the *Chicago Tribune,* Abend for the *New York Times,* Sokolsky for the *Ledger-Post* service, and Millard for the *New York Herald* and later, from 1925 to 1941, for the *New York Times.* Elliston was a stringer for the *New York World* in the 1920s, as well as for the British papers noted, and Linton Wells also wrote from China for that paper in 1911-31. Charles Dailey and Frederick Smith had written for the *Chicago Tribune,* Harrison Forman and A. J. Billingham for the *New York Times,* as had Archibald T. Steele, although he was later with the AP and then the *Chicago Daily News.* Nathaniel Pfeffer and Thomas Steep wrote for the *New York Tribune* prior to 1924, and Victor Keen became Shanghai correspondent for the *New York Herald Tribune* in 1929.

Foreign reporters who went to the Siberian border in 1929 to report the clash of arms there between the Nationalist and Soviet troops included Goette of INS, Bess of UP, and two experienced correspondents temporarily in the Far East, Wilbur Forrest of the *New York Herald Tribune* and William Philip Simms of the Scripps-Howard Newspapers.

Many of these and other correspondents moved in a complex pattern of assignments in China, Japan, and elsewhere between 1920 and 1930. That pattern was even more complex after 1931, as China became a major center for events of world importance and concern, with the number of correspondents and the volume of news greatly increased.

PART II
The Media: 1920–1940

News Agencies of the World: 1939

(Listing is by country, agency and logo, date of origin, operating base, and sponsorship. An asterisk indicates Ring Combination membership in 1934, the year the Ring organization suspended.)

Afghanistan	Bakhtar; 1939; Kabul; Official.
Argentina	Agencia Noticiosa Saporitii (ANS); 1900; Buenos Aires; Commercial.
Australia	Australian Associated Press (AAP); 1935; Melbourne; Cooperative.
	Australian United Press, Ltd. (AUP); 1930; Sydney; Commercial.
Austria	*Amtliche Nachrichtenstelle (AN); 1920; Vienna; Official.
Belgium	*Agence Télégraphique Belge (BELGA); 1920; Brussels; Semi-official.
Brazil	Agência Meridional (AM); 1931; Rio de Janeiro; Commercial.
Bulgaria	*Bulgarska Telegrafitscheka Agentzia (BTA); 1898; Sofia; Official.
Canada	*Canadian Press, Ltd. (CP); 1917; Toronto; Cooperative.
	British United Press (BUP); 1922; Montreal; Commercial.
China	*Central News Agency (CNA); 1924; Nanking/Chungking; Official.
	New China News Agency (NCNA); 1937; Yenan/Peking; Official (Communist).
Czechoslovakia	*Cëskoslovenska Tisková Kancelár (CTK, CETEKA); 1918; Prague; Independent.
Denmark	*Ritzaus Bureau (RB, RITZAU); 1866; Copenhagen; Independent.
Estonia	*Eesti Telegraafi Agentuur, A.S. (ETA); 1920; Tallinn; Independent.
Finland	*Suomen Tietotoimisto-Finska Notisbyrån (STT-FNB); 1887; Helsinki; Semi-official.
France	*Agence Havas (HAVAS); 1835; Paris; Semi-official.
	Agence Télégraphique Radio (Radio); 1918; Paris; Independent.
Germany	*Deutsches Nachrichten Büro (DNB); 1933; Berlin; Official. (Formed by Nazi merger in 1933 of *Wolff'sche Telegraphen Büro–Conti-Nachrichten Büro (WTB-CNB), 1849, and Telegraphen-Union Internationaler Nachrichtendienst (TU), 1913.)
Greece	*Agence d'Athènes (AA); 1905; Athens; Semi-official.
Hungary	*Magyar Távirati Iroda (MTI or IRODA); 1881; Budapest; Semi-official. (Replaced *Ungarische Telegraphen Bureau (UTB), 1861, in 1920.)

India	*Associated Press of India (API); 1905; Calcutta; Independent. (Controlled by Reuters, Ltd., after 1915.)
Iran	Pars News Agency (PARS); 1938; Teheran; Official.
Israel	Israeli News Agency (INA); 1923; Tel Aviv; Semi-official.
Italy	*Agenzia Stefani (Stefani); 1853; Rome; Official.
Japan	*Domei Tsushin-sha (DOMEI); 1936; Tokyo; Semi-official. (Formed by government merger in 1936 of *Nippon Shimbun Rengo-sha (RENGO), 1925, and Nippon Dempo Tsushin-sha (DENTSU), 1901.)
Latvia	*Latvijas Telegrafa Agentura (LETA); 1920; Riga; Independent.
Lithuania	*Litauische Telegraphen-Agentur (LTA); 1920; Kaunas; Independent.
Mexico	Agencia Noticiosa Telegrafica Americana (ANTA); 1935; Mexico City; Semi-official.
Netherlands	*Algemeen Nederlandsch Persbureau (ANP); 1934; The Hague; Independent. (Replaced Reuters affiliate, Nederlandsch Telegraaf Agentschap (ATP).)
New Zealand	New Zealand Press Association (NZPA); (1878); Wellington; Cooperative.
Norway	*Norske Telegrambyrå (NTB); 1867; Oslo; Independent.
Poland	*Polska Agencja Telegraficzna (PAT); Warsaw; Official.
Portugal	*Agence Havas (branch); Lisbon; Semi-official.
Rumania	*Agence Orient Radio (RADOR); 1919; Bucharest; Official.
South Africa	*South African Press Association (SAPA); 1938; Johannesburg; Cooperative. (Replaced *Reuter South African Press Association (RSAPA).)
Spain	*Agence Espagñol et International; 1926; Madrid; Official. (Replaced *Agencia Telegrafica Fabra, 1867.) Agencia Efe (EFE); 1938; Madrid; Official.
Sweden	*Tidningarnas Telegrambyrå (TT); 1921; Stockholm; Cooperative, Semi-official. (Replaced *Svenska Telegrambyrån (ST), 1867.)
Switzerland	*Agence Télégraphique Suisse (ATS); 1894; Berne; Independent. Agenzia Telegrafica Svizzera (ATS) (Italian section). Schweizerische Depeschenagentur (SDA) (German section).
Turkey	*Andolu Ajansi (AA); 1920; Ankara/Angora; Semi-official.
USSR	*Telegrafnoie Agenstvo Sovietskavo Soyuza (TASS); 1925; Moscow; Official. (In 1925 replaced Rossiyskoye Telegraphnoye Agenstvo (ROSTA), 1918 and 1894.)
United Kingdom	*Reuters, Ltd. (REUTERS); 1851; London; Independent. *Press Association, Ltd. (PA); 1868; London; Independent. (In 1925 acquired control of majority of shares in Reuters, Ltd.) *Exchange Telegraph Co., Ltd. (EXTEL); 1872; London; Independent.
United States	*Associated Press (AP); 1848; New York; Cooperative, Independent. United Press Associations (UP); 1907; New York; Commercial, Independent. International News Service (INS); 1909; New York; Commercial, Independent. Transradio Press Service (TP); 1934; New York; Commercial, Independent.
Yugoslavia	*Agence Avala (AVALA); 1919; Belgrade; Semi-official.

News Agencies and Syndicates 12

The return of peace in 1918 made it possible for news agencies to resume an exchange of reports on a world-wide scale across frontiers and through the Ring Combination as they had done prior to the four-year wartime interruption. The original Big Three among world agencies basic to the Ring Combination provided the nucleus as before around which smaller national agencies were grouped to receive and deliver reports. Also as before, each of the Big Three had its own exclusive territories in the world for distribution of the full report. The three were Reuters, Ltd., based in London, the Agence Havas in Paris, and Wolff'sche Telegraphen Büro-Conti-Nachrichten-Büro in Berlin.

The national agencies associated with these three world agencies gave the Ring Combination a total membership of twenty-eight by the mid-1920s, the largest number since the group was organized in 1870. Some were new, having been established in war-born countries, a few were reorganized and retitled, and others had been formed in the years from about 1835. The Associated Press in the United States, second only to the Agence Havas in age, but still counted as a national agency within the Ring organization, had advanced in its scope of coverage since 1900 so that it was equal in status by the 1920s to any one of the Big Three world agencies.

As before the war, there were other news agencies operating independently of the Ring Combination. Most of them were small and often specialized in the subject matter reported, which might be politics, finance and commerce, sports, or religious interests. Other independent services, as well as news agency subsidiaries, were in the nature of syndicates, providing a variety of feature material, entertaining as well as informative, and including photo services.

Two of the independent news agencies established in the United States in the first decade of the century had grown so vigorously during the war years, including subscribers in other countries, that they also could be classified as world agencies by the 1920s. These were the United Press and the International News Service.

Many agencies were private enterprises, and a few were cooperative nonprofit services, owned and controlled by member newspapers. In either form, financial existence required a subscribing national press large enough and prosperous enough to provide adequate support. Where such support was insufficient, the alternative was either financial support from private or political sources or government subsidy. With support from such sources, the agency or any medium so assisted might be expected to respond to the wishes and interests of its beneficiary, possibly to the point of following a propaganda line. These several varieties of control were represented in news agency ownership throughout the world.

A major change came in the relationship between news agencies in 1934 when the Ring Combination ceased to exist. This change, discussed later, meant an end to exclusive territories for the distribution of any services—also considered limited territories—except as such limitation might be set by a government. With that same limitation, it also meant that any or all agencies after 1934 might operate as independent organizations.

Postwar News Agency Changes

The end of the war brought the end of the Austrian K. K. Telegraphen Korrespondenz-Büro (Korrburo) and of its Hungarian subsidiary, the Ungarische Telegraphen Korrespondenz-Büro, both of which had been in close relationship with the Wolff agency in Germany. The new Austrian republic established an official government news agency in 1922. This was the Amtliche Nachrichtenstelle Agentur (ANA) based in Vienna.

The new government of Hungary took over an existing private agency established in Budapest in 1881, the Magyar Tavirati Iroda (MTI or IRODA), and made it official. In 1920, it was released from government control. Its direction was vested instead in a holding company also operating an MOT Telegraph Agency, a new Hungarian Broadcasting Company, an advertising agency, and a Film Bureau producing newsreels and advertising films. The agencies in Austria and in Hungary continued to receive the Wolff reports. The new republic of Czechoslovakia formed a new agency, the Cëskoslovenska Tisková Kancelář (CTK or CETEKA) agency, with headquarters in Prague. The new Kingdom of Yugoslavia formed a semi-official agency in 1919, the Agence Avalar (Avala), with headquarters in Belgrade. It later was made an official government agency. Bulgaria formed an official agency at Sofia in 1919, the Bulgarski Telegrafitscheka Agentzia (BTA), titled also in French as the Agence Télégraphique Bulgare (ATB).

Turkey, after passing through an internal change of government in 1920, formed the Anadolu Ajansi, or Agence d'Anatoli (AA), with its main office in the new capital, Angora, and a branch office in Constantinople. (In 1930, these cities became Ankara and Istanbul, respectively.) A semi-official agency originally, with 45 per cent of its shares owned by the government, it became a private company in 1925, but with a government subsidy, comparable in that respect to France's Agence Havas.

Rumania formed an official agency in 1919, the Agence Orient Radio (Rador), in Bucharest. Ownership, vested in the National Bank of Rumania, itself an arm of the government, passed to the control of the Ministry of Foreign Affairs in 1924 and became recognized in 1926 as semi-official, with 60 per cent of the stock owned by the government and the remaining 40 per cent owned jointly by the National Bank and the Bucharest Chamber of Commerce.

In the north of Europe, the new republics of Poland, Latvia, Lithuania, and Estonia were formed in whole or in part from areas formerly parts of czarist Russia and Germany. All four established new official agencies. Poland formed the Polska Agencja Telegraficzna (PAT), also using the French version of the name, the Agence Télégraphique Polonaise, with its headquarters in Warsaw. Latvia formed the Latvijas Telegrafa Agentura (Leta), or Agence Télégraphique Lettone, of Riga. Lithuania formed the Litauische Telegraphen-Agentur (LTA), or Agence Télégraphique Lithuanienne, of Kaunas. Estonia formed the Eesti Telegraafi Agentur, A.S. (Eta), or Agence Télégraphique Esthonienne, of Tallinn.

The Soviet government in 1918 had supplanted the two prerevolutionary Russian agencies with an official Rossiyskoye Telegraphnoye Agenstvo (Rosta), or Russian Telegraph Agency, of Moscow. This was reorganized in July 1925 and became the Telegrafnoie Agenstvo Sovietskavo Soyuza (Tass). The name in that full version, although rarely used, was variously transliterated from the Cyrillic script. It also appeared as the Telegrafnoye Agenstvo Sovietskogo Soiuza, as the Telegrafnoje Agenstvo Ssojusa, and as the Telegrafnoe Agenstvo Soyuza. In some versions the agency became "agentstvo."

With the outbreak of World War I, the Wolff service had ceased to go to the Russian press, but continued to go to neutral Norway, Sweden, and Denmark. Swedish publishers and editors, offended by a bias injected into the Wolff wartime reports, chose to form a new cooperative agency owned by the Stockholm newspapers, with no Wolff participation such as had existed in the Svenska Telegrambyrån, a virtual subsidiary of the German agency. In 1920, therefore, a new Tidningarnas Telegrambyrå (TT) was formed in Stockholm. The Swedish provincial newspapers also formed their own cooperative, Presstelegrambolaget, but it was merged with TT in 1922 to form a general agency owned by the press of the country.

Wolff's association with the Ritzaus Bureau of Denmark ended with the war. Havas and Reuters also lost their joint monopoly position in Belgium in 1920 when the reestablished Belgian government formed a new Agence Télégraphique Belge (Belga) based in Brussels. It continued to receive the Havas report, however. In Holland, the Reuters affiliate, the Nederlandsch Telegraaf Agentschap (NTA), with the associated Vas Dias and Belifante domestic services, were supplanted in 1934 by a new cooperative Dutch agency, the Algemeen Nederlandsch Persbureau (ANP).

The Havas association with the Stefani agency of Italy ended in 1924 when Stefani became an official arm of the Italian Fascist government. A Havas financial interest in the Agencia Telegrafica Fabra in Spain also ended in 1926 when that service was sold to a Spanish banking group and retitled the Agence Espagñol et International. The Havas reports continued to be received by both agencies for use.

The Ring Combination membership included those European agencies that had survived wartime or immediate postwar change, as in Belgium, Holland, Italy, Spain, Denmark, Norway, Sweden, Finland, Switzerland, and Greece.

A series of changes occurred in Japan. The Kokusai agency gained its independence of Reuters in 1923, although it continued to receive the report. In 1925 Kokusai absorbed the Toho service, but was itself reorganized in 1926 to become the Rengo agency. In 1927 Rengo absorbed the Teikoku agency and in 1934 added AP reports to those of Reuters. It also sent correspondents of its own abroad. Then in 1936 the new army-dominated government of Japan forced a merger of Rengo and Dentsu, with an official Domei agency resulting.

In China, the Kuomintang in 1924 formed the first news agency in that country at Canton, the Chung Yang Sheh, or Central News Agency (CNA). In 1928 its headquarters was moved to Nanking, the new capital of the Nationalist government. It became the official government agency, directed by Yu Wei-yi, but soon succeeded by Tung-tze Hsiao. Branch offices were established not only at Canton, but at Shanghai, Peiping, Tientsin, and Hankow. Staff or stringer correspondents were named in those cities and others within China, in Hong Kong, and in some major capitals of the world. The CNA became a member of the Ring Combination, with exclusive rights to the Reuters service.

Reorganizations brought the formation of the Canadian Press (CP) in 1923 and the South African Press Association (SAPA) in 1938. An Australian United Press, Ltd. (AUP) was organized in 1932, a merger of small services owned by individual newspapers, and concerned with domestic news distribution. With headquarters in Sydney, the AUP established offices in Melbourne and in Canberra, which had become the active capital in 1927, and stringers were engaged in other cities. It exchanged news with the British United Press (BUP), formed in Canada in 1922, and with the Exchange Telegraph agency of London. The Australian metropolitan papers formed a second agency in 1935, the Australian Associated Press (AAP), a cooperative, with its headquarters in Melbourne and offices in London and New York. The Ring Combination by then no longer existed, but the AAP did arrange to receive the Reuters service.

Central News, Ltd. (CN) and the Exchange Telegraph Company (Extel), both of London, were among the oldest of non-Ring services. Since 1908 more than half the shares in Central News were owned in the United States. In 1937, however, Melvin J. Woodworth of New York, the second largest shareholder, sold his interest to Extel, which then was working closely with the Press Association, Ltd.

Among those writing for Central News during its postwar years from 1920 to 1938 were W. J. Deeth in Paris, and H. V. Wallace King in Berlin, where he also wrote for the London *Daily Herald* and for the *Detroit News*. For Extel, André Glarner, formerly of the UP, wrote from Paris from 1912 until his retirement in 1952, and also wrote from Geneva. James Gallagher in Paris and A. E. Ruttle in Berlin also wrote for Extel.

In France, the Agence Télégraphique Radio (Agence Radio), established in 1918, entered into a news exchange with the United Press. In 1929, however, it came under the control of the Agence Havas, and under its full direction in 1932 through an interlocking stock ownership. In 1937 a new arrangement gave the French Ministry of Foreign Affairs an influence over its output. An exchange arrangement between the Agence Radio and Extel continued until 1940, however. Two other older French agencies also dealt with business and financial information, the Agence Fournier and the Agence Économique et Financière.

In Italy, under the Fascist government in the years after 1922, an Agenzia di Roma became a semi-official service specializing in political and business reports. An Agenzia Volta also provided political and business service. A privately owned service, l'Informazione, operated from 1925 to 1938, with correspondents in Italian cities, in a few European capitals, and in Buenos Aires. Its reports were circulated in mimeographed form to newspapers and embassies in Rome, and to private subscribers in Italy and some other countries.

In Spain, the Agencia Mencheta, dating from 1882, specialized in sports news. Logos, established in Madrid in 1928 by the newspaper *El Debate* but later converted to a cooperative enterprise, distributed a specialized report primarily of Catholic news.

In addition to Logos, two other special Catholic news services were established in 1920. One was the Katholischer Internationale Presse-agentur (KIPA), with headquarters in Fribourg, Switzerland, serving German-language Catholic papers in Europe. The other was formed in the United States, the National Catholic Welfare Conference News Service (NCWC), with headquarters in Washington, D.C.

A Jewish Telegraph Agency, Inc. (JTA) began in London in 1919 to provide matter of special interest to Jewish or Hebrew newspapers throughout the world. Its headquarters was moved to New York in 1936, and it was reorganized as a nonprofit service, with support from Jewish groups and individuals in the United States, Great Britain, and elsewhere. The JTA and the *Jewish Daily Forward*, established in New York in 1897, were jointly represented in Berlin by Jacob Lestschinsky until 1933. He then was arrested by the new Nazi government and forced to leave. The JTA continued to be represented in London by Alexander Puninasky and in Rome for a time by Edouard Kleinlerer.

Other specialized European agencies formed after World War I included two in Norway. One was Bull's Presstjanst, established by Cornelius Bull in 1927 at Halden, but with its headquarters moved in 1929 to Stockholm, thus becoming technically a Swedish agency. It specialized in news of the Scandinavian countries for distribution in those countries. The other was Press Telegraph (PT), established at Oslo in 1938. A private agency, it offered a financial and commercial service, with stringer correspondents in Norwegian cities, exchange arrangements with financial services in other countries, and distribution in Norway, Sweden, and Denmark.

In Sweden, the Svensk-Internationalla Pressbyram of Stockholm and the Svensk-Americansa Nyhetsbyrån of Stockholm and New York provided special reports. In Finland, there was the Presscentralen of Helsinki and also the Työväen Sanomalehtien Tietotoimisto (TST), a Social Democratic service for newspapers of that political persuasion in the country.

A financial service, Agence Cosmographique, was formed in Switzerland. Interbalkan of Bucharest was concerned with news of southern Europe. In Austria, a Korrespondenz Wilhelm was established as a semi-official political service. A Slovak News Agency (ZAS) had its headquarters in Bratislava, Czechoslovakia. Three small agencies were formed in Poland, the Agencja Telegraficzna Espress (ATE), the Agencja Eschodnia, and the Polska Informacja Polityczna (PIP), a semi-official agency concerned with political topics, attached to the Ministry of Foreign Affairs.

There were regional agencies in the Soviet Union handling the distribution of the Tass service in the republics after 1925, and also returning local and regional reports to Tass in Moscow. Among them were the Radio-telegrafnoe Agenstvo Ukrainy (RATAU), (Ukrainian Radio-telegraphic Agency), and Zakavkaspoe Telegrafnoe Agenstvo (ZAKTAG) (Transcaucasian Telegraph Agency).

As the ANP was formed in Holland in 1934, a new cooperative agency, so in the Dutch East Indies an Algemeen Nieuws en Telegraaf Agentschap (ANETA) service was formed at Batavia in the same year. Receiving news by wireless from Holland, allied to ANP, and returning reports to Amsterdam, it also became known as Aneta-Holland. A smaller agency, Kantorberita Antara (ANTARA), was formed at Batavia in 1937.

In India, the Associated Press of India (API) was the only agency serving the press of that country after World War I. A Reuters subsidiary, it distributed that report. Also receiving some financial support from the government of India, it was commonly regarded as both semi-official and pro-British.

The upsurge of nationalist sentiment in India brought a demand for a new agency more likely to reflect the public aspirations for independence. A Free Press of India (FPI) was established in 1927 as a new service, with headquarters in Bombay. It was an agency sponsored by Dr. Annie Besant, British-born founder of the Central Hindu College at Benares, and by other followers of Gandhi, with S. Sadanand as managing editor. An office was opened in London and a stringer correspondent was engaged in New York. To provide a sure outlet for FPI reports, an English-language daily, the *Free Press Journal,* was started at Bombay in June 1930, an *Indian Express* at Madras, and others were planned for several large cities, to be published in the Gujarati and Marathi languages, as well as in English.

The FPI and its associated newspapers encountered obstacles, however. Reuters and the API had a near-monopoly on telegraphic news communications facilities in India. This alone made distribution of the FPI reports almost impossible. Further, some Indian nationalists themselves already publishing newspapers objected to having a news agency sponsoring newspapers of its own. In addition, the British government and the vice-regal government of India were disturbed by viewpoints put forward in some FPI reports. The result was that the FPI was forced to suspend in 1935, although the Bombay and Madras newspapers continued.

The disappearance of the FPI might have left the nationalist newspapers again without a special service. In 1933, however, a United Press of India (UPI) had been formed, with headquarters in Calcutta and a branch office in Lahore. More moderate in the tone of its reports than the FPI, it nevertheless was a nationalist enterprise. The active figures in its operation were Dr. B. C. Roy, managing director of *Forward* of Calcutta, and B. Sen Gupta, who had directed the FPI office in Calcutta. The UPI began with sixteen Calcutta and Lahore newspapers as subscribers. It depended for its reports almost entirely upon stringers, including a half dozen outside India. The agency was to gain strength during World War II.[1]

In Iran, the first news agency, Pars, was formed in 1934. It was an official service operated by the Ministry of Foreign Affairs in Teheran In Afghanistan the first agency was formed in 1939 at Kabul. Known as Bakhtar, it was a division of the government Press Department, and therefore official. It served the limited number of publications in the country, the state-operated radio, government ministries, and diplomatic missions. It engaged a few stringers abroad, but depended for world reports primarily upon contract services from other agencies.

In China, the official Central News Agency (CNA) of Nanking was supplemented by two small semi-official services, Kuo Wen of Canton and Kuo Min of Shanghai. A Communist service called the Nationalist News Agency in translation existed briefly in Hankow, and a Japanese propaganda agency Shun Shih was in Shanghai in 1937. All except CNA itself were short-lived.

In the Western Hemisphere, the British United Press (BUP) had been formed in Montreal in 1922, with Charles F. Crandall, a Canadian citizen, as principal owner. A branch office was established in London in 1924. Herbert Bailey, formerly in Petrograd and in France during the war for the *Daily Express* and the *Daily Mail,* was director of the BUP from 1924 until his death in 1939. He was succeeded by Francis Hoult (Frank) Fischer who had been with the agency for ten years.

Independent of the United Press, the BUP had its own correspondents throughout much of the British Empire and Commonwealth, and elsewhere, plus an exchange arrangement with the Australian United Press after 1932. The BUP nevertheless distributed the UP service as a part of its total report reaching newspapers in Canada, Australia, Great Britain, and other areas. It also established a feature syndicate, British United Features, which originated material but also distributed the output of the United Features Syndicate of New York, a UP subsidiary.

---

1 The UPI in India was suspended in 1958, the same year the unrelated UPI was formed in the United States as a merger of the UP and the INS.

The Latin American press was served with world news reports chiefly by news agencies of other countries, notably the Agence Havas, the United Press, the Associated Press, and to some extent by the International News Service. Individual Latin American newspapers had their own staff or stringer correspondents abroad, however. The small and specialized Agencia Noticiosa Saporiti (ANS) of Buenos Aires, established in 1900, was the only service that seemed able to survive, and it went only to provincial newspapers in Argentina.

A somewhat more ambitious service was formed in Brazil in 1931, the Agencia Meridional, Ltda., of Rio de Janeiro. It was sponsored by the Diarios Associados newspaper group conducted by Assis ("Chatõ") Chateaubriand. It gathered domestic news only, largely through an exchange based on the content of the Chateaubriand newspapers, and its reports were directed exclusively to those newspapers and radio stations also forming part of the considerable Chateaubriand empire. There were two other independent Brazilian services, the Agencia Brasiliera and the União Telegráfica Brasiliera. Both were small and limited.

In 1935, with the Ring Combination at an end, the Agence Havas established a subsidiary in China. It proved impossible to maintain, however, in view of Japanese military advances there. Another Havas subsidiary, the Agencia Noticiosa Telegrafica Americana (ANTA), was established in Mexico City in 1935, with support from the Mexican government. Although semi-official in character, it was regarded as having prospects of success. The forced suspension of the Agence Havas itself in 1940, however, as a result of the wartime German occupation of France, brought an end to ANTA as well, although it lingered until 1943, with support from the Reuters agency.

Wolff and German Agency Changes

Among the world agencies, the greatest change in the 1920s and 1930s was that affecting the Wolff agency of Germany. Operated since 1865 as Wolff'sche Telegraphen Büro-Conti-Nachrichten-Büro (WTB-CNB), it was a limited stock company owned primarily by the private Bleichröder bank of Berlin, but with government financing that made it at least a semi-official agency.

The Wolff agency, as it was commonly known, had come under the control of the German government in 1917, in the midst of the war. With the collapse of the monarchy in 1918, it reverted to the control of the Bleichröder bank, of which Paul Schawabach then was senior part-

ner. The agency was directed, as it had been since 1887, by Dr. Heinrich
Mantler. Its activity was curtailed for a time after the war when the
Allies maintained a temporary *cordon sanitaire* around Germany.
These restrictions were eased in 1923, as the Weimar Republic became
fully operative. Wolff no longer had exclusive rights in Central
Europe for news distribution, however, but shared those rights with
Reuters and Havas, except in Germany itself.

By 1930, the technical direction of the agency rested with its domestic
division, officially known as the Continental Telegraphen-Compagnii.
The WTB–CNB as a unit was capitalized at 800,000 Reichsmarks
($200,000). In addition to its Berlin headquarters, it had district of-
fices in Hamburg, Frankfurt-am-Main, Cologne, Leipzig, and more
than fifteen other cities in Germany. To these offices it distributed
about 30,000 words of foreign and domestic news each day, redistrib-
uted to about 2,100 newspapers and other subscribers, including radio
stations. Hellschreiber wireless-activated tape printers were used to
provide service to 350 of the larger papers, a Siemens teleprinter network for others, while smaller papers were served by telephone or
messenger. By 1932, a limited multiple-address wireless system was introduced at a special low rate.

The Wolff service never had a staff or stringer representation
abroad approaching that of Reuters or Havas in size. The greatest original Wolff coverage outside of Germany existed during the 1930–33
period. In those years the agency had staff representatives not only in
London and Paris as before, but in Rome, Vienna, Moscow, Prague,
Amsterdam, Berne, Geneva, Brussels, Budapest, Madrid, Copenhagen, Helsinki, Istanbul, Sofia, New York, Washington, and Shanghai.
There were stringers in Oslo, Stockholm, Riga, Tallinn, Ankara,
Cairo, Tokyo, and elsewhere. Notable among its staff correspondents
were Siegfried Horn and W. Stellbogen in Paris, Wilhelm Klein in
Geneva, and Emil Klaessig and Kurt Sell in Washington. Klaessig was
president of the Association of Foreign Correspondents in the United
States in 1930–31.

The Wolff agency also sponsored a number of supplementary and
specialized services. Among them were the Deutsche Diplomatische-
Politische Korrespondenz and the Aussenpolitische Korrespondenz,
both dealing with foreign affairs and both edited by Dr. Edgar Stern-
Rubarth, a director and last editor of the Wolff agency itself. Another
was the Berliner Berichte Dienst (B. B. Dienst), providing reports
from Berlin for the German provincial papers. A *Berliner Lokalnach-
richten* also provided Berlin reports. Other Wolff services included
Reichstag reports, commercial news and stock market reports, sports
news, and a distribution of prepared editorials for use by any paper.

Contrary to earlier years, Wolff–CNB had substantial competition in Germany after the war from an independent agency. Known as the Telegraphen-Union Internationaler Nachrichtendienst, G.m.b.H., with headquarters in Berlin, it had been formed in 1913, owned jointly by Dammert-Verlag and Patria Literarischer Verlag, two publishing organizations producing industrial and agricultural periodicals.

In 1917, ownership of the Telegraphen-Union, or TU as it was commonly known, was acquired by Dr. Alfred Hugenberg, an executive with the Krupp steel and munitions enterprises. He became an influential figure in the German press world during the fifteen years following, owning newspapers, a feature syndicate, an advertising agency, and UFA, the leading film company.

The Telegraphen-Union, capitalized at 1,325,000 Reichsmarks (about $330,000) and with Otto Mejer as editor, was mainly concerned with the news of Germany. It arranged to receive a world report from the United Press of New York and the service of Exchange Telegraph in London. It also had about thirty staff and stringer representatives abroad. These included H. W. von Doemming in London and later in Washington; F. H. Glimpf also in London; Nicholas V. Grote in Rome; W. von Hahn in Geneva; and E. von Mensenkampff and O. Fierman-Kruyth in Paris.

In 1928, the TU absorbed two old, independent Berlin agencies, the Herold Depeschen Büro dating from 1862 and the Telegraphisches Büro Louis Hirsch formed in 1868. It gained subscribers throughout Germany and some in Central European countries. It also provided specialized services comparable to some of those produced by Wolff–CNB. Independent of the Ring Combination, it was more active than the Wolff agency.

Another German agency, noncompetitive with the Wolff–CNB or TU because of its special character, was the Transozean Nachrichten. Dating from 1913 and closely associated with the German Ministry of Foreign Affairs, it distributed without charge news and information by wireless during the war years for use by foreign publications. In this, its mission was propagandistic. In continuing after the war, Transozean gained a reasonably good reputation for its service, limited though it was, and its reports were used by some newspapers in the Balkans, Latin America, and Asia. It had a few correspondents abroad, among them Helmut Gansser in Geneva and J. Plaut in Shanghai.

When the National Socialist party gained control in Germany in 1933, the entire press and radio organization within the country was forced into the service of the regime. One of the first acts of the new government was to create its own official agency, replacing services previously maintained by the National Socialist party to distribute information and propaganda. These had been the Nationalsozialistische Partiekorrespondenz (NSK) and the Verein deutsche Zeitungswert (VdZ).

The new agency was the Deutsches Nachrichten Büro (DNB). Both the Wolff–CNB and the Telegraphen-Union were immediately required to merge with it. Their offices, bureaus, equipment, and staff were taken over. Otto Mejer, who had directed the TU, became managing director of DNB. Dr. Mantler, who had served some forty-five years as director of the Wolff–CNB organization, was retired and died soon after. Stern-Rubarth, chief editor, was dismissed because he was Jewish, as were many others throughout the German press and media organizations.

The DNB operated in close association with the Ministry of Foreign Affairs and, more particularly, with the new Ministry of Public Enlightenment and Propaganda, the first government ministry of any country to bear a name so frankly descriptive of its purpose and giving recognition to the unabashed use of information as a tool in shaping public opinion. Dr. Joseph Goebbels, heading the ministry, was outspoken on that issue. It administered a censorship as well as a program of propaganda exceeding in scope anything previously known.

The DNB provided a general news report to the press and radio of Germany. The Deutsche Diplomatische-Politische Korrespondenz, one of the former Wolff services, was continued under that name, although with different direction and as a channel through which to distribute matter reflecting the policies of the new government on foreign affairs. A Dienst aus Deutschland (Service from Germany), somewhat comparable to the former Aussenpolitische Korrespondenz, was created to distribute abroad without charge selected materials supportive of the Nazi government.

The DNB sent more correspondents abroad than Wolff ever had, but the results added nothing to the quality of news coverage. Kurt Sell, who had been in Washington for Wolff, remained for DNB, but was soon succeeded by H. W. von Doemming, formerly there for TU. Wolf Dietrick Langan, who had followed von Doemming in London for TU, remained there for DNB.

The Transozean Nachrichten service survived the Nazi assumption of power in Germany, but was reconverted to a propaganda purpose under the Ministry of Public Enlightenment and Propaganda. It disseminated news and information by shortwave radio, especially to the Far East and Latin America, and had offices in other countries including the United States. Such offices served as cover for propaganda activities and espionage.

The Agence Havas grew in the years between the wars, but ended its existence in 1940, after 105 years, when the World War II German occupation of France made it suddenly impossible to continue.

Charles Lafitte, director of the agency in Paris since 1897, held that position until 1924. He was succeeded by Léon Renier until the mid-1930s, and then by Charles Houssaye, formerly director of the South American service and successor during the 1914–18 war to his uncle, Henri Houssaye, as director of the news service itself. Pierre Guimier directed the advertising division. Léon Rollin, correspondent in Vienna in 1914, and later in Madrid, South America, and Washington, and diplomatic correspondent in Paris, directed the foreign news service during much of the postwar period. He then became inspector-general for the agency in 1934.

Even though some Paris dailies had correspondents abroad, the dependence of the press, radio, and the people of France upon Havas for news was almost total. The service was distributed nationally over a 4,000-kilometer network of telegraph lines activating teleprinters, and it provided a telephone and messenger service in Paris. The advertising division, introduced in 1852, represented more than 200 newspapers.

The Havas service was almost equally important in some other countries, notably those in Latin America. It went to the Swiss ATS agency and the Agence Belge of Belgium; to French overseas areas in Africa and the Pacific; to Indo-China; to areas mandated to France under the League of Nations, such as Syria and Lebanon; to the Agence Télégraphique Monaco, which it controlled; to the Agenzia Telegrafica Stefani of Italy, which it controlled until 1924; and to the Agencia Telegrafica Fabra of Spain until 1926. Even with those changes, the Italian and Spanish agencies continued to receive the Havas report, as did also the press of Portugal. It formed part of the Ring Combination exchange with Reuters, and Wolff/DNB.

Utilizing the new shortwave transmitter erected in 1931 at Pontoise near Paris, and with the financial aid of the French government, Havas introduced the multiple-address system of transmission to make news more widely available in Latin America and other areas of the world at a rate lower than any other agency or service could match at the time. By January 1934 the reports were reaching more than 2,000 newspapers in many countries.

In 1934, with Ring Combination limitations ended on distribution of service, Havas established its short-lived subsidiary agency in China, and in 1935 joined with the Mexican government in sponsoring the Agencia Noticiosa Telegrafica Americana (ANTA) in Mexico City. From 1929 until 1937, Havas also controlled the Agence Télégraphique Radio (Agence Radio) established in Paris in 1918. After 1937 that agency was reorganized, and was believed to have become subject to the control of the Ministry of Foreign Affairs.

The close relations that had existed between the Agence Havas and the French government almost from the time of its formation continued after 1920. Government funds were made available to the agency on a larger scale than ever from 1926 to assist in extending coverage and news distribution, and especially after 1930 to finance a counter-propaganda service as Italian and then Nazi shortwave propaganda became increasingly aggressive. This included support for the multiple-address transmissions.

It was public knowledge that Havas was receiving generous payments from the government. Havas insisted that this did not make the agency official, but that the benefits were to meet the cost of reports sent to French colonial areas where existing papers were small and rarely able to afford a service out of their limited resources, and where it was important to have news made available. The benefits were provided to Havas through several government ministries, most of which had secret funds (les fonds sécrete) in their annual budgets. This was common practice in European, Latin American, and Middle Eastern countries. The funds also were used by the government to make payments to publishers, editors, and journalists of the country, and of other countries, and so to assure support for government policies or to assist in making that support possible by indirection. It was a system tantamount to bribery or blackmail, depending upon the motivation of the party which initiated action resulting in the payment.

In 1926 at least 8 million francs (then about $225,000) were budgeted to Havas from the Ministry of Foreign Affairs. Funds also were provided through the Ministries of the Interior, Colonies, Public Works, and Fine Arts. Debates on budget appropriations in the Chamber of Deputies revealed that from these various sources the Agence Havas received the equivalent of about $1 million in 1931, and $1.5 million in 1936. With such facts on the record, and secret funds still unaccounted for, it was at least understandable that Havas assertions on independence of government favors were received with skepticism by those aware of an historic and demonstrated venality on the part of French publications, especially some of the Paris dailies and weeklies.

There never was reason to question the loyalty of the Agence Havas to the French government or to France itself. The professional competence of the best French journalists also was equal to any, and often considered superior in terms of literary style. Some of the French provincial dailies were regarded as better made than any Paris daily, and certain periodicals were properly admired throughout the world. Even so, a number of dailies and weeklies in Paris were subject to influences making them doubtful sources of information; others were so politically partisan as to be unreliable. A few whose policy was for sale or which were conducted as blackmail sheets were referred to at times as the "gutter press."

Havas was equipped and staffed to gather and distribute the news effectively. If it had faults, they were to be ascribed chiefly to the topmost management shaping policy in sensitive areas of the news and misusing its secondary power in the field of newspaper advertising, not highly developed in France. The public tended to believe that if a product or service was good there was no need to advertise it. Further, there were so many newspapers in Paris that advertisers scarcely knew where to place their messages. They could not afford to use all of the papers, or even most of them. In practice, Havas, through its advertising division, determined the placement of much of the newspaper advertising, with the greatest volume quite understandably assigned to five or six information papers of larger circulation. Even then, the advertising volume was small and the papers therefore also were small, rarely more than twelve pages, and were offered to readers at prices lower than in London or New York.

The limited revenue from either sale of copies or sale of advertising space accounted in part for the acceptance by French papers of funds from government, from political parties, and from business and industry. The special interests of any of these contributors could be reflected in the news and editorial content or policy, without any sure awareness of such influences by readers. A shortage of revenue from normal sources also explained why some papers sought funds through blackmail directed at prominent persons, business firms, and foreign governments. Whether blackmailed or not, governments often paid to assure editorial support for their policies or to forestall editorial attacks. These might be direct payments or might take the form of travel advertising or foreign product advertising. A country whose government was unwilling to follow such procedure might become the target of abuse. This was true, for example, of the United States, which refused payments and was therefore attacked or maligned in some Paris dailies.

The Soviet government, following World War I, published documents found in the archives of the czarist government indicating payments to newspapers, journalists, and statesmen in France by Alexander Isvolsky during his years as Russian ambassador in Paris from 1906 to 1910. These records and letters from Isvolsky were republished in 1924 in *l'Humanité,* the Communist party paper in Paris. Yet the general practice had not ceased at that time.

Robert Dell, for some years Paris correspondent for the *Manchester Guardian,* described in 1929 how the Ministry of Foreign Affairs used its secret funds to shape press policies. Writing in the *Nation,* he said:

> The French people know only what their government and the press under its control allow them to know. Facts are suppressed or distorted; the actions of foreign governments are misrepresented. . . . The French government can in a few weeks, through the press, entirely change what passes for public opinion, work up a panic or quiet it down, make one country popular or another unpopular.[2]

The same observation was made a few years later by A. J. Cummings, respected political editor of the London *News-Chronicle.* Writing in *The Press and a Changing Civilization* (1936), he said that where French interests are concerned the Ministry of Foreign Affairs puts out the word, and

> the newspapers in sheep-like obedience execute the official order and sing their patriotic chorus until they receive the 'cease fire.' Again, if the Government wishes to prepare public opinion for some unpleasant official decree it calls in the aid of the press to soften the blow and can be infinitely surer of a willing response than in the case of an English government seeking to win over the English press. [P. 93]

Kent Cooper, general manager of the Associated Press, in 1930 told the AP board of directors that

> Havas holds the French press in bondage because of its advertising department. A paper that does not take the Havas service cannot get advertising. But the news service of Havas is so inferior that it is not worth considering.[3]

French journalists were at least as critical. Pierre Dénoyer, New York correspondent in 1931 for *Le Petit Parisien,* then the leader among Paris dailies in circulation and perhaps the best information paper, told a conference at Princeton University that

> to alienate Havas may mean for a newspaper the loss of practically all of its advertising. This power . . . is of tremendous importance for the press and for the public, for it is known that in several cases advertising patrons have objected to editorial policies and interfered directly or indirectly with them, stopping campaigns and tabooed subjects.[4]

---

2   Robert Dell, "The Paris Press Scandal," *Nation* (January 30, 1929), 129-31.

3   See Cooper's *Barriers Down* (1942), p. 194.

4   See *Conference on the Press.* Princeton University, April 23-25, 1931. (Washington, D.C., 1931).

This view, along with that of Cummings, was supported by another French writer, Alfred Fontenoy, citing an occasion when Pierre Guimier, advertising director of Havas, called upon all French dailies to withhold certain details about the 1934 "Stavisky affair" insurance scandals involving important persons, and all did so except the Socialist and Communist papers.

Neither Cummings nor Fontenoy mentioned the use of secret funds as a key to the effective control of the French press. But they wrote in a period when Italian government funds were used to purchase French press support for Italy's campaign in Ethiopia.

With reference to Guimier's influence, however, Fontenoy added that

> if a newspaper tried to be independent and publish undesirable information, it would lose not only its advertisers but be barred from the [Havas] news service, and this would be a terrible blow, since only a few French publications have their own reporters and correspondents. This explains why even the left-wing bourgeois papers obey Havas.[5]

The "orders" were given discreetly, Fontenoy conceded, by merely prescribing "moderation" in the expression of opinions, permitting " 'comments in principle' but no attacks on those who subsidize them," and rarely criticizing, but offering instead " 'well meant advice and stimulation.' " The results, nevertheless, tended to be as Havas wished them to be.

Jean Galtier-Boissière and René Lefebvre writing in Paris in the mid-1930s presented evidence that Havas itself had yielded to French government requests that certain information be reported only within France, through special communiqués, and that if reports were sent abroad on the subjects the dispatches were to be marked "Privat," with the Havas *cachet* or logotype omitted. The agency also was said to have carried some reports as trial balloons to enable the government to test public reaction to a contemplated move.[6]

The only serious trouble the Agence Havas had with the French government, so far as known, occurred in 1936. The agency, at that time, held a financial interest in three or four Paris dailies, *Le Journal, l'Echo de Paris, l'Oeuvre,* and perhaps *Le Petit Journal.* Guimier himself was the active director of *Le Journal,* one of the more sensational morning dailies. The papers published attacks on Roger Salengro, minister of the interior in the then current Popular Front government, a coalition headed by Léon Blum, Socialist party leader. The attack in

---

5 Alfred Fontenoy, "The Power of a News Agency," *Magazine Digest* (February 1937). Trans. from *Die Neue Weltbühne* (Prague), November 26, 1936.

6 See Galtier-Boissière and Lefebvre in *La Crapouillot* (June 1934), p. 90.

Le Journal was especially virulent, and Salengro committed suicide. He had been a close personal friend of Premier Blum, who believed the attacks in all of the newspapers had been originated and shaped by Guimier. The premier therefore insisted that either the advertising division of the Agence Havas must be completely separated from the news division, or that Guimier must resign as a director of the agency, which he did.

Two leading French journalists added devastating postscripts to the story of the manner in which the Agence Havas used its power. Both wrote after the agency had ceased to exist in 1940.

Pierre Lazareff, editor of *Paris-Soir,* an afternoon paper and the most widely circulated French daily in the late 1930s, wrote in *Deadline: The Behind-the-Scenes Story of the Last Decade in France* (1942), that Havas had helped obstruct an effort in 1923 to establish *Le Quotidien* as an honest and objective Paris daily. He also said that it had conspired against *L'Ami du Peuple* as a new paper in 1928, and had otherwise misused its position even as Fontenoy and others had asserted.

André Géraud, respected as a political journalist long associated with *l'Echo de Paris* and writing under the name of "Pertinax," also referred to Havas in his book, *Gravediggers of France* (1940). He placed the agency "at the hub of the wheel" by which the press was made subservient. He too placed responsibility particularly upon Guimier, but also upon Léon Renier, as general director from 1924 until the mid-1930s. The two men were described as "servile and conniving." A phone call from the office of either one, he said, was enough to assure that "some piece of news embarrassing to a particular minister or to a certain financial interest would . . . be passed over in silence by the great dailies. Usually an official denial, a hint of dreadful consequences to come were quite enough to bring those who dared open their mouths back into line."

Apart from such faults as may have rested with the top management of the Agence Havas, and despite Cooper's disparaging reference of 1930, the agency's organization for coverage of the news probably was better in that decade than it ever had been. The foreign department was headed by Léon Rollin, an admirable professional journalist who assigned and recruited correspondents in the world service.

One such recruit was Camille Lemercier, who had started his news career as an assistant in the Paris bureau of the *Chicago Daily News* in 1927. He was sent to New York in 1930 as manager of the Havas bureau. He headed the Berlin bureau from 1932–33, but returned to New York as manager of the North American service, including relations with the Canadian Press (CP) and the Havas-sponsored ANTA agency in Mexico City. Lemercier died in New York in 1936 and was succeeded by Henri Barde. He was formerly in Shanghai and returned there in 1937. Guy Fritsch-Estrangin, who had served in Berlin with Lemercier, then headed the New York office. Others in the New York bureau at various periods included Robert Rémy in the late 1920s; Roger Dapoigny, who became secretary-treasurer of the Foreign Press Correspondents Association in 1933-35; and André Péron, Robert Gueydan, Albert Grand, Jean Legrange, and Albert Rocchia. Percival H. Winner, an American citizen who had served in European posts for the AP and the *Philadelphia Public Ledger,* was a member of the New York bureau in 1934-36.

In Washington, the agency had Jeanne Pierre Bernard and Jean Baubé. Count Raoul de Roussy de Sales was chief diplomatic correspondent there from 1937 to 1940, writing under the name of "Jacques Fransalés." He had started work in the United States in 1932 as a correspondent for the periodical *Revue de Paris,* and also had written for *Paris Midi* and *Paris Soir.* He served as president of the Foreign Press Correspondents Association in 1931-39.

Chief of the London bureau in 1932-33 was Paul Louis Bret, followed by Jean Baubé, formerly in Washington, and Pierre Maillaud in 1939-40. Others in the bureau included Robert Battefort, Fernand Moulier, Gaston Gerville-Réache, Pierre Jennerat, Yves Morvan, Jacques Duchêsne, and Jean Oberlé.

In Berlin, the Havas bureau had been headed in 1932-33 by Lemercier, temporarily absent from New York. He was followed by Paul Ravoux in 1933-37, when he became the nineteenth correspondent expelled since the Nazi government gained power in 1933. Fritsch-Estrangin also was in the bureau in 1933-37, when he went to New York. Others there were Roger Maffré, Etienne Journiac, André Hesse, and Emil Winck, who was executive secretary in 1930-31 of the Foreign Press Association in Berlin.

In Rome, Jean Allary was bureau chief from 1931-38. He was succeeded by Roger Maffré, formerly in Berlin, but head of the Bucharest bureau just before moving to Rome. Reports from Geneva were provided by Henri Ruffin and Honorio Roigt, among others. Anatole Visson, Russian-born and French-educated, wrote from Brussels. In Moscow, Havas was represented at various times by Jean Fontenoy, Jean Chamenois, Léon Bassée, and Robert Gilles. Maurice Negré was in Warsaw.

Jacques Deladot, in Buenos Aires, directed coverage in South America, with Philippe Berthelot and Martial Bourgeon also assigned there, and other staff and stringer correspondents at capitals throughout the continent.

Henri Barde was director of services in the Far East, based in Shanghai from 1932 to 1936, and then in New York for a year. Jean Fontenoy, formerly in Moscow, served in Shanghai pending Barde's return in 1937. Others there included Jacques Marcuse and Michel Bréal.

Other correspondents recruited by Rollin and serving in various parts of the world or on roving assignments included Géraud Jouve, Louis Joxe, Maurice Schumann, and Robert Guillain.

Reuters

As it had become known in the 1916 reorganization, Reuters, Ltd., provided the broadest international news coverage and service through the 1920s, but was rivalled during the 1930s by the Agence Havas and, even more particularly, by the Associated Press and the United Press.

Sir Roderick Jones, managing director since 1915, continued in that position until his retirement in 1941. Frederick W. Dickinson, chief editor since 1902, died at his desk in 1922. Douglas Williams, son of the former chief editor, George Douglas Williams, might have succeeded to the post, and did occupy it briefly, but preferred to return to New York, where he had been chief correspondent since 1920. Sir Roderick himself therefore acted also as chief editor temporarily until 1923, when Herbert Jeans, formerly chief parliamentary correspondent, took over and continued until his death in 1931. He was succeeded then by Bernard Rickatson-Hatt, who had been personal aide to Sir Roderick, but had been in the New York bureau for the previous year.

The close relationship of Reuters to the British government during the Great War had led some to assert erroneously that it was an official agency. The death of Herbert de Reuter in 1915 also had raised concern at the time lest control of the agency pass to persons who might compromise its traditional independence and objectivity. The best procedure to meet both of these issues, in Sir Roderick's view, was for the British press itself to own Reuters, as the Associated Press was owned by its member papers in the United States. Other members of the board of directors accepted this view.

Under the arrangements concluded in 1916 to safeguard the agency, Sir Roderick owned 60 per cent of the stock in Reuters, Ltd., and was trustee for the remaining 40 per cent. This, as he wrote later, "enabled me without interference to pave the way for the attainment of my ideal, namely to bring the newspapers of the United Kingdom into the proprietorship of Reuters and to place the control beyond the life limitations of one individual ownership, and also beyond the objections arising from ownership by an ordinary public stock company.''

The attainment of this ideal was to take time, however. In 1925, Sir Roderick proposed that ownership of Reuters should be transferred, jointly and equally, to the Press Association, Ltd., an agency already owned by the British provincial newspapers and with which Reuters had worked closely since its formation in 1868, and to the Newspaper Proprietors' Association, which represented the London daily and Sunday newspapers.

The Newspaper Proprietors' Association was not prepared to accept the proposal at that time. The Press Association, Ltd., then directed by H. C. Robbins, was receptive, however, and in 1926 acquired the 60 per cent of the shares owned by Sir Roderick. In 1930, it bought most of the remaining shares and was to acquire the final block of stock when Sir Roderick retired from the chairmanship and managing directorship of Reuters in 1941. Even though operating separately, Reuters as a world agency and the PA as a domestic agency, they exchanged news, coordinated their operations, occupied the same building, and were administered through a single board of directors.

During the twenty-five years that Sir Roderick Jones directed Reuters, it extended and improved its world coverage and service, with correspondents and bureaus in every strategic news center and stringers elsewhere. It was both a general news service and a service providing every sort of commercial and financial report.

The commercial service, the first to be established when the agency began in 1851, returned more revenue proportionate to staff requirements than the general news service. Separately operated as a Reuters' Trade Service in 1920 and later as a Commercial Telegraphic Bureau (Comtelburo), it was directed by Cecil Fleetwood-May. As the Ring Combination began to ease its restrictions, the commercial reports went out after 1932 in a beam wireless, multiple-address "Reuterian" service to Cairo, Capetown, Bombay, Shanghai, Tokyo, and later to South America. The service was accepted as authoritative in determining commodity and general market prices in most of the world. Special features also were distributed through a subsidiary, Atlas Despatches.

Reuters was under some financial strain even after World War I, with the necessities of greatly extended coverage raising costs. Some revenue also was lost when the Agence Télégraphique Belge was formed in 1920, responsive to the wishes of the Belgian government. The agency bought the Reuters-Havas office long operated in Brussels. Further revenue was lost when the Kokusai Tsushin-sha agency in Japan bought its independence of Reuters in 1923. In Holland the

Algemeen Nederlandsche Persbureau replaced the Reuters-owned Nederlandsche Telegraaf Agentschap in 1934, and the Reuter South African Press Association was taken over by the South African and Rhodesian press in 1938. There was some compensation remaining in those situations, except for Belgium, because the Reuters service continued to go to the others on a contract basis.

Competition arose in Japan and China, however, with the United Press and International News Service providing alternative service in what had been an exclusive Reuters territory. The British United Press established in Canada in 1922 and independent of the Ring Combination was able to seek clients even in the United Kingdom, as well as in Canada and Australia. In addition, Reuters felt indirect financial pressure because Havas, Wolff, and the new Tass agency of Soviet Russia all benefited through financial support from their governments.

On the other hand, after the British Broadcasting Corporation was formed in 1927 as a government-controlled operation, it became a client of the Reuters service, paying £8,000 (nearly $40,000) for a limited news service during its first year. It ultimately became the largest single customer of Reuters, and used the reports in preparing BBC news broadcasts for home and overseas programs. The commercial "Reuterian" service was profitable. The agency's income was somewhat bolstered by the provision of government funds to meet the cost of a special service of daily telegrams for the information of British civil and military officials in parts of the Commonwealth where daily newspapers were absent or inadequate. From 1923 to 1936, the Canadian government also paid $32,000 annually to help compensate Reuters for its news service reaching dailies there through the Canadian Press, Ltd., and to underwrite a cable dispatch of 10,000 words a month from Canada to London, plus a mail service, for use in the United Kingdom and elsewhere to create an interest in Canadian affairs.

The growth of Reuters required its move in 1923 from offices occupied since 1870 at 24 Old Jewry to a large remodeled building on the Thames Embankment near Blackfriars. This was outgrown within another decade, and plans were drawn for a new building to be shared with the Press Association, Ltd., by then under the direction of Edward Davies, successor to Robbins. That large modern structure was erected at 85 Fleet Street and occupied early in 1939. The Agence Havas and some other agencies with which Reuters had exchange arrangements also occupied space in the building.

The years understandably brought personnel changes in the Reuters organization. Beyond those mentioned, S. Carey Clements, secretary of Reuters since 1915 and third to occupy that position after John Griffiths and W. F. Bradshaw, retired in 1932. The work of his office then was divided to meet the needs of a larger organization. Two new London positions were created. William Ledebur Murray, with Reuters since 1899, became European general manager, and William Turner was appointed overseas general manager, bringing experience as director of agency coverage during the Paris Peace Conference, followed by eleven years in Shanghai (1920–31) as general manager for the Far East.

Reuters coverage, which had started in Europe, remained strong there. William J. Moloney, with the agency since 1908, was in Berlin immediately after the war. Maurice Lovell, an able linguist and a roving correspondent, spent considerable periods in Germany, Austria, Hungary, Rumania, and France. Paris coverage was provided by Martin Herlihy, who was later in Cairo, and by R. N. Neale, Josselyn Hennessy, John Pigg, Gordon Waterfield, and Lovell. Correspondents in Rome included C. F. Whittall, Dariel Brindley, and Cecil Squire Spriggs, formerly of the *Manchester Guardian*. W. H. G. Werndel, a veteran of Reuters service, became permanent correspondent in Geneva in 1920. On his retirement in 1932, he was succeeded by Fergus Ferguson, also a veteran, who continued until 1938. Each of these correspondents served Reuters for a half century.

Hubert D. Harrison, who had written from the south of Europe since 1924 for the *Manchester Guardian,* the *Daily Express,* and other papers, became Reuters correspondent in the Balkans in 1937. His service was brief, however. He had scarcely established himself in Belgrade when he was expelled in December,[7] after which he represented the *News-Chronicle* and the *New York Times* in Berlin. Joseph Swire was in Greece and Bulgaria for Reuters in 1932 and 1935. Desmond Tighe was in the Balkans in 1939, and the area was visited by Ferguson and Lovell.

Samuel Rodman was in Moscow for Reuters in the 1930s and wrote also for the Sunday *Observer.* Robin Kinkead, an American, also was in Moscow at this period, and Ian L. Fleming was second man in the bureau from 1933 to 1935.[8]

---

7 Harrison's expulsion from Yugoslavia was one of the more unusual episodes of its kind. He had sent a routine report of a government order banning publication of a Mickey Mouse cartoon strip in *Politika,* the leading Belgrade daily. The cartoon showed Mickey Mouse masquerading as a prince, with the prince's uncle conspiring against the real prince. This was interpreted by Yugoslav officials as having a reference to the boy, King Peter, who had succeeded to the throne after the assassination of his father, King Alexander, in Marseilles in 1934, and to his cousin, Prince Paul, the chief regent. A London newspaper using Harrison's dispatch drew the conclusion independently, but Harrison was mistakenly held responsible by the Yugoslav officials and expelled.

8 Fleming declined an agency appointment in the Far East and entered banking instead. In later years he wrote for the *Daily Telegraph,* but already was publishing a series of suspense-fiction novels about the adventures of James Bond, 007 agent in the British secret service. Some of the novels were made into motion pictures.

Gerald Delaney was Cairo correspondent, having succeeded David Rees on his death in 1915. Valentine Williams, in Berlin before the war, then had joined the *Daily Mail,* but returned to the Reuters' staff to go to Egypt in 1923-24. There he reported the excavations at the newly discovered tomb of King Tut-ankh-amen, a major archeological event, and one of the first of the sort to receive world-wide press attention.

At the opposite end of the African continent in Capetown, James S. Dunn, son of Nicol Dunn, a former editor of the *Morning Post,* had succeeded Roderick Jones as Reuters general manager for South Africa in 1915 when Jones returned to London just prior to assuming direction of the agency. Dunn continued in that position until his retirement in 1940. He presided over a small staff, but also was concerned with the direction of the Reuters South African Press Association, a subsidiary, until 1938, when it became the independent cooperative South African Press Association (SAPA).

In India, China, and Japan Reuters coverage was substantial. Sir Edward Buck represented the agency from 1915 to 1933 in Calcutta, Simla, and New Delhi. Upon retiring, he was succeeded by James Strachey Barnes. William J. Moloney also made India his administrative base from 1932 to 1937 as general manager for the Far East.

William A. O'Neill in Hong Kong was Reuters manager for South China, and was succeeded in 1933 by A. Patrick Perry, formerly in New York. The mainland China representation was strong, with about twenty-five in the Shanghai bureau alone in 1927 and later. Many were Chinese nationals. The director of the bureau was William Turner, general manager for the Far East from 1920 to 1932, when he returned to London.

Others in Shanghai through the years included A. Bernard Moloney. A younger brother of William J. Moloney, he began service with the agency in Amsterdam in 1916, but was in Shanghai from 1919 to 1922, followed by eleven years in London, when he was assigned to New York. There were Thomas Ming-heng Chao, Frank Oliver from 1927 to 1937, and James Melville Cox, with long experience in Asia. The agency also was served by H. G. W. Woodhead, editor of the *Peking and Tientsin Times,* a stringer for Reuters, among others, from 1912 to 1930, and by John Jack in Nanking in 1927.

From Tokyo, J. Russell Kennedy, Irish-born but a naturalized American citizen, with long prior experience with the AP, was both director of the Kokusai news agency and Reuters correspondent in 1914-25. He was succeeded by Malcolm Duncan Kennedy (unrelated) serving Reuters in Tokyo until 1934.

Reuters had been represented in New York since 1892 by S. Levy Lawson. He was succeeded in 1920 by Douglas Williams, former Berlin correspondent, who remained until 1930, except for several months during 1922–23 when he acted as chief editor in London and.then chose to return to the New York post.

Williams resigned from his Reuters position in 1930 to enter a New York brokerage firm. Bernard Rickatson-Hatt arrived from London to replace him, but remained only a year, returning then to London to assume the chief editor's post himself following the death of Herbert Jeans in 1931. A. Patrick Perry served as chief correspondent in New York in 1931–33, at which time he went to Hong Kong, with A. Bernard Moloney, formerly in Shanghai and London, succeeding him.

Moloney presided over a New York bureau staff of about twenty-five, many of them concerned with reporting business and financial news for Reuters' commercial service. He also supervised one or two men in Washington and some seventy-five stringers throughout the United States. He became president of the Association of Foreign Correspondents in the United States in 1936. Alan O. Trower, also of Reuters, was secretary-treasurer of that association in the late 1930s.

Among other members of the Reuters staff in New York during the 1920s and 1930s were David Brown, D. Kimpton Rogers, A. Frank Tinsley, Alaric Jacob, A. G. Field, T. A. Dixon, Douglas Towley, J. C. Talbot, H. E. Astley Hawkins, and Lawrence de Neufville.

Associated Press

The three news agencies of the United States, the Associated Press, the United Press, and the International News Service, gained positions of leadership in world news reporting. They were well supported by members or subscribers in the United States and in some other countries. Many U.S. newspapers and radio stations received service from two of the agencies, and sometimes from all three. Each had its subsidiary services or syndicates distributing features and photos.

The Associated Press extended its organization vastly after 1920. Melville E. Stone, general manager for nearly twenty-eight years, retired in 1921, and was succeeded by Frederick Roy Martin, assistant manager since 1912 and a former editor of the *Providence Journal* in Rhode Island. Martin resigned in 1925, and Kent Cooper, with the agency since 1910 as traffic manager and as assistant general manager under Martin, became general manager. He served until his retirement in 1948.

With 894 member papers in the United States in 1914, and with a virtual end to restriction on membership, that number had grown to

1,437 in 1939. Others were receiving service in other countries. Radio stations also became subscribers in the U.S. A leased wire network of 64,800 miles serving the member papers in 1920 and activating teleprinters in bureaus, radio stations, and newspaper offices became a network of 285,000 miles by 1939, plus a 10,000-mile network developed since 1935 in an AP Wirephoto service. A supplementary mail service had been added in 1928 to distribute feature material. Reflecting greater world coverage and a staff increase to match, the agency's annual operating budget grew from $5,191,143 in 1920 to $11,081,321 in 1939. For foreign news gathering alone, the costs had soared from $30,362 in 1914 to $1,013,897 in 1939.

The New York headquarters office, long on Madison Avenue, was moved in December 1938 to a large new AP building in the Rockefeller Center grouping. The Canadian Press (CP) and other agencies maintained offices in the AP building. There was a large AP bureau in Washington, a division headquarters bureau in Kansas City, other important bureaus in Chicago, Atlanta, Denver, Los Angeles, and San Francisco, and representatives in member newspaper offices in other cities of the United States. There were large bureaus in London, Paris, and some other major capitals of the world, and smaller bureaus in many others.

The Washington bureau grew steadily in importance in the years between the wars, through the administrations of Wilson, Harding, Coolidge, Hoover, and Roosevelt. Among correspondents at various times were Edwin Milton Hood, who began as an office boy in 1875 and occupied every position, including that of bureau chief and division superintendent to the time of his death in 1923; Charles Stephenson Smith and Joseph E. Sharkey, although they were overseas much of the time; Kirke L. Simpson, who was awarded a Pulitzer Prize in 1922; Milo H. Thompson, Charles P. Williamson, Byron Price, Stephen T. Early, who became press secretary for President Roosevelt; and Andrue H. Berding, formerly in the Rome bureau.

Jackson S. Elliott, active in the direction of the AP foreign service in New York during the war, was followed in that position in 1919 by Charles Thaddeus Thompson, with the agency since 1892. He was its first correspondent in Paris, beginning in 1902, correspondent in France and Italy throughout the war, and director of coverage during the Paris Peace Conference. Upon his death in 1925, he was succeeded by Charles Stephenson Smith, most recently London bureau chief. Returning to Washington in 1930, Smith was followed as foreign editor in 1930–31 by Alexander H. Uhl, by Smith Reavis in 1931–33, DeWitt Mackenzie in 1933–36, and John Evans in 1936–43. All were men with extensive foreign experience.

The Associated Press had entered into the provision of news to papers in Canada and Mexico since 1893, and in South America and Central America since 1918. In 1939 a subsidiary, La Prensa Asociada (LPA) was formed in Buenos Aires,[9] and another, Teleradio Brasiliera in Rio de Janeiro, to handle the distribution of AP reports in those areas of Latin America.

Two other subsidiaries had been formed in 1930, the Associated Press of Great Britain, Ltd., in London, and the Associated Press, G.m.p.H., in Berlin. These were photo syndicates. The German subsidiary was forced to cease operations in 1933 as the new Nazi government denied foreign-based organizations the right to do business in the country. When the Ring Combination ended in 1934, the British subsidiary became free to seek subscribers to the AP news service in the United Kingdom, but did not do so until early in 1939.

Lloyd Stratton headed the British subsidiary until 1936. He was succeeded by Gideon Seymour, who had been bureau chief in Buenos Aires in 1931. Stratton traveled during the next four years on agency business to South Africa and Australia, and then was in the New York office. Seymour maintained his base in London until 1937, and was succeeded by William F. Brooks.[10]

The London bureau, the key point for foreign coverage, had been headed by Robert M. Collins in 1905–20, Charles Stephenson Smith in 1920–25, DeWitt Mackenzie in 1925–33, Frank H. King in 1933–37, and J. Clifford Stark to World War II. Bureau members at various times between 1920 and 1940 included Smith Reavis, Percival H. Winner, James Pomeroy Howe, Charles P. Nutter, James Carlisle MacDonald, Fred Vanderschmidt, Oscar Emil Wade Werner, Andrue H. Berding, Melvin K. Whiteleather, Drew Middleton, Thomas W. Morris, Rader Winget, Frank T. Hollowell, Witt Hancock, Roy Porter, Guy Moyston, Victor G. C. Eubanks, Harry H. Romer, Martha Dalrymple, James B. Reston, and Robert Bunnelle. Many of these correspondents had served in other bureaus, or would do so later.

The Paris bureau was almost equally important, with much the same movement of correspondents. Elmer E. Roberts, with the AP since 1897 and in Europe for the agency since 1900, had taken charge of the Paris bureau in 1911 and remained until his retirement in 1929. He was followed by Joseph E. Sharkey, formerly chief of bureaus in

---

9   Not to be confused with a German-sponsored propaganda agency of the same name in Buenos Aires during World War I.

10   Seymour left the AP in 1939 to become president and executive editor of the *Minneapolis Star* and *Tribune*.

Tokyo and Geneva, to which he returned in 1933. John Evans, in Paris as early as 1919, and chief of the Rome bureau in 1931-33, followed Sharkey in Paris from the latter year until he became foreign editor in New York in 1936. John Lloyd, with the AP since 1925, but chiefly in Latin America, and Moscow bureau chief in 1935-36, acted as Paris bureau head in 1936-37 and again in 1938-40, with Charles P. Nutter filling in during the 1937-38 interval. Henry Cassidy took over from Lloyd early in 1940, but closed the bureau when Nazi troops occupied Paris in June.

Members of the Paris bureau included Thomas J. Topping and Samuel F. Wader, both there during World War I, Hudson Hawley, who then had been a member of the *Stars and Stripes* staff, French-born Georges Langelaan, and Frederick K. Abbott, formerly of INS. Several moved from the London bureau, among them Smith Reavis and his wife, Hazel Benjamin Reavis. They returned to New York in 1930, with Reavis taking charge of Latin American news processing, and then serving as foreign editor in 1931-33. Others moving to Paris were Winner, Nutter, MacDonald, Whiteleather, Hollowell, and Porter. Still others in the bureau included Alexander H. Uhl, after his stint as foreign editor in New York in 1930-31, Richard G. Massock, Hal Lehrman, Stuart Moroney, Edward G. Angly, Charles Foltz, Jr., Edward Kennedy, Louis Nevin, Taylor Henry, Harold E. Walker, and two fashion writers, Adelaide Kerr and Alice Maxwell.

The Rome bureau had been directed since its formation in 1903 by Salvatore Cortesi, a stringer there from 1895. He retired in 1931.[11] The activities of the Fascist government from 1922, and the personality of Benito Mussolini, made Rome a major news center. John Evans, formerly in Paris, succeeded Cortesi as bureau chief in 1931-33, when he returned to Paris in the same capacity. He was succeeded in Rome by Andrue H. Berding, formerly in Paris, but second man in the Rome bureau since 1928. As bureau chief, Berding served in 1933-35 and again in 1936-37, after an interval during which he covered the Italo-Ethiopian War. He went to the AP bureau in Washington in 1937. John Lloyd, former bureau chief in Moscow and Paris, followed Berding in Rome in 1937-38, when he returned to Paris, followed in turn by Richard G. Massock. In Europe since 1932, Massock had covered the Spanish Civil War in 1936-37 and headed the Moscow bureau in 1937-38. He remained in Rome until 1941, where he was interned along with other U.S. correspondents in Italy when the United States entered World War II, and was held until repatriated in 1942.

---

11   His son, Arnaldo Cortesi, was Rome correspondent for the *New York Times* in 1921-38.

Members of the Rome bureau in those years also included others coming from Paris and London. Among them were Winner in 1924–28, when he joined a new overseas service of the *Philadelphia Public Ledger–New York Evening Post,* Hollowell, until 1926, when he joined the *New York Herald Tribune,* Hawley, Kennedy, Walker, and Charles H. Guptill.

The Berlin bureau was important throughout the years. S. Miles Bouton returned in 1920 to his prewar assignment as head of that bureau. He was assisted by another prewar member, Guido Enderis. A Swiss citizen who had resided for some years in the United States, but who chose to remain in Germany even after 1917, Enderis kept a protective watch on AP property. He became bureau chief in 1924, but resigned in 1928 to join the *New York Times* staff in Berlin, and was succeeded by Louis P. Lochner. A native of Wisconsin, Lochner had joined the AP bureau in Berlin after brief service in Europe for the Federated Press, a small New York agency established in 1919 to provide special coverage for labor news. As AP bureau chief from 1928 to 1941, Lochner also served as president of the Foreign Press Association (Verein der Ausländischen Presse) from 1928 to 1931, and again in 1934. He was awarded a Pulitzer Prize in 1939 for his correspondence from Germany during the previous year. As with Massock and the correspondents in Italy, Lochner and other U.S. correspondents in Germany were interned in December 1941 and repatriated in 1942.

Other members of the AP Berlin bureau in those years included Whiteleather and Werner, both formerly in London, Edward Shanke, G. O. Beukert, John A. Bouman, Preston Grover, Lynn A. Heinzerling, Alvin J. Steinkopf, Ernest G. Fisher, Rudolf Josten, Robert F. Schildbach, Mary Bainbridge Hayden, and Alex Dreier, until he became one of the first U.S. radio correspondents, serving the National Broadcasting Company in Berlin.

In Vienna, Robert Atter, prewar AP correspondent there, returned briefly after the war, but was followed by Charles E. Kloeber, with the agency since 1897, serving in Washington, China, New York, and elsewhere, and as a correspondent in France in 1918.[12] Kloeber was succeeded as bureau chief in 1934 by Wade Werner, formerly in London

---

12 In Vienna in 1919, as Oliver Gramling reports in *AP: The Story of News* (1940), Kloeber "found himself covering Sir William A. Goode," then a member of the British reparations commission for Austria, but "the same 'Billy' Goode whom [Charles S.] Diehl, [assistant general manager for the AP] had assigned to Admiral Sampson's flagship back in the days of the Spanish-American war." Goode, then a correspondent for the Associated Press of Illinois, later was assistant to Cortesi in the new Rome AP bureau in 1903. Subsequently, he returned to England, his native country, and entered upon a career in diplomacy.

and Berlin, with Schildbach, also formerly in Berlin, as an assistant. In 1938 Alvin J. Steinkopf moved from Berlin to Vienna to succeed Werner, with A. D. Stafford and Louis Matzhold also in the bureau. The three reported the Nazi seizure of Austria in March of that year. Steinkopf presently opened a new AP bureau in Budapest, to report the Balkans from there. He was succeeded several months later by Robert B. Parker, Jr.

In St. Petersburg, following Stone's visit of 1903-04, the Associated Press had coverage from 1904 to 1917. From then until 1924 its news of the USSR was received chiefly through countries adjacent to Russia. A few press representatives had reached Moscow in 1919-20, including Mrs. Marguerite Harrison, formerly of the *Baltimore Sun* but also accredited to the AP. She was imprisoned when the Soviet officials learned that she was making reports to the U.S. Army intelligence branch. James P. Howe, a freelance writer in China as early as 1913, but in the AP London bureau in 1921, entered Soviet Russia at that time with the first group of correspondents. Charles Stephenson Smith, in that country during the war years, also returned that year, moving from the London bureau. Neither man remained for long, however.

James C. Mills, with the AP since 1910, had resigned in 1917 to work with the American Red Cross during the war, first in France and then in Italy, the Balkans, and the Crimea. Rejoining the AP in 1922, he covered the Lausanne conference between Turkey and the Allies which resulted in a revision of the 1919 Treaty of Sèvres. He then reported the conflict between Turkey and Greece, but in 1924 he went to Moscow to reinstitute regular coverage for the agency and remained until 1927.

Walter A. Whiffen, a correspondent for the AP in Petrograd in 1914-17, and wounded while with Russian troops, was readmitted in 1927, even though he also had been a correspondent with Allied forces in Siberia in 1918. He replaced Mills in Moscow. There, however, he died a few weeks later, after twenty-six years with the agency. William Reswick, formerly with INS, then became AP chief in Moscow for a time.

Stanley P. Richardson, in Moscow for the AP from early in 1931 until 1935, was followed by John Lloyd, previously in Latin America. A year later Lloyd was moved to the Paris bureau, with Charles P. Nutter heading the Moscow bureau in 1936-37, when he also went to Paris, followed in Moscow by Richard G. Massock until 1938, Wade Werner to 1939, and Witt Hancock to 1940. Nutter returned to Moscow in 1940 with Robert Magidoff as assistant.

Geneva, headquarters for the League of Nations, became an important news center from 1920. Correspondents moved there, usually from Paris, to cover meetings of the Council and Assembly or special conferences. Some, however, were on permanent assignment in Geneva. Joseph E. Sharkey, with the AP since 1898 and widely experienced, was resident correspondent in Geneva from 1923 to his retirement in 1937, except for 1932-33, when he headed the Paris bureau. In those years he covered League-sponsored conferences in such other places as Genoa, The Hague, Lausanne, and Washington. Hudson Hawley moved from Paris to Geneva when Sharkey was away, until 1929, when he transferred to the INS staff. Plautus I. Lipsey, Jr., formerly of INS, served in Geneva in the year Sharkey was in Paris. Melvin K. Whiteleather followed him in Geneva in 1937-38, and Charles Foltz, Jr., was there in 1938-39.

In Madrid, Robert E. Berry, with long previous experience with the AP, became correspondent after the war. He was succeeded in 1929 by Clarence DuBose, previously with the United Press in Tokyo and Mexico City, but DuBose died there in 1931. Alexander H. Uhl was Madrid bureau chief in 1935-38, followed by Nutter. John P. McKnight, also with previous service in Latin America, was Lisbon bureau chief.

General coverage of Europe and other areas was maintained through the years by shifting men about as the news seemed to require. Sharkey and Smith, Lloyd and Evans, Cassidy and Nutter, and some others were greatly on the move.

Topping, of the Paris bureau, and Clifford L. Day, later with the United Press, went into the Ruhr for the AP with French troops in 1923, and Topping also was in Morocco and Syria between 1925 and 1927. Mackenzie, although primarily in London, also moved about Europe. Even after serving as foreign editor in New York in 1933-36, he was back in 1938 and in charge of AP coverage of the Czech crisis, assisted by Steinkopf, Porter, and others.

Some of the AP correspondents in Europe were equally familiar with the Far East and Latin America, both areas where the agency's coverage gained strength from the time of the war. Sharkey had been in Tokyo from 1914 to 1921, Smith had been in Shanghai, and Whiffen had been in Peking and Tokyo between 1919 and 1927. James P. Howe knew China as a freelance, returning there for the AP in 1928, after an interval in Calcutta, and was Peiping correspondent until 1930. In India again in 1930-32, he opened an AP bureau in Calcutta to report events relating to the strong nationalist movement under Mahatma Gandhi, and then was in China once more in 1932 at Shanghai.[13]

---

13 Howe was the son of E. W. (Ed) Howe, highly individualistic editor-publisher of the *Atchison Globe* in Kansas, and brother of Gene Howe, almost equally famed as publisher of the *Amarillo News and Globe* in Texas.

James A. Mills, an experienced and mobile correspondent for the AP, following his period as bureau chief in Moscow in 1924-27, pioneered a new part of the world for the agency in 1930 by going to Addis Ababa, Ethiopia, to report the coronation of Emperor Haile Selassie. He moved directly to India in that same year to report the salt rebellion in which followers of Gandhi dramatized their struggle for independence. In this, Mills and Howe were among the first U.S. correspondents to give direct coverage to events in India, so long reported almost exclusively through the Reuters agency. In 1931 Mills accompanied Gandhi to London for the All-India Roundtable Conference of that year.

Late in 1931, Mills was in Manchuria to report the Japanese military move in that area. He was in India again in January 1932, when Gandhi was arrested by British authorities, and once more in mid-1933, when Gandhi was released. Mills was in Manchuria again in 1932.

Glenn Babb was a third correspondent greatly on the move for the AP, chiefly in the Far East. The Associated Press representation in that part of the world had begun in Manila in the 1898-1903 period, and had placed Martin Egan and Robert M. Collins in Tokyo from about 1902 until 1907. J. Russell Kennedy, former assistant to Melville E. Stone in New York, followed until 1913. He was succeeded by Sharkey, who left in 1921 to accompany the Japanese delegation to the Washington Naval Conference of 1921-22.

The Tokyo bureau was directed from 1921-24 by George Denny. He had arrived in Japan in 1904 to help report the Russo-Japanese War for the AP, served briefly in the St. Petersburg bureau in 1905, but then had returned to the Tokyo bureau as second man under Egan, after Collins left to head the London bureau, and remained under J. Russell Kennedy and Sharkey.

Babb himself had gone to Tokyo in 1915 after being graduated from the University of Missouri School of Journalism. He worked on the staff of the *Japan Advertiser*. In 1917-18, he served in the U.S. Army, but returned in 1920 to his former position in Tokyo. From 1922 he was correspondent there for the *Philadelphia Public Ledger-New York Evening Post* service until joining the AP in 1924.

Many U.S. correspondents in the Far East moved back and forth between Japan and China, and Babb was one who did so. He directed the AP bureau in Tokyo in 1924-25, went to the New York office in 1925-26, but was back in the Far East in 1926 as chief of the Peking bureau, where he remained until 1928. Meanwhile, Victor G. C. Eubanks, formerly in the London bureau, was Tokyo chief from 1925 to 1928. Babb returned there from 1928 to 1930, but assumed direction of the Shanghai bureau in 1930–32. In that time he gave direct coverage, along with Mills, to the Japanese invasion of Manchuria. He was in Tokyo once again in 1932 and remained until 1936, when he returned to New York to handle foreign cables.

Howe had succeeded Babb in Peking in 1928 and remained until 1930, when he went to India to open the Calcutta bureau. Mills, who had been in Manchuria in 1931 and again in 1932, succeeded Babb in Tokyo in 1936 for a year.

New figures joined in the staff moves. Morris J. Harris, who had worked with Babb on the *Japan Advertiser* in 1921, and remained there until 1924, then joined the AP. He was assigned first to Peking but became bureau chief in Shanghai in 1925. He remained in China until 1941, not necessarily as bureau chief, but covered the Kuomintang extension of power, the Manchurian invasion, the war with Japan, and related subjects up to the time of Pearl Harbor in 1941. Archibald T. Steele, a correspondent in China for the *New York Times* in 1932–33, also served the AP there in 1933–35, but then joined the *Chicago Daily News* as China correspondent.

Others representing the Associated Press in China through the years began with Robert M. Collins and Charles E. Kloeber reporting the Boxer affair in 1900. Frederick Moore, later a propagandist for Japan, wrote as a stringer for a time. H. G. W. Woodhead, editor of the *Peking and Tientsin Times*, was an AP stringer from 1912 to 1930, as he was also for Reuters and several newspapers. Charles Stephenson Smith was in Shanghai during the early part of World War I, but relieved Whiffen in Petrograd early in 1917. Whiffen himself, after reporting the Allied expedition entering Siberia in 1918, along with Sharkey, remained in Peking and Tokyo in 1919–27. Thomas Steep was in Peking for the agency in 1922–23, and later with the *New York Herald Tribune*. L. E. Claypoole, coming from the AP Manila bureau in 1927, wrote from China, and so did W. H. Hubbard, H. L. Felton, J. L. McCartney, and H. C. Vezey in that same decade.

Latin American affairs received growing attention. John Lloyd was a member of the staff of the English-language *Havana Post* from 1920 to 1925. He then joined the AP staff and in 1927 moved from Cuba to Chile, Peru, Bolivia, and Mexico. There he headed the AP Mexico City bureau in 1928–33. He was in Europe for the following seven years, heading the bureaus in Moscow, Rome, and Paris.

John P. McKnight, in Cuba for the AP in 1931–32, then was bureau chief in Mexico City from about 1936 to 1938, when he was reassigned to Lisbon as bureau chief.

Gideon Seymour was bureau chief in Buenos Aires in 1931. Other AP staff correspondents in that capital and elsewhere in South America included Rafael Ordorico, Milo H. Thompson, and Charles T. Guptill. Thompson was reassigned to London in 1938 as general executive for Europe, and Guptill was assigned to Rome.

Most AP coverage in Latin America was provided by stringers. The volume of news transmitted was far below that from Europe and Asia. The AP world report distributed to newspapers in Latin America was substantial in volume, however.

United Press Associations

The United Press was directed from 1908 to 1920 by Roy W. Howard. He then turned his attention to the group of papers at that time officially redesignated as the Scripps-Howard Newspapers. Howard was succeeded as president of the UP by William W. Hawkins, who had been assistant manager. In 1923, however, Hawkins also became identified with the newspaper group and Karl A. Bickel, with the UP since its formation and already its general manager, became president from 1923 to 1935. Retiring in the latter year, he was succeeded by Hugh Baillie, former Washington news chief and then an executive in the New York headquarters. Earl J. Johnson became general news manager under Baillie, and both continued in those positions for more than ten years.

The substantial growth of the UP during the war years included rapid extension of its service to Latin American dailies after 1916. By 1930 it rivaled the Associated Press and Reuters as a world agency, both in gathering news and in its distribution. It was serving newspapers in countries in Latin America, Asia, and Europe, as well as throughout the United States.

Originally intended to serve afternoon newspapers and the Sunday morning editions of such papers as might have them, the UP soon was called upon to provide news reports to morning papers also. In 1919 it sought to make this official by designating its morning service as the United News. This name was dropped in 1927, however, with the UP service going to both morning and afternoon papers.

Unlike the AP, the UP made its news service available to radio stations and networks in the United States. It established a subsidiary in Latin America, the Prensa Unida based in Buenos Aires, to handle service there. In 1937 it established a division in Peru, the Prensa Unida Peruvian (PUP), financed by *El Comercio* of Lima, to serve that newspaper alone.

The UP had had an exchange relationship with the Dentsu agency of Japan since 1909; with Rosta in the Soviet Union since 1919, and with Tass after its formation in 1925; with Extel in London from 1920; and with the Agence Télégraphique Radio in Paris from the time of its formation in 1918 until it was merged with Havas in 1929. The British United Press (BUP), established in Canada in 1922 as an independent agency, also entered into an exchange relationship with the UP and distributed the UP service in Canada, in Australia through the Australian United Press, and later in the United Kingdom. A feature syndicate, British United Features, also distributed the output of the United Feature Syndicate, a UP subsidiary in New York.

The UP was related within the Scripps organization to the Newspaper Enterprise Association (NEA) based in Cleveland since 1902 and reorganized as NEA Features, Inc., in 1921, with a New York office and overseas representation. A Scripps-Howard Newspaper Alliance (SHNA) formed in 1918 and based in Washington prepared and distributed special articles and editorials for the Scripps newspapers. The United Feature Syndicate (UFS) was established in New York in 1919, reincorporated in 1923, and in 1930 purchased and absorbed a Metropolitan Newspaper Service dating from 1919. In 1931 the Scripps-Howard Newspapers purchased the *New York World,* morning and evening, and the World Feature Service was added to the UFS. Meanwhile, a Scripps-sponsored Science Service had been established in 1921, with a telegraphic report introduced in 1927. A United News Picture Syndicate was established in 1928, and in 1936 was combined with NEA to become NEA-Acme, Inc., handling both features and photos for general syndication. All were under the corporate umbrella of the E. W. Scripps Company of Cincinnati.

The growth of the United Press proceeded in a manner to provide sharp competition with the Associated Press. As the postwar period began, Baillie was in charge of the Washington bureau, with Armistead L. Bradford and Robert Bender as his chief aides. With his move to New York, he was succeeded in the capital bureau by Carl D. Groat, formerly in Paris and Berlin, but then editor of the *Cincinnati Post,* a key Scripps-Howard paper. Paul R. Mallon was bureau chief in the late 1920s, with Kenneth Crawford as an assistant. Raymond Clapper was director in the early 1930s, followed by Lyle Wilson. Washington bureau members through the years also included Thomas L. Stokes, Frederick C. Othman, H. O. Thompson, Virgil Pinkley, Merton T. Akers, William J. McEvoy, Richard L. Harkness, and Harrison E. Salisbury.

New York was the headquarters and the center for the UP leased wire network that extended for 154,000 miles in the United States by the mid-1930s linking sixty-nine bureaus, Washington included, and with a major division point in Chicago. A world report, coming and going, also centered in New York. There James H. (Barney) Furay was foreign editor in 1918–19 and again in 1920–24, when he became vice-president in charge of the foreign news department until 1937. Louis F. Keemle was cable editor. Joseph L. Jones, with service in various UP bureaus since 1921, followed Furay as foreign editor from 1924 to 1937 and then as vice-president. Miles W. Vaughn had been foreign editor in the 1919–20 interval, and Joe Alex Morris held that post in 1938–43.

Edward L. Keen had been in London and Paris for the UP since 1910, European manager until 1925, and a vice-president of the agency from 1919 until his retirement in 1940. He was followed in London as European manager by Webb Miller, a UP correspondent since 1916. Miller was Paris bureau chief in 1921–25, based in London from 1930, but also constantly on the move to follow the news wherever it led. Clifford L. Day, formerly of the AP, was in the London bureau from the early 1930s and became assistant European manager in 1939.

James Irvin Miller (unrelated to Webb Miller) had been in Buenos Aires since 1918, where he helped win acceptance of the UP service by *La Prensa* and other dailies. He became vice-president in charge of South American service in 1923 and remained there until 1930. He then was succeeded by Armistead L. Bradford, formerly in Washington but with experience in Buenos Aires in the early 1920s and as chief of the Paris bureau in 1925–30.

In the Far East, with a base either in Tokyo or Shanghai, the news service was directed from 1920, successively, by Miles W. ("Peg") Vaughn, former foreign editor in New York, Raymond Gifford (Ray) Marshall, John R. Morris, and H. O. Thompson, formerly in Washington.

UP staff correspondents in London, the key point for European coverage and service through the 1920s and 1930s, included Joseph L. Jones, later foreign editor and vice-president in New York; Keen, Miller, and Day, as mentioned; Henry Tosti Russell and Charles McCann; Arch Rogers, formerly in South America for the agency; Ralph H. Turner, formerly in Tokyo and Mexico City; Joseph Grigg, Jr., formerly of the *New York Evening Sun* bureau in London; and Robert L. Frey, later an assistant to Hugh Baillie.

Still others in London were Alex Dreier, later in Berlin for the AP and then NBC correspondent there; Charles L. Collingwood, who also entered radio reporting in later years for CBS; Herbert S. Moore, to become founder of Transradio Press in 1934; Robert Couch, Robert C. Dowson, and Keith James; Harry L. Percy, George Chandler, and Laurence Meredith; Charles Hallinan, Herbert G. King, and Byron Taves; Peter C. Rhodes and Homer Jenks. Further,

Frederick C. Oechsner, Everett R. Holles, Virgil Pinkley, formerly in Washington, and Wallace Carroll were to play important roles in London and elsewhere, as was Harry R. Flory, former INS bureau chief there. London and Paris both were capitals from which correspondents moved on assignments to all parts of the world, as well as within the AP organization.

In Paris, the staff representation included Henry Wood, in Europe for the UP since 1912. Webb Miller was a war correspondent and bureau chief in 1921–25. Bradford, bureau chief in 1925–30, was followed by Ralph E. Heinzen, in the bureau earlier and its chief from 1930 to 1940. Harry Flory and Wallace Carroll, both mentioned for their attachment to the London bureau, also served in Paris.

Others in the Paris bureau at various times included Gabriel Curtail; Carl D. Groat, later in Washington; John T. Burke and Thomas Cope; Edwin Ware Hullinger, formerly in Moscow; Samuel S. Dashiell, formerly of the *New York World;* Pierre Salarnier and Hugo Speck; Wilfred Fleisher, both earlier and later in Tokyo with the family-owned *Japan Advertiser;* Henry T. Gorrell, Mary Knight, Llewellyn (Johnny) White, and William Downs; Laurence E. (Larry) LeSueur and Eric Sevareid, both later to become radio and television correspondents.

In Berlin, the first postwar bureau head was Carl D. Groat, following his participation in the Paris Peace Conference coverage. He was succeeded in 1925–33 by Frederick Kuh.[14] Frederick C. Oechsner, formerly in Berlin for the INS, had joined the UP London bureau in 1932, but returned to Berlin in 1933 to replace Kuh. Joseph Grigg, Jr., moving from London to Berlin in 1939, became bureau head in March 1941 when Oechsner was appointed Central European manager.

Other Berlin bureau members at various times included Frank J. Taylor, later known as a frequent contributor to the *Saturday Evening Post;* Gus Oehm and Ferdinand C. M. Jahn; John Graudenz, later of the *New York Times* bureau; Harold A. Peters and H. C. Buurmann, later manager in Amsterdam; Edward W. Beattie, Jr., later UP European business manager; Clinton Beach (Pat) Conger, son of Seymour Beach Conger, AP correspondent in Berlin prior to and during the first years of World War I; Dana Adams Schmidt and Jack Fleischer; Howard K. Smith and Richard G. Hottelet, both later in radio and television news reporting.

Hugh Baillie visited Berlin in 1935 shortly after becoming president of the UP and obtained an interview with Adolf Hitler. Richard McMillan represented both the UP and the BUP in Berlin about 1930, as he

---

14 Not to be confused with Ferdinand Kuhn, Jr., of the *New York Times* London bureau at this period.

did also in other years in Paris and Vienna.

In Rome, the first postwar bureau chief was Henry Wood,[15] already greatly experienced, including wartime coverage in Italy. He served from 1919 to 1921, when he went to Paris and then to Geneva in 1923. His successor in Rome was Thomas B. Morgan, in Italy for the AP during and after the war, but present there for the UP as bureau chief in 1922–35. Morgan reported the first decade of the Fascist regime. He made himself an authority on Vatican affairs and was the first newsman to obtain an interview with Pope Pius XI after his consecration in 1922. Following Morgan as bureau chief in Rome were G. Stewart Brown in 1935–36, and Boston-born Aldo Forte in 1936–39.

Others in Rome for the UP through the years included New York-born Camille M. Cianfarra, whose father had been an assistant in the bureau until he joined the *New York Times* staff there in 1935; Henry T. Gorrell, and Ralph E. Forte (son of Aldo Forte), a representative of the *Chicago Daily News* until he joined the UP in 1937; Samuel S. Dashiell and Virgil Pinkley at certain periods; and Hugo Speck.

Spain was an active news center through the 1920s and far more so in the 1930s. Jean DeGandt was chief representative for the UP in Madrid. The civil war years of 1936–39 brought an influx of correspondents covering both sides.

In Geneva to report League activities, Henry Wood, formerly in Rome and Paris, served from 1923 to 1932, when he resigned. He was replaced by G. Stewart Brown, followed by Frederick Kuh, formerly in Berlin. John G. McNaughton, an assistant in the bureau, was killed in 1936 while mountain climbing. Other correspondents went to Geneva as news developments seemed to require, usually from the Paris bureau.

Junius B. Wood was in Prague in 1938, followed by the husband-wife team of Reynolds and Eleanor Packard, who were later in Rome. Edward J. Bing was in Budapest, and Robert H. Best was in Vienna from 1920 to 1938. He served there also as president of the local branch of the Anglo-American Press Association in 1935.

The United Press maintained early and strong coverage in the Soviet Union. Frank J. Taylor of the Berlin bureau went to Moscow in 1919 before correspondents were officially admitted, but did not remain. The first permanent UP representative there was Edwin Ware Hullinger, who assumed the post in 1921. He also served the *Chicago Daily News*. John Graudenz of the Berlin bureau went to Moscow in 1923. Hullinger was forced to leave in 1924 when his visa was not renewed.

---

15   Not to be confused with Junius B. Wood of the *Chicago Daily News* but also with the UP.

He was replaced by Frederick Kuh, U.S.-born, formerly in southern Europe for the London *Daily Herald*. Kuh served in Moscow in 1924–25, then became chief of the Berlin bureau as previously noted.

The UP was unrepresented in Moscow from 1925 to 1927 except by a former woman secretary in the bureau, a Soviet citizen. The Rosta agency, reorganized in 1925 as the official Tass agency, had been represented in New York at least since 1923, and had a news exchange relationship with the UP. Eugene Lyons, an American who had worked in the Rosta-Tass office in New York for the previous four years, was assigned to Moscow as UP correspondent in 1927 and remained until 1936. In 1930 he obtained the first interview given to any western correspondent by Joseph Stalin.

Karl Bickel, president of the UP in 1923–35, visited Moscow in 1925, when the UP relationship with Rosta was interrupted, and he also visited Rome on several occasions. There he had informal talks with Benito Mussolini, but these produced no news reports.

Roy Howard, former UP president and chairman of the board of the Scripps-Howard Newspapers in 1936, visited Moscow in March of that year and gained an interview with Stalin. The text was released for distribution not only by the UP, but by the AP and INS as well. By that time, other news correspondents had interviewed Stalin, but Howard's interview nevertheless was viewed as important.

Before Lyons left Moscow in 1936, he had gained Henry Shapiro as an assistant, and Shapiro succeeded him as chief of the UP Moscow bureau. Shapiro served from 1936 until his retirement in 1973, a period of thirty-seven years. For many years, he was dean of the foreign press corps in Moscow, a recognized authority on Soviet affairs, and helpful as an instructor to numerous other correspondents.

Rumanian-born, Shapiro had been brought to the United States at age fourteen. He was educated in New York, graduated from the Harvard Law School in 1932, and was admitted to the New York State bar. After practicing law in New York City for two years, he went to Moscow to make a study of Soviet law. In the two years following, he also wrote special articles for the *New York Herald Tribune* and the London *Morning Post*, and became a stringer both for Reuters and the United Press before succeeding Lyons and turning from law to a career in journalism. Meyer S. Handler was his first assistant. Fluent in the language and perceptive, Shapiro earned awards for his reporting. His Russian-born wife, Ludmilla Nikitina Shapiro, as fluent in English as he was in Russian, also wrote from Moscow for the London Sunday *Observer* and other newspapers and periodicals.

As with the Associated Press, a number of the United Press correspondents were almost constantly on the move in Europe and other parts of the world. Webb Miller, even though chief of the Paris bureau in 1921-25 and the London bureau in 1925-35, including direction of the European service, was one of the most mobile members of the staff. Other UP "swing men" included Hullinger, after he left Moscow in 1924; Otis Peabody Swift, formerly of the *New York Tribune* and the *Chicago Tribune,* who was in some twenty countries in the brief period of 1922-23, and who returned then to New York as cable editor; Waverly Root, also formerly of the *Chicago Tribune;* and Leon Kay, who joined the UP in 1923. Both the latter traveled almost constantly over a long period. Edward W. Beattie, Jr., joined the UP in Washington in 1931 and was sent abroad in 1933 where he moved almost without respite between London, Berlin, Tokyo, Shanghai, and other places. Virgil Pinkley did very much the same. Both men assumed administrative duties with the agency.

The position of the UP in Latin America as established in 1916 was strengthened and directed from Buenos Aires, where its subsidiary, Prensa Unida, had its headquarters. James Irvin Miller and Armistead L. Bradford, as managers between 1918 and 1938, presided over a staff and stringer representation throughout South and Central America. Joseph L. Jones, formerly in London, served in Buenos Aires, Rio de Janeiro, Lima, Santiago, and Caracas before returning to New York as foreign editor and as an executive vice-president. J. B. Powers, manager in Buenos Aires, also returning to New York, became an independent advertising representative there for Latin American newspapers.

Others in Latin America included William L. F. Horsey, who joined the UP staff there in 1923 and remained for many years, directing the Santiago bureau from 1937 to 1948. U. Grant Keener directed the Rio de Janeiro bureau, with Charles Kinsolving as an assistant. James Alan Coogan and Daniel A. Campbell were in the Brazilian capital later. Ricardo Leon and Horace Fusoni were in Lima. Lester Ziffren and Arch Rogers, both in Buenos Aires, later were in Spain. Clarence DuBose, formerly in Tokyo, reported from Mexico City, but moved to Madrid for the AP in 1929 and died there in 1931. Ralph H. Turner, also formerly in Tokyo and Mexico City, later moved to the London bureau, but left the agency to become publisher of his own newspaper in California. Jacques Armand and John R. Morris, formerly on the *Japan Advertiser* staff in Tokyo, both served as bureau chiefs in Mexico City, and both later assumed administrative posts with the agency. Morris later returned to the Far East.

Activities in the Middle East and Asia resulted in a strong development of UP coverage. Jacob Simon, an artist as well as a writing correspondent, represented the agency in Jerusalem from 1929 until his death by drowning early in 1942. Carl Crow, a U.S. businessman in the Far East from 1910 to 1937 conducting an advertising agency, also had a financial interest both in the *Shanghai Evening Post* and the *Japan Advertiser* of Tokyo. He also reported from both cities for the UP. The agency director in Tokyo in the early 1920s was Clarence DuBose, later in Mexico City. Miles W. Vaughn, foreign editor in New York in 1919–20, became Tokyo correspondent in 1924 and directed the Far Eastern coverage from there until 1934.

In China, Raymond Gifford (Ray) Marshall[16] was in Peking for the UP from 1921 to 1925 and, after assignments in New York and San Francisco, he returned to China in 1932 as chief of the Shanghai bureau. In 1934 he transferred to Tokyo, succeeding Vaughn as director of the Far Eastern service. Harold O. Thompson, formerly in Washington, assisted Marshall there and was his successor in 1939. Henry Misselwitz, a member of the *Japan Advertiser* staff, joined the UP Tokyo staff in 1927, but went to the Shanghai bureau almost immediately. He remained there until 1930, when he moved to the New York bureau.

Both John R. Morris, on the *Japan Advertiser* staff in the early 1930s, and Randall Gould, managing editor of the *Japan Times* in 1923-24, were active for the UP. Morris became chief of the Mexico City bureau but returned to Shanghai in 1933 as bureau chief and succeeded Marshall as manager of the Far Eastern service in 1936.[17] Milton Chase was night editor in the Shanghai bureau at that time, and staff members included Robert Bellaire, Weldon James, John Goodbody, and Paul Feng.

Randall Gould in joining the UP took charge of the bureau in Peking in 1925, succeeding Ray Marshall, and remained until 1927. At that time he went to Manila as bureau chief until 1928. He was succeeded in Peking by Demaree Bess, who had been in the Far East since 1923, first with the *Shanghai Times,* then with the *Japan Advertiser* and, from 1925 to 1927, as Tokyo representative of the *Philadelphia Public Ledger-New York Evening Post* service. He remained in Peking for the UP from 1927 to 1932.

Meanwhile, Bert L. Kuhn was in charge of the Shanghai bureau. He was succeeded by Herbert R. (Bud) Ekins, who had joined the UP in 1927 as Honolulu bureau chief. Ekins was in Manila in 1928-29, and took charge in Shanghai in 1930. In 1932 Gould was back in China as

---

16 Not to be confused with James D. (Jim) Marshall of *Collier's,* also in China in the 1930s.

17 John R. Morris is not to be confused with Morris J. Harris in Japan and China for the AP in 1924–41, and also a former *Japan Advertiser* staff member.

Shanghai bureau head. He remained there until early 1941. Through the later years of that period, he was editor of the *Shanghai Post & Mercury,* rather than a UP staff member, and was also Shanghai correspondent for the *Christian Science Monitor.* Bellaire succeeded Gould as Shanghai bureau chief in 1936, followed in 1937 by Robert T. Berkov, briefly, and then by Earl Leaf, former Tientsin correspondent.

Ekins replaced Bess in Peking (Peiping), a less important center since Nanking had become the capital. Bess not only left Peiping, but left the UP to succeed Gould temporarily as Shanghai correspondent for the *Christian Science Monitor.* A year later, in 1933, he went to Geneva as correspondent for the *Monitor.*

In 1936 Ekins was replaced in Peiping by Robert McCormick. At that time, Ekins went to report the closing months of the Italo-Ethiopian War, and then became night news editor at UP headquarters in New York. In September-October of that year, however, he undertook a special assignment for the *New York World-Telegram* and other Scripps-Howard newspapers, setting a new record for flight around the world by commercial air transport. Traveling aboard the German zeppelin Hindenburg from Lakehurst, New Jersey, to Frankfurt and by airplanes from there eastward to Asia, back across the Pacific and the United States, he landed at Lakehurst again eighteen and one-half days later, having covered 25,654 miles. He lectured on the subject throughout the United States before returning to the Far East for the UP in 1937 to report upon the war then in progress in China. In 1939 he returned to Europe as bureau chief in Rome, but was expelled soon after assuming that post.

The growing crisis in the 1930s also brought UP correspondents to the Far East as resident staffers and as visitors. Frederick Kuh, then Berlin bureau chief, made the journey to Manchuria in 1931. Reynolds Packard, Edward W. Beattie, Jr., and Virgil Pinkley were other visitors. UP correspondents in Shanghai in those years included F. M. (Mack) Fisher, George Hogg, Alfred Hicks, Derrell Berrigan, Fritz Silber, and Jack Belden. Some went frequently to Nanking. Doris Ruebens wrote from Hankow in 1930. Harold Guard, a British-born newsman, represented the UP in Hong Kong.

Manila received regular coverage, with 1934 especially important because independence for the Philippines was approved by the United States in that year, and scheduled to become effective in 1945. William B. Juhns was Manila correspondent in 1925-27. Gould and Ekins headed the UP bureau there between 1927 and 1929. Reuel S. Moore, formerly in the Honolulu bureau, served in 1930-36. He was succeeded by Richard C. Wilson, formerly in Mexico City for INS. In

Honolulu, Moore was followed by Daniel A. Campbell, and was succeeded in turn by Wendell Burch. Robert Waite was in Singapore in this period, and Charles P. Arnot became correspondent in Australia in 1939.

Through the 1920s and 1930s, the UP correspondents, as a group, tended to be young and aggressive and highly competitive in coverage. While there were exceptions, most of them also were American citizens, appointed for overseas service on the assumption that they would be best able to view events and write of them in a manner to interest readers in the United States. This, in fact, applied in general to agency and newspaper representation for all services, with nationals of the countries directly represented outnumbering others.

By 1939, the United Press had more than fifty bureaus in the United States, including extensive New York and Washington operations, and thirty-five overseas bureaus, of which the London office was the most active. The agency's total annual expenditure for news-gathering then was close to $8 million. About 150,000 words of domestic and foreign news were being distributed each day over a leased wire network serving 975 morning and evening newspapers in the United States, and virtually all radio stations, by then numbering about 800. In addition, service was going to 486 clients in other countries.

The International News Service (INS), forming part of the Hearst organization, was more limited in scope than the other two U.S. agencies. It was, nevertheless, active and enterprising, grew rapidly, and gained status for world coverage by 1936.

From 1917 to 1928 INS served afternoon newspapers only, but Hearst introduced a Universal Service in 1918 to provide a news report to morning papers. After 1928, the INS reports went to both, with Universal Service operating as a separate feature agency until 1937, when it was suspended.

The agencies were directed from New York, INS by Moses Koenigsberg, who also headed the Hearst-owned King Features Syndicate (KFS) created in 1914, and Universal Service by H. H. Stansbury. The services went to the Hearst newspapers, numbering thirty-five morning and evening dailies in nineteen cities by 1935, but also were available to other papers. Thus a total of 900 dailies in the United States were receiving the INS reports in 1936, plus many radio stations, as well as newspapers in Latin America, Asia, and Europe. Its domestic leased wire network grew from 24,500 miles in 1918 to 60,000 miles in

International News Service

1936, with bureaus from coast to coast, and in London, Paris, Berlin, Buenos Aires, Tokyo, and other world cities. The INS operating budget in 1936 was about $2 million.

In addition to KFS, one of the larger syndicates, International News Photos (INP) was formed in the 1930s. Eight radio stations were Hearst-owned, as well as *Cosmopolitan* and a number of other magazines, and the newsreel, Hearst-Metrotone News.

As with the AP and UP, the INS maintained a strong Washington bureau. London was its main bureau in Europe. Earl Reeves, INS wartime chief there, remained until 1921. Frank E. Mason, former magazine editor but military attaché at the U.S. embassy in Berlin after the war, and then INS correspondent there in 1920–21, succeeded Reeves in London and was director of the agency's European service. He moved to the direction of the Paris bureau in 1925, but returned to New York in 1927, first as business manager and then, following Koenigsberg, as general manager and president of the INS in 1928. In 1931, however, he resigned to become vice-president of the National Broadcasting Company, where he continued until 1945.

With Mason's departure, Joseph V. Connolly headed the INS from 1931 until his death in 1945. Barry Faris, formerly of the *Indianapolis Sun* and a member of the UP staff in New York, had become chief editor of INS in 1916, and continued as vice-president, editor-in-chief, and associate general manager of the agency until 1956, at which time he became international editor of the more simply titled Metrotone News.

Hobart C. Montee, with seven years as a correspondent in the Far East, including a period as editor of the *Manila Times,* was director of the foreign service in New York until 1934, followed by John C. (Jack) Oestreicher, who had succeeded Mason as London bureau chief and director of the European service in 1926–34. For Universal Service, Plautus I. Lipsey, Jr., was foreign editor in New York until 1932, when he joined the AP, with assignment to Geneva.

Harry R. Flory, who had gone to Europe in 1922 to direct a bureau in Paris, went to London instead. He succeeded Mason as bureau chief in 1925–26. He was in Paris in 1926–28, but then returned to head the London bureau. When he left London for Paris in 1926, Flory had been replaced by Oestreicher, who headed the bureau until 1928 but continued there until 1934 as director of the European service, returning then to New York as foreign editor.

Flory resigned in 1931 as INS London bureau chief to join the UP staff. Succeeding him was Otto D. Tolischus, a Balt by birth but in the United States since his youth, and managing editor of the *Cleveland Press* from 1916 to 1923. In 1923 he went to Berlin for INS, and remained until 1931. Again London bureau chief from 1931 to 1933, Tolischus then joined the *New York Times* staff and returned to Berlin. He was succeeded in London for INS by Harry K. Reynolds in 1933–34, followed by William Hillman until 1938, when he joined the *Collier's Weekly* staff. Hillman was succeeded in turn by J. Kingsbury Smith, who had joined the INS London bureau in 1928 after two previous years with the agency in New York, and a year on the UP cable desk there.

Others in London for INS at various times included Russell F. Anderson, Thomas C. Watson, and David M. Church; Charles A. Smith, formerly of the *New York Times* bureau; Pierre J. (Pete) Huss, formerly in Mexico City; David Sentner and Jack Lait; Frank Gervasi, who left also to join *Collier's;* and Robert J. Nixon, formerly of the Washington staff.

George R. Holmes, chief of the INS bureau in Washington, was in London in 1930 to report the Naval Conference of that year. Wythe Williams, who was in London for the *New York World* in 1910–12 and in Paris for the *New York Times* in 1913–17, wrote for *Collier's,* the *Philadelphia Public Ledger,* and the *Saturday Evening Post* between 1918 and 1927, and again with the *New York Times* in 1927–31. He was with the Hearst newspapers after 1931, however, and directed Universal Service in London in 1934–36. He then returned to the United States to become editor of the *Greenwich Time* of Greenwich, Connecticut.[18] Inez Calloway Robb, a special writer on the New York staff of the INS, was in London in 1937 to help report the coronation of George VI.

The INS Berlin bureau, following Mason's move to London in 1921, was headed by S. Dunbar Weyer until his suicide in 1928. Tolischus, present since 1923 and Central European manager, took charge. When he became chief of the London bureau in 1931, he was followed as Berlin bureau chief by Edward L. Deuss, formerly in Moscow. Deuss, like Kuh of the UP, felt the pressure of the Nazi government in 1933 and left Berlin. To succeed him there, Arno Dosch-Fleurot was sent from the Paris bureau.

Dosch-Fleurot had been in Europe for the *New York World* from 1914 to 1931, when that paper, morning and evening, was sold to the Scripps-Howard group and ceased to exist. He then joined the INS Paris bureau. Quentin Reynolds of the *New York Evening World,*

---

18 During his long career, Williams was at various times president of the Anglo-American Press Association in Paris (1922), of the International Association of Journalists Accredited to the League of Nations in Geneva (1928), and both a founder and first president of the Overseas Press Club of America in New York (1939). He was decorated by the French government as a Chevalier of the Legion of Honor.

also a victim of that sale, became an assistant in the INS Berlin bureau at that time.

Hudson Hawley, formerly with the AP in Paris, Rome, and Geneva, had joined the INS bureau in Paris in 1929. He moved to Berlin in 1934 as Central European manager, but proceeded to London in the same year to succeed Oestreicher as European news manager. Tom Wilhelm, also formerly of the AP, assumed Hawley's briefly held post in Berlin. Pierre J. Huss, who had joined the Berlin bureau in 1932 after about a year in London, was the first U.S. correspondent to obtain an interview with Adolf Hitler after the Nazi party leader became chancellor in 1933.

Two other INS Berlin correspondents occupied special positions, even though holding no bureau titles. These were Karl H. von Wiegand and Hubert Renfro (Red) Knickerbocker. Von Wiegand, German-born but U.S.-raised, had gone to Europe for the UP in 1911 after prior news experience that included service with the AP in San Francisco. He was UP correspondent in Berlin when the war began in 1914, but returned to New York in 1915 to work for the *New York World*. There he switched to the INS in 1916, to the *New York Sun* shortly after, but rejoined the Hearst service in August 1919. Back in Berlin, he was European director for the Universal Service until its demise in 1937. He was assisted for a number of years by Charles L. Flick. His daughter, Charmion von Wiegand, also wrote for the Hearst newspapers from Russia in 1930. With unusual sources of information in Germany and central Europe, von Wiegand produced special reports for the Hearst papers, distributed through the INS. Occasionally, he traveled to other parts of the world, notably on special flights of the Graf Zeppelin and the Hindenburg in the 1920s and 1930s.

Knickerbocker, going to Europe to study medicine, was diverted to a news career in Berlin in 1924-25 when acting as an assistant to Dorothy Thompson, then correspondent for the *Philadelphia Public Ledger-New York Evening Post* service. Transferring to INS in 1925, he served the agency in Moscow and Berlin until 1928. In the latter year he returned to the *Public Ledger* as its Berlin correspondent, succeeding Dorothy Thompson (who had become Mrs. Sinclair Lewis), and continued until 1933. His work in 1930 won him a Pulitzer Prize awarded in 1931. With the suspension of the *Public Ledger* and its service in 1933, Knickerbocker returned to the INS on a roving assignment that took him to Ethiopia, Spain, and China for war coverage, and to other centers of news activity until 1941. In that year he joined the newly established *Chicago Sun* as director of its prospective foreign news service.

Other members of the INS or Universal Service staffs in Berlin included Walter Dietzel, Frederick C. Oechsner, later with the UP,

Robert Barry, formerly of the *Public Ledger* service, and William L. Shirer, formerly of the *Chicago Tribune* and writing for Universal Service from 1935 to 1937, at which time he became radio correspondent for the Columbia Broadcasting System. Dr. Max Jordan, an American formerly acting in New York as a stringer for the *Berliner Tageblatt*, did some work for INS in Central Europe in the 1920s, but joined the National Broadcasting Company early in the 1930s as its representative in the same general area.

In Vienna, INS was represented by Alfred Trynauer from 1927 to 1938, when Austria was seized by the Nazis. Charles L. Flick was in Vienna and had been in Berlin earlier. Frazier (Spike) Hunt, formerly with the *Chicago Tribune,* joined INS in 1919 and roved much of the world as a special writer until he became more particularly associated with the Hearst magazines, with London as a base. Ernest Hemingway, writing in Paris and elsewhere in Europe for the *Toronto Star* in 1922-23, also wrote for INS and Universal Service. Max Perlman was in Bucharest for INS in the late 1920s. General F. A. Sutton, a British soldier and adventurer, provided some correspondence from Russia, and also from China, during that decade. Anatole Visson, Russian-born and French-educated, was in Brussels in the late 1930s, writing for the Agence Havas as well as INS, but later joined the staff of *Time* magazine.

The INS Paris bureau was headed by Mason in 1922-26, Flory in 1926-28, and successively by William Parker, later with Reuters, Frederick K. Abbott, later with the AP, Lindesay Parrott, Michael Wilson, and from 1937 by Kenneth T. Downs, arriving from New York. Universal Service was represented there by Philip Lemont and Seymour Berkson, formerly of the AP. Stanton B. Leeds, Henry Cavendish, formerly of the *New York Herald* Paris edition, and Carol Weld were among bureau members.

Other INS staffers in Paris included Basil Woon, Hudson Hawley, formerly of the AP, and Arno Dosch-Fleurot, until the latter two went to the Berlin bureau. Still others were William Lee Dickson, Thomas Grandin, until he joined the Columbia Broadcasting System, Edward Hunter, formerly in London and Manchuria for the agency, and Harold J. T. Horan. A former tutor for William Randolph Hearst, Jr., and for John Hearst, Horan also wrote from Geneva and Rome at times. He and the elder William Randolph Hearst acted jointly in 1928 to obtain an exclusive account of an Anglo-French naval agreement. The outcome was that Hearst himself was expelled from France.

Moscow was covered for INS by Isaac Don Levine, formerly of the *Chicago Daily News,* from 1922 to 1925, with William Reswick as an assistant until he joined the AP. Edward L. Deuss was in Moscow from 1925-31, when he went to Berlin. Knickerbocker was in Moscow as well as Berlin for extended periods between 1925 and 1928, and again later. Deuss was followed as INS staff correspondent in Moscow in 1931-32 by Kendall Foss, formerly in London and Berlin for the *New York Times*. He was succeeded in 1932-34 by Linton Wells, who had worked for the *China Press* in Shanghai as early as 1911 and was something of an adventurer.[19] Lindesay Parrott, Scottish-born and educated in England, Switzerland, and the United States, followed Wells in Moscow in 1934. Parrott also served in Paris and Rome between 1933 and 1937.

The Rome bureau was headed from 1925 to 1935 by Guglielmo Emanuel, who became dean of the press corps in that capital during the decade. An Italian citizen, he was arrested in 1935 on political charges and held incommunicado. Hudson Hawley moved from London to fill in until he was replaced by Frank (Henry) Gervasi, who had been in Madrid since joining the foreign staff in 1934 after earlier experience with the AP in New York and as diplomatic correspondent in Washington for Universal Service. Gervasi remained in Rome until 1939, and then moved to the London bureau.

Succeeding Gervasi in Rome at that time was Percival H. Winner, possessing perhaps the most varied experience of any correspondent. He had been in Rome a decade before for the AP, and then for the *Philadelphia Public Ledger* service in 1928-33. He was in New York for the Agence Havas in 1934-36, and with both NBC and CBS during 1936-38. He returned to Rome for the INS in 1938. For Universal Service, prior to its suspension, Prince Pignatelli was in Rome in 1930, followed by William W. (Bill) Chaplin.

Latin American coverage for INS was directed from Buenos Aires, with Daniel Carey and Percy Forster among the correspondents. Leo Reisler was in Havana, and William Flythe was in Mexico City for about a decade. Richard C. Wilson and Pierre J. Huss also served in Mexico City, with Wilson as chief of the bureau. When Huss was transferred to London in 1931 to begin a long career in Europe, he was succeeded in Mexico City by Arthur Constantine. Wilson transferred to the UP in 1936, with an assignment in Manila.

In the Far East, Duke N. Parry based in Tokyo was manager of the service in that part of the world in 1922. He switched briefly to the *Philadelphia Public Ledger* service, but was back with INS in 1923, and in New York in 1924. Luther A. Huston, in Tokyo in 1927, was moved to China later in the year, but was in New York in 1930 as

---

19   With the *New York World* in 1926, Wells and Edward S. Evans had established a new record by circumnavigating the globe in twenty-eight-and-a-half days, by train, auto, ship, and plane. With the suspension of the *World* in 1931, he joined INS, and in 1936 the *New York Herald Tribune* to report the Italo-Ethiopian War.

director of sales for INS until he joined the *New York Times* for long service in Washington.

James R. (Jimmy) Young, a former personal secretary to E. W. Scripps and a nephew of Paul Patterson, publisher of the *Baltimore Sun,* had worked for that papèr and for the UP prior to 1927. In that year he joined the staff of the *Japan Advertiser* in Tokyo. In 1929 he became manager there for INS and Universal Service and later for International News Photos as well, and represented them in Japan until 1940.

In China, INS coverage began in 1922 when Edna Lee Booker (later Mrs. John Stauffer Potter), with earlier news experience in Los Angeles and San Francisco, began work for the *China Press* in Shanghai. She also wrote for INS and continued to represent the agency through 1943, moving in the later years to Chungking.

Lloyd (Larry) Lehrbas, formerly with the Hearst-owned *Chicago Evening American,* began fourteen years of work for the INS in China in 1923. In the period he became one of a group of foreigners captured and held by bandits in a holdup of the Peking Express, running between Shanghai and Peking. Lehrbas later joined the AP and was reassigned to Europe in 1937.

John Goette joined the INS in China in 1924 after previous news experience in India. With Peking as his base, he remained until 1941, by then long dean of correspondents there. He moved out regularly, however, and was in Manchuria in 1929 to report Russo-Chinese hostilities along the border between the two countries, and again in 1931. He was in Shanghai in 1932 at the time Japanese forces were in occupation there.

Dixon Hoste became Shanghai correspondent for INS and Universal Service in 1925, following two years of travel in the interior of China, and served for more than a decade. Alfred Meyer was in China for INS in 1927, and Burt L. Kuhn of the *China Press* also served the agency until switching to the UP.

Theodore O. (Ted) Thackrey, formerly editor of the *Cleveland Press,* associate editor of the *New York Telegram,* and editor of the *Buffalo Times,* all Scripps-Howard newspapers, went to China in 1929 as director of the *Shanghai Evening Post & Mercury* and of its vernacular edition, *Ta Mei Wan Pao.* He also wrote for INS, and remained until the mid-1930s. At that time he returned to the United States to become executive editor of the *New York Post.*

Edward Hunter joined the INS staff in 1931. He had been a *Japan Advertiser* staff member in 1927, acting editor of the English-language *Hankow Herald* and *Peking Leader,* and a Peking correspondent for the *New York Evening Sun.* For the INS, he was in Manchuria for eighteen months following the Japanese invasion of 1931, but transferred to the INS London bureau in 1933. The agency was represented in China in the late 1930s by M. C. (Henry) Ford, also of the *Shanghai Evening Post & Mercury*.

The early syndicates and special services prior to and during the period of World War I, with their materials going to newspapers, continued in the years following, although with changes and with their numbers increasing, particularly in the United States. Some were sponsored by newspapers, or they distributed reports produced by newspaper staff members, as had been true since 1900 and earlier. Some were sponsored by news agencies, while others were independent commercial enterprises.

Continuing after 1920 were the McClure Newspaper Syndicate, the Scripps-owned Newspaper Enterprise Association (NEA), and the Hearst-owned King Features Syndicate (KFS), among others. The Wheeler syndicate was merged into the Bell Syndicate, also created by John N. Wheeler in 1916.

The NEA, operating from Cleveland since its establishment in 1902, was directed from that time until his retirement in 1929 by Robert F. Paine, previously of the *Cleveland Press*. Reorganized in 1921 as NEA Service, Inc., a New York office opened in 1929, directed by Fred S. Ferguson, formerly of the UP and successor to Paine in the general managership. It had a number of writers abroad, including Milton Bronner in London, Minott Saunders in Paris, and at various times E. Percy Noël, Linton Wells, and Peggy Hull (Mrs. Eleanor Goodnough Kinley until her remarriage in 1933 to Harvey V. Duell, then managing editor of the *New York Daily News*). Acme Newspictures, formed as a subsidiary in 1925, became NEA-Acme ten years later.

The Scripps organization also established a Scripps Editorial Board in 1918, a United Feature Syndicate in 1919, and a Science Service in 1921. Following the reorganization that transformed the former Scripps-McRae Newspapers into the Scripps-Howard Newspapers in 1920, the Scripps Editorial Board became the Scripps-Howard Newspaper Alliance (SHNA), based in Washington and directed by William Philip Simms, wartime Paris correspondent for the UP. It distributed news features, articles, and editorials to the Scripps newspapers.

The United Feature Syndicate in New York began as a subsidiary of the UP to distribute special articles by statesmen, public figures, and "big name" writers. Directed by Monte Bourjaily in 1928-36, it grew greatly in the variety of material distributed. It added a United News Pictures subsidiary. It acquired in 1930 a Metropolitan Newspaper Service, originated in 1919 as a venture of the *Metropolitan Magazine,* and a part of the Bell Syndicate until 1922. When the *New York World* was purchased by the Scripps-Howard Newspapers in 1931, it acquired the World Feature Service, in existence since 1896.

Science Service was formed in recognition of the growing importance and public interest in science. Designed by E. W. Scripps, in consultation with Professor William E. Ritter, zoologist, of the University of California, Berkeley, and also director of the Scripps Institution for Biological Research, La Jolla, Science Service was directed from New York by Dr. Watson Davis. At first going to Scripps newspapers, it became available to others.

A service resembling a news agency but operating as a syndicate was organized in Washington in 1919 by David Lawrence, formerly a correspondent in the capital for the Associated Press and for the *New York Evening Post.* Known as the Consolidated Press Association (CPA), and backed by the *Chicago Daily News,* the *New York Sun,* and other papers, it distributed a wire service of special reports, including some from abroad, to subscribing newspapers in the United States. In addition to Washington reports by Lawrence and by Frank Kent of the *Baltimore Sun,* as well as reports from New York, other writers included William Bird in Paris, A. G. Gardiner in London, Francis M. Mansfield in Geneva, and Edgar P. Snow in China. Horace Epes as editor kept the service in good order. The CPA also distributed the Washington and overseas reports of the *Chicago Daily News* until 1929, the evening *New York Sun* reports in the 1929-32 period, and the *Daily News* service again in 1932-33. At that time, the CPA was absorbed by another service, the North American Newspaper Alliance (NANA) of New York.

A cooperative service, the Associated Newspapers (AN), was formed in 1912 under the sponsorship of Jason Rogers, publisher of the *New York Globe,* an afternoon paper (1904-23). With twenty-eight afternoon papers included, it was active during the war and after in originating news and feature material.

The successful operation of Associated Newspapers inspired the formation of a service formed in 1922 by the *New York Times.* This was the North American Newspaper Alliance (NANA), with a number of other large city morning dailies sharing in the operating expenses. It was directed at the outset by John N. Wheeler, even then heading the Bell Syndicate, and with its headquarters in the *New York Times* building. The purpose was to arrange coverage of important predictable events at home and abroad, and to handle the distribution of special articles, and the serialization of important current books on public affairs, including biographies and autobiographies. The NANA absorbed the Associated Newspapers group after 1923 and in 1933 also absorbed the Consolidated Press Association, with its editors of that time, Bertram G. Zilmer and George M. Bond, becoming editors of the NANA service.

The NANA began by distributing reports by Lemuel C. Parton, in Europe in 1923 and in Labrador in 1924 to cover the landing there of U.S. Army fliers who had circled the globe in amphibious planes. Lawrence Wilson wrote from China in 1927. Among major reports given special distribution was Charles A. Lindbergh's personal account of his solo Atlantic flight to Paris in 1927, written exclusively for the *New York Times*. Also handled were accounts of Richard E. Byrd's expedition to the Antarctic and the South Pole, as reported in 1929 by Russell Owen of the *New York Times*, with daily shortwave radio transmissions from Little America on the Polar ice cap to New York in a coverage that gained Owen a Pulitzer Prize in 1930. The memoirs of General John J. Pershing, for which NANA paid what then was a record price of $270,000, were serialized in 1930. In the early 1930s also, NANA distributed special news-related articles by Junius B. Wood and John Gunther, both formerly of the *Chicago Daily News*, and others by Vincent Sheean and Jay Allen, both formerly of the *Chicago Tribune*. Ernest Hemingway reported aspects of the Spanish Civil War for NANA from 1937–38, an experience that also was to produce his books, *Spanish Earth* (1938) and *For Whom the Bell Tolls* (1940).

The need for photographs, a more urgent requirement for newspapers from the 1920s, produced new services or syndicates not only in New York, but in London, Paris, and other world centers. Certain such services were independent and commercial, others were affiliates or subsidiaries of newspapers or news agencies. The Reuters and Wolff agencies entered the field. Acme Newspictures became a subsidiary of NEA, and United News Pictures a subsidiary of the United Feature Syndicate. An A.P. Picture Service formed by the Associated Press in 1928 became AP Wirephoto in 1936. A Wide World Photos syndicate organized in 1919 as a subsidiary of the *New York Times* was sold to AP Wirephotos in 1941. International News Photos, a subsidiary of the International News Service, was organized as a syndicate in 1935. As technology permitted, the distribution of pictures originally dependent upon the mail service moved to airmail and then to transmission by wire. As with AP Wirephoto, the other news agencies adopted that method, as did NEA-Acme.

Individual newspapers in the United States had entered into the syndication of their special news services and features, either directly or through an existing syndicate, or by mail or leased wire. Such distribution was utilized by the *New York Herald* and, to some extent, by the *New York Tribune* in 1900 or earlier, and was continued following the merger of those papers in 1924 by a New York Herald Tribune Syndicate. The *Chicago Daily News* distributed its world news service from 1899, either directly or through the CPA or other syndicates. A New York Sun News Service of earlier date became the Laffan News Bureau in 1897–1916, and evening *Sun* reports later were moved by the CPA in 1929–32.

A Hearst Syndicate of 1895 became the King Feature Syndicate (KFS) in 1914, proceeding to great size and variety. Opéra Mundi, a Paris syndicate established in 1928 by Paul Winkler, a French newsman, became the European outlet for KFS. The *New York World* service of the 1890s also became the World Syndicate in 1905, and continued until absorbed in 1931 by the Scripps UP-related United Feature Syndicate. A *Chicago Tribune* syndication, beginning in 1910, was transformed after 1920 to become the Chicago Tribune–New York News Syndicate, Inc.

The *Philadelphia Public Ledger,* purchased in 1913 by Cyrus H. K. Curtis, established its own syndicate in 1915. Curtis also bought the *New York Evening Post* in 1923, with a combined Ledger-Post news service available through syndication from that time until Curtis's death in 1933, with the morning *Ledger* itself then soon suspended and the *New York Evening Post* sold to a new owner, J. David Stern.

The *Des Moines Register and Tribune* formed a Register & Tribune Syndicate in 1924, distributing photos and other materials, and later handling the *Chicago Daily News* service distribution. The *New York Times,* with a greatly increased Washington, national, and foreign news service, had entered upon independent syndication of that service from the time of World War I. It also had sponsored Wide World Photos in 1919 and the NANA in 1922.

Several other daily newspapers in the United States with foreign representation did not distribute those reports. The *Christian Science Monitor,* circulating nationally and internationally, could not offer exclusive territories for use of its material and therefore could not consider syndication in the usual form. It was much quoted, however. The one other U.S. daily that did enter syndication later was the *Baltimore Sun,* with a small but high-quality service of its own.

There were many other commercial syndicates, but most of the matter distributed was feature or entertainment material. Of approximately 100 syndicates in the United States in 1925, about one-third joined in forming an Association of Newspaper Syndicates. By 1936 there were more than 200 syndicates operating. No such number existed in other countries. A few, however, offered their services abroad. This was true of two or three London newspapers, and of photo syndicates in London and Paris.

The general syndication of material in the United States did include news and photos, news-related cartoons, special articles, and even weekly magazine supplements. In addition, there were comic strips and Sunday comic supplements in color, all in great variety, often imitative, and rarely comic, in fact. There were public affairs columns and other columns in great variety, offering New York and "Broadway" items, "Hollywood" information or gossip about persons whose names were generally familiar, sports commentary, fashion reports, cooking, home-making, literary, and humor columns, and a great many more to meet every sort of interest. There were even syndicated editorials as well as fiction, until that was made pointless by the easy availability of stories to be heard on radio and by inexpensive paperback books gaining distribution in the 1930s.

The syndicates distributed material either as a total package, with a variety of material, or by selling particular features. Newspapers in the United States, Canada, and some other countries found in this system a source of material to attract, entertain, and hold readers. If a feature or group of features was popular it had value to the newspaper. For this reason, a particular feature might go to the highest bidder among newspapers appearing in the same city or circulation area.

It was generally understood that the price of a syndicated feature or package was to be scaled to the size of the city and to the circulation and general prosperity of the newspaper. It also was understood that a paper buying a feature would have the exclusive right to that feature in its city or circulation area. Yet if a particular feature was popular, other syndicates were quick to find writers and artists to produce something very similar for sale to competing papers. Thus there was duplication and imitation in the field.

A trend toward the use of entertainment features in newspapers in the years following the war, and perhaps especially in the United States, led to the growth in the number of syndicates and the size of some. With about 1,700 daily papers, and many more weekly papers, there was a great market for syndicated features. Even though the price of most features and syndicate packages was moderate, the return to the syndicate and to the more popular artists and writers could be substantial.

World Press Patterns: The British Style 13

Daily and weekly newspapers continued as the major sources of current information for most persons during the years between the two world wars. Radio was playing an important role, however, by the 1930s. Magazines also became more active in reporting upon topics of the day. News magazines gained readership in the United States. Restyled picture magazines attained popularity, stressing prompt and effective photographic reporting and exerting notable impact.

In reporting the news of its own community, each newspaper provided an unmatchable service. The years since 1900 had seen many reach out to develop independent or supplementary regional, national, and sometimes foreign coverage, even though also receiving news agency reports and syndicated services.

The quality newspapers held to a sober presentation of the most significant news, adding serious commentary and guidance in editorials and in special articles. But some of the popular papers also were active in both respects.

The character of the newspaper press throughout the world, in terms of general appearance, was marked by three prevailing patterns. These related to typography and format, primarily, but were not without significance as bearing upon content and policy. The first pattern was exemplified by most of the London and British dailies, the second by Paris dailies and the French press in general, and the third by New York dailies and the U.S. press in general. One or another of these patterns was found in use by the press of other countries.

What this meant was that in the British pattern the first and last pages of most papers were occupied by advertising. On page one this might be a full-page advertisement, it might be two or more large advertisements, or it might be what would be called classified advertising in U.S. terminology, "smalls" in British usage, or *petite annonces* in French. The back page would be given over to a number of advertisements of various sizes, or what might be called "classified display" in the United States.

This prominent placement of advertising, especially on page one, justified a high rate for the sale of space and therefore was profitable. At the same time, the practice had a certain advantage in protecting what otherwise might have been news pages from tears and smudges, with annoyance to readers. The lack of a page-one display of news also prevented passersby on the street or persons in shops from catching the essentials of the news by glancing at the headlines, without buying a copy of the paper. This, of course, was irrelevant as it affected persons receiving the paper by subscription or delivery. Since for others a headline display on page one was the newspaper's "show window" to capture attention and so sell copies, it might equally be said that the use of advertising instead of news on page one had a negative value.

To compensate for the absence of that page-one headline display as a stimulus to street or shop sales, every newspaper produced separate "contents bills" for each edition. These were full sheets, equal to a standard-size page, printed in colors and type designs distinctive for each paper. Such a bill, posted outside a shop, on a fence or wall, or carried in a clip stick by a news vendor in the streets, was visible and readable from a distance. Each bill informed of some one report in the edition. It was not a headline, but used a few words in block type revealing no essential facts, yet indicating the subject matter in a manner intended to pique interest and create sales. Since London dailies included some of the largest circulation in the world, it must be assumed that the method was effective. Even those few papers using news on page one used contents bills.

In this typical British pattern of the 1920s and 1930s, the two facing middle pages of the day's edition of a morning newspaper, in particular, were used with the main news page on one side, and the leader or editorial page facing it on the other. These pages were free of advertising, if one excepts a column listing current theatrical, musical, and cinema attractions. The leader page, in addition to two or three columns of editorials, commonly presented one or two special articles, a selection of letters to the editor, and possibly a Court Circular. This was the nearest thing to a "society" column, such as almost certainly would appear in a U.S. daily, although not in a British newspaper. But it was limited almost exclusively to mention of appointments and ceremonies involving the royal family, activities of members of the nobility, of the cabinet, visiting leaders of state, and members of the diplomatic corps.

The main news page, whether on the left or right, was comparable to the first page of a newspaper made in the U.S. pattern or that of a Paris information paper in that it presented the major news stories of the day. Each such story was complete in itself, however, with no continuation or "jump" to another page, as in a U.S. paper, but often briefer for that reason. Headlines tended to be more in the nature of labels than informative, and usually no more than a column in width. Photos were rarely used on the page; such news photos as appeared usually were grouped on a later page, surrounded by advertising.

Except on infrequent occasions, when a special supplement might be added, the British paper formed a single section of some thirty to forty pages. It was usually departmentalized in the sense that the reader would know that secondary national and world news reports would be in the same general position each day, and the same with news of Parliament, the law courts, business and finance, sports, theatrical and musical reviews, and other subjects. Except for the two middle pages, advertisements appeared throughout the paper.

The most obvious difference between newspapers made in the British pattern and those in the Paris or U.S. patterns was typographical. Both of the latter used news on page one, usually with headlines summarizing the subject of each story, sometimes large and occasionally with color used to gain greater attention. The headlines were more informative in the U.S.-style paper than in the Paris or French paper. Contents bills were not used with either.

The British and U.S. dailies stressed the news of the day, and thus were information papers. So also was the French provincial press, generally. But the Paris press, setting its distinctive pattern, was divided between information papers and political papers, or journals of opinion. The lack of advertising volume in the Paris and French newspapers meant that they had proportionately less space for news and editorial matter than newspapers made in either of the other patterns. Those following the U.S. pattern in particular, and many British papers also, in presenting more advertising, had relatively more space for news, photographs, articles, and entertainment features. Many in the U.S. pattern were published in two sections, more in larger Sunday editions.

The British provincial papers tended to resemble the London press, and U.S. dailies were generally similar in appearance throughout the country. The French provincial papers were comparable to the Paris information papers, but the Paris political papers were a rather separate variety. Many of them, because they were small in circulation, as well as size, were printed commercially rather than in publishing plants of their own.

By the 1920s, newspapers made in the British pattern were found throughout much of the world, particularly in the Commonwealth countries, China, and Argentina. Papers made in the Paris pattern were common throughout the European continent, in most of Latin America, and parts of Africa, the Middle East, and Asia. The U.S. pattern was followed, at the time, in Canada, Cuba, and the Philippines. Beginning in the 1930s, however, the U.S. pattern was adopted more widely in Mexico, South America, and parts of Asia, due in part to the growing use in those areas of U.S. news agency services. There was, however, a general tendency to borrow features of any one of the three patterns for use anywhere else in the world, with the character of all modified accordingly.

British Press: United Kingdom

The Times

The *Times* of London, with the longest tradition among daily papers for world news reporting, entered the immediate postwar period high in prestige, prosperous, and with a respectable circulation for a quality paper. Its reporters or correspondents, although writing anonymously, were well received wherever they might be, while other newsmen sometimes might be turned away.[1]

In 1920, the *Times* had been for a dozen years under the control of Lord Northcliffe as chief proprietor, with John Walter V, a member of the founding family, as coproprietor since 1910. Howard Corbett, managing director since 1911, yielded that post in 1920 to Campbell Stuart (later Sir Campbell Stuart), with William Lints Smith continuing as associate manager. Stuart also was managing editor of Northcliffe's *Daily Mail.*

Geoffrey Dawson, editor of the *Times* since 1912, had resigned in 1919 because of differences with Northcliffe. He was replaced by Henry Wickham Steed, then head of the paper's imperial and foreign department. Northcliffe's health suffered in 1921 and he went on a world cruise, hopeful of recovery, but returned to die in his London home in August 1922, aged fifty-seven. Steed resigned in November, his approximate three-year term the shortest for any editor in the paper's history. Dawson, a close friend of Walter's, returned to that position in December.

The *Times* entered a new period at this point. With Northcliffe's death, John Walter V sought to regain the chief proprietorship, but

---

1 This was a circumstance not unmatched elsewhere. In Boston, for example, the *Boston Transcript* (1830–1938) was so respected that the story, perhaps apocryphal but still indicative, was told of a butler in a Beacon Hill household informing his master that "there are several reporters who wish to speak with you, sir, and a gentleman from the *Transcript."* It also has been common for reporters from less respected newspapers to pose as representing the *Times,* the *New York Times,* and other leading papers.

was unable to obtain the unconditional financial backing he desired to permit purchase of the controlling shares in the company inherited by Lady Northcliffe. Financial assistance did come, however, from Major John Jacob Astor, second son of the late Viscount Astor of Hever Castle.

A contest between persons and groups seeking those shares in the *Times* forced the final sales figure to £1,680,000 (in excess of $8 million at the time). This was more than £500,000 beyond what Walter had anticipated, and more than he could manage. Major Astor, however, produced £1,580,000 of the total sum, and became chief proprietor in October 1922. The remaining £100,000 was provided by Walter, giving him a 10 per cent interest and a position as coproprietor of the paper, as before under Northcliffe.

The entrance of Major Astor into the chief proprietorship of the *Times* was neither the first nor the last participation by members of that family in journalistic activity and public affairs in England and in the United States.

John Jacob Astor, born at Walldorf, Germany, in 1763, was a resident of the United States from 1783 until his death in 1848. He made a fortune as a fur trader with interests extending to Canada and the Oregon coast, as a participant in the China trade, as a merchant, financier, and as owner of tracts of land on Manhattan Island. He left three daughters and two sons, William B. Astor and John Jacob Astor II.

William B. Astor, to the time of this death in 1875, added to the family fortune, further advanced by his son, John Jacob Astor III, and by his grandson, William Waldorf Astor. John Jacob Astor's younger son, John Jacob Astor II, sired another branch of the family carried forward by his son William, his grandson, John Jacob Astor IV, and his great grandson, Vincent Astor. In 1912, John Jacob Astor IV (1864–1912) was lost in the sinking of the *Titanic*. His son (William) Vincent Astor, then twenty-one, became head of the New York branch of the family.[2]

William Waldorf Astor (1848–1919), great grandson of John Jacob Astor, was graduated from the Columbia University Law School in 1875. He served in the New York state legislature in 1878–81, was U.S. minister to Italy in 1882–85, and wrote three books stemming from that experience. In 1890 he chose to live in London, accompanied by his wife and two young sons. With a fortune estimated at about $100 million, he also became active in ownership there of a Waldorf Hotel. In 1893 he purchased the *Pall Mall Gazette* and established the *Pall*

---

2 In 1933, Vincent Astor and W. Averell Harriman financed the establishment of *Today* magazine in New York. It was merged in 1937 with *News-Week* and retitled as *Newsweek,* with Astor as president.

Mall Magazine. In 1899 he and his wife were naturalized as British subjects. In 1911 he bought the Sunday *Observer* from Lord Northcliffe. In January 1916, as the war was in progress, he was made Baron Astor of Hever Castle, and in June 1917 a viscount. He died in 1919.

Lord Astor's sons were Waldorf Astor Astor and John Jacob Astor V. Born in New York, they were eleven and four years old, respectively, when the family settled in London in 1890. Both were educated at Eton and Oxford and chose, also, to become British subjects.

Waldorf Astor, the elder, on leaving Oxford became active in public affairs. In 1910, when thirty-one, he was elected to Parliament, representing the Sutton division of Plymouth, near which he established his estate, Cliveden. In 1906 he married the former Nancy Langhorne. Virginia-born, she had been divorced in 1903 from Robert Gould Shaw; she also became a British subject.

During the war, Astor became parliamentary secretary to Prime Minister Lloyd George and served in other government posts until 1921. When his father died in 1919, he inherited the title, becoming the second Viscount Astor of Hever Castle. The *Pall Mall Gazette* and the *Pall Mall Magazine* had ceased to exist by that time, but Lord Astor became publisher of the *Observer,* edited by J. L. Garvin. He also became a member of the House of Lords, and Lady Astor took his seat in Parliament, the first woman ever to occupy such a position, where she served actively until her retirement in 1945.

John Jacob Astor V, second son of the first Viscount Astor, had entered military service in 1906, when he left Oxford. He became aide-de-camp to the viceroy of India, Lord Hardinge of Penshurst, from 1911 to 1914. This was an active period in India, during which the capital was moved from Calcutta to Delhi, and one during which King George V visited that part of the realm. Astor served gallantly in France throughout World War I, was twice wounded and emerged with rank as major. He was elected to Parliament in 1922, representing the Dover division of Kent. Late in the same year he bought control of the *Times.*[3]

Campbell Stuart, manager of the *Times* since 1920, became a director of the paper for life in the sale of 1922, and William Lints Smith, former associate manager, became manager until his retirement in 1937. He was succeeded by Christopher Shotter Kent, assistant manager in the intervening years. Under his regime, the *Times* was more prosperous than it had been even under Northcliffe.

Although the prestige of the *Times* had been based largely upon the quality and performance of its staff correspondents in various parts of

---

3   See Virginia Cowles, *The Astors* (1980), for the complex history of the family.

the world, Geoffrey Dawson, having returned to the paper as editor in 1922, was not primarily interested in international affairs. National and empire issues and politics were of greater concern to him, and he had a predilection for taking a personal role in such affairs. This was not a wholly happy augury for the paper in a period during which international affairs were to be of the utmost importance.

When Steed became editor of the *Times* in 1919 he was succeeded as head of the imperial and foreign department by Dr. Harold Williams, long with the paper. Hugh McGregor, formerly chief sub-editor in the foreign room, became assistant foreign news editor. He resigned in 1921, and Williams died in 1928. At that time, Dawson himself assumed all responsibility for foreign news coverage and for the appointment of correspondents, and in 1929 he abolished the position of foreign editor.

Even though foreign affairs were not Dawson's first interest, the paper did continue to provide excellent coverage in that respect. A concern for a strong leader page caused Dawson to give opportunity to a group of writers with special knowledge of the world. Among them was Sir Valentine Chirol. He had retired as foreign editor in 1912, but remained active. From 1922 until his death in 1929 he wrote again for the *Times*. J. W. Flanagan, with the paper since 1886, was another called upon, but he also died in 1929.

These losses were balanced by a return to the staff at that time by Dudley Disraeli Braham, with the paper in 1903–13 as a correspondent, leader writer, and interim foreign editor, but he had been in Australia since then on business unrelated to the *Times*. Robert M'Gowan Barrington-Ward, a foreign sub-editor in 1913–14, then in wartime military service and subsequently with the *Observer*, also returned to the *Times* in 1927 to write leaders on foreign affairs. William Francis Casey, with the paper since 1913 and a correspondent after the war in several capitals, rejoined the London staff in 1928 to write on foreign subjects.[4]

Although there was no foreign editor after 1929, the paper was well staffed in London by men experienced in foreign affairs, and the direction of foreign and imperial news coverage was largely yielded by Dawson to two such men, Ralph Deakin and Philip G. Graves. They were in constant communication with correspondents deployed throughout the world—about thirty staff representatives and about sixty stringers, of whom perhaps twenty were active enough to be on retainer fees. Despite Dawson's lukewarm interest in foreign affairs, the *Times* retained its position in international reporting.

---

4 Barrington-Ward became editor of the *Times* on Dawson's retirement in 1941. Casey succeeded Barrington-Ward when he died in 1948.

At least a half dozen correspondents of high competence left the staff during the years of Dawson's editorship, some certainly because of direct differences reflecting no credit upon him. Among them were B. H. Liddell Hart, the paper's military correspondent from 1925 to 1929, when he resigned; Vladimir Poliakoff ("Augur"), diplomatic correspondent from 1924 to 1936, when he moved to the *Evening Standard;* Norman Ebbutt, Berlin correspondent from 1925 until 1937, when Dawson made no protest against his unwarranted expulsion; G. E. R. Gedye, in Central Europe from 1922 to 1928, when he switched to the *Daily Express;* and Douglas Reed, also in Central Europe from 1927 until he left the paper in 1938.

Staff coverage for the *Times* in European capitals after World War I was continued by some who had been active previously. But changes were not long in coming. In Paris, George Jeffreys Adam was succeeded as bureau chief in 1922 by Hubert Walter, son of John Walter III of the paper's founding family, who had been in Brussels. He was joined by Sisley Huddleston, formerly of the *Daily Mail* and *Continental Daily Mail,* but also writing for the *Christian Science Monitor.* Huddleston left the *Times* in 1924, although remaining in Paris as correspondent for the *Monitor.* Walter continued there until 1927, when his health caused him to return to London where he died in 1931, aged sixty-one. He was followed in Paris successively by H. G. Daniels, formerly in Berlin and Paris for Reuters, William Francis Casey, and David Scott. In a bureau usually numbering three men, others at various times included Ralph Deakin, formerly in Berlin, Thomas Cadett, Victor Cunard, and Robert Wright Cooper.

Deakin had reopened the Berlin bureau after the war, followed by Daniels, returning from Paris. In 1925, Norman Ebbutt became bureau chief until 1937. He was succeeded by James Holburn, who had been second man in the bureau. Ewan Butler and Arthur Ernest Baker also served in the Berlin bureau at various times, as did Douglas Reed from 1927 to 1935. He then became a roving correspondent for the paper, based in Berlin until 1938, when he joined the *News-Chronicle.*

G. E. R. (George Eric Rowe) Gedye, of British nationality, had served both the *Times* and the *New York Times* as a stringer in the Ruhr and the Rhineland between 1922 and 1927. He then went to Vienna for the *Times* but switched to the *Daily Express* in 1928, and then to the *Daily Telegraph* in 1929. Hugo A. Newman was in Vienna for the *Times* in 1935, and Reed from 1935 to 1938.

In Rome, the *Times* was represented from 1915 to 1920 by William K. McClure (later Sir William McClure). He became press attaché at the British Embassy in Rome in 1921. There until his death in 1939, he was at all times helpful to correspondents of various countries.

Vernon Bartlett succeeded McClure as Rome correspondent for the *Times*. Previously a member of the Reuters staff at the Paris Peace Conference and later in Central Europe, Bartlett also had represented the London *Daily Herald* in Paris for a short time. He then became secretary to Henry Wickham Steed, editor of the *Times*, but soon was made a correspondent for the paper at Geneva, and also covered the Kapp putsch in Berlin in March 1920, and the Russian-Polish "civil war" of that year before going to Rome. There he remained until 1922, when he joined the Secretariat of the League of Nations. In 1927, while in that position, he also began a period of six years as a broadcaster on foreign affairs for the BBC, attaining considerable repute. He gave up both posts in 1933 to join the *News-Chronicle* staff and was back in Rome.

When Bartlett left the *Times* post in Rome in 1922, he was replaced by Colin R. Coote, who remained until 1926. Following him, and serving successively, were Maxwell H. Macartney, one of the paper's correspondents during the war, A. O. Roberts, and G. D. R. Lumby.

Joseph Swire wrote for the *Times* from Albania early in the 1930s, but joined Reuters. Patrick Maitland became correspondent in the Balkans and Eastern Europe in 1938. Arthur Ernest Baker was variously in Berlin, Warsaw, Vienna, and the Balkans, and then diplomatic correspondent in London until he joined the BBC in 1938. Walter Burton Harris, correspondent in Tangier and Morocco since the 1880s, continued there until his retirement in 1933, after about fifty years with the *Times*.

Lawrence E. Fernsworth, U.S.-born, and also serving the *New York Times*, wrote from Madrid for the *Times* before and during the Spanish Civil War. George Lowther Steer, formerly with the *Capetown Argus* in South Africa, and also with the *Yorkshire Post* of Leeds, joined the *Times* in 1935 and reported both the Italo-Ethiopian War and the first year of the Spanish Civil War, when he switched to the *Daily Telegraph* staff. His place was taken in Spain by Harold A. R. (Hal or Kim) Philby, previously writing from there for the London General Press, a small British agency.[5] Henry Buckley also wrote from Spain during the war.

In Washington, Arthur Willert (later Sir Arthur Willert), resident correspondent from 1911, returned to London in 1920 and soon became head of the press section in the British Foreign Office. He was

---

5 Only much later did it become known that Philby, since his student days at Cambridge in 1933, had been acting as an agent and informant for the Communist government in Moscow, where he ultimately took refuge in 1962. See: E. H. Cookridge, *The Third Man* (1968); William Stevenson, *A Man Called Intrepid* (1976); Andrew Boyle, *The Fourth Man: The Definitive Account of Kim Philby, Guy Burgess, and Donald Maclean and Who Recruited Them to Spy for Russia* (1980).

succeeded in Washington by Willmott Harsant Lewis (later Sir Willmott Lewis).

Lewis, Welsh-born, had completed his formal education at Heidelberg and the Sorbonne. In Shanghai in the first years of the century, he became editor of the *North China Daily News,* but also reported both the Boxer uprising and the Russo-Japanese War for the *New York Herald,* and later was editor of the *Manila Times.* There he became acquainted with John J. Pershing, then a brigadier general, serving a second tour of duty with the U.S. Army in the Philippines. As general in command of the U.S. Expeditionary Forces in France in 1917–18, Pershing enlisted Lewis's services as an information specialist, and Lewis remained in France in 1919 as a correspondent for the *New York Tribune* during the Peace Conference.

In March 1920, Lewis joined the staff of the *Times* and was sent to Washington. One of his first concerns was coverage of the Naval Conference of 1921–22. He remained in Washington as *Times* correspondent from 1920 until his retirement in 1947. For a short period in his first years, he had William Francis Casey as an assistant. Long before his retirement, he had become dean of the foreign press corps in Washington, had earned the informal title as "Britain's ambassador incognito," and had been recognized with a knighthood in 1931. He was a familiar figure at the National Press Club, respected and admired by his colleagues.

In New York since 1914, Walter Fred Bullock, representing the *Times* and the *Daily Mail,* both Northcliffe papers, was replaced for the *Times* under its new ownership in 1923 by U.S.-born Louis E. Hinrichs. Frank Basil Riley, Australian-born and a Rhodes scholar, was his assistant in 1924–27, when he was reassigned to China. Ewan Butler was among later members of the New York staff, prior to assignment in Berlin. Claud Cockburn, another assistant in the late 1920s, also substituted for Lewis in Washington in 1930–31.

In China, Dr. George Ernest Morrison, assuming a post as adviser to the first president of the new Chinese Republic in 1912, after seventeen years in Peking for the *Times,* was replaced by David Fraser, in Shanghai for the paper for more than a decade. He remained as chief correspondent until after World War I, followed by Colin Malcolm MacDonald, Peter Fleming, and then by Frank Basil Riley, transferred from New York in 1927. Riley helped report the move of Nationalist forces northward from Canton to Nanking, but he had been in China only a few months when, on a journey to meet Feng Yuhsiang, the so-called "Christian general," one of a number of warlords contesting for power, he vanished somewhere near Chanchow, Manchuria, and was believed to have been murdered. He thus became the second *Times* correspondent lost in reporting disorders in China; the other, Thomas William Bowlby, had been captured and killed there in 1860.

In Japan, the *Times* was served in the early 1920s by Frank H. Hedges, who also then represented the *Daily Mail*, the *Christian Science Monitor*, and other publications, and was for a time editor of the *Japan Advertiser*. He was followed by R. Lewis Carton, also editor of the *Japan Advertiser* in 1922–23, and then by Hugh Byas. A British newsman, Byas had joined the *Times* staff in London in 1908, but went to Japan in 1913 as managing editor of the *Japan Advertiser*. In 1925 he became Tokyo correspondent both for the *Times* and for the *New York Times*, serving them equally until his retirement in 1941.

In India, Sir Stanley Reed at Bombay coordinated the activities of a group of correspondents for the *Times* throughout the subcontinent. Sir Alfred Watson, for one, editor of the *Statesman* of Calcutta also represented the *Times* there from 1924 to 1932. Sir Harry Perry Robinson, a member of the paper's wartime staff in France, accompanied the Prince of Wales on a journey to India in 1920. Robinson also was in Egypt in 1922, and the first correspondent to enter the newly discovered tomb of Tut-ankh-amen in the Valley of the Kings. Alexander Inglis, a member of the London bureau of the *Christian Science Monitor*, joined the *Times* in 1932 and accompanied Geoffrey Dawson to Canada to report the Ottawa Economic Conference, which was concerned with empire trade, and he then went on to India in 1933. Stringers served the paper elsewhere in Asia, Africa, and South America.

The *Times* correspondents, leader writers, and special contributors were a rare group, well informed and able to call upon the most authoritative persons and sources for information and answers to questions. They were served by, and themselves contributed to an excellent reference library, or intelligence department (ID) in the London office in Printing House Square. The paper had 200,000 circulation in 1939, its highest ever to that time.

The competition to gain stock control of the *Times* in 1922 had caused concern lest, on some future occasion, control of the paper should pass to persons who might fail to maintain its standards and traditions. It was the same issue that had arisen with reference to the protection of the Reuters news agency in 1915–17, following the death of Herbert de Reuter, and an issue remaining of concern to Sir Roderick Jones in 1922 and later. After due consideration, a Times Holding Company was formed as the new ownership of the paper became established in 1923. It provided for a voting trust under which any future transfer of shares would require the approval of that company and, specifically, would need the unanimous approval of a committee of five for the transfer of shares held by Astor and Walter.

Indicative of the concern felt for the sure preservation of the *Times* standards was the personnel of that committee, representative of the highest judicial, academic, scientific, and financial elements in the United Kingdom. Specifically, they were to be those individuals holding office as Lord Chief Justice of England, Warden of All Souls College at Oxford, President of the Royal Society, President of the Institute of Chartered Accountants, and Governor of the Bank of England. The purpose was to ensure, "so far as humanly possible, that the ownership of *The Times* shall never be regarded as a mere matter of commerce to be transferred without regard for any other circumstance to the highest bidder, or fall, so far as can be foreseen, into unworthy hands."[6]

The Daily Telegraph and *Morning Post*

The *Daily Telegraph* emerged from the war in a somewhat weakened position financially, but as an active and respected quality newspaper. Making some concessions to popular interest and selling at half the price per copy, its circulation was larger than that of the *Times*. The Honorable Harry Lawson, director since 1903, became proprietor upon the death of his father in 1916, when he also inherited the title, becoming the second Lord Burnham. In 1919 he was made a viscount.

In 1927, Lord Burnham sold the *Daily Telegraph* to Sir William E. Berry, in association with his younger brother, James Gomer Berry, and with Sir Edward Iliffe. These three already were well established in publishing. William Berry had started the *Advertising World* as a business publication in 1901. In 1915 he had acquired the *Sunday Times,* dating from 1822, and then near collapse. It was soon restored under his direction to become a quality paper.

With his brother, and sometimes in association with Iliffe, owner of the Coventry *Midland Daily Telegraph* and other publications, further papers were acquired in the 1920s and 1930s, among them the *Fi-*

---

6   This procedure was not quite followed when the *Times* was sold in 1966 to Canadian-born Roy Thomson, by then Lord Thomson of Fleet. In May 1966 news had been put on page one for the first time. Between then and the summer, the Astors and presumably the Walters as well had invited Thomson, already a fabulous figure in journalism, to take over the *Times.* The members of the committee of five, as proposed in 1923, apparently were notified "as a matter of courtesy." A Monopolies and Mergers Act, passed by Parliament earlier, called for an investigation of the transfer of ownership of the paper by a Monopolies Commission. Under the chairmanship of A. W. Roskill, Q.C., it eventually approved the sale of the newspaper to the Thomson Organization for £3,300,000, more than three times the 1922 valuation, to be spread over ten years, and accounting for an 85 per cent interest in the company. See Francis Williams, *The Right to Know: The Rise of the World Press* (1969), pp. 181-90.

nancial Times, the *Daily Graphic,* and the *Daily Sketch,* all of London, the *Sunday Chronicle* and Sunday *Empire News,* both of Manchester, and other provincial papers. William Berry had been knighted in 1921, and Gomer Berry was knighted in 1928. Iliffe and both Berry brothers were raised later to the peerage.

The *Morning Post,* dating from 1772, was a notably conservative quality paper. Faced with the competition of three other morning quality papers, the *Times,* the *Daily Telegraph,* and the *Manchester Guardian,* and feeling inroads upon its readership also from the *Daily Mail* and *Daily Express,* both popular morning dailies, the *Post* was purchased and merged with the *Daily Telegraph* in 1937.

The direction of the Berry-Iliffe publications, including other provincial papers, was divided. Some were suspended, some acquired, and some resold as the years passed. Iliffe became publisher of certain directories, important for reference. The Berry brothers concentrated primarily upon newspaper publishing, but with some business periodicals and popular periodicals as well.[7] From 1915 until 1937, William E. Berry edited and directed the *Sunday Times,* following which Gomer Berry did so. From 1937, in this switch, Sir William took full direction of the *Daily Telegraph.* The *Telegraph* in 1939 had a circulation of 884,602, more than four times that of the *Times,* successful as it was judged to be.

The *Daily Telegraph* and the *Morning Post* before the 1937 merger had reported domestic and foreign news with care. Arthur Watson, editor of the *Daily Telegraph* since 1924, remained in that post until his retirement in 1950. N. F. Newsome was foreign editor in the 1930s and presided over the efforts of a considerable staff.

Maurice Low for the *Post* and Percy Sutherland Bullen for the *Telegraph* had been in the United States as correspondents since the first years of the century, and both continued actively until shortly before the 1937 merger. Low was knighted in 1922. Bullen was president of the Association of Foreign Correspondents in the United States in 1921–22, and was honored by the University of Missouri School of Journalism in an annual Journalism Week awards ceremony in May 1930. A medal commemorated his years of service and recognized him "for clearness and fairness in interpreting the life of one people to another and kindred people, for skill and sympathy and understanding in reporting international affairs, and for maintaining with signal distinction the finest traditions of a long line of British journalists."

Sydney J. Clarke also was in New York for the *Telegraph* in the 1920s, and Martin Moore was in Washington early in the 1930s. Alex

---

7 Gomer Berry acquired an interest in 1933 in the Condé Nast U.S. high-fashion publication *Vogue* and added a British edition.

268 Crisis and Conflict

J. Faulkner became New York correspondent in 1934 when Bullen retired, and he became president of the Association of Foreign Correspondents in 1943-44. Douglas Williams, formerly of Reuters, joined the New York bureau in 1937 after a seven-year interval with a New York brokerage firm. Roger Machell accompanied King George VI and Queen Elizabeth on a royal tour of Canada and a visit to the United States in the summer of 1939.

In Paris, the *Morning Post* was represented prior to the merger by Lester Lawrence, formerly of Reuters, by Gordon Knox, G. A. Martelli, Alfred Bach, John Pollock (later Sir John Pollock), and by Darsie R. Gillie, who also had represented the paper in Berlin in 1929-33. He remained in Paris after the merger as a correspondent for the *Yorkshire Post* of Leeds.

The *Daily Telegraph* correspondents in Paris in the same period included David Loch as chief of bureau in the 1920s and until 1934, with J. D'Arcy Morrell and Herbert Routh as assistants, and also with Alex J. Faulkner for four years prior to his assignment to New York in 1934. Edwin H. Wilcox, formerly in Berlin, succeeded Loch in Paris in 1934, and served until his retirement in 1938. He then was followed by Eustace B. G. Wareing, also formerly in Berlin. Julian Grande, formerly in Geneva, and C. J. Martin were assistants in the bureau in Paris, although Martin soon joined the *Daily Mail.*

In Berlin, Wilcox had been bureau chief for the *Telegraph* until his transfer to Paris in 1934. He was succeeded by Wareing. Noel Panter in Munich was expelled in 1933. B. Pembroke Stephens, formerly in Paris for the *Daily Express,* had become a member of the *Telegraph* bureau in Berlin, but also was expelled by the Nazi government in 1934, going to Spain and then to China.

Wareing, taking charge in Berlin in 1934, already had been with the *Daily Telegraph* for forty years in various assignments, including an earlier tour of duty in Berlin. Assistants there were Hugh Carleton Greene and Anthony Mann.

The *Morning Post,* prior to its absorption by the *Telegraph,* had been represented in Berlin in 1929-33 by Darsie R. Gillie, formerly in Warsaw in 1926-29 and also then representing the *Chicago Daily News.* Going to Paris in 1933, Gillie served the *Post* until the sale. In Berlin he had been replaced in 1933 by Karl Robson, formerly in Vienna. In 1936 Robson went to cover the Spanish Civil War and remained there for the *Telegraph* after the merger.

Bernard Moore was in Geneva for the *Morning Post* prior to the merger, but then switched to the *Daily Herald,* while A. R. Cushden took over for the combined papers. Previously, the *Telegraph* had covered Geneva by dispatching men from its Paris bureau. The *Post* had Ion S. Munro in Rome, but he switched to the *Daily Mail* at the time of the merger and remained until joining Reuters in 1938. He had been succeeded in Rome for the *Telegraph* by A. Beaumont.

The *Daily Telegraph* was represented in Vienna from 1929 until 1938 by G. E. R. Gedye, also serving the *New York Times* after 1931.

Alfred T. Cholerton, who had gone to Moscow in 1921 for the London *Daily News*, after several years with the British government Intelligence Service, soon switched to the *Daily Telegraph*. He remained in Moscow for the paper for nearly twenty years. His Russian-born wife and daughter were in Sweden and England after the early 1930s, but he stayed on in Moscow and reported actively, although he was not well. Notably outspoken, he was warned repeatedly because of his reports, but he was not expelled.

John Harold Watson was in Turkey for the *Daily Telegraph* from 1925 to 1940, when he died in Istanbul. George Lowther Steer, formerly of the *Times,* joined the *Daily Telegraph* in 1937. He toured Africa in 1938–39, producing new and useful information, but left the paper when the European war began in 1939 to join the British forces.

Karl Robson and Henry Buckley, switching from the *Times,* reported the Spanish Civil War for the *Daily Telegraph,* as did Alan Dick, who had been in Ethiopia previously. British-born René Mac-Coll, with earlier experience on the *Baltimore Sun* staff in the United States, joined the *Telegraph* in 1929. He had represented the paper on assignments in India in 1932, in Albania in 1938, and was in Spain in 1938–39.

B. Pembroke Stephens was in Germany in 1934, then in Spain, and in China in 1937. There he was killed in a Japanese bombing attack on Shanghai. Ronald Monson went from London to replace him. Representation for the *Daily Telegraph* in China prior to 1931 had been provided by George Gorman, and for the *Morning Post* by L. Impey and by H. G. W. Woodhead, editor of the *Peking and Tientsin Times.* Woodhead was a stringer for Reuters, the AP, and others.

Ellis Ashmead-Bartlett, a staff correspondent for the *Daily Telegraph* since 1897, continued to move about the world on assignments. He also served as a Member of Parliament in 1924–26. From 1920, he was at various times in the Soviet Union, China, and India, as well as in Europe. He died in Lisbon in 1931.

Sir Percival Phillips, U.S.-born, was engaged in foreign news reporting from 1897. He joined the *Daily Telegraph* staff in 1934 after having been with the *Daily Express* from 1901 to 1922 and with the *Daily Mail* from 1922–34. For the *Telegraph* he covered the Italo-Ethiopian War of 1935–36. He was in Tangier in 1936 reporting the beginning of the Spanish Civil War when he was taken ill. Brought back to London, he died there in January 1937 in his sixtieth year.

The *Daily Telegraph* had the services of B. H. Liddell Hart as military correspondent prior to 1925, when he joined the *Times* in the same capacity. He was succeeded by Major General A. C. Timperley, who resigned in 1939, followed in turn by Major General Sir Charles Gwynn. Hector C. Bywater was naval correspondent. Maurice Gerothwohl was diplomatic correspondent for a time. So also was Vladimir Poliakoff until he joined the *Times* in 1924.

The *Daily Telegraph,* despite its acquisition of the *Morning Post* in 1937 and its strong circulation, suffered perhaps an unprecedented loss of experienced men for any comparable period, mostly in the 1930s. This included the retirement of Bullen, Loch, and Wilcox, the departure from the staff of Gedye, Steer, Martin, Hart, Timperley, and Poliakoff, and the deaths of Walton, Stephens, Ashmead-Bartlett, and Phillips.

The Manchester Guardian

The *Manchester Guardian* was the only non-London daily newspaper to receive national distribution, although two Manchester Sunday papers did so, the *Empire News* and the *Sunday Chronicle.* It was the only provincial paper to undertake any consistent original coverage overseas. That coverage was not extensive, but it was significant. The *Guardian* was considered a "writers' paper" in that correspondents were selected with special care, and it was expected that most of what they wrote would appear without cuts or changes. The reports were marked by solid substance, background interpretation, and writing style.

The *Guardian* usually was described as liberal in editorial policy. As a quality paper, its circulation was not large, but it reached an important segment of the national readership and was regarded by some as the best newspaper in the United Kingdom, and even in the world.

Edited with distinction by Charles Prestwich Scott through fifty-seven years from 1872 to 1929, he also was its chief proprietor after 1905. C. E. Montague, Scott's son-in-law, was chief leader writer after World War I. The *Manchester Evening News* established in 1868 was acquired by the *Guardian* in 1924. It became so prosperous, even as a local paper in the Manchester area, that it bolstered the *Guardian*'s financial capacity to report the news more widely. From the mid-1920s the *Evening News* was edited by William Haley; later he became director of the BBC and then editor of the *Times.*

Robert Dell, who had represented the *Guardian* in European capitals before the war and in Paris during the war period, served there and in Berlin after the war, but was chiefly in Geneva from 1920 until his death in 1940. Eric O. Siepman also was in Geneva for the paper.

In Russia at the time of the 1917 revolution, Morgan Phillips Price, David Siskice, and Michael Farbman were writing for the *Guardian.* Farbman was in Petrograd and Moscow as late as 1920, writing also for the *Chicago Daily News.* Francis McCullagh, who had written for the *Guardian* from St. Petersburg since 1904, covered the Russo-Japanese War, writing for the *New York Herald* as well. He remained in Moscow until jailed and expelled in 1919. Arthur Ransome, in Petrograd for the *Guardian* during the war and revolution, returned to the Soviet Union in 1921 as chief correspondent. Malcolm Muggeridge also spent most of 1922–23 in Moscow, and Alexander Werth was there longest for the paper, from 1931 to 1937.

William Bolitho Ryall, born in Capetown, had served with South African forces in France during the war and narrowly escaped death in the Somme battle of 1916. After a long period of hospitalization, and unfit to return to military duty, he joined the *Guardian* staff in Paris and helped cover the Peace Conference, writing under the name of William Bolitho. He remained until 1923, except for excursions to Berlin, and then joined the Paris bureau of the *New York World.* John G. Hamilton succeeded Bolitho in Paris, but died in 1926. He was followed by Dell, moving temporarily from Geneva, and by Alexander Werth and F. A. Voight.

Werth, former Paris correspondent for the *Glasgow Herald,* represented the *Guardian* there from 1929–31, when he went to the Moscow bureau. He returned to Paris in 1937–40, then also writing for the *Sunday Times.* Voight, in Berlin for the paper from 1920–28 and again in 1930–33, wrote from Paris from 1933–39, but at the same time traveled widely, sending reports from the Soviet Union, Poland, Hungary, Turkey, Spain, and Czechoslovakia.

Henry W. Nevinson, active as a correspondent from the first years of the century, chiefly for the *Daily Chronicle,* represented the *Guardian* at the Washington Naval Conference of 1921–22, also writing for the *New York World* and the *Baltimore Sun.* He reported from Germany for the *Guardian* in 1923, and later from Palestine.

Cecil Squire Spriggs was in Germany for the paper in the early 1920s, and then in Rome, where he soon joined Reuters to begin a long career with the agency. Hubert D. Harrison, in Belgrade as a student, wrote from there as a stringer for the *Guardian,* and also for the *Daily Express* and the *Daily Herald* until 1937, when he joined Reuters.

Marcel W. (Mike) Fodor, Hungarian-born engineer and linguist, was a resident of England throughout the years of the war. He represented the *Guardian* in Vienna during the 1920s and 1930s. One of the most knowledgeable correspondents in Europe, he also acted as Vienna correspondent for the *Philadelphia Public Ledger-New York Evening Post* service from 1925-34, and for the *Chicago Daily News* from 1935-38. During more than fifteen years in Vienna he was one of the most respected members of a group of correspondents of various nations who made the Café Louvre a regular meeting place. He was a friend, informal guide, and mentor for a considerable number of correspondents later to attain reputations of their own, among them Dorothy Thompson and John Gunther. Fodor was in Paris for the paper in 1938-40, after the Nazi seizure of Vienna and annexation of Austria.

H. N. Brailsford moved about Europe for the *Guardian*. He also represented the *Daily Herald* in 1919-20, before becoming editor of the weekly *New Leader*. Alfred P. Wadsworth was one of several correspondents covering the troubles in Ireland in the 1920s, and served the *Guardian* in other capacities, later to become its editor. Geoffrey Theodore Garratt reported the Italo-Ethiopian War.

A. Wyn Williams was correspondent for the *Guardian* in New York in the 1930s. T. M. Young journeyed to the United States on a special news mission, and Nevinson's presence in Washington in 1921-22 has been mentioned. The paper also received reports from several stringers in the United States, among them Percival H. Winner, who was experienced as a correspondent in Europe for the AP and other services, and Bruce Bliven, editor of the weekly *New Republic* in New York.

British-born Herbert B. Elliston represented the *Guardian* in China as well as the *New York World* during the 1920s, shortly after leaving Cambridge. He wrote as a stringer for the *Guardian* and also for the *Observer* from the United States during the decade of the 1930s while serving as financial editor of the *Christian Science Monitor* in Boston.

Through the 1920s and 1930s, John B. Powell, owner and editor of the *China Weekly Review* of Shanghai, and H. J. Timperley both wrote from China for the *Guardian,* with Powell also writing for the *Chicago Tribune* and the London *Daily Herald*. A. Morgan Young, editor of the British-owned *Japan Chronicle* of Kobe, wrote from there for the *Guardian* during part of the 1930s. J. T. Gwynn was in India. G. Lowes Dickinson produced reports on a special journey in the Far East. Guenther Stein, formerly of the *Berliner Tageblatt* and the *Frankfurter Zeitung,* but a victim of the Nazi press purge, also wrote from China for the *Guardian* in the late 1930s, and for the *News-Chronicle* as well.

The News-Chronicle

The *Daily News* and the *Daily Chronicle,* London morning dailies dating from 1844 and 1877, respectively, and each having had its periods of distinction, were merged in 1930 as the *News-Chronicle,* also a six-day morning paper. The *News-Chronicle* promptly gained recognition as a daily of liberal views and high standards of responsibility, yet with sufficient popular appeal to attain a national circulation exceeding a million by 1939.

The *Daily News* in 1902 had come into the effective control of the Cadbury family, manufacturers of cocoa and chocolate products. They were Quakers, reflecting the humanitarian and pacifist inclinations of that group. The paper was directed successively until 1930 by George Cadbury, Henry Taylor Cadbury, and Edward Cadbury. In 1912, the afternoon *Star* was acquired, and continued under the Cadbury direction. The *Morning Leader* also was purchased in 1912, but was merged with the *Daily News.* This was true likewise of the *Westminster Gazette,* a paper that had possessed importance under the editorship of John Alfred Spender between 1896 and 1922, but became part of the *Daily News* in 1928.

The *Daily Chronicle* had been ably edited from 1904-18 by Sir Robert Donald. It was then acquired by a group including Prime Minister Lloyd George, but resold in 1926, and resold again in 1928 to William Harrison of the Inveresk Paper Company, Ltd. Harrison also gained stock control of the *Daily News* in 1930, and it was by his action that the two papers were merged in that year as the *News-Chronicle.* In 1936, however, Harrison sold his interest in the paper to the Cadburys, again giving them full control.

The *News-Chronicle* after 1930 was directed by Lawrence J. Cadbury and Sir Walter Layton (later Lord Layton); the latter served as chairman of the board of directors of that paper and of the afternoon *Star.* From 1937, Layton was at the same time editor of the *Economist,* authoritative weekly in the field of business and finance, but with important reference to public affairs as well. A. J. (Arthur John) Cummings was political editor of the *News-Chronicle* and wrote a "Spotlight" column of comment. Vernon Bartlett, formerly of the *Times* and of the League of Nations Secretariat, and for six years broadcasting on foreign affairs for the BBC, became diplomatic correspondent in 1934, and a Member of Parliament in 1938. The paper developed a limited, quality foreign service, retaining a number of correspondents who had served the papers separately.

For the *Chronicle,* Cummings had written both from Berlin and Moscow. Sir Philip Gibbs, a correspondent with the paper before and during the war, had turned to the writing of fiction, but had ended his time as a correspondent with a series of articles in 1921 based on a journey to Greece and another to the Soviet Union in company with Leonard Spray and other journalists newly admitted to that country at the time. Martin H. Donohoe, long in Paris for the *Chronicle,* died there in 1927. He was replaced by George Renwick, formerly in Berlin. Denis Weaver was an assistant. J. W. Harding was in New York. The *Daily News* had J. C. Segrue in Paris after the war, followed by H. W. Smith. Segrue went to Berlin, where he also wrote for the *New York Tribune.* H. Wilson Harris and S. J. Jennings were in Geneva. There Harris was the first president of the International Association of Journalists Accredited to the League of Nations. He left daily journalism in 1932 to become editor of the *Spectator,* a London weekly of opinion. Philip W. Wilson was in New York in the early 1920s, followed by Wilson Midgley. Mrs. L. T. Beddow wrote from China for the *Daily News* in 1926–27, and Paul Winterton was in Moscow in 1928–29.

For the combined *News-Chronicle* after 1930, Denis Weaver remained in Paris until 1932, when he replaced Segrue in Berlin, and was joined there by Ian C. Colvin. Frank Hillier took the Paris post. Vernon Bartlett gave up his role with the BBC in 1933 and returned to Rome for the *News-Chronicle.* Back in London as diplomatic correspondent in 1934, he was replaced in Rome by David Woodward.

Both Weaver and Colvin were expelled from Berlin by the Nazi government in September 1938. Hubert D. Harrison, expelled from Yugoslavia as a Reuters correspondent in December 1937, joined the *News-Chronicle* Berlin bureau in February 1938. He also wrote for the *New York Times,* and replaced Weaver as Berlin bureau chief. Colvin returned to Berlin. Douglas Reed, in Berlin and Central Europe for the *Times* since 1927, also joined the *News-Chronicle* Berlin bureau in 1938.

The spring of 1939 brought Harrison's expulsion from Berlin, and Colvin left with him. Woodward, recently expelled from Rome, took Harrison's post in Berlin, with P. B. Wadsworth assigned as second man in the bureau. Reed was in Prague when German forces entered in the spring of 1939. Harrison was reassigned to Moscow in the summer of that year, but was soon succeeded by American-born John Scott, who had worked in a Russian factory and had written from the Soviet Union for the Agence Havas.

Robert Bernays wrote from India early in the 1930s and then from Germany and from Austria. In Spain, during the civil war, the paper was represented by Philip Furneaux Jordan, William Forrest, and Hungarian-born Arthur Koestler, who had been associated with the Jewish-owned Ullstein papers of Germany, which were promptly taken over by the Nazis in 1933.

In China, German-born Guenther Stein, in addition to writing for the *Manchester Guardian,* represented the *News-Chronicle.* Yet another refugee from Nazi Germany, Viktor Weisz, arrived in London in 1939 and became an effective political cartoonist for the *News-Chronicle,* signing his panels with the name "Vicky."

In the United States, Robert J. (Robin) Cruikshank was New York correspondent for the *News-Chronicle* in the early 1930s. He served as president of the Association of Foreign Press Correspondents in 1934–36, and was honored with the first life membership in the association. He returned to London in 1937 to become editor of the *Star* and, a few years later, was made a director both of the *News-Chronicle* and of the *Star.*

Raymond Gram Swing, U.S.-born newsman of long European experience, became New York correspondent for the *News-Chronicle* in 1937, succeeding Cruikshank, but he resigned late in that same year to give full attention to an assignment as a radio news commentator for the Mutual Broadcasting System, and as American commentator for the BBC. He was followed as New York correspondent for the *News-Chronicle* by Robert (Charles Harry) Waithman.

The Daily Mail

Three London morning dailies vied for circulation leadership in the years between the wars. All were nationally distributed popular newspapers, offered at a price lower than that for the quality papers. These were the *Daily Mail,* the *Daily Express,* and the *Daily Herald.*

The *Daily Mail* led in circulation in 1920. The *Daily Express,* in offering special inducements to subscribers, overtook and passed it. The *Daily Herald,* adding further inducements, passed both temporarily in the mid-1930s. In 1939 the *Daily Express* again led, with 2,557,963 daily; the *Daily Herald* stood at 2,000,000; and the *Daily Mail* exceeded 1,500,000. Several tabloid and Sunday papers exceeded these figures, and all formed a "mass circulation" press.

The three popular dailies provided independent coverage of national and international news. The *Daily Mail* was enterprising in this respect from the time of its establishment in 1896. Its staff also represented the *Sunday Dispatch.* These two Northcliffe papers were served after 1908, when he also bought the *Times,* by some of the same correspondents, especially in New York, Berlin, and St. Petersburg. His three other papers, the London *Evening News,* the tabloid *Daily Mirror,* and the *Continental Daily Mail* of Paris, gave little or no staff coverage to world affairs, although the Paris edition provided some.

After Northcliffe died in 1922 his publications underwent changes. The *Times* was sold. A group of provincial dailies and magazines were retained and directed by Northcliffe's brother and associate, Viscount Rothermere (formerly Harold Harmsworth). In 1938, Rothermere passed control of the papers to his son, the Honorable Esmond Harmsworth, who was to become the second Viscount Rothermere on his father's death in 1940.

Thomas Marlowe, editor of the *Daily Mail,* played an important role in its success. Douglas Crawford, in Paris for the paper during the Peace Conference, was foreign editor in London through most of the 1920s and 1930s, followed by F. W. (Frank) Memory.

Walter Fred Bullock, in New York for the paper since 1906, remained until his retirement in 1936. He also represented the *Times* throughout the period of its Northcliffe ownership, 1908–22. Bullock was a founding member of the Association of Foreign Press Correspondents in the United States in 1917, and its first president. He was succeeded in New York in 1936 for the *Daily Mail* by Lionel G. Short and then by Don Iddon, formerly a member of the New York bureau of the *Daily Express.* The *Daily Mirror* was not notable for its foreign reporting, but it was represented in New York by T. Walter (Skipper) Williams, followed by John B. Walters, formerly his assistant. In 1939 Iddon added that representation to his assignment for the *Daily Mail.*

George Ward Price, with the *Daily Mail* since 1912, had a roving commission after the war, but spent considerable time in Rome. Ion S. Munro, *Morning Post* correspondent there, switched to the *Daily Mail* following the merger of the *Post* with the *Daily Telegraph* in 1937, but soon after joined Reuters and went to India. John Bannister wrote from Vienna in the 1930s.

Sir Percival Phillips, with the *Daily Express* from 1902 to 1922, joined the *Daily Mail* staff in that year and remained until 1934, when he moved to the *Daily Telegraph.* He was in China for the *Daily Mail* in 1927, wrote a series of reports from his native United States in 1933, and visited other parts of the world for the paper. Joseph M. N. Jeffries, who had served as a war correspondent for the *Daily Mail,* continued as a staff member until 1933. Ferdinand Tuohy, son of James Tuohy, London correspondent for the *New York World* from 1899 to 1922, and himself Paris correspondent for the *World* in 1922, switched to the *Daily Mail* at that time and covered foreign assignments.

Harold G. Cardozo and C. J. Martin, formerly of the *Daily Telegraph,* were in Paris for the *Daily Mail.* Rothay Reynolds was in Berlin until expelled in September 1938. He was succeeded there by Ralph Izzard. Fred A. Mackenzie, who had represented the paper in Berlin before the war, was in Moscow from 1921–25, also writing for the *Chicago Daily News.* Richard Eaton entered the Soviet Union by way of Estonia in June 1923, representing both the *Daily Mail* and *Le Matin* of Paris, but was arrested and expelled in 1924. H. Challiner

James was in Geneva. Noel Monks, Tasmanian-born and formerly of the *Melbourne Herald* and the *Daily Express,* joined the *Daily Mail* staff in May 1939, based in Paris. Major General John F. C. Fuller was in Ethiopia as a military correspondent for the *Daily Mail* during the Italo-Ethiopian War. Cardozo went from Paris as one of several representatives of the paper in Spain during the civil war. Others there included Randolph Churchill, son of Winston Churchill. Frances Davis, a young American woman, wrote for the *Chicago Daily News.*

In China, L. Impey wrote of the 1926–27 Kuomintang advance for the *Daily Mail* and also for the *Morning Post.* In Peking, John Goette wrote for the *Daily Mail,* as well as for the INS. In Japan, Frank H. Hedges wrote both for the *Daily Mail* and the *Times* prior to 1922, with Vere Redman later representing the *Daily Mail.*

The Daily Express *and* Evening Standard

The *Daily Express,* established in 1900 by Cyril Arthur Pearson, came into the control of Canadian-born Max Aitken (William Maxwell Aitken) in 1915 when it was at a low ebb. Unlike most London papers, it had used news on page one from the time of its establishment, and had been made and priced as a popular morning newspaper. The *Daily Express* was revitalized by Aitken, with the important assistance of Ralph D. Blumenfeld and, later, of Arthur Christiansen.

Blumenfeld, a U.S. newsman, had gone to London originally for the *New York Herald* in 1890, and again later in the decade. He joined the *Daily Mail* staff in 1900, but moved to the *Daily Express* in 1902. He remained with that paper until his retirement in the early 1930s, and was editor during most of the period. He was followed by Christiansen, formerly in the paper's Manchester office.

A *Sunday Express* was established in 1921. Aitken, who had become Lord Beaverbrook in 1917, also acquired the *Evening Standard* in 1922, and added the *Evening Citizen* of Glasgow. He held a dominant control over the papers virtually to the end of his life in 1964.

The *Daily Express,* vigorous in its coverage of national and international affairs, took a strong conservative editorial position. Distributed nationally, it was a circulation leader. Serving successively as foreign editors between the wars were Crossley Sutcliffe, A. L. Easterman, and Charles Sutton, presiding over a considerable staff.

American-born Percival Phillips was one of the first correspondents for the *Express,* joining the staff its first year in 1901. Originally from Pittsburgh, where he began news work, he had reported the Greco-Turkish War of 1897 for the *Chicago Inter-Ocean* when he was only twenty. He remained with the *Daily Express* until 1922, and was by then a British citizen and knighted for his work as a correspondent during World War I. As Sir Percival Phillips, he moved to the *Daily Mail* staff in 1922 and in 1934 to the *Daily Telegraph* staff, and continued in international reporting until his death in 1937.

Henry J. Greenwall became a member of the paper's Paris bureau during World War I, after earlier work there for the *Continental Daily Mail*. He served the paper on a roving assignment which took him to Germany, Italy, Spain, Portugal, Ireland, Austria, Switzerland, Belgium, the Balkans, Soviet Russia, Turkey, North Africa, China, Japan, and India. He went to Washington in 1926-27, and to the United States again in 1929 and in 1932-33.

Frank Dilnot and Don Iddon represented the *Daily Express* in New York in the early 1920s, with Iddon transferring later to the *Daily Mail* bureau there. J. W. T. (Warren) Mason was New York correspondent for nearly twenty years, followed in 1933 by C. V. R. (Cecil Vincent Raymond) (Tommy) Thompson. While still a member of the London staff in 1931, Thompson had received the Selfridge award for descriptive writing. In 1934 he married Dixie Tighe, a New York newspaper women and also a member of the *Daily Express* bureau there in the 1930s. Both Dilnot and Thompson served as presidents of the Association of Foreign Press Correspondents in the United States.

Nicholas R. Bodington was in Paris for the *Daily Express*. B. Pembroke Stephens also served in Paris, but later went to Berlin, where he switched to the *Daily Telegraph*. Denis Sefton Delmar, in Berlin prior to the arrival of Stephens, had a long career with the paper. Patrick Murphy also was in Berlin in 1934. Australian-born Selkirk Panton, formerly in Vienna, was successor to Stephens in Berlin in 1934 and remained until the outbreak of war in 1939 required his departure.

Edward H. Strutt was in Rome. G. E. R. Gedye, formerly of the *Times,* was in Vienna for the *Daily Express* in 1928-29, but then switched to the *Daily Telegraph*. Hubert D. Harrison wrote from Belgrade from 1934-37, then switched to Reuters. Geoffrey Cox and William Morrell were in Prague in 1938. Rhea Clyman was in Moscow in 1932, but was expelled. Delmar, formerly in Berlin, was in Moscow later in the 1930s.

E. O'Dowd (O.D. or "Odie") Gallagher, an Australian, joined the *Daily Express* staff in the 1930s. He covered the Italo-Ethiopian War, the Spanish Civil War, and also was in China. Sydney Monks was another engaged in reporting the war in Spain. Noel Monks, also an Australian, based in Paris for the paper from 1935-39, covered both of those wars prior to switching to the *Daily Mail* with his wife, Mary Welsh, then likewise in the Paris bureau of the *Express*. An American formerly with the *Chicago Daily News,* Mary Welsh had become a protégé of Lord Beaverbrook. She was to become a member of a new London *Time* magazine bureau in 1940. In 1946 she became the third wife of Ernest Hemingway.

In China, U.S.-born George E. Sokolsky, reported from Shanghai from 1920 to 1930, at the same time he was writing for the *Philadelphia Public Ledger–New York Evening Post* service, as well as others. J. W. T. Mason, so long in New York for the paper, moved to Japan in 1933. Hessell Tiltman also wrote from Tokyo.

The *Daily Express* had Sidney Strube as a political cartoonist on the London staff, producing effective treatments of current news subjects.

Lord Beaverbrook's *Evening Standard* had no active correspondents overseas, but it nevertheless occupied an unusual position in foreign affairs, especially for an afternoon paper. Even though lacking representatives in other countries, George Slocombe, formerly of the *Daily Herald,* assumed title as foreign editor in 1931, and he traveled where news of international significance seemed to warrant. David Low, New Zealand-born political cartoonist, produced incisive panels several times a week, often on international themes, and these became syndicated world-wide in the 1930s.

The *Standard* also had two quite remarkable columnists. Robert H. Bruce Lockhart (later Sir Robert Lockhart), writing anonymously, produced the "Londoner's Diary," a leader-page feature in which he gave special attention to international subjects, drawing upon an unusual personal background of experience and exceptional sources of information. Vladimir Poliakoff ("Augur"), equally informed, was formerly with the *Times* and the *Daily Telegraph.* He was with the *Evening Standard* from 1937–45, and his reports, distributed by the Provincial Newspapers, Ltd., of the United Kingdom, also were used by the *New York Times.*

Poliakoff's effectiveness was demonstrated when a group of British conservatives, worried about the ominous course of European affairs late in 1937, arranged for cabinet member Lord Halifax to go informally to Germany to discuss with Hitler means to ease the situation. Prime Minister Chamberlain approved the plan, but Anthony Eden, then foreign secretary, threatened to resign unless assured that any such talks would be merely exploratory, with no commitments made. Ferdinand Kuhn, Jr., then London correspondent for the *New York Times,* was able to present an exclusive account of this critical conflict within the cabinet. Poliakoff, however, was able to go farther and reveal the terms Hitler himself intended to present to Halifax if they met. This he obtained through Italian sources, then concerned lest an Anglo-German agreement should endanger the existing Rome-Berlin Axis.

Hitler's terms provided that he should be given complete freedom of action with reference to Czechoslovakia, which in fact he was to seize in 1938 and 1939. Poliakoff's revelation of these terms in the *Evening Standard* in 1937 caused sharp reaction in Great Britain, presaging as it did an appeasement of Hitler, if accepted by Halifax. Astor of the *Times* and Geoffrey Dawson its editor had been represented in the discussions leading to the proposal that Halifax meet with Hitler, and Dawson undertook to discredit Poliakoff's story, using the columns of the *Times* to do so. Eden, on the other hand, through the medium of the old and important *Yorkshire Post* of Leeds, owned by his wife's family, was able to substantiate Poliakoff's report.

The Halifax-Hitler talks took place in November 1937. What followed led to Eden's resignation from the cabinet in February 1938. Germany annexed Austria in March, part of Czechoslovakia in September and the rest in March 1939. Meanwhile, two Chamberlain-Hitler meetings and the Munich Conference, all in September 1938, had sealed the fate of Czechoslovakia, very much in accordance with Poliakoff's report in 1937.

The Daily Herald

The *Daily Herald* became a daily on March 31, 1919, following wartime years of weekly publication. It had been originally a daily from 1912 to 1914, established to give the Labour party a voice in the public press, although it was not an official party paper. George Lansbury, a Labour party leader, had been editor through the war and continued until 1923. His enthusiasm was such that he was able to win financial support for the paper from trade unions, the Cooperative Movement, and private individuals. It gained a circulation of 330,000 by 1920, a respectable figure for so specialized a publication, but its advertising volume and revenue were low.

This difficulty was partially solved in 1923 when the Labour party itself and the Trade Union Congress agreed to take over the *Daily Herald* as an official party paper. Hamilton Fyfe became editor, bringing experience as a long-time member of the *Daily Mail* staff, as a war correspondent, as editor of the *Daily Mirror* in its first year, and as an associate of Lord Northcliffe. Fyfe had joined the Labour party after the war, and was editor of the *Herald* until about 1930.

Through those years, the *Daily Herald* became a substantial newspaper, advancing the Labour party views on problems of the time, but also providing excellent coverage of political, financial, industrial news, and sports, while adding coverage from abroad. There were problems, however. With its price at two pence, twice that of the popular papers, its circulation was only about 250,000, and the volume of advertising was still too low to meet costs. With Labour party approval, a new company was formed in 1929, the Daily Herald, Ltd. The Odhams Press of London, publishing the long-established *Illustrated London News* and other newspapers, periodicals, and books and directed by Julius Salter Elias (later Lord Southwood), gained 51 per cent of the stock. The remaining 49 per cent was held by the General Council of the Trade Union Congress, which was given representation on the directorate of the Odhams Press, with control of the *Daily Herald* editorial policy.

The business direction of the paper was vested in the Odhams Press, with Elias proceeding on the theory that proper management and promotion could produce at least a million daily circulation for the paper, so making it an attractive advertising medium and solving its financial problem. It did not quite do that, but not because Elias failed to try. The *Daily Herald* was doubled in size, and photos and features were added. Printed on the same presses as the popular Sunday *People,* also owned by the Odhams Press, it used the same type face, giving it a somewhat sensational appearance. A second printing plant also was set up in Manchester to speed national distribution, as was done by other popular papers.

In March 1930, seven months after the Odhams connection began, the *Daily Herald* attained a million circulation. It still was not enough to meet costs, however. Even though advertising volume increased, the rate was lower because of a presumed working class readership, with less purchasing potential. Elias did not retreat, however. He introduced a strong circulation campaign in which readers were offered supplementary gifts with subscriptions to the paper. Other newspapers had done the same, but Elias engaged 50,000 canvassers throughout the country, and added prizes in easy contests. Using Odhams book-publishing resources, he also offered sets of books as inducements. The result was the attainment of a two million circulation figure for the *Herald* in 1933, the largest for any daily newspaper in London or the world at that time.

The *Daily Express, Daily Mail,* and *News-Chronicle* had joined in the contest for circulation. While protesting the Elias campaign, they also spent fortunes in the provision of special inducements to "buy" readers. It was a campaign that ended in the mid-1930s. By 1937 the *Daily Express* led, with 2,329,000, the *Herald* held to about two million, and the *Daily Mail,* previously in the lead, stood third. Francis Williams, in *Dangerous Estate* (1957), summarized by saying that the costly "newspaper war" of the 1930s did succeed, however, in "permanently increasing newspaper readership," that "a surprising number of the bought readers stuck," and that "all over the country people who had never read newspapers before were doing so" and were to "go on reading them in increasing numbers."

When the *Herald* had resumed daily publication in March 1919, George Slocombe covered the Peace Conference for it and remained as its correspondent in Paris until 1931, when he became foreign editor of Beaverbrook's *Evening Standard.* During those years, he reported nearly all the important postwar conferences in Europe and also was on a roving assignment that took him to Italy in 1922, Russia in 1926, the United States in 1927, Geneva and Spain on several occasions, and to India in 1930. A serious and well-informed correspondent, he was rewarded by the friendship and confidence of statesmen and leaders in many countries, and was able to provide the *Herald* with notable reports. He was president of the Anglo-American Press Association in Paris in 1927–28.

Contributing also to the paper in those years were such known writers as H. M. Tomlinson, E. M. Forster, W. J. Turner, Harold J. Laski, Aldous Huxley, Walter de la Mare, Havelock Ellis, and George Bernard Shaw. H. N. Brailsford wrote as a correspondent from various parts of Europe in 1919–21, while also contributing to the *Manchester Guardian.* M. Phillips Price, who had covered the Russian revolution for the *Guardian,* became Berlin correspondent for the *Herald.* Griffin Barry was in Moscow after 1921. Vernon Bartlett wrote from Paris in 1921 just before joining the *Times.* Frederick Kuh, U.S.-born, took his first foreign assignments as correspondent for the *Herald* in Vienna. He was in the Balkans in 1920–24, and then joined the United Press for assignment in Moscow. Hubert D. Harrison wrote from Belgrade in 1924–37, and for the *Guardian* and *Daily Express,* before switching to Reuters.

The change that overtook the *Daily Herald* in 1930 resulted also in staff changes. Fyfe was succeeded as editor, with his two immediate successors serving rather briefly until 1935. Then, serving longer, came Francis Williams (later Lord Francis-Williams), formerly of the *Liverpool Courier,* the *Sunday Express,* and financial editor of the *Evening Standard.* He had joined the *Daily Herald* in 1930 as financial editor (city editor in British usage), and developed unusual sources throughout the business and government establishment, including the Bank of England. In 1936 he was named editor of the *Daily Herald,* and served until entering wartime government service in 1940.

W. N. Ewer was diplomatic correspondent in London. Will Dyson, Australian-born political cartoonist, provided powerful art for the paper. William Towler was foreign editor in the late 1930s, and A. L. Easterman, formerly of the *Daily Express,* held title as chief foreign correspondent and moved about Europe. Harold Butcher became New York correspondent in 1930, while also writing for the *Liverpool*

Echo. Jack Sandford, succeeding Slocombe, served in Paris through the 1930s. Carlo a'Prato, formerly of *Il Mondo* in Rome, and a refugee from the Fascist government, wrote from Geneva during the 1930s both for the *Herald* and for the *New York Times.* Victor Schiff, formerly of *Vorwärts,* Berlin Socialist daily suppressed by the Nazis in 1933, had a roving commission in parts of Europe after that time for the *Herald.*

Dr. Friedrich Sheu wrote from Vienna. Bernard Moore, formerly in Geneva for the *Morning Post,* became *Herald* correspondent there in 1937 following the *Post* merger with the *Daily Telegraph.* Alexander Hamilton, formerly in Berlin for Reuters, was in Prague for the *Herald* in 1938. H. V. Wallace King, who had written from Berlin for Central News of London and for the *Detroit News,* became *Herald* correspondent there and remained until forced out by the European war in 1939. Keith Scott-Watson, in Danzig briefly in 1939, was expelled. Ronald Mathews was in Moscow.

In the Far East, John B. Powell, editor of the *China Weekly Review* in Shanghai, wrote for the *Herald* as well as for the *Manchester Guardian* and the *Chicago Tribune.* Edgar P. Snow, U.S.-born, became Far Eastern correspondent for the *Herald* in 1932, and chief of its service in China in 1937, while also writing for the afternoon *New York Sun* in the 1934–37 period, and for the *Saturday Evening Post.* Snow was the first correspondent to present first-hand reports on the Chinese Communist group centering at Yenan, and whose leaders he learned to know personally and well. His book, *Red Star Over China* (1938), became a classic.

Despite the large circulation it attained by the mid-1930s, the *Daily Herald* was not a popular paper in the usual sense. It treated the news as seriously as a quality paper. Also, even though a Labour party paper and technically a political paper, it was hardly more partisan in its editorial position than the "liberal" *Manchester Guardian* or *News-Chronicle,* or the "conservative" *Times* in theirs. It was more responsible than the *Daily Mail* or *Daily Express,* which reflected the very personal and sometimes eccentric interests of Lord Rothermere and Lord Beaverbrook.

Sunday and Provincial Press
    The British Sunday newspapers held a position in journalism scarcely paralleled in any other country. Apart from the *Sunday Dispatch* published as a weekend paper by the *Daily Mail,* and the *Sunday Express* by the *Daily Express,* other nationally distributed Sunday papers were independent ventures. Published in London and Manchester, all were larger than a weekday paper, but still produced in a single section and more costly to buy.

The *News of the World,* established in 1843, became the Sunday paper of largest circulation in the world, about four million in 1939. (It rose as high as eight million in the 1950s.) The paper's direction from 1891 was in the hands of George Riddell, a barrister, with a former interest in the *Western Mail* of Cardiff, and then in other newspaper and publishing properties. He was knighted in 1909, became a baronet in 1918, played a prominent role in British information matters at the Paris Peace Conference and later, and was raised to the peerage in 1920 as Lord Riddell of Walton Heath. Upon his death in 1934, the direction of the paper passed to Sir Emsley Carr, editor since 1891.

The high readership of the *News of the World* was based upon its human interest content, prize contests, and especially upon crime stories told in their most lurid details. It did present some substantial subject matter. Henry Noble Hall, an experienced and serious British correspondent, wrote from the United States for a time, and there were others. What won the paper attention, however, was sensation and entertainment.

Two quality papers appearing in London on Sundays more than compensated for the trivialities of the *News of the World,* but their circulations, even though also national and acceptable in size for quality papers, were understandably fractions of the other. These were the *Sunday Times* and the *Observer,* dating from 1822 and 1791.

William Ewart Berry directed the *Sunday Times* from 1915 until 1937, followed then by his younger brother, Gomer Berry. Under the Berrys' direction the *Sunday Times* gave careful attention to the range of public affairs at home and abroad, as well as to literature and the arts. It was not to be expected that the staff representation of a weekly would be so large as for a daily, but the *Sunday Times* had distinguished contributors on all subjects and stringers abroad. Thus it received reports through the years from, among others, Maurice Lovell of Reuters, who moved about Europe, Alexander Werth in Paris and Moscow, J. A. Ford in Berlin, and Virginia Cowles, an American, in Spain and other parts of Europe.

The *Observer,* long a serious paper, had gained high respect under the editorship since 1908 of James L. Garvin, after his earlier association with the *Daily Telegraph.* Garvin also edited the afternoon *Pall Mall Gazette* from 1912 until its suspension in 1915, and was editor-in-chief of the *Encyclopaedia Britannica* fourteenth edition in 1926–29. His articles on political subjects gave the *Observer* importance and influence. With the death in 1919 of Viscount Astor, its owner since 1911, the paper continued under his elder son, Waldorf Astor Astor, the second viscount and the paper's actual proprietor since 1915.

As with the *Sunday Times,* special writers served the *Observer* at home and abroad. Among many others, Philip Carr wrote from Paris, as did Sisley Huddleston, also representing the *Christian Science Monitor* there; Marguerite Wagner wrote from Berlin; Herbert B. Elliston, formerly of the *Manchester Guardian,* wrote from the United States; Sonya Chamberlin (Mrs. William H. Chamberlin) wrote from Moscow, where Chamberlin was *Monitor* correspondent in 1922–33; and Ludmilla Shapiro (Mrs. Henry Shapiro) later did the same, with Shapiro as UP correspondent there.

Other Sunday papers include the *People,* established in 1881 but acquired by the Odhams Press and published both in London and Manchester. It used much the same appeal as the *News of the World,* with its circulation rising from about 250,000 in the early 1920s to two million in the 1930s. Its weekly circulation reached about five million in the 1950s.

The *Sunday Pictorial,* established in 1915 as a weekend edition of the *Daily Mirror,* also was to reach millions. The *Empire News* of Manchester, dating from 1884, circulated two million, as did the *Sunday Chronicle* of Manchester. The *Sunday Graphic* of London circulated more than a million. *Reynold's News,* dating from 1850, a somewhat specialized publication of the cooperative movement but nationally distributed from London, had about 625,000.

The *Sunday Express* and the *Sunday Dispatch,* weekend editions of the *Daily Express* and the *Daily Mail,* with mid-century circulations of about 3.25 million and 2.5 million respectively, were more important for their news and editorial content than any except the *Sunday Times* and the *Observer.*

Many of the British provincial dailies provided their readers with a good budget of news, but all were in competition with the nationally distributed London papers and the *Manchester Guardian.* Apart from the *Guardian,* the only other provincial dailies with any representation abroad at some period in the 1930s would seem to have been the *Western Mail & South Wales News* of Cardiff, with Dermot MacDermot in Paris; the *Yorkshire Post* of Leeds, with Darsie R. Gillie in Paris; the *Glasgow Herald,* with Alexander Werth in Paris; and the *Liverpool Echo,* with Harold Butcher in New York.

Australia and New Zealand

In Australia and New Zealand, both with many daily and weekly newspapers, it was natural that the most active should be in the larger cities, notably in Sydney, Melbourne, Adelaide, Brisbane, Perth, and

The British Press: The Commonwealth

in Canberra, the capital since 1927. In New Zealand they were in Auckland, Christchurch, and Wellington, the capital.

The *Sydney Morning Herald* and the *Melbourne Argus* as early as 1873, when the first cable reached Australia, had joined to share the cost of maintaining a correspondent in London to prepare a special news report based upon the full Reuters file. From that time, the press of Australia never ceased to have special representation in London, and the New Zealand press soon was equally represented. From the 1890s, newsmen of both dominions were present on world news fronts, and also became identified with the press of the United Kingdom itself.

The first Australian press correspondent in the United States from 1916 was William W. Davies, formerly representing that press in London. In 1920, Davies also became New York correspondent for *La Nación* of Buenos Aires, while continuing to serve the Australian Consolidated Press, an association of papers. He had been a charter member of the Association of Foreign Press Correspondents in the United States, formed in 1917, and served as president of that body.

A. D. Rothman, representing the *Sydney Morning Herald* and the Australian Associated Press (AAP), also was in New York in the years between the wars. Other representatives of that agency, and of the New Zealand Press Association, as well as of individual newspapers, were in residence through the years in London. Sir Keith Murdoch of the *Melbourne Herald* and Rupert Henderson of the *Sydney Morning Herald* exercised great influence. Murdoch, as a director of the Australian Associated Press, worked increasingly in cooperation with Reuters and also established a family interest that was to extend widely within the country and eventually to London and New York.

Canada

For the press of Canada, the Canadian Press (CP) was formed as an agency in 1923, a reorganization of the earlier Canadian Press, Ltd. It had its representatives in the Associated Press headquarters in New York to provide some coverage, while also processing a news exchange with the AP and Reuters. Among them were Hugh Raine, Alex Pringle, Kenneth S. Clark, formerly in Washington, Don Gilbert, and Glasgow-born S. S. (Sam) Robertson. George Hambleton established a London bureau in 1927, later enlarged, with Edwin S. Johnson in charge in the late 1930s. He was joined in 1939 by Robertson, moving from New York, and D. Ernest Buritt, moving from the agency's Montreal headquarters. Guy Rhoades and Jack Brayley in the London bureau later moved to New York and Montreal. Gillis Purcell, general superintendent in Montreal since the 1920s, was succeeded in that position in 1940 by Charles Bruce, who had been in New York following Robertson's transfer to London.

Among newspapers in Canada, the *Toronto Daily Star* directed by Joseph E. Atkinson, and the country's largest in circulation, was perhaps also most active in original coverage in the United States and Europe in the years between the wars, with substantial reports also from Ottawa and other domestic points. It published a *Star Weekly* in a magazine format.

Ernest Hemingway, a native of Illinois, following brief experience on the *Kansas City Star,* had worked for the *Toronto Star* in 1919-20 in Toronto. He served it as a roving correspondent in Europe in 1921-23, and occasionally thereafter until 1926. With Paris as his base, he provided an interview in 1922 with Georges Clemenceau, France's wartime premier, then just returned from a tour of the Far East and a visit to the United States. From Istanbul, he produced reports of the closing period of the Greco-Turkish War in 1922-23, and covered the Lausanne Conference of 1923, where the 1919 Turkish peace treaty was revised and a Turkish-Greek agreement concluded. He went then to Germany to do a series on the extension of the French occupation in the Ruhr and on the runaway inflation in the country. He also wrote during 1923 for Hearst's Universal Service, but returned to Toronto at the end of the year to work again for several months in the *Star* office. He was writing short stories, sketches, and poems in this same period, and the success of his first novel, *The Sun Also Rises* (1926), brought a turn away from newspaper correspondence, except briefly at the time of the Spanish Civil War, when he wrote for the North American Newspaper Alliance.

The *Toronto Star* also had sent Gregory Clark to report the Washington Naval Conference in 1921, to France in 1926, to London in 1937 to report the coronation of George VI, and to Rome in 1939 for the election of Pope Pius XII. The paper received reports from Europe from David Rogers and Pierre Van Paassen, also writing for the *New York World* until its suspension in 1931. Matthew H. Halton was in London for the *Star* from 1932 to 1940. Henry Somerville was in London and Moscow in the 1930s. Frederick Griffin was in the Soviet Union in 1932. He reported the early part of the Spanish Civil War in 1936 and also was in Mexico and the United States on assignments. Gordon Sinclair was in Europe and other parts of the world.

The *Star* received the Canadian Press service, and also the syndicated services of the *Chicago Daily News* and the *New York Herald Tribune.* Its own writers supplemented these reports with background material, human interest reports, and aspects of the news with special meaning to Canadian readers.

The *Toronto Globe and Mail,* a merger of those two morning papers brought about in 1936 by C. George McCullagh, provided special coverage from Ottawa, New York, and London. The *Toronto Evening Telegram,* also represented in Ottawa, had C. H. J. Snider in England and Ireland in 1920 and in London later, where he reported the major events through the coronation of George VI in 1937. W. T. Cranfield also was in London for the paper. Robinson MacLean covered the Italo-Ethiopian War, and C. B. Pyper, the Spanish Civil War. The *Evening Telegram* was acquired by the *Globe and Mail* in 1948.

The *Montreal Star,* owned by Hugh Graham (Lord Atholstan) from 1870 until his death in 1938, and then by J. W. McConnell, had a limited foreign service, with E. J. Poole, for one, in London. Both the *Star* and the *Toronto Globe and Mail* also received the full *New York Times* service.

Two groups of papers had some special representation outside Canada. The Southam papers, including the *Ottawa Citizen, Winnipeg Tribune, Hamilton Spectator, Calgary Herald, Vancouver Province,* and *Edmonton Journal,* received reports from Lukin Johnston in London from 1928 until 1933, when he was drowned; from A. C. Cummings, also in London; Charles O. Smith in Washington; and Pierre Briquet, of the *Journal de Genève,* writing from Geneva. The Sifton papers, including the *Winnipeg Free Press,* the *Regina Leader-Post,* and the *Saskatoon Star-Phoenix,* had Grant Dexter, J. B. McGeachy, and Francis Stevens in London at various periods.

For the French-language press of Montreal, *La Presse* had Joseph Bourgeois in New York; *La Patrie* had Joseph de Valdor, also in New York; and *Le Devoir* had a correspondent in Geneva.

Correspondents for the British and U.S. agencies and newspapers reported regularly from Ottawa, and the Ottawa Imperial Economic Conference of 1932 brought an influx of correspondents from London and from Commonwealth countries.

The British United Press (BUP), formed in 1922, based in Montreal, and owned by Charles F. Crandall, was directed from 1924 to his death in 1939 by Herbert Bailey and then by Francis Hoult Fischer. It provided a substantial supplementary service to newspapers in Canada, Australia, and later in Great Britain. It also had a close and developing relationship with the United Press in the United States.

India

In India, the important dailies included the *Statesman* of Calcutta, with a New Delhi edition added in 1924; the *Times of India* in Bombay; and the English-language *Amrita Bazar Patrika* of Calcutta. The Bengali-language *Ananda Bazar Patrika* began in Calcutta in 1922;

the *Sunday Standard* in Bombay in 1936; the *Hindustan Standard*, in the Hindi language, in Delhi in 1933, with an English-language edition in Calcutta in 1937; and the *Hindustan Times* in Delhi in 1924. Some of these papers had stringers in London and other capitals. These papers were provided with a world news service chiefly through the Associated Press of India, a subsidiary of Reuters.

South Africa

For South Africa and Rhodesia, the Argus South African Newspapers included nine daily and Sunday papers in the Union of South Africa and five in Rhodesia. Five of these papers were represented by correspondents in London, and one or two by stringers in New York. These were the *Argus* of Capetown; the *Star* of Johannesburg; the *Friend* of Bloemenfontein; the *Daily News* of Durban; and the *Diamond Fields Advertiser* of Kimberley.

Others in the group included the *Cape Herald* and the *Cape Times*, both of Capetown; the *Rand Daily Mail* and the *World* of Johannesburg; the *Pretoria News* of Pretoria; the *Eastern Province Herald* and the *Evening Post* of Port Elizabeth; two papers in the Afrikaans language, *Die Burger* of Capetown and *Die Volksblad* of Bloemfontein; and the *Rhodesia Herald* of Salisbury.

The Reuter South African Press Association served these papers. It was reorganized in 1938 under the ownership of the newspapers themselves and more simply titled the South African Press Association (SAPA). It continued to distribute the Reuters world report.

Newspaper Services
in the United States   14

Seven services providing active domestic and foreign news coverage were sponsored by newspapers of the United States in the decades of the 1920s and 1930s. They were associated with the *New York Times,* the *New York Herald Tribune,* formed in a merger of those two separate newspapers in 1924, the *Chicago Daily News,* the *Chicago Tribune,* the *Christian Science Monitor,* the *New York World* morning and afternoon until both were suspended in 1931, and a combined *Philadelphia Public Ledger–New York Evening Post* service operating from 1919 to 1933.

All of these services except that of the *Monitor* became available for use in other cities of the United States, and sometimes in other countries, through syndication. The *Monitor* service was excepted because the paper itself circulated nationally and internationally, which meant that it was not possible to assign exclusive areas of syndication.

Some other news-related material was available through commercial syndicates in the United States, or feature services sponsored by news agencies, or through special associations formed by newspapers.

Limited services of domestic and international news also were presented through the afternoon *New York Sun,* which survived the suspension of the morning *Sun* in 1920, the *Baltimore Sun,* the *Brooklyn Eagle,* the *Detroit News,* the *Kansas City Star,* and the *Washington Star.* The *Wall Street Journal* and the *New York Journal of Commerce* both extended their coverage of business and finance after 1920. Specialized reports also were produced by the Fairchild Publications, Inc., of New York. These included the *Daily News Record,* the *Women's Wear Daily,* and *Men's Wear.* Matching these were two high-fashion magazines, *Vogue* and *Harper's Bazaar.* There also were a number of technical publications, including *Aviation,* produced by the McGraw-Hill Publishing Company of New York. They received world reports, largely from stringers or freelance writers. With the exception of the *World* and the *Ledger-Post* services, the others continued through the 1940s.

The *New York Times* established a position of leadership among newspapers in the United States in terms of news coverage at home and abroad. As a quality newspaper, its circulation did not match some others, but it increased about 60 per cent between 1920 and 1939 to attain a weekday figure of 474,277 (more than twice that of the *Times* in London), and 788,997 on Sundays. It was a large newspaper, both in news and advertising volume, published in two sections, and in multiple sections on Sundays.

Because of the size of the country, it was impossible for any newspaper in the United States to have national distribution on the date of publication, as in Great Britain and some other nations of less area. The *New York Times* did come as close as any, however, to being a newspaper of national distribution, even though late in delivery in most areas, and rivalled only by the *Christian Science Monitor* and the *Wall Street Journal,* which had the same delivery delays. Concentrated in the New York metropolitan area, it also circulated widely on a Boston-Washington axis, and westward to Buffalo, Cleveland, and Pittsburgh. Beyond that, copies went to every part of the country, especially the Sunday edition, with a magazine supplement and book section added to much else. Dependent upon mail delivery in this period, any one of the three papers mentioned was up to four days late when it reached the most distant parts of the country. Air mail reduced this time, but at a cost that added little to circulation.

The *New York Times* had entered upon a new period in 1896 when it was purchased by Adolph S. Ochs. Then handicapped, financially and competitively, it made a quick recovery and by the time of World War I was in a strong position. Ochs brought together a remarkable group of executives. Louis Wiley came from the *New York Sun* to direct the business affairs of the *New York Times.* The paper was edited through the years from 1900 to 1940 by Charles R. Miller, Rollo Ogden, Dr. John R. Finley, and Charles Merz. Carr V. Van Anda was managing editor from 1904 to 1925, followed by Frederick T. Birchall to 1932, and then by Edwin L. James. Ochs himself died in April 1935, aged seventy-seven, and was succeeded as publisher by his son-in-law, Arthur Hays Sulzberger, then forty-four.

Enterprise in communications was important to the growing preeminence of the *New York Times* in those years. Experiments in transatlantic wireless were conducted jointly for news purposes by the *New York Times* and the London *Times* between 1900 and 1907, and was used before and after the war. The *New York Times* also played a part in the formation of Press Wireless, Inc., and Fred E. Meinholtz, communications specialist, contributed greatly to the paper's organization.

The *New York Times* also had introduced rotogravure printing in the United States just before World War I, providing a superior means for the reproduction of photographs. It had established the *Mid-Week Pictorial* as a separate gravure photo magazine as the war began. It sought out photos and in 1919 had established Wide World Photos as a subsidiary to obtain photos and make them available by syndication. By 1925 about a hundred photographers and assistants were at work throughout the world, and continued until the service was sold to the Associated Press in 1941. The *New York Times* had become a paper of record, regularly indexed for reference from 1913 and had published *Current History* magazine from 1914 to 1936. In 1922 it was instrumental in the formation of the North American Newspaper Alliance (NANA) to handle special reports and their distribution.

Following somewhat in the path of the *New York Herald* and the London *Daily Telegraph* during the previous century, the *New York Times* gave its support to exploration and science, including Peary's journey to the North Pole in 1909, Lindbergh's Atlantic flight in 1927, the Byrd expedition to the South Pole in 1928–29, and others. Van Anda, whose interests were almost limitless, was one of the first news executives to insist that science be reported prominently and accurately. Accordingly, the paper gave special notice to the first reports from Germany in 1921 of Albert Einstein's calculations on the "theory of relativity" and to his meetings with scientists in the United States soon after. Van Anda himself was one of the few laymen who understood Einstein's mathematics.

The *New York Times* gave great space to the discoveries in the tomb of Tut-ankh-amen in Egypt in 1922. Sir Harry Perry Robinson of the London *Times* was the first correspondent to enter the tomb, and his reports appeared in full in the *New York Times,* along with all the photographs available, with the paper's rotogravure facilities used to provide the finest reproduction.

In 1930, the *New York Times* gave detailed reports of the attempts to scale Mount Kanchejunga, a 28,146 foot Himalaya peak, third highest in the world. Frank S. Smythe, a British newsman, provided reports on the expedition between March and June of that year. In 1931 the

New York Times and the *Times* of London jointly sponsored an expedition headed by British explorer Bertram Thomas in the so-called "Empty Quarter" of southern Arabia, one of the remaining unmapped areas of the world. In the same year, the ascent of Swiss physicist August Piccard into the stratosphere in a balloon provided another story of scientific pioneering given special handling and page-one attention.

Meanwhile, advances in aviation received intensive coverage in the *New York Times*. In 1926 staff members Russell Owen and William Bird accompanied two expeditions seeking to cross the North Pole by air. They had an assist from William C. Lyon, Seattle stringer correspondent, who proceeded to Alaska on the story. Owen covered the first expedition, in which Roald Amundsen, Norwegian Arctic explorer, along with Lincoln Ellsworth and Umberto Nobile, flew over the North Pole in the dirigible *Norge*. Bird covered another expedition in which his near-namesake Lieutenant Commander Richard E. Byrd and pilot Floyd Bennett flew over the Pole in a tri-motored Fokker plane, with special articles by Byrd appearing on page one. In addition to news coverage of the *Norge* flight, the *New York Times* ran a series of page-one articles by Federick Ramm, a Norwegian aboard the dirigible. Thanks to the development of radio, his account appeared only seven hours after the flight, as contrasted to the 153 days that had elapsed between Peary's attainment of the Pole in April 1909 and the publication of his first message.

Not only did the *New York Times* have exclusive rights to Lindbergh's own account of his Paris flight in May 1927, but it had special coverage on other aerial ventures. These included a flight from New York to Germany in June 1927 by pilot Clarence D. Chamberlain and Charles A. Lavine, the first transatlantic air passenger, and a flight from New York to the coast of France, also in June, by Navy Commander Richard E. Byrd, accompanied by Bert Acosta, George Noville, and Bernt Balchen. There followed the Byrd expedition to the Antarctic in 1928–29, where he flew over the South Pole on November 28, 1929, from his base at "Little America," with Balchen at the plane's controls and Harold I. June as radio operator. Russell Owen accompanied this expedition, with his reports reaching New York by radio in a system organized by Fred E. Meinholtz, the paper's communications specialist.[1]

---

1 Russell Owen was awarded the Pulitzer Prize in 1930 for his two years of reportage from the Antarctic, characterized as "the greatest assignment in newspaper history," and compared to the Henry Morton Stanley assignments in Africa in the 1870s.

An incident of the reporting, illustrative of communications advances, related to an occasion when Meinholtz was listening to Owen's news report from the Antarctic on a

In national news coverage, the *New York Times* had Richard V. Oulahan in charge of its Washington bureau from 1912 until his death in 1931. He was only absent when he directed the *New York Times* staff at the Paris Peace Conference in 1919, and when he went to the Philippines, China, and Japan in 1923–24. The growing importance of Washington as a world capital brought a marked increase in general press coverage. The *New York Times* bureau there became the largest representing any one newspaper, with about twenty-five reporters in the 1930s, plus technical and clerical personnel.

Oulahan was succeeded as chief of the bureau in 1931 by Arthur Krock, a member since 1927 of the paper's board of editors in New York formulating news and editorial decisions. Before that he had been a Washington correspondent in 1911–15 for the morning *Louisville Courier-Journal* and the afternoon *Louisville Times,* a correspondent for both papers at the Paris Peace Conference, and editor-in-chief of the *Louisville Times* from 1919 to 1923. He then became an editorial writer for the *New York World* and director of the editorial page following the death of Frank I. Cobb in that year. Krock also assisted Ralph Pulitzer, the *World* publisher. He switched to the *New York Times* in 1927.

Krock directed the paper's Washington bureau from 1931, demonstrating his talents as a reporter, analyst of political and public affairs, and as a bureau administrator. He became the author of one of the early signed special columns from the capital, started in 1933 and titled "In the Nation." It appeared three times a week on the editorial page. He also wrote a signed column in the Sunday "Editorial Section," regarded as important reading for those seeking an understanding of national and world events and trends. In 1937 Krock obtained the only personal interview ever granted a correspondent by President Franklin D. Roosevelt. He received Pulitzer Prizes for Washington correspondence in 1935 and 1938, with an added special citation in 1951, in addition to other recognition. Members of the Washington bureau included William H. Lawrence, Felix Belair, Harold Hinton, Turner Catledge, and Samuel Thurston Williamson, until he left to participate in the establishment of *News-Week* magazine in 1934.

In New York, the entire staff also grew after 1920, with specialists among its members, both in the news and among the editorial page

---

receiving set in his home. The dispatch was interrupted by a personal message to Meinholtz, relayed from the *New York Times* office in Manhattan to Little America and back, asking him to hang up the receiver on his home telephone so that he could be reached from the *New York Times* office a few miles away. Meinholtz discovered that his small son had left the receiver off.

writers. Waldemar Kaempffert, for example, joined the paper in 1927 as a science specialist, followed in 1930 by William L. Laurence (not to be confused with William H. Lawrence of the Washington bureau). Hanson W. Baldwin, a U.S. Naval Academy graduate of 1924, joined the staff after several years of sea duty and became naval and military correspondent moving about the world on assignment.

Apart from writers on politics, finance, labor, and sports, regional correspondents were appointed. For example, Lawrence E. Davies, a former Oregon newsman, and more recently with the Paris edition of the *New York Herald,* was assigned to Philadelphia in 1927 to cover the Middle Atlantic states. In the late 1930s he was reassigned to San Francisco to report the western states, plus Alaska and Hawaii, and continued there until his retirement in 1969. Regional correspondents operated in other parts of the United States. They were in constant telephone and teleprinter contact with the New York office. This gave the *New York Times* original coverage of important developments in every part of the country, with daily reports, Sunday roundup stories in the "Editorial Section," and special articles.

The *New York Times* staff abroad had been growing since 1908 and was substantially extended during the period of World War I. The first Pulitzer Prize for "meritorious public service" was awarded to the *Times* in 1918 in recognition of its war reporting through 1917. Charles A. Selden and Edwin L. ("Jimmy") James, among those representing the paper in Paris during the war, both remained in active service. Selden returned to New York and left the paper temporarily, as it turned out. James became Paris bureau chief in 1919, and also director of the paper's European service. This he administered from Paris until 1929 and then from London until 1930, when he returned to New York, first as assistant managing editor and then managing editor from 1932.

In Paris in 1922, Ochs discussed with James details and costs that would be involved in the development of a news coverage both in Europe and the rest of the world designed to produce the most comprehensive reports available to any newspaper, and supplementing the news agency services also received. James estimated that it would cost $500,000 a year, and Ochs gave the word to go ahead.

Adding the great file of news from its bureaus in Washington, Albany, and regional centers, plus the New York staff contributions, and reports received from the AP, UP, INS, and Reuters, the *New York Times* was publishing a very large newspaper each day. Naturally, there was duplication in the reports from the paper's own correspondents and from the news agencies, so that a selection of material had to be made by the editors in New York. Normally, the reports by the paper's own correspondents were used most prominently, many under bylines. When great events justified it, entire pages of advertising were omitted from a day's edition to permit the use of space for the most complete news coverage, including the full texts of important public addresses and documents. This policy, dedicated to the best service of information, won recognition for the *New York Times* as one of the great newspapers of the world.

The development of the overseas and Washington staff was brought into a new focus through a Sunday "Editorial Section" of about twelve pages conceived by Sunday editor Lester Markel to provide what he called "the deeper sense of the news." It included reports specially prepared by the paper's correspondents throughout the United States and abroad. A "News of the Week in Review" page was added later. The Sunday paper also included a separate rotogravure section from 1913 until about 1935, a book review supplement, and a magazine supplement, both of the highest quality and under Markel's close supervision. A large Sunday financial section dealt with business and commerce around the world, and other special sections were authoritative in their fields, contributing to Sunday editions totalling 300 to 500 pages. Unlike most other U.S. newspapers, the *New York Times* used no syndicated matter and no comic strips or Sunday comic sections, which were deemed no proper part of a quality newspaper. As with the *Times* of London, a crossword puzzle was its only popular feature.

Between the end of World War I and 1940, the *New York Times* developed the largest foreign staff of any newspaper in the world. Charles M. Lincoln, former news executive with the *New York Herald* but with the *New York Times* since 1907, became foreign editor in 1926, a post he occupied until 1941. Eugene J. Young, who had been foreign editor of the *New York World,* also joined the *New York Times* after the *World's* suspension in 1931 and helped supervise the growing volume of international news. The correspondents were not stinted on the volume of material they might send. Quality was desired, and completeness was considered an essential element, whether in foreign or domestic reports.[2] The paper noted that its cable costs for 1926–27 had been $500,000, or as much as James had estimated in 1922 for an entire world service. Those costs rose steadily, totalling more than $1 million for foreign communications charges alone in 1940, without reference to staff, travel, and bureau costs, and with

---

2   The volume of news along with the style of writing in the 1920s became a subject of some criticism, epitomized by the complaint that "the *Times* never reported the news in one paragraph when it could just as well use five."

5,338,119 words received during the year from representatives around the world.

European coverage was administered through the Paris bureau until 1929, and the staff there grew. With James in charge, other early members included British-born Walter Duranty, in journalism since leaving Cambridge in 1906 and with the *New York Times* in Paris from 1913 to 1921, and Percy J. Philip, also British, with the London *Daily News* as a war correspondent, then with the *New York Times* in Paris from 1920 and bureau chief there from 1932. He also broadcast from Paris for the BBC from that time.

Others in the Paris bureau included Harold Callender, Louis B. Kornfeld, James Graham, and Harold B. Hinton, later in the Washington bureau. Lansing Warren, formerly of the *Chicago Tribune,* joined the bureau in 1927. J. Carlisle MacDonald, formerly of the *New York World, New York Herald,* and the AP, was in the bureau in 1928-31, when he entered the field of industrial relations as assistant to the chairman of the board of the U.S. Steel Corporation. William P. Carney, formerly of the Paris edition of the *New York Herald,* joined the bureau in 1925. Gaston Hanet Archambault, editor of the Paris edition of the *New York Herald* from 1905 to 1924, except for wartime service in the French army, joined the bureau in 1933. Of French nationality but London-educated, he also had edited the English-language afternoon *Paris Times* during its brief existence from 1924 to 1929, and then had been in the Paris bureau of the *New York Sun* until 1933. Jules Sauerwein, foreign editor of *Le Matin* and after 1932 of *Paris Soir,* both leading Paris dailies, also wrote for the *New York Times.*

The London bureau of the *New York Times* had been the administrative center prior to the war for the paper's coverage of Europe. British-born Ernest Marshall had taken direction of that bureau in 1908 when the *New York Times* entered seriously upon the organization of independent foreign reporting, and he remained until 1927. Charles A. Selden was a member of the bureau, although in Paris during the war and bureau chief there before his departure in 1919.

Allen Raymond, formerly of the *New York Sun,* replaced Marshall as London bureau chief in 1927 and served until 1930, when he joined the *New York Herald Tribune.* It was in 1929 that James moved from Paris to London to direct the *New York Times* European service from there. Charles H. Grasty, former publisher of the *Baltimore Sun,* but with the *New York Times* on a roving commission since 1916, including coverage of the Peace Conference, was an editorial correspondent in the London bureau from 1920 until his death there in 1924. Others in the bureau in the 1920s included Harold B. Hinton, between Paris and Washington bureau assignments, Charles A. Smith and Kendall Foss, both later with INS, Thomas R. Ybarra, formerly in Berlin, Henry Charles Crouch, and Ferdinand Kuhn, Jr.,[3] who joined the bureau in 1928.

Charles A. Selden, who had returned from Paris to New York in 1919, left the *New York Times* in 1920 to become European correspondent for the *New York Evening Post,* and later wrote for magazines, moving about much of the world. In 1927, however, he rejoined the London bureau of the *New York Times.* When Raymond left in 1930, he became bureau chief until his retirement in 1937. Harold Callender, long in the Paris bureau, moved with James to London in 1929 to direct the European content of the paper's Sunday "Editorial Section." With the departure of James for New York in 1930, Callender returned to the Paris bureau.

In 1936, Selden became ill and Kuhn was named as acting head of the London bureau. When Selden retired in 1937, Kuhn was confirmed in that position and served until 1939. He was president of the Association of American Correspondents in London in 1937-38. He returned to New York in 1939 as an editorial writer and special writer for the paper.

Kuhn's departure from London in 1939 brought the appointment of Raymond Daniell as bureau chief. Also a member of the bureau since 1928, he had had previous experience with the *New York Herald,* the Associated Press, the *New York Evening Post,* and had been in Mexico City for the *New York Times.*

Others in the London bureau in the 1930s included Tania Long, formerly in Berlin for the *New York Herald Tribune,* who became Mrs. Raymond Daniell, but continued as a correspondent; Walter F. Leysmith, an Australian; James B. ("Scotty") Reston, formerly of the AP bureau in London; Robert P. Post, Drew Middleton, and James (Jamie) MacDonald. Vladimir Poliakoff, then writing for the London *Evening Standard,* also wrote special political articles for the Sunday "Editorial Section" of the *New York Times* under his pseudonym of "Augur."

The other major capitals of Europe were regularly covered by *New York Times* staff correspondents. Cyril Brown was in Berlin from 1921 to 1925. He also had been in London and Berlin for the paper in the 1914-17 period, but had switched to the *New York World* in 1917-21. Brown left the *New York Times* again in 1925 to join Fox Movietone News, but then moved to Paramount News in 1929, serving as a newsreel interviewer and narrator.

---

3 Not to be confused with Frederick Kuh of the UP.

Brown was succeeded in Berlin in 1925 by Lincoln Eyre, who had been a war correspondent for the *New York World,* then became Berlin correspondent for the *New York Herald,* and later for the afternoon *New York Sun.* Eyre died in 1928, succeeded in Berlin for the *New York Times* by Wythe Williams. Williams had been a correspondent for the paper in Europe before and during the war, but had moved to *Collier's Weekly* in 1918, and in 1919 to the service of the *Philadelphia Public Ledger* and the *Saturday Evening Post,* both Curtis publications. In 1927, however, he rejoined the *New York Times* as Geneva correspondent. He was in Berlin for the paper from 1928 to 1931, when he left again to become chief correspondent in Europe for the Hearst newspapers and director of Universal Service, with headquarters in London. In 1936, he returned to the United States to become editor of *Greenwich Time* of Greenwich, Connecticut. Guido Enderis, in Berlin for the Associated Press before and after the war, joined the *New York Times* bureau there in 1929. He succeeded Williams as its chief from 1931 to 1941.

Frederick T. Birchall, managing editor in New York since 1925, yielded that post to Edwin L. James in 1932. By his own choice, he went to Berlin as a special writer for the paper and moved about the continent until 1939, although his headquarters was in London after 1937. He was awarded the Pulitzer Prize in 1934 for correspondence from Germany during 1933, the first year of the Hitler regime.

Others in the Berlin bureau included Boston-born Thomas R. Ybarra in 1924–25, when he went to the London bureau; John Graudenz, formerly of the UP; Louis Hamburg of Wide World Photos, a *New York Times* enterprise; and Irish-born Robert Crozier Long, a financial specialist also writing for the *Economist* of London. Two who joined the Berlin bureau in 1933 were C. Brooks Peters and Otto D. Tolischus, formerly chief of the INS bureaus in Berlin and London. Tolischus was to remain in Berlin for the *New York Times* until 1940, when the Nazi government "invited" him to leave because of his reports. In that same year he was awarded the Pulitzer Prize largely on the basis of those very reports in his 1939 correspondence from Berlin, the substance of which also appeared in his book, *They Wanted War* (1940). Summoned to New York, Tolischus was reassigned to Tokyo.

In Vienna, Clarence K. Streit served as correspondent in 1925–28. A Montanan, a Rhodes scholar, and a student at the Sorbonne, Streit had been in Paris and elsewhere for the *Philadelphia Public Ledger* from 1920–25 when he joined the *New York Times.* He was assigned briefly first to North Africa. John S. Macormac followed Streit in Vienna from 1929–31. Then assigned to Ottawa, Macormac was succeeded in Vienna by G. E. R. Gedye, who had been in the service since 1927 of the *Times*, the *Daily Express*, and the *Daily Telegraph*, all of London. He continued in Vienna for the *New York Times* until 1938, was in Prague until that city also was seized by the Nazis in March 1939, and then in Moscow. Stephen K. Swift had been in Vienna prior to March 1938 as a representative of Wide World Photos.

In those years, Emil Vadnay, Hungarian-born and based in Prague, covered central and southeastern European affairs for the *New York Times* from 1926 to 1939, when he died. British-born Hubert D. Harrison, in Belgrade since 1924 serving various British papers, was briefly representative there for Reuters and for the *New York Times* in 1937, but was expelled from the country and went to Berlin for the *News-Chronicle*. George Weller, studying at the University of Vienna following graduation from Harvard, became a member of the *New York Times* staff in 1932, reporting the Balkans until 1936, when he joined the *Chicago Daily News* European service.

The *New York Times* was sympathetic to the purposes of the League of Nations from the time of its establishment in 1920. In its early years, the League activities were reported for the paper by members of the Paris bureau going to Geneva as the news seemed to require. In 1926, however, Robert Neville became resident correspondent there for the paper. Wythe Williams, rejoining the *New York Times* in 1927 succeeded Neville. When Williams moved to Berlin in 1928, he was replaced, in turn, by Streit coming from Vienna.

Streit remained as Geneva correspondent for the *New York Times* for ten years, serving also in 1931 as president of the Association of Journalists Accredited to the League of Nations. He was assisted for a time by Carlo a'Prato, formerly of *Il Mondo* of Rome, also writing for the *Daily Herald* of London. Articles a'Prato wrote in 1937 for the *Journal des Nations*, a Geneva publication dealing with League activities, brought a formal protest from the Italian Fascist government. The Swiss government, in an unusual response, ordered him to leave the country, contending that his articles tended to disturb the foreign relations of Switzerland. Streit's own departure from Geneva came in 1939 and, after a short period in the *New York Times* Washington bureau and the publication of his book, *Union Now* (1939), he left the paper but remained in Washington as a writer and advocate of Atlantic Union. He was followed in Geneva for the *New York Times* in 1939 by Warren Irvin.

In Rome, the *New York Times* was effectively represented from 1921 by Arnaldo Cortesi, son of Salvatore Cortesi, stringer and then correspondent there since 1902 for the Associated Press until his retirement in 1931. The younger Cortesi served the paper from 1921 to

1938. The Italian Fascist government then issued a decree prohibiting Italian citizens from working for foreign agencies or newspapers. As a consequence, Arnaldo Cortesi became correspondent for the paper in Mexico City in 1939, succeeded as bureau chief in Rome, temporarily, by Camille M. Cianfarra. New York-born, Cianfarra was brought up in Rome, where his father was an assistant in the United Press bureau, and where the son also worked for a year before joining the *New York Times* staff in 1935 until 1941. In April 1939, Herbert L. Matthews became chief of the Rome bureau, with Cianfarra remaining primarily as a specialist on Vatican news. Matthews was expelled from Italy in October 1940, but was permitted to return in November and continued until Italy joined Germany in a declaration of war on the United States on December 11, 1941.

An important personality in the *New York Times* organization began her association with the paper in Rome in 1921. Mrs. Anne O'Hare McCormick, in Europe with her husband, Francis J. McCormick, an importer of Dayton, Ohio, mailed several articles to Van Anda in New York. They were used in daily and Sunday editions of the paper. She wrote well and demonstrated an understanding of a new postwar generation in Europe. This included Benito Mussolini whom she identified as the prospective ruler of Italy a year before he and his Fascist party gained power in 1922.

In that year, Mrs. McCormick was made a member of the *New York Times* staff, with a roving commission in Europe. As a correspondent, she wrote from various countries and conducted substantial interviews with leading figures in government and politics. In 1936 she became the first woman on the editorial board of the *Times* in New York, and in 1937 began to write an editorial page column appearing three times a week. Called "In Europe," then "Affairs of Europe" and ultimately merely "Abroad," it alternated with Krock's Washington column, "In the Nation." Also, in 1937, Mrs. McCormick was awarded the Pulitzer Prize for foreign correspondence in the preceding year. Described by Meyer Berger in his centennial *Story of the New York Times* (1951) as "the most honored newspaperwoman in the world," she continued abroad and in the United States as a writer for the paper until her death at seventy-three in 1954.

Coverage for the *New York Times* in the Soviet Union began in November 1921 with Walter Duranty, formerly in the Paris bureau, entering with the first group of correspondents officially admitted. He remained Moscow representative until 1934. Duranty became one of the most knowledgeable correspondents on Soviet affairs. He had two interviews with Stalin, was awarded a Pulitzer Prize in 1932, and returned to Moscow on several occasions between 1934 and 1939.

302 Crisis and Conflict

Edwin L. James, before returning to New York in 1930 as assistant managing editor for the *New York Times,* went from his London post to Moscow and, after leaving, wrote an uncensored series of six substantial articles published on the editorial page and also distributed through syndication for wider use. Robin Kinkead substituted in Moscow in 1932 when Duranty was on holiday, but later left the paper to enter public relations with Pan-American Airways.

When Duranty left the Moscow post in 1934 he was succeeded by Harold Norman Denny, who remained until 1939. Denny had joined the *New York Times* bureau in Paris in 1922. There he had worked since just after the war for the *Chicago Tribune* Paris edition. For the New York paper he went from Paris to Morocco and the Sahara in 1926, to Nicaragua in 1928, Cuba in 1930, and then had been in the New York office. His five-year assignment in Moscow was interrupted when he covered the early phase of the Italo-Ethiopian War in 1935 and again in 1937, and when he went to Paris to write a series of uncensored articles on Soviet life and affairs and, surprisingly, was permitted to return. Denny left Moscow for other assignments in the spring of 1939. He was succeeded by G. E. R. Gedye, formerly in Vienna and Prague for the paper.

In the growing world crisis of the 1930s, the Italo-Ethiopian War was covered for the *New York Times* by Herbert L. Matthews, formerly of the Paris bureau; by Gedye, leaving his Moscow post temporarily; by George Lowther Steer, also writing for the *Times* of London; and by Joseph Isreals, Jr., reporting from Addis Ababa.

In Spain, the paper had been represented during the 1920s by correspondents moving chiefly from the Paris bureau. From 1931 to 1938, Lawrence A. Fernsworth, formerly of the Paris edition of the *New York Herald,* was in Barcelona writing also for the London *Times.* Frank L. Kluckhohn was in Madrid in 1931, followed by William P. Carney of the Paris bureau, and another former Paris *Herald* staffer.

The *New York Times* was represented in southern Europe and the Middle East late in the decade by Cyrus L. Sulzberger. A nephew of Arthur Hays Sulzberger, publisher of the *Times* since 1935, he had worked for the *Pittsburgh Press* following his graduation from Harvard in 1934, then moved to the United Press bureau in Washington, to the London *Evening Standard,* and back to the UP, again, in Europe. He joined the *New York Times* staff there in 1939.

In Tokyo, Hugh Schuck, then managing editor of the *Japan Advertiser,* acted as a stringer for the *New York Times* in the 1920s. From 1923 to 1925 the paper was represented there by Wilfrid Fleisher, then also business manager of the *Japan Advertiser.* In 1925, he moved to the *New York Times* Washington bureau. With his departure from Tokyo, British-born Hugh Byas became the paper's correspondent in Japan, while also writing for the *Times* of London. He represented both papers in Tokyo until his retirement early in 1941, and was replaced then by Otto D. Tolischus, formerly in Berlin.

In China, Harrison Forman wrote for the *New York Times* from the early 1920s. Thomas F. Millard and Frederick Moore, both "old China hands" since about 1900, also served during that decade. Millard served from 1925 to early 1941. William Finch wrote for the paper in 1931. Archibald T. Steele, Canadian-born but U.S.-naturalized, represented the paper in Manchuria and North China in 1932-33. He joined the AP staff in Shanghai in 1933, and in 1935 became correspondent in China and the Far East for the *Chicago Daily News.*

Hallett E. Abend, after news experience in Spokane, Los Angeles, and Honolulu, and a year as a freelance writer in China, joined the *New York Times* staff there in 1927, first in Peking and then in Shanghai. He remained in China as a correspondent until May 1941. The Chinese Nationalist government in Nanking had tried unsuccessfully to have Abend deported from China in 1929, and he later had trouble with the Japanese in Shanghai. Anthony J. Billingham also represented the *New York Times* in Shanghai in 1937. Frank Tillman (Till) Durdin, who had been a reporter for the *San Antonio Express* in his native state, and for the *Los Angeles Times,* joined the *Shanghai Evening Post* in 1930. He was managing editor of the *China Press* of Shanghai in 1932-37. In the latter year he joined the *New York Times* as correspondent in Nanking, and succeeded Abend as chief correspondent for the paper in China in 1941.

In Latin America, George H. Corey wrote from Brazil in 1930-31, and John W. White,[4] formerly of the *Chicago Daily News,* was in Argentina then and later. Raymond Daniell had been *New York Times* correspondent in Mexico City before his transfer to London in 1928. Frank L. Kluckhohn, forced to leave Spain in 1936, soon became Mexico City correspondent but was expelled in 1939, following which he was in Buenos Aires, along with White. Arnaldo Cortesi, leaving Rome in 1938, succeeded Kluckhohn in Mexico City. In 1941 he exchanged places with White, who took the Mexico City post as Cortesi went to Buenos Aires.

---

4   Not to be confused with James D. White of the AP staff in China, or with Lewellyn (Johnny) White of the UP.

The *New York Herald Tribune* was formed in 1924 in a merger of the *New York Herald* and the *New York Tribune,* each an important daily in its own right for more than eighty years. The merger was an element in changes in the New York newspaper field brought about by Frank A. Munsey, who earned the dislike of many working journalists put out of jobs by his activities as the "great executioner of newspapers." Beginning his working career as a telegrapher in his native state of Maine, and then manager of the Western Union office in Augusta, Munsey at twenty-eight went to New York in 1882. There he established a magazine, the *Golden Argosy* (1882) (later the *Argosy*), and in 1889, *Munsey's Weekly* (later *Munsey's Magazine,* a monthly). By 1905 they were yielding him an annual income of $1 million. He also established a successful chain of Mohawk grocery stores, one of the first, and became active in banking, hotels, and real estate.

As early as 1903, Munsey believed the time was near when most of the publishing in the United States would be done by three or four concerns. He was himself then engaged in attempting to create a chain of newspapers in the eastern states. In 1891 he had acquired the New York *Star* (1868) and turned it into a tabloid retitled the *Continent,* which stressed pictures and human interest material. The public did not respond, and the paper was suspended after four months with a loss of about $40,000. In 1901, he tried again by buying the *Washington Times* (1894) and the New York *Daily News* (1855). In 1902 he bought the Boston *Journal* (1833), and in 1908 he acquired the Baltimore *Evening News* (1872), published by Charles H. Grasty since 1892, and he established the Philadelphia *Evening Times* as a new paper.

These ventures were not generally successful. Munsey disposed of the New York *Daily News* in 1904 at a reported loss of $750,000, and the paper ceased to appear two years later. The Boston *Journal* was sold at a loss in 1913 and was merged in 1917 with the Boston *Herald.* The Philadelphia *Evening Times* was suspended in 1914. The *Washington Times* was sold in 1917 to Arthur Brisbane, who in turn sold it to William Randolph Hearst. Munsey bought the Baltimore morning *American* and evening *Star* in 1921. He merged the *Star* with the *Evening News,* and sold that paper to Hearst in 1922, and in 1923 the morning *American.* This brought an end to one phase of his involvement with newspapers, and with his attempt to form a chain.

Meanwhile, Munsey had embarked upon a separate undertaking in New York, based upon the belief that there were too many papers in the city, and that consolidations would mean greater profits for the survivors. He purchased the *New York Press* in 1912 for $1 million, intending at the time to make it a part of his "chain." Established in

1887, it had been a generally successful morning paper. In 1916, Munsey also was able to buy the morning *New York Sun* and the *Evening Sun,* including the related Laffan News Bureau.

Charles A. Dana, editor and publisher of the *Sun* newspapers from 1868, had died in 1897, and direction of the papers was taken over by William M. Laffan, formerly business manager. Laffan died in 1909 and in 1911 ownership of the papers was gained by William C. Reick.

Reick had been with the *New York Herald* in 1888–1906 and became president of the New York Herald Company in 1903. From 1907 to 1912 he had held a substantial interest in the *New York Times* and also had joined with Adolph S. Ochs, owner-publisher of that paper, in ownership of the *Philadelphia Public Ledger.* After buying the *New York Sun* papers in 1911, Reick disposed of his interest in the *New York Times* in 1912, and in 1913 he and Ochs sold the *Public Ledger* to Cyrus H. K. Curtis. In 1916, with the circulations of the *Sun* papers lagging, Reick sold those papers to Munsey for nearly $2.5 million. Reick then became president of the New York *Journal of Commerce,* a business paper dating from 1827. Reick died in 1924, and the paper was sold in 1927 to Herman Ridder, active since 1890 in New York publishing.

The *Sun* papers had lost their membership in the New York Associated Press in the conflict with the old United Press in 1892, and Laffan, by then publisher, had established the Laffan News Bureau in 1893 as a special service. Munsey abolished that bureau on buying the *Sun* papers in 1916. He merged the *New York Press,* owned since 1912, with the morning *Sun,* so gaining the AP membership of the *Press* for the *Sun.* To gain a membership for the evening *Sun,* Munsey failed in an effort to buy the *New York Evening Post,* but he was able to buy the *New York Evening Globe,* dating from 1904, for $2 million, and this he merged with the evening *Sun* as a way to gain the desired AP membership.

Munsey spent an additional $2 million in the 1916–20 period to bolster the circulation of the *Sun* papers and to increase the advertising volume and revenue. He had small success with the morning *Sun.* The evening *Sun,* however, was almost doubled in circulation, and its advertising revenue increased by more than 30 per cent. Ervin Wardman, former editor of the *New York Press,* was publisher, and Keats Speed, also formerly of the *Press,* was managing editor.

The *New York Herald,* meanwhile, had been losing its earlier preeminence since the 1890s, challenged in the morning field especially by the *New York World,* the *New York Journal,* and the *New York Times.* Its publisher, James Gordon Bennett, Jr., also had attempted a London edition of the *Herald* in 1889–90, and an edition in Caracas,

Venezuela, in 1900–04, but both failed. Bennett died in May 1918, leaving no heir. With a payment of $4 million, Munsey soon acquired the *New York Herald,* its companion afternoon paper, the *Evening Telegram,* and the Paris edition of the *New York Herald.* In 1920, he merged the morning *Sun* with the morning *Herald.* The *Evening Sun* was retitled the *Sun* and continued. In 1924, he purchased the evening *Mail* (1882) for $2.2 million, a paper with the recent dubious distinction of having become a vehicle for German propaganda during World War I. This he merged with the *Evening Telegram.*

Thus between 1891 and 1924 Munsey had reduced the number of daily newspapers in New York by six, the *Star,* the *Daily News,* the *Press,* the morning *Sun,* the *Globe,* and the *Mail.* In 1924, he sought to buy the morning *New York Tribune,* intending to merge it with the *Herald.* However, Ogden Reid, publisher of the *Tribune,* refused to sell. He and his wife, Helen Rogers Reid, a participant in the direction of the paper, then entered upon long negotiations with Munsey and bought the *Herald* (with which the old *Press* and *Sun* were incorporated) and its Paris edition for $5 million. The result was the establishment of the *New York Herald Tribune,* thus reducing the number of Manhattan newspapers by one more.

Munsey retained the former Bennett afternoon paper, the *Evening Telegram,* and also retained the *Sun* as an afternoon paper. Late in 1925, Munsey was negotiating for the purchase of another afternoon daily—the *Chicago Daily News*—following the death in August of Victor F. Lawson, its publisher. He is said to have offered $10 million for the paper. In December 1925, however, Munsey himself died at seventy-one.[5] His estate was appraised at $20 million and, with no heir, went mostly to the Metropolitan Museum of Art. The *Evening Telegram* and the *Sun* were sold by the estate to Munsey's business associate, William T. Dewart.

In 1927 Dewart sold the *Evening Telegram* to the Scripps-Howard Newspapers, thus giving that group its first New York paper, among twenty-four afternoon dailies from coast to coast. In 1931 the morning *New York World* and the *Evening World* also were sold to Scripps-Howard. The morning *World* ceased to exist. The *Evening World* was merged with the *Evening Telegram* to make the *New York World-Telegram,* a more important paper than either had been individually.

---

5   William Allen White, normally a man of compassion, reflected the common feeling among news people in an editorial page commentary in his *Emporia Gazette.* It read:

"Frank A. Munsey contributed to the journalism of his day the talent of a meat-packer, the morals of a money-changer and the manners of an undertaker. He and his kind have about succeeded in transforming a once-noble profession into an eight per cent security. May he rest in trust!"

The *Sun* continued as an afternoon paper under the control of the Dewart family.

The loss of six New York dailies through Munsey's action, and another in the *Herald* merger with the *Tribune,* plus the loss of the *World* newspapers in 1931, was not the whole story. The *New York Daily News,* unrelated to that with which Munsey had been identified in 1901-04, had been established in 1919 as a morning tabloid by Joseph Medill Patterson and Robert R. McCormick. Its success induced Hearst to introduce his own morning tabloid in New York in 1924, the *Daily Mirror,* which also succeeded but led to the suspension in 1937 of his morning *American.* Bernarr Macfadden, already successful as publisher of *Physical Culture, True Story,* and other magazines, followed Hearst by a few months in 1924 and introduced the New York *Evening Graphic* as a third New York morning tabloid. More extreme in content than either of the others, it ceased to appear in 1932.

Until the morning *Sun* was merged with the *Herald* in 1920, it had substantial coverage in Washington and abroad, and the evening *Sun* also was well represented. Laurence Hills, morning *Sun* capital correspondent, who also had reported the 1919 Paris Peace Conference, was named by Munsey to direct the Paris edition of the *New York Herald.*

The evening *Sun* after 1920 had the veteran correspondent Joseph Grigg in London, where Herbert Bailey also wrote for the paper as well as for the *Daily Mail* prior to becoming director of the British United Press in 1924. Percy H. Winner was in Paris in 1922. Edgar P. Snow wrote from China in 1934-37, and others provided limited coverage from foreign places.

The *New York Herald* and the *New York Tribune* each had had its representation in news centers prior to the merger of the two papers in 1924. The *Herald* had John McHugh Stuart in London. Francis McCullagh in Moscow in 1919 and writing also for the *Manchester Guardian* was jailed, but he left the Soviet Union before the official admission of correspondents began in 1921. Sanford Griffith and Raymond E. Swing (Raymond Gram Swing)[6] were in Berlin in 1921. Swing was among correspondents admitted to Moscow that year, but did not remain for long. He joined the *Wall Street Journal* as London representative in 1922.

Louis Seibold, a veteran *New York World* correspondent awarded a Pulitzer Prize for an exclusive interview with the ailing President Wilson in 1920, joined the *Herald* soon after receiving that award in 1921, and traveled about the world on special assignments. William Henry

---

6   He incorporated his wife's maiden name as part of his own.

Donald, *Herald* correspondent in China as early as 1911, later became an adviser to Sun Yat-sen, to Marshal Chang Hseuh-liang, and then to Chiang Kai-shek.

Gaston H. Archambault, managing editor of the Paris edition of the *Herald* both before and after the war, left that paper in 1924 to edit a new afternoon *Paris Times,* but when it suspended in 1929 he went to the Paris bureau of the New York evening *Sun,* and then to the *New York Times* bureau in 1933. British-born Eric Hawkins, in Paris since his youth, and already in news work before joining the Paris *Herald* staff in 1915, succeeded Archambault as managing editor. May Birkhead was with the paper from 1912 until 1926, after which she switched to the staff of the Paris edition of the *Chicago Tribune.*

For the *New York Tribune,* Arthur Draper had been in London since 1915 and directed the paper's European coverage from there until 1925. Harold E. Scarborough, formerly of the *Baltimore Sun,* joined the London bureau in 1920, following a period with the International Red Cross at its headquarters in Geneva. John Elliott, recently out of Princeton, also joined the London bureau.

Ralph Courtney was Paris correspondent. Wilbur Forrest, wartime correspondent there, was temporarily in Mexico and Haiti in 1920–21. In the latter year, Courtney became Rome correspondent, and Forrest returned to Paris to head that bureau. In Berlin, the paper had William C. Dreher, Joseph Saxe, Elias Tobenkin, and J. C. Segrue, who also wrote for the London *Daily News* and then for the *News-Chronicle* as it became in 1930. Otis Peabody Swift, later of the UP, ranged over Europe for the *Tribune.* Nathaniel Pfeffer wrote from China.

Washington was covered for the *Tribune* by Carter Field, Grafton Wilcox, and Theodore M. Knappen. In New York, Frank H. Simonds wrote syndicated interpretative articles on international subjects, as he had during the war. The paper used political cartoons by J. N. Darling of the *Des Moines Register* since 1906. His work, signed "Ding," was syndicated and gained him Pulitzer Prizes in 1924 and 1943.

The *New York Tribune,* founded and edited by Horace Greeley from 1841 to his death in 1872, then became the property of Whitelaw Reid, a staff member since the time of the Civil War. From 1889 until his own death in 1912, Reid served almost constantly in diplomatic posts in France and Great Britain. Meanwhile, the paper was run editorially by a so-called "regency" group. In 1908, Reid's son, Ogden Mills Reid, then twenty-six and educated at the University of Bonn and at Yale and just admitted to the New York state bar joined the staff as a reporter, later moving to various positions. In 1911 he married Helen Rogers, a native of Wisconsin and graduate of Barnard

College. Upon his father's death in 1912, Ogden Reid became editor and publisher of the *Tribune* and began a process of rebuilding and revitalizing the paper that proceeded through the war years and after. It was a process in which Mrs. Reid participated actively. A thoroughly modern building was completed in 1923 and in 1924 the Reids purchased the *New York Herald.*

The *New York Herald Tribune* thus came into being, and staff changes followed. Armstead R. Holcomb moved from night editor to managing editor. Wilcox came from Washington as assistant, and became Holcomb's successor in 1931. Stanley Walker was city editor. David Rogers developed a strong reference library for use by all members of the staff. Arthur Draper returned from London in 1925 as foreign editor, and then became assistant editor of the paper from 1926 to 1933, when he resigned to become editor of the weekly *Literary Digest.*

Scarborough succeeded Draper in London as bureau chief and director of the European service. A strong staff was created in New York and Washington, and a larger and more active foreign staff developed. The Paris edition of the *Herald* was continued under the direction of Laurence Hills and Eric Hawkins. In 1927 a Sunday magazine supplement was added, edited by Mrs. William Brown Meloney, a former editor of the *Delineator* magazine. The supplement continued after 1935 as *This Week,* still under her direction, and was distributed with many other Sunday newspapers throughout the country. Thus the magazine alone circulated more than ten million copies each week.

By 1930 the *New York Herald Tribune* was firmly established as a newspaper of quality, in many ways matching its chief morning competitor, the *New York Times,* but more readable and typographically more attractive. Politically, it provided an editorial voice for the Republican party, whereas the *New York Times,* although taking an independent position, commonly supported the Democratic party.

Walter Lippmann, who had succeeded Frank I. Cobb as editor of the morning *World* upon his death in 1923, joined the *Herald Tribune* after the *World's* suspension in 1931. He wrote a tri-weekly column, "Today and Tomorrow," dealing with national and international affairs. It was published on the editorial page or the "op ed" (opposite editorial) page and widely syndicated. Five years later in 1936, Dorothy Thompson, then married to novelist Sinclair Lewis, but formerly in Berlin as chief of the central European news service of the *Philadelphia Public Ledger-New York Evening Post,* also joined the *Herald Tribune* to produce an "On the Record" column concerned almost exclusively with international affairs. This appeared in alternation with Lippmann's column and was also widely syndicated.

In Washington, with Wilcox moving to the New York office in 1924 after sixteen years in the capital for the AP, the *Chicago Tribune,* and then the *New York Tribune,* Carter Field took over as chief of the *Herald Tribune* bureau. In 1929, however, he became Washington correspondent for the Bell Syndicate. He was succeeded by Theodore C. Wallen, former editor of the *Hartford Courant,* but in Washington for the *Herald Tribune* since 1927. Wallen's death in 1936 brought Albert C. Warner into the post of bureau chief until 1939, when he became a radio commentator for the Columbia Broadcasting System, succeeded in turn by Joseph F. Driscoll, formerly bureau chief in London.

Other members of the Washington bureau at various times prior to 1940 included Theodore M. Knappen, John O'Brien, and Ernest K. Lindley, until he joined *Newsweek* magazine in 1937 as Washington correspondent. Joseph W. Alsop, Jr., and Robert E. Kintner also left the bureau in 1937 to conduct a column of capital information distributed by the North American Newspaper Alliance.

Direction of the *New York Tribune* European service had centered in London since George W. Smalley established it in 1866. The *New York Herald* service, by contrast, had centered in Paris. Apart from a business office on the Avenue de l'Opera, the news activities were at 38 rue du Louvre, also the office of the Paris edition of the *Herald,* adjacent to Les Halles and near the rue de Rivoli. In 1930, all of these functions in Paris for the *New York Herald Tribune* and the Paris *Herald* were moved to a new, specially designed building at 21 rue de Berri, near the Champs d'Elysées. The Paris edition of the *Chicago Tribune* was purchased in 1934 by Ogden Mills Reid and suspended. It then became possible, without confusion, to retitle the Paris *New York Herald* to make it accord with the parent paper in New York. Thus, it became the European edition of the *New York Herald Tribune,* a seven-day morning newspaper distributed throughout Europe and beyond.

The *Herald Tribune* concentrated its European direction in Paris in 1935. John Elliott, in Berlin for the paper since 1926, was placed in charge. Scarborough, who had directed the service from London since 1925, was reassigned to New York.[7] It was then that Joseph F. Driscoll of the New York staff was assigned to replace him as London bureau chief until 1939. He was assisted by Arthur E. Mann, formerly of the *Chicago Tribune* and of the London bureau of the *New York World* until that paper was suspended in 1931.

---

7 Scarborough wished to remain in London and chose to resign after visiting New York. Upon returning to England and obviously deeply dejected, he took his own life by dropping overboard as the ship entered Southampton waters.

In Paris, Wilbur Forrest, chief *Tribune* correspondent from 1920 and for the *Herald Tribune* until 1927, then went to the Washington bureau, and visited China and Japan in 1929. In 1931 he became executive assistant to Ogden Reid in New York, a director of the paper, and in 1939 assistant editor.

Forrest was succeeded in Paris by Leland (Lee) Stowe, who had prior experience on the *Worcester Telegram* in Massachusetts, the *New York Herald,* with Pathé News, and on the *Tribune* New York staff. Arriving as second man in the bureau in 1926, some months before Forrest's departure, he remained until 1935. He then began four years as a roving correspondent for the paper in North and South America, but returned to Europe to cover parts of the Ethiopian and Spanish wars. When based in Paris between 1927 and 1935, Stowe also moved out to cover stories in Geneva, Spain, Germany, and elsewhere on the continent. He was awarded a Pulitzer Prize in 1930 for correspondence relating to the coverage of the Young Reparations Conference in Paris during the previous year. He also was made a member of the French Legion of Honor.

With Stowe's departure from Paris in 1935, he was succeeded as *Herald Tribune* correspondent there by Walter B. Kerr,[8] formerly in Berlin. Other members of the bureau in the years between 1929 and 1940 included Ralph W. Barnes, a native of Oregon and a graduate of Harvard who joined the staff of the Paris edition of the *New York Herald* in 1926 and became an assistant to Stowe in 1929 as a correspondent for the parent paper, Sonia Tomara engaged as a second assistant, and James M. (Don) Minifie.

The Paris edition of the *New York Herald* (the *New York Herald Tribune* from 1934), had been a paper of limited news value during Bennett's lifetime, reflecting some of his prejudices and giving considerable space to the social life in Paris. Under the news direction of Hawkins, it gained substance, content, and circulation in the 1920s and 1930s. Apart from staff coverage, the paper received a daily roundup of news by cable from New York. Its direct coverage of the Lindbergh arrival in Paris in 1927 was notable. But it also did well in coverage in the same period of the Gertrude Ederle channel swim; the wedding of Belgium's Prince Leopold and the Princess Astrid of Sweden in Brussels; the Byrd Atlantic flight, with a landing on the channel coast of France; handling of the Dempsey-Tunney heavyweight championship fight in Philadelphia; the Stavisky "affair" in France in 1934; and other stories bringing a greater professionalism into the columns of the paper.

---

8 Not to be confused with Walter F. Kerr, drama critic for the *Herald Tribune* from 1951, and a playwright and author.

In the period from 1920, Paris *Herald* (or *Herald Tribune*) staff members included Gaston H. Archambault, managing editor before the war and after his return from French army service until 1924. Reuben Briggs Davenport was an editorial writer from 1920 until his death in 1932, probably the last of the original *New York Herald* staff members with service for the paper dating back to coverage of the American Indian Wars in 1872. John Jeffery and Lewis Glynn were British newsmen with the paper since before the war.

There were early arrivals on the staff after the war, some of them U.S. Army veterans who had married French girls and either had remained in or returned to Paris. They included Robert W. (Tommy) Thompson, with postwar experience on the *Milwaukee Sentinel,* who returned to Paris in 1924; Ralph Heinzen, later with the United Press; and Louis Harl. Joining the staff in 1920 was Vincent (Booge) Bugeja, Maltese-born and Cambridge-educated. Other arrivals in the early 1920s included Don Donaldson, formerly of the *Evening Telegram,* who remained more than ten years and later joined the *New York Times* in New York; Martin Sommers, later foreign editor of the *Saturday Evening Post;* Al Laney, a war veteran returning in 1924 after working on the *New York Mail* until its demise, but returning to the *New York Herald Tribune* in New York in 1935 as a bylined sports writer; Lawrence E. Fernsworth, night editor in 1924–25, and later in Spain for the *Times* of London and the *New York Times;* Lawrence E. Davies was with the paper in 1924–26 and later with the *New York Times;* William P. Carney soon went to the INS and then also to the *New York Times;* Wilfred Courtney (Will) Barber and Robert Dickson were both later with the *Chicago Tribune.*

The latter half of the 1920s brought others to the staff, among them Ralph W. Barnes, later with the parent paper; Edwin G. Skinner, later with the *New York Mirror;* Reginald Coggeshall, out of Harvard but with Boston news experience, who later returned to university instruction; Elliott Paul, later going to the Paris *Tribune* and becoming a novelist; Robert W. Desmond, formerly of the *Milwaukee Journal* and later with the *Christian Science Monitor* and the *New York Times* and in university faculty positions; Henry Cavendish, later with Universal Service; Leland Case, later editor of the *Rotarian* magazine; Jack Pickering, a former Chicago newsman; Kenneth N. Stewart, an experienced U.S. newsman, later returning to the *Herald Tribune* in New York and also in university teaching; Raymond Lawrence, later of the *Oakland Tribune;* Allan Finn and Larry Dame, both experienced professionals; and Llewellyn B. (Johnny) White, formerly of the AP. There were also Whit Burnett, formerly with papers in Salt Lake City and Los Angeles, and Martha Foley, who later were to be married and to work together in Vienna for the *New York Sun* and there to establish *Story* magazine.

The 1930s saw others come and go in the *Herald* office. Among them were Fred Abbott, formerly with INS; Paul Archinard, who went to NBC; Edgar (Ned) Calmer, formerly of the *Chicago Tribune* and later of CBS; William L. Shirer, formerly of the Paris *Tribune,* of the *Chicago Tribune* itself, briefly with the *Herald,* then with Universal Service and with CBS; Eric Sevareid, formerly of the *Minneapolis Star,* later with the UP and also with CBS; George Polk, a fourth, to go later to CBS. Still others included Rex Smith, later of *Newsweek* and then vice-president of American Airlines; Dean Jennings, San Francisco newsman, later in government work and magazine writing; Paul Ghali, later with the *Chicago Daily News;* Taylor Henry and Mel Most, both later with AP; Kenneth Downs, later with INS; William Hillman, later with INS and *Collier's Weekly;* Charles Wertenbacker, later with *Time* magazine; Frank Kenney, later in the *Herald Tribune* London and Washington bureaus and a war correspondent; and Robert N. Sturdevant, former AP correspondent and in radio, as well as coauthor of the written history of the Paris *Herald.*[9]

Looking beyond Paris, the *New York Herald Tribune* received reports from Rome after 1926 from Frank T. Hollowell, formerly a member of the AP bureaus in London and Paris. In 1930, he was followed in Rome by Ralph W. Barnes, who had demonstrated high competence as Stowe's assistant in Paris since 1929. Barnes moved in 1931 to Moscow to open the paper's first bureau there, and later to Berlin and London.

Joseph B. Phillips succeeded Barnes in Rome. He had arrived from the New York office to serve in the London bureau in 1929–31, and remained in Rome from 1931 to 1935. John T. Whitaker, a member of the New York and Washington staffs, and then in Geneva from 1931 to 1935, followed Phillips in Rome. He went in 1936 to report the latter part of the Italo-Ethiopian War. Sonia Tomara, who had been in the Paris bureau, succeeded to the Rome post, but soon went to points in the Balkans and Middle East. She was followed in Rome by James M. (Don) Minifie, who remained until 1940, when he went to the London bureau.

Geneva and the League of Nations activities were reported for the *Tribune* and *Herald Tribune* until the late 1920s by Ralph Courtney,

---

9 One of the stars of the *Herald* between the wars was W. H. (Sparrow) Robertson. With the paper from about 1920 to 1940, he was a sports columnist and a rare character, but hardly concerned with news. For the story of Sparrow see Eric Hawkins and Robert N. Sturdevant, *Hawkins of the Paris Herald* (1963), and Al Laney, *Paris Herald: The Incredible Newspaper* (1947).

Wilbur Forrest, and Leland Stowe traveling from the Paris bureau. In 1929, however, Reginald Wright Kauffman became a resident correspondent there, succeeded by John T. Whitaker in 1931–35. Coverage then was provided from Paris again.

Stowe returned to Europe in 1936 and went to cover aspects of the Italo-Ethiopian War. Like Whitaker, he obtained his first experience as a war correspondent, and they both added to that experience in Spain. Linton Wells, most recently in Moscow for INS, also reported the Ethiopian War for the paper. Vincent Sheean, formerly of the *Chicago Tribune* and a writer for NANA, reported aspects of the war in Spain for the *Herald Tribune*. Walter B. Kerr, then of the Paris bureau, was in Prague in 1938 and with insurgent forces in Spain in 1939.

From Moscow, the *Herald Tribune* received reports in the 1920s from Maurice G. Hindus, born in Russia in 1891 but raised and educated in the United States from 1905. Henry Shapiro, prior to taking a permanent post for the UP in Moscow, also wrote for the *Herald Tribune*. Ralph W. Barnes, transferred from Rome in 1931, opened the paper's first bureau there. Four years later, Barnes was moved to Berlin and succeeded in Moscow by Joseph B. Phillips of the Rome bureau.

Phillips remained in Moscow from 1935 to 1937, when he left the paper to return to the United States as foreign editor of *Newsweek* magazine. The post in Moscow then was taken by Joseph Barnes,[10] who had joined the *Herald Tribune* staff in New York in 1935 after three years with the Institute of Pacific Relations, in the course of which he had visited Russia and the Far East. He remained in Moscow from 1937 to 1939. The sources of information there became so restricted by 1939, and the censorship so onerous, that the *Herald Tribune* closed its bureau, as the *New York Times* was to do later in the year, and Barnes went to Berlin.

John Elliott, who had gone from the London bureau to Berlin in 1926, went to Paris in 1935 to become director of the paper's European service, even as Walter B. Kerr, second man in the Berlin bureau, then replaced Stowe as Paris correspondent and bureau chief. It was at that time that Ralph W. Barnes succeeded Elliott in Berlin and remained there from 1935 to 1939. An experienced and dedicated correspondent, his persistence in seeking information led to his expulsion by the Nazi government. He then was placed in charge of the London bureau, succeeding Joseph F. Driscoll, who was reassigned to the Washington bureau.

---

10   Not to be confused with Ralph W. Barnes.

Joseph Barnes, upon closing the Moscow bureau in 1939, had succeeded Ralph Barnes in Berlin. He was there when the European war began in September. A month later he returned to New York as foreign editor of the *Herald Tribune,* succeeded in Berlin by Clinton Beach (Pat) Conger with Russell Hill as second man.

Conger had been born in Berlin in 1912, son of Seymour Beach Conger, Associated Press correspondent there in 1911-17. The younger Conger had served in the United Press bureau in Berlin for a time in the early 1930s. He became director of the *Herald Tribune* bureau there in October 1939, but he was expelled six weeks later, leaving Hill in charge. Conger went to Amsterdam, then to Paris as assistant to Kerr and Elliott, and later to Rome.

In addition to its substantial reporting of European affairs, the *Herald Tribune* was represented in Latin America and the Far East. Jack Starr-Hunt, editing *Excelsior* in Mexico City, was stringer there for the paper, and also for the *Christian Science Monitor* and the *Wall Street Journal.* Leo J. Reisler, once a secretary to E. W. Scripps, was resident correspondent in Havana in the early 1930s. Leland Stowe visited and wrote from South America after leaving Paris in 1935.

Roy Bennett of the *Manila Herald* became a stringer for the *Herald Tribune* in the Philippines in 1924, with others to follow. In China, Nathaniel Pfeffer was in Peking for the *Tribune* before the 1924 merger and continued until 1926 for the *Herald Tribune.* For the year following, Thomas Steep traveled in China for the paper. He had entered news work at sixteen, writing from Cuba in 1896 for the Scripps-McRae newspapers, and at eighteen became the youngest correspondent covering the Spanish-American War. He wrote from St. Petersburg in 1905, was a member of the *Daily Mail* staff in London, an AP correspondent in Mexico in 1911-14, in the Scandinavian countries in 1914-15, served the *New York Tribune* at the Washington Naval Conference in 1921-22, worked again for the AP in Peking in 1922-23, and was in the Philippines for the *Herald Tribune* in 1926 before taking Pfeffer's post in Peking. In 1927 he returned to New York and entered the public relations field.

Victor Keen became Shanghai correspondent for the *Herald Tribune* in 1929 and manager of its Far Eastern service. A member of the *Japan Advertiser* staff in Tokyo from 1923 to 1928, Keen had written from there for the *Herald Tribune* and also for the *Chicago Tribune* before transferring to Shanghai. Willard D. Price also wrote for the paper from Japan, Manchuria, and China from 1933 to 1937, and moved about the Pacific area. Wilbur Forrest, returning to the United States from the Paris bureau in 1927, had gone to China and Japan in 1929.

Wilfrid Fleisher became correspondent for the *Herald Tribune* in Japan in 1931, and was its Tokyo representative until 1940. Son of Benjamin Wilfrid Fleisher, publisher of the *Japan Advertiser,* he had represented that paper and also the *New York World* as a correspondent with U.S. forces in Siberia in 1918–19, then twenty-one years old, and had been with the UP in Paris and Geneva in 1921–23. In Tokyo as business manager of the *Japan Advertiser* in 1923–25, he also had acted as correspondent for the *New York Times,* and then had been a member of the *Times* bureau in Washington in 1925–28. Back in Tokyo, he served from 1929 to 1940 as managing editor of the *Japan Advertiser* and began his representation for the *Herald Tribune* in 1931. In 1940, going to the paper's Washington bureau, he was succeeded in Tokyo by Joseph Newman.

By 1935 improved telephone facilities in Europe were being used increasingly to move dispatches from such centers as Geneva, Vienna, Rome, and Berlin to be recorded on a disk or wire, usually in Paris, transcribed, and relayed from there to London or New York. The Press Wireless, Inc., organization by then was in operation, with transmission facilities available in Paris to serve the press exclusively. This was one reason the *Herald Tribune* moved the direction of its European service from London to Paris in 1935. Radiotelephonic service, as well as cable telephony, was by then also in commercial operation between Europe, North America, and South America.

Radiotelephonic service between Tokyo and New York became available in 1936. Fleisher in Tokyo provided the first major news report transmitted in that fashion in November. Read into the telephone in Tokyo at a normal conversational rate of speed, it was recorded on a disk in the *Herald Tribune* office in New York, published under a slugline, "By Telephone to the Herald Tribune," and bore a Tokyo dateline. It reached the New York office on a direct connection, and without the censorship then in effect on cable and radiotelegraphic connections out of Tokyo.

References have been made to the extensive use of the radiotelephone by the *Herald Tribune,* beginning experimentally in 1927 and developing so that by 1940 the paper was receiving about 90 per cent of all reports from correspondents abroad by direct connections to the New York office. It also reached its correspondents by direct calls from New York or Paris. This system of coverage was expensive, costing about $5,000 a month in 1940, but even this was estimated as about $2,000 less than it would have cost to move the same messages by cable or radiotelegraph, while it had the added advantgage of avoiding delays and, in some cases, eliminating censorship complications.

The *Chicago Daily News* service, providing both Washington and international coverage, was long established by 1920, its beginnings dating from 1900 or before. The quality of its reports was such that the service was syndicated, going not only to other newspapers in the United States, but to some in Canada and to the *Daily Telegraph* in London. Its announced purpose was

> to give a brief but vigorously human account of great world events and to record those happenings, movements and ideas which seem likely to influence the destinies of nations or which reveal the characteristics of one people to another. . . . The key words of the service are *significance* and *interpretation*. . . . Our endeavor is perhaps not so much to tell what has happened—the news agencies do this—as to tell how and why it happened, and what it means.

In this concept of its task, the *Daily News* service was ahead of most others. It was a concept set by Victor F. Lawson as publisher and by Charles H. Dennis as editor. Lawson died in 1925 and Dennis retired. A group headed by Walter A. Strong, business manager of the paper, bought the *Daily News*. The Lawson-Dennis concept remained unchanged, with news coverage strengthened at home and abroad.

The dean of the *Daily News* foreign service in 1920 was Edward Price Bell. In London for the paper since 1900, he remained until 1923. Returning then to Chicago, Bell continued actively with the paper until his retirement in 1932. Bearing the title of "editorial commissioner," he began by traveling throughout much of the world in 1924 interviewing leaders of government. One of his later missions occurred in 1929 when, in London temporarily, he persuaded British Prime Minister Ramsay MacDonald to visit Washington for a conference with president Hoover, establishing the basis for a London Naval Conference in 1930.[11]

With Bell's departure from London in 1923, the European direction of the *Daily News* service was transferred to Paris under Paul Scott Mowrer, correspondent and bureau chief there since 1910. Director of the paper's World War I coverage, Mowrer was made a member of the French Legion of Honor in 1918 and an officer of the Legion in 1933, and also was president of the Anglo-American Press Association in 1924. In 1928 he was awarded the Pulitzer Prize for "foreign correspondence" in the previous year, the first award in that precise category.

Edgar Ansel Mowrer, like his elder brother, had been graduated from the University of Michigan and, after postgraduate work at the

---

11 James D. Startt, *Journalism's Unofficial Ambassador: A Biography of Edward Price Bell, 1869-1943* (1979).

University of Chicago, had been studying at the Sorbonne in Paris when the war began. From that time, he had been a correspondent for the *Daily News*. In Rome since 1915, he was reassigned to Berlin in 1923.

Ben Hecht, a member of the paper's Chicago staff, had become the *Daily News* resident correspondent in Berlin in December 1918 and remained until 1920, when he returned to Chicago. George R. Witte followed him in Berlin in 1920–23. Edgar Mowrer, serious and highly respected, was president of the Foreign Press Association in Berlin during his last year there in 1932–33. His reporting did not please the new Nazi regime, nor did his book *Germany Puts the Clock Back,* which was based on his dispatches in 1932 and published in the spring of 1933. Those same dispatches won him the Pulitzer Prize for foreign correspondence, but he was forced to leave Germany because of Nazi government-originated threats against his life if he remained.

Hal O'Flaherty, Constantine Brown, Junius B. Wood, and Hiram K. Motherwell were other members of the *Daily News* European staff in those years. O'Flaherty had been in the *New York Sun* London bureau in 1916–17, and returned in 1919 after wartime service in the U.S. Army Air Force, but he joined the *Daily News* bureau in December. In 1920 he went to cover aspects of the Russian-Polish civil war and then was stationed in Stockholm reporting the Scandinavian and Baltic countries until 1922. He became London bureau chief when Bell returned to Chicago in 1923. Three years later, when he was president of the Association of American Correspondents in London, he returned to Chicago to become foreign editor of the *Daily News,* a post formerly held by Dennis in his joint capacity as editor of the paper. Henry Justin Smith, formerly news editor, became managing editor at this time. In 1932 O'Flaherty was assistant managing editor, and in 1936 succeeded Smith as managing editor, a post he occupied until his retirement after World War II.

Constantine Brown, although U.S.-born, had reported aspects of World War I for the *Times* of London. He became resident correspondent in Turkey for the *Chicago Daily News* after the war. He was named as O'Flaherty's successor as London bureau chief in 1926 and remained until 1930, when he left the paper to become foreign affairs editor for the *Washington Star,* with his writing syndicated.

Junius B. Wood,[12] with the *Daily News* since 1907, had covered the U.S. punitive expedition in Mexico in 1916–17, the war in France in 1918, and the Allied move into Siberia in 1918–19. Between 1920 and

12 Not to be confused with Henry Wood of the United Press, although Junius B. Wood also later joined the UP service.

1925 Wood was in China, Japan, the Philippines, and India for the paper, except for coverage of the Washington Naval Conference in 1921. He was ostensibly resident correspondent in Moscow in 1925–32, but actually in Geneva for a period in 1926, and in places as widely separated as Latin America and Scandinavia and the Baltic area in 1929–30. He returned to the Far East in 1932, reporting from Tokyo and Manchuria. Late in 1933 he took the Berlin post vacated by Edgar Mowrer, but left the paper in 1934, and wrote for the North American Newspaper Alliance in 1935–38. It was in the latter year that he became a United Press representative in Prague.

Hiram K. Motherwell was a member of the *Daily News* European staff from 1919 to 1927. He replaced Edgar Mowrer in Rome in 1923 and remained until 1927, when he returned to the United States to become a magazine editor.

Louis Edgar Browne, a World War I correspondent for the *Daily News,* was on a roving assignment in Europe during the 1920s. A. R. Decker, who had covered the Balkans since 1914, was in Vienna until 1930. Darsie R. Gillie, also representing the *Morning Post* of London, wrote from Warsaw in the late 1920s.

Three new correspondents joined the *Daily News* service in Europe in the 1920s under rather unusual circumstances. They were (James) Negley Farson, John Gunther, and William H. Stoneman. In 1910, when Paul Scott Mowrer, a youthful member of the Chicago staff, was offered the assignment to Paris, Henry Justin Smith told him he would be making a "terrible mistake" if he accepted the appointment and would put himself in a kind of limbo. By the 1920s, that attitude had changed completely, with an appointment to almost any foreign bureau regarded as a plum. Smith himself, indeed, substituted for Mowrer in Paris at one time, and a new generation of young newspapermen sought such assignments. Agencies and newspapers with foreign staffs generally ruled, however, that any appointments must be made by the home office, and from among members of the home staff. This was by then specified for *Daily News* appointments, and the opportunities came rarely. Farson and Gunther, in particular, were able to triumph over that barrier to a foreign appointment, as was Stoneman in his own way.

Negley Farson, growing up in the Chesapeake Bay area, led a varied and adventurous life. This included a period of business in England and in Petrograd during the first years of World War I and through the revolution. He then joined the British Royal Flying Corps, with service in Egypt in 1918. There he was seriously injured and during his convalescence began to write. Some of his freelance material on Russia appeared in the *New York Sun* and the *New York Herald.*

Again in business after the war and in Chicago, Farson presented to Victor F. Lawson a proposal for a series of special articles for the *Daily News* describing experiences while trying to "sail across Europe" in a small boat with his wife, a member of an aristocratic Russian family, victims of the revolution. Lawson accepted his proposal and in 1924 Farson at thirty-four turned to journalism as a new career. A boat was outfitted in Rotterdam, and the Farsons sailed up the Rhine and the Main rivers, through Ludwig's canal "over the roof of Europe" from Bamberg into the Altmuhl, to Kelheim on the Danube, down that river to Vienna, and to the Black Sea. The journey required eight months.

This exploit, with a readable series of articles and also the publication of a book, *Sailing Across Europe* (1926), gave Farson a place in the *Daily News* organization. Nominally attached to the London bureau in 1925, he traveled almost constantly for the next six years, sometimes on dangerous assignments taking him to the Middle East, Italy, the Balkans, Sweden, Ireland, the Soviet Union, India, Egypt, and Poland. At length, however, he was able to settle in London in 1931, succeeding Constantine Brown as chief correspondent. He was president of the Association of American Correspondents in London in 1933-34. In 1935 he left the *Daily News,* but remained in London while continuing to travel widely and to write.

John Gunther, the second to bypass the approved road to foreign assignment, joined the *Daily News* staff in 1922 following graduation from the University of Chicago. After two years as a reporter in the home office, he sought an overseas appointment but received no encouragement. Gunther thereupon resigned, went to London at his own expense, and applied to Hal O'Flaherty, then chief of the bureau, for a place in that office. O'Flaherty was obliged to refer the matter to Mowrer, director of the European service in Paris. Neither Mowrer nor O'Flaherty was unsympathetic to Gunther's aspiration. With no current staff needs in Europe, however, and aware of the attitude in Chicago, Mowrer was obliged to say that he could not approve any "immediate appointment" and cited the confusion that might arise by setting any precedent for letting "our people go on appointing themselves in this way."

Meanwhile, Gunther was in London. O'Flaherty gave him an occasional assignment, and then found him a place in the United Press bureau. By late in the year, however, it became possible to make him a regular member of the *Daily News* bureau in London. There he was based in 1924-26. In that time, he moved widely to cover stories or to assist where needs arose. This took him to Paris, Moscow, Berlin, Rome, Geneva, Stockholm, Warsaw, Athens, Vienna, Spain, and the Middle East.

In 1926, Gunther was assigned as second man in the Vienna bureau, then headed by A. R. Decker, whom he was to succeed as bureau chief in 1930–35. Again, however, he moved about the Balkans and Central Europe, including a brief period in Berlin late in 1933 between the departure of Edgar Mowrer and the arrival of Junius B. Wood as his replacement. Gunther was president of the Anglo-American Press Association in Vienna in 1931–32. In 1935 he replaced Farson as head of the London bureau, where he had started eleven years earlier.

During his later years in Vienna, Gunther had written some magazine articles, chiefly for *Harper's* monthly, including an anonymous factual report of the Nazi-organized assassination of Austria's Chancellor Englebert Dollfuss in July 1934. Also anonymously, he had written parts of a book, *Not to Be Repeated: Merry-Go-Round of Europe* (1932), presenting an unusually frank appraisal of men and issues, and patterned after the highly successful *Washington Merry-Go-Round,* published in the previous year, also anonymously but actually by Drew Pearson and Robert Allen.

In somewhat the same vein, but stemming more particularly from his by-lined articles for *Harper's,* Gunther was persuaded to write a comprehensive and serious book under his name about Europe's problems, leaders, and governments. After some hesitation, he began work on such a volume in Vienna early in 1935 and continued it under great pressure after assuming the responsibilities as head of the *Daily News* London bureau in April. It was published in London in February 1936 under the title *Inside Europe,* and in New York a few weeks later. An immediate success in both countries, the work was translated into other languages.

The book's contents were so topical that each new print order required updating. To meet those demands, Gunther resigned from the staff of the *Daily News* in September 1936 and returned to New York to give attention to the book. He was replaced in the London bureau by William H. Stoneman.

In writing *Inside Europe,* Gunther depended not only upon his own experience and observation, but he was greatly assisted by *Daily News* colleagues and others, as he acknowledged in a small book, *A Fragment of Autobiography* (1961). Not only did he prepare four completely revised editions of *Inside Europe* between 1937 and 1940, but began work on an *Inside Asia* in 1937, published in 1939 and revised in 1942. He wrote other "inside" books later on Latin America, Africa, U.S.A., and Russia. He produced other books and also wrote for the North American Newspaper Alliance, as well as filling radio and later television assignments on international affairs.

William H. Stoneman, who followed Gunther in London in 1936, was the third man to win his way to foreign assignment through purposeful effort and ingenuity. He had joined the *Daily News* staff in Chicago as a reporter in 1925, a recent graduate of the University of Michigan. In 1927, he learned that the appointment of a resident correspondent in Stockholm was being contemplated and promptly applied. He also arranged to take a room with a Swedish family in Chicago so that he might learn the language. While he did not precisely "appoint himself," he earned appointment by that enterprise and determination and went to Stockholm in 1928–29.

In the latter part of 1929, with the world economic crisis just beginning, one of the first European industrialists to be affected was Ivar Kreuger, the so-called Swedish "match king" who had built a complex international monopoly since the war by operating 250 factories in forty-three countries. This empire began to collapse, bringing losses to stockholders in many parts of the world. In March 1932 Kreuger killed himself in Paris. In Stockholm, Stoneman was able in 1929 to reconstruct Kreuger's operation in full and personal detail. This was a matter of importance in the financial community, and of general interest as well. His effective reporting recommended him for appointment to head the paper's Rome bureau in 1929–32, succeeding Carroll Binder. He then was in Moscow in 1932–35, was briefly in Berlin, reported the Italo-Ethiopian War, wrote a series of articles from Palestine, was in Paris, and then succeeded Gunther in London in 1936, where he remained for ten years.

The *Daily News* had received reports from Moscow after the revolution from Michael Farbman, also writing for the *Manchester Guardian;* from Edwin Ware Hullinger in 1921–24, while also serving the United Press; and, in the same period, from F. A. Mackenzie, also writing for the *Daily Mail.* Junius B. Wood became *Daily News* correspondent in Moscow in 1925 succeeding Mackenzie and held that appointment technically until 1932, even though he was away from Moscow much of the time. Other *Daily News* correspondents filled in for him there during such intervals, including Gunther and Farson, and also Carroll Binder and Gene Morgan, both formerly of the Chicago staff. Stoneman followed as resident correspondent from 1932 to 1935.

Carroll Binder had reported a Nicaraguan revolution for the *Daily News* in 1926–27. When Motherwell left Rome in 1927, Binder took charge of that bureau until replaced by Stoneman in 1929. He then was in Moscow in 1929–30 and in London in 1930–31, but returned to Chicago at that time to serve more than three years as assistant to a new publisher of the paper.

Walter A. Strong, with the paper since his youth, had taken control of the *Daily News* after Lawson's death in 1925. Strong died suddenly in May 1931 at forty-seven, and the controlling interest in the paper was sold to Colonel Frank Knox, who had been a member of Theodore Roosevelt's "Rough Riders" in the Spanish-American War. He had been general manager of the Hearst Newspapers in 1928-30 and then publisher of the *Manchester Union-Leader* in New Hampshire. Knox was associated there and also in the purchase of the *Daily News* with Theodore T. Ellis, former publisher of the *Worcester Telegram-Gazette* in Massachusetts.

As publisher, Knox was somewhat cool in his attitude toward the *Daily News* foreign service, which then cost approximately $350,000 a year to maintain. He also felt that some of the correspondents had been so long out of the United States that they had lost their perspective. Accordingly, he transferred the administration of the foreign service from Paris to Chicago. It was at this time that Edward Price Bell retired and Hal O'Flaherty, previously foreign editor, became assistant managing editor and Binder assistant to Knox.

Whatever reservations Knox may have had in 1931, the *Daily News* foreign service proceeded in full strength. The gravity of the international situation became increasingly apparent from that time, with Japanese forces moving into Manchuria and China and the Nazi regime taking control in Germany in 1933. There, Edgar Ansel Mowrer was forced to leave Berlin before the end of the year. It was intended that he should go to Tokyo for the paper, after a vacation in the United States, but instead was made Paris bureau chief. His brother, Paul Scott Mowrer, in Paris since 1910 and bureau chief was recalled to Chicago in 1934 as associate editor and chief editorial writer, and was made editor of the paper in 1935.

In 1934, Theodore T. Ellis died at sixty-seven, and Knox became the sole publisher of the *Daily News*. Also that year, Binder went to Japan as a correspondent, returned to Europe in 1936 to report the growing crisis there, and then was back in Chicago, becoming director of the foreign service at a time when O'Flaherty became managing editor upon the retirement of Henry Justin Smith.

A third member of the Mowrer family joined the Paris bureau in 1932. Richard Mowrer, son of Paul Scott Mowrer and nephew of Edgar Ansel Mowrer, and who was brought up in France, had become a member of the Paris bureau of the *Philadelphia Public Ledger* but switched to the *Daily News*. He remained attached to the Paris bureau until 1939, but was in Spain during much of the 1936-39 civil war period. In January 1939 he was assigned to Rome but was expelled in April. He was in Warsaw in September when the German attack there opened the European war.

Wallace R. Deuel was another among active new members of the foreign staff during the 1930s. A 1926 graduate of the University of Illinois, and then an instructor in political science and international law at the American University in Beirut, he joined the *Daily News* staff in Chicago in 1929 as an editorial writer and assistant to O'Flaherty, then foreign editor. In 1930 he was sent to New York to take charge of the paper's office there, one to which foreign reports came from Europe and elsewhere to be processed for relay to Chicago and to newspapers receiving the *Daily News* service by syndication. In 1931-32 he was in the paper's Washington bureau.

Deuel's first foreign assignment for the paper came in 1932, when he was dispatched to direct the Rome bureau as Stoneman was reassigned to Moscow. Ralph E. Forte, formerly Madrid correspondent, was second man in the Rome bureau and took charge in 1934 when Deuel went to Berlin to succeed Junius B. Wood, who left the paper at that time. Deuel remained in Berlin until 1940, except for an absence in 1935 to report the early phase of the Italo-Ethiopian War and another in 1939 when he went on home leave. He was relieved on those occasions, first by Stoneman, coming from Moscow, and then by Frank G. Smothers, formerly in the Far East but in Rome since 1937.

Forte, in charge in Rome since 1934, joined the United Press in 1937. He was succeeded by Smothers, experienced in Shanghai and Tokyo. Smothers was expelled in November 1938, however, and was replaced by Richard Mowrer. He, in turn, was expelled four months later as "unfriendly," and was replaced by John T. Whitaker, previously with the *New York Herald Tribune,* but with the *Daily News* since 1937.

In joining the *Daily News,* Whitaker held a roving assignment, and covered the growing storm in Europe in 1937-38. In the winter of 1938-39 he went to Peru to cover the Eighth Pan American Conference at Lima, and then visited Argentina, Brazil, Mexico, and other Latin American states. He interviewed leaders and studied the situation in a part of the world where Italian and German propaganda efforts by then warranted special investigation.

Back in Europe, Whitaker occupied the Rome post from mid-1939 to February 1941, when he was expelled. At that time, the difficulties of coverage had become such in Rome that the paper closed its bureau, depending upon news agency service from that capital.

Another *Daily News* correspondent in the 1930s was Jay Cooke Allen, who was in Spain for the paper in 1934-35, but who returned to the staff of the *Chicago Tribune* with which he had been identified previously. Three women joined the staff at that general period, Frances Davis, Helen Kirkpatrick, and Mary Welsh. With earlier experience in Boston and as a writer for the *Daily Mail* during the first months of the Spanish Civil War, Frances Davis also wrote from Spain for the *Daily News* in 1937-38. Helen Kirkpatrick joined the

London bureau in 1939. She had been a representative in Geneva for the Foreign Policy Association of New York, and also had written from there for the *New York Herald Tribune*, the *Manchester Guardian*, the *News-Chronicle*, and the *Daily Telegraph*. In London, she had prepared a weekly news digest, the *Whitehall News Letter*. As a member of the *Daily News* staff, she became diplomatic correspondent. Mary Welsh began as a writer in the society department after a time as a student at Northwestern University. By 1936 she had opportunities to help cover general news stories. Early in 1937 she took a vacation trip to Europe, where she was encouraged to approach Lord Beaverbrook in London and ask for a job on the *Daily Express*. A year later, after a second meeting with Beaverbrook in New York, she was hired and worked in London and Paris for the *Daily Express* and *Time* magazine through the war years. During that time she met and married Ernest Hemingway.

George Weller, in the Balkans for the *New York Times* since 1932, joined the *Daily News* staff in 1936 for service in the same area. When Gunther moved to London in 1935, he was succeeded in Vienna by Reginald Sweetland, who had been in the Far East for the paper since 1924. Sweetland was replaced in 1936 by Frank L. Hayes from the Chicago office, but who returned there in 1937. His successor was the richly experienced Marcel ("Mike") Fodor, who had represented the *Manchester Guardian* in Vienna since the early 1920s, and was regarded as an authority on European affairs. Fodor was forced to leave Vienna with other correspondents in March 1938 when the German army occupied Austria. He was in Prague when that capital also was occupied by the Germans in 1939, and then went to Amsterdam, to Paris, and to Washington.

Apart from its extensive European coverage, the *Daily News* provided reports from the Far East and from Latin America. J. Russell Kennedy, with long experience in Japan for the AP and Reuters, and as director of the Kokusai news agency, wrote from Tokyo from 1923 until his death in 1925. James L. Butts wrote from China in the 1920s, as did Paul Wright from 1925. Reginald Sweetland was in Shanghai from 1924 to 1933, and in Tokyo in 1933–35, when he transferred to Vienna. He was succeeded in Tokyo by Don Brown, as he had been succeeded in Shanghai by Frank G. Smothers. Smothers moved to Tokyo to replace Brown in 1936, but became correspondent in Rome in 1937.

Archibald Steele, with the *New York Times* in China since 1932, switched to the *Daily News* in 1937 in Peiping, but soon covered China more widely. Robert J. Casey of the Chicago staff made an adventurous journey to Southeast Asia for the paper in 1927. Junius B.

Wood was in Tokyo and Manchuria in 1932, and Carroll Binder was in Japan in 1934–35.

John W. White, who had been in Buenos Aires for the *Chicago Tribune,* went on a journey around South America for the *Daily News* in 1927. He later joined the *New York Times* as Buenos Aires correspondent. John T. Whitaker was in Peru and throughout much of South and Central America in 1938–39.

Chicago Tribune

The *Chicago Tribune* in 1920 claimed the largest morning newspaper circulation in the United States with about 440,000 and more than 700,000 on Sundays. With a regional distribution extending through much of Illinois and into adjacent states in every direction, the figures rose higher through the 1920s and 1930s. Before 1930, however, the national circulation leadership had passed to the tabloid-format *New York Daily News* under the same corporate ownership as the Chicago paper.

Robert R. McCormick and his cousin Joseph Medill Patterson were copublishers of the *Tribune* from 1914 to 1920. Enterprising and profitable, the *Tribune* had established the Army Edition in Paris in 1917. By agreement reached in France during the war by the cousins, the *New York Daily News* began publication in 1919 with Patterson in charge, while McCormick directed the *Tribune.* A Chicago Tribune-New York News Syndicate, Inc., based in New York, distributed news and feature material originated by the two papers. By 1930, with both financially successful, elaborate new buildings had been erected in Chicago and New York to house them. The "Tribune Tower" was one. In New York, the United Press, previously with its headquarters in the *New York World* building on Park Row, moved into the *New York Daily News* building on East 42nd Street.

In 1924 the *Tribune* established a major Chicago radio station. The call letters, WGN, were derived from the paper's slogan, "The World's Greatest Newspaper." In 1934 that station and WOR, Newark and New York, formed the nucleus of the Mutual Broadcasting System (MBS), a third national radio network in the United States, with as many as 560 affiliated stations at one period, and the largest in that sense. *Tribune* correspondents in Europe became its representatives. The *Daily News* later established WPIX as a New York radio station.

In 1924, Patterson and McCormick also sponsored *Liberty* magazine, which became a popular weekly, but sold it in 1931 to the Macfadden Publications, Inc. In 1934, after seventeen years of publication, the Paris edition of the *Chicago Tribune* was sold to the *New York Herald Tribune* and merged with the Paris edition of the *New York Herald,* as mentioned earlier.

Two others of the Patterson family entered the news field. Joseph Medill Patterson's sister, Eleanor Medill Patterson, in 1939 bought the *Washington Times* and the *Washington Herald,* afternoon and morning dailies, from William Randolph Hearst. Previously operated since 1930 or later on a lease basis, she merged them as the *Washington Times-Herald,* an all-day paper. His daughter, Alicia Patterson (Mrs. Harry F. Guggenheim), in 1940 established a tabloid, *Newsday,* as a Long Island suburban afternoon paper published at Garden City. It became highly successful.

The *Daily News* built its circulation on a policy of sensationalism in the news and by its use of photos. Firmly established and with more than a million copies being sold by 1930, Patterson gave it a new direction, recognizing that the economic depression then beginning meant that the public interest related to survival. While still a popular paper, the *Daily News* became more serious. It provided original coverage in Washington, but left foreign and national coverage to the news agencies and to the service received through the Chicago paper.

The character of the *Chicago Tribune* under McCormick's direction, changed from what it had been prior to 1914. The paper was widely criticized for news and editorial-page content viewed as reflecting McCormick's personal prejudices and eccentricities. Its entertaining features, aggressive news coverage, and campaign for circulation gave it leadership in competing in the Chicago area primarily with Hearst's morning *Examiner.* To win and hold readers, both papers depended upon agents who used strong-arm methods. After 1920, when national prohibition became law, some of these agents turned to bootlegging liquor and introduced gangsterism into the Chicago area under such leaders as Al Capone, whose influence extended to violence in labor relations and some business operations.

However McCormick and the *Tribune* may have been criticized, the paper was well made, professionally and technically, by a loyal and energetic staff. Its circulation grew throughout that part of the Midwest referred to by the paper as "Chicagoland," and its advertising volume and revenue mounted with its circulation. The paper was typographically attractive and was imitated by others in that respect. Its news coverage in Washington and abroad was extended. The *Tribune* and Joseph Pierson, its cable editor, were active just after the war in using wireless to brings news directly from France to the Chicago office and in establishing Press Wireless, Inc., as a new service to transmit international news reports.[13] With his own concentration on that venture, Pierson was followed as cable editor or foreign editor of the *Tribune* successively by George Scharschug, Paul Jacoby, and Donald Starr.

The *Tribune* postwar staff in 1919 included Arthur Sears Henning, Arthur M. Evans, and later Walter Trohan, all in Washington. Floyd Gibbons was in Paris as chief of the European service from 1919 to 1924. Others in that bureau then included Henry C. (Hank) Wales as second man, and Frederick A. Smith, Spearman Lewis, and Betty Van Benthuysen. Percy Hammond, the paper's drama critic, was in Europe temporarily, and John T. McCutcheon, cartoonist-correspondent, there during the war, made another visit.

Richard Henry Little was in Berlin as postwar correspondent, but went to report the Russian civil war early in 1919. With White Russian forces near Petrograd, he was wounded and returned to Chicago after his recovery. Gibbons, who had been with Little on the first part of this adventurous journey, reached Moscow and remained briefly. Rhys C. Thackwell was in Danzig in 1919, Arthur E. Mann was in Rome, and Thomas Stewart Ryan was in Fiume at the time of the d'Annunzio *coup* there, but then moved on to Warsaw. Parke Brown from the Chicago staff was with U.S. occupation forces in Germany. Henry M. Hyde, also of the Chicago staff, was in London, as bureau chief.

Other moves occurred in the 1919–20 period, both abroad and at home. Two Chicago staff members traveled widely in the United States. Philip Kinsley, later to write an official history of the *Tribune,* was with President Wilson on his final speaking tour in the western part of the country in 1919. He also was with Warren Harding on his 1920 presidential campaign tour, and in 1921 went to the Philippines with General Leonard Wood, who assumed the post there as governor-general. The paper was represented successively in Canada by Charles Bishop, Frank Phillips, and Roy Carmichael.

In Europe, staff members were moved about. Spearman Lewis went from Paris to Milan on a brief assignment. John Clayton replaced Thackwell in Danzig. Arthur E. Mann moved from Rome to Stockholm. Parke Brown and Colonel Henry J. Reilly were in Berlin. Paxton Hibben was in Smyrna, and Ladislas Czapski was on the Black Sea coast in the south of Russia. Frazier Hunt, who had been with Allied forces near Archangel in 1918, made a fifteen-month world trip in 1919–20, cabling some 75,000 words, with his reports going to thirty-eight newspapers in the United States and Canada. He resigned from the staff in January 1921.

---

13   See Desmond, *Windows on the World,* pp. 458–64.

Larry Rue, formerly on the *Duluth News Tribune* staff and then with papers in Minnesota and Michigan, joined the *Tribune* just after the war, during which he had served in the U.S. Army Air Force. His first assignment was to the Balkans. Paul Williams also had joined the *Tribune* soon after the war, during which he had been an officer in the AEF. With the Allied forces entering Russia, he traveled in the Ukraine with the White Russians under General Anton Denikin. In making a forced landing in Rumania while on a flight intended to take him to Warsaw, and remaining overnight in a hut, he contracted an eye infection. It did not yield to treatment and he returned to the United States for further attention. Upon recovery, he became a representative in New York for the Paris edition of the *Tribune.*

Gibbons, on returning from his visit to Moscow in 1919, resumed direction of the Paris bureau, headed in his absence by M. (Merle) Farmer Murphy, who had been correspondent for the *Tribune* in New York from 1897 to 1917. Murphy then went to Vienna as central European correspondent from 1919 to 1921. At that time he left the paper to join the American Relief Administration Expedition working in Central Europe as well as Soviet Russia. In 1923, he returned to the United States and joined the staff of the *Baltimore Sun,* which he served in the United States and abroad until 1934, when he joined the staff of the U.S. Department of State.

Gibbons and Wales both moved about Europe from their base in Paris. Gibbons returned to Moscow in 1921, entering the Soviet Union in August of that year, three months before the general group of correspondents was admitted. He did not remain for long, but produced a volume of copy. Clayton had managed to reach Moscow late in 1919, but was expelled. George Seldes, who had been in Berlin for the paper since 1920, succeeding Little in covering Central Europe, became resident correspondent in Moscow in November 1921. Expelled in 1923, he returned to Berlin. Parke Brown, who had been there in the absence of Seldes since 1921, was reassigned to Rome, but Seldes soon followed him.

After the expulsion of Seldes from Moscow the *Tribune* had no permanent staff representative in the Soviet capital. Larry Rue was there briefly in 1923, but was expelled, and Wales was there for a short time in 1931. From 1923 until 1940, most of the *Tribune* staff reports relating to Russia came from Donald Day in Riga, Latvia, where he could write without censorship.

Day had arrived in Riga in 1919 representing INS and hoped to proceed to Moscow. Since no visas then were being given to correspondents, he remained in Riga, but switched to the *Chicago Tribune* staff in 1920 while also serving as a stringer for the London *Daily Mail.* His reports were based upon matter culled from the Soviet press and upon travelers' tales.

Although the *Times* of London was likewise dependent upon Riga for its news of the Soviet Union, its correspondent R. O. G. Urch was better qualified than Day by reason of earlier residence in Russia and a thorough knowledge of the language. The *Tribune* reports by contrast tended to be unreliable, but continued until Latvia was occupied by Soviet forces in 1940 and Day was expelled. Instructed by the *Tribune* to return to the United States, he made his way instead to Stockholm and Helsinki, leaving the paper's service.

Developments in Italy during the early 1920s were reported for the *Tribune* by Arthur E. Mann and Thomas Stewart Ryan. Ryan soon went to Warsaw. Mann switched to the *New York World* in 1923 and was replaced for the *Tribune* by Parke Brown, who arrived from Berlin. Larry Rue was in Rome in October 1922 a day after the Fascist takeover of the Italian government, but he did not remain. Vincenzo De Santo, an Italian citizen, was second man in the bureau in 1923–24. Seldes came from Berlin in 1924 to replace Brown. With his expulsion in 1925, Seldes was succeeded in Rome by Clayton, and Clayton by David Darrah in 1927.

Correspondents for the *Tribune* were among the first to be expelled by postwar authoritarian governments. Clayton, Rue, and Seldes had been expelled from Moscow between 1919 and 1923, and Seldes from Rome in 1925. Out of Rome, Seldes went to Syria to report a French military action there. He then went to Mexico, returned to Europe, but left the *Tribune* in 1927.

The *Tribune* bureau in London had been headed during the war by Philip H. Patchin. Henry M. Hyde of the Chicago staff replaced him early in 1919, but left in September to join the *Baltimore Sun* bureau in Washington. He was succeeded by John S. Steele, who was no stranger to London. Irish-born and U.S.-naturalized, he had been with the *New York World* in New York. In London through the war, he represented the U.S.-based Edward Marshall Syndicate of newspapers. Transferring to the *Tribune*'s London bureau in 1919, he remained as its chief until 1935. He then retired but reappeared almost at once as London representative of the Mutual Broadcasting System, in which the *Tribune* held a major interest.

The campaign for home rule and independence in Ireland that had attained serious proportions during the Easter rebellion in Dublin in 1916 was a matter of news importance for the London bureau of the *Tribune,* as for other papers and agencies. Steele went from London to Ireland in 1920 soon after taking charge of the bureau. He won the confidence of Arthur Griffith, advocate of full independence for southern Ireland. Griffith later sent an emissary to meet with Steele in London, although without admission of his part in doing so. The emissary, proceeding with equal caution, conveyed Griffith's wish to reach a settlement with the British Crown and so to end the long strife in Ireland, yet with independence for the south.

Responding to this private message, Steele arranged for Philip Kerr (later the Marquess of Lothian and British ambassador to the United States in 1939–40), then private secretary to Prime Minister Lloyd George (1916–22), to initiate conversations that were to continue over a period of six months. Some were in Steele's office and others at the prime minister's Downing Street office. These talks led to a peace treaty and the establishment of the Irish Free State in December 1922. Ironically, Griffith himself had fallen dead on the way to his Dublin office the previous August 12.

Sigrid Schultz, who had become an assistant in the *Tribune* Berlin bureau from 1914 to 1917, returned there after the war. With Seldes's departure for Rome in 1924, she served as bureau chief until 1939. One of the first women to occupy so important a post or for so long a period, she also represented the Mutual Broadcasting System in Berlin in her later years there.

A change also occurred in the Paris bureau in 1924, with Wales taking over its direction while Gibbons moved about Europe. As an assistant, Wales had Lansing Warren, who had joined the bureau in 1923 and remained until 1927, when he switched to the *New York Times* bureau there. Gibbons left the *Tribune* staff in 1929 to become involved with radio broadcasting. Most of his work then was in the United States, but he did travel abroad, including visits in Japan, Manchuria, and China in 1931–32. He also provided some coverage of the Italo-Ethiopian and the Spanish Civil wars in 1935 and 1936. He wrote on those occasions for INS as well as reporting by radio. He died in 1939 at fifty-two.

Larry Rue, with the *Tribune* since 1919 and based originally in Vienna, covered southern Europe, the Middle East, and North Africa in the first years. He was in Rome in 1922 when the Fascist party took over the government. In Munich in November 1923, he witnessed the "beer hall putsch" that gave first major publicity to Adolf Hitler and the Nazi party. In Moscow briefly, he was expelled. Having been a wartime flier, Rue persuaded the *Tribune* to provide him with his own small plane for greater mobility to cover assignments in 1929–30. In that latter year, however, he left the paper to become associated with Gibbons in radio broadcasting in New York. A year later, he joined the *Tribune's* sister publication, the *New York Daily News*. In 1939 he returned to Europe as a correspondent for both papers.

One of a group of young Americans migrating to Paris after the war was (James) Vincent (Jimmy) Sheean, a Chicagoan who had worked as a reporter for about a year on the staff of the *New York Daily News.* He paid his own way to Europe in the spring of 1922, toured France and Italy and returned to Paris in October. There Wales hired him to help in his own office and in the office of the Paris edition of the *Tribune.* In the spring of 1923 Sheean became a full assistant. He went in November 1923 to report the Lausanne conference, which was called to draft a new peace treaty between Turkey and Greece. He covered a part of a League of Nations Assembly session in Geneva, and was in the Ruhr Valley in the winter when French and Belgian troops moved in, seeking to enforce German reparations payments. In 1924 he was in Rome, then in Madrid, in London for several months, in the Rhineland area, in Geneva again for another League Assembly, and in Spain once more.

In December 1924, Sheean went to Morocco to report the Riff War then in progress, with native forces under Abd el-Krim contesting the Spanish and French presence in the area. Establishing a personal relationship with the Riff leader and others in the group, he produced a series of articles that gained him wide recognition. Even after that he remained in the Riff country and in Tangier for about two months. During that time he was completely out of touch with the *Tribune,* which could not be certain he had survived the risks attached to his venture. Back in the Paris office he was lauded for his news stories, but a minor disagreement a few weeks later resulted in his polite dismissal from the staff.

Returning to New York, Sheean completed a book, *An American Among the Riff* (1926). Before its actual publication, he went again to Morocco, where France had joined with Spain to subdue the tribesmen, as they did in May. By then, Sheean was under contract to the North American Newspaper Alliance, for which he wrote from North Africa and later from other parts of the world, including China and Russia. Out of these experiences came four more books, and then another. This latter was an autobiographical *Personal History* (1935), perhaps the first best-seller by a newspaper correspondent since Henry Morton Stanley's *How I Found Livingstone* (1872). Sheean covered part of the Spanish Civil War for the *New York Herald Tribune,* and he continued to write on a freelance basis, resulting in other books.

The Paris bureau of the *Tribune* and the Paris edition of the paper formed a kind of staging area for some of the paper's correspondents in Europe and elsewhere. As with the *Japan Advertiser* in Tokyo and the Paris edition of the *New York Herald,* the *Tribune* edition included and produced newsmen and women active in the coverage of international affairs.

David Darrah, with experience on the *Cleveland Plain Dealer,* joined the Paris edition of the *Tribune* in 1919 after army service, and was managing editor in 1922–26. The paper itself then was published in the plant of *La Petit Journal* at 5 rue Lamartine. Other staff members at that time included Ralph Jules Frantz, with the paper from 1925 and managing editor in 1930–34; Bernhard Ragner, night editor; and Spencer Bull, city editor. Jack Hummell was publisher in the 1933–34 period.

Vincent Sheean worked for the Paris *Tribune* in 1923, but then went to the parent paper as a correspondent until 1925. Jay Allen (Jay Cooke Allen, Jr.) joined the staff in 1924, but began a career as a roving correspondent in Europe in 1925 for the parent paper and for others. James L. Thurber, who had worked in the American Embassy in Paris during the Peace Conference, then as a reporter on the staff of the *Columbus Dispatch* in his native Ohio, returned to Paris in 1924 and was on the Paris *Tribune* staff until 1927. He returned to the United States that year, first as a reporter on the *New York Evening Post,* but within a year began a long career as writer, editor, and artist for the *New Yorker* magazine.

Other Paris *Tribune* staff members in the mid-1920s included Harold Stearns and Alex Small, perhaps longer with the paper than any others. Others were Eugene Jolas, Waverly Root, Elliott Paul and Henry Miller, both to become novelists, Virgil Geddes, Harold Ettlinger, Will Barber, Don Skene, and William L. Shirer, newly graduated from Coe College, Cedar Rapids, Iowa, where he also had worked for the *Cedar Rapids Republican.*

Still other staff members of the Paris *Tribune* included Percival H. Winner in 1920–21, who was later with the New York *Sun,* the AP, and other papers and services; Harold Norman Denny, who moved to the *New York Times* staff in 1922; Otis Peabody Swift, later with the UP; O.W. (Tom) Riegel in 1925–27, who was later with the *New York Daily News* and then a professor at Washington and Lee University; May Birkhead, formerly of the Paris *Herald;* Irene Corbally (Mrs. Bert L. Kuhn), later to join the UP in China where she wrote as Irene Kuhn, with Bert Kuhn a member of the UP Shanghai bureau; and Morrill (Bill) Cody, Frank Wills, Ned Calmer, and Eugene Rosetti.

Edmond L. Taylor, a former St. Louis newspaperman, joined the Paris *Tribune* in 1927 and was assistant managing editor in 1928–30. At that time he became a member of the parent paper's Paris bureau, and bureau chief in 1933. Shirer also had joined the parent paper in 1927. Hugh Curran and E. R. Noderer both moved from the Paris paper to posts for the *Tribune* in Dublin and in Rome, respectively. David Darrah moved to the London bureau in 1926, later to Rome, was in South America in 1930–31, then back to Rome, where he was expelled in 1935 because of dispatches bearing on the Ethiopian War. In London again, he became bureau chief when John L. Steele retired. Darrah held that post until 1940.

Jay Allen transferred from the Paris *Tribune* to the parent paper's staff in 1925 and covered stories in France, Belgium, and Spain. He established the *Tribune*'s first bureau in Madrid in 1931. Allen also was in Italy, Austria, Poland, the Balkans, and Germany through a period of nine years. He left the *Tribune* to become a correspondent in Spain for the *Chicago Daily News* in 1934–36. When the civil war began there, he returned to the *Tribune* in 1936–37 and then wrote for the Esquire Features Syndicate of New York.

William L. Shirer's experience was comparable to Allen's in that he moved about Europe for the parent *Tribune* from 1927 to 1933, but was much in Vienna and London. During that period, he also made two journeys to India. The first was in 1930, on one of the early British Imperial Airways commercial flights to Asia. From India he also rode through the Khyber Pass to Kabul, where he was the only correspondent to report the enthronement of Nadir Khan as King of Afghanistan. He was in India again in 1931 when Gandhi was released from imprisonment following his "salt march" of April 1930 so that he might attend the second Indian Roundtable Conference in London. In Vienna once more in 1932–33, Shirer then left the *Tribune.* Back in Paris, he worked for the Paris *Herald* until 1934, at which time he joined the Berlin bureau of Universal Service. When that Hearst agency was suspended in 1937, Shirer was engaged by Edward R. Murrow, European director for the Columbia Broadcasting System, then buildings its service. Shirer thus began a career as a radio news broadcaster and commentator, first in Vienna and then in Berlin. Ned Calmer of the Paris *Tribune* also later joined the CBS.

Henry (Hank) Wales, in the *Tribune* Paris bureau since the war years, and moving about Europe after 1919, had succeeded Gibbons as chief of the bureau in 1924. Gibbons left the paper in 1929 to follow his new career in radio. Wales left in 1933 to become a script writer in Hollywood. He was succeeded as Paris bureau chief by Edmond L. Taylor, who had switched from the Paris *Tribune* in 1930 to become second man in that bureau.

From 1933 to 1939 Taylor not only headed the Paris bureau of the *Chicago Tribune,* but also traveled to other parts of Europe as the news required, including Vienna, Munich, and Prague during the critical days of 1938. During his term as bureau chief, the Paris edition of the *Tribune* was sold in 1934 to the *New York Herald Tribune* and merged with the Paris edition of the *New York Herald.* The *Tribune* had been considering such a sale since 1930, when its circulation was lagging. When the sale finally was made in 1934 it is possible that the *Tribune* may actually have been leading. Both papers were in the 20,000 circulation range. The *New York Herald* Paris edition thus became known as the *New York Herald Tribune,* at last taking the name of its parent paper in New York after ten years. Ralph Jules Frantz, managing editor of the Paris *Tribune,* and Don Skene went to the parent paper in New York. Staff members Robert Sage and Kenneth (Dick) Glen went to the Paris *Herald-Tribune.*

The *Chicago Tribune* European staff at that period in 1934 had Taylor in Paris as bureau chief. Darrah was in Rome but soon went to London. He was followed by Noderer in Rome. Sigrid Schultz was in Berlin. Sam Pope Brewer, a graduate of Yale and the Sorbonne, also joined the Paris bureau in 1936 and moved about Europe. Jay Allen returned to the paper, after two years with the *Chicago Daily News,* and covered the Spanish Civil War in 1936–37.

Taylor resigned from the *Tribune* at the end of 1939 because of a disagreement over the paper's treatment of the news, in what amounted to a direct confrontation with the publisher, Colonel McCormick, over policy. He became a radio correspondent for the Columbia Broadcasting System and also produced a timely and well-received book, *The Strategy of Terror: Europe's Inner Front* (1940). As Taylor left, Larry Rue returned to Europe for the *Tribune,* after eight years with the *New York Daily News,* and took the Paris post.

Although the *Tribune* had its greatest foreign coverage in Europe, it also was represented in Asia and Latin America. Frederick A. Smith, assistant director of the *Tribune* service in France when the war ended, was the first correspondent to reach Berlin after the armistice, arriving by plane as one of the so-called "run-away" AEF correspondents. He went soon after to Japan, Siberia, and China. From Shanghai, he went to seek and rescue a missionary, a Dr. Shelton, who had been captured by bandits. Smith himself became ill, and returned to Chicago, where he switched to the staff of the *Chicago Herald and Examiner.*

Henry Mercer wrote for the *Tribune* from Calcutta after the war. Frazier Hunt's world journey in 1920–21 included the Far East. Shirer was in India in 1930 and again in 1931, and visited Afghanistan on the first occasion. Roderick O. Matheson, formerly editor of the *Honolulu Advertiser,* became identified with the *Japan Advertiser* in Tokyo and wrote from there for the *Tribune* from 1921 to 1928. He cabled the first eye-witness account to reach the United States of the disastrous Japanese earthquake of 1923. Prior to his death in 1928, he had become dean of the correspondent group in Tokyo and president of the R.T.P. Club, formed in 1923 as the first *bona fide* overseas correspondents' association in Japan. St. Clair McKelway, former Washington and New

York newsman with the *New York World* and the *New York Herald Tribune,* succeeded Matheson as *Tribune* correspondent in Tokyo in 1929-30. He edited the *Bangkok Daily Mail* in 1930-31, prior to returning to New York to become a staff writer for the *New Yorker* magazine and its managing editor in 1936-39. Honolulu-born Kimpei Sheba also was writing from Tokyo for the *Tribune* in 1937 and continued after McKelway's departure.

Charles Dailey, formerly of the *Louisville Courier-Journal,* joined the *Chicago Tribune* staff in 1920 in Chicago. He went to China in that same year aboard a ship bearing relief supplies to assist in meeting famine conditions there. He remained there as Peking correspondent for the *Tribune* for more than ten years.

John B. Powell represented the *Tribune* in Shanghai from 1917 until 1937. He had gone to China to help Thomas F. Millard, formerly *New York Herald* correspondent there, in conducting his weekly *Millard's Review of the Far East.* The publication came under Powell's management and ownership in 1923 and appeared from then until 1941 as the highly respected *China Weekly Review.* First as a stringer and then as a regular staff member, Powell also served the *Tribune,* the *Manchester Guardian,* the London *Daily Herald,* and occasionally the *New York Herald Tribune* and the Associated Press. He had assistants, including Donald Patterson and Edgar P. Snow.

Snow, like Powell, a graduate of the University of Missouri, had been a member of the *Kansas City Star* staff before his arrival in China in 1929, when he was twenty-four. Between 1930 and 1934 he also wrote for David Lawrence's Consolidated Press Association from China, Manchuria, Burma, and India. This included coverage of the new Nationalist government of China, its relation to the Communist wing of the Kuomintang party, and the Sino-Japanese conflict as it escalated. He became a correspondent for the London *Daily Herald* from 1932, for the *New York Sun* from 1934, and a lecturer at Yenching University in Peiping.

Snow's writing and the hospitality he extended in his home at Peiping to students sympathetic to the Communist element in the internal Chinese situation, along with a friendship with Sun Yat-sen's widow (the elder sister of Mme. Chiang Kai-shek), who had joined the Communists, combined to bring Snow to the attention of Mao Tse-tung and other leaders of that group. It was arranged for Snow to meet with them. With Huang Hua, one of his students (later foreign minister in the Communist Chinese government), Snow went in 1936 from Peiping to Sian and to Paoan, near Yenan in north Shensi province, and so to Lochuan. There he remained for several months, the first correspondent to enter the area controlled by the Communist Chinese. Speaking some Chinese, Snow learned more. He was with Mao Tse-tung much of the time, and also established friendly relations with Chou En-lai, Chu Teh, and others, whom he interviewed and photographed.

Upon returning to Peiping at some risk, his reports and a book, *Red Star Over China* (1937), cast light on an otherwise confusing situation in China and earned added respect for Snow himself. Continuing as a correspondent through the years in China, in other parts of Asia, and in Russia, he wrote chiefly for the *Saturday Evening Post* and produced a number of books.

For the *Chicago Tribune,* John Powell was almost alone in providing special correspondence from China for that paper after 1929, since even Dailey's reports from Peiping ended no later than 1930, and Snow was writing for the New York evening *Sun* and the London *Daily Herald.*

The activities of the new Nationalist government produced subjects deserving of attention, but China was increasingly harassed by Japan's moves in Shantung, Manchuria, and in the north. With full-scale war beginning in 1937, Powell ceased to represent the *Tribune* in China. In that year Maxwell M. Corpening, a former U.S. Army officer, appeared in Shanghai as correspondent for the paper but was actually a spokesman for Colonel McCormick. He informed Powell that McCormick had concluded that "China is no longer important as a source of news" because it soon would be taken over by the Japanese and the news could be reported from Tokyo. From that time, *Tribune* coverage of China and Japan alike was provided through Tokyo with Kimpei Sheba as correspondent.

The *Tribune* was only thinly represented in Latin America. Reports were provided from Mexico City from 1920 by John Cornyn, who had been with the *New York Press* prior to its merger with the *New York Sun* in 1916. Gerald Martin was in Panama. Frederick Wright, George Seldes, and John Clayton were among *Tribune* correspondents in Mexico City for brief periods during the 1920s and 1930s. John W. White represented the *Tribune* in Buenos Aires as early as 1923, but switched to the *Chicago Daily News* and then to the *New York Times.* David Darrah was in South America in 1930–31, temporarily absent from his post in Rome.

The *Christian Science Monitor* completed its first decade as a six-day afternoon newspaper in 1918. From 1918 to 1922 it was published as a morning newspaper, but then returned to afternoon publication. It

Christian Science Monitor

was the only afternoon newspaper, other than the *Chicago Daily News,* to undertake an original and substantial national and international coverage of the news.

A small part of the *Monitor* circulation was in Boston, its place of publication. Delivery elsewhere was by mail and almost exclusively to subscribers, rather than by sale of individual copies. Most readers in the United States and Canada received the paper from one to four days after the date of publication, and others a week or more after that date. This included a substantial distribution in Europe and elsewhere. In 1917 it was subtitled as "An International Daily Newspaper," and that is what it became quite literally in news and general editorial emphasis, in advertising content, and in readership.

The ownership and direction of the *Monitor* was vested in the Board of Directors of the Mother Church, the First Church of Christ, Scientist, in Boston. Management rested more directly, however, with the Board of Trustees of the Christian Science Publishing Society. Technically a "religious newspaper," its religious content was minimal, and confined to a short daily article on an inside "Home Forum" page, otherwise largely literary in subject matter. The original and continuing purpose of the *Monitor* was to provide a service of substantive news and information for a general readership beyond the limitations of church membership. It offered an alternative to a triviality and sensationalism that had become increasingly common in the urban press of the United States in the years prior to the *Monitor*'s establishment in 1908. The staff membership of the paper was professional in the best sense, adhering to the highest standards and producing a well-made quality publication.

The *Monitor* was edited from 1921 to 1927 by Willis J. Abbot, who had been a news executive and editorial writer for nearly ten years with the Hearst newspapers in New York and Chicago. He also had been formerly with the *Chicago Times,* the *New York Sun, Collier's Weekly,* and a Washington correspondent for newspapers in the Midwest. With a law degree from the University of Michigan, his interests had turned to politics and international relations. Abbot gave special attention to the *Monitor*'s news coverage of such matters and to government administration. He traveled widely throughout the United States and abroad with his observations reflected in special articles and in an editorial page column, "Watching the World Go By."

Abbot's assumption of the editorship in 1921 marked the beginning of a new and more vigorous period in the *Monitor*'s coverage. In a further reorganization in 1927, justified by the growth of the paper, an editorial board was made the active agency for the general direction of news and editorial policy. Its first members were Abbot, as editor; Roland R. Harrison, formerly of the *New York Herald,* as executive editor; Frank L. Perrin, formerly of the *St. Louis Globe-Democrat* and other newspapers, as chief editorial writer; and Charles R. Heitman, former associate editor of the *Monitor,* but at this time manager of the Publishing Society. The membership of the board changed from time to time, and other editors and staff members were invited to join in its daily meetings. These meetings were in effect editorial conferences to discuss among other things the prospective news budget for the day and the manner in which it was to be presented. It was a kind of conference later to be adopted by other major dailies.

Full Associated Press and United Press agency services reached the *Monitor.* A London bureau had been established in 1908, and a Washington bureau in 1909. Other bureaus were established early in New York, Chicago, San Francisco, and Los Angeles. Stringers were appointed in other cities in the United States and Canada. Under Abbot's direction, an overseas service reaching beyond London was established in the decade after 1922, with bureaus also in Paris, Rome, Berlin, Geneva, and Moscow, and stringers in China, Japan, India, Australia, New Zealand, and Mexico.

The *Monitor* bureau in Washington was directed from its beginning in 1909 until 1915 by W.W. Germane, followed briefly by R. Eddy Matthews, by Charles D. Warner in 1915–19, and by Thomas Dawson and A. J. Montgomery until 1922. In the latter year, Cora Rigby, formerly in Washington for the *New York Herald,* became bureau chief until 1930. One of the first women correspondents in the capital, she had helped establish the Women's National Press Club in 1919, and was its president for a number of years. The bureau during the 1920s also included Demarest Lloyd, Frederic William Wile, Andrew Russell (Drew) Pearson, Robert S. Allen, Mary J. Hornaday, and Richard L. Strout.

Lloyd was a stockholder in the *Chicago Tribune* through inheritance from his maternal grandfather, William Bross, one of the incorporators of the Tribune Company in 1861. Lloyd was himself a director of the company in 1926–31. Independently wealthy, he was remarkable among working newsmen, known in Washington and later also as a member of the London bureau for covering stories in his own chauffeur-driven Rolls Royce.

Wile, in returning to the United States after the war and bringing experience as a correspondent since 1900 in Berlin and London, was head of the *Philadelphia Public Ledger* Washington bureau and then with the *Washington Star* after 1922. He also wrote for the *Monitor* and was one of the first to broadcast news from the capital.

Drew Pearson, educated at Exeter and Swarthmore College, had been director of the American Friends Service Committee in the Balkans in 1919-21, a lecturer at the University of Pennsylvania in 1921-22, and at the same time reported the Washington Naval Conference for newspaper syndication. He traveled and wrote from Australia and New Zealand, Japan, China, Siberia, and Europe in the 1921-25 period, and also lectured at Columbia University. In 1925 he married Felicia Gizycka, daughter of Eleanor Medill Patterson, of the *Chicago Tribune* family. They were divorced in 1928. It was at about that time that Pearson, covering the Department of State for the *Baltimore Sun,* also wrote for the *Monitor.* Abroad, he reported the Geneva Naval Conference in 1927, the Pan American Conference at Havana in 1928, the signature of the Kellogg-Briand peace pact in Paris that same year, the London Naval Conference in 1930, and Cuban disorders in 1931.

Meanwhile, Robert S. Allen, formerly with newspapers in Wisconsin and with the United Press, Mary J. Hornaday, daughter of James F. Hornaday, long a respected Washington correspondent for the *Indianapolis News,* and Richard L. Strout became active in the *Monitor* Washington bureau. Strout, following graduation from Harvard, had worked for the *Sheffield Independent* in England in 1919 and had worked also for the *Boston Post* until he joined the *Monitor* in 1921. He served in the Washington bureau for more than fifty years as a correspondent of the highest competence and wrote for the *New Republic* under the pseudonym of "TRB." Greatly honored for his work, he received a Pulitzer Prize in 1978.

Following the death of Cora Rigby in 1930, Allen became Washington bureau chief for the *Monitor.* A native of Kentucky, he had been educated at the University of Wisconsin, the University of Munich, and George Washington University. He had worked for the *Capital Times* in Madison, the *Milwaukee Journal,* and the United Press before joining the *Monitor.* In 1929 he married Ruth Finney of the United Press staff in Washington. She was regarded as one of the ablest capital correspondents.

Allen left the *Monitor* in 1932 after it was revealed that he and Drew Pearson were coauthors of the anonymously published book, *Washington Merry-Go-Round* (1931). Although highly successful, it dealt with affairs and personalities in Washington in a manner somewhat derisive and often considerably at odds with *Monitor* views and with reports that had emanated from the Washington bureau under Allen's direction."[14]

---

14 Allen and Pearson soon began a daily syndicated column from the capital, also called "Washington Merry-Go-Round." Widely used, it continued for many years. Allen withdrew in 1942, called into wartime service as an army reservist. He lost an arm in combat in Europe and was much decorated. He resumed independently as a columnist after the war and produced other books. Pearson, meanwhile, continued the "Wash-

With Allen's departure in 1932, the direction of the *Monitor* Washington bureau was assigned to Erwin D. (Spike) Canham. A Phi Beta Kappa graduate of Bates College in his native Maine, Canham had joined the *Monitor* staff in Boston in 1925 before he went to Oxford as a Rhodes scholar. Between that time and 1932 he worked in Europe for the *Monitor,* covering League of Nations Assembly sessions in 1926, 1927, and 1928. He reported the London Naval Conference in 1930 and was Geneva correspondent in 1930–32. In 1933, he returned to London temporarily to cover the World Economic Conference.

In Washington, Canham presided over a staff including Strout and Mary Hornaday and augmented by three dedicated reporters. Joseph C. Harsch had joined the *Monitor* staff in Boston in 1929 following graduation from Williams College and two years at Cambridge University. He joined the Washington bureau in 1931. Tully Nettleton and Neal Stanford, both with prior news experience and coming originally from Oklahoma and Illinois, brought added strength to the bureau. Nettleton in 1937 was national president of Sigma Delta Chi, professional journalistic society.

In 1939 an exchange between Boston and Washington made Roscoe Drummond director of the bureau. Canham went to Boston where he later became editor of the *Monitor* and served in many public service appointments.[15]

Drummond had joined the *Monitor* staff in Boston in 1924 following his graduation from Syracuse University. Moving through various positions, he was assigned to London in 1930 as European editorial manager, and returned to Boston in 1933 as executive editor. He directed the Washington bureau from 1939 to 1953, when he became a syndicated columnist in the capital for the *New York Herald Tribune.*

Under Willis Abbot's general direction the *Monitor* foreign service was firmly established. In London, he conferred in 1922 and 1923 with John Sidney Braithwaite, a gentleman of broad experience and competence, on the recruiting and placement of staff correspondents. Braithwaite was given charge of the London bureau and administered the service there and in the rest of Europe until after World War II.

The London bureau had provided most of the *Monitor's* original foreign reports between 1908 and the end of World War I. Beginning in 1919, Sisley Huddleston, formerly representing the *Daily Mail* in Paris, began to write from there for the *Monitor,* as he did for the

ington Merry-Go-Round" column to the time of his death in 1969, assisted in the later years by Jack Anderson, who inherited his role and the column.

15   Canham wrote the paper's definitive history, *Commitment to Freedom: The Story of The Christian Science Monitor* (1958).

Westminster Gazette, the *Observer,* and in 1922–24 for the *Times* of
London. From 1924 until 1939 he wrote exclusively for the *Monitor.*
Crawfurd Price, who had represented the *Times* in the Balkans, also
was a regular contributor to the *Monitor* from 1919 to 1928.[16]
    The *Monitor* had purchased special articles from nonstaff members
in various parts of the world prior to 1919, and it continued to do so.
In London, H. W. Massingham, former editor of the *Daily Chronicle,* the *Star,* and the weekly *Nation,* wrote a column, "A British On-
looker's Diary," which appeared in 1922–24. R. A. Scott-James, formerly assistant editor of the *Daily Chronicle,* wrote for the *Monitor* in
1930–34. Philip Kerr (later the Marquess of Lothian), who was closely
identified with British public affairs, contributed an editorial page column, "The Diary of a Political Pilgrim." Henry Wickham Steed,
former correspondent and editor of the *Times,* contributed a weekly
editorial column for several years. V. S. Pritchett, later known as a
critic and novelist, did some of his first writing for the *Monitor,* with
sketches from Ireland and Spain.
    Other articles were purchased from two Americans, Stanley High
and Reuben Henry Markham. High, as a theological student at Boston University, joined the *Monitor* staff in 1923. Subsequently, he
wrote articles rather than news from China and from the Soviet
Union. He left the staff to enter work for the Methodist Church, but
continued to write for magazines and newspapers. Between 1936 and
1952 he wrote political campaign speeches for Franklin D. Roosevelt,
Thomas E. Dewey, and Dwight D. Eisenhower, and served as a senior
editor of the *Reader's Digest.*
    Reuben Markham, Kansas-born and an ordained minister, had
gone to Bulgaria in 1912 for the American Board of Commissioners
for Foreign Missions of the Congregational Church. Returning to the
United States in 1917, he was sent by the U.S. Army to Archangel in
1918 and then to France, but was back in Bulgaria in 1920, again for
the church. Pressure from the Bulgarian government ended his missionary activities, but he remained in Sofia and published a vernacular
weekly, *Svet* (World). In 1927 he became a stringer for the *Monitor*
and soon was a staff correspondent covering the Balkan area. By then
a recognized authority on that part of Europe, his writing also conveyed a vivid sense of color and human values, touching upon much
beyond the news itself. Except for some months in Ethiopia in 1935
prior to the Italian invasion of that year, he remained in southern

---

16   Canham tells of Price's enterprise when the walnut crop in the Balkans failed one
year shortly after the war, and Price bought as much of the Spanish walnut crop as he
could manage financially. The profit was such that he was able to buy "a hotel or two"
in London.

Europe until the European war began in 1939, and then went to Palestine to write a series of articles.

William Henry Chamberlin, a graduate of Haverford College and formerly a staff member of the *Philadelphia Press* and the *New York Tribune*, went to Moscow in 1922 with his wife, Sonya Trosten Chamberlin, who spoke Russian. Chamberlin contributed articles to the *Monitor*, which engaged him as a staff correspondent in 1923. He remained in Moscow until 1934. Sonya Chamberlin also wrote for the *Observer* of London. Chamberlin left Moscow to complete a fourth book, *The Russian Revolution, 1917–1921* (1935), based on his observation and research. He then also was in Tokyo and later in Paris for the *Monitor*.

Hugh Spender, a brother of J. A. Spender, editor of the *Westminster Gazette*, joined the *Monitor* London staff in the mid-1920s and was sent to Geneva to report League of Nations activities. Canham, then at Oxford as a Rhodes scholar, assisted him during the summers and succeeded him as resident correspondent in Geneva in 1930–32 before being reassigned to Washington.

Supporting Huddleston's coverage from Paris, the *Monitor* in 1929 named Lewis Rex Miller to that bureau. A Kansan, like Markham and, like Canham, a Rhodes scholar, he had served with a British-Indian Expeditionary Force in Mesopotamia during the war. He also had taught for several years at Harvard, his alma mater, and had been a foreign service officer with the U.S. Department of Commerce. From Paris, Miller moved to Geneva to succeed Canham in 1932, but returned to Boston in 1933 as editor of a new gravure magazine supplement concerned largely with public affairs and published weekly with the *Monitor*. In 1936 he moved to San Francisco as Pacific coast correspondent for the paper, succeeding Courtland Holdom.

Among the earlier *Monitor* staff correspondents in Europe, Dr. Paul Cremona, a native of Malta and a British citizen, established a Rome bureau in 1921 and served there until 1938. By then he was dean of the foreign press corps in that capital. He was expelled in 1938 under a new Italian Fascist government decree, following the German Nazi lead, designating foreign journalists of the Jewish faith as "undesirable." This was doubly absurd because Cremona was a member of a family that had been Catholic for at least three centuries.

In Paris, Mallory Browne, formerly of the Boston staff, succeeded Miller in 1932 and remained until 1939. In Rome, Cremona was succeeded in 1938 by Saville R. Davis, who had gone from the Boston office to report the Spanish Civil War. He returned to Boston in 1939, and was followed in Rome by Joseph C. Harsch from the Washington bureau. Harsch soon transferred to Berlin, and Joseph G. Harrison of the Boston staff took the Rome post.

344 Crisis and Conflict

Welsh-born J. Emlyn Williams began a long career in Berlin as central European correspondent for the *Monitor* in 1931, with Howard Siepen as an assistant in the bureau. A. Godfrey Lias, a British citizen primarily associated with the London bureau, was also a specialist on central European affairs and spent some time based in Prague. Edward B. Hitchcock of the Boston staff also was in Prague in 1937.

Williams provided coverage from Vienna and Prague in the early 1930s. He was replaced in Berlin by Charles E. Gratke, experienced as a newsman in Oregon and Michigan and as an executive in the Boston office. Gratke suffered personal violence at the hands of Nazi hoodlums in 1933 following his coverage, along with Williams, of a Hitler address in Berlin, and was soon moved to the London bureau as editorial director, succeeding Drummond. Williams then returned to Berlin but was obliged to leave with other British citizens when the European war began in September 1939. He was replaced by Harsch of the Rome bureau.

Meanwhile, Demaree C. Bess, who had served the United Press in China and had been *Monitor* correspondent in Shanghai in 1932, moved to Geneva in 1933 to succeed Miller. In 1934, he transferred to Moscow when Chamberlin left and remained there until 1938, when he resigned to become Paris based European correspondent for the *Saturday Evening Post.*

There followed a hiatus in *Monitor* reporting from Moscow, where the difficulties of coverage had become greater than ever for the media and were to become worse. Indirect coverage was resumed from Riga in 1939, with Edmund (William) Stevens, only recently come from Moscow, named as a stringer there to cover the Baltic countries as well. Stevens had spent part of his youth in Italy. He was graduated from Columbia University in 1932, studied at the University of Moscow in 1934, and learned Russian and acted as a translator for a Moscow publishing organization. He also began a distinguished journalistic career by writing from Moscow for the *Manchester Guardian* and the *Daily Herald* and substituting for the Reuters correspondent, Samuel Rodman, in the summer of 1938. He left Moscow early in 1939.[17]

Through the years, the *Monitor* London bureau continued as the major center, not only for coverage of British news but as the point through which reports were channeled to the paper in Boston from the European continent, Africa, the Middle East, and some parts of Asia. Braithwaite was in general charge, with European editorial managers

---

17 Stevens married Nina Añdreyevña Bōnareñko in Moscow in 1935. They departed at a time when it was still possible for him to leave the country with his wife. This later became a problem for several western correspondents whose wives were Russian-born.

assigned from Boston. Drummond occupied that position in the bureau then located on Adelphi Terrace, overlooking the Thames, from 1930 to 1933. He was followed by Gratke until 1935. Scottish-born Walter W. Cunningham, previously foreign editor in Boston, succeeded Gratke, with the bureau moved to a location near Whitehall and Parliament Square. Cunningham was editorial manager in 1935-38. He was followed by Hitchcock in 1938-39, and then by Mallory Browne, moving from Paris.

Members of the London bureau in those years included Godfrey Lias, diplomatic correspondent; Peter Lyne, parliamentary correspondent; Everard Cotes, who had been in India as editor of the *Statesman* of Calcutta and cofounder of the Associated Press of India (API), and who sold his interest to Reuters in 1915; Colonel H. G. Kennard, political writer; and Harold Hobson, drama critic. Others were Ronald Maillard Stead, John Allen May, Melita Spraggs (later Mrs. Knowles), and Alexander Inglis, until he joined the *Times* and went to Ottawa and later to India. All were special writers and all were British citizens. Others attached to the bureau at various times included Demarest Lloyd, Erwin D. Canham, Robert W. Desmond, news editor in 1936, and J. Emlyn Williams, after leaving Berlin in 1939.

In the Middle East, Gershon Agronsky wrote for the *Monitor* from Jerusalem for many years. He established the *Jerusalem Post* in 1932. Martin Agronsky, a nephew born in Philadelphia, was a staff member of that paper in 1936-37. He later became an NBC radio correspondent in New York and elsewhere.

From the Far East, the *Monitor* arranged to receive by mail reports written by stringers. Staff correspondents were appointed later. Bert Crane was a stringer in China before 1927. Frank H. Hedges, writing from Tokyo for the *Times* of London until 1925 and later for the *Daily Mail,* opened the first *Monitor* bureau in that capital in 1927 and served as correspondent until 1931. Demaree Bess, in China and Japan after 1924 and writing for the United Press, became *Monitor* correspondent in Shanghai in 1932. Randall Gould, editor of the *Shanghai Post & Mercury,* succeeded him from 1933 until 1941. Chamberlin, following his departure from Moscow in 1934, was correspondent in Tokyo from 1934 to 1939. He then returned to Europe to succeed Browne in Paris, who went to London. Marc T. Greene, an "old China hand," wrote as a freelance for the *Monitor* from many parts of the Far East through these years, as well as for the *Providence Journal.*

For Latin American coverage, the *Monitor* received reports from Mexico City through Jack Starr-Hunt, who also edited *Excelsior* and wrote for the *New York Herald Tribune* and the *Wall Street Journal.* Betty Kirk wrote from Mexico after 1936, as well as for other publications in the United States and the United Kingdom. Roland Hall Sharp of the Boston staff, with a doctorate in international relations from the University of Geneva, made several extended journeys in South and Central America in the late 1930s. Traveling by commercial airlines, then recently beginning service and giving mobility to correspondents, Sharp produced substantial background reports from many countries. From Canada, Lloyd Roberts wrote from Ottawa, followed by Bruce Hutchinson of the *Victoria Daily Times.*

In Boston, the *Monitor* in the 1930s was directed by its editorial board. Following Abbot's death in 1934, the members included Harrison, a trustee of the Publishing Society; Perrin, who assumed some of Abbot's responsibilities; Drummond, executive editor; Donovan M. Richardson, a former Rhodes scholar and director of the editorial page; and Paul S. Deland, American news editor, and with the paper since its beginning. Cunningham was foreign editor until taking charge of the London bureau in 1935. British-born Henry Sowerby was his assistant. Gratke, returning to Boston from London in 1935, succeeded Cunningham.

Herbert B. Elliston, British-born and Cambridge-educated, formerly correspondent in China for the *Manchester Guardian* and the *New York Herald,* and an economic adviser to the Chinese government in 1923-27, was financial editor of the *Monitor* in 1930-40. He also wrote some editorials and acted as a stringer for the *Observer* of London. Elliston left the *Monitor* in 1940 to join the *Washington Post* as associate editor and chief of the editorial page until 1953.

Miller, editor of the new weekly gravure supplement from 1933, moved to the San Francisco bureau in 1936. Direction of the magazine section passed to Ernest C. Sherburne, who had been with the *Monitor* since its earliest days and long in New York as drama critic. Desmond, with the *Monitor* in 1931, wrote for the paper in London in 1932-33 and became associate editor of the magazine section. He was a member of the editorial page staff in 1934-36, along with Donovan, Perrin, and Carlyle W. Morgan. In London as news editor in 1936, he was then on roving assignment until 1938. At that time, he became a visiting professor at Stanford University and then left to join the faculty at Northwestern University.

The *Monitor* bureau in New York, with a considerable staff of its own, was directed from 1924 to 1945 by Alexander H. Williams, a former *New York Herald* staff member and Mexico City correspondent. Frederick W. Carr was in charge of the Chicago bureau from 1914 until the late 1930s. He was then succeeded by Ralph W. Cessna, formerly in Boston. Courtland Holdom conducted the San Francisco bureau, assisted by Royal Arch ("Rags") Gunnison, formerly of the Boston staff, until Holdom was succeeded by Miller in 1936. Gunnison entered upon assignments in 1940 for *Collier's Weekly* and the Mutual Broadcasting System. Bruce Buttles was in Los Angeles. The paper had representation also in Atlanta, Miami, Detroit, Dallas, and Seattle.

Abbot, with the *Monitor* from 1921–34, did much to add depth, breadth, and professionalism to its news and editorial content. Through his own activity in interviewing leaders of government and industry at home and abroad, he made the paper known more widely. He was among the founders and a director of the American Society of Newspaper Editors (ASNE) in 1922. Abbot was also a vice-president of the Pan American Congress of Journalists, out of which grew the Inter-American Press Association (IAPA). Further impetus toward professionalism and public appreciation of the *Monitor* came through Rufus Steele, former San Francisco newspaperman and magazine writer, who conducted a page-one column, "The March of the Nations," from 1931 until his death in 1935.

By the decade of the 1930s, the *Monitor* was recognized as one of the great newspapers of the world. In a sense, this was symbolized by the completion and occupancy of an almost palatial modern publishing house adjacent to its former home and to the Mother Church in Boston. Its coverage of the news in Boston was as thorough as in Washington or London, and its general writing style was such that the inevitable delays in delivery of the paper throughout the nation and the world did not detract from its readability or informative value. Certain taboos that had placed inhibitions upon coverage of such matters as crime and disaster in earlier years, reflective of the church sponsorship of the paper, were modified. As Canham notes in his *Commitment to Freedom,* by the 1930s there was "no subject of public importance . . . which could not be treated effectively and helpfully in the *Monitor.* The test of social significance is the only genuine test that needs to be applied. Items which are only scandalous and trivial are merely ignored. There must be a valid social reason for printing anything. . . . In every case, all efforts must be made to give the story depth and significance beyond the bare news." This is a standard, actually, for any quality newspaper.

The advances that came to the *Monitor* in general content and treatment represented the thinking of many of those already mentioned: Abbot, Steele, Harrison, Braithwaite, Lord Lothian, Heitman, Drummond, Perrin, Richardson, Deland, Sherburne, Gratke, and Canham. Another was Volney D. Hurd. With the paper since his youth, and a flier during World War I, he made the paper a source of information on aviation and on radio as it developed. For the latter, he originated a daily script for broadcast, "The Monitor Views the News." When radio was still young, the script went without cost for use by some 400 radio stations throughout the United States. Sports received careful attention in the paper, as well as books, music, and drama. Herbert Nichols became one of the first serious reporters in the field of natural science. Hurd, Gratke, and Deland trained a group of young reporters who moved on to responsible posts in New York, Washington, and foreign capitals in the late 1930s and later. Among them were Saville R. Davis, Joseph G. Harrison, Royal Arch Gunnison, William H. Stringer, Henry S. Hayward, Robert R. Mullen, John Beaufort, Gordon Walker, Nate White, and others. Gordon Converse, a photographer for the *Monitor,* brought a new dimension to that art for newspaper use. With its emphasis on background in the news, the *Monitor* also developed one of the finest special libraries or reference departments attached to any newspaper. It was directed by Blanche L. Davenport through the 1930s.

New York World

The *New York World* was greatly successful as a morning and Sunday newspaper under the direction of Joseph Pulitzer between the time he acquired it in 1883 and his death in 1911. The *Evening World,* established in 1887, and the *St. Louis Post-Dispatch,* which he had put together in a merger in 1878, were also successful.

The *World* had been criticized by some for what seemed sensationalism in certain aspects of news treatment. This unquestionably was true in the 1895-1900 period when W. R. Hearst, in entering the New York newspaper field by purchasing the *New York Journal,* challenged the circulation leadership of the *World.* The *World* responded by fighting fire with fire through the period of the Spanish-American War. Pulitzer himself, virtually blind since 1890, and none too robust, was perhaps not wholly aware of the extremes to which this contest carried both papers, typographically as well as otherwise. After the war, Pulitzer put the *World* back on the more sober and responsible news and editorial course that he favored. Even after his death, his ideas and ideals were respected by editors of his papers.

Those ideals also were reflected in Pulitzer's will. For one thing, it provided for a $2.5 million endowment to establish what became the Graduate School of Journalism at Columbia University in New York. Opened in 1912, its objective was to prepare men and women specifically for professional careers in journalism in accordance with ideas Pulitzer had outlined in an article published in 1904 in the monthly *North American Review,* then edited by George Harvey, a former managing editor of the *World* and later U.S. ambassador to Great Britain.[18]

Pulitzer's will also provided for the award of annual Pulitzer Prizes in recognition of high performance in journalism and writing, with the awards made by the trustees of Columbia University on recommendation of an Advisory Board. A major prize was to go to a U.S. newspaper, when warranted, for "disinterested and meritorious public service." Other prizes were for reporting, editorial writing, fiction, drama, history, biography, or autobiography. Still other classifications were added later, including Washington or foreign correspondence, national and international reporting, news photography and cartoons. The first awards were made in 1917 for accomplishments of the preceding year. Since then prizes have been announced in that fashion annually about May 1 of each year.

The *New York World* was edited from 1904 by Frank I. Cobb, and the paper maintained a strong Washington bureau. Its original coverage from abroad was limited until 1914, although it was represented during the Spanish-American War in Cuba and the Philippines. Irish-born James M. Tuohy had been London correspondent since 1899. Joseph Grigg became an assistant in that bureau at the time of World War I, as did Wythe Williams, until he switched to the *New York Times.* The *World* at that time received the service of the *Daily Mail,* but developed wartime coverage of its own. Eugene J. Young was foreign editor.

Wartime reports were received from Germany between 1914 and 1917 from D. Thomas Curtin, E. Alexander Powell, Gustav C. Roeder, Karl H. Von Wiegand, formerly of the UP, and notably from Herbert Bayard Swope, awarded one of the first Pulitzer Prizes in 1917 for his reports from the fronts in 1916. From Belgium and

---

18 Perhaps the first university to offer instruction in journalism was Washington College (now Washington & Lee University) at Lexington, Virginia. Robert E. Lee, commander of Confederate forces during the Civil War, was president of that college in 1869. He believed a good press could be helpful in solving the reconstruction problems in the southern states in that period, and scholarships were provided for fifty young men in a program directed by the editor of the *Lexington Gazette.* One or two courses in journalism were introduced at the University of Missouri in Columbia, Missouri, in 1878 and 1884, with a School of Journalism established there in 1908. The Wharton School of Business at the University of Pennsylvania in Philadelphia introduced five courses in journalism in 1893-94. A chair of journalism was established at the University of Zurich, Switzerland, in 1903. Between 1905 and 1912, courses in journalism were introduced at the state universities in Wisconsin, Kansas, Oregon, and Washington, and others followed, some inspired by Pulitzer's proposal of 1904. Universities in Germany, Japan, and China began to give attention to journalism after 1920, some with stress on its historical, sociological, and legal aspects.

France, war reports came from Henry Noble Hall, Arno Dosch-Fleurot, Irvin S. Cobb, also writing for the *Saturday Evening Post*, Henry Wales, later of INS and the *Chicago Tribune*, Lincoln Eyre, later with the *New York Times*, and British-born William Cook. J. Carlisle MacDonald joined the paper in 1917 as a war correspondent in France, and Cyril Brown, formerly of the *New York Times*, did the same.

Swope became executive editor of the *World* in New York after the war, serving from 1920 to 1929, when he resigned to pursue other interests. James W. Barrett was city editor through the years to 1931. Franklin P. Adams, writing as "F.P.A.," conducted a "literary" editorial page column, "The Conning Tower." Heywood Broun moved from sports writing to the conduct of another general column of commentary, "It Seems to Me." Alexander Woollcott was drama critic until he switched to the *New York Times* in the same role. Rollin Kirby, editorial page cartoonist, was awarded three Pulitzer Prizes, in 1922, 1925, and 1929. A reporting prize went to John J. Leary, Jr., in 1920, as one of the first labor news specialists, and to Louis Seibold, long in the Washington bureau, in 1921 for an interview with President Wilson in 1920. The *World* itself was awarded the top prizes for "meritorious public service" in 1922 and 1929, and the same award went to the *Evening World* in 1929. Two such awards went to the Pulitzer *St. Louis Post-Dispatch* in 1926 and 1927.

In staff changes, Samuel G. Blythe, an earlier head of the Washington bureau, switched to the *Saturday Evening Post* as a political writer. Seibold, long with the paper, moved to the *New York Herald* in 1921. Charles Michelson, Washington bureau chief from 1917, resigned in 1929 to become director of public relations for the Democratic party and was effective in bringing about the nomination and election of Franklin D. Roosevelt as president in 1932.

Walter Lippmann and Charles Merz, both formerly with the *New Republic*, joined the *World* in 1921. Merz went as a special correspondent to India and the Far East, but switched to become a staff correspondent in 1922–23 for *Collier's Weekly* and the *Century* magazine. Frank I. Cobb died in 1923, although only fifty-four. Honored in 1924 by a special posthumous Pulitzer Prize citation, he was followed as director of the editorial page by Lippmann. Merz then rejoined the *World*, working again with Lippmann on the editorial page until 1930, when he went to the *New York Times*, of which he became editor in 1938. Maxwell Anderson and Laurence Stallings, also editorial writers, later left the paper, having turned to playwriting. Frank Sullivan, successful as a feature writer and columnist, left the paper to write for the *New Yorker* magazine.

Changes occurred also in the *World*'s foreign representation. Tuohy, London bureau chief, became ill in 1922 and died in 1923. John L. Balderston became acting director and then director of the bureau. A former Philadelphia newsman, Balderston had been a wartime correspondent based in London for the McClure Newspaper Syndicate and also director in Great Britain and Ireland for the U.S. government Committee on Public Information. He remained in London after the war as editor of the *Outlook* and as a member from 1921 of the *World* bureau. In that capacity, he sometimes moved to the continent and as far as Egypt on stories. A novelist and playwright as well, he became widely known as the author of the play, "Berkeley Square," staged in London and New York in 1929 and later produced as a motion picture.

Arthur E. Mann, formerly of the *Chicago Tribune,* joined the *World* bureau in London in the 1920s. Carlisle MacDonald, with the paper during the war, and then with the *New York Herald* and the AP between 1919-23, briefly rejoined the *World* and then joined the *New York Times* before turning to work in corporate public relations. Cyril Brown followed wartime service for the paper by opening a bureau in Berlin, but in 1921 he rejoined the *New York Times,* which he had represented in London and Berlin in 1914-17. Dosch-Fleurot succeeded him in Berlin, covering Germany and Central Europe until the mid-1920s, when he became Paris bureau chief. He was made a member of the French Legion of Honor in 1929.

Alfred Murray was a member of the Paris bureau, Beatrice Baskerville reported from Rome, and Albin E. Johnson was resident correspondent in Geneva. Samuel Spewack represented the *World* in Moscow in 1922, and was in Italy in that same year to cover the Genoa Conference, which was concerned with relations between Soviet Russia, Germany, and France, and with world economic matters. Original *World* reports from the Far East were few, and nonexistent from the Middle East, Africa, and Latin America. Charles Merz was in India and the Far East for the paper in 1921, however, and George E. Sokolsky and Linton Wells both wrote as stringers in China.

William Bolitho Ryall, wounded while a member of South African forces during World War I, became Paris correspondent for the *Manchester Guardian.* Still writing in Paris, he switched his tri-weekly column on European affairs bearing his by-line, "William Bolitho," to the *New York World* in 1923. In 1928 he transferred to New York temporarily, but returned to Paris and wrote from there until his death at thirty in 1930, never fully recovered from his wartime wounds.

Bolitho gained a reputation as a brilliant analyst of public affairs and as a literary stylist. Walter Duranty of the *New York Times,* who had known him as a close friend in Paris, paid Bolitho special tribute in his book, *I Write As I Please* (1935). He credited Bolitho with teaching him "nearly all about the newspaper business that is worth knowing. I have never met anyone," he wrote, "who could see further through a brick wall than he could, or who was better, to use a newspaper phrase, at 'doping out the inside facts' of any situation." Editor of the *World,* Walter Lippmann, who had known Bolitho both in New York and Paris, supported this view. "In his presence," Lippmann said, "it was easy to believe that one had a private revelation of those great concerns which in prosaic living seem verbal and remote." Sharing space with Auguste Rodin's bronze and marble bust of Pulitzer, a memorial bust of Bolitho also was placed in the Graduate School of Journalism at Columbia University in 1921.

The *Evening World,* although commercially successful, undertook virtually no original coverage outside of New York City. One exception was in the work of Dutch-born Pierre Van Paassen, who contributed special articles from many parts of Europe and elsewhere. These were published in an editorial page column titled "World's Window."

Despite much excellent original news and editorial material published in the *New York World,* and despite a high sense of tradition and dedication on the part of most staff members, the paper faced growing problems through the 1920s. In contrast, the *St. Louis Post-Dispatch* was successfully operated after Pulitzer's death in 1911 by Joseph Pulitzer, Jr., with O. K. Bovard as managing editor. In St. Louis and Washington the staff included some of the nation's most respected newsmen. Among them were Charles G. Ross, Paul Y. Anderson, Marquis Childs, Raymond P. Brandt, and Irving Dilliard. Daniel R. Fitzpatrick was a political cartoonist. The paper gained four Pulitzer Prizes between 1926 and 1941 and recognition as one of the best in the country.

The *New York World,* however, lost ground both because Ralph and Herbert Pulitzer appeared to lack strong interest in the paper, and because of the special competitive situation then existing in the New York morning newspaper field. The result was the sale in 1931 of the morning and evening *World* to the Scripps-Howard Newspapers. Their suspension was regarded as doubly tragic coming at a time when the national economic depression meant sudden unemployment for hundreds of staff members of all departments.

Some of the *World* staff members remained with the Scripps-Howard *New York World-Telegram,* an afternoon paper. Lippmann joined the *New York Herald Tribune* as an editorial page columnist on public affairs. Arthur E. Mann in London also joined the *Herald Tribune.* Eugene Young, the foreign editor, went to the *New York*

Times. Dosch-Fleurot remained in Paris but transferred to INS and Universal Service. Linton Wells in China was another who joined INS and was assigned to Moscow. Albin E. Johnson remained in Geneva for a time, writing for the *Kansas City Star* and doing some special articles for the *New York Times.* Barrett and Adams turned to the radio field. Van Paassen became a roving correspondent for the *Toronto Star* and wrote a best-selling book of personal reminiscences, *Days of Our Years* (1939). Heywood Broun turned to politics, helped establish the American Newspaper Guild in 1933, and served as its president. He died in 1939.

Philadelphia Public Ledger–New York Evening Post

These two papers came under common ownership in 1922 and conducted a joint Washington and foreign news service available through syndication until 1933 as a Ledger-Post report.

The *Philadelphia Public Ledger* was established as a morning paper in 1836. It was owned from 1902 to 1913 by Adolph S. Ochs, publisher of the *New York Times* and the *Chattanooga Times* of Tennessee. In 1913, it was purchased by Cyrus H. K. Curtis of the Curtis Publishing Company in Philadelphia, already producing the successful and profitable *Saturday Evening Post,* the *Ladies Home Journal,* and the *Country Gentleman,* weekly and monthly magazines. In 1914 Curtis also established an *Evening Public Ledger.* Between 1918 and 1925 he bought the Philadelphia *Evening Telegraph,* and the morning papers, the *Philadelphia Press* and the *Philadelphia North American.* These he merged with the *Ledger* papers, morning and evening. In 1930, Curtis also bought the morning *Philadelphia Inquirer,* dating from 1829, following the death in 1929 of Colonel James Elverson, Jr., whose family had owned it since 1899. The *Inquirer* was continued as a separate newspaper. Other surviving daily newspapers in Philadelphia after this Curtis operation were the highly successful evening and Sunday *Bulletin,* established in 1847, the morning *Record,* dating from 1870, and the evening *News,* a tabloid established in 1925.

In 1922 Curtis also had purchased the *New York Evening Post,* dating from 1801 and one of the oldest surviving newspapers in the United States. Owned since 1881 by Henry Villard (1835–1900) and his son, Oswald Garrison Villard (1872–1949), it had been sold for $1 million in 1918 to Thomas W. Lamont of the J. P. Morgan Company, a Wall Street banking firm. Lamont had been a reporter for the *New York Tribune* in 1892–94. He had turned over the *Post's* operation to a syndicate including Edwin F. Gay, former dean of the Harvard Graduate School of Business Administration, as editor, Franklin D. Roosevelt, George W. Wickersham, and Owen D. Young. Curtis bought it from that syndicate in 1922 for $1.6 million, or more.

The *New York Evening Post,* mentioned earlier in this volume, had provided good coverage from Washington for many years. For foreign reports it had depended chiefly upon news agency service, but did undertake limited original coverage, purchased special articles, had staff members journeying abroad at times, used the services of a few stringers, and those of a few staff correspondents. At the time Curtis purchased the paper, César Saerchinger had been its correspondent in Berlin since 1919. Stoddard Dewey, long in Paris as a freelance writer and stringer for various newspapers, had served the *Post* there.

The *Public Ledger,* represented in Washington during the war years with Lincoln Colcord as bureau chief, had received the service of the *Times* of London, used reports from Dr. Emile Joseph Dillon of the *Daily Telegraph,* and published articles by leading writers and statesmen of several countries. Raymond Carroll went from the Washington bureau to France as a war correspondent in 1917–18 and remained to report the Peace Conference.

In the autumn of 1919 Curtis undertook to develop a Washington and foreign service for the *Ledger* that would be equal to the best and be made available to other newspapers through a Ledger syndicate, formed at that time. The paper also joined with the *Chicago Tribune* and the *New York Times* in those experiments for direct reception of news from Europe by wireless that were to result in the formation of Press Wireless, Inc. Frederic William Wile, correspondent in Europe since 1900 for the *Chicago Daily News,* the *Daily Mail,* and the *New York Times,* returned to the United States to become chief of the *Ledger* Washington bureau, which included Colcord, Carroll, and Robert Barry. He left the bureau in 1922 to conduct his own news service in the capital, to write a column for the *Washington Star,* and to become one of the early radio news commentators on national and foreign affairs. Barry replaced him as bureau chief.

Wythe Williams, in Europe for the *New York World* in 1910 and later for the *New York Times* and *Collier's Weekly,* and also writing for the *Times* and the *Daily Mail,* was engaged to organize a European service for the *Ledger,* with headquarters in Paris. Henry Craven became foreign editor in Philadelphia. News exchange arrangements were made with the *News Chronicle* of London and *Le Petit Parisien,* with Philippe Millet of its staff as a special writer.

Williams recruited a staff to report the news in Europe, many beginning work in Paris and reassigned from there. The members included Samuel Dashiell and Jacob Leary, both from the *Ledger* staff in Philadelphia; E. Percy Noël, who had served the *Chicago Daily News* during the war; Seymour Beach Conger, chief of the AP bureau in Berlin before the entrance of the United States into the war and returned there for the *Ledger;* Carl W. Ackerman, previously in Europe for the UP and the *New York Times* and assigned to London; Clarence K. Streit, a student at the Sorbonne in 1919 and at Oxford as a Rhodes scholar in 1920-21; and Dorothy Thompson, a graduate of Syracuse University who had entered upon study at the University of Vienna in 1919 and was attempting freelance writing. By 1921 the *Ledger* foreign staff totalled twenty-eight persons. It also included stringers George E. Sokolsky in China and Glenn Babb in Tokyo.

The Curtis purchase of the *New York Evening Post* in 1922 brought a joint operation with the *Ledger* in Washington. Saerchinger, in Berlin for the *Post,* moved in 1925 to the London bureau of what became a Ledger-Post service, even though the foreign personnel was almost entirely *Ledger* and the service was distributed through the Ledger Syndicate. Johannes Steele was named as foreign editor of the *Post.* John C. Martin, son-in-law of Curtis, took a part in the administration of the *Ledger* and *Post,* along with the *Evening Public Ledger* and the *Philadelphia Inquirer,* all sometimes then referred to as the Curtis-Martin Newspapers.

Staff changes occurred as the years passed, some even before the purchase of the *Post.* Ackerman left London in 1921 for corporate public relations with the General Motors Corporation, but in 1931 he became dean of the Columbia University Graduate School of Journalism. Sidney Thatcher, formerly of the AP, replaced him in London. Wile left the Washington bureau in 1922. Craven resigned as foreign editor in Philadelphia in 1926. In Europe, Streit went from the Paris bureau to represent the Ledger-Post service in Rome in 1921-23, in Istanbul in 1923-24, and in Paris again in 1924-25, when he joined the *New York Times* service, assigned first to Vienna and then to Geneva.

Raymond Swing joined the *Ledger* bureau in London in 1924. Swing's experience as a correspondent had started in Berlin as a representative of the *Chicago Daily News* in 1913-17. After wartime service in Washington with the War Labor Board, he returned to Berlin for the *New York Herald* in 1919-22, and then directed a new foreign service in London for the *Wall Street Journal* in 1922-24. With Thatcher's departure in 1926, he assumed direction of the Ledger-Post service, assisted by Morris Gilbert and Saerchinger until 1930. Saerchinger then became London and European manager for the Columbia Broadcasting System.

Conger, in Berlin for the *Ledger* since 1919, left in 1924 to join the Booth Newspapers of Michigan as an executive editor in Detroit. He was succeeded by Dorothy Thompson, who had been *Ledger* correspondent in Vienna since 1920. She was succeeded there by Marcel W. (Mike) Fodor, also of the *Manchester Guardian,* who had coached her when she began her assignment in Vienna.

During her time in Berlin from 1924 to 1928, Thompson became acquainted with Adolf Hitler and other members of the growing Nazi party. She made a journey to Soviet Russia, and earned a reputation for effective and substantive reporting. Sigrid Schultz was Berlin bureau chief for the *Chicago Tribune* at the same time. It was the only capital to have two women directing coverage for news services, and both were held in high esteem for their efforts.

A member of the Berlin bureau working with Conger and then with Thompson was Hubert Renfro ("Knick" or "Red") Knickerbocker. With earlier experience on newspapers in Newark, New Jersey, and in New York, including the *Evening Post,* Knickerbocker had gone to Munich in 1923 to study medicine. He acted as a stringer there for the United Press and had reported the beer hall putsch of November 1923, marking the beginning of the National Socialist movement and the appearance of Hitler as a political figure. This led to Knickerbocker's appointment as an assistant to Conger in Berlin, where he remained as an assistant to Dorothy Thompson in the Ledger-Post bureau until 1925. Knickerbocker then joined the INS staff and was in Moscow for two years, but returned to the Ledger-Post service in Berlin. In 1928 Dorothy Thompson married novelist Sinclair Lewis. They returned to the United States, where she continued her career as a writer and commentator on international affairs.[19]

Knickerbocker succeeded Dorothy Thompson in 1928 as Ledger-Post bureau chief in Berlin and as central European correspondent, with his mandate extending to the Soviet Union as well. His assistant in the bureau was Albion H. Ross, a Dartmouth graduate studying in Berlin, and who was later with the *New York Times.* Possessed of initiative and intelligence, Knickerbocker scored a number of successes. In 1929 he exposed an effort by Vladimir Orloff, former counselor of state in the Imperial Russian government, along with an associate, to sell counterfeit documents, some purporting to show that U.S. Senators William E. Borah and George W. Norris had accepted $100,000 from the Soviet government to gain their support for U.S. diplomatic recognition of the USSR, a recognition actually not accorded until 1933.

---

19 In 1934, Dorothy Thompson, upon revisiting Germany, was promptly expelled, having written and spoken unflatteringly of Hitler. In 1936 she was invited by Mrs. Helen Rogers Reid of the *New York Herald Tribune* to contribute a tri-weekly column for publication in that newspaper. Titled "On the Record," and dealing with international affairs, it was widely syndicated. In 1937 she and Lewis were separated and were divorced in 1942.

In 1930, Knickerbocker spent seven weeks in the Soviet Union, with an unusual opportunity to travel widely. Fluent in Russian, he obtained considerable information and after his return to Berlin he reported his findings in twenty-four articles written in the manner of the French *grand rapportage*. It was a comprehensive study of the first Russian five-year plan and a survey of economic conditions. Included was an interview with Stalin's mother at Tiflis, presenting personal information not previously known about the head of the Soviet government. Also published in New York as a book, *The Red Trade Menace* (1931), and in London as *The Soviet Five-Year Plan and Its Effect on World Trade,* the articles won Knickerbocker a Pulitzer Prize in 1931.

Knickerbocker made a comparable journey about Europe in 1931 to study the commercial relations of the Soviet Union with other countries, resulting both in articles and a second book, *Soviet Trade and World Depression* (1931). Further, in the winter of 1931-32 he prepared a study of the situation in Germany itself during "its hardest winter in 100 years." James E. Abbe, also known as a news reporter and photographer, traveled with him. Another series of twenty-four articles illustrated with Abbe's photos were widely syndicated and republished in a third book, *The German Crisis* (1932).

The Ledger-Post service was not limited to European coverage. Percival H. Winner, experienced as a correspondent for a variety of papers and services, joined the New York staff of the *Evening Post* in 1929 as an editorial writer on foreign topics. In the Far East, Sokolsky, a writer for the *Ledger* in 1929, continued for the combined Ledger-Post service, as well as for other papers. Frank H. Hedges, also serving other papers, had opened a Peking bureau for the *Ledger* in January 1922, but returned to his former base in Tokyo as Ledger-Post service correspondent there. Duke N. Parry, formerly with INS, took charge in Peking for a year, but returned to INS, with Hedges then resuming the Peking position. Glenn Babb covered Tokyo from 1920 to 1924, although on leave in 1922 and relieved by Benjamin G. Kline. In 1924 Babb joined the AP as bureau manager in Tokyo, while Demaree Bess, formerly of the *Minneapolis Tribune* and *Los Angeles Times,* then became Ledger-Post manager in the Far East, with headquarters in Tokyo until 1927, when he joined the United Press.

One of the most mobile members of the service and outlasting it was E. Percy Noël, one of the first appointees of Williams in the Paris bureau. Indeed, his experience extending over the years from World War I to World War II was not only extensive but as varied as that of any correspondent. For the Ledger-Post service, Noël went from Paris to Moscow in 1922-23, to London and Berlin, and to Tokyo in 1928-29. There he also wrote for the NEA and worked as a staff mem-

ber for the English-language edition of the *Mainichi* of Osaka. Back in
Paris in 1931, he was assigned to Geneva, but then left the service to
join the AP. His pilgrimage did not end there. In 1932–33 he was
writing from Paris for the *St. Louis Post-Dispatch,* in 1933–36 he was
Paris manager for the Columbia Broadcasting System, and in 1936–39
he was again in Japan as a columnist for the *Japan Times* and correspondent for the Paris afternoon paper *l'Intransigeant.* He returned to
Paris in 1939 and became correspondent for the Philadelphia *Evening
Public Ledger,* more or less bringing him full circle since joining the
morning *Public Ledger* in 1919.

The death of Cyrus Curtis in 1933 at eighty-three brought an almost
immediate reorganization of the Curtis-Martin newspapers and an end
to the Ledger-Post news service and of the Ledger Syndicate as well,
after about thirteen years of operation. The morning *Public Ledger*
ceased publication. It was merged into the *Philadelphia Inquirer,*
which Curtis had purchased in 1930. The *Evening Public Ledger* was
continued as a Curtis-Martin paper, but the *New York Evening Post*
was sold for less than $1 million to J. David Stern, already publisher
of the morning *Philadelphia Record* since 1928, and also of two dailies
in nearby Camden, New Jersey, the morning *Post* and the evening
Courier.

Staff members of the morning *Public Ledger* and of the Ledger-
Post service were confronted with much the same problem in the matter of employment in a continuing period of economic crisis that had
confronted members of the *New York World* newspapers two years
before. Some of the morning *Public Ledger* staff continued with the
evening *Public Ledger,* particularly in the Washington bureau of the
latter paper; some went to the *Philadelphia Inquirer* staff; and some
went to the *New York Evening Post* or to Stern's Camden papers.

Stern, simplifying the name of that paper in 1934 to make it merely
the *New York Post,* retained some members of the Ledger-Post foreign service in a limited *Post* service, with their reports used also in the
Philadelphia Record and in his Camden papers, but otherwise without
syndication. Johannes Steel continued as foreign editor in New York
until 1939, when he became a radio news commentator. George
Seldes, formerly of the *Chicago Tribune,* reported part of the Spanish
Civil War for what had become the Stern newspapers. Theodore O.
(Ted) Thackrey, formerly with the Scripps-Howard newspapers, but
in China since 1929 with the INS and as director of the Shanghai
Evening Post & Mercury, returned to the United States as editor of the
New York Post. In 1939, Stern sold the *New York Post* to George
Backer, a New York millionaire liberal active in the ownership of the
Jewish Telegraph Agency. In 1932 he had married Dorothy Schiff,

daughter of the late Mortimer L. Schiff, former partner in the New York banking firm of Kuhn, Loeb & Co. and a director in several major enterprises, including the Western Union Telegraph Company. Backer retired in 1942 because of illness. The Backers were divorced in 1943, and Mrs. Backer, taking over the paper as publisher, married Thackrey, then managing editor. He was her third husband.

Most correspondents in the Ledger-Post service moved to other assignments. Swing, in London, returned to the United States to represent the London *News-Chronicle* and to broadcast to the United Kingdom for the BBC, as he would continue to do until 1945. He soon began also a new career as a radio news commentator for the Mutual Broadcasting System. Knickerbocker in Berlin returned to the INS, which he had served there previously in 1925–28. Albion Ross, his assistant, joined the *New York Times* bureau in Berlin. Fodor in Vienna continued for the *Manchester Guardian,* but wrote also for the *Chicago Daily News.* Samuel Dashiell in Paris joined the United Press staff. Barry in Washington became a member of the Universal Service staff in Berlin. George Sokolsky in China had returned to the United States in 1932 with a new book, *The Tinder Box of Asia,* and remained as a writer of a syndicated column on foreign affairs.

When owner Colonel James Elverson, Jr., of the *Philadelphia Inquirer* since 1911 died in 1929 control of the paper passed to his daughter Eleanor, the widow of Jules Patenôtre, former French ambassador to the United States in 1891–93. She tried to conduct the paper for a time, but it was sold to Curtis in 1930 for a reputed $18 million. Even though the morning *Public Ledger* had been merged with it shortly after the death of Curtis in 1933, the 1930 sale was renegotiated in 1934, with the paper reverting to Patenôtre ownership.

An element in the renegotiation was the fact that Eleanor Patenôtre's son Raymond, born in the United States but grown to manhood in France, had become a publisher there. Although also a textile industrialist, a member of the Chamber of Deputies, and the holder of portfolios in several cabinets, he gained an interest in two newspapers in 1924 when he was forty. The funds received from the sale of the *Inquirer* in 1930 had been used to advance those other interests.

John C. Martin, Curtis' son-in-law, was prepared to reconsider the sale of the *Inquirer* for private reasons, and the ownership of the paper was returned to Eleanor Patenôtre. In 1936 she resold it for $13 million to Moses L. ("Moe") Annenberg. Formerly circulation director of the Hearst newspapers, Annenberg had been the owner since 1922 of the New York *Morning Telegraph,* a theater and racing paper, and of the *Daily Racing Form.* He was also the operator of a national leased wire service providing horserace results, and was the publisher of several popular magazines.[20]

With the second sale of the *Inquirer,* Raymond Patenôtre became the successful owner and publisher before 1940 of fifteen dailies in France. They included *Le Petit Journal, l'Oeuvre, Le Quotidien,* and *La République,* all of Paris; *Le Petit Niçoise* of Nice, *La Sarthe* of Le Mans, *Le Petit Var* of Toulon, and others, all making him a respected figure in journalism.

Other U.S. Newspaper Services

The number of daily newspapers in the United States supplementing news agency reports from Washington through special representation of their own in the capital increased greatly in the years between the wars. Some maintained staff correspondents and perhaps even a bureau. Others shared a correspondent with another newspaper. Still others received reports from stringers. With the addition of radio and magazine correspondents, photographers, some foreign correspondents, plus those writing for the Washington newspapers and serving the enlarged news agency bureaus, the journalistic population in Washington grew enormously. The National Press Club, as a center for all such persons, found it appropriate and possible to erect a large office building conveniently located at 13th and F Streets, with the club itself occupying the two top floors, while many of the correspondents and bureaus had office space on the floors below.

The cost of foreign coverage beyond that provided by the three U.S. agencies was such as to restrain most newspapers. Coverage on any major scale was restricted to those dailies to which reference has been made in the foregoing pages, and two of those services did not survive the period, that of the *New York World* and that of the Ledger-Post.

Several U.S. dailies, however, did maintain limited services. The New York evening *Sun* was one. Published after 1925 by William T. Dewart, who had been president of the Sun Company prior to Munsey's death, it received reports from a number of correspondents abroad, and also maintained a Washington bureau. It was represented in Paris by William Bird, formerly of the *New York Times* domestic

---

20   The *Philadelphia Inquirer,* under Moses L. Annenberg, advanced to a new high point in circulation. Along with his other enterprises in what became Triangle Publications, Inc., he prospered. In 1939, he was assessed $9.5 million in back taxes and interest due the Internal Revenue Service, and also sentenced to three years in prison. Paroled in 1942, he died in that same year. His business was carried on by his son, Walter H. Annenberg.

staff, but a Paris representative prior to 1933 for the Consolidated Press Association, which had distributed the *Sun* service to other newspapers. Joseph W. Grigg, long in London for the morning and evening *Sun* papers, was assisted in 1925–27 by his son, Joseph W. Grigg, Jr., who was later with the United Press. Frederick C. Oechsner was in Berlin for the *Sun* from 1929 to 1932, when he joined the UP. Whit Burnett, formerly of the Paris edition of the *New York Herald*, was in Vienna. Edgar P. Snow wrote from China from 1934 to 1937, while also serving other publications. Edward Hunter also was in China for the *Sun* until he joined INS in 1931. Newton Edgers was in Tokyo.

The *Baltimore Sun* was strongly represented in Washington and in 1924 established what was to become a limited, but high quality foreign service. M. Farmer Murphy, formerly in Europe for the *Chicago Tribune,* and Frederic Nelson were in London. S. Miles Bouton was in Berlin, where he formerly had represented both the Associated Press and the *New York Times,* and where he also wrote for the *Brooklyn Eagle.* He left Germany in 1934, after a warning as to his safety if he remained. Bouton later became an editorial writer for the *Jamestown Post* in New York. The *Brooklyn Eagle* had Guy C. Hickok in Paris during the war and for several years after. E. K. Titus was in Moscow for the paper briefly in 1922.

Marcel Wallenstein began a long career in London as a correspondent for the *Kansas City Star,* and Albin E. Johnson, in Geneva for the *New York World,* remained there for the *Star* for a time after the *World* suspended in 1931.

The *Wall Street Journal,* entering direct foreign coverage, had G. V. Ormsby and G. F. Nash writing from London. Raymond Swing directed a foreign service for the paper from that capital in 1922–24 until he joined the Ledger-Post service.

The *Detroit News* was represented in London in 1925 by Jay Hayden. Philip A. Adler went to Moscow in 1929, to the Far East in 1935–36, and to various parts of Europe in 1937 and again in 1939. British-born H. V. Wallace King in Berlin wrote also for the *News,* for the London *Daily Herald,* and for Central News. Cyril Arthur Player, a member of the staff of the *News* in the 1920s and early 1930s, wrote regularly of foreign subjects and traveled abroad occasionally. In 1934 he went to the staff of the *Wall Street Journal.*

Stoddard E. Dewey, dean of U.S. correspondents in Paris at the time of his death in 1933, had written from there for more than fifty years for various publications, including the *New York Evening Post* prior to its purchase by Curtis in 1922, the *New York Journal of Commerce,* and the *Washington Star.* Sterling Heilig also was a stringer in

Paris in the 1920s for U.S. papers. The two men, personal friends, kept afternoon "office hours" at the Café de la Paix.

The *Washington Star* acquired the services of Frederic William Wile in 1922, but he became a radio news commentator after 1930. Constantine Brown, London bureau chief for the *Chicago Daily News* in 1926–30 and then a writer for the McClure Newspaper Syndicate, became foreign editor of the *Star* in the mid-1930s, made some journeys abroad, and wrote regularly for the paper on international affairs.

The *Chicago Times,* established in 1929 as an afternoon tabloid, added to its coverage and early in 1939 named Irving B. Pflaum as foreign editor. Pflaum had gone to Europe in 1932 for the *Chicago Evening Post* shortly before that paper was suspended. He remained there for the United Press, covering part of the Spanish Civil War, and then working for a time in New York for Transradio Press.

Newspapers in France
And Other Countries 15

Some of the best daily papers in France continued to be published in   *France*
cities other than Paris. Staff representation outside the country, aside
from the Agence Havas, was exclusively for papers appearing in the
capital. These also were the papers to which foreign correspondents
and diplomatic personnel gave closest attention.

The nearest thing to a quality paper in Paris in the 1920–40 period
probably was *Le Temps,* a dull but respected and informative morning
daily. Its political articles came from such well-informed writers as
André Tardieu, a career journalist but also a member of various cabinets. The paper used the Havas reports in such a manner typographically that it required an experienced and patient reader to find and sift
the wheat from the chaff. *Le Temps* also had its own able correspondents writing from other capitals. Among them in the years between
the wars Robert L. Cru was in London, Paul Gentizon in Rome, Jean-
Emile Laya in Geneva, and René Lauret in Berlin, where he was president of the Foreign Press Association in 1937.

Robert Guillain wrote from Shanghai, and George Lucianni from
Moscow. Lucianni left Moscow in the early 1930s for a visit home to
Paris and was denied a re-entry visa. Indicative of the importance of
Le Temps, the French government itself responded by informing Moscow that unless Lucianni was permitted to return to Moscow all Soviet
correspondents in Paris would be expelled. The Soviet government re-
lented, and Lucianni returned.

The *Journal des Débats,* a second high-quality paper, had Paul Vil-
lars in London and Edouard Bauty in Geneva. Writing for *l'Echo de
Paris,* R. Lacoste was in London and Albert Huard in Berlin. André
Geraud, formerly in London, but writing in Paris under the name
"Pertinax," dealt informatively with foreign affairs in almost daily
articles, but moved late in the 1930s to the weekly, *l'Europe Nouvelle.*
For *l'Oeuvre,* a political paper dating from 1893 but acquired by Ray-

mond Patenôtre and put on a new course, the foreign editor in the late 1930s was Mme. Geneviève Tabouis. She was extremely well connected in France, and wrote interpretations of international subjects under the name of "Cassandra."

Le Matin and *Le Petit Parisien,* among nationally distributed Paris dailies, were circulation leaders until the mid-1920s. Both might have been classified as "popular" papers, with *Le Journal* as a third. For *Le Matin,* Jules Sauerwein was foreign editor prior to 1932 when he moved to *Paris Soir.* Sauerwein also wrote for the *New York Times.* He traveled about the world for *Le Matin* producing *grand rapportage* typical of the larger Paris journals of information. Edmond Streider was in Berlin for the paper, Edouard Sommer in Geneva, Leonce Levy in New York, and Richard Eaton in Moscow, where he also represented the *Daily Mail* in 1923–24.

Le Petit Parisien, leading in circulation among French papers through much of the period, also offered what was generally regarded as the best foreign report. The paper was served by Jean Massip in London, Camille Coutre in Berlin, Paul De Bochet in Geneva, and Théodor Vaucher in Rome, where he was president of the Foreign Press Association for two terms in 1937 and 1938. Pierre Denoyer and André Peron were in New York and Washington for the paper. Phillipe Millet of the Paris staff wrote effective reports on international subjects, and also provided special articles for the Ledger-Post service in the United States.

For *Le Journal,* a popular paper controlled by Agence Havas, and one of the more sensational, H. Claude-Drenon was in London, M. de Marsillac in Moscow, Georges Blum in Berlin, Robert Guyon and Jacques Gachet in Rome, Rony Roche in Geneva, and Bernard Musnik and Fernand J. J. Merckx in New York. Aspects of the Italo-Ethiopian War were reported for the paper by two women correspondents, Edith Marie de Bonneuil and Margareta de Harreros.

The afternoon *Paris Soir* made its small beginning in 1920 as a left-wing paper and was sold in 1930 to Jean Prouvost of a textile-manufacturing family, with Patenôtre also holding an interest. By the late 1930s it had gained the largest circulation in France, about two million, with a national readership. An information paper directed by Pierre Lazareff, and with Sauerwein added to its staff in 1932, *Paris Soir* was given added news substance by Count Raoul de Roussy de Sales as Washington correspondent until he joined the Havas staff there in 1937. Walter Bing was in Berlin and Jean Deveau in Rome for the paper, although both were expelled. Allou Cherie covered the Italo-Ethiopian War for the paper, and Louis Delaprée died of wounds received while covering the Spanish Civil War.

For *l'Intransigeant,* another afternoon paper of substantial circulation, also Prouvost-controlled and larger in advertising volume and size than most, M. J. Auffret was in London and John H. Simon in New York. E. Percy Noël wrote for the paper from Japan between 1936 and 1939. *Excelsior* was largely devoted to social life but received reports on the Spanish Civil War from Edmund Demaitre, a special correspondent. Equally unusual, *La Volonté,* although a political paper, had David G. Lewy as a Geneva representative, and *Le Petit Dauphinois* of Grenoble, a provincial daily, had correspondent Marius Berthet in Geneva. A Paris business daily, *Le Journée Industrielle,* also chose Geneva as a place suitable for coverage by Fernand Fournier. The Fournier family had operated the Agence Fournier as a Paris-based business and financial service since 1879. It had E. Changeat as a correspondent in London between the wars.[1]

Soviet Union

In the Soviet Union, restraints of the czarist regime had survived the revolution. They were manifested in controls exercised over the Communist press and information structure, and over foreign press representatives, barred until 1921. The press and radio of the Soviet Union were deliberately shaped to advance the program of the Communist party at home and abroad. The administration also sought to control what correspondents reported.

The Rosta news agency, formed after the revolution, sent its first correspondent abroad in 1922 to China. The agency was reorganized in 1925 as Tass, and included regional subsidiaries within the Soviet Union. It was directed from Moscow by Polish-born Joseph Doletzky, who had been managing director of Rosta from 1921, and later by Nikolai G. Palgunov. Constantine Umansky was foreign editor. Its representation abroad was relatively limited until after World War II, but it did have correspondents and bureaus in some major news centers.

Rosta formed a news exchange relationship with the United Press, and this was continued with Tass. Exchange arrangements with other agencies followed. For Tass, this was informational because no foreign reports were used directly in the Soviet Union, although some were referred to leaders of the government. Agencies and newspapers of other countries, by contrast, often credited Tass for reports ema-

---

1 See Kenneth E. Olson, *The History-Makers: The Press of Europe From Its Beginning Through 1965* (1966), for a major study of the European press.

366 Crisis and Conflict

nating from Russia, not infrequently on the basis of the broadcast of its reports by the official Radio Moscow station.

After the 1925 reorganization, the Tass representation in China was extended from its original base in Peking to include Canton, at a time when Moscow advisers were working with the Kuomintang, and then to Hankow, and later to Shanghai. Until 1927 the service had been made available for use without cost to any publication in China wishing to receive it. From that time, however, following the split within the Kuomintang the service was officially banned, but there was still some secret distribution. Vladimir Rogoff, Michael Yakshasnin, and S. Slepack were Tass correspondents in China at various times.

The Soviet newspapers, *Pravda,* which represented the Communist party Central Committee, and *Izvestia,* which represented the Politburo, both sent correspondents abroad. In London, Andrew Rothstein was an early representative of Rosta and *Pravda* and also went to Geneva. He was born in Britain of Russian parents and was a British citizen. From 1927 until after World War II he headed the Tass bureau in London, and also served at one period as president of the Foreign Press Association there. Other Tass representatives in London in those years included Leonid Bondarenko and Alexander Sverlov.

In Paris, Tass correspondents included Palgunov, later director of the agency, and Vladimir Romm, formerly in Tokyo, and later in Geneva and Washington. Boris Mikhailov was in Paris for *Pravda.* Vittorio Kin was in Rome for Tass. The USSR did not join the League of Nations until 1934, when three additional Soviet correspondents appeared in Geneva, one of them Miloye M. Sokitsch of *Pravda.*

In Berlin, Tass was represented by Andrei Smirnov, later Soviet envoy to Iran, by Julia Annenkowa, and by Andreas Rosinger, who was expelled by the Nazi government in 1933. Both Abram Gartman and Ilja Tschernjak of *Pravda* left Germany voluntarily at that time, but did so because they were under pressure from the Nazi government. In September 1933, Ivan Bespalow of Tass and Dr. Lili Keith of *Izvestia* were arrested in Leipzig and expelled. On that occasion, Moscow responded by withdrawing all remaining Soviet correspondents in Germany, and also ordered four German correspondents to leave Russia, among them Arthur Just of the *Kölnische Zeitung* and Karl Gerbing of the *Berliner Lokal-Anzeiger.*

Kenneth Durant, an American citizen, was head of the Rosta bureau in New York before 1925, and continued as director of the Tass bureau until his retirement in 1944. Eugene Lyons, also an American citizen, was Durant's chief assistant until assigned to Moscow as correspondent for the United Press in 1927-36. Stephen Naft and Harry Freeman, also U.S. citizens, were in the Tass bureau for many years.

Vladimir Romm, after experience in Tokyo, Paris, and Geneva, became Washington correspondent for Tass in 1934 and remained until 1937. In that year he was recalled to Moscow to face trial during the great purge of the period. Despite intervention on his behalf by colleagues of the Washington press crops, he was among the victims. Another was Doletzky, director of the Tass agency, who was arrested and attempted suicide. He was succeeded as head of the Tass service by Nikolai G. Palgunov, formerly in the Paris bureau, who continued until 1960. In Washington, following Romm's departure, the Tass bureau was headed until World War II by Laurence Todd, an American citizen.

Tass never was included in the Ring Combination, but after that combination ended in 1934 it formed news exchange arrangements to include not only the United Press, but Reuters, Havas, the Associated Press, and the new official DNB agency of Nazi Germany. Again, so far as Tass was concerned, this was for information only within the agency and Politburo.

Italy

The leading daily of Italy at the time of World War I was *Il Corriere della Sera* of Milan. It was represented by Dr. Salvatore Aponte in Paris, always a major news center for the Italian press. In the 1930s, Pietro Pupino-Carbonelli was in London, Dr. Christano Ridomi in Berlin, Alberto Bargelesi in Vienna, Guilio Caprin in Geneva, and Count Leone Fumasoni Biondi in New York.

La Stampa of Turin, rivalling the Milan paper in quality and circulation, also had its correspondents abroad. *La Tribuna* of Rome was represented in New York by A. Arib-Costa, who served as president of the Association of Foreign Correspondents in the United States, and who was made a life member of that organization.

Benito Mussolini, active as a journalist before World War I and founder of *Il Popolo d'Italia* as a Milan morning daily in 1914, returned to that paper following wartime service. He used its columns to rally support for a program intended to solve postwar economic and political problems in Italy, to gain greater recognition for the country's interests than had been accorded in the Paris Peace Conference settlements, and to advance his concepts for what became a National Fascist party.

At the Cannes Conference in January 1922, where the Allies acted to regulate international loans, Mussolini appeared as a correspondent for his paper, but even more as a leader of the new Fascist party formed in 1921. The Fascists gathering in Rome in October 1922 had enough strength to warrant King Victor Emmanuel inviting Mussolini to form a new cabinet.

With Mussolini heading the government, his newspaper *Il Popolo d'Italia* presumably had superior sources of information and spoke editorially with special knowledge and authority. Mussolini's brother, Arnaldo, directed the paper in Milan until his death in 1931, after which Vito Mussolini, a nephew, assumed that role. Carlo Camagna in London for the official Agenzia Stefani also represented *Il Popolo d'Italia* there. Enrico Massa and Aldo Gini were in Paris for the paper, with Antonio Pirazzoli present for *Il Popolo* and *Il Messaggero* of Rome.

Mussolini's paper never overtook *Il Corriere della Sera* in circulation or in general prestige. The Crespi brothers, who were textile manufacturers, owned that paper and had embraced fascism, but they did not interfere with its direction by Senator Luigi Albertino, who had edited it with distinction since 1908. The paper's independence nevertheless offended the Fascist leadership, which forced its suspension in November 1925. This was a pretext for Albertino's dismissal, despite his contract with the Crespis. Aldo Borelli, formerly of *La Nazione* of Florence, was appointed editor, along with an almost entirely new editorial staff. The paper then was permitted to resume. It retained national circulation leadership, even though a quality newspaper. *Il Corriere* stressed information rather than political ideology, and was permitted a greater freedom of expression than any other Italian paper.

From 1931, Luigi Barzini served the *Corriere* as London correspondent. His father, also Luigi Barzini, was the respected correspondent for the paper in China at the time of the Sino-Japanese War of 1894 and later. He was also in Europe reporting World War I. The younger Barzini was brought up in the United States and graduated from Columbia University in 1930. From that time until 1940, he represented *Il Corriere della Sera*. He reported the Italo-Ethiopian War in 1935–36. Sandro Sandri, of *La Stampa* in Turin, was with him during that war coverage, and both were together again in China in 1937 to report the second Sino-Japanese War. They were aboard the U.S. gunboat *Panay* on the Yangtze River near Nanking when it was fired upon and sunk by Japanese air action in December of that year. Sandri was killed in the attack and Barzini was wounded.

La Stampa, owned by the Fiat motor company, was a morning daily of quality. It also had suffered suspension in September 1925 and, as in Milan, had been permitted to resume only after its staff membership had been changed to make it more acceptable to the Fascist regime. In addition to Sandri, its correspondents included Emmanuel Ceria and Concetto Pettinato in Paris and Guido Tonella in Geneva.

Il Mattino of Naples, another leading paper, was required to make changes comparable to those forced upon *Il Corriere* and *La Stampa.* The practice was quite general throughout Italy after 1924. One of the papers giving early support to the Fascist cause, with no change required, was *Il Messaggero* of Rome. It was a popular daily viewed by some as a scandal sheet, edited and published from 1921-26 by Dr. Virginio Gayda. The paper was later represented in Paris by D. Russo and Antonio Pirazzoli, writing also for *Il Popolo,* and in London by Carlo Camagna, likewise writing for *Il Popolo* and for Stefani. Filipo Bojano represented the same three in Berlin.

In 1926, Gayda became editor in Rome of *Il Giornale d'Italia,* established in 1900 by Alberto Bergamini and conducted as a respected morning daily until he was forced to sell to a Fascist party member in 1922. When Gayda was editor, his office was shared with a great bronze effigy of Romulus and Remus, the legendary twin founders of Rome, and he made the paper a voice for Mussolini in matters of foreign policy. Achille Saitta represented the paper in Paris.

The Agenzia Stefani, long a subsidiary of the Agence Havas, was transformed into an official Italian agency reflecting the Fascist government policy conducted after 1924 by Manlio Morgagni, a wealthy Milan friend of Mussolini. Arturo Léone headed a Stefani bureau in Paris, G. Onnis was in Geneva, Camagna in London, and Bojano in Berlin, where he also was president of the Foreign Press Association.

The press in Germany experienced a drastic change in the decade following the war. The establishment of the National Socialist regime in 1933 signaled another sweeping reorganization affecting both the news agencies and the newspapers.

Between 1920 and 1933, the Verlag Ullstein, a Berlin publishing house dating from 1877, published four dailies, four weeklies, and a dozen specialized periodicals and directories, as well as books. The dailies included the *Vossische Zeitung,* founded in 1704 and often likened to the *Times* and the *New York Times* as a quality paper; the *Morgenpost,* the *B.Z. am Mittag (Bezett am Mittag* or *Berliner Zeitung am Mittag),* and the *Berliner Allgemeine Zeitung,* all of Berlin. These dailies were represented in London by Count Albrecht Montgelas, in Paris by Hermann Berg, in Rome by Mario Passarge, in Geneva by Georg Bernhard and Julius Becker, and by Wilhelm Schulze in New York and later in Tokyo. Hungarian-born Arthur Koestler was assistant chief editor and foreign editor of the *B.Z. am*

Mittag. He was then in Moscow for the papers in 1932–33 and in Paris until 1936, when he separated himself from Nazi journalism and switched to the London *News-Chronicle* to cover the Spanish Civil War and begin a new career.

Another Berlin publishing group headed by Hans Lackmann-Mosse published the highly regarded liberal daily, the *Berliner Tageblatt,* several other papers, reference books, and owned an advertising agency. The papers were represented by Walter Schindler in London, Egon Kaskeline and Paul Block in Paris, W. Ruppel in Geneva, Joachim Friedenthal and Herbert Kluge in Rome, and Paul Scheffer in Moscow. Dr. Max Jordan, U.S.-born but German-educated, was in New York for the paper until the early 1930s, when he went to Europe for INS and later moved into radio broadcasting with the NBC. Frau Vogel Sternberg was representative in Shanghai, where her husband represented the *Hamburger Fremdenblatt,* an important daily. Guenther Stein was a member of the staff in Berlin and also went to the Far East.

Two other dailies of special quality and prestige were the *Kölnische Zeitung* of Cologne and the *Frankfurter Zeitung* of Frankfurt-am-Main. The Cologne paper was represented in London through the pre-Nazi period by Dr. H. Roering, in Paris by Eugène Feihl and Walter-J. Frings, in Rome by Filippo Hiltebrandt, and in Moscow by Arthur Just. The Frankfurt paper was represented in London by Dr. F. Sieburg, Wolff von Dewal, and Rudolf Kircher, in Paris by D. Reifenberg, in Rome by Nikolas Benckiser, in Geneva by Eugène Tung, in Moscow by Hermann Poerzgen, and in New York by Dr. H. A. Mattefeldt. It also received some reports from China from Agnes Smedley, an American.

The *Deutsche Allgemeine Zeitung* of Berlin, among other significant papers, had Karl Silex in London, F. Silberstein in Paris, and Max Beer in Geneva. The *Berliner Lokal-Anzeiger* and the *Hamburger Nachrichten,* both owned by Alfred Hugenberg, among other Berlin and provincial papers, plus the Telegraphen-Union news agency and other properties, had correspondents in European capitals. The Hamburg paper had Dr. A. K. Abshagen in London. The *Lokal-Anzeiger* had Werner von Heimburg in Paris, Gustav Eberlein in Geneva, Karl Gerbing in Moscow, and Captain E. von Salzmann, Werner von Crome, and Franz Otto Wrede in London.

The *Berliner Börsen Kurier,* a business paper, was represented in London by George Popoff. Dr. Kurt Ihlefeld wrote from Paris for the *Hannoverscher Kurier* of Hanover and other papers. In Geneva, Gustav Herbert represented the *Deutsche Tageszeitung* of Berlin, and Carl Hillekamps served the *Münsterischer Anzeiger* of Munich. Alfred Dang also was in Geneva for the Sozialdemokratischer Presse-dienst, a service going to the Social Democratic party papers. Jost Görgen wrote from there for the Deutscher Zentrumsdienst, also a service for political party papers so long as they were permitted to exist prior to the Nazi assumption of power.

Changes came in 1933 when Communist and Socialist publications and services were promptly suppressed. As in Italy, owners of newspapers unrelated or unsympathetic to the ruling party were under pressure to dispose of their papers to party members, which meant in effect to the Eher Verlag publishing firm established by Max Amann for the National Socialist party publications. In Germany, Jewish-owned publications were immediate targets, and the Verlag Ullstein and the Mosse publishing firm were instantly affected. The *Vossische Zeitung,* an Ullstein publication, disappeared in spite of its prestige. The *Berliner Tageblatt,* a Mosse publication, was placed under the editorship of Paul Scheffer, who had been its Moscow correspondent and had earned a reputation as an authority on Soviet affairs. Denied a re-entry visa to the Soviet Union after an absence in 1929, he was reassigned to London for the paper. As editor of the *Tageblatt,* he was under such pressure to follow an official party line that he contrived to gain a reassignment as correspondent for the paper in New York. Guenther Stein left Germany and became a correspondent in China for the *Manchester Guardian* and the *News-Chronicle.* Koestler left the Ullstein-owned *B.Z. am Mittag* to cover the Spanish Civil War for the London *News-Chronicle.*

The Nazi government permitted some papers known for their liberalism to continue as showpieces. The *Frankfurter Zeitung,* for one, was taken over from its Jewish ownership and placed under the editorship of its former London correspondent, Rudolf Kircher. In the same fashion, the *Deutsche Allgemeine Zeitung* was placed under the editorship of its former Berlin correspondent, Karl Silex. Both men were friends and admirers of Great Britain and the British but, unlike Scheffer, they turned those other once-great papers to the propaganda service of the Nazi party and government.

Three correspondents for the *Berliner Lokal-Anzeiger,* remaining in London after 1933, were expelled by the British government in 1937 because of political activity unrelated to legitimate news work. They were von Salzmann, von Crome, and Wrede. The Nazis, in retaliation, expelled Norman Ebbutt, Berlin correspondent for the *Times.* Earlier in 1933, Gerbing of the *Lokal-Anzeiger* and Just of the *Frankfurter Zeitung* were expelled from Moscow in retaliation for the arrest of two Soviet correspondents in Germany.

Other changes that occurred in the German press following the Nazi assumption of power bear a relation to the crisis leading to the outbreak of war in Europe in 1939 and need not be reviewed here, other than to refer to the merger of the Wolff and Telegraphen Union news agencies in 1933 to form the official DNB agency.[2]

Holland and
Northern
Europe

The countries of northern Europe, whose people were literate and alert, had more strong and active newspapers in proportion to their size and population than most.

Language differences meant that those papers were little read beyond the boundaries of their own lands, but they often were quoted. They tended to be well made information papers, read throughout the relatively small countries of publication. Some were enterprising in their coverage of news abroad. There also were papers sponsored by political and religious groups.

In Holland, *De Telegraaf* of Amsterdam had Arnold Vas Dias variously in London, New York, and Washington in the years between the wars. G. J. M. Simons also was in New York, H. Van den Bergh was in Paris, and H. Van der Elst in Geneva. J. M. Goedemans was in Berlin until he was expelled in 1933. Dr. Johann Gerhard van Massdijk replaced him. The Amsterdam *Algemeen Handelsblad* had J. E. A. Reyneke Van Stuwe in London, Max Blokzijl and Bert Wessel in Berlin, M. C. M. Voorbeytel in Paris, and Mlle. L. Haakmann in Geneva.

The highly regarded *Nieuwe Rotterdamsche Courant* (NRC) of Rotterdam was represented in London by Dr. P. N. Van Eyck, in Berlin by H. J. Noordewier, in Paris by H. Van Loon, in Geneva by B. de Jong, and in New York by Mrs. Albert Boni. The *Rotterdamsch Nieuwsblad* had A. K. Van Riemsdijk in London, and *De Maasbode* was represented there by J. H. Boas.

The *Vaderland* of The Hague had W. F. A. Roell in Paris. The *Haagsche Courant* there was served in London by Dr. Freiherr de Marees van Swinderen, who also wrote for other Dutch papers. Henry-A. Th. Lesturgeon served it from Paris. Jan Houbolt in New York wrote for a group of papers in Holland.

In neighboring Belgium, the Agence Télégraphique Belge had Charles Bronne in Paris, largely to maintain news exchange arrangements with the Agence Havas, and René Gérard was in Geneva. Among Brussels newspapers, *Le Soir* had Albert G. de Gobart in

---

2   See, however, Robert W. Desmond, *The Press and World Affairs* (1937), pp. 236–43; and William L. Shirer, *The Rise and Fall of the Third Reich* (1960), pp. 244–48. See also chap. 17 below.

Paris, with Emile Fourvel as an assistant, and *l'Independence Belge* had Léo Vermassen in Berlin and Paul Prist in Paris. *L'Étoile Belge* had August Nadél in Paris, and *La Dernière Heure* had Maurice de Waleffe in Paris and Armando Zanetti in Geneva. The Flemish-language *Het Laatste Nieuws* had Karl A. Mayer in Paris.

The languages of the Nordic or Scandinavian countries of Denmark, Norway, Sweden, and Finland were sufficiently related to make possible a considerable exchange of news and some sharing of correspondents. For the press of Denmark, *Politiken* of Copenhagen had E. Christiansen in London, Ernest Goldschmidt, Andreas Vinding, and Sven Tillge Rasmusen in Paris, and Thorwalls Steinthal in Berlin, where he also represented the *Stockholms Tidningen*. The *Berlingske Tidende* of Copenhagen had E. Munck in London, Ole Winding in Paris, and Allen Jensen in New York. For the *Nationaltidende* of Copenhagen, Hendrick C. B. Bendz was in Berlin. He also represented the *Dagens Nyheter* of Stockholm. Oskar Jörgensen of *Social-Demokraten* of Copenhagen was another in Berlin. Ole Just represented the Danish Ritzaus bureau in Geneva.

For the press in Norway, three Oslo dailies were represented in other capitals. The *Morgenpost,* commonly considered the leading nationally distributed paper of the country, had Reider Oeksnevad in Paris. Doery Smith was in London for the *Aftenposten.* The *Norges Handels og Sjöfartstidende,* a business paper, had Axel Thorstad writing from Berlin, F. Wering from Paris, and M. Martinsen from London, where he also represented the *Nya Dagligt Allehanda* of Stockholm.

In Sweden, five newspapers in Stockholm and one in Gothenburg were represented abroad. The important *Dagens Nyheter* had Pers Federspiel in London, Nils Widstrand in Paris, and H. C. B. Bendz in Berlin. Bendz also wrote for the *Nationaltidende* of Copenhagen. The *Stockholms-Tidende* had S. Lönnberg in London, Gunnar de Ceder-schiöld and later Viscomte Nicolas de Rochefort in Paris, and Thorwalls Steinthal in Berlin. The latter also wrote for *Politiken* of Copenhagen.

The *Social-Demokraten* was represented by Paul Olberg in Berlin, where he also wrote for papers in Gothenburg and Helsingfors. *Svenska Dagbladet* had Eric Swenne and Dr. K. G. Bolander in London, and Nils Nillson and Karl Albert Damgren in Berlin. *Nya Dagligt Allehanda* had Victor Vinde in Paris and M. Martinson in London, where he also wrote for the *Norges Handels og Sjöfartstidende* of Oslo. *Aftonbladet* had Helge Hellroth in Paris.

The *Göteborgs Handels-och Sjöfartstidning* of Gothenburg, a business paper of high general quality, received reports from Gustaf Sjösteen in London, and Gustaf Adolph Nilsson in Berlin. Paul Olberg, in

Berlin for that paper, wrote also for *Social-Demokraten* of Stockholm, and for *Suomen Sosialdemokratti* of Helsingfors. Bertil Svahnström was in Berlin for the Tidningarnas Telegrambyrå (TT) agency. In Finland, the *Suomen Sosialdemokratti* was served in Berlin by Olberg and by Steinthal, both writing also for papers in Gothenburg, Copenhagen, and Stockholm. Two other Helsinki dailies were represented abroad, the *Helsingen Sanomat*, with Lüsi Karttunen in Rome, and *Ussi Suomi*, with Dr. Ada Norna in Berlin. Five of these Nordic correspondents were expelled from their posts in Berlin between 1933 and 1935.

Among newspapers of Poland, all in Warsaw, the *Kurjer Warszawski* had F. B. Czarnowski in London and Marie Mecinska in Berlin. The *Gazeta Warszawska* had Jerzy Drobnik in Berlin. Four papers had representation in Geneva, Georges Kweytmann for *Glos Porany,* M. Kahany for *Novy Dziennik*, A. Bregman for *Kurjer Porany,* and Felixs Chrzanowski for the *Courrier de Varsovie.* Chrzanowski also represented the Polska Agencja Telegraficzna (PAT). That agency also had Wenceslas Oryng in Geneva, Dr. Stefan Litauer in London, Paul Kleczkowski in Paris, Pietro Gorecki in Rome, Jan Ostrowski-Naumoff in Berlin, and Dr. A. Moravski-Nawench in New York, where he served a term as president of the Association of Foreign Press Correspondents in the United States.

Switzerland and Southern Europe

The *Neue Zürcher Zeitung* (NZZ) of Zurich, Switzerland, a serious quality daily, was one of very few newspapers of the smaller European countries to be widely circulated and read beyond its national frontiers. Published in German, it was represented at this time in Berlin by Josef Halperin, among others, by Eric Kessler in London, Max Muller and J. Gerszuny in Paris, and Robert J. Hodel in Rome, with stringers elsewhere.

Der Bund of Berne, was another quality daily. It was represented in Berlin by Dr. Emil Schultz, by Jean R. de Salis in Paris, Guenther Rheinhardt in New York, and others. A third German-language daily, the *Basler Nachrichten* of Basle, had Herman Boschenstein in Berlin until he was expelled in 1937, Hans Morf in Paris, and George Popoff in London, also writing there for the *Berliner Börsen Kurier* and for other papers.

For the French section of Switzerland, the *Gazette de Lausanne* had Maurice Muret and Gaston Riou in Paris. For the *Tribune de Genève,*

Marcel Rouff wrote from Paris, and Pierre Berhus for the *Journal de Genève*. William Martin, editor of the latter paper, wrote effectively on international subjects, and both Geneva papers rather naturally gave close attention to League of Nations affairs.

In Austria, the most respected daily of the country was the *Neue Freie Presse* of Vienna. It was represented in London by Dr. Maximilian Bach and in Paris by E. Janstein. Nicholas Basseches was in Moscow for several years but was expelled in 1937. The paper had Dr. Paul Goldmann in Berlin for many years prior to 1938. Assisted for some of the period by Dr. Edwin Kondor, Goldmann became dean of the foreign press corps. He died in Berlin in 1939.

The *Neues Wiener Journal* had E. Salzer in London, the *Arbeiter Zeitung* had J. Diner-Denes in Paris, and the *Wiener Tag* had Bruno Heilig in Berlin. Erwin Wassbaeck represented the official Austrian news agency, Amtliche Nachrichtenstelle, in Berlin from 1922 until 1935, when he was expelled in retaliation for the expulsion from Vienna of German press representatives there. With the seizure of Austria by Nazi forces in 1938, the entire Austrian press underwent changes comparable to those that had occurred in Germany itself since 1933, and foreign correspondents left by request.

In Czechoslovakia, the press was centered in Prague and scarcely active outside the country. The *Prager Presse,* however, had J. Stavik in Paris, and M. Kolarz in Berlin. Kolarz was expelled in 1936, the paper's second representative there to be so treated within a period of six months. The *Lodivé Noviny* had Dr. Rudolf Frucht in Berlin. The same fate that befell the Austrian press in 1938 overtook that of Czechoslovakia in 1938 and 1939.

In Hungary, the Iroda news agency had Nicolas Ajtay in Paris to handle its news exchange with the Agence Havas. Those Hungarian dailies with any representation beyond the country were all published in Budapest. The *Pester Lloyd* and *Pesti Tozsde* both were represented in London by T. A. Weber. George Popoff, writing from London for *Pesti Tozsde,* also wrote for papers in Berlin and Basle. For *Az Est,* Emeric Seidner was in Geneva and Ladislaus Ráskay was in Berlin. Ráskay also wrote for *Pesti Napló* and for *Magyaroszàg*. Dr. Dezsoe Vertesi was in Berlin for *Budapesti Hirlap*.

For Rumania, the Rador agency had Mlle. Rachel Chaies in Geneva. Pompiliu Paltanea wrote from Paris for the *Universul* of Bucharest. For Greece, Christos Kessary represented *Ethnos* of Athens in London.

Most world news reached the press of the Balkan countries through the Agence Havas, and the same was true for the press in Spain and Portugal. Several papers in the latter countries sought to supplement those reports through correspondents of their own, and the Fabra agency of Spain had José Aguirre in Paris to maintain its relationship with the Havas agency. All such efforts for the press of Spain, in particular, virtually ended with the civil war of 1936-39, and the Fabra agency came to an end in 1938.

Among Madrid dailies prior to 1936, *A.B.C.* received reports from A. Bolin in London, and from E. Uhthoff and Monte Cristo de la R. Escalera in Paris. For *La Nación*, J. Ugidos wrote from London. *La Epoca* had C. Botella in Paris. *El Débate* had A. Solache writing from Paris and Creta Daffina from Rome. *Ahora* had Eugeni Xammar in Berlin, who also wrote for *Publicitat* of Barcelona. Jean Aramburu was in Paris for *El Sol* and its afternoon edition, *Voz*, and also wrote for *Dia Grafica* of Barcelona. A weekly, *Crisol*, had Pedro Rossello in Geneva. *El Noticiero Sevillano* of Seville received reports from J. Royer-Deloche in Paris. Through the period of the 1936-39 civil war it was impossible for the Spanish press to proceed in any normal fashion.

In Portugal, the Lisbon press was represented in Paris. There Albert de Monsarez and Mme. Irène de Vasconcellos wrote for the *Diario de Lisboa,* P. Osorio served the *Diario de Noticias,* and Mme. de Almada-Negreiros represented the *Jornal do Comercio* and some other publications.

Middle East, Africa, and Asia

Few countries in these areas of the world had a press sufficiently advanced in the 1920-40 period to undertake direct news coverage beyond their own frontiers. Few had national news agencies of their own. Such world news as they received reached them through the Havas and Reuters agencies. The extension of radio and radio news broadcasting lagged behind other parts of the world. Where exceptions to these circumstances existed, as in Egypt, South Africa, India, and Australasia, they have been described in references to British Commonwealth countries.

Another exception was Japan, to which reference also has been made. There the press developed actively in the years between the wars, as did radio. As previously described, the Nippon Shimbun Rengo-sha (Rengo) agency was formed in 1925 in a merger of the earlier Kokusai Tsushin-sha and Toho agencies, with the even older Teikoku Tsushin-sha also absorbed in 1927. The Nippon Dempo Tsushin-sha (Dentsu) agency also operated from 1907 until 1936, at which time the Rengo and Dentsu agencies were merged by government edict to become an official agency, Domei Tsushin-sha (Domei).

Through the years, the agencies had exchange arrangements in some combination with Reuters, the AP, and the UP. Kokusai, Dentsu, and then Rengo and Domei all showed enterprise in original coverage at home and elsewhere. Inosuke Furuno, with Kokusai since its establishment in 1914, became Rengo correspondent in Peking after 1925, and became director of Domei in 1939. Chuzo Hagiwara represented the Domei agency in New York after 1936. Other representatives were in Washington, London, and Paris.

Japanese newspapers also reached out after 1920, beginning with coverage of the League of Nations and the Washington Naval Conference of 1921–22. The Osaka *Mainichi* sent M. Fusi to Moscow in 1921. Toshio Nagano wrote from Berlin for the *Mainichi* and also for *Nichi Nichi* of Tokyo. Those two papers were represented in Paris by Toshio Eito and in Rome by Schichiro Ono. The *Asahi* of Tokyo was represented in London by Y. Chiba, in Paris by R. Sighetokuo, in Berlin by Dr. M. Okanouye, and in Moscow by Maso Soma. Newspaper as well as news agency coverage was regularly maintained in Geneva and Washington.

In China and the British Crown Colony of Hong Kong, the Chinese vernacular press grew in the years between the wars. The Kuomintang or Nationalist party, in establishing a new government at Nanking in 1928, also established the official Chang Yang Sheh or Central News Agency (CNA). It introduced its own staff and stringer representation not only in China itself, but in Hong Kong, Tokyo, London, Paris, and New York. An official Kuomintang party daily, *Chung Yang Jih Pao* (Central Daily News) appeared in Nanking.

Earlier restrictions on the vernacular press in China were removed. In addition to such vernacular papers as had grown up in the shadow of the English-language press and some other European newspapers in the treaty ports, the 1930s produced more independent dailies. By that time, *Ta Kung Pao* of Tientsin was a successful quality paper circulating widely. It received reports from Mme. S. Rosen Hoa in Paris and from other writers abroad. *Shin Pao,* also of Tientsin, and *Shun Pao* and *Sin Wan Pao,* both of Shanghai, were successful vernacular papers. They received reports from Cheng Yin Fum and Daisy Leigh Wang in Paris, from Ernest K. Moy in New York, and from a few others.

News reports reaching newspapers in Hong Kong and the treaty ports of China, cities in southeast Asia, the Dutch East Indies, and the Philippines were provided by Reuters, Havas, UP, AP, INS, the Dutch ANP agency, the related ANETA service in Batavia (Aneta-Holland), and the ANTARA agency also at Batavia after 1937. None of the papers published in those areas had any resident staff correspondents abroad, but some received stringer reports. As with some of the papers in India, this would have been true for the *South China Morning Post* of Hong Kong, the *Shanghai Post & Mercury,* and the *Manila Bulletin.* Editors and staff members of such newspapers traveling abroad also wrote special dispatches or series of articles.

The press of the Middle East, including Egypt, depended upon Reuters and Havas for world news reports. A few papers arranged to receive supplementary news reports, usually from Paris. *Al Ahram* of Cairo received reports from Robert Vaucher in Paris, and B. Khalifa Boubli wrote from Paris for various Egyptian publications. *Al Akhbar* and *Al Gomhouria,* both important Cairo dailies, received reports.

For the developing Turkish press, Eddin Zya-Mattle wrote from Paris for the *Journal d'Orient,* a French-language daily of Istanbul, and I. Loufti reported from Paris for *Cumhuriyet,* also of Istanbul. The leading daily of Teheran, Iran, *Ettela'at,* received reports from Paris from A. Amani. Both Lebanon and Syria were under French mandates. Pierre Bustany wrote from Paris for *Lissan-Ul-Hal* of Beirut, and *Al Vatan* and *Al Oumran* of Damascus received reports respectively from Emile Bouery and Michel Nahas.

Latin
America

The press organization of Latin America remained greatly dependent for world news upon the Agence Havas, but it also received reports through the UP, AP, INS, and Reuters. A considerable number of newspapers in South and Central America also had their own staff or stringer representation in other capitals of the hemisphere and the world after 1920, and published reports by traveling staff members.

The two quality morning dailies of Buenos Aires, *La Prensa* and *La Nación,* the most prosperous and respected newspapers of Latin America, were especially enterprising. They received reports from their special representatives throughout Argentina, and also from writers elsewhere in the Western Hemisphere and in Europe. In the 1930s, *La Prensa* had R. Laenz Hayes in Paris as director of the paper's European service. Others in the Paris bureau included E. Villareal, Ventura Garcia Calderon, and Ramon da Franch. Harold Neill was in London, Felix Bagel in Berlin, and Romeo Roncini in New York. For *La Nación,* F. Ortiz Echagüe in Paris directed the paper's European service. Other Paris bureau members were Y.-E. Yndart, Ad. Frago Mitra, and M. Gabrieli. Patrick D. Murphy wrote from London. Honorio Roigt went to Geneva as the first permanent Latin

American correspondent at League of Nations headquarters. He later joined the Agence Havas to specialize on service from Geneva to the agency's Latin American clientele. William W. Davies was in New York also serving the Australian press, and Albert Caprile, Jr., was another representative in New York.

La Razon of Buenos Aires had V. Verdera, F. M. Salazar, Mme. L. Diaz, and N. R. da Souza in Paris and R. E. Ṁ. Casares in London. Seven other Argentine dailies also had representatives in Paris. Five were Buenos Aires papers: *El Mundo,* with A. de Ugarte, *El Diario,* with Carlos Del Carril, *La Calle,* with Robert Salabery-Cahen, *Crítica,* with José-G. Antune, and the English-language *Standard,* with J.-A. Mulhall and Marcos Sastre. Beyond that, *La Capital* of Rosario had C.-G. Sarti in Paris, and *Los Andes* of Mendoza had F.-J. Trianes.

The press of Brazil was equally represented in Europe, again with Paris as the major news center. The Diários Asociados, a group of more than twenty dailies, plus magazines and radio stations owned by Assis de Chateaubriand ("Chatto"), was well represented. Chateaubriand himself, in the 1920s, had conducted special interviews with leading European personalities. The key paper in the group was *O Jornal* of Rio de Janeiro, with the *Diario da Noite,* a São Paulo afternoon paper, as perhaps second in importance. From 1931, all of the papers were linked to form an exclusive domestic news agency, the Agencia Meridional. Nicolas Assi of the São Paulo paper was a resident correspondent in Paris, with his reports going to all in the group.

Other newspapers of Brazil with Paris representatives included six in Rio de Janeiro and four in São Paulo. Those in the capital were the *Correio da Manhã* represented by Paulo de Bittencourt, later a director of the paper, and Augusto Shaw; *O Paiz,* by G. Géville; the *Gazeta de Noticias,* by S. de SaValle; the *Gazette de Brésil,* by M.-P. Muscat d'Orsay, a director of the paper as well as of a South American information service; the *Jornal do Comercio,* by E. Montarroyos; and *O Globo,* by Olavo Freire. For the São Paulo papers, Freire also represented the important *Folha da Manhã,* André Lassalle, the *Jornal de São Paulo,* and J.-G. Drummond, *A Gazeta. O Estado de São Paulo,* the oldest, also was represented.

Three dailies in Chile had European representation. *La Nación* of Santiago had G. Biessy in residence in Paris, *La Union* of Santiago had W.-B. Morgan there, and *El Mercurio* of Santiago and Valparaiso, with afternoon papers in both cities, had H. Farini Fynn in Paris and Alva Valdosa in London.

For the press of Uruguay, and specifically of Montevideo, L.-S. Pierotti, Carlos Masanes, and H. D. Barbagaleta all wrote from Paris for *El Imparcial,* Pedro Nadal for *El Dia,* Mlle. Maillard for *La Mañana* and *El Diario.* Jorge Messer wrote for both of the latter papers from Berlin.

The press of Colombia had representatives in Paris, all writing for Bogotá papers. These were *El Tiempo,* with Dr. Enrique Santos and J. R. Vejarano as correspondents, and with Vejarano also writing for *Imparcial* of Madrid; *El Debate,* with A. de Romero Cubides; and *Mundo al Dia,* with P. de La Cruz. H. Perea wrote for four Bogotá papers, *El Tiempo, Diario Nacional, La Prensa,* and *El Relator.*

The Mexican press received reports from Paris by L. Lara Pardo representing *Excelsior* of Mexico City and four other papers, and from Manuel Ugarte, M.-S. Valencia, and Carlos Serraño writing for *El Universal* of Mexico City and other Latin American papers. A. Algar was in New York for *El Universal.* Enrique de Lasala provided a general service from Paris for Mexican and Latin American papers.

For the press of Cuba, E. Ramirez Avilez wrote from Paris for *El Pais* of Havana, and C.-D. de Battemberg wrote from there for the *Diario de La Marina,* also of Havana.

News Broadcasting, Magazines, and Photography   16

The 1920s and 1930s brought the advance of radio throughout the world as a medium of entertainment and information. At first a novelty, it developed rapidly both technically and in its contributions to a public awareness and understanding of current affairs at home and abroad. By the late 1930s, it rivalled the daily newspaper in the service of current information to many, used news agency reports as a basis for its reports, but also broadcast accounts and commentaries by many of its own correspondents.

Electrical communication had advanced in the previous century, with special contributions by scientists in France, Germany, Italy, Great Britain, the United States, and Canada. Radio was in that direct line of advance and continued to benefit by the extension of broadcasting to the high frequency (short wave) transmission bands. Linked to medium-wave stations for general broadcasts, and with the stations joined to form networks in the larger countries, the peoples of the world were able to hear history-in-the-making.[1]

The broadcasting of news was accomplished originally by reading brief news reports over the air, as taken directly from a newspaper and then from a news agency report. The next step was to assign a radio staff member to act as a reporter to provide a running account of a special event as it occurred. This account might be broadcast by one station or any number, forming a network. If not describing an event as it unfolded, the broadcaster might describe a situation or present an analysis of a circumstance of public concern. Those who were selected to read the news, to prepare the texts for reading, and to report or analyze events, were almost always experienced newsmen or women. Their voices became familiar to those who heard them on local stations in many countries. Where they were identified by name, those

---

1   See Desmond, *Windows on the World* (1980), ch. 18.

names also became familiar. In countries where stations were joined in networks, broadcasters so widely heard attained fame over a period of time.

For the British Broadcasting Corporation, Vernon Bartlett, formerly of the London *Times,* broadcast from Geneva from 1927 to 1933 and was heard also in the United States in later years. Raymond Gram Swing, formerly of the *Chicago Daily News* and other papers, spoke regularly from the United States in an "American Commentary" broadcast by the BBC. For the BBC, Arthur Ernest Baker, formerly of the *Times,* became overseas news editor. Percy J. Philip, Frederick Whyte, S. K. Ratcliffe, and other British newsmen in Europe broadcast the news, and Richard Dimbleby was heard from London and overseas points for the BBC in the 1930s.

For the three major U.S. radio networks, NBC, CBS, and MBS, broadcasts were made from New York or Washington, as well as from Europe and Asia by such veteran newsmen as Frederic William Wile, William Hard, and later by Floyd Gibbons, Lowell Thomas, H. V. Kaltenborn, and others. Edward R. Murrow, taking charge of the CBS bureau in London in 1937, made changes that placed William L. Shirer in Berlin, Eric Sevareid in Paris, and later added Charles L. Collingwood, Howard K. Smith, Walter Cronkite, Richard G. Hottelet, and others. Swing joined the MBS network as a news commentator before 1939, and so did several other newsmen.

The decade of the 1930s was bright with magazines in the United States, including four varieties that were novel if not wholly new, but all of which added substance to the available portrayal of world events. These varieties included the digest and pocket magazine, represented by *Reader's Digest* established as a monthly periodical in 1922 and published without advertising. There followed the weekly newsmagazine, with *Time* appearing in 1923 and gaining such success as to invite imitations in *Business Week* in 1929, *News-Week* (later *Newsweek*) in 1933, and the *United States News* in the same year. Third came the city magazine symbolized by the *New Yorker,* a weekly started in 1925, and lush monthlies, also rich in advertising, illustrated by *Fortune,* a product of Time, Inc., started in 1930, and *Esquire,* begun in 1933. The fourth variety was characterized by *Life,* an elaborate photo magazine started in 1936 as another publication of Time, Inc. It invited imitations by reason of its success, with *Look,* a product of the Cowles Publishing Co., Des Moines, started in 1937, as one of them.

The United States was not alone in responding to these trends in the 1930s. As radio was a matter of international interest and development, so was photography soon after, and imitation of successes in such matters, as well as in the field of the news magazines, was to be expected.[2] *Life* was imitated in England with *Picture Post* and in France with *Match,* and soon elsewhere.

The new stress on photography had been spurred by the postwar success of the *New York Daily News,* an illustrated tabloid, and by a parallel advance in public favor for the London *Daily Mirror* (1903) as well as newly established tabloids. Syndicates providing photos for all newspapers grew in numbers and size. Transmission of photos by airmail and then by electronic means made them available for use as promptly as the news itself.

As sound and color had come to motion pictures in the late 1920s and early 1930s, so photography was advanced by the general availability of flash bulbs replacing powder; color films supplementing black and white; and the introduction of the small 35-millimeter camera with a short focal-length lens permitting photography under adverse light conditions, which resulted in candid camera views. Having originated in Germany in the late 1920s, this new combination of camera-film-and-lens changed photography throughout the world within the next few years. It resulted in the development of elaborate photo departments attached to daily newspapers and magazines in many countries.

Although photographers had earned reputations in earlier times, many more became known after 1930 for their work. Among them were Dr. Erich Solomon, first to produce candid camera pictures, and Alfred Eisenstaedt, both of Germany, Hungarian-born André Friedmann (Robert Capa), and Levon West (Ivan Dmitri), Margaret Bourke-White, James Abbe, and Carl Mydans among U.S. photographers.

---

2 Desmond, *Windows on the World* (1980), chs. 19, 20.

The Ring Combination Abandoned 17

The first five news agencies to be established, all before 1860, were the Agence Havas in France (1835), the New York Associated Press in the United States (1848), the Wolff agency in what then was Prussia (1849), the Reuter service in England (1851), and the Stefani agency in Piedmont (1853) before the unification of Italy.

Wolff and Reuter began by providing commercial reports only to their clients. By 1860, however, all five were general news agencies, and their services were enriched by a mutual exchange. Between 1860 and 1870, a dozen agencies were formed in other countries. Telegraph and cable lines by then existed to facilitate the gathering and the distribution of reports over wide areas and at rates within the means of most daily papers.

Of approximately seventeen agencies existing in 1870, Havas, Wolff, and Reuter were particularly well established. In that year, Paul Julius Reuter promoted a formal arrangement with the other two whereby each might gather news wherever it wished; the three would exchange their reports, but each would have specified areas of the world where it might distribute that news or sell its service to national news agencies without competition from either of the others. No national agency then was sufficiently developed to match any one of the "big three" in gathering news beyond its own frontiers and thus benefited by receiving a service of world news.

This association was the beginning of a League of Allied Agencies (les Agences Alliées) variously titled but commonly referred to as the "Ring Combination." The member national agencies by contractual agreements or treaties, received a world report from some one of the big three. In return each made its own national report available to be exchanged and integrated into the world report distributed by each of the big three agencies. Because the national agency received a world report so far transcending the limited domestic report provided through its own efforts, it also made a differential payment to the world agency, while binding itself to refrain from distributing its own service beyond its own country.

In the years between 1870 and 1932 new agencies were formed in countries where none had existed. Some joined the combination; some were replaced or reorganized. Although periodic renewal of the contractual arrangements occurred, with some modifications, the essential agreement remained fundamentally unchanged. In 1930, when the Ring Combination was sixty years old, it included twenty-eight member agencies, the largest number ever in the group.

The considerable power of the big three was rarely challenged among the agencies in what sometimes was called a cartel controlling the presentation of world news. Reuters was dominant in the association because it had the largest staff representation for original coverage of world news, because its exclusive territory for news distribution included areas yielding especially important and interesting reports, because British-controlled communications facilities brought information to London in great volume, and because a strong subsidiary dealing in commercial news added a special value to its service and prosperity. Further, unlike Havas and Wolff and some of the national member agencies, Reuters was independent of government and its service therefore had greater credibility.

The first shadow to fall over the monopoly position of the big three as world agencies within the Ring Combination came in 1902–04 when the Associated Press (originally the New York Associated Press), introduced its own vigorous coverage of news in Europe and the Far East. It was the first national agency of the group to do so. At that time, however, its enterprise actually added strength to the Ring Combination because its reports also could be incorporated in the total world service through its association with Reuters.

What disturbed the Ring Combination more seriously arose from the refusal of the Agence Havas and of Reuters, as World War I began in 1914, to carry the German war communiqués. The Havas refusal proved especially important because its service went to South America, an exclusive territory, where the important Buenos Aires daily *La Nación* appearing in neutral Argentina found that refusal objectionable. It invited the Associated Press as an active agency in another neutral country to provide a supplementary service that would include the German and Austrian communiqués. As a member of the Ring Combination, however, the AP was obliged to decline.

La Nación then turned to the United Press for such a service. Still a young agency, but one that had demonstrated enterprise, the UP was independent of the Ring Combination and was able to respond affirmatively. Special UP reports were moving to *La Nación* by 1915, and soon to other Latin American dailies as well. Even though the AP was a cooperative, nonprofit agency, as contrasted to the UP, a commercial agency, its directors nevertheless were unhappy about being obliged to refuse the invitation from *La Nación*. They also saw the competitive UP gain a position of strength through its freedom to do what was denied to the AP. They were further disturbed to learn that the Havas agency was injecting an anti-U.S. bias into some of its reports to South America.

The AP sought a compromise agreement with the Agence Havas so that it might be able to share South America, as it already shared Central America and Canada under Ring Combination treaties. It was the summer of 1918, however, after the United States itself had entered the war, before a compromise was approved by Havas. The AP then joined the UP in introducing service to newspapers in South America.[1]

This move did not please Reuters, which had not been consulted in the matter. Further, by 1920 the AP had gained a postwar position strong enough in South America to be disturbing also to Havas.

Meanwhile, the United Press reports were going to the prestigious *La Prensa* of Buenos Aires and many other papers. The International News Service, equally free of Ring Combination ties, also was finding clients on the continent, and both agencies were by then moving likewise into Asia and Europe. The British United Press, although a Canadian corporation, had close relations with the UP and distributed its service in Canada, Australia, and later even in Great Britain. These developments bothered both Havas and Reuters, and also caused new dissatisfaction among the directors of the Associated Press.

The UP, INS, and BUP all found advantage in their independence of the Ring Combination. The official or semi-official character of the Havas and Wolff agencies and of most of the associated national agencies in the Ring Combination had become of concern to newspapers of some other countries receiving the world service provided through the group. The independent agencies were gaining clients as a result. Even where received as supplementary to a Ring Combination service, the reports of the independent agency often were used by preference.

It had been the practice, since the formation of the Ring Combination, for the directors of the associated agencies to meet at intervals of five or ten years to review the contracts or treaties and sometimes to make adjustments. From the end of World War I such meetings occurred more frequently. It was at such a gathering at Berne in June 1924 that questions were raised in private conversations, for perhaps the first time, as to the value of the exclusive territories provision in the contracts. A year later, a Conference of Telegraphic News Agencies sponsored by the League of Nations met in Rome, and the issues

---

1 For details of the negotiations see Desmond, *Windows on the World* (1980), ch. 13.

by then bothering a number of the Ring agencies were raised even more pointedly and in open discussion. By 1927 the topic tended to dominate a Ring Combination meeting at Warsaw, and also dominated a League-sponsored Conference of Press Experts meeting soon after at Geneva.

In April 1927 Kent Cooper, general manager of the AP, had persuaded his board of directors to approve a formal notice to Reuters, Havas, and Wolff that the Associated Press wished to terminate entirely the arrangement for reserved territories or spheres for the exclusive distribution of news. It was not terminated, but a compromise agreement was reached at the Geneva meeting in August whereby certain adjustments of those territories were to be made.

The Associated Press by that time was contributing as much as Reuters or any other agency to the exchange of world news through its own extended coverage. It ceased to pay any differential to Reuters, with the agencies making an even exchange of their reports. Effective in 1928, it also was agreed not only that the AP was to have a free hand to distribute its service in Canada and Mexico, as it had since 1893, but its right to share South America with Havas was given first official recognition by Reuters. The AP also was now to share Cuba and the West Indies with Reuters. In return for these concessions, Havas as well as Reuters gained the right to sell service in Canada, which had been exclusive to the AP since 1893, although shared with Reuters in the 1917–23 period.[2]

These modifications operative in the Western Hemisphere still did not meet the total problem. The independent UP and INS were finding new clients in the Far East, which had been exclusive territory for Reuters. The news agency reorganization of 1926 in Japan had transformed the Kokusai into the Rengo agency, patterned after the AP as a nonprofit, cooperative service. Rengo also absorbed the Teikoku agency in 1927. It sought the right in 1928 to make an independent contract to receive the AP service, in addition to that from Reuters, and further to distribute a world news service in China, part of the Reuters territory. Reuters rejected both proposals and proposed to increase its differential charge to Rengo from £6,000 to £10,000 a year (roughly, from $20,000 to $48,500). Rengo renewed its contract with

---

2 The AP had helped to bring the Canadian Press, Ltd., into existence in 1911 as a nonprofit, cooperative agency formed on the same basis as the AP itself, and receiving its world service through the AP. From 1917 to 1923, however, that agency also received the Reuters service, with the Canadian government providing a subsidy of $50,000 a year as a differential payment. This arrangement ended in 1923 when the Canadian Press, Ltd., was reorganized, known more simply as the Canadian Press (CP). Still owned by the newspapers of the country, but rejecting any further government subsidy, it was again receiving world news through the AP alone until the compromise of 1928.

Reuters for one year, but privately urged the AP to seek a general revision of agency relationships so that it could receive that service. The AP was prepared to make this effort.

Reuters, for reasons of its own, was hardly more satisfied than the Associated Press with the contracts as they existed in the 1928-30 period. It was keenly aware of the UP, BUP, INS competition in its territory, as well as in others. The development of radiotelegraphic news transmission, although largely of its own creation, reduced the value of British-controlled cables, previously so important in providing a flow of news and general information into London. Nor was Reuters any more pleased than Havas or the AP by 1930 and 1931 to note the degree to which certain Ring Combination agencies were lending themselves to growing propaganda efforts by their governments. This was so not only for Stefani in Italy, but for those in Germany, the Soviet Union, and Japan.

The outlook for the Ring Combination reached a crisis point in 1931. The Associated Press then repeated its 1927 move, which had been cancelled, and gave notice again of its intention to terminate in 1932 the contract with the big three so far as it related to reserved territories for news distribution. The AP also had announced its intention to establish overseas subsidiaries and did so in 1931. It formed in London the Associated Press of Great Britain, with a branch in Paris, and the Associated Press in Berlin. Both were photo services and handled no news. With the announced change of 1932, however, there was no assurance that these subsidiaries might not also introduce a distribution of news in all three countries.

A further potential threat to the concept of exclusive territories arose in 1931 as Havas introduced the distribution of its report through the system of multiple transmission. Reuters undertook to do the same in 1932, and Press Wireless was prepared to adopt the method, with economies in prospect. The ease of transmitting a service widely by this means made any control of its reception unrealistic.

With all of these circumstances in the background, a meeting occurred in London in February-March 1932, with Sir Roderick Jones as host to Kent Cooper of the Associated Press, Charles Houssaye of Havas, and Dr. Heinrich Mantler of Wolff-CNB. Their conversations resulted in another compromise. The big-four agencies, as they now were, would continue to exchange news. But each agency was to be free to serve clients in any part of the world, with no further concern for reserved territories. This, of course, would be a major change.

The first action following this agreement was the acceptance by the Associated Press of a request from Yukichi Iwanaga, director of the Rengo agency in Japan, for the provision of an AP world news report to that agency beginning July 1, 1933.

Despite the London agreement, this so irritated Sir Roderick Jones that he declined to permit continuation of the Reuters service to Rengo. On behalf of Reuters, he also notified the Associated Press, and Havas and Wolff as well, that the contracts providing for the exchange of news between the big four would be terminated, so far as Reuters was concerned, upon the date of their expiration, March 31, 1934.

It had not been the wish of Cooper or the Associated Press to end the news exchange with Reuters or the other agencies, but merely to end the exclusive territories provision for news distribution. What had become a breach in AP-Reuters relations by Sir Roderick's action was of concern to all agencies in the Ring Combination suddenly faced with a prospective interruption in the established flow of a full world news report.

In response to a letter from Cooper, H. C. Robbins, general manager of the Press Association, Ltd., which held the controlling stock interest in Reuters, indicated that he "deplored" the break, and his intervention, in the end, helped to heal the breach. Cooper also wrote to Houssaye proposing that the AP and Havas, at least, continue a news exchange. Houssaye agreed, but also added his voice to that of Robbins in seeking to prevail upon Sir Roderick to reconsider his position.

Meanwhile, the Wolff-CNB agency in Germany had been suddenly swallowed up early in 1933 in the new Nazi government official agency, the Deutsches Nachrichten Büro (DNB), which inherited Wolff's position in the Ring Combination. Otto Mejer, formerly head of the independent Telegraphen Union, was managing director of DNB. Succeeding Mantler, of Wolff's, Mejer added his persuasions to those of Robbins and Houssaye. The Canadian Press and Rengo also urged a reconciliation between Reuters and the Associated Press. The result was a visit by Sir Roderick Jones to New York early in 1934, where discussions proceeded with Cooper and with Frank B. Noyes, publisher of the *Washington Star* and president of the Associated Press.

In the interval between the time Sir Roderick Jones agreed to journey to New York and the time of his arrival, some concern arose in Cooper's mind that the Reuters agency director might be coming with the intent of bringing the United Press into the Ring Combination and of forcing out and replacing the AP. He was aware that the late Herbert de Reuter had discussed such a change in 1912 with Roy Howard, then heading the five-year-old UP, and that Howard had considered it seriously enough to make a special trip to London to meet with the Reuters board of directors. Howard had decided against an alliance with the British agency at that time, but Cooper could not be certain that a new proposal would be rejected.

Relations between Cooper and Howard had been cordial on the personal level, but Howard no longer headed the UP. Hugh Baillie was acting president of the agency in 1933–34, and became president in 1935. The UP had become far more competitive with the AP since 1912, and Baillie was known as an aggressive executive. Both Cooper and Baillie believed strongly in a free flow of news in the world. The UP had formed its own bilateral agreements with non-Ring agencies, and also was serving many AP papers in the United States. UP executives had indicated they considered the agency fortunate to be out of the Ring because of the limitations such membership would place upon its growing world distribution of news, and because of the official and semi-official character of some Ring agencies. But, again, Cooper was not certain this view would survive a new invitation from Sir Roderick, including the concessions already agreed upon at London in 1932.

To forestall the possibility of any such Reuters-UP relationship, Cooper proposed a contract between the AP and the UP, with the INS free to join if it wished. The agreement was that neither agency "would make a contract with any European agency to the exclusion of the other, or have relations with an agency which refused to serve them both." Such an agreement was signed on February 8, 1934, two days before Sir Roderick's arrival in New York.

As it happened, there was no need to use that contract to block any Reuters proposal to the UP. No such proposal was made. Even if it had been, it is doubtful that the UP would have been interested, despite Cooper's unease. When the AP-UP contract expired in 1939, the entire situation had changed and there was no occasion for its renewal.

The 1934 meeting in New York between Sir Roderick, Cooper, and Noyes actually led to a prompt agreement on February 12. It provided for continuation of a direct and even exchange of news between the Associated Press and the Reuter-Press Association combination. It also was agreed that the AP or Reuters could make an agreement with any other agency in any country, or provide service to individual newspapers or other possible clients in any country. The same advantages were extended to the Canadian Press.

The Agence Havas was not happy about these agreements. They meant that the AP, at least, would have no objection to Reuters joining in the distribution of news in South America. This it would have been entitled to do, in any case, since the concept of exclusive territories had been ruled out at the London meeting of March 1932, at which Havas was represented. The Havas agency carried considerable weight with some of the European agencies, and might have tried to enlist their opposition to the bilateral AP-Reuters agreement. It did not undertake to do so, however. Neither did the new DNB agency, inheriting the Wolff position in the Ring Combination, advance any sort of opposition. The New York agreement therefore was ratified soon after at a meeting of Ring agency directors at Riga. It was the last such meeting.

Even the Riga ratification was academic because the four-party contracts of 1932 between Reuters, Havas, Wolff, and the Associated Press, the four world agencies and the core of the Ring Combination, were due to lapse on March 31, 1934. As of April 1 that year, the Ring Combination came to an official end after sixty-four years.

The effectiveness of the Ring Combination had been under erosion since the period of World War I. The growth after 1920 of the UP, INS, and BUP as independent competitive world agencies was a major factor. The injection of official propaganda into some services after 1930 was another, and the ultra-official character and policy of the German DNB agency in itself would have made the end inevitable. The introduction of multiple-address transmission by Havas in 1931 and Reuters in 1932 also made exclusive territories potentially unrealistic.

The end of the Ring Combination was followed immediately by the conclusion of a series of bilateral treaties between agencies to provide for a continuing exchange of world news. In anticipation of that end, the Stefani agency of Italy signed bilateral contracts in January 1934 with Havas, Reuters, and the Associated Press. In February a bilateral agreement was signed between Reuters and the AP. Cooper of the AP went to Paris and Berlin soon after and negotiated contracts with Havas and the DNB. Proceeding to Moscow, he conferred with Jacob G. Doletzky, then managing director of Tass, and by November Tass had signed bilateral contracts with AP, Reuters, and Havas.

Foreign-originated news reports were not published within the USSR, however, nor within Nazi Germany. The AP, Reuters, and Havas services, as received by Tass and DNB, therefore were for information only, and for the attention of top officials in the governments of those countries. The same became true in Fascist Italy after 1935, in Japan after 1936, and in Spain after 1939.

Apart from the barriers to international exchange of news erected by the totalitarian governments, the press and peoples of other countries had a wider choice of news services after 1934 than they had had earlier. Not only was the AP service made available in Japan and the United Kingdom and elsewhere, so enabling that agency to overtake the UP, INS, and BUP, but the Reuters and Havas services were made available in the United States and Canada. The official and propagandistic qualities of the DNB and Tass reports limited their acceptance and use. Other national agencies lacked world coverage and therefore were not competitive.

The entire relationship between world and national agencies was complicated after 1934, however, by the mounting tensions of the period. The technical advances in communications were misused in campaigns designed to advance the interests and purposes of authoritarian and military regimes in Europe, Asia, and Latin America. Large and small news agencies in Italy, Germany, and Japan were made instruments of aggression. News agencies in Great Britain, France, and the United States, while laboring to maintain services clear of propaganda, were under official pressure to counter the propaganda of the other agencies. This left many agencies in smaller countries with an awareness of vulnerability soon to be proved very real.

PART III
The End of an Era

Toward the Abyss: The 1930s 18

Hope persisted through the 1920s that peace and order might be assured in a world recovering from war. Some events of that decade were constructive, among them positive actions taken through the League of Nations. But some other events were disheartening, including the trend toward authoritarianism in government and the accompanying restraint affecting the media of information.

By 1929, two major problems appeared to be approaching solution. Serious economic dislocations that had existed in some countries had eased, or gave promise of easing. This was true in Germany and, significantly, bore upon the second major problem: that country's ability to meet the reparations payments called for under the terms of peace set in 1919. Already modified through provisions of the Dawes Plan in 1924, further modifications of those terms were specified by the Young Plan agreements reached in the summer of 1929, and Germany was expected to have no further difficulties in making the payments. Beyond that, world trade, industry, and travel were advancing. Arms reduction agreements had been reached, and a world disarmament conference was in prospect. The general outlook seemed favorable, at last.

Unfortunately, this proved to be a mirage. What had been a political tinder box in 1914, with a shot fired at Sarajevo setting the world aflame, became an economic tinder box exploding in October 1929 on the New York stock market. Events from that time were to draw the peoples of most countries toward an abyss in whose depths nearly all were to become engulfed by 1941. Gunfire began in 1931 and from that time until 1945 a second Great War proceeded, more than twice as long as the first and more disastrous.

It is beyond the scope of this volume to tell the story of World War II and its coverage. But because the media and the news personnel of the 1920s and 1930s have been introduced, and were directly involved in that sequence of events, the circumstances must be examined here in a kind of overview.

The place to begin this aspect of the story is in the United States. After a recession following the 1914–18 war, the U.S. economy began to revive in 1922 and, until 1929, the nation enjoyed a period of prosperity. There were problems, but commerce and industry grew, led by automotive and textile production, petroleum and rubber, chemicals, electrical equipment, construction, and a strong market for consumer goods, including imports. There was also an active tourist business. Operating under a Federal Reserve System established in 1913, U.S. banks and investment trusts offered loans at low interest rates. Some economists spoke of a new era in which those cyclical downturns and panics of earlier times were no longer to be feared. Gains in stock market quotations and in real estate values induced thousands of persons to seek profit in both of those areas of investment, often buying stocks on margin and buying properties heavily mortgaged.

A downturn came at the end of 1926 with the collapse of a spectacular land boom in Florida,[1] scarcely noted elsewhere in the country. The eyes of others were on the New York stock and bond market. The quotations on almost anything bought seemed to rise, and speculators bought more, counting their "paper profits" even as they held on for further gains.

What few recognized or understood was that the quotations bore no relation to the value of the stocks based on earnings, or that the economy had gone far into debt through mortgaging of properties and installment-buying, or that bank loans were over extended. They ignored the fact that weak currencies in France and other countries, and lagging economies, might be reflected in the United States. In the end, they failed to notice that bumper crops in Europe in 1929 had created surpluses that depressed the agricultural market and reduced farm income in the United States.

Economic Disaster

An awakening from this dream world came suddenly on October 23, 1929, with a sharp drop in New York stock market prices. The following day, "Black Thursday," brought a further decline, with thirteen million shares changing hands, a vast number at that time. Sixteen million shares were sold in the Tuesday following. Those who had

---

1 Despite fantastic prices as sandy bits of ground were sold and resold, the term "boom" was specifically barred from use in such Florida newspapers as the *Miami Herald,* for example, fat with advertisements for property in what was presented as a sound development in a new Utopia.

been buying stocks on margin, or partial payment, were immediately affected, and many were forced to sell at a great loss. Reassurances even from some persons considered most knowledgeable and reliable in the financial world proved meaningless. Recovery did not come. Within a month, $30 billion in the previous market value of listed stocks was lost, and the Great Depression began in the United States. By mid-1932 the market loss stood at $75 billion. The low point came in March 1933. It was not just those who had been playing the market as speculators who suffered. Industry was operating at less than half capacity. Hundreds of businesses had failed. Numberless mortgages had been foreclosed on homes and farms. One-third of all banks in the country were closed, with savings and deposits lost. In a population of 123 million, fifteen million were unemployed, with many homeless and rootless.[2]

The New York market crash of 1929 was felt almost immediately in other parts of the world. Foreign investors in U.S. securities sold out at whatever prices they could get. Foreign funds in New York banks were recalled. U.S. funds abroad also were recalled. U.S. travel and purchases abroad dropped sharply, with losses seriously felt in many countries.

Most immediately significant in Europe was the virtual halt by U.S. institutions, banks, and private investors in the purchase of German government bonds, and there was some effort to dispose of such bonds already held. The purchase of these bonds, secured by a mortgage on the German state railways, had been the key element in enabling Germany to meet reparations payments under the terms of the 1924 Dawes Plan. The expectation had been that such purchases would continue under the provisions of the recently concluded Young Plan.

With bond purchases suddenly interrupted, Germany clearly would be unable to make reparations payments. This made the Young Plan potentially ineffective. France nevertheless insisted that an unconditional 660 million Reichsmarks ($157 million), a minimum specified under the Young Plan, be remitted through the new Bank for International Settlements at Basle, even though an agreement also existed providing that such a minimum payment might be returned to Germany as a loan, if necessary to support that nation's economy.

The situation was further complicated by the fact that reparations payments were linked for certain European nations to the repayment of funds lent to them as Allied governments by the United States dur-

---

2 For a concise summary and analysis of the "1929 Crash and the Great Depression," see Samuel Eliot Morison, *The Oxford History of the American People* (1965), pp. 940–47.

ing and just after the war. Those loans were estimated in February 1922 at something over $11.5 billion, bore a low interest rate, and were payable over a sixty-two-year period.

The United States was ineligible to receive any reparations payments because the Senate had refused to ratify the Treaty of Versailles. The government in Washington had consistently stated there was no relationship between the reparations received by other nations and the debts they owed to the United States. France, however, insisted in 1930 that if it was not to receive reparations payments from Germany, neither would it make any debt payments to the United States nor to Great Britain, from which it also had received loans.

Great Britain had made war loans of about $10 billion before the United States entered the war, and in 1918 had proposed a mutual cancellation of all debts between the Allies. France then was agreeable, but President Wilson had rejected the proposal for the United States, to which Great Britain then owed more than $4.2 billion, and France more than $3.4 billion. In 1922, Lord Balfour, on behalf of the British government, proposed that all claims for war debts and reparations together be cancelled and a general settlement made to end what he called "the economic injury inflicted on the world by the present state of things." France by that time did not wish to compromise on German reparations payments, and the United States held to its position on the debts. The matter figured once again in discussions leading to the drafting of the Dawes Plan in 1924, but with no change.[3]

As the issue arose for a fourth time in 1930, it caused sharp anti-U.S. feeling in France, with Uncle Sam depicted prominently as "Uncle Shylock." By 1931 the reparations-war debts impasse had become such that in June President Hoover proposed a one-year moratorium on payments both of debts and of reparations. Since there seemed no alternative, this was accepted by all nations involved. Before that moratorium year had passed, other problems had arisen and no further German reparations payments ever were made, and only a small proportion of the war debts.[4]

In the fateful sequence of international events, the next major crisis arose in Vienna in March 1931. Austria had been in almost unceasing difficulties since its establishment as an independent republic in 1919. Some improvement had come by 1929, but the Wall Street crash had been felt there in a prompt downturn of trade and travel. This brought

---

3   President Coolidge's observation that "They hired the money, didn't they?" was ill-received abroad and precluded any change.

4   Finland, with a debt of $8.2 million to the United States incurred after the war, was the only country to make full payment.

a fresh proposal for an Austro-German customs union or *Anschluss* such as had been rejected before, but the idea now was advanced by both countries on March 21, 1931. The usual objections followed but the concept was not abandoned. As a means to force an end to the idea, France withdrew substantial funds standing to its account in the Kreditanstaldt of Vienna, the central bank of Austria. The result was that despite efforts by the Bank of England, the Bank for International Settlements at Basle, and other financial institutions, the Kreditanstaldt failed and closed its doors on May 11, 1931.

A panic was caused in other countries, especially Germany, where a third crisis arose in the sequence leading to disaster. The Darmstäder und Nationalbank of Darmstadt failed in July 1931. The bank had branches in 120 cities of Germany, owned 143 buildings, and was represented in the management of more than a thousand companies, including some of the most important. Its failure therefore had far-reaching results. All banks in Germany were closed for two days to avert complete financial chaos. Banks in the United States and other countries recalled their short-term loans in German banks, making the situation that much more difficult.

The repercussions were felt throughout the world by banks, corporations, and governments concerned both by prospects of bankruptcy and of public uprisings. President Hoover's June proposal for a year's moratorium on all intergovernmental debts and reparations payments was accepted. A formal Austro-German renunciation of the proposed *Anschluss* was made, intended to ease tensions further. A six months' extension of foreign credits to Germany was granted to help the situation there.

None of these actions reversed the economic trend. The U.S. crisis and depression was rapidly becoming a world depression, largely because of a shrinkage of trade. A collapse of coffee prices disruptive of Brazil's economy brought a revolt there in October 1930. Stresses in, the sugar market produced another revolt in Cuba. A *coup d'état* in Argentina was followed by others in Latin America. There were trade declines and rising tensions in Czechoslovakia and other European countries.

Great Britain, a world financial and banking center for at least a century, with the pound sterling a basis for exchange, was forced off the gold standard in September 1931. Japan also abandoned that standard in December, and the United States followed in April 1933. In Germany by early 1932 six million were unemployed in a population of about sixty-four million, a currency crisis continued, there were food shortages, public discontent was deep, and fears existed of a Communist takeover.

The effects of the Wall Street crash were felt in Japan as early as in Germany, though for different reasons. The country had not fully recovered from the 1923 earthquake disasters. Industrial recovery had proceeded, however, and the merchant marine had grown. The state of the postwar European economy was such that Japan's markets there were limited. The market in the United States after 1922 was far better, especially for silk, and also in parts of Latin America, but both began to shrink in 1930. A great potential market existed near at hand in China. But the advances of the Kuomintang and the establishment of a Nationalist government at Nanking in 1928, with a program of unification and development in progress, caused concern in Japan lest its trading position there be adversely affected by the creation of a competitive domestic industrial economy. To forestall any such thing and to block the military forces of the Chinese Nationalists from reaching Peking and also entering Manchuria, Japanese troops already had been moved into Shantung province in 1927. Because of British objection and also because the occupation had brought a serious Chinese boycott of Japanese-manufactured goods, the troops were withdrawn in 1929 following a face-saving tariff agreement with the Nanking government.

The timing was such at this period, however, that Japan soon found its trade declining in the United States and in other parts of the world, resulting in an alarming rise in unemployment in Japan. The nation's population then was approaching ninety million, nearly three times what it had been as the Meiji period began in 1868, and it was growing at a million a year. Space and revenue were required to maintain a nation of that size. Korea had been annexed in 1910, and interests had been established in Manchuria since the Russo-Japanese War of 1904–05. These were regarded in Tokyo as areas open to emigration and settlement by Japanese, as sources of raw materials, and as markets for goods.

Although a part of greater China, Manchuria had been a kind of Japanese protectorate since 1905. The South Manchurian Railway was Japanese-owned, and ownership of the Chinese Eastern Railway was shared, first with the czarist government of Russia and then with the Soviet government. Under the weak Manchu Empire prior to 1912 and under the equally weak Chinese republic existing from that time, Japan's control of these Manchurian interests had been possible. Many Japanese were engaged in agriculture and business enterprises there. This situation involved Japan in an uneasy relationship with the Chinese warlord, Chang Tso-lin, nominally ruling the northern provinces constituting Manchuria. He also had become the major figure in a triumverate heading the Chinese Republic at Peking. It was not without significance that Chang was killed, undoubtedly assassinated, when his private railway car was bombed near Mukden in 1928. The Japanese were believed to have been responsible because he had opposed certain proposals favored by Tokyo.

Chang Hseuh-liang, known as the young marshal, succeeded his father as military governor of Manchuria, but instead of supporting the Republic, he was in accord with Generalissimo Chiang Kai-shek, president since 1928 of the Nationalist government at Nanking, contesting for total control of the country. Marshal Chang joined formally with the Nationalists in what proved an unsuccessful 1929 military action to gain control of the Chinese Eastern Railway, involving an affray with Soviet troops. With Chiang Kai-shek he discussed a campaign to force the Japanese out of the lower areas of Manchuria, but both felt they lacked the power to do so at the time.

Since 1920 in Japan there had been a strong movement under the monarchy toward the establishment of democratic practices. Some Japanese believed that this trend needed to be curbed to allow for an expansion of the economy in Manchuria through military action. While the assassination of Chang Tso-Lin was perhaps an unofficial move by extremists in this direction, the government did support a larger plan backed by industrial leaders and the army to oppose the 1929 Chinese Nationalist interest in Manchuria. Yuko Hamaguchi became prime minister in July 1929, but was viewed by the independent extremists as standing in the way of the expansionist program and was assassinated in Tokyo in November 1930. Reijiro Wakatsuki, the new prime minister, was in fear of this growing exercise of power by the army element in particular and permitted them to assume virtual control of policy so long as he was in office.

During the summer of 1931 two incidents inflamed the situation. Chinese landlords in Kirin province in Manchuria became engaged in a controversy in June with Korean immigrants seeking to settle there with Japanese support. Serious anti-Chinese riots followed in Korea at Seoul and elsewhere. Chinese patriotic societies in Shanghai and other cities responded by charging that Japanese authorities had fostered those demonstrations, and a new boycott was instituted against Japanese goods in China.

The second incident followed closely when Chinese troops in Manchuria on June 27 arrested and executed Major Nakamura, a Japanese officer travelling there. The Japanese government protested and also charged that the Chinese first sought to deny responsibility in the matter, and then failed to keep a promise to find and deal with those who might have been responsible for the execution. An effort in Japan to withhold news of the Nakamura execution failed, public emotions rose, and the army leaders had further ammunition for pressing a demand at home for vigorous action against China and in Manchuria itself. On the night of September 18–19, 1931, according to the Japanese army, Chinese troops near Mukden attempted to destroy the tracks of the Japanese-owned South Manchurian Railway, and had in fact blown out a section. Japanese troops protecting the right-of-way responded by attacking the Chinese garrison at Mukden and took control of the city of 250,000. Then the Japanese forces moved northward to seize other cities, and by the end of 1931 military control had been established over all of Manchuria.

It may be said that from June 1931, when Wakatsuki was in the midst of his term as prime minister, a military group headed by General Sadao Araki, the minister of war, was piloting Japan on a course from which there was to be no retreat. The goal was the formation of what became known as the Greater East Asia Co-prosperity Sphere in which Japan would be dominant over much of Asia. No opposition or interference was to be tolerated at home or abroad in its organization or conduct.

The Mukden Incident of September 18, 1931, was seen as a pretext for the Japanese seizure of Manchuria. Unrecognized as such at the time, it was the first action in what was to become World War II, lasting almost fourteen years until the Japanese surrender ceremony in Tokyo Bay on September 2, 1945.

Hitler and the Rome-Berlin Axis The economic pressures which brought extremist elements increasingly to power in Japan after 1930 were matched in Germany with the abandonment of the democratic process in that country. Former Field Marshal Paul von Hindenburg had been president of the German Republic since 1925. Parties of the right were strongly represented in a coalition government formed in March 1930 by Chancellor Heinrich Brüning of the Center party. Allied troops in occupation of the Rhineland, the Ruhr, and Saar areas of western Germany all were removed by the end of that year in conformity with the provisions of the Young Plan of 1929 relating to the payment of reparations.

Economic pressures stemming from the New York market crash were seriously felt in Germany by 1930, and a budget bill submitted by the Brüning government was denied approval in the Reichstag. When President Hindenburg nevertheless authorized it by decree, his action was condemned by the Reichstag. Brüning thereupon dissolved it, effective in July, citing emergency powers under Article 48 of the Constitution. New Reichstag elections were scheduled for that fall.

In the September 1930 elections, all of the moderate parties lost seats in the Reichstag. The Socialists held 143 seats and were in a strong position. To the alarm of many, the Communists held 77 seats. Most significant, however, was the National Socialist (Nazi) party gain of 107 seats, as compared to only 12 seats previously held since the election of 1928. The party had been regarded as unimportant since the fiasco of the Munich beer hall putsch of 1923, and seemed to have been made irrelevant by the growing prosperity of the country in the 1925–29 period.

As leader of the Nazi party, Adolf Hitler had persisted after his release from prison in 1924 in the advocacy of a party program based on views outlined in his book *Mein Kampf*. As economic difficulties fed discontent in 1930, he and his party associates gained support among the people and also among some leaders of industry displeased by the government's acceptance of the Young Plan in August 1929, despite its greater moderation in reparations demands. The Nazi party program was opposed to all provisions of the Versailles Treaty. This meant opposition to reparations payments in any form, to limitation on German military forces, to the existence of the "Polish corridor" through what had been a part of Prussia, and to the designation of the port of Danzig as a free city under the administration of the League of Nations.

With its greater strength in the Reichstag after September 1930, the Nazi party gained a major position in the government structure. In the worsening economic climate of 1931, following the denial of a German-Austrian customs union, the collapse of the Austrian Kreditanstaldt and of the German Darmstäder und Nationalbank, and growing unemployment, more people responded to the Nazi party promises and demagoguery.

In March 1932 a new presidential election took place in Germany, followed by new Reichstag elections in July. Hindenburg ran for re-election, but was opposed by Hitler of the National Socialist party, and by Ernst Thälmann of the Communist party. Because Hindenburg fell slightly short of a clear majority, a run-off election took place in April. He then was returned for a second term, but with only a slim plurality over Hitler. In the Reichstag elections of July, the National Socialist representation rose to 230 seats, making it the majority party. Prior to the Reichstag elections, President Hindenburg asked Franz von Papen to assume the chancellorship, with Constantin von Neurath as foreign minister, and General Kurt von Schleicher as minister of defense in the cabinet.[5]

---

5 Von Papen was military attaché in the German embassy in Washington in 1915 and was recalled upon demand of the United States government for engaging in propaganda activities and possible sabotage.

Much as Mussolini had advanced the cause of fascism in Italy in 1919–22 by the formation of armed squads (Squadre d'Azione) wearing black shirts, so Hitler and the Nazi party had formed their Storm Troops (Sturmabteilung) as "Brownshirts." A ban had been placed upon their activities by the Brüning government, but one of von Papen's first acts as chancellor was to remove that ban. Such disorders followed, with attacks on Jews and Communists in the streets, that martial law was introduced in July. Even that did not assure order. The great unemployment by then existing, along with both food and currency problems, caused a deadlock in the Reichstag which resulted in adding Nazi power to that body in the July elections.

With the National Socialist majority in the Reichstag, President Hindenburg invited Hitler to serve as vice-chancellor under von Papen, which he refused. Neither the Nazis nor the Communist party, with the smallest representation in the Reichstag, would agree to join in a coalition government. In the circumstances, von Papen was forced to resign as chancellor in November 1932. Hitler again refused the chancellorship because he was unwilling to accept conditions set by Hindenburg. At the president's request, General von Schleicher formed a new cabinet in December. He was unable to conciliate or reconcile the existing party groups, however, and resigned in January 1933.

President Hindenburg, with no alternative left, named Adolf Hitler chancellor, and he took office on January 30, 1933. Von Papen became vice-chancellor. Alfred von Hugenburg, Krupp executive and owner of the Telegraphen Union news agency and other media, was included in the cabinet, along with two members of the Nazi party, Hermann Goering and Wilhelm Frick. Hitler refused to compromise with leaders of the still-strong Center party, Brüning among them. Hitler also brought about the dissolution of the Reichstag, with new elections set for March.

The campaign for the March election of members to the Reichstag was interrupted on February 27, 1933, by a fire that destroyed most of the Reichstag building. The fire was believed to have been set by the Nazis to help justify new laws and regulations soon to be introduced.[6] The elections gave the Nazi group added power. The passage of legislation in the weeks following gave legal authority to what amounted to a Nazi dictatorship in Germany. Significantly, this began with legislation providing for full control of the press and public information.

An opening move in information-manipulation had come within a week of Hitler's assumption of the chancellorship in a Nazi-drafted

---

6   The Nazis attributed the fire to a Dutch Communist, a known half-witted arsonist, Marinus van der Lubbe, who was "found guilty" and decapitated.

"Decree for the Protection of the German People," signed by President Hindenburg on February 3, 1933. As with many dictatorial moves, it pretended to high purpose and legality, explained as being necessary to prevent the publication of "false news" and "malicious" reports. Within a month, the decree resulted in the suppression of more than 200 newspapers and periodicals.[7]

A second decree came immediately after the Reichstag fire, again signed by Hindenburg. It suspended all articles of the Weimar Constitution protecting civil rights, so ending freedom of speech, freedom of the press, freedom of association, and freedom of assembly. Mail might be opened, telegrams examined, telephone conversations monitored and recorded, homes searched, and property confiscated. Of two further decrees in March, one provided for the establishment of a government Ministry of Public Enlightenment and Propaganda (Reichsministerium für volksaufklärung und propaganda). A euphemism, this also was so self-contradictory as to be laughable. Yet it also was the first frank pronouncement of propaganda as a function of government. Dr. Paul Joseph Goebbels, one of the first members of the Nazi group, held this ministerial portfolio throughout the Nazi regime.

It was Goebbels who said at this time that "The mission of the press should be not merely to inform, but also to instruct. The press of Germany should be a piano upon which the government might play. The press must therefore cooperate with the government, and the Government with the press." In this, he was borrowing from the Soviet concept that the press should serve an instructional purpose in support of party policies, and he also produced a variation on the musical theme originated by Mussolini in 1926 when he said he considered the "Italian Fascist journalism like an orchestra."

A decree of September 22 established a Reich Culture Chamber (Reichkulturkammer), also headed by Dr. Goebbels, with seven separate divisions to exercise full control over press, radio, theater, music, the arts (painting and sculpture), writers, and motion pictures. Each operated under its own president and directorate appointed by Goebbels. For example, the Reich Press Chamber (Reichpressekammer), under a detailed press law (Schriftleitergesetz), converted the German press into a "public institution." It determined who might work as journalists, all to be classified as semi-state officials, and responsible solely to the State rather than to their publishers, editors, or other pri-

---

7 The Society of German Newspapers (Verein der Deutsche Zeitungs Verlager) had a membership of 2,060 daily newspapers, about half the nation's total. It did not even try to contest this action in order to protect the freedom, staff, or ownership of newspapers. As this writer was told in Berlin at the time by an official of the organization, "This is not a matter of right. It is a matter of force."

vate interests. All were to join a German Press Federation with an honor court supervising the observance of the law and authorized to punish an "errant" journalist by fine, imprisonment, or expulsion from the profession.

The president of the Press Chamber was Max Amann, the leader Wilhelm Weiss. Amann had served in the same regiment with Hitler during the war and already headed the National Socialist Publishing Association (Zentral Verlag der NSDAP) of Munich, which had produced Hitler's book *Mein Kampf* in 1925. Weiss was chief editor of the official Nazi party paper, the *Völkischer Beobachter* (National Observer), started in Munich but with a Berlin edition added in 1933.

To assure fulfillment of its assigned mission, the press was made subject to daily instructions provided through the Propaganda Ministry. Recognizing that this might make each paper resemble the others, thereby sacrificing reader attention, Goebbels specified that the press "should be unified in purpose and complex in the execution of that purpose," that it should be "monoform in will, but polyform in the expression of that will." This proved a difficult standard to attain because editors learned to be cautious about departing from instructions. The result was that newspapers did, in fact, look and read very much the same, and loss of readership brought a decline in the number of papers as the years passed.

An added important control over information in Germany was made effective in December 1933 through an order that brought a merger of the Wolff-CNB news agency and the younger and independent Telegraphen Union (TU). Out of this came the Deutsches Nachrichten Büro (DNB) as an official agency of the Nazi government. Dr. Heinrich Mantler, long director of the Wolff-CNB agency, retired. Otto Mejer, who had headed the Telegraphen Union, became director of the new DNB. The world Ring Combination of news agencies, of which Wolff had been an original member, also came to an effective end in 1933 and an official end in 1934.

On August 2, 1934, President Hindenburg died at age eighty-seven. In a plebiscite a fortnight later the German public approved by an eighty-eight percent vote the combination of the presidency and the chancellorship under Hitler. He chose Der Führer (the leader) as the title to be used. New Reichstag elections in November 1933 had permitted no candidates in opposition to the Nazi party, which meant that the legislative body was no more than a rubber stamp for party policy. As Der Führer, Hitler held an absolute dictatorship after August 1934 over what then became known as the Third Reich, succeeding the Empire of 1871–1919, and the Republic of 1919–34.

The dictatorship had been effective since Hitler assumed the chancellorship in January 1933. The Nazi Storm Troopers, many of them otherwise unemployed young men, were used without compunction to advance party purposes. This included persecution of Jews, to be eliminated as competitors with so-called "Aryans" in the business and professional community. Hitler gave secret orders in May 1933 looking toward the beginning of rearmament. The Nazi regime took Germany out of the League of Nations in October, after seven years of membership. A "People's Court" was created in May 1934, empowered to try cases in secret. Its wide powers were supported by concentration camps to which thousands were assigned without trial, and where gas chambers beyond were used to execute millions before 1945.

In June 1934 Hitler met in Venice with Mussolini. There was no immediate result, but it marked a first step toward formation of a close working relationship, or Rome-Berlin Axis, in October 1936, extended in November as a Rome-Berlin-Tokyo Axis. On June 30, a fortnight after the Venice meeting, there occurred in Germany a so-called "Blood Purge" in which seventy-seven members of the Nazi party were murdered, including some leading figures, allegedly because they had plotted against Hitler. Actually the purge was a means of solidifying his control of the party and nation. Among the victims were religious leaders resisting integration into the new political regime, and General von Schleicher, former chancellor, and his wife. Von Papen, who had recently spoken out against the loss of freedom under the Nazis, escaped execution only narrowly by committing himself wholly to the Nazi cause.

In Austria, Nazi agitation supported from Germany grew locally in 1933. In Vienna, the government headed since May 1932 by Chancellor Englebert Dollfuss used dictatorial methods to restrain the local Nazi agitation, but conflict only escalated within the country. On July 25, 1934, a month after the blood purge in Germany, a Nazi-supported putsch in Vienna resulted in the assassination of Dollfuss. A Nazi seizure of the country might have followed, but Italy and Yugoslavia massed forces on the Austrian frontier. For the time, this led to a denial by the German Nazi regime of any part in the action, and Dr. Kurt Schuschnigg, a Dollfuss associate, formed a new government in Vienna.

Since August 1934, Nazi agitation had proceeded in the Saar basin south of Luxembourg, a part of prewar Germany adjacent to France, but made a part of France in the Paris peace settlement. The League of Nations arranged for a plebiscite in the area, allowed under the Versailles Treaty, providing for the right of self-determination. In the vote returned on January 13, 1935, the people indicated a ninety percent desire for a reunion with Germany, and that occurred on March 1.

This move strengthened Hitler's position vis-a-vis France and Britain. In March he made a formal denunciation of the Versailles Treaty provision for a permanently disarmed Germany, and he also denounced the provisions for reparations payments. This was protested by France and Britain and also by Italy, but no further reparations ever were paid. The only related German concession was a promise that any German navy would be at only thirty-five percent of the strength of the British navy. This gave reassurance to Great Britain, false reassurance, as it turned out, but was at the time a precedent for later British efforts to appease the Hitler regime in seeking other compromises.

The Nazi government, having succeeded in regaining the Saar and denouncing the Treaty of Versailles without contest, also denounced on March 7, 1936, the Locarno treaties of 1925 guaranteeing among other things the French-German and Belgian-German frontiers. On that same date, German military forces created and rearmed since 1933, contrary to the treaty terms, moved into the Rhineland area of Germany adjacent to the French border.

This was a defiant action by the Nazi regime and raised the spectre of a new war in Europe. There was speculation later that the German forces, perhaps insufficiently prepared to risk a confrontation, particularly with a rather strong French army, might have withdrawn if France and Great Britain had seriously challenged the action. Once in the Rhineland, however, the German military position became static and the first alarms subsided.

Mussolini: Italy and Ethiopia

Even as the German move into the Rhineland occurred in 1936, Italy was engaged in its own military venture to gain control of Ethiopia. That already had created a crisis occupying the attention of all nations and placing stress on the League of Nations. Complications existed also in a growing unrest in the new Spanish republic, while problems relating to the general world economic dislocation remained critical. In the circumstances, no country was prepared to force the issue over Ethiopia or the German military move into the Rhineland. In what had been a test of wills and a test of strength, the position of Hitler and the Nazi government was advanced. From that time, there was no effective check on the aggressive actions of Germany, Italy, or Japan. A test of strength between the League of Nations and Japan following its invasion of Manchuria and adjoining areas of China in 1931–32 had resulted only in Japan's withdrawal from the League. By March 1936, Japanese military forces were deep in China, and the battle there would be fully joined in 1937.

Fascist Italy, which had been rearming and thinking in terms of empire, clashed with Ethiopian forces on the Italian Somaliland frontier in December 1934. Italy had concluded an agreement with France in January 1935. This was seen in Paris as a reassurance against Nazi aggression, but provided also a French recognition for Italy's claims in Africa. On that basis, Italy proceeded in what became a full invasion in October 1935 of Ethiopia from Italian Eritrea, as well as from the Somaliland. Great Britain and other countries protested, and the League of Nations objected, but France did not, nor did Germany or Japan. An Italian victory in May 1936 was followed by its formal annexation of Ethiopia, and also by its withdrawal in December from the League of Nations.

Spanish Civil War 1936–39

Meanwhile in Spain, the republic formed in 1931 was so conducted as to offend segments of the population, beginning with royalists, property owners, and the clerical elements, but also including many in the middle and professional classes, most members of the military, and many others. The result was civil war beginning in July 1936 and continuing until March 1939.

Italy and Germany joined in support of the Insurgents led by the army's General Francisco Franco, while Soviet Russia assisted the Republican side. Religious and political emotions became involved world-wide, with volunteers going to Spain to join the Republican side in particular. A victory for the Insurgents resulted in the establishment of a new authoritarian, right-leaning, fascist-type government under the Falangist party headed by General Franco.

These wars of 1931–39 in China, Ethiopia, and Spain were somewhat comparable to the Balkan wars of 1910–13 in providing testing grounds for men and equipment to be used in the greater conflict to follow.

Austria Overrun 1938

In the same period, Nazi demonstrations had continued in Austria, with aid and encouragement from Germany. Schuschnigg, successor to Dollfuss in 1934, was at length summoned to a conference with Hitler at his Berchtesgaden retreat in February 1938. There he was abused and threatened and forced to yield to Nazi demands. This meant that he appointed Arthur Seyss-Inquart, Austrian Nazi leader, as minister of the interior and also gave full recognition to the Austrian Nazi party. Schuschnigg's regime lost standing as a result and he was forced to resign as chancellor on March 11, with Seyss-Inquart replacing him. The following day, German troops marched across the border into Austria without resistance. On March 13 Seyss-Inquart proclaimed Austria's union with Germany, and on March 14 Hitler arrived in Vienna to take formal possession. A plebiscite on April 10 was reported to have produced a popular vote within Austria of 99.75 per cent in favor of the union.

England and France ineffectively protested the Austrian seizure. Italy accepted the result. The League of Nations took no action, and negative opinion in the United States and other countries also was ineffective. Schuschnigg was arrested and placed in confinement.[8] Others in Austria either accepted the new situation, so different from the Anschluss sought in 1931 and earlier, or were placed in concentration camps. Jews suffered under the same restraints existing in Germany and beginning to be felt in Italy. Some persons were able to escape, and some others committed suicide.

Munich and Czechoslovakia

Even before the Austrian seizure, attention also had been turned to Czechoslovakia as another target of Nazi aggression. In 1935, with Germany rearming, France signed a five-year alliance with Soviet Russia in which each agreed to aid the other in the event of unprovoked aggression. Czechoslovakia joined in this mutual assistance pact. The latter action brought its own reaction in Berlin, and led to a vote in the Sudeten area of Czechoslovakia, a German-speaking section in the northwestern part of the country adjacent to Germany. That vote gave a Sudeten Nazi party a position of strength in the Prague government.

In 1936, Czechoslovakia was accused by the Nazis of giving the Soviet air force rights on Czech soil. Nazi agitation continued through 1937 both in Germany and in the Sudeten area itself. In 1938, following the Austrian annexation, a full crisis arose over a possible German

---

8 Schuschnigg was kept under house arrest in Vienna from March 12 to May 28, 1938, at Gestapo headquarters for seventeen months following, and at the Dachau concentration camp until May 1, 1945. He was moved with other selected prisoners to a mountain village in the Tyrol and due to be executed to prevent rescue by the Allies, but they were liberated by U.S. troops on May 4. Seyss-Inquart, who was captured, was among those tried for war crimes at Nuremberg. Sentenced to death, he was executed in October 1946. See Schuschnigg's own *Austrian Requiem* (1946), and William L. Shirer's *The Rise and Fall of the Third Reich* (1946), pp. 352–53.

occupation of the Sudetenland, and it was not overlooked that Germany by then surrounded Czechoslovakia on three sides. Konrad Henlein, leader of the Sudeten Nazi party, made new demands and German troops were massed on the Czech frontier.

Great Britain and France reacted to these moves. With Austria freshly in mind, Britain's Prime Minister Neville Chamberlain flew to Berchtesgaden to confer with Hitler, then to Godesberg for another meeting, and then to Munich for a third, all between September 15 and 29 of 1938.

The Munich conference on September 29 captured world attention and brought Chamberlain and France's Premier Edouard Daladier together with Hitler and Mussolini, along with their foreign ministers, Joachim von Ribbentrop and Galeazzo Ciano. Czechoslovakia was unrepresented. It was agreed that the Sudetenland was to be given to Germany, but the independence of the rest of the country would be preserved; that Hitler would make no further territorial demands in Europe; and that Great Britain and France would guarantee the new Czech frontiers. Chamberlain returned to London to assure the British people that "peace in our time" had been assured by the agreement. Daladier did much the same in Paris.

Czechoslovakia had no choice but to accept the settlement and German troops moved into the Sudetenland on October 1. On October 5, President Beneš resigned in protest.[9] The country had lost 16,000 square miles of territory and five million in population. Germany was placed in a position to dominate the entire Danube area. France and Great Britain had lost prestige. Persecution of Jews was extended to Czechoslovakia. On November 30, Emil Hacha, judge of the high court, was elected president to succeed Beneš.

A new crisis arose in Czechoslovakia in March 1939. The Hacha government in Prague deposed Monsignor Joseph Tiso, a prelate who had become premier of the region of Slovakia, in the east, for allegedly working for separation of the territory. Tiso appealed to Hitler, who summoned Hacha to Berlin and invited him to "place the fate of the Czech people . . . trustingly in the hands of the Führer." The alternative, he said, would be the destruction of Prague by bombing. With no choice, all of Czechoslovakia became a German "protectorate." German troops moved in on March 15 and Hitler made the announcement in Prague the day after. Thus, Czechoslovakia, like Austria, became a part of the German Reich. The Czech armed forces were disbanded and resistance to Nazi authority was punished by death or work in a labor force.

---

9 Beneš became a visiting professor at the University of Chicago, but was in France and England during the war years heading a Czech government-in-exile. He returned to Prague after the war.

President Roosevelt appealed to Hitler and Mussolini, following the Munich conference, seeking assurances of peace. As with Chamberlain, Hitler denied any aggressive intentions. This was part of the "big lie" technique forming an element in his propaganda program. Some British government leaders and members of the establishment had hoped since 1935 that a policy of appeasement would take Hitler to a point where, if granted certain concessions, he would be satisfied. With his seizure of all of Czechoslovakia on March 15–16, 1939, even those who had supported the appeasement concept were disillusioned, as were leaders in France. This disenchantment was reenforced by a German annexation on March 21 of the Lithuanian seaport of Memel and new demands on Poland. Britain and France were further disenchanted when Italy invaded Albania in April 1939.

Both Britain and France began serious defensive military preparations, and concluded mutual aid treaties with Poland, Rumania, Greece, and Turkey. The Nazi regime from the outset had been hostile to the Soviet Union. One result was a so-called Anti-Comintern Pact standing against the efforts of the Communist International organization to advance the cause of communism in the world. It was signed in 1936 by Germany, Italy, and Japan, making for a Rome-Berlin-Tokyo Axis. The pact was renewed in April 1939, with the new Franco government in Spain and that of Hungary joining in.

*Poland
Invaded
1939*

Great Britain, after signing mutual aid treaties with Poland and other countries in 1938 and 1939, attempted in the latter year to persuade the Soviet Union, a target of Nazi propaganda, to join in such an agreement. Moscow rejected the proposal. What no others then knew was that the Nazi government, contrary to its earlier position but for its own reasons, had opened secret negotiations with Communist party leaders in Moscow at least as early as May 1939.

The world was astounded when it learned on August 21, 1939, that a German-Soviet seven-year trade agreement had been signed two days before in Moscow. An even more surprising ten-year non-aggression treaty was signed by the two countries on August 23. These documents, of course, made the Anti-Comintern Pact of 1936–39 meaningless. The other signators, Italy, Japan, Spain, and Hungary, were left in a kind of limbo. Members of the Communist party in countries other than the Soviet Union also were shaken by the willingness of Moscow to ally itself with the National Socialist regime, previously regarded as the greatest enemy of communism, and it caused some defections from Communist ranks.

Coming so unexpectedly and marking so complete a reversal of Nazi Germany's anti-Soviet propaganda, the "Communazi" pacts, as some called them, were promptly recognized as providing assurance to both signators that they might proceed with their own military plans, each without interference by the other.

Conclusion of the treaties was followed almost immediately by a reassertion of German demands upon Poland. Without waiting for a reply, but announcing that the demands had been rejected, a long-planned German attack on Poland was launched September 1 on land and in the air. Soviet troops also moved into parts of Poland on September 17, dividing the country with Germany. Within another month, Russia gained control of the Baltic republics and invaded Finland in November. For this action it became the only member-country to be expelled from the League of Nations. Events themselves soon brought an end to the League itself.

Europe at War

Great Britain and France, having concluded mutual-aid treaties with Poland in March, declared war on Germany on September 3. Thus Europe was at war, with action extending immediately to the Atlantic, where German submarines took early toll. German armies were massed in the west, facing French and British forces, with Belgium and Luxembourg standing between, but there was relatively little action on that front through the winter of 1939–40.

Poland was conquered and occupied by German and Soviet forces by the end of September 1939. The Polish corridor was wiped out, East Prussia was reunited with its western part, and the port city of Danzig was annexed by Germany. Soviet forces held control in the Baltic states and the war with Finland ended with that country's surrender in March 1940.

That new year brought sweeping German campaigns. Norway and Denmark were occupied in April 1940. Holland, Belgium, and Luxembourg were overrun in early May, followed by a quick drive into France. British and French forces along the Channel coast were trapped, with some 335,000 of both armies almost miraculously transported from the Dunkirk beaches to safety in England, although minus their equipment. Italy declared war on France and Great Britain on June 10, with its forces entering southern France. France signed an armistice on June 22, with German forces occupying most of the country, including Paris. A French government was established in July at Vichy in the south, administering an unoccupied zone but subject to German direction. A rival "Free French" government was formed in London.

The French defeat left a greatly weakened Britain to face Germany and Italy alone. It had support from Commonwealth countries. Its navy was intact and it had a limited but sturdy air defense. It also was to receive ships, supplies, and some assistance, actually beyond what strict neutrality permitted, from the United States. The United Kingdom suffered severely, nevertheless, through the winter of 1940–41 from German air attack and submarine action.

The power of the German military forces was turned elsewhere, as well, in 1940. By the end of the year Rumania and Hungary had been brought into Axis control and support, as was Bulgaria by early 1941. Greece, under Italian attack, and Yugoslavia both became centers of battle in that year and were forced to surrender. The fighting spread to the Mediterranean and Africa, where Italian forces based in Libya had become active in 1940. In a cynical disregard of the 1939 treaties, June 1941 also brought a German invasion of Soviet Russia.

Across the world, Japan had pursued its war against China with special vigor since 1937, forcing the Nationalists to leave Nanking and establish a new capital at Chungking in 1939. It also had signed a mutual aid pact with Italy and Germany in 1940.

In December 1941, Japan attacked Hawaii and the Philippines, thus bringing the United States into the war, both in the Pacific and in support of Great Britain and the Soviet Union in Europe. Japan's attack on Hong Kong and other British positions as well brought Great Britain and Commonwealth forces into action in the Pacific. Thus the Asian war that began in 1931 and the European war of 1939 became literally a world war, involving North America, a vast area of Africa, and indirectly South America. It continued in that framework until 1945.

Radio had joined with the newspaper and magazine press by the 1930s in providing the peoples of all developed countries with a service of current information. Both radio and press were themselves served by news agencies and syndicates. The value of the media as a source of information was determined by the degree of freedom, reliability, and professionalism under which they were conducted. The availability of sources generally, and the independence with which foreign correspondents might write or broadcast, shaped the content and quality of their reports on public affairs. The extent to which propaganda or censorship might be used as an instrument of policy by governments also affected the understanding of peoples.

As the 1930s began, international reporting was proceeding with almost complete freedom except in Soviet Russia, Fascist Italy, and Spain. This was a decline from 1920, when greater freedom existed in the latter two countries. Domestic press controls also had been added in some others by 1930, but as yet with relatively little effect on international news reporting. The serious decline in freedom of information began with the armed conflict between Japan and China in 1931, and with the Nazi assumption of power in Germany in 1933.

As crisis turned to military action and to war, some correspondents who had been reporting general news and substantive affairs became war correspondents. They did not necessarily need to go off to some far scene of action; the war often enough came to them.

Where their own countries were involved, correspondents serving abroad sometimes were caught in what had become enemy territory. Normally, in such cases, they were repatriated along with diplomatic representatives of their countries. Representatives of the media of neutral countries commonly remained in countries at war, often at risk and always under censorship. But neutral countries did not all remain neutral, and some that were neutral also were invaded.

As that sequence of events already outlined began with the Japanese aggression against Manchuria and China in 1931, there were no Chinese correspondents in Japan. Japanese correspondents in China either were in the protected international zones of Shanghai, Tientsin, or Peiping, or in Hong Kong, or they accompanied Japanese troops as war correspondents. Neutral correspondents in Japan and China were all representatives of the U.S., British, or European press and were able to remain until the Japanese attack on Pearl Harbor and Hong Kong in December 1941. Even then, Axis correspondents remained in Tokyo, while U.S. and British correspondents remained in Chungking. Japanese correspondents left the United States and Great Britain. United States and British correspondents left Asian and Pacific areas under Japanese control if they could, although some could not.

As the growing crisis brought war to Ethiopia in 1935–36 and to Spain in 1936–39, correspondents reported the action. The fateful events in Vienna, Munich, and Prague in 1938 and 1939 drew them, along with photographers, to those places. In the same years from 1933 to 1939, neutral correspondents were expelled in growing numbers from Rome, Berlin, and Moscow. Further, restrictions and censorships induced others to depart voluntarily from those three capitals and from Tokyo.

As full-scale war began in Europe in September 1939, there was a mutual withdrawal by correspondents of the belligerent countries, leaving only neutral reporters, these including U.S. media representatives. The year 1940 was not far advanced when the German move into Norway, Denmark, and Holland brought further withdrawals. The French surrender in June removed even the neutral correspondents from Paris by German demand. Some moved to Vichy, the new capital of unoccupied France. Other withdrawals proceeded in the south of Europe through 1940. The last moves came in 1941, first in response to the German turn against Soviet Russia in June and then in response to the Japanese attacks in Asia and the Pacific in December.

Italy

Fascist Italy, the second country following Japan to resort to open warfare, invaded Ethiopia in 1935. It had been building its military organization from 1930 and had departed from the course of international amity by using the still young radio medium from about that same time for propaganda purposes. The media of the country were brought under a tighter control, as described earlier. An amended press law in May 1932 required that the director or responsible editor obtain what amounted to an annual license for his publication. It provided penalties for violation of directives to the media, with two violations grounds for dismissal of the director or editor, and possibly for suspension of the publication itself.

The Nazi regime borrowed measures already introduced in Italy for media control, and Italy soon borrowed some of the German innovations. The establishment in Berlin of a frankly designated Ministry of Public Enlightenment and Propaganda, for example, produced changes in Italy. The first move occurred after Galeazzo Ciano, publisher of *Il Telegrafo* at Leghorn and also Mussolini's son-in-law since 1930, succeeded Lando Ferretti in August 1933 as director of the Press Office in the Ministry of the Interior. About a year later, on September 6, 1934, that office was transferred to the Ministry of Foreign Affairs (Ministerio degli Affari Esteri), retitled the Undersecretariat of State for Press and Propaganda, and its scope extended to include four divisions. On June 24, 1935, the undersecretariat was transformed to give it full ministerial status as the Ministry of Press and Propaganda (Il Ministerio per la Stampa e la Propaganda), well housed in the Via Veneto, and a new point of contact and accreditation for foreign correspondents. Ciano, as director of the ministry, attained cabinet status in addition to holding membership in the Fascist Grand Council. He soon departed the ministry, however, to head a bomber squadron in the Ethiopian War and was succeeded by Dino Alfieri. Ciano became minister of foreign affairs in 1936–43.

The name of the ministry still did not reflect the full scope of its activities, which were comparable to those of the German Propaganda Ministry. In recognition of this, it was renamed again on June 1, 1937, becoming the Ministry of Popular Culture (Ministerio della Cultura Popolare). Alfieri remained as director until 1940, when he became ambassador to Germany. He was succeeded by Alesandro Pavolini.

Lando Ferretti, while still director of the original Press Office in the Ministry of the Interior in 1930, had outlined the role of the Italian press at that time. He said:

> The Fascist press, following the pioneer example of Signor Mussolini's own newspaper, *Il Popolo d'Italia,* opened a new cycle in the history of the press, in which newspapers are no longer the organs of conflicting parties or of contending interests but rather the means of propaganda and advance of the new state in which everyone works in disciplined accord for a common aim and ideal. Hence the necessity of a new legislation based on the principle of responsibility.[1]

---

1 *Editor & Publisher* (January 3, 1931).

This was much the same concept as advanced in the Soviet Union with reference to its own press. Dr. Gayda, as editor of *Il Giornale d'Italia* of Rome, also following that concept, contended that "the freest press in the world is the Italian press." He reasoned:

> Elsewhere newspapers are under the command of plutocratic groups, of factions, and individuals; elsewhere they are reduced to the meagre task of purchase and sale of exciting news. . . . Elsewhere newspapers are nowadays grouped in the hands of a very few persons who consider the newspaper as a mere industry, just as in the iron or leather trade. The Italian press is free because it serves only one cause, one regime.[2]

From 1933, however, the Italian press became increasingly subject to control and manipulation by the Fascist leadership, and that leadership became more closely identified with Nazi leaders and policy in Germany. This had its effect upon foreign correspondents in Italy. Their outgoing reports had been subjected to an unacknowledged censorship virtually from the beginning of the Fascist regime in 1922, but it was not intolerable or beyond avoidance, and news sources remained reasonably open, particularly in contrast to the Soviet Union.

All this began to change in 1933, and in December 1934 an official censorship was authorized in a decree signed by Mussolini, acting not only as the leader and premier, but in his capacity as minister of war, navy, and air. Under fourteen heads, the decree listed subjects, military and otherwise, not to be mentioned by the domestic press or radio, or by foreign correspondents. From about the same time, interviews with Mussolini became rare, and then perhaps arranged as a favor or a reward to a correspondent who was deemed to have earned it by writing in a manner pleasing to the regime or to Mussolini personally. This system of rewards was an Italian contribution to the methodology of political propaganda. A second contribution was the establishment in Rome by the government of a Circolo, or club, where correspondents acceptable to the regime might enjoy the amenities and dine well at moderate cost. Both of these devices for dealing with correspondents were borrowed by the Nazi government and by some others.

It was not immediately apparent at the time, but the censorship introduced in Rome in December 1934 was intended to throw a security blanket over Italian preparations for the campaign against Ethiopia that began tentatively on the Somaliland frontier at that period and proceeded with full force from October 1935. As the Mukden incident of September 1931 marked the beginning of a separate story of war in-

---

2 *Editor & Publisher* (November 26, 1932).

volving Japan and China, the Ethiopian invasion of 1935 marked such a beginning with reference to Italy and the related press coverage there.

Events centering in Germany and Spain from 1935 and 1936 as they bore upon the media proved even more significant, in retrospect, than those described as having occurred in Italy. They exerted an influence upon France, Great Britain, the Soviet Union, the United States, and nearly every other country of the world.

-- *Germany*

The Nazi regime in Germany, no less than the Soviet or Italian Fascist regimes, undertook to shape the minds of its people and those of other countries, so far as possible. This meant a control of the domestic media, and it meant the exclusion of uncontrolled media of other countries. In addition to suppressing many newspapers in the first days of the National Socialist government in 1933, a ban was placed almost at once upon the importation of 254 specified foreign newspapers and periodicals, with 77 more to be added to that forbidden list in 1938. It was a punishable offense for any German to possess a copy of any such publications of more than twenty countries, or clippings from them, or material taken from them and duplicated in typewritten or any other form.

As in Italy, means were found to control the ownership of newspapers and periodicals in Germany. Editions of the official Nazi party paper, the *Völkischer Beobachter* (National Observer), were published in Munich, Berlin, and after 1938 in Vienna. *Die Illustrierte Beobachter* of Munich was an illustrated weekly edition of the daily. For members of the Hitler Youth organization, *Die Hitlerjugend* was published in Berlin, and *Der Arbeitsmann* was for those included in the Reich Labor Service.

A number of Nazi leaders had their own papers. Dr. Goebbels conducted *Der Angriff* (The Attack), a Berlin daily tabloid, and much later established *Das Reich* as a quality weekly journal. Hermann Goering controlled *Der Essener National Zeitung* of Essen. Heinrich Himmler, head of the police service, had *Das Schwarze Korps* of Berlin, official paper of the Schutzstaffel, the S.S. or Elite Guard storm troopers. Robert Ley had the *Westdeutscher Beobachter* of Cologne; and Julius Streicher had *Der Stürmer* of Nuremberg. The major party publisher, however, was Max Amann, director of two publishing companies, the official Zentral Verlag der NSDAP and the Franz Eher Verlag.

A decree of April 1935, specified (1) conditions under which non-party members might continue to operate newspapers or periodicals in Germany, (2) provided that non-Nazi publications might be suppressed in favor of party publications as a means "to eliminate unhealthy competitive situations," and (3) provided for the suppression of "the scandal press." Under this decree, Amann was able to gain control of most of the nonparty newspapers of Germany, with Hitler himself sharing in the prosperity of the publishing companies Amann directed. The suppression of the "scandal press" did not extend to Streicher's *Der Stürmer,* notorious for its vulgarity and abusiveness.

Foreign correspondents in Germany had worked under favorable conditions between 1920 and the first month of the Nazi regime in 1933. From 1931, the Ministry of Foreign Affairs occasionally tried to "straighten out" a correspondent on some subject. Through 1932, however, correspondents reported the growing signs of trouble without serious restraint. This changed promptly after the Nazi government was established in January 1933. The Reichstag fire followed. Jews and Jewish-owned publications were immediate targets of persecution, and it came as no surprise to foreign correspondents when they were informed late in February 1933 that "the parliamentary democratic time in Germany has passed." A day or two later they were told further that action would be taken against correspondents whose dispatches "maliciously oppose the government."

Correspondents soon realized that they were under surveillance, that their office and home telephones were being tapped or monitored, and that their German friends and news contacts were being watched. When they visited the Foreign Ministry or other government offices in what had been the normal course of their work, they began to receive suggestions as to how they should treat the news, then warnings, and sometimes threats of possible physical violence or of expulsion if their reports failed to meet standards deemed acceptable by the government.

A supervision, as it was called—actually a censorship—was instituted over outgoing dispatches. If a dispatch was rejected, in whole or in part, officials notified the correspondent, as specified in Article 7 of the International Radio-Telegraph Convention concluded at Madrid in 1932. That notification was not necessarily prompt, however, which meant that a correspondent never could be certain of the immediate fate of a dispatch, or have opportunity either to change it to save its coherence or to know that it reached its destination in time for use while still retaining its news value.

Although monitored, telephone connections remained unaffected by the supervision. It thus remained possible for a correspondent to continue what had become a common practice in the preceding year or more to talk directly by telephone with his office or with a bureau in another capital, usually Paris, or to read a dispatch to be recorded for use, as in London, or perhaps to be forwarded to New York.

The first member of the foreign press corps to feel direct personal action under the Nazi regime was Jacob Lestschinsky, a Lithuanian Jew acting as Berlin correspondent for the Jewish Telegraph Agency (JTA), a New York organization, and also for the *Jewish Daily Forward* of New York. He was arrested in March 1933 and held incommunicado for several days. Through the intervention of the Foreign Press Association, he was released and left Germany. Under the terms of an existing German-American trade agreement, it still remained possible for correspondents working independently to send news to the London office of the JTA and to a number of other subscribers. The Berlin bureau in July 1933 was ordered to cease news-gathering activities, but it continued to produce reports until November 1937 when it was closed.

Dr. Goebbels, propaganda minister, William Frick, minister of the interior, Hermann Goering, then minister for air, Hitler, and other Nazi officials spoke then and later about the portrayal of German affairs in the foreign press. Typical was a Goering comment in a speech to international press representatives in Berlin on March 25, 1933, in which he objected to what he called "exaggerated reports."

In that same month, the government announced three measures to prevent the publication abroad of "false atrocity stories" from Germany or about Germany. These called for German diplomatic representatives to protest to the government of any country in which they served concerning the publication there of stories judged to be of that variety. A ban was placed on the distribution in Germany of foreign publications using such stories, and action was proposed against correspondents "who persisted in sending such reports."

Members of the foreign press corps in Berlin did not bow meekly to the government's efforts to control what was reported and what was published. Truth and accuracy were not sufficient for the Nazi leaders, and objectivity was no more respected than in Moscow. Correspondents noted that Goering in his March 25 talk did not deny that Nazi party members had participated in beatings and killings, or that German journalists, Jewish and otherwise, were among the victims. But he contended that such incidents were few, considering the revolutionary times, and therefore might be considered "false atrocity stories" published abroad.

Protests by the foreign press group about interference with their work and their reporting had small result. More than a dozen correspondents left Germany before the end of 1933, either by demand or because they felt it prudent to do so. Between 1933 and 1937 no less than nineteen were expelled, five others left under threat, and thirteen left voluntarily because they were Jewish and felt unwelcome, unsafe, and professionally handicapped. This was in contrast to six expulsions from Moscow in the same approximate period of five years at the outset of the Communist regime, and only two expulsions from Rome in the first thirteen years of the Fascist regime.

The most striking incident among the early departures related to Edgar Ansel Mowrer, Berlin representative of the *Chicago Daily News* since 1923. As president of the Foreign Press Association in 1933, he took a leading role in defending correspondents arrested by the Nazis or faced with expulsion. In the Pulitzer Prize awards announced in May of 1933, he received recognition for the best foreign correspondence based upon his reports from Germany in 1932. Most of these reports appeared in his book *Germany Puts the Clock Back,* published in London and New York in 1933, almost coincidentally with Hitler's assumption of the chancellorship. The book revealed accurately the forces behind the National Socialist development, but it placed Mowrer in disfavor with the party leadership.

Summoned to the Foreign Press Section of the Ministry of Foreign Affairs in March 1933, at a time when he was getting about on crutches as a result of a skiing mishap, Mowrer was asked to resign as president of the Foreign Press Association, ostensibly for reasons of health. He declined, and reported the matter to the membership of the association, which upheld his refusal. Goebbels then threatened to abolish the Foreign Press Association, and that possibility was pending through much of the summer.

In August, Mowrer was notified by the government that his "false" reports had caused so much "righteous wrath" among "good Germans," that the government "could not hold itself responsible for his safety" if he chose to remain in the country. This was equivalent to a warning that his life was in danger if he did remain. The United States ambassador in Berlin, William E. Dodd, advised Mowrer to leave, as a matter of discretion. He did so in September, the thirteenth correspondent to depart under some form of pressure during the first seven months of the Nazi regime.

Re-established in Paris as *Chicago Daily News* bureau chief, Mowrer pointed out that the Nazi government was not persecuting and expelling correspondents because they wrote "false" or "malicious" reports as asserted, but because the truths they reported were unpleasant and inexpedient. This could be said with rare exceptions for correspondents forced out of any country during the years since international news reporting began in the mid-nineteenth century.

Frederick Kuh, Jewish chief of the United Press bureau in Berlin since 1925 and also under threat, was another of the correspondents to leave. Others departing voluntarily included Edward L. Deuss, chief of the International News Service bureau since 1931; Miles Bouton, then representing the *Baltimore Sun;* Oskar Jorgenson, *Social-Demokraten,* Copenhagen; Adolfph Nilsson, *Göteborgs Handelstidningen,* Gothenburg; Erst H. Regenburger, *Neue Zürcher Zeitung;* Erwin Kondor, *Neue Freie Presse,* Vienna; Abram Gartmann and Ilja Tschernjak, both of *Pravda,* Moscow; Andreas Hecht, UP; and Charles E. (Chuck) Gratke, the *Christian Science Monitor,* after he had been beaten by Nazi hoodlums setting upon him as he left the Sportspalast in Berlin following a Hitler address.

Visiting correspondents were not exempt from harsh treatment or denial of entrance to the country. John Walter, Jr., twenty-six, son of John Walter V, coproprietor of the *Times* of London, and Rolf Kaltenborn, sixteen-year-old son of H. V. Kaltenborn, CBS radio commentator, while traveling together suffered violence from the Nazis in Berlin. Dorothy Thompson, Berlin bureau chief in 1924–28 for the Ledger-Post service, upon returning to Germany in August 1934 as a writer for the *Saturday Evening Post* was promptly ordered to leave "because of numerous anti-German references" in her writing.

Resident correspondents expelled in 1933 included Ivan Bespalow of the Soviet Tass agency and Lili Keith of *Izvestia,* following their arrest in Leipzig in September. Noel Panter of the London *Daily Express* was expelled in October. Based in Munich, his apartment was searched and his papers confiscated. His reporting of a Hitler speech to storm troopers was judged to have been disrespectful. B. Pembroke Stephens also of the *Daily Express* was expelled in 1934 on charges of "news distortion."

Others expelled between that time and 1937 included Andreas Rosinger of Tass; Bertil Svahnstrom of the Swedish TT agency; Erwin Wasserbaeck of the official Austrian Amtliche Nachrichtenstelle agency; Patrick Murphy, a third *Daily Express* staffer; Karl Robson, *Morning Post;* Theodor Steinthal, *Politiken,* Copenhagen; and even an Italian correspondent, Mario da Silva of *Il Lavoro Fascista,* Rome. The last three expelled in 1937 were Norman Ebbutt, in Berlin for the *Times* since 1925; Paul Ravoux, a resident journalist in Berlin since 1919 and chief correspondent there for the Agence Havas since 1933; and Herman Boschenstein, of the *Basler Nachrichten* of Basle, Switzerland.[3]

---

3 A full list of the correspondents expelled from Germany to 1937, with some further details, appears in Vernon McKenzie's *Through Turbulent Years* (1938), pp. 237–38 and passim. See also *Editor & Publisher* (April 6, 1935).

The expulsion of Norman Ebbutt of the *Times,* the seventeenth ordered to leave the country, was a *cause célèbre* matching the earlier departure of Mowrer. It came as a Nazi response to the unprecedented expulsion by the British government of three German correspondents and an office secretary in August of 1937.

The German press was represented in London at that time by about 100 accredited correspondents, contrasted to about fifteen British correspondents in Berlin. There was reason to believe that many, and probably most were engaged in something other than journalistic activities, including espionage and propaganda, and as agents watching some 15,000 German refugees then in the United Kingdom.

The British government, persuaded that this was the case, and presumably with specific information, gave notice through the Home Office to four that their alien permits to reside in Great Britain would be suspended two weeks later, meaning that they would be required to leave the country. The four were Werner von Crome, chief correspondent for the *Berliner Lokal-Anzeiger;* Franz Otto Wrede, assistant correspondent, and a woman secretary in that office; and Wolf Dietrick Langen of the official DNB agency. Rather surprisingly, Langen had previously been expelled from Italy.

The Nazi government reacted immediately by expelling Norman Ebbutt, the highly respected and able correspondent for the *Times* and a recent president of the Foreign Press Association in Berlin. Ebbutt was attacked in the German press in terms that would have been unprintable in Anglo-Saxon newspapers or most others. His expulsion was announced officially as having been based on lying and biased reports, which was completely untrue.[4]

The difficulties of gathering information, and sorting fact from fantasy increased for correspondents in Germany from 1933. There was no opposition press and objective sources were few. After the 1934 blood purge, if not before, correspondents who had been in Germany for years found that German friends were afraid to be seen with them lest they be suspected of giving information to the foreign press and penalized. The government made every effort to channel the news through official sources that could be controlled, and discouraged efforts by correspondents seeking information from other sources, or departing from a portrayal of events acceptable to Nazi officialdom.

---

4 Whereas the *Times* in earlier periods had defended its correspondents, resisted their expulsion, and sometimes forced governments to cancel or apologize for expulsions, nothing of the sort was even attempted in Ebbutt's case. Geoffrey Dawson, editor of the *Times,* was so dedicated to appeasing the Hitler government that he made no protest whatever. Ebbutt was crushed, and Dawson and the *Times* were demeaned in the eyes of those aware of the circumstances.

News conferences for foreign reporters were instituted early in the regime both at the Ministry of Public Enlightenment and Propaganda and at the Ministry of Foreign Affairs. The Foreign Ministry, long a source of information, continued to be referred to in press reports as "Wilhelmstrasse," by reason of its location, just as it was convenient at times to refer to the British Foreign Office as "Whitehall," to the French Ministry of Foreign Affairs as "the Quai d'Orsay," to the Italian Foreign Ministry as the "Chigi Palace," and the Soviet Foreign Commissariat as "the Kremlin."

The Foreign Ministry conferences, together with the controlled German press, provided much of the raw material for news dispatches sent abroad, although with careful attribution to those sources and some clue usually given to their credibility or lack of it. Information still was to be gleaned from courageous individuals and from embassies and consulates. Correspondents also retained considerable freedom of movement. Some possessed sufficient background knowledge and experience and used their eyes, ears, and minds to such purpose that they were able to arrive at accurate conclusions not always in accord with the official line. Whether they then could report without concern for censorship or official repercussions was, of course, another matter. As in the Soviet Union and Italy, it became necessary for some correspondents to leave the country if they were to write fully and freely.

In September 1936, Frederick Oechsner, Berlin manager for the United Press, expressed the personal view that foreign correspondents in Germany were freer to report the news than German journalists. This probably was true, so far as it went, since the German journalists had ceased to have any freedom or independence whatever. Oechsner added that the government rarely objected to a report, even if it could be viewed as harmful, so long as it also was accurate. This opinion was hardly shared by other correspondents. Also, he spoke immediately after the summer Olympic Games of 1936 in Germany during which a special temporary hospitality was extended to visiting press representatives.

The Nazi regime began to give even closer attention to the manner in which correspondents reported German affairs. Signalizing that trend and coming at a time when restraints also were rising in Soviet Russia and Fascist Italy, Adolf Hitler addressed the Reichstag on January 30, 1937, the fourth anniversary of the National Socialist government. In the course of lengthy remarks, he presented a kind of ultimatum to correspondents. There could be no lasting peace among nations, he said, so long as "an international clique is allowed to poison the wells of public opinion." He therefore proposed the crea-

tion of what soon were referred to as "nonaggression press pacts" between nations. Under such agreements, the form of a nation's government, the manner of its administration, and the manner in which the
press functioned within its borders would be the concern of that nation alone. Such matters would not be permissible for comment—much
less unfavorable comment—by the press or radio of another nation.

The Nazi government concluded such nonaggression press pacts
during 1937 with Italy, Hungary, Austria, Poland, and a less formal
one with Yugoslavia. The existence of the pacts did not restrain the
German press itself, however, from commenting adversely when it
chose to do so. Even though Austria and Poland had signed pacts with
Germany, they became particular targets of German abuse. One was
invaded and annexed within a year, and the other was attacked in 1939.

Hitler's theme of January 1937 was heard again in September at an
elaborate National Socialist Party Congress at Nuremberg. There Dr.
Goebbels and Dr. Otto Dietrich, Reich press chief (Reichspressechef)
and one of Hitler's oldest personal friends, both made charges that the
press of other lands was "warmongering" and poisoning public opinion, and that individual correspondents were misrepresenting Germany. Freedom of the press, Dietrich said, was "a mask behind which
modern bandits, war-mongerers and vultures who feed on mankind
hide their faces."

Later in the year, the Foreign Press Association sent out invitations
to its annual ball at the Adlon Hotel. Quite contrary to the response in
all previous years, German government officials, clearly following instructions, unanimously declined the invitations. So the gauntlet was
down, with the Nazi regime in a clear adversary relationship to the
foreign press and radio representatives in Berlin. The problems that
had beset correspondents became even more serious.

The year 1938 was critical. Germany, Italy, and the Soviet Union
were participating in the Spanish Civil War. German aggression
brought Austria and much of Czechoslovakia within the boundaries
of the Reich, and the continent moved to the brink of war, perhaps
only forestalled by the Anglo-French concession on Czechoslovakia at
the September Munich Conference. The foreign press corps remained
large in Berlin. Those correspondents who had been expelled or otherwise departed had been more than replaced in numbers, because it was
obvious that the Hitler government held the key to peace or war.

A new attempt to place shackles on the foreign press came early in
1938. In what was for him a rather conciliatory speech, Hitler, in the
Reichstag on February 20, had returned to the subject of "nonaggression press pacts," as originally advanced twelve months before. In referring to Germany's relations with Great Britain and France, he said
that "the only thing that has poisoned and thus injured the common

life of these two countries is the utterly unendurable press campaign which . . . has existed under the motto 'freedom of personal opinion.' " He went on to say:

> I do not understand it when I am told by foreign statesmen and diplomats that there are no legal possibilities in these countries of putting an end to the lies, for private matters are not at stake. It concerns the problems of the common lives of the peoples and the States.
>
> We cannot shut our eyes to the consequences of these campaigns, for it could so easily come to pass that in certain countries contemptible international lie manufacturers could generate such violent hatred against our country that gradually hostile public opinion would be created against us which the German people would not be able to resist.
>
> This is a danger to peace. I am no longer prepared to tolerate unanswered this unbridled slander. From now on we shall answer back and do so with National Socialist thoroughness.[5]

This was a remarkable statement, coming from the leader of a party, government, and nation whose controlled press and radio in five years had earned a reputation for inaccuracy, abusiveness, and falsehood in references to other nations and peoples. It was in keeping, however, with the bold concepts expressed in Hitler's *Mein Kampf,* involving what became known as the "big lie" technique and also as the "mirror image" wherein an object or a subject is viewed in reverse.

The Hitler speech, of which the portion dealing with press matters was only a small part, was regarded as so important in a time of mounting crisis that it was reported extensively throughout the world. The United Press transmitted the full text of 18,000 words, the longest to that date. That text, made available in advance through the Propaganda Ministry, was translated, checked back for accuracy, broken into seventy-five "takes" or parts, sent on double-trunk teleprinter circuits from Berlin to London, relayed by cable and radiotelegraph circuits to New York, and thence to Buenos Aires, with further distribution from both places.

What the Nazi regime wanted, so far as press matters were concerned, was a general signature of the nonaggression press pacts, treaties that not only would stifle "criticism," but halt the reporting, however true, of information viewed in Berlin as tending to create an unfavorable impression of Nazi policy. Such reporting did not constitute a "press campaign," as Hitler implied, but neither did it match the control maintained by the Nazi government over its own media.

As a follow-up to Hitler's February speech, Dr. Otto Dietrich again spoke on March 7, this time to a gathering of diplomats and of both

---

5 *New York Times,* February 21, 1938.

German and foreign newsmen meeting in Berlin. By this time undersecretary in the Propaganda Ministry and in charge of press matters, Dietrich said, among other things:

> We see it as the duty of the foreign correspondent to give his fellow-citizens an unprejudiced and truthful picture of a foreign land and its people. Whoever has this conception of his profession can always be sure of our support. We shall not deny him the right of factual criticism.
>
> Whoever, however, has personal feelings of dislike or even hatred for the land of which he is a guest that will bring him into conflict and, perhaps, make impossible objective reporting, should not come to us. By his tendentious writings he harms not only our country but his own also, and becomes the object of a distrust that must eventually lead to a break.
>
> In such cases we have employed expulsion, which is not a National Socialist discovery, but is employed wherever journalists ignore their duty and abuse hospitality. In such cases we have in the past employed expulsion and will employ it in the future.
>
> However, we understand the particular difficulties under which journalists work. We do not believe that every journalist who does not write like a National Socialist is a swine. We recognize that as a member of another people he thinks and feels differently from us, just as we expect Germans abroad to remain constantly conscious of their Germanism.[6]

Magnanimous as he was in conceding that a foreign journalist might not be "a swine" merely because he did not write like a Nazi, Dietrich reverted to his 1937 Nuremberg speech in which he described "liberty of the press" as "one of the hollowest of all empty phrases that ever befogged the human mind."

"If newspapers everywhere would not only talk peace, but also keep the peace themselves," he said, "an atmosphere of mutual respect and understanding would be created that, within a few months, would accomplish what decades of futile efforts failed to accomplish in making a peaceful world." He cited the nonaggression pacts already signed by Germany with Italy, Austria, Poland, Hungary, and Yugoslavia. Such pacts, he said, would be negotiated with other countries whenever the opportunity appeared. He compared them with agreements intended to halt the smuggling of cocaine. Short of such agreements and world-wide "press peace," he warned, the Reich would not hesitate to retaliate in kind whenever it was the victim of "mud-slinging from abroad."

The Hitler-Dietrich proposals, recognized as devices to muzzle the press, were received scornfully in the United States and almost equally so in Great Britain and France. The German invasion of Austria on

---

6   *New York Times,* March 8, 1938; March 13, 1938, sec. E, p. 5.

March 12, five days after Dietrich spoke, underlined the justification for that scorn. The reaction in the United States was epitomized in a cartoon by Max P. Milians showing an armed Nazi climbing the Statue of Liberty, a bludgeon at his belt and a lash protruding from his pocket, as he invited Miss Liberty to sign a "suggested press censorship pact." The Nazi was saying to her, "You stop telling the truth about me—and I won't print any more lies about you! Is it agreed . . .?"

Published comments in Great Britain were milder, so far as they appeared at all. The "appeasement" concept then was being advanced by Dawson of the *Times,* by Lord Astor of the *Observer,* as well as by Prime Minister Chamberlain and others.[7] They chose to believe that Hitler was prepared to make the conclusion of such a pact a condition for the settlement of differences, and a peaceful settlement quite naturally was desired.

In that context, Great Britain did not protest the German invasion and annexation of Austria. In the same month, it showed a readiness to compromise over German demands for control of the Sudeten area of Czechoslovakia by sending a mission to Prague to try to negotiate instead of standing firmly in opposition to Hitler's territorial claims.

Contrary to the situation in the United States, there was a precedent in Great Britain for withholding press publication of information on matters deemed "not in the public interest." Although counted as having a free press, the self-restraint of the newspapers, for example, in a unanimous omission of reports on the relationship between King Edward VIII and Wallis Warfield Simpson until a few days before it culminated in the king's abdication in December 1936 illustrated what might be done in its control. Nor had the public been informed of serious differences between Prime Minister Chamberlain and Foreign Secretary Anthony Eden, rooted in Eden's objections to the appeasement of the Nazi government, until Eden actually resigned in February 1938.

The British government did say in response to the Hitler-Dietrich addresses that there was no intention or possibility on its part of interfering, as suggested, with the freedom of the nation's press. Yet the press itself had shown a willingness to accept restrictive guidance as a demonstration of responsibility in seeking appeasement. It also operated under the shadow of the Defense of the Realm Act (DORA) dating from the period of World War I, and of the Official Secrets Acts

---

7   At a small meeting attended by the writer late in 1937, Lord Astor presented an appeasement view that it might be possible to reach an agreement with Hitler, but the passage of time, producing more dedicated Nazis in Germany, would make any such later agreement less likely.

as passed and amended by Parliament between 1889 and 1939, with its provisions invoked at times. All of this combined to shape a milder British expression with reference to the Nazi proposals by which the foreign press might be brought under a curb.

As for France, the third important free press country surviving among the larger world powers in 1938, its newspapers often had demonstrated a readiness to accept payment to shape their policies, as most recently at the time of the Italo-Ethiopian War. Both the Agence Havas and some newspapers were subsidized by the French government itself.

In these circumstances, there was some reason for the Nazi leaders to believe there might be a basis for success in their desire for non-aggression press pacts. Yet it was a false expectation, actually. Beyond that, it was ill-timed. The invasion of Austria, an exercise in brute power against one of the countries that had signed a nonaggression press pact earlier, and coming so soon after Dietrich and Hitler had spoken, raised a storm of disapproval in most countries of the world. As promised, the Nazi government and press responded with "National Socialist thoroughness," which meant with violence and vituperation, and with no modification of policies.

German pressure on Czechoslovakia continued, leading to the Munich conference where Great Britain and France further appeased Hitler by yielding to his demand for control of the Sudetenland, followed almost predictably by the seizure and annexation of all of Czechoslovakia in March 1939. Soon after the Munich conference, the results of which brought outraged protests throughout the world, Prime Minister Chamberlain, speaking in the House of Commons, remarked that "it is not one of the characteristics of the totalitarian states to foul their own nests!"

Whether properly or not, this statement was taken by some to mean that he felt that a substantial portion of the British press, to say nothing of the press of the United States and many other countries, was behaving less admirably than the German press in news and editorial treatment of the Munich settlement made at Czech expense. Yet, within the British press itself, and apart from the shabby treatment accorded Ebbutt, two respected correspondents were dismissed because they ventured to write books critical of British government policy at Munich. These were Douglas Reed, correspondent with the *Times* since 1927, who wrote *Insanity Fair: A European Cavalcade* in 1938, and G. E. R. Gedye, correspondent for the *Daily Telegraph* since 1929, who wrote *Fallen Bastions* in 1939 (published in the United States as *Betrayal in Central Europe*).[8]

---

8   Reed remained active with the more liberal *News-Chronicle,* and Gedye with the *New York Times.*

The French press and radio omitted many references to Germany that might have offended the Nazi leadership, and did so presumably at the request of Premier Daladier, another architect of the Munich settlement. Germany itself spent substantial sums, particularly between March and November 1938, to buy the support of venal French journals and journalists, even as the Italian Fascist government had done during its Ethiopian venture of 1935-36.

Concession to German pressure, based on fear of retribution rather than venality, followed protests from Berlin over publication in the Copenhagen *Berlingske Tidende* of a speech by a member of the British House of Commons concerning Nazi atrocities against the Jews. Even so, on that occasion the newspaper made an apology and its foreign editor, Nicolas Blaedel, was sent on a long vacation. Other vulnerable European newspapers published in countries adjacent to Germany yielded to direct or implied warnings and were understandably cautious about what they published. Some newspapers and some governments even as far removed as Latin America were responsive to German and Italian propaganda and financial manipulation. The media of Italy, Spain, and Japan, as well as of the Soviet Union, subject to their own government restraints and reflecting the problems and objectives of those governments, were not disposed to be critical of Germany.

This left the press and radio of the United States as the most independent and most outspoken in the world, as well as the most informative about Nazi government activities and policies and those of other totalitarian states. It was matched in this respect by much of the British Commonwealth press, and hardly less by the media of the United Kingdom, allowing for the appeasement element. This was an important segment of the world media structure and remained as an irritant to the Nazi regime.

From the time of the total annexation of Czechoslovakia in March 1939, the denouement in Europe was not long in coming. The Spanish Civil War ended in that same month. Fascist Italy invaded Albania in April. Great Britain began a program of serious rearmament, and unrealistically joined with France in assuring support to Poland in the event of a German attack, and then also unrealistically pledged the same to Rumania and Greece as well. Meanwhile, those secret negotiations had been proceeding between Nazi Germany and Soviet Russia, with trade and nonaggression treaties concluded in August. On September 1 Germany invaded Poland, and on September 3 France and Great Britain, honoring their assurances of aid to Poland, both declared war on Germany.

The media, already reporting a war in Asia since 1931, and also having reported wars and crises since 1935 in Ethiopia, Spain, the Rhineland, Austria, and Czechoslovakia, now became engaged in reporting a war destined to overspread the European continent.

The Soviet Union, because of its governing political ideology and deliberate self-containment, was less directly affected by the economic dislocations sweeping much of the world in the early 1930s. Its commercial and financial relations with other nations were limited—those aspects of capitalism standing contrary to communist policy. The domestic economy was stimulated by the 1928 Five Year Plan and proceeded in a program of construction and industrialization providing employment opportunities. Indeed, foreign engineers and specialists were invited to participate in the work.

There was great interest throughout much of the world in the Five Year Plan as an imaginative undertaking, with a successful result possibly to bring the Soviet Union into a more normal and friendly relationship within the international community of nations. Although foreign correspondents in Moscow were rarely given opportunity to see the projects under way, the subject was nonpolitical and the concept so generally favorable in purpose that they were able to write about it without transgressing restrictions of censorship.

All was not well within the country, however. Problems emerging even from the Five Year Plan itself were included among others that placed correspondents at cross purposes with the censorship. For one thing, the great costs of dams, power plants, and factories were met largely by dumping Russian oil, grain, timber, and other materials in foreign markets in such quantities and at such prices as to contribute to the disruption of some of those markets already suffering from the world depression. This invited counter measures, including tariff rate increases. The value of the ruble in markets at home and abroad was adversely affected, instituting an inflationary trend. The progress of the Five Year Plan was uneven, and the quality of the work often faulty. These were not subjects correspondents were encouraged to investigate or report.

Further, much of the work of the Five Year Plan was remote from settled areas, offering virtually no employment for city dwellers. The concentration on requirements under the Plan also meant that the production of consumer goods, already in short supply, was slighted. The general standard of living therefore declined in a considerable reversal from the period of the New Economic Policy in effect for some years prior to 1926. This caused public discontent, if not hardship. Here again correspondents were restricted in obtaining reliable information, or reporting what they did learn.

Agriculture was another sensitive area. A return to farm collectivization involved confiscation of the property of independent farmers, or *kulaks*, with many deported, put to forced labor, or relocated to work on the collectives. The program was so inefficient that food shortages were common. Grain was being exported, and a great famine occurred in 1932–33, more serious than that which had brought the American Relief Administration into the country in 1921.

Rumors of the famine centering in the Ukraine reached Moscow, with estimates that it had taken five million lives. It was a topic not mentioned in the Soviet press and was barred from foreign correspondents' reports, so far as possible. Only after a good harvest had corrected the situation in the fall of 1933 were several correspondents at last permitted to visit the Ukraine. There they learned that the gravity of the famine had not been exaggerated, but they still could not tell the full story.[9]

In discussing the problem, William Henry Chamberlin, who left the country after ten years as Moscow correspondent for the *Christian Science Monitor,* was able to explain that the very word "famine" never would have been passed by the censorship. If the food situation was "acute," and if mentioned at all, it might be referred to as "difficult." If really "desperate," only then might "acute" be acceptable, but other phrases more likely to pass the censorship would include a reference to "a food shortage" or "food stringency," "belt-tightening" or "diseases of malnutrition."

In the Ukraine, Chamberlin talked with as many persons as possible. As Litvinov in 1921 had said that "food is a weapon," so the president of a district Soviet Executive Committee, responding to questions in 1933, said that to have attempted to avert the loss of life in 1932 by importing grain from abroad "would have been injurious to our prestige," while to have stopped the requisition of the peasants' grain would mean that "they never would have worked hard again because they would always expect the Government to come to their aid." So, he said, "the Government went on the path it chose consciously."

The population of the USSR in 1930 was estimated at about 157 million. Of these, no more than a million were counted as members of the Communist party. Josef Stalin, consolidating his powers as head of the party and of the government, was not only dictatorial but para-

---

9 In northern China, south of the Gobi desert, at about the same time, famine also took about five million lives. This also went unreported. Annual Yellow River floods, enormously costly to life and property, also went unreported. In China, however, this was not because of censorship, but because of a lack of organized coverage and communication.

noic in the projection of his policies, and he was psychotic in his suspicion of others. These were years of terror, and by Stalin's direction there were numberless arrests by the secret police.[10]

Even so highly placed a Communist party member as Leon Trotsky was ousted and exiled in 1929 along with others. He was later murdered in Mexico. Persons arrested were relocated, exiled, or executed. There were mass deportations, even of entire village populations, to forced labor camps in Siberia, the Solovetzky Islands, and the Marin territory in the Arctic. Millions were affected and often required to live under subhuman conditions, as described by Alexander I. Solzhenitsyn in *The Gulag Archipelago, 1918–1956* (1973).[11]

A general purge of the Communist party membership in the Soviet Union began in 1933, preceding the Nazi party blood purge of 1934. Stalin's suspicions turned first, however, to four British engineers connected with the Metropolitan Vickers organization in Russia to aid in the Five Year Plan construction program. Arrested and brought to trial in Moscow in April 1933, they were charged and found guilty of complicity in a plot to sabotage the new Dneprostroi hydroelectric plant. When the British government protested and placed an embargo on Soviet goods, the engineers were permitted to leave Russia.

Others were less fortunate. The assassination in December 1934 of Serge Kirov, a close associate of Stalin's, led to the arrest of many party members. Four of them, all former members of the Politburo, were Grigori Zinoviev, Aleksei Rykov, Nikolai Bukharin, and Lev Kamenev. Tried for treason and conspiracy in January 1935, they were sentenced to from five to ten years in prison. In 1936, Zinoviev, Kamenev, and fourteen others were back in court being tried as "Trotskyites" and "enemies of the people," and charged with plotting against the regime. To the surprise of foreign observers, they confessed to most of the charges and were convicted and promptly executed.

Through 1937, trials of other party leaders continued, among them Karl Radek, Joseph Doletzky, director of the Tass agency, and Vladimir Romm, former Tass correspondent in Geneva and Washington, where he was well liked and gained a voluntary but ineffective defense from his colleagues there. No less than thirteen more party leaders

---

10   The secret police were variously known through the years under the acronyms for the changing organizations, among them the GPU, Cheka, OGPU, MVD, MGA, KGA, and KGB.

11   Again, Chamberlin indicates that the euphemisms for "mass deportation," "forced labor," or "labor camps," if permitted at all, might become "state-assisted migration," "labor of prisoners," and "state-supported colonization of unsettled areas."

were executed following trials in that year; others in 1938 included Rykov and Bukharin.

Charges also were brought in 1937 against officers in the Red Army and members of the Soviet diplomatic corps accused of conspiring with Germany and Japan. One of them, Marshal Ian Borisovich, apparently committed suicide. Marshal Mikhail N. Tukhachevski and seven other generals were tried in a secret court-martial and executed.

The liquidation of such leaders of the Communist party itself, along with numberless others, and the expulsion of about 350,000 party members between 1933 and 1939, made Stalin and the Soviet Union greatly despised throughout the world and reversed any earlier hope that the Soviet Union might become a respected member of the world family of nations. Andre Y. Vishinsky, chief prosecutor for the government, shared in this general opprobrium. Except for the army court-martial, the trials were open to foreign correspondents.

Despite these negative events and a dubious result of the much-publicized Five Year Plan, there were certain advances to be reported during the 1930s. The diplomatic recognition of the Soviet Union by the United States came in November 1933. Trade relations were opened, and William C. Bullitt became the first U.S. ambassador in the country since before the revolution. His presence, along with members of the embassy staff, was reassuring and helpful to U.S. correspondents. Bullitt immediately introduced weekly news conferences, and John Wiley, embassy counsellor, was available at other times as a source of information. What the existing British, French, and other embassies had meant to correspondents for the media of their countries now was matched for the U.S. correspondents, and added a source available for others as well.

Although there was an inflationary problem in the Soviet Union, and a strong campaign against religious orders, there also was a curtailment in the earlier aggressive program of proselyting for communism throughout the world by the Third International. There was at that time no military build-up in the nation, and Soviet representatives were sent to the 1932 Geneva Disarmament Conference, while non-aggression treaties were signed with Poland, Finland, Estonia, Latvia, and France, and later with Rumania and Czechoslovakia. These moves all reduced international tensions. Tensions with China, arising from the expulsion of Soviet advisers from the Kuomintang in 1927 and a contest centering around the Chinese Eastern Railway in Manchuria in 1929 also were eased. In 1935, the Soviet Union sold its interest in that Manchuria railway to Japan, removing another thorny issue.

The formation of the Nazi regime in Germany in January 1933, with its consistent expression of hostility toward the Soviet Union, became a reason for Moscow to reverse its own former rejection of the League of Nations and to enter into membership in September 1934. It also turned the Third International to the support of the western democracies and against the German and Italian Fascist regimes. Further, the Soviet Union formed alliances with France and Czechoslovakia. It then began a program of armament and gave military support to the Spanish Republic in 1936 in that country's civil war, while Italy and Germany supported the Insurgents in opposition to the Republic.

These various changes in the Soviet Union could have made matters easier for the foreign press group in Moscow. Actually, except for the establishment there of a U.S. Embassy, things became more difficult because of the growing terror within the country. The foreign press corps in 1934 numbered twenty-five or thirty, of whom seven were representatives of the U.S. press. Chamberlin had left permanently in 1934, after a decade in Moscow, Duranty of the *New York Times* also left in 1934, and Louis Fischer of the *Nation,* a third veteran, left in 1935.

The last more or less favorable reference by any correspondent to the censors in the Press Department was made in 1934 by Harold N. Denny, who had just succeeded Duranty there for the *New York Times.* He said that the censors were "competent and courteous, and sometimes surprisingly liberal." Recognizing that every correspondent had encountered "troubles with dispatches he considered entirely innocent," Denny also said that at times "censors have been of positive help." Beyond that time, such statements were not heard.

It had been conceded earlier that the need to depend on euphemisms to satisfy the censors might deprive some news reports both of impact and accuracy and, to that extent, leave readers less than well informed. The hope was, however, that the careful reader sufficiently interested to turn to books and other sources, and aware of the correspondent's problem, would understand the euphemisms, would read between the lines, and would establish a perspective or perhaps a belated comprehension. While this expected a good deal of the average reader, even more had to be expected of him after 1934.

Difficult as things had been previously for the correspondent, his dependence upon the Press Department of the Commissariat of Foreign Affairs increased. The censorship centered there, as did arrangements for permits to travel, to visit institutions, or to meet officials. Restrictions became greater in all respects, and individual Soviet citizens aware of the terror were more cautious than ever about speaking to foreigners.

The actual transmission of press dispatches and the handling of telephone service and radio broadcasts by correspondents was the function of the Office of Post and Telegraph, controlled by a Commissariat for Communication.

The correspondent was greatly dependent on Soviet publications for information and subject matter. Such publications, along with Soviet radio and photographs, were subject to domestic censorship. This domestic control rested with the Chief Administration of Affairs of Literature and Publishers (Glavnoye Upravleniy po Delam Literatura u Izdatelstv), commonly referred to as "Glavlit," and technically attached to the Commissariat of Education.

Directives to the Soviet press and media were channeled through the Administration of Propaganda and Agitation (Otdel po Propaganda i Agitataii), usually spoken of as "Agitprop," and itself a division of the Communist party's high-level Central Committee.

With many agencies each exercising its own degree of control over what a correspondent was able to learn and then to dispatch, and with increased tensions under the terror, the correspondent was under so severe a squeeze that there was very little left for him to report each day. Particularly for a special correspondent of a newspaper seeking background to add depth and substance to his reports, the restrictions by 1936 became such that he could send no more than a news agency correspondent whose function it was to adhere to basic facts only; and he had trouble enough obtaining them. But for a newspaper to maintain a special correspondent in Moscow at great expense, merely to duplicate the substance of news agency dispatches that the paper would receive, in any event, was a waste of time, talent, and money. For that reason, some special correspondents left Moscow at that period.[12]

Denny of the *New York Times* was able to write a series of reports relating to the treason trials of 1937 and have them carried out of Russia for publication. Surprisingly, there were no repercussions. In the autumn of 1937, he also went on leave to Paris. There he wrote another series of articles about Soviet life and affairs, again without censorship, yet was granted a re-entry visa, and returned to Moscow in the spring of 1938. There he learned that his Russian secretary, Valentina Snigirsvskaya, who had made transcripts of the trials, had been arrested in March, shortly before Denny returned. She was not to be heard from again.

---

12 One of the very few exclusive and exceptional stories by any correspondent during those years came in October 1936. There had been rumors that Stalin was dead, or dying, or was to make a journey to the United States for a serious operation. Charles P. Nutter, then chief of the Associated Press bureau in Moscow, submitted a written query to the Kremlin. He received a reply written and signed by Stalin himself, in blue pencil, and addressed to Nutter personally. In it, Stalin invited the world to believe that he was dead and "not to disturb me in the calm of the other world."

Two circumstances relating to censorship occurred early in 1939. The first was a suggestion presented in *Izvestia* in March that control should be relaxed over the writing of those worker-peasant correspondents, or *rab'selkor,* in the preparation of their letters to certain of the Soviet newspapers citing faults in factories and on the farms. Such correspondents, *Izvestia* noted, were obliged to submit their reports to the district party Executive Committee secretary before they were sent along to the newspapers. The secretaries, it was pointed out, had no wish to have shortcomings in their districts given publicity, and tended to cut and amend a report until it lost its point. Yet the purpose of the system was to reveal faults so that corrections might be made.

"It is because of this widespread censorship," applied at the district level, *Izvestia* objected, "that so much unlawful activity is allowed to go unchecked. It is a scandalous state of affairs." This was a comment on method, rather than policy. Coming from the government newspaper, and presumably reflecting a high-level party view, it might have foreshadowed a change. Yet no such change occurred. When *Izvestia* referred to the issue again, it was only to say that the paper had "erred gravely" in its observation. That was the final word.

The second event was of greater importance, significant in more ways than one. It began on May 3, 1939, with an announcement that Maxim Litvinov was replaced as foreign commissar by Vyacheslav Molotov, the one regarded as relatively liberal, the other a hard-line old Bolshevik. The change was reported as being made at Litvinov's request, for reasons of health. Few believed this, and soon were persuaded that Litvinov knew nothing of the change until the last moment.

On May 4, correspondents were summoned to a night meeting at the Foreign Commissariat. There the chief of the Press Department and supervisor of censorship informed them that by Molotov's instructions "from today the preliminary censorship of messages to the foreign press is abolished." The censorship at the Press Department, in effect since 1921, thus ended—temporarily as it turned out.

There was a qualification in the new ruling in that censorship itself was not abolished, but there would be no preliminary censorship as previously. Instead all dispatches were to be filed at the Post and Telegraph Office for direct transmission. Telephone connections and radio broadcasts could be made there as before, also without the earlier requirements of prior censorship. The qualification existed in a warning to correspondents that they would be held personally responsible if subsequent examination of their dispatches or a monitoring or recording of their telephone conversations or transmissions or of their radio broadcasts indicated that they had overstepped the line of propriety previously drawn by the censorship and had sent matter deemed hostile to the USSR or injurious to its prestige. In such case, the correspondents were told, "the Soviet government without delay will deprive such correspondent of his right to stay within the borders of the Soviet Union"

This marked the first use anywhere of a form of control under which a correspondent was in effect made responsible for censoring his own copy. It was referred to by correspondents as a "responsibility censorship." In practice, it meant that the correspondent might exercise an even stricter control than the official censor, lest he be expelled. This raised the question as to his own possible future assignment and also the prospect that his replacement, lacking a familiarity with the situation, would be in an even more difficult position.

The reason for this sudden change of censorship method remained a puzzle for some time. One almost immediate result was that the *Times* of London, always unwilling to accept a preliminary censorship, appointed its first resident correspondent in Russia since 1917. James Holburn, formerly in Berlin for the paper, arrived in Moscow in the late spring of 1939.

The responsibility censorship remained in effect for eight months, from May 4 until December 29, 1939. The reason for the sudden replacement of Litvinov by Molotov in the Foreign Commissariat in May became clear after the announcements in late August that nonaggression and trade treaties had been concluded between the Soviet Union and Nazi Germany. Molotov, it appeared, had been the chief Soviet negotiator in the matter, dealing directly with Germany's Foreign Minister von Ribbentrop, with Litvinov unaware of the exchange.

As suddenly as the responsibility censorship had been announced in May, a full censorship preliminary to transmission of reports was reestablished on December 29. This action was explained "first, because of general international conditions and, second, because, in the Soviet government's view, results of the abolition of censorship have not been satisfactory to them." During the nearly eight months that had intervened, two or three correspondents had been cautioned by the Press Department because of alleged factual errors in dispatches. But there had been no expulsions, and no incidents to explain what the government might mean in saying that the results had not been satisfactory.

International conditions unquestionably had changed, however. When Germany attacked Poland on September 1, 1939, Soviet forces soon moved into eastern Poland and eastern Czechoslovakia. In November, Red Army troops also moved against Finland in a campaign that continued until March 1940, when Finland was obliged to surrender, yielding some 16,000 square miles of territory to the USSR. In

June 1940 Soviet forces also moved into occupancy of the three Baltic republics of Latvia, Estonia, and Lithuania, and into the Bessarabian area of Rumania.

From September 1939, no foreign correspondent was permitted to go from Moscow to report on Red Army action in any of the areas in which it became involved. Aside from formal communiqués, the only news coverage of the Russo-Finnish War from November to March came from correspondents on the Finnish side; the Soviet press itself had little to say about the campaign. Coverage from Riga also ceased to be possible from the time the Red Army entered Latvia in June 1940.

The German official DNB news agency had been represented in Moscow from the time of its establishment in 1933, replacing the Wolff agency. The signing of the Communazi pacts in August 1939 also brought to Moscow representatives of the official *Völkischer Beobachter* and other German dailies with close Nazi party ties, including the *Hamburger Fremdenblatt,* the *National Zeitung* of Essen, and the *Neuste Nachrichten* of Leipzig. They seemed to receive favored treatment. For example, as the war began in September 1939, the telephone ceased to be available for Anglo-American correspondents in Moscow to contact their bureaus or offices outside the USSR; even their service messages, entering or leaving the country, were subject to delay or stoppage. The German correspondents, however, met no such restrictions; they telephoned reports to their papers, and their service messages moved freely.

Through the responsibility censorship period, the substance of the news became even more difficult to obtain in Moscow. The reinstituted preliminary censorship became still more restrictive, and there appeared to be special discrimination against Anglo-American correspondents, perhaps because they were most persistent in seeking to report the news, and perhaps because the media of those countries showed sympathy with the victims of Soviet aggression, especially Finland. The attack on that country resulted in the expulsion of the Soviet Union from the League of Nations.

The preliminary censorship was resumed on December 29, 1939, and returned to the Press Department, but it no longer was an open censorship, with the correspondent meeting directly with a censor. Now the censor acted independently. With the Soviet Union at war, correspondents were reminded that any references affecting the security of the country would be stricken. Yet it was denied as being in any way a military censorship. Objective criticism was not to be barred, correspondents were assured, but neither was any definition offered to indicate what might or might not be regarded as objective. The only concession was a recognition of the international regulations approved at the ITU conference of 1932 and made effective in 1934, whereby a sender was to be notified of any change in a message sent. Elsewhere, that notification often was delayed, as it commonly was in Berlin. But in Moscow, if a censor had objection to some reference, he notified the correspondent by telephone. Usually a compromise then was reached, but the correspondent had the right to withdraw the dispatch if he considered the changes seriously harmful to the substance or coherence of the story.

The end of the open censorship introduced two other circumstances that changed the character of Moscow coverage, again adversely. Previously, censors with appropriate language qualifications had examined correspondents' copy. Under the new, impersonal arrangement this no longer was necessarily so. Previously, censors also had been available at almost any hour, except from 2 A.M. to 10 A.M. This now became 1 A.M. to 10 A.M., subtracting another hour in a capital where news often originated and needed to be dispatched in the very early morning hours.

The first of these circumstances meant that references in stories, even though accurate and unobjectionable, were sometimes cut because they went beyond a censor's vocabulary or understanding.[13] The second circumstance came to be regarded as a deliberate move under which official communiqués during the Russo-Finnish War, and other important releases from government departments, were issued at about 3 A.M. Moscow time, intentionally held to permit their first distribution in an official Soviet version in Tass shortwave broadcasts via Moscow Radio.

This latter procedure worked well, from the Soviet point of view. The Radio Moscow broadcasts were monitored around the world, and became the basis for news reports in virtually all countries. The Moscow broadcast at 3 A.M., for example, was 8 P.M. of the previous date in New York and 5 P.M. in San Francisco. It thus became the basis for late afternoon and evening radio news broadcasts in the United States, Canada, and Latin America, and for news reports in

---

13 Gedye of the *New York Times,* following his departure from Moscow, cited three examples. The word "dyestuffs" was cut from a routine list of products Russia was to receive from Germany under the provisions of the 1939 trade treaty. The censor explained: "Foodstuffs means stuff for food. Dyestuffs means stuff for dying. I am not going to pass an insinuation that the Soviets will import poison gas from Germany." A reference to the "secretaryship of the Comintern" was suppressed "because the Comintern has no ships." A reference to the "Baltic division" of the Foreign Ministry was suppressed "because there are no Soviet troops in the Baltic now—not even a battalion, let alone a division. Besides, the Red Army is not under the Foreign Affairs Commissariat."—*Time,* September 23, 1940.

some afternoon papers in the western sections of the hemisphere, as well as for the morning papers of the following day. The same Moscow broadcast was too late for the morning papers of that date in western Europe, but suitable for morning news broadcasts and for the first editions of afternoon papers. It also provided the first reports for Asia, the Middle East, and Africa.

The result was that no other disinterested reports on the same subjects could be filed by correspondents in Moscow until long after the official Tass versions had been circulated world-wide. Even then, any such reports might not be used because another news cycle could have produced later developments. Edwin L. James, managing editor of the *New York Times,* cited this Moscow procedure as "a squeeze play" by which correspondents in that capital were denied the opportunity to report the news while it was still news.

The special correspondent in Moscow had been under a disadvantage since 1936, and was even more handicapped by these developments in 1939. In the circumstances, the *New York Times* chose to close its Moscow bureau in March 1940, after more than eighteen years. "Things became so pestiferous we got fed up," James said, adding that "the Russians would be pleased if all foreign correspondents got out. It is undignified to keep a correspondent there under those conditions."

The *New York Herald Tribune* had reached the same conclusion even earlier, and had closed its Moscow bureau in 1939. The *Christian Science Monitor* had done the same early in 1940, after seventeen years. The *Times* of London followed suit, withdrew Holburn late in September 1940, after about a year of representation within the Soviet Union. Gedye, the last *New York Times* correspondent, summarized the situation, writing from a new post in Istanbul:

> The Government of the Soviet Union has been and is pursuing a policy of the starkest realism. . . . Moscow remains today one of the most important political centers of the world. As a news center it has ceased to exist and every correspondent still there knows that his work is entirely valueless. It is even misleading, for he is able to present only that version of events which the Soviet authorities desire to be accepted abroad. Correspondents have been reduced to precis-writers to Tass and the official press. More exactly, they are allowed to summarize only such portions of the Moscow statements as it is thought desirable for the outside world to know.[14]

When Gedye wrote, the western correspondents remaining included Holburn of the *Times,* who left a few days later; A. T. Cholerton for

---

14   *Editor & Publisher* (September 14, 1940), p. 6.

the *Daily Telegraph;* John Scott for the *News-Chronicle;* and news agency representatives. These included Henry Shapiro of the United Press; Henry C. Cassidy for the Associated Press, with Robert Magidoff as assistant; Maurice Lovell, who had replaced John Wallis, for Reuters; and Jean Champenois, who had represented the Havas agency until it became a casualty of the war, with France's surrender in June 1940. It remained as a new Free French agency based in London, the Agence L.E.F. (for "liberté, egalité, fraternité").

The interval between September 1940 and June 1941 was the most difficult in the history of foreign press reporting of Soviet affairs since correspondents had been officially admitted to that country in 1921. It was a period during which a half dozen men maintained little more than a technical presence in Moscow, representing primarily the United Press, the Associated Press, and Reuters. This was to change only after June 22, 1941. On that date, with the objective of his 1939 non-aggression treaty attained, as he believed, Hitler turned his armies against Russia. Stalin, equally cynical and equally pragmatic, reversed the Communist party policy toward the foreign media, and sought to enlist them in his own support.

U.S.A.

The step by step descent of the world into the abyss of war during the decade of the 1930s was touched off by the New York stock market crash of October 1929. Japan fired the first shots in Manchuria in 1931. Ten years later, in December 1941, the United States became the last major nation to be drawn into the war, with Japan again the aggressor.

President Hoover, in the White House from March 1929 until March 1933, was confronted throughout most of that period by the problems of the national and world economic depression. His administration found no solution nationally. His chief contribution, internationally, undoubtedly was his proposal of 1931 for a year's moratorium on the payment of reparations and war debts. Renominated as the Republican party candidate in the presidential campaign of 1932, he was confronted by so deep a public discontent arising from the national economic dislocation that, not surprisingly, he lost his bid for re-election in a landslide vote going to Franklin D. Roosevelt, the Democratic party candidate.

Inaugurated March 4, 1933, Roosevelt found the country at its lowest ebb. He promised an administrative policy dedicated to a restoration of the economy. A "bank holiday" was proclaimed immediately, with all financial institutions closed for several days. During a special session, Congress promptly granted unprecedented emergency powers to the president. A succession of measures referred to as the "New Deal" and intended to put the country on a recovery course soon began to receive congressional attention.[15] The gold standard was abandoned in April 1933, and banks by then appeared under firm control. A "Good Neighbor" policy was introduced to improve relations with Latin America. A World Economic Conference meeting in London in June-July was supported, but had little useful result because Roosevelt himself disapproved the priority of currency stabilization on its agenda. Diplomatic recognition was extended by the U.S. to the Soviet Union in November. In December the twenty-first amendment to the Constitution was ratified, permitting resumption of the manufacture and sale of alcoholic beverages, halted in 1920 under provisions of the eighteenth amendment.

Important in the Roosevelt administration also was another "new deal" in press relations at the White House itself. Under President Hoover, presidential news conferences had become infrequent, and ceased altogether after the election of November 1932. This changed promptly under Roosevelt. His first news conference met in the White House office four days after inauguration. In that first week, he also addressed the people of the country in a first informal radio "Fireside Chat."[16]

Roosevelt entered the presidency with long experience in meeting reporters and correspondents. Active in politics since his youth, he had been a member of the New York State senate, assistant secretary of the navy during the Wilson administration, Democratic vice-presidential candidate in the 1920 campaign, and governor of New York State for two terms from 1929 to 1932. Like his kinsman, former President Theodore Roosevelt, he had a keen sense of press relations and procedures and, like President Wilson, a feeling for what might be accomplished by reaching the people of the nation and of the world through the medium of the press and of the radio as well.

Upon taking office, Roosevelt named the first full-time presidential press secretary, Stephen T. Early, an experienced Associated Press correspondent in the capital. He abandoned the practice of requiring

---

15   These measures provided for legislation dealing with agriculture, banking, home financing, monetary policy, relief, unemployment, security markets, labor-management relations, industry, public utilities, and other matters. They were not universally approved, and two acts passed by Congress were found unconstitutional by the Supreme Court, but they did combine to help restore the nation.

16   The term was suggested by Harry C. Butcher, then director of the CBS radio station WTOP in Washington.

written questions, submitted in advance of conferences, as required since the Harding administration, and was able to deal skillfully and informatively with questions as they were presented orally. Direct quotations, however, were still to be used only with permission.

From the outset, Roosevelt held two news conferences each week, usually on Tuesdays at 4 P.M. and Fridays at 10:30 A.M., thus giving equal opportunity for first publication of the news to morning and afternoon papers in the eastern and possibly in the central time zones. Afternoon papers in the mountain and Pacific time zones also could use reports from the Tuesday conferences in their late editions, while radio news broadcasts could include matter originating at either conference.

When the president was in Washington, the conferences took place in his office at the White House, in what later became known as the oval office. Steve Early and others were at the president's side, and sometimes officials, advisers, and guests. Among them were Marvin H. McIntyre, former city editor of the *Washington Star* and a member of the secretarial staff, and Louis McHenry Howe, for fifteen years Albany correspondent for the *New York Herald* and a close personal friend and confidant of the president. To such persons he might turn for supplementary remarks and information by way of response to questions asked. An official transcript was always made.

A vast amount of news came from the White House conferences of twenty or thirty minutes duration. They were well attended, sometimes with 200 or more filling the room, all standing. Occasionally, conferences were transformed into what amounted to seminars of longer duration, as when an administration budget was about to be presented to Congress. Chairs then were brought in so that the correspondents might be seated, hear the items discussed, consult related documents, view charts prepared for the meeting, and make careful notes.

When the president went to his own home at Hyde Park, up the Hudson River from New York, as he did frequently, or later to his retreat at Warm Springs, Georgia, or when he made visits to other parts of the country or of the world, he was accompanied by senior correspondents for the three U.S. news agencies, AP, UP, and INS. News conferences continued on such occasions. They met, with rare exceptions, on a twice-a-week basis, throughout Roosevelt's twelve years in office. His Fireside Chats, although less frequent than news conferences, numbering only eight during his first four years, for example, reached more persons than ever before addressed by any head of state, thanks to the radio medium. The same was true for his public addresses, with the texts also usually available to the press in advance and sometimes published in full.

At the White House, correspondents gathered in advance of the hour appointed for conferences. When the president was ready and seated at his desk, they would enter and stand in a semicircle. He opened the conference by making such announcements and comments as he wished, and then invited questions.

Roosevelt's relations with correspondents, in and out of the White House, were amiable and mutually useful. They respected his open and informative responses and his impartiality. He learned to know them as friends, addressing many on a first-name basis. He gained information from them, as they did from him. There were moments of irritation, but they were rare, far outbalanced by times of shared amusement and laughter. No president, before or since, has had such a consistently good relationship with the media representatives.

So much news developed at the White House through the hours of every day that Early, as presidential press secretary, required a staff of his own and, after 1936, conducted his own daily and then twice-daily news conferences in his office in the executive wing of the mansion. He and his assistants were available to correspondents, foreign as well as domestic, both directly and by telephone at almost any time.

Mrs. Eleanor Roosevelt played a far more active role than any previous first lady. Of great personal capability and possessing wide interests, she was constantly active and traveled far afield at times, frequently acting as "eyes and ears" for the president. She required her own press secretary, Malvina (Tommy) Thompson, who also assisted as Mrs. Roosevelt conducted a weekly news conference to speak of her observations and interests and to respond to questions. These meetings, held in the Monroe Room on the second floor of the White House, tended to be informal, with an exchange of ideas and information. Except on one occasion, when she had returned from a foreign journey, they were open only to women correspondents. This circumstance helped to establish women firmly as essential members of the Washington press corps. From 1935, Mrs. Roosevelt wrote of her activities in a short daily column, "My Day," which was widely syndicated.

The beginning of the Roosevelt administration in 1933 marked the beginning of a distinct new period in the history of the United States and of the information media as well. The task of the administration was to try to solve the economic and social problems besetting the country, and those besetting the world could not fail to enter the equation. The complexities and urgency of these nation-wide problems required matching action on a scale that could only be provided by the national government.

The president had to find men and women of special qualifications, if solutions were to be found. The problems seemed so desperate in

1933 that the members of the Congress had been willing to grant him extraordinary emergency powers. The group he brought together was referred to, partly in jest, as "the brain trust." Perhaps not since the time of the constitutional convention of 1787 had so dedicated a group addressed itself to the welfare of the nation. Even as the concept of press freedom had concerned those others, leading to the Bill of Rights in 1791, so a concern for full public information was greatly present in 1933.

Relations of the press in Washington with the legislative and judicial branches of the government were, by tradition, excellent, as they were also with the executive branch, and in 1933 the relations with the White House moved to a new high level. Beyond that, every department and agency, if it had not already done so, appointed a suitably qualified public information officer and staff to assist media representatives. As the president conducted his news conferences, cabinet officers also met with correspondents.

The complexity of affairs from 1933 was such that those men and women of the press and radio assigned to Washington, or otherwise reporting substantive news, needed to possess an understanding of economics, finance, social issues, and international relations beyond what had been expected in the past. They obviously needed to be able to comprehend the subjects demanding attention if they were to make them comprehensible to the public. Some news people were prepared to meet this requirement and more rose to the occasion.

Prior to 1930 or 1933, reports from Washington had tended to be heavily political and sometimes partisan, concentrating on national, regional, and even local issues, considerably personalized and sometimes trivial. General news, local and otherwise, tended often to be superficial. The gravity of the national and world depression changed that, bringing a concern for serious issues examined in depth and increasingly within a world context. This gave a new maturity to the media. It was not easy for some publishers and editors to grasp the fact that a transformation was being forced upon all peoples. Contributing, however, was a generation of journalists, many of them young, and some very recently out of colleges and universities.

The greater concern with substantive news after 1933 was reflected in the United States also by the appearance of a growing number of foreign correspondents in New York and Washington. They were concerned with the New Deal program for whatever it might mean in producing solutions to social and economic problems also affecting their own various countries. Further, the critical events transpiring on all continents had repercussions in Washington that made it a major world capital in every sense, requiring attention by the media of all lands.

The prevailing spirit in Washington, and no less in New York, seemed to be that everybody was working together to accomplish a most urgent healing of a national and international economic and social malaise. The correspondents were as sincerely involved as any. The caliber of the Washington correspondents at the time was revealed in a careful analysis conducted over a period of sixteen months in 1935-36 by Dr. Leo C. Rosten, working under a fellowship from the Social Science Research Council of New York. The results were presented in a classic volume of its kind, *The Washington Correspondents* (1937).[17]

Robin J. Cruikshank of the London *News-Chronicle,* representative of the best among overseas reporters in New York and Washington, saw the United States at that period as "the political and economic laboratory of the western world." He wrote:

> The gigantic experiments now being made in the political test tubes of Washington are being followed with as much attention on the other side of the Atlantic as on this. The outcome of these experiments is bound to affect parties and policies in other lands. This is one reason why the work of foreign correspondents here is more important today than it has ever been before. It is a privilege to assist in the making of history, but it also is a responsibility. It needs a trained intelligence, a patient understanding and an instinctive sympathy. The pace at Washington is so fierce these days that the foreign correspondent, like Alice in Wonderland, has to run at top speed in order to keep on the same spot.[18]

It was precisely to assist correspondents in keeping pace with the course of events that all branches of government provided what help they could. The appointment of information officers and the ready availability of published texts and documents brought some accusations that the administration was engaging in self-serving publicity and propaganda. This was hardly to be taken seriously, because there were so many other news sources in Washington and elsewhere in the country to which correspondents could turn to check the accuracy of information received, while other sources also would be quick to make such corrections as they deemed appropriate.

News relating to the national economic situation and to crisis and war elsewhere in the world dominated in press and radio coverage in the United States throughout the 1930s. Great attention went also to

---

17 Almost coincidentally, *The Press and World Affairs* (1937), a first comprehensive study of international news reporting and originally a doctoral dissertation at the University of London School of Economics and Political Science, was published in London and New York by Robert W. Desmond.

18 See *Editor & Publisher* (April 7, 1934), p. 16.

the three presidential campaigns of 1932, 1936, and 1940, with Roosevelt elected and then returned for a second and an unprecedented third term, and indeed a fourth in 1944. There were strong winds of change blowing in the areas of labor-management relations and social and educational concepts.

The first Roosevelt administration included an elaborate Century of Progress Exposition in Chicago in 1933. That became an occasion for the flight of an Italian air squadron of twenty-four planes from Italy to Chicago and return. The squadron was under the command of General Italo Balbo, also prominent in the direction of the Fascist party and government. The flight was significant in marking the great advance that had by then occurred in aviation.

The 1920s had produced a dramatic evidence of that progress, much of it already mentioned, having included Charles A. Lindbergh's solo flight across the Atlantic in 1927, with others following; the flights of Richard E. Byrd over the North Pole in 1926, across the Atlantic in 1927, and over the South Pole in 1929; and the flight of the first woman, Amelia Earhart, across the Atlantic in 1928. In the Pacific, Lieutenants Lester J. Maitland and Albert F. Hegenberger, U.S. Army pilots, had flown from Oakland, California, to Honolulu in June 1927, and Sir Charles Kingsford-Smith and a crew of seven flew from Oakland to Brisbane, Australia, in June 1928. Dirigible balloons also were in the air. The *Graf Zeppelin,* based at Friedrichshafen, Germany, and commanded by Hugo Eckener, became notable in crossing the Atlantic to Lakehurst, New Jersey, in 1928; in flying 21,700 miles around the world by way of Japan in 1929; and by 1937 in the completion of 500 flights, of which 144 were ocean crossings, carrying 13,110 passengers, plus mail and freight.

These advances in air transport continued in the 1930s, with commercial services introduced. The U.S.-based Pan American Airways began Key West–Havana flights in 1927, which were extended to the West Indies and South America in the early 1930s. Using flying boats and retitled Pan-American World Airways in 1935, a "China Clipper" service began between San Francisco, Honolulu, and Manila. It was soon extended to Hong Kong. A "Dixie Clipper" service began in June 1939 between New York and Lisbon.

Meanwhile, a British Imperial Airways in 1929 began a commercial air service between England and India, later extended to Australia and Hong Kong. Commercial airlines introduced service in the mid-1920s between cities in Europe, and in the 1930s also in the United States, Canada, Latin America, and China. Germany's *Hindenburg* airship, twice the size of the *Graf Zeppelin,* made its first flight from Friedrichshafen to Lakehurst in August 1936, crossing the Atlantic in just over fifty-one hours. It was used in regular commercial service in the following nine months, carrying more than 1,000 passengers in some luxury on ten round-trip flights.

This new "air age" was not without its disasters, however. The last flight of the *Hindenburg* provided a notable example. Landing at Lakehurst on May 6, 1937, with ninety-seven passengers and crew, it burst into flames and was completely destroyed, with thirty-six lives lost. Photographers present to record a routine landing obtained dramatic pictures of the burning aircraft. Herbert Morrison, holding an open microphone to describe the arrival, broadcast a famous and emotional description of the tragedy on a national radio network hookup.

In other air disasters, the British dirigible *R-101* crashed at Beauvais, France, in October 1930, with forty-seven killed; the U.S. dirigibles *Akron* and *Macon,* and the Soviet dirigible *Maxim Gorky,* were lost, the first in 1933, with seventy-five killed, and the others in 1935. Wiley Post, who had flown the Atlantic in 1929 and again in 1931, was killed with Will Rogers, the actor, humorist, and syndicated columnist, when their plane was lost near Point Barrow, Alaska, in August 1935. Amelia Earhart, who had married New York publisher George Palmer Putnam in 1931, had flown the Atlantic again in 1932 and the Pacific, from Honolulu to Oakland, in 1935. On June 1, 1937, she left Miami on a projected flight around the world, with Fred Noonan as navigator. Both were lost when their plane vanished after leaving New Guinea on July 2.

In addition to the advances in aviation in the 1920s and 1930s, mediumwave and shortwave radio, recordings, and motion pictures, to which sound and color had been added, were working great changes in the way of life in the U.S. and the world. In transport, too, rail services were improved and new luxury liners and cargo vessels constructed since the war were in service on all the seas. The French Line had the *Normandie* and other ships on the North Atlantic run in 1935. The British Cunard-White Star Line put the *Queen Mary* in service in 1936 and the *Queen Elizabeth* later. These two ships, the largest afloat, set new records of less than four days for the crossing. The *Queen Mary* crossed in 1938 in 3 days, 20 hours, and 42 minutes. The Italian Line placed the *Rex* in service, and Germany had both the *Bremen* and *Europa.* Such U.S. ships as the *Leviathan* on the North Atlantic service, and the "president" liners on the San Francisco–Shanghai crossings were joined by others.

On a less happy note, gangsterism did not end in the United States with the repeal of prohibition. The Federal Bureau of Investigation (FBI), having had its origin in 1908, was renamed and reorganized in

1935 under the direction of J. Edgar Hoover, and received much attention for its successes in combatting crime. It could not have prevented the kidnapping on March 1, 1932, of the infant son of Charles A. Lindbergh and Anne Morrow Lindbergh, already much in the news because of their joint ventures in aviation, including a flight to the Orient in 1931. The kidnapping and death of the child shocked the nation and the world. In 1934 Bruno Richard Hauptmann, a German immigrant, was arrested for the crime. He was tried and convicted, and in 1935 executed.

Other varieties of trouble arose in the United States. The sit-down strike, which became an element in violent labor confrontations with management in 1936, continued to be used, particularly in the automotive and steel industries. These events and a long conflict with the International Longshoremen's Union beginning in San Francisco in 1934 interfered with the recovery program. Yet the strength of union organizations was advanced as a part of that very program and included the formation of an American Newspaper Guild (ANG), bringing new security and improved working conditions to news personnel.

Disasters of nature also overtook the country in the 1930s, with drought and floods, landslides and tornadoes, and in 1938 a tropical hurricane causing damage as far north as New England. Droughts in the Midwest, at their worst in Arkansas, Oklahoma, and Kansas in the summer of 1934 ruined crops over that broad area, and winds blew the topsoil away in great "dust storms." A Soil Conservation Act in 1935 provided for a program to restore the land, but thousands of families already had lost their homes and property. Many sought new lives in California and other western states which were themselves suffering from the general depression and did not at the time welcome the influx of poverty-stricken immigrants.[19]

From 1935 the growing crisis in Europe was felt increasingly in the United States, and the crisis in China also had its impact. In 1937 the president signed a Neutrality Act prohibiting the export of arms and munitions to belligerent nations, by then meaning Japan, Italy, Germany, and Spain. Volunteers from the U.S. at that time were joining the forces of the Spanish Republic in the civil war then in progress, with a sharp division of opinion in the United States over the issues involved, over the position of the Church in the conflict, and concern over the participation of Italy, Germany, and Soviet Russia in the confrontation.

Before 1937 ended, the U.S. gunboat *Panay* had been sunk by Japanese air action over the Yangtze River, China's Nationalist govern-

---

19 The hardships of this situation and of the western migration are well told by John Steinbeck in *Grapes of Wrath* (1939).

ment had been forced out of Nanking and was moved inland to
Chungking. In 1938 Austria's annexation by Nazi Germany, the
Munich conference, and the seizure of an important segment of
Czechoslovakia led Roosevelt to ask appropriations to add strength to
the U.S. armed forces.

Since 1930, and particularly from 1937, Italian, German, and Japanese radio broadcasts, slanted to achieve a propaganda effect, were
directed in appropriate languages to the Middle East, Asia, and Latin
America. Efforts were being made by the Axis powers to subvert and
control newspapers in Latin America. This had been of early concern
to France and Great Britain, which had undertaken to counter the
propaganda assault by introducing their own foreign-language broadcasts. From 1937, the United States also became concerned because it
was being misrepresented in Latin America, and its good neighbor
policy was being undermined. The United States joined with Great
Britain in establishing listening posts to monitor the Axis broadcasts
to learn more precisely what was being said about them.

In 1938 the United States established a Division of Cultural Relations in the Department of State. Headed by Dr. Ben Cherrington of
the University of Denver, its announced purpose was to facilitate an
inter-American cultural exchange intended to defuse the Axis propaganda. Financial and technical aid also was extended to private broadcasters directing programs to Latin America, and to monitoring services associated with the Princeton University School of Public and
International Affairs in the east, and Stanford University in the west.

As 1939 began, more than 500 correspondents represented the
domestic media in Washington, and ten or more foreign countries had
staff or stringer correspondents present, totalling more than twenty
individuals. These were new high figures. Accredited foreign correspondents long had attended State Department news conferences. They
were entitled to attend White House conferences, and sometimes did
so, but by common agreement did not ask questions.

Most foreign correspondents in the United States still remained in
New York, but journeyed to Washington more frequently, and occasionally to other parts of the country. Difficult as it might seem to
cover so large a country as the United States from a city on the eastern
seaboard, with newsworthy events and situations arising in various lo-
cations, the correspondents were able to do so with reasonable effectiveness. The news flowed into New York, in any event. Correspondents could use the telephone to follow up special interests almost anywhere. Commercial airline services developing in the 1930s gave them
added mobility. Radiotelephone service by then also enabled them to
report directly to their home offices in almost any part of the world if
that seemed desirable.

News coverage had become ever more intensive, and the structure of government more complex. Some system was required to bring names, facts, and statistics together in convenient form, and to keep lists of offices and personnel constantly up to date for media reference and for the government itself.

A Division of Press Intelligence (DPI) was formed as early as August 1933 to provide a regular review of the national press in order to learn how the country was responding to the government's program. In July 1935 this became a division of a National Emergency Council (NEC). Both were headed by Charlotte J. Hatton. By 1939 the government had become so large that a new agency was created as a clearing house for information. This was the Office of Government Reports (OGR), directed by Lowell Mellett, former editor of the *Washington Daily News*. Its function was to collect and disseminate information to serve the president, other officials, and members of Congress in their relations with state and local governments, and with groups and citizens. The OGR absorbed the DPI, which was withdrawn from the NEC. To the OGR also was added a United States Information Service (USIS) headed by Harriet Root. It provided a clearing center in Washington for inquiries concerning all branches of the government and its *U.S. Government Manual* was a directory of all departments, divisions, agencies, and personnel of the national government, which was updated three times a year. The long established *Congressional Directory* and the *Statistical Abstract of the United States,* both published annually, also listed most sources and made much information conveniently available.

Despite the critical events in progress in Asia and Europe, two impressive world fairs were opened in 1939 in San Francisco and New York, and both reopened in 1940. Britain's King George VI and Queen Elizabeth visited Canada and the United States during May and June of 1939, and were guests at the White House. Their tour was covered by many reporters and correspondents, including Richard Dimbleby of the BBC accompanying the party. They had hardly returned to London when the German-Russian nonaggression and trade treaties were signed and the European war began on September 1.

U.S. sentiment had been strongly opposed to the Italian and German military aggression manifested since 1935. The Italian move into Albania in April 1939, followed by the German and then Soviet Russian attacks on Poland in September, led Congress to amend the 1937 Neutrality Act, which ended an embargo on the sale and shipment of arms abroad and was clearly intended to permit such material to go to Great Britain and France. Contributing to this change of policy was the fact that thirty American citizens had been drowned on the first day of the war when a German submarine sank the British ship

Athenia in the Atlantic. In October, all U.S. ports and waters were ruled closed to belligerent submarines, which then meant only German undersea craft. The U.S. defense program undertaken in 1938 also was extended.

The beginning of the war in Europe resulted in a cautious closing of some doors in Washington, and certain security precautions were introduced. Even so, President Roosevelt continued his news conferences. Steve Early and Mrs. Roosevelt did the same. At the Department of State, Secretary Cordell Hull conducted conferences attended by from ten to thirty domestic and foreign correspondents, and Michael McDermott and staff assistants also remained available as information officers there to meet with media representatives.

Special tensions arose in New York, however, among members of the Association of Foreign Press Correspondents in the United States, then an organization of 113 active members and fifty-four associate members commonly meeting in the Lotos Club. Correspondents of countries at war were set at odds. German correspondents, forbidden by the Nazi government to belong to foreign organizations, already had technically withdrawn. But an article by Ernest A. Hepp of the DNB agency, nevertheless appeared in the association's monthly mimeographed newssheet, the *Foreign Press,* of January 15, 1940. It was regarded by some as blatant German propaganda, and others wondered why it had been published at all. A number of members and officers of the association resigned in protest. Italian members were out of the association by September. In October 1941, the association was reorganized, becoming more simply the Foreign Press Association (FPA). With Japanese members also formally dropped after the Pearl Harbor attack of December 7, the membership in January 1942 stood at seventy-seven with forty-four associates.

The gravity of the war situation following the surrender of France in June 1940 brought the first peacetime military selective service law in the United States in September to aid in building a new army. It was extended in August 1941. A more aggressive German propaganda campaign directed at Latin America brought the formation of a U.S. Council of National Defense on August 16, 1940, and a replacement of the State Department Division of Cultural Relations with an Office for the Coordination of Commercial and Cultural Relations Between the American Republics.

Considering the aggression of the Nazi regime and the sentiment among much of the U.S. adult population, there was concern as to how the United States might maintain its neutrality in the war. This was an issue in the 1940 presidential campaign. All aliens in the country were required to register and abide by strict new regulations. German submarine activity in the Atlantic and close to U.S. shores was such that President Roosevelt arranged for fifty over-age U.S. destroyers to be given to Great Britain. They were in exchange for leases on air and naval bases for U.S. use in Newfoundland and the West Indies. The U.S. Navy also provided a technically limited assistance to British ships and convoys in the Atlantic.

President Roosevelt was re-elected to his third term in November 1940. At that period, Great Britain was fighting alone against Germany and Italy. Its forces were limited, the British Isles were under heavy air attack, and German submarines were causing heavy losses at sea. In March 1941, the U.S. Congress voted a so-called lend-lease act, providing that goods and munitions might be available to democratic governments in return for other goods and services. This permitted shipment of every sort of aid to Great Britain.

An unlimited national emergency was declared in May 1941, giving the president even greater powers. In June, all German and Italian assets in the United States were declared frozen, along with all assets belonging to European countries occupied by German and Italian forces. German consulates in the United States were ordered closed, along with the New York office of the Transozean Nachrichten, a propaganda organization.

On July 31, the State Department office concerned with German and Italian propaganda efforts in Latin America was again modified. It became the Office of the Coordinator of Inter-American Affairs (CIAA), headed by Nelson A. Rockefeller. Its function was the formulation and execution of programs to further national defense and strengthen bonds between the nations of the Western Hemisphere through radio, press, film, and other appropriate means. Following the U.S. entrance to the war in December 1941, this became more simply still the Office of Inter-American Affairs (OIAA), still directed by Rockefeller, and with much the same purpose as before.

In August of 1941, President Roosevelt met with Britain's Prime Minister Churchill at sea, off Newfoundland. There an understanding was formulated on war aims in the Atlantic Charter. By that time also, the U.S. Navy was providing increased aid to British convoys, and British ships suffering war damage were being repaired in U.S. shipyards. The *Robin Moor,* a U.S. freighter, was torpedoed off the Cape Verde Islands in May 1941, but without loss of life. In October, two U.S. destroyers were lost, the *Kearny,* off Iceland, and the *Reuben James* in the Atlantic, with 100 men drowned.

As the United States became more directly involved in the issues of war, correspondents in Washington looked for information not only to the news conferences held by the president and by Secretary Hull, but to those of Henry L. Stimson, secretary of war, and to Frank Knox, secretary of the navy. Knox, also publisher since 1931 of the *Chicago Daily News,* had been the vice-presidential candidate with Alfred Landon on the Republican party ticket in 1936. He was named to a coalition cabinet in 1940. Correspondents now also met with Henry A. Wallace, secretary of agriculture, Harry Hopkins, secretary of commerce, Harold L. Ickes, secretary of the interior, and James A. Farley, postmaster general.

The war in Asia had become of great concern in Washington in 1940, as the Japanese extended their forces beyond China in September to what had been French Indo-China and poised a threat to other areas. The German attack on Soviet Russia in June 1941 held the possibility that Japan, an ally in the Rome-Berlin-Tokyo Axis, might even direct an attack upon Russia by way of Manchuria. In any event, Roosevelt in July 1941 ordered an embargo on the shipment from the United States of scrap iron and gasoline to Japan, both essential to that country in the conduct of its war.

Admiral Kichisaburo Nomura, who had arrived in Washington in February as newly appointed ambassador from Japan, entered an official protest to the embargo. A graduate of the U.S. Naval Academy at Annapolis and often in the country, Nomura was fluent in English. On November 15 he was joined by Saburo Kurusu, who flew directly from Japan. He was formerly Japanese consul in Chicago, and his wife was an American. These two officials joined in negotiations at the State Department to seek a reversal of the embargo.

The negotiations were continuing when, according to plan, Japanese air and naval forces combined in an attack on the major U.S. Pacific naval base at Pearl Harbor, Hawaii, early on Sunday, December 7, 1941 (December 8 in Japan and other places west of the International Date Line). This attack was coordinated with Japanese assaults on the Philippines, Guam, Midway Island, Hong Kong, and Malaya. Congress voted a formal declaration of war on Japan the next day, as did the British Parliament. Germany and Italy declared war on the United States December 11. Thus in little more than twenty years since the end of World War I, the cycle of events had come full circle.

In terms of public information, national and international, the people of the United States may be said to have been better served than any others during those intervening years of the 1930s. The media were active, strong and competitive, the reporters competent and dedicated. Most important, as neutrals the reporters or correspondents were free to move almost as they wished through ten years of crisis and war. In a media service in no way limited or distorted by any domestic censorship, general partisanship, propaganda, venality, or even a disposition to appease a hostile foe, the people of the United States were almost overwhelmed by the volume of information available to them.

The End of an Era   20

News executives in the free countries of the world could not escape a realization by the 1930s that more was required than in any previous decade to make clear to the public the greater complexities of the period. The windows of the world were never open wider, providing the peoples of those free countries, at least, with a view of their broad environment.

Newspaper and news agency reporting was deep and extensive. It was supported by radio news coverage, magazine contributions, excellent photographs, newsreels, and special film documentaries relating to public affairs. Newspaper and magazine circulations rose, radio news broadcasts and commentaries gained great audiences, and book sales mounted.

But this advance in the 1930s came too late to reverse a downhill momentum then in progress. The open windows of the free world, and the improved media performance, were offset by a closing of windows in other parts of the world overrun by a creeping totalitarianism, accompanied by negative media practices, sharp censorships, and organized propaganda campaigns. Had the concentrated effort to advance public understanding been undertaken with full vigor in the 1920s when the climate was right, the course of history might have been quite different.

Of course, this can be no more than a matter of speculation. There were many, however, who spoke out in the 1920s for sanity and reason. They did not prevail. Yet neither can it be demonstrated that even in the 1930s enough persons understood clearly what was transpiring in the world to reverse the course of events. Most remained preoccupied with their personal affairs. If they bought more newspapers, magazines, and books and listened to the radio, most sought from them chiefly diversion and entertainment. In retrospect, also, there was no effective public demand for a wiser, more realistic leadership. On the contrary, the response, world-wide, often was strongest to apostles of intolerance and demagoguery.

The news of the day was almost ceaselessly depressing in the 1930s. Whatever good there was to be reported tended to be overshadowed by news of crisis, violence, disaster, and disorder, or by the tragedy of men, women, and children caught in an economic maelstrom or in the backlash of military action. Critics of the media sometimes protest that dismal reports receive unwarranted emphasis to the point of a contrived sensationalism, because the sense of drama and suspense involved will sell papers.

Granted that there have been examples of improper sensationalism at times, but this was hardly a legitimate complaint with reference to international news in the 1930s. At any time, the bad news must be presented with the good or distortion results. The bad news often is of such importance as to warrant prominent display, and is sensational enough in itself. This was commonly the case in the 1930s.

No normal person welcomes bad news, and media personnel themselves would prefer pleasant news. Bad news does not, in fact, necessarily sell papers. In any event, to hold the media at fault for the dissemination of bad news suggests the fable of the ancient ruler who killed the messenger who ventured to bring him unwelcome tidings.

As in any period of human experience, that which is reported as good or bad news on any day is a postscript to what has gone before, and a prelude to an unpredictable tomorrow. So those hopes of 1920 for a world of permanent peace and general well being for all mankind had been progressively reversed through the 1930s, and the battle was about to be fully joined. Not only were the lamps going out in Europe, as Sir Edward Grey put it in 1914, but by 1941 windows throughout the world were closed and shuttered. It was the end of an era of hope for peace following World War I.

Bibliography

Abend, Hallett. *Chaos in Asia.* New York, 1939.
_____. *Japan Unmasked.* New York, 1941.
_____. *My Life in China, 1926-1941.* New York, 1943.
_____. *Ramparts of the Pacific.* New York, 1942.
Abrams, Alan E., ed. *Journalist Biographies Master Index: A Guide to 90,000 References to Historical and Contemporary Journalists in 200 Biographical Directories and Other Sources.* Detroit, 1979.
Alcott, Carroll. *My War With Japan.* New York, 1943.
Allen, Frederick Lewis. *Since Yesterday.* New York, 1940.
Andrews, Sir Linton and H. A. Taylor. *Lords and Laborers of the Press.* Carbondale, Ill., 1970.
Baillie, Hugh. *High Tension.* New York, 1959.
Barnouw, Erik. *A History of Broadcasting in the United States.* 3 vols. New York, 1966-70.
Barns, Margarita. *The Indian Press.* London, 1940.
Barzini, Luigi. *O America, When You and I Were Young.* New York, 1977.
Beals, Carleton. *The Crime of Cuba.* Philadelphia, 1933.
Beattie, Edward W., Jr. *"Freely to Pass."* New York, 1942.
Bellanger, Claude, with Jacques Godechot, Pierre Guiral, and Fernand Terrou. *Histoire Général de la Presse Française.* 5 vols. Paris, 1969-76.
Benjamin, Robert Spiers, ed. *Eye Witness.* New York, 1940.
_____. *The Inside Story.* New York, 1940.
Bentley, Nicholas, ed. *Russell's Despatches From the Crimea, 1854-1856.* London, 1956.
Berger, Meyer. *The Story of The New York Times, 1851-1951.* New York, 1951.
Bernhardt, Ludwig. *Der Hugenberg-Konzern.* Berlin, 1928.
Bienstock, Gregory. *The Struggle for the Pacific.* New York, 1937.
Birchall, Frederick T. *The Storm Breaks: A Panorama of Europe and the Forces That Have Wrecked Its Peace.* New York, 1940.
Bisson, T. A. *Japan in China.* New York, 1938.
Blumenfeld, Ralph D. *All in a Lifetime.* London, 1931.
Bojano, Filippo. *In the Wake of the Goose-Step.* Chicago and New York, 1945.

Booker, Edna Lee. *News Is My Job: A Correspondent in War-Torn China.* New York, 1940.
_____. *Flight From China.* New York, 1945.
Boorstin, Daniel J. *The Americans: The Democratic Experience.* New York, 1973.
Bourke-White, Margaret. *Portrait of Myself.* New York, 1963.
Boveri, Margaret. *Mediterranean Cross-Currents.* London and New York, 1938.
Boyle, Andrew. *The Fourth Man: The Definitive Account of Kim Philby, Guy Burgess and Donald Maclean and Who Recruited Them to Spy for Russia.* New York, 1980.
Briggs, Asa. *History of Broadcasting in the United Kingdom.* 2 vols. Oxford, 1961–65.
Brown, Charles H. *The Correspondents' War.* New York, 1967.
Brown, Francis James et al. *Contemporary World Politics: An Introduction to the Problems of International Relations.* 2d ed. New York, 1940.
Brucker, Herbert. *Freedom of Information.* New York, 1949.
Bryan, J. III and Charles J. V. Murphy. *The Windsor Story.* New York,.1979.
Burnham, Lord (Edward Frederick Lawson). *Peterborough Court: The Story of the Daily Telegraph.* London, 1955.
Byas, Hugh. *Government by Assassination.* New York, 1942; London, 1943.
Caldwell, Louis G. *The American Press and International Communications.* New York, 1945.
Camrose, Viscount. *British Newspapers and Their Controllers.* London, 1938; rev. ed. 1948.
Canham, Erwin D. *Commitment to Freedom: The Story of the Christian Science Monitor.* Boston, 1958.
Capa, Robert. *Slightly Out of Focus.* New York, 1947.
Chamberlin, William Henry. *Confessions of an Individualist.* New York, 1940.
_____. *Japan Over Asia.* New York, 1937; rev. ed. 1939.
Chao, Thomas Ming-Heng. *My Fifteen Years as a Reporter.* London, 1944.
Chaplin, W. W. *Blood and Ink: An Ethiopian War Diary.* New York and Harrisburg, Pa., 1936.
Charnley, Mitchell V. *News by Radio.* New York, 1948.
Chester, Edmund A. *A Sergeant Named Batista.* New York, 1954.
Childs, Harwood L. and John B. Whitton. *Propaganda and Short Wave.* Princeton, 1942.
Childs, Marquis. *Sweden, The Middle Way.* New York, 1936.
_____. *Washington Calling.* New York, 1937.
_____. *This Is Democracy.* New York, 1938.
Clapper, Raymond. *Watching the World, 1934–1944.* Ed. by Mrs. Raymond Clapper. Introd. by Ernie Pyle. New York, 1944.

Close, Upton (Josef Washington Hall). *Behind the Face of Japan.* New York, 1942.

Cockburn, Claud. *A Discord of Trumpets.* New York, 1956. Published in London as *In Time of Trouble: An Autobiography.*

Cookridge. E. H. *The Third Man.* New York, 1968.

Cooper, Kent. *Barriers Down: The Story of the News Agency Epoch.* New York, 1942.

_____. *Kent Cooper and The Associated Press: An Autobiography.* New York, 1959.

Cowles, Virginia. *The Astors.* New York, 1980.

_____. *Looking for Trouble.* New York and London, 1941.

Darrah, David. *Hail Caesar!* Boston, 1936.

Davis, Frances. *My Shadow in the Sun.* New York, 1940.

Defense of Freedom. New York, 1952. (Ed. by staff of *La Prensa,* Buenos Aires.)

DeForest, Lee. *Father of Radio: The Autobiography of Lee DeForest.* Chicago, 1950.

Delmar, Sefton. *Trail Sinister: An Autobiography.* London, 1961.

Denny, Harold. *Behind Both Lines.* New York, 1942.

Desmond, Robert W. *The Press and World Affairs.* New York, 1937; reprint 1972.

_____. *The Information Process.* Iowa City, 1978.

_____. *Windows on the World.* Iowa City, 1980.

Deuel, Wallace. *People Under Hitler.* New York, 1942.

Digby, George. *Down Wind.* New York, 1939.

Drewry, John E., ed. *Post Biographies of Famous Journalists.* Athens, Ga., 1942.

Driberg, Tom. *Beaverbrook: A Study in Power and Frustration.* London, 1956.

Duranty, Walter. *Duranty Reports Russia.* New York, 1935.

_____. *I Write As I Please.* New York, 1935.

Ebenstein, William. *Fascist Italy.* New York, 1939.

Eliot, Major George Fielding. *The Ramparts We Watch.* New York, 1939.

Elson, Robert T. *Time, Inc.: The Intimate History of a Publishing Enterprise, 1923-1941.* New York, 1968.

Emery, Edwin and Michael C. Emery. *The Press and America: An Interpretative History of the Mass Media.* 4th ed. Englewood Cliffs, N.J., 1978.

Ettlinger, Harold. *Fair, Fantastic Paris.* Indianapolis, 1944.

Faber, John. *Great Moments in News Photography.* New York, 1960.

Farago, Ladislas. *Abyssinian Stop Press.* London, 1936.

Farmer, Rhodes. *Shanghai Harvest: A Diary of Three Years in the China War (1937-1940).* London, 1945.

Farson, Negley. *Behind God's Back.* New York, 1941.

_____. *A Mirror for Narcissus.* New York, 1956.

_____. *Transgressor in the Tropics.* New York, 1938.

_____. *The Way of a Transgressor.* London, 1936.

Fenton, Charles A. *The Apprenticeship of Ernest Hemingway: The Early Years.* New York, 1954.

Fielding, Raymond. *The Newsreel.* New York, 1972.

Fischer, Heinz-Dietrich and John C. Merrill, eds. *International and Intercultural Communication.* Rev. ed. New York, 1976.

Fischer, Louis. *Men and Politics: An Autobiography.* New York, 1946.

_____. *Soviet Journey.* New York, 1935.

Flannery, Harry W. *Assignment to Berlin.* New York, 1942.

Fleisher, Wilfrid. *Volcanic Isle.* New York, 1941.

Fodor, Marcel W. *The Revolution Is On.* Introd. by Dorothy Thompson. Boston, 1940.

Forbath, Alex, ed. *Europe Into the Abyss.* London, 1938.

Ford, Hugh. *The Left Bank Revisited.* New York, 1972.

Fredborg, Arvid. *Behind the Steel Wall: A Swedish Journalist in Berlin, 1941-1943.* Stockholm and New York, 1944.

Frédérix, Pierre. *Un Siècle de Chasse aux Nouvelles: De l'Agence d'Information Havas à l'Agence France-Presse, 1835-1957.* Paris, 1959.

Friedrich, Carl Joachim. *Foreign Policy in the Making—The Search for a Balance of Power.* New York, 1938.

Furman, Bess. *Washington By-Line: The Personal History of a Newspaperwoman.* New York, 1949.

Furuno, Inosuke, ed. *Tsushinsha shi kankokai.* Tokyo, 1958. (History of news agencies.)

Fyfe, Hamilton. *Sixty Years of Fleet Street.* London, 1949.

Garraty, John A. and Peter Gay, eds. *The Columbia History of the World.* Fwd. by William McGill. New York, 1972.

Gates, Gary Paul. *Air Time: The Inside Story of CBS News.* New York, 1978.

Gauvreau, Emile. *My Last Million Readers.* New York, 1941.

Gayn, Mark J. *Journey from the East: An Autobiography.* New York, 1944.

Gedye, G. E. R. *Fallen Bastions.* London, 1939. Published in New York as *Betrayal in Central Europe.*

Gellhorn, Martha. *A Stricken Field.* New York, 1940.

_____. *The Trouble I've Seen.* New York, 1936.

Géraud, André ("Pertinax"). *Gravediggers of France.* New York, 1944.

Gibbons, Edward. *Floyd Gibbons, Your Headline Hunter.* New York, 1953.

Gies, Joseph. *The Colonel of Chicago.* New York, 1979. (Biography of Robert R. McCormick of the *Chicago Tribune.*)

Gill, Brenden. *Here at the New Yorker.* New York, 1975.

Goebbels, Joseph. *Final Entries 1945: The Diaries of Joseph Goebbels.* Ed. with introd. by Hugh Trevor-Roper. Trans. by Richard Barry. New York, 1978.

Goldhurst, Richard. *The Midnight War: The American Intervention in Russia, 1918-1920.* New York, 1978.

Gollin, A. M. *The Observer and J. L. Garvin, 1908-1948.* Oxford, 1960.

Gould, Randall. *China in the Sun.* Garden City, N.Y., 1946.

Gramling, Oliver. *AP: The Story of News.* New York and Toronto, 1940.

Grandin, Thomas. *The Political Use of Radio.* Geneva, 1939.

Greenwall, Harry J. *Round the World for News.* London, 1936.

Griffin, Frederick. *Soviet Scene.* Toronto, 1933.

_____. *Variety Show.* Toronto, 1936.

Gunnison, Royal Arch. *So Sorry, No Peace.* New York, 1944.

Gunther, John. *A Fragment of Autobiography.* New York, 1962.

_____. *Inside Asia.* New York, 1939.

_____. *Inside Europe.* New York and London, 1936. Annual rev. eds. 1937-40.

_____. *Inside Latin America.* New York, 1941.

Hanighen, Frank C., ed. *Nothing But Danger.* New York, 1939.

Harris, Henry Wilson. *Life So Far.* London, 1954.

Harsch, Joseph C. *Pattern of Conquest.* New York, 1941.

Hartwell, Dickson with Andrew Rooney, eds. *Off the Record: The Best Stories of Foreign Correspondents.* Garden City, N.Y., 1953.

Hauser, Heinrich. *Time Was: Death of a Junker.* Trans. by Barrows Mussey. New York, 1942.

Hawkins, Eric and Robert N. Sturdevant. *Hawkins of the Paris Herald.* New York, 1963.

Heaton, Herbert. *A Scholar in Action: Edwin F. Gay.* Cambridge, Mass., 1952. (Re.: *New York Post,* 1918 period.)

Hecht, Ben. *Child of the Century.* New York, 1954.

Hemingway, Mary Welsh. *How It Was.* New York, 1976.

Herd, Harold. *The March of Journalism: The Story of the British Press from 1622 to the Present Day.* London, 1952.

Herndon, Booton. *Praised and Damned: The Story of Fulton Lewis, Jr.* New York and Boston, 1954.

Herrmann, Lazar (pseud. Leo Lanis). *Today We Are Brothers: The Biography of a Generation.* Trans. by Ralph Marlow. Boston, 1942.

Hicks, Wilson. *Words and Pictures: An Introduction to Photojournalism.* New York, 1952.

Hill, Max. *Exchange Ship.* New York, 1942.

Hills, Lee and Timothy J. Sullivan. *Facsimile.* New York, 1949.

Hindle, Wilfred. *The Morning Post.* London, 1937.

_____, ed. *We Were There: By Twelve Foreign Correspondents.* New York, 1939.

Hindus, Maurice G. *Moscow Skies.* New York, 1936.

History of The London Times, 1785-1948, The. 5 vols. London and New York, 1935-48.

Hitler, Adolf. *Mein Kampf.* 2 vols. Munich, 1925-27. English trans., New York, 1939.

Hobson, Harold with Philip Knightley and Leonard Russell. *The Pearl of Days, An Intimate Memoir of The Sunday Times, 1822-1972.* London, 1972.

Hoge, Alice A. *Cissy Patterson.* New York, 1966.

Hohenberg, John. *Foreign Correspondence: The Great Reporters and Their Times.* New York, 1964.

Hunt, Frazier, *One American and His Attempt at Education.* New York, 1938.

Huss, Pierre J. *The Foe We Face.* New York, 1942.

Huth, Arno. *Radio Today: The Present State of Broadcasting In the World.* New York, 1942.

Ito, Masanori. *The Japanese Press—Past and Present.* Tokyo, 1949.

Iyenger, A. S. *All Through the Gandhian Eye.* Bombay, 1950.

Jeffrey, William H. *Mitre and Argentina.* New York, 1952.

Jones, Sir Roderick. *A Life in Reuters.* London, 1951.

Kaltenborn, H.V. *I Broadcast the Crisis.* New York, 1938.

———. *It Seems Like Yesterday.* New York, 1956.

Kaplan, Justin. *Lincoln Steffens: A Biography.* New York, 1974.

Kemsley, Viscount. *The Kemsley Manual of Journalism.* London, 1950.

Kendrick, Alexander. *Prime Time: The Life of Edward R. Murrow.* Boston, 1969.

Kiplinger, W. M. *Washington Is Like That.* New York, 1942.

Kirk, Betty. *Covering the Mexican Front: The Battle of Europe Versus America.* Norman, Okla., 1942.

Kirkland, Wallace. *Recollections of a Life Photographer.* Boston, 1954.

Kisch, Egon. *Sensation Fair.* Trans. by Guy Endore. New York, 1941.

Knightley, Philip. *The First Casualty: From the Crimea to Vietnam: The War Correspondent as Hero, Propagandist and Myth Maker.* New York and London, 1975.

Knoblaugh, H. Edward. *Correspondent in Spain.* London and New York, 1937.

Kobler, John. *Luce, His Time, Life and Fortune.* New York, 1968.

Koenigsberg, Moses. *King News: An Autobiography.* New York, 1941.

Koestler, Arthur. *Arrow in the Blue: An Autobiography.* 2 vols. New York, 1952-54.

Kruglak, Theodore E. *The Two Faces of Tass.* Minneapolis, 1962.

Kuhn, Irene. *Assigned to Adventure.* Philadelphia, 1938.

Laney, Al. *Paris Herald: The Incredible Newspaper.* New York, 1947.

Langer, William L., ed. *An Encyclopedia of World History.* 5th ed. Boston, 1972.

Lawrence, David. *Diary of a Washington Correspondent.* New York, 1942.

Lazareff, Pierre. *Deadline: The Behind-the-Scenes Story of the Last Decade of France.* Trans. by David Partridge. New York, 1942.

Lee, Alfred McClung. *The Daily Newspaper in America: The Evolution of a Social Instrument.* New York, 1937.

Lendt, David L. *Ding: The Life of Jay Norwood Darling.* Ames, Iowa, 1979.

Levine, Isaac Don. *Eyewitness to History.* New York, 1973.

———. *Red Smoke.* New York, 1952.

Lewis, Alfred Allen. *Man of the World, Herbert Bayard Swope: A Charmed Life of Pulitzer Prizes, Poker and Politics.* New York, 1978.

Lindsley, Charles Frederick. *Radio and Television Communication.* New York, 1952.

Lochner, Louis P. *Always the Unexpected: A Book of Reminiscenses.* New York, 1956.

———. *What About Germany?* New York, 1942.

Lockhart, R. H. Bruce. *British Agent.* Introd. by Hugh Walpole. New York and London, 1933.

———. *Comes the Reckoning.* London, 1947.

Low, David. *Low's Autobiography.* London and New York, 1957.

———. *Years of Wrath. Cartoon History: 1931–1945.* Text by Quincy Howe. New York, 1946.

Lowenstein, Karl. *Brazil Under Vargas.* New York, 1942.

Lyons, Eugene. *Assignment in Utopia.* New York, 1937.

———. *Moscow Carrousel.* New York, 1935.

———. *The Red Decade.* Indianapolis, 1941.

———, ed. *We Cover the World.* New York, 1937.

MacColl, René. *Deadline & Dateline.* London, 1956.

MacLean, Robinson. *John Hoy of Ethiopia.* New York, 1936.

Macmahon, Arthur W. *Memorandum on The Postwar International Information Program of the United States.* Department of State Publication 2438. Washington, D.C., 1945.

MacNeil, Neil. *Without Fear or Favor.* New York, 1940.

Manevy, Raymond. *Histoire de la Presse, 1914 à 1939.* Paris, 1945.

Marcosson, Isaac F. *Before I Forget: A Pilgrimage to the Past.* New York, 1959.

Markham, James W. *Voices of the Red Giants: Communications in Russia and China.* Ames, Iowa, 1967.

Martin, Ralph G. *Cissy: The Extraordinary Life of Eleanor Medill Patterson.* New York, 1979.

Massock, Richard G. *Italy From Within.* New York, 1943.

Mathews, Joseph J. *Reporting the Wars.* Minneapolis, 1946.

Matthews, Herbert L. *Education of a Correspondent.* New York, 1946.

———. *Eyewitness in Abyssinia.* London, 1937.

———. *Two Wars and More to Come.* New York, 1938.

McCormick, Anne O'Hare. *The World at Home: Selections from the Writings of Anne O'Hare McCormick.* Ed. by Marion Turner Sheean. Introd. by James B. Reston. New York, 1956.

McCutcheon, John T. *Drawn from Memory.* Indianapolis, 1950.

McKenzie, Vernon. *Through Turbulent Years.* New York, 1938.

Merrill, John C. *The Elite Press: Great Newspapers of the World.* New York, Toronto, and London, 1968.

Merrill, John C. and Harold A. Fisher. *The World's Great Dailies: Profiles of 50 Newspapers.* New York, 1980.

Miller, Webb. *I Found No Peace: The Journal of a Foreign Correspondent.* New York, 1936.

Minney, Rubeigh James. *Viscount Southwood.* London, 1954.

Mitarai, Tatsuo. *Shimbun Taiheiki.* Tokyo, 1950. (History of the press in Japan.)

Moats, Alice-Leone. *Blind Date With Mars.* Garden City, N.Y., 1943.

Monks, Noel. *Eye-Witness: The Journal of a World Correspondent.* London, 1955.

Morgan, Thomas B. *The Listening Post: Eighteen Years on Vatican Hill.* New York, 1944.

―――. *A Reporter at the Papal Court.* New York, 1938.

―――. *Spurs on the Boot: Italy Under Her Masters.* Philadelphia, 1941.

Morgagni, Manlio. *L'Agenzia Stefani.* Milan, 1930.

Morison, Samuel Eliot. *The Oxford History of the American People.* New York, 1965.

Morris, Joe Alex. *Deadline Every Minute, The Story of the United Press.* Garden City, N.Y., 1957.

Morris, John. *Traveler from Tokyo.* New York, 1944.

Mosley: Leonard. *Down Stream: The Uncensored Story of 1936-1939.* London, 1939.

Mott, Frank Luther. *American Journalism: A History of Newspapers in the United States Through 260 Years, 1690 to 1950.* Rev. ed. New York, 1950.

Mowrer, Edgar Ansel. *The Dragon Awakes.* New York, 1938.

―――. *Immortal Italy.* New York, 1927.

―――. *Triumph and Turmoil: A Personal History of Our Times.* New York, 1968.

Mowrer, Lilian T. *Journalist's Wife.* New York, 1937.

Mowrer, Paul Scott. *The House of Europe.* Boston, 1945.

Muggeridge, Malcolm. *Winter in Moscow.* Boston, 1934.

Munro, Ion. *Through Fascism to World Power.* London, 1933.

Nevinson, Henry W. *Fire of Life.* London, 1935.

Newman, Joseph. *Goodbye Japan.* New York, 1942.

Nichols, M. E. *(CP) The Story of The Canadian Press.* Toronto, 1948.

Oechsner, Frederick et al. *This Is the Enemy.* Boston, 1942.

Oestreicher, J. C. *The World Is Their Beat.* New York, 1945.

Olson, Kenneth E. *The History Makers: The Press of Europe From Its Beginnings Through 1965.* Baton Rouge, 1966.
Ortega y Gasset, José. *The Revolt of the Masses.* New York, 1932.
Owen, Russell. *South of the Sun.* Fwd. by Roy Chapman Andrews. New York, 1934.
Packard, Reynolds and Eleanor Packard. *Balcony Empire.* New York, 1941.
Paley, William S. *As It Happened: A Memoir.* Garden City, N.Y., 1979.
Patmore, Derek. *Balkan Correspondent.* New York, 1941.
Paulu, Burton. *British Broadcasting: Radio and Television in the United Kingdom.* Minneapolis, 1956.
Pers, Anders. *Newspapers in Sweden.* Stockholm, 1954.
Phillips, Cabell, ed. *Dateline: Washington.* Garden City, N.Y., 1949.
Pilat, Oliver. *Drew Pearson: An Unauthorized Biography.* New York, 1973.
Pitcairn, Frank. *Reporter in Spain.* London, 1936.
Poliakoff, Vladimir ("Augur"). *Europe in the Fourth Dimension.* New York, 1939.
Pollard, James E. *The Presidents and the Press.* New York, 1947.
Powell, John B. *My Twenty-Five Years in China.* New York, 1945.
Price, G. Ward. *Extra-Special Correspondent.* London, 1957.
———. *I Know These Dictators.* London, 1938.
———. *Year of Reckoning.* London, 1939.
Price, Morgan Phillips. *My Three Revolutions.* London, 1969.
Price, Warren C., comp. *The Literature of Journalism: An Annotated Bibliography.* Minneapolis, 1959; rev. ed., 1977.
Reed, Douglas L. *Disgrace Abounding.* London, 1939.
———. *Insanity Fair.* London and New York, 1938.
Reigel, O.W. *Mobilizing for Chaos.* New Haven, 1934.
Reith, Lord. *Into the Wind: His Autobiography.* London, 1947.
Report on the British Press. London, 1938. (By Political and Economic Planning, PEP.)
Robinson, Thomas F. *Radio Networks and the Federal Government.* New York, 1943.
Rosenstone, Robert A. *Romantic Revolutionary.* New York, 1975.
Ross, Albion. *Journey of an American.* Indianapolis, 1957.
Ross, Ishbel. *Ladies of the Press: The Story of Women in Journalism.* Fwd. by Stanley Walker. New York and London, 1936.
Rosten, Leo, *The Washington Correspondents.* New York, 1937.
Rue, Larry. *I Fly for News.* New York, 1932.
Saerchinger, Cesar. *Hello America! Radio Adventures in Europe.* Boston, 1938.
Salisbury, Harrison E. *Black Night, White Snow: Russia's Revolutions 1905-1917.* Garden City, N.Y., 1977.
Sanders, Marion K. *Dorothy Thompson: A Legend in Her Time.* Boston, 1973.

Scarborough, Harold E. *England Muddles Through.* New York, 1932.

Schechter, Abel A. and Edward Anthony. *I Live on Air.* New York, 1941.

Scheffer, Paul. *Seven Years in Soviet Russia.* Trans. by Arthur Livingston. New York, 1931.

Schlesinger, Philip. *Putting 'Reality' Together: BBC News.* Beverly Hills, 1979.

Schramm, Wilbur, ed. *Mass Communications,* Urbana, 1949.

Schuman, Frederick L. *International Politics.* Rev. ed. New York, 1937.

Scott, John. *Beyond the Urals: An American Worker in Russia's City of Steel.* Boston, 1942.

_____. *Duel for Europe.* Boston, 1942.

Seldes, George. *Sawdust Caesar.* New York, 1935.

_____. *Tell the Truth and Run.* New York, 1953.

_____. *The Vatican: Yesterday, Today, Tomorrow.* New York, 1934.

_____. *World Panorama, 1918–1933.* Boston, 1933.

Servan-Schreiber, Jean-Louis. *The Power to Inform; Media: The Business of Information.* New York, 1974. Published in France as *Le Pouvoir d'Informer,* 1972.

Seton-Watson, R. W. *Britain and the Dictators.* New York, 1938.

Sevareid, Eric. *Not So Wild a Dream.* New York, 1946. Rev. ed., with new fwd. 1976.

Sharp, Roland Hall. *South America Uncensored.* New York, 1945.

Sheean, Vincent. *Not Peace But the Sword.* New York, 1939.

_____. *Personal History.* New York, 1935. Published in London as *In Search of History.*

Shirer, William L. *Berlin Diary: The Journal of a Foreign Correspondent, 1934–1941.* New York, 1942.

_____. *End of a Berlin Diary.* New York, 1947.

_____. *Gandhi: A Memoir.* New York, 1979.

_____. *Midcentury Journal: The Western World Through Its Years of Conflict.* New York, 1952.

_____. *The Rise and Fall of the Third Reich: A History of Nazi Germany.* New York, 1960.

_____. *20th Century Journey: A Memoir of a Life and the Times of William L. Shirer, The Start, 1904–1930.* New York, 1976.

Siepmann, Charles A. *Radio, Television and Society.* New York, 1950.

Simon, André. *J'Accuse! The Men Who Betrayed France.* New York, 1940.

Simon, Lord (Ernest D. S. Simon). *The B.B.C. From Within.* London, 1953.

Simonds, Frank L. and Brooks Emeny. *The Great Powers in World Politics.* Rev. ed. New York, 1937.

Sington, Derrick and Arthur Weidenfeld. *The Goebbels Experiment: A Study of the Nazi Propaganda Machine.* New Haven, 1943.

Slater, Michael. *Dickens on America and the Americans.* Austin, Texas, 1978.

Slocombe, George. *A Mirror to Geneva.* London and New York, 1938.

_____. *The Tumult and the Shouting.* New York, 1936.

Smedley, Agnes. *Battle Hymn of China.* New York, 1943.

Smith, Howard K. *Last Train from Berlin.* New York, 1942.

Snow, Edgar. *Battle for Asia.* New York, 1941.

_____. *Far Eastern Front.* New York, 1934.

_____. *Journey to the Beginning.* New York, 1958.

_____. *Red Star Over China.* New York, 1937.

Snow, Lois Wheeler. *Edgar Snow's China.* New York, 1981.

Snyder, Louis M., ed. *Masterpieces of War Reporting.* New York, 1962.

Snyder, Louis L. and Richard B. Morris, eds. *A Treasury of Great Reporting: "Literature Under Pressure" from the Sixteenth Century to Our Own Times.* Pref. by Herbert Bayard Swope. New York, 1949.

Sokolsky, George E. *The Tinder Box of Asia.* Garden City, N.Y., 1932.

Southworth, Herbert R. *Guernica! Guernica!* Berkeley, 1977.

Stanhope, Aubrey. *On the Track of the Great: Recollections of a Special Correspondent.* London, 1914.

Startt, James D. *Journalism's Unofficial Ambassador: A Biography of Edward Price Bell, 1869–1943.* Athens, Ohio, 1979.

Steer, George. *Caesar in Abyssinia.* Boston, 1937.

_____. *Tree of Gernika.* London, 1938.

Steffens, Lincoln. *The Autobiography of Lincoln Steffens.* 2 vols. New York, 1931.

_____. *The Letters of Lincoln Steffens.* Ed. by Ella Winter Steffens and Granville Hicks. 2 vols. New York, 1938.

_____. *Lincoln Steffens Speaking.* New York, 1936.

Stevens, Edmund. *Russia Is No Riddle.* New York, 1945.

Stewart, Kenneth N. and John Tebbel. *Makers of Modern Journalism.* New York, 1952.

Stokes, Thomas L. *Chip Off My Shoulder.* Princeton, 1940.

Stone, Shepard and Hanson Baldwin, eds. *We Saw It Happen: The News Behind the News That's Fit to Print.* New York, 1939.

Storey, Graham. *Reuters: The Story of a Century of News-Gathering.* London and New York, 1951. Published in London as *Reuters' Century, 1851–1951.*

Stowe, Leland. *Nazi Means War.* New York, 1933.

_____. *No Other Road to Freedom.* New York, 1941.

_____. *They Shall Not Sleep.* New York, 1944.

Strong, Anna Louise. *I Change Worlds: The Remaking of an American.* New York, 1935.

Sulzberger, Cyrus L. *A Long Row of Candles: Memoirs and Diaries, 1934-1954.* New York, 1969.

_____. *Seven Continents and Forty Years: A Concentration of Memoirs.* Fwd. by André Malraux. New York, 1977.

Swanberg, W. A. *Citizen Hearst: A Biography of William Randolph Hearst.* New York, 1961.

_____. *Luce and His Empire.* New York, 1972.

Swing, Raymond Gram. *How War Came.* New York, 1939.

_____. *Preview of History.* New York, 1937.

Tabouis, Genevieve. *Blackmail or War.* London, 1938.

_____. *They Called Me Cassandra.* New York, 1942.

Tardieu, André. *France in Danger.* London, 1935.

Taylor, A. J. P. *Beaverbrook.* London, 1972.

Taylor, Edmond. *The Strategy of Terror: Europe's Inner Front.* Boston, 1940.

Tebbel, John. *An American Dynasty, The Story of the McCormicks, Medills and Pattersons.* Garden City, N.Y., 1947.

Templewood, Lord. *Nine Troubled Years.* London, 1954.

Tentative International Bibliography of Works Dealing with Press Problems. Paris, 1954 (Unesco publication.)

Thomas, Lowell. *Good Evening Everybody: From Cripple Creek to Samarkand, An Autobiography.* New York, 1976.

_____. *Magic Dials.* New York, 1939.

_____. *So Long Until Tomorrow: From Quaker Hill to Kathmandu.* New York, 1977.

Thompson, C. V. R. *I Lost My English Accent.* New York, 1939.

Thompson, Dorothy. *Let the Record Speak.* Boston, 1939.

Timperley, H. J. *Japanese Terror in China.* New York, 1938. Published in London as *What War Means: The Japanese Terror in China. A Documentary Record.*

Tolischus, Otto D. *They Wanted War.* New York, 1940.

_____. *Through Japanese Eyes.* New York, 1945.

_____. *Tokyo Record.* New York, 1943.

Tomlinson, John D. *The International Control of Radio-Communications.* Ann Arbor, 1945.

Tong, Hollington K. *Dateline China: The Beginning of China's Press Relations with the World.* New York, 1950. Published in Taiwan as *China and the World Press.*

Turner, Timothy. *Bullets, Bottles, and Gardenias.* Dallas, 1935.

Ullstein, Hermann. *The Rise and Fall of the House of Ullstein.* New York, 1943.

Valdés, Miguel Valasco. *Historia del Periodismo Mexicano.* Mexico City, 1955.

Van Paassen, Pierre. *Days of Our Years.* New York, 1939; rev. ed., 1941.

Vaughn, Miles W. *Covering the Far East.* New York, 1936. Published in London as *Under the Japanese Mask.*
Villard, Oswald Garrison. *Fighting Years: Memoirs of a Liberal Editor.* New York, 1939.
Weddell, Alexander W. *Introduction to Argentina.* New York, 1939.
Wells, Linton. *Around the World in Twenty-eight Days.* New York, 1926.
_____. *Blood on the Moon.* Boston and New York, 1937.
Wendt, Lloyd. *Chicago Tribune: The Rise of a Great American Newspaper.* New York, 1979.
Werth, Alexander. *France in Ferment.* London and New York, 1934.
Whitaker, John T. *Americas to the South.* New York, 1939.
_____. *And Fear Came.* New York, 1936. Published in London as *Fear Came on Europe.*
_____. *We Cannot Escape History.* New York, 1943.
White, John W. *Argentina: The Life Story of a Nation.* New York, 1941.
White, Llewellyn. *The American Radio.* Chicago, 1947.
White, Llewellyn and Robert D. Leigh. *Peoples Speaking to Peoples.* Chicago, 1946. (Report on International Mass Communications from The Commission on Freedom of the Press.)
White, Paul. *News on the Air.* New York, 1947.
White, Theodore H. *In Search of History: A Personal Adventure.* New York, 1978.
_____ with Annalee Jacoby. *Thunder Out of China.* New York, 1946.
White, William. *By-Line: Ernest Hemingway.* New York, 1977.
Wildes, Harry Emerson. *Japan In Crisis.* New York, 1934.
Wile, Frederic William. *News Is Where You Find It: Forty Years' Reporting at Home and Abroad.* Indianapolis, 1939.
Williams, Francis. *Dangerous Estate, The Anatomy of Newspapers.* London and New York, 1957.
_____. *Nothing So Strange, An Autobiography.* London, 1970.
_____. *The Right to Know: The Rise of the World Press.* London, 1969.
_____. *Transmitting World News.* Paris, 1953. (Unesco publication.)
Windsor, Duke of. *A King's Story: The Memoirs of the Duke of Windsor.* London and New York, 1951.
Wolff, Theodor. *Through Two Decades.* Trans. by E. W. Dickes. London, 1936.
Wolseley, Roland, ed. *Journalism in Modern India.* Bombay, 1953.
Wood, Alan. *The True Story of Lord Beaverbrook.* London, 1965.
Wood, James Playsted. *Magazines in the United States.* 2d ed. New York, 1956.
Woods, Frederick, ed. *Young Winston's Wars.* New York, 1973.

Woodhead, Henry George W. *Adventures in Far Eastern Journalism: A Record of Thirty-Three Years' Experience.* New York, 1935. Published in London as *A Journalist in China.*
_____. *A Visit to Manchoukuo.* Shanghai, 1932.
Woodward, J. L. *Foreign News in American Morning Newspapers.* New York, 1930.
Wrench, John Evelyn. *Geoffrey Dawson and Our Times.* London, 1955.
Wyant, Hubbard. *Fiasco in Ethiopia: The Story of a So-Called War by a Reporter on the Ground.* New York, 1936.
Ybarra, Thomas H. *America Faces South.* New York, 1939.
_____. *Young Man of the World.* New York, 1942.
Young, Eugene J. *Looking Behind the Censorships.* New York, 1938.
Young, James R. *Behind the Rising Sun.* New York, 1941.
Young, Kenneth, ed. *The Diaries of Sir Robert Bruce Lockhart.* Vol. 1, 1915-38. London and New York, 1973.

Index

Berrigan, Derrell, 242
Berry, Sir Gomer, 266, 267, 267n, 284
Berry, Robert E., 231, 247
Berry, Sir William, 266, 267, 284
Berthelot, Philippe, 219
Berthet, Marius, 365
Besant, Dr. Annie, 88, 207
Bespalow, Ivan, 366, 423
Bess, Demaree, 179, 180, 196, 241, 242, 344, 345, 357
Best, Robert H., 238
Bethlen, Count Stephen (István), 19
Beukert, G. O., 229
Bickel, Karl A., 135, 136, 234, 239
Billingham, Anthony J., 196, 303
Binder, Carroll, 145, 322, 323, 326
Bing, Edward J., 238
Bing, Walter, 364
Bing-shuey, Edward, 194
Biondi, Count Leone Fumasoni, 367
Birchall, Frederick T., 149, 291, 299
Bird, William, 251, 360–61
Birkhead, May, 69, 69n, 308, 333
Bishop, Charles, 328
Bittencourt, Edmundo, 153
Bittencourt, Dr. Paulo, 153, 379
Bittencourt, Silvia de ("Majoy"), 153–54
Black Sea, 53, 320, 328
Blaedel, Nicolas, 431
Bleichröder Bank (Berlin), 209
Bliven, Bruce, 135, 272
Block, Paul, 370
Blokzijl, Max, 372
Blood Purge (Germany), 407, 424
Blum, Georges, 364
Blum, Léon, 217, 218
Blumenfeld, Ralph D., 277
Blythe, Samuel G., 350
De Bochet, Paul, 364
Bodington, Nicholas R., 278
Bohigas, Angel, 151
Bojano, Filipo, 369
Bolander, Dr. K. G., 373
Bolitho, William, 271, 351–52
Bolivia, 147, 161, 165, 233
Bolsheviks, 22, 23, 26, 29, 33, 48, 438. See also Communists
Bombay, 88, 207, 221, 265, 288, 289
Bonarenko, Nina Andreyevna, 344n
Bond, George W., 252
Bondarenko, Leonid, 366

Boni, Mrs. Albert, 372
De Bonneuil, Edith Marie, 364
Booker, Edna Lee, 196, 249
Booth Newspapers, 355
Borah, William E., 356
Borelli, Aldo, 109, 368
Boris III, King (Bulgaria), 61, 62, 63
Borisovich, Marshal Ian, 435
Borodin, Michael, 182, 183, 186
Boschenstein, Hermann, 374, 423
Boas, J. H., 372
Boston, 258n, 272, 338, 341, 343, 344, 345, 346, 347
Boston Evening Transcript, 131, 258n
Boston Herald, 304
Boston Journal, 304
Boston Post, 340
Boston University, 342
Botha, General Louis, 89
Boubli, D. Khalifa, 378
Bouery, Emile, 378
Bouman, John A., 229
Bourgeois, Joseph, 288
Bourgeon, Martial, 219
Bourjaily, Monte, 251
Bourke-White, Margaret, 383
Bouton, S. Miles, 299, 361, 423
Bovard, O. K., 352
Bowlby, Thomas William, 265
Boxer Rebellion, 192, 233, 264
Bradford, Armistead L., 161, 235, 236, 237, 240
Bradshaw, W. F., 222
Braham, Dudley Disraeli, 261
Brailsford, H. N., 272, 282
Braithwaite, John Sidney, 341, 344–45, 347
Brandt, Raymond P., 352
Brayley, Jack, 286
Brazil, 5, 106, 147, 152–57, 159, 161, 209, 240, 303, 324, 379, 399
Brazilian Newspaper Assn. (ABI), 156–57
Bréal, Michel, 220
Bret, Paul Louis, 219
Brewer, Sam Pope, 335
Briand, Aristide, 16, 16n
Brindley, Dariel, 223
Briquet, Pierre, 288
Brisbane (Australia), 83, 285, 449
Brisbane, Arthur, 304
British Broadcasting Corp. (BBC), 222, 263, 270, 273–75, 297, 359, 382, 453

484   *Index*